D0266609

Statistics For Management

A Practical Introduction To Statistics

By

Dr. B. J. Mandel

*Professor Emeritus of Statistics and
Former Chairman of Statistics Department,
School of Business, Industry and Management,
University of Baltimore*

*Former Director, Office of Statistical Programs
and Standards, U. S. Postal Service*

Currently, Statistical Science Consultant and Educator

and

Dr. Robert E. Laessig

*Professor of Management,
College of Business and Administration,
Drexel University, Philadelphia, PA*

Consultant, Robert E. Laessig, Ph.D. and Associates

DANGARY PUBLISHING COMPANY
Baltimore, Maryland 21206-4902
1996

ISBN 0-910484-00-7

Printed in the United States of America by
Dangary Publishing Company
6260 Frankford Avenue
Baltimore, Maryland 21206-4902

Library of Congress Catalog Card No. 95-83928
ISBN 0-910484-00-7

Sixth Edition, 1996

Foreword

by
Steven M. Bajgier, Ph.D.
Department Head, Department of Quantitative Methods
College of Business and Administration
Drexel University
Philadelphia, PA 19104
January 1996

....

It is my pleasure to write a foreword for the newly revised textbook, *Statistics for Management*, by Drs. Mandel and Laessig.

In writing this remarkable textbook, the authors have drawn extensively on two different kinds of experience. The first type of experience that the authors bring to the book is that of practicing statisticians. The authors have dealt extensively with statistical problem solving as researchers and consultants to government and industry over many decades. The second type of experience is that of teaching statistical principles, methods, and applications to individuals, both in traditional classroom settings as well as the setting of continuing professional education workshops and special training courses. The combination of these two types of experience has produced an outstanding book. It is simultaneously understandable, interesting, and extremely practical.

This book is very far from an abstract, theoretical treatment of statistical principles and formulas. This is a book that really explains statistical thinking, and gives readers practical guidelines for the application of statistics to the most frequently encountered problems. The emphasis in this text is on the understanding of concepts and the statistical methods related to them, as well as the rationale underlying each statistical method. Formulas are illustrated with numeric examples so the distractions caused by symbols are minimized.

Foreword

The previous editions of this fine textbook have helped a great many students and managers to understand statistical thinking. This revision has resulted in a significantly improved text in many ways, and I recommend this book without reservation as an introductory treatment of statistics where the primary goals are to introduce concepts as well as to excite readers about the way that statistical problem solving can enhance and improve decision making and management.

I am sure you will enjoy the book and realize tremendous benefits from its use.

Preface

This is the sixth edition of *Statistics For Management — A Practical Introduction to Statistics* and the 40th year of its service to students and instructors of introductory courses in statistics. There must be something good in a textbook that has lasted this long.

Former editions were written on the premise: *To teach, you must simplify and not overwhelm.* This objective continues to be the basic approach in the sixth edition. However, some significant additions and improvements have been made to the previous edition. Many more additional practical uses of statistics are included. To help the reader quickly determine the primary improvements in the textbook we are briefly listing below the main changes.

One of the primary changes is an expansion of the meaning, practical usefulness, and the major principles which underlie random sampling. The four previous chapters, (Chapters 7, 8, 9, and 10) have been expanded to cover, with demonstrations, 15 different ways of selecting random samples; four ways of determining the "appropriate" size of sample; how to derive unbiased estimates by extending the sample to the level of the universe of interest; how to measure the reliability of the estimates and present them in a simple, communicative, and meaningful way to recipients of the results; and how to make reliable comparisons using significance testing. In fact, the chapters on sampling may be considered the equivalent of a short text on *an introduction to sampling principles, concepts, methodology, and applications.* Detailed demonstrations are given of each of these elements.

The text now includes a new chapter entitled Statistical Process Control (SPC), an essential part of Total Quality Management (TQM). Chapter 11 covers the main concepts, principles and techniques of improving quality and maintaining satisfactory levels of quality. It includes the Pareto Method of detecting the primary sources and causes of quality problems and the allocation of resources to solve these problems; it includes an extensive coverage of the control chart approach to measuring quality on a continuing, periodic basis, and improving quality and productivity of products or services.

The third main improvement is in Chapter 12 — Introduction to Correlation and Regression Analysis. This chapter demonstrates two ways of deriving the forecasting equation — the forward and backward methods. It also uses simulation to demonstrate the main concepts in the field and it includes a substantial variety of novel uses of correlation and regression analysis, such as detection of possible fraud or abuse, improving productivity by a regression control chart, and establishing a productivity index.

Another unique feature of this book is that in Chapter 3, on frequency distributions, we pay considerable attention to the normal frequency distribution and explain the four conditions or factors which tend to create normal distributions. A detailed step-by-step demonstration is given on how to plan and construct frequency distributions and use them effectively.

The coverage of each chapter is in the Contents section which follows this Preface. A main feature of each chapter is the emphasis it gives to practical uses and to demonstrating in detail, step by step, the methods of computing and using the various statistical tools covered. Another feature is the variety of challenging problems in the Problems section, with solutions given to many of these problems in Appendix F.

What is also new about the text is that I have had the benefit of Dr. Robert E. Laessig's knowledge and experience, as he joined me in preparing this edition of *Statistics For Management*. Dr. Laessig currently holds the rank of Professor of Management in the College of Business and Administration at Drexel University, Philadelphia, PA.

B.J. Mandel
Educator and Consultant

Washington, D.C.
January, 1996

Acknowledgments and Dedication

....

This book has been a labor of love based on the conviction that an adequate, practical understanding of statistical applications can make a difference in management and decision making. However, the book could not have been revised to its current level without the support of some very dedicated and capable people. We thank them all and dedicate this book to them and to our loved ones all over the world.

We especially appreciate and acknowledge Dr. Steven Bajgier of Drexel University for his thoughtful and helpful critique of the book's technical content. He also provided substantial assistance in drafting most of the charts and figures in the book. Extra pains were taken to assure that they are accurate and correctly shaped — e.g., normal curves are really normal. Thus, the reader is given an accurate impression of the points being made in each of the charts and figures in the book.

In addition, Dorothy Lasky, of Dot 2 Design, Baltimore, MD, put the book into final galley for printing. She transformed our rough-looking draft into the readable and quality product before you. Her patience with the many so-called minor revisions and her commitment and competence are appreciated.

Rosemarie Foglia-Polidoro was instrumental in typing the many drafts that preceded the typesetting for publication. Her dedication and competence are appreciated. In addition, we thank Margaret Coyle for the many courier-trips she walked between the authors and the typist. Vickie Bethea also helped with manuscript typing. Other people helped with data collection, editing, and the various other activities needed to complete the book. They include Robert McMurray, Joshua Lubeck, and our very helpful secretary Sandra Narinesingh. We thank them, and all the others who contributed to the successful completion of this project.

Of course, any and all errors remain the responsibility of the authors, but we have tried diligently to eliminate them and to make this book as readable and comprehensible and useful as possible. We hope we have succeeded.

Finally, though most importantly, we acknowledge the patient and constant support we received from our families. It seemed like it would never end, but they stuck with us throughout the arduous process. We dedicate this book to them and to all those who will use it to try to make this world a little better place in which to live.

B.J. Mandel and R.E. Laessig

January, 1996

Main Contents
by Chapter

1 The Field of Statistics 1

Meaning and Scope of Statistics 2
Meaning and Scope of Management 2
Objectives of the Book 3
Some Principles of Statistics 5
Analytical Tools 7
Some Cautions in the Use of Statistics 10
Variety of Uses of Statistics 13
   In the private sector 13
   In government 15
Universal Application of Statistics 17
Summary 18
Problems 19

2 Conducting a Statistical Survey 23

A Statistical Problem and How To Deal with It 24
Steps in Conducting a Survey 25
Quick Summary of Steps 32
Methods of Quantifying a Process or Problem 33
Elements of Good Questionnaires 38
Problems of Accuracy in Collecting Data 40
Comparative Advantages of Mail Questionnaire
   and Personal Interview 41
Summary 42
Problems 44

3 Organizing Data for Analysis — Frequency Distributions 47

Frequency Distribution Defined 47
Uses of Frequency Distributions: A Problem 48
Organizing a Variable for Analysis 52
Other Frequency Distributions 59
Graphic Patterns of Frequency Distributions 60
The Normal Frequency Distribution
    and Some of Its Uses 66
Summary 72
Problems 74

4 Averages and Their Uses 77

What is an Average? 77
Several Concepts of an Average 79
How to Derive the Mean, Median, and Mode 80
Uses of Averages in Management Problems 89
Which Average to Use 91
Averages and the Normal Distribution 94
Special Sections —
    Short-Cut Methods of Computing the Mean .. 95
    How to Compute a Weighted Mean 100
Summary 101
Problems 102

5 Variation — Its Measurement and Analysis 107

Universal Existence of Variation 107
Quantitative Concept of Variation 108
Methods of Measuring Variation 110
    The verage deviation 111
    The standard deviation 112
    The range 116
Uses of the Standard Deviation 116
Some Additional Applications of $\bar{X}$ and σ_x
    to Normal Distributions 126
Calculating the Standard Deviation
    from Frequency Distributions 132

Special Section —
  Short-Cut Method of Computing
  the Standard Deviation 133
Summary 135
Problems 137

6 Probability — The Foundation of Statistics and Guided Decisions 145

The General Concept of Probability 145
Fields of Application of the Theory of Probability . 146
The Measurement of Probability 147
Deeper Meaning of Probability 148
Different Ways of Determining Probability 150
Basic Rules of Probability 156
Special Section — Probability and
  the Binomial Distribution 159
Summary 166
Problems 167

7 Random Sampling — A Short-Cut to Fact Finding 173

The Meaning of Random Selection 173
Confidence in Results 175
Practical Value of Sampling 175
Six Elements of a Sampling System 178
Five Basic Methods of Random Selection 184
Stratified Random Selection 196
Other Methods of Selection 202
Summary 203
Problems 205

8 Some Principles and Concepts of Sampling 209

Management and Knowledge
  of Sampling Principles 209
The Concept of Error in Data 210
The Nature of Sampling Error 211
A Controlled Experiment in Sampling 214

Sampling and the Three Fundamental
   Frequency Distributions 224
Summary 228
Problems 231

9 Estimation and Sample Size Determination 233

Estimation Procedures 234
Measuring the Precision of Estimates 236
Presenting Sample-Derived Estimates 242
Determining the Appropriate Size of Sample 250
Stratified Random Sampling 264
Summary 268
Problems 269

10 Significant and Insignificant Differences 277

Decisions with Known Risk 278
Nine Ways of Determining Significant Differences . 281
Assumptions Underlying Significance Tests 294
Significance Tests for Percentages (Large Samples) . 296
One-Sided and Two-Sided Tests 301
Logical Steps in Tests of Significance 304
The t-Test of Significance (Small Samples) 310
The Chi-Square Test of Significance 314
Summary 321
Problems 324

11 Statistical Process Control 329

Total Quality Management and Statistics 329
Statistical Tools and Key Words 330
Measurement of Quality 333
The Pareto Method of Quality Improvement 336
The General Concept of a Control Chart 340
Constructing and Using a Control Chart
   for Averages ($\overline{X}$ Chart) 342
The Range Chart (R Chart) 353
By-Product Uses of the $\overline{X}$ and R Charts 356

Control Chart for Fraction Defectives (p Chart) ... 362
Control Chart for Number of Defectives
    (np Chart) 369
Control Chart for Number of Defects
    Per Unit (c Chart) 370
Other Control Charts 371
Summary 373
Problems 376

**12 Introduction to Correlation and
Regression Analysis** 381

Definitions 382
Applications of Correlation and
    Regression Analysis 383
Elements of Correlation Analysis 385
Elements of Linear Regression Analysis 395
Correlation and Regression Analysis, Method #1 .. 397
Correlation and Regression Analysis, Method #2 .. 405
Some Additional Practical Uses of
    Correlation and Regression Analysis 408
Cautions in Use of Correlation
    and Regression Analysis 410
Summary 415
Problems 417

13 Times Series and Forecasting 425

Uses of Time Series 426
Elements of Times Series 427
Methods of Time Series Analysis 432
Some Cautions in Time Series Analysis 443
Summary 445
Problems 446

**14 Presenting Statistics in
Graphs and Tables** 449

Tabulation of Data 450
Methods of Presenting Data 450
    Graphic presentation of statistical data 450

Tabular presentation or statistical tables 462
Four different types of tables 469
Summary 470
Problems 471

15 A Summary of the Book 475

Objectives of the Book 475
Principles Underlying Statistics 477
Statistical Methods 477
Variety of Uses of Statistics 481
Conclusion — The Power of Statistics 482

Appendix A
Principle Statistical Formulas, By Chapter 485

Appendix B
Properties of One Half of the Normal Curve 494

Appendix C
The t-Distribution . . . . . , ... 495

Appendix D
The Chi-Square Distribution 496

Appendix E
Values of the Simple Linear Correlation Coefficient
Needed for Significance at Given Levels 497

Appendix F
Answers to Problems 499

Index 533

Chapter 1

The Field of Statistics

"The scarcest material of all is not tin, not mercury, not tungsten, but statistical knowledge....The proper use of statistical theory is a problem of management. A new profession in business administration has grown up. It might be called statistical administration. Those who practice the new profession require intimate knowledge of statistical principles and of the uses of theoretical statistics, not as technicians, but as administrators who know where, when, and how to put statistical theory to use in their companies." *

....

Statistics is a field whose time has finally arrived. This science is concerned with all problems of mankind on which it can shed light, especially the management of people, the most precious resource of the world. It involves the collection, processing, analysis, and presentation of objective numeric data to guide behavior in every activity of life, and for every one of us. One of the most recent accomplishments related to statistics is the improvement of quality and productivity in many organizations. This book offers everyone an opportunity to appreciate the power of statistical reasoning and understand how to use it advantageously.

In this chapter we first define the study of statistics and then discuss the meaning and scope of management. This is followed by illustrations of a variety of actual statistical applications made to management problems, with the resulting benefits thereby achieved. Thus, it indicates implicitly why an understanding of statistics is essential for all managers (both present and future) and all analysts, such as management analysts, program analysts and budget analysts, in order that they may reap the benefits that the use of statistics offers. These benefits are equally achievable by all persons, whether in managerial, professional, technical, or support positions.

---

* W. Edwards Deming, *A Career In Statistical Administration*, August 1953.

Meaning and Scope of Statistics

Statistics has different meanings, and probably for this reason many people beginning the study of statistics do not have a full grasp of its scope. Of the many beginning students in our statistics classes who were asked at their first session "What is your understanding of the study of statistics?," some believed statistics to be a study of numbers; others, an analysis of figures to make predictions; still others, a showing of facts in graphs and charts; some even said facetiously, a jumble of symbols and formulas. By assembling the many incomplete answers, however we can get a fairly good idea of the meaning of statistics. A comprehensive definition is contained in the following key words (italicized): *Statistics* is a large body of *principles* and *methods* used to *collect, process, analyze,* and *present quantitative* data for *use* in making objective decisions.

Meaning and Scope of Management

Throughout this book reference is made to "management." The following definition of management is offered. We claim no particular credit for this definition. It is based partly on statements by authors of books on management and partly on suggestions made by participants in our various statistics and management courses. It goes as follows: *Management is the efficient, effective, and humane handling of the resources for which it is responsible to carry out the objectives and mission of the organization.*

These resources are quite diverse and may be classified under the following headings:

1. People, the most important resource, and their minds, treated humanely
2. Money wisely used
3. Time
4. Machines
5. Material
6. Space
7. Nature's bounties of air, water, etc.
8. Methods of management
9. Information

The primary point is that management involves decision-making, and many decisions can be improved by the use of statistical data, properly collected, tabulated, analyzed and presented.

Objectives of the Book

This book has several objectives. Its primary objective is to present and describe in as simple a manner as possible some of the more frequently used statistical techniques and to do so by demonstrating the many places and problems to which they can be applied; for this reason, the subtitle of this book is "A Practical Introduction to Statistics."

Recognition by management

Associated with this primary objective is the hope that this introductory study of statistics, from a practical viewpoint as opposed to a purely methodological viewpoint, will instill in its readers — both managers and students (our future managers) — an appreciation for the science of statistics as a powerful way of thinking and doing things. All too often in our modern world, men and women in executive or various management positions in business, industry, and government do not understand what statistics can do for their organization, and therefore do not use it. This is consistent with a powerful statement made by our past President Thomas Jefferson: "Men of good will often destroy that which they do not understand." Not only do such persons not use the science of statistics and its resulting information to provide a basis for better management, but they frown upon others in the organization who suggest its use. These individuals would rather keep busy making decisions the old fashioned way, right or wrong, than take a little time out to quantify problems, collect data, and act on the basis of the facts they reveal. Therefore, if this book only wins the appreciation of the reader for the value of statistics and the statistical viewpoint it will have achieved a major purpose, for our reader of today can become a more efficient and effective manager of tomorrow — one who will be in a position to gain new information and insight from appropriate statistical applications as a basis for rational action.

Methods of collecting, analyzing, and presenting data

Since one important element of scientific management is the collection of facts, this book aims to teach some of the methods of collecting statistics, particularly through the use of random sampling methods. Depending on the problem, there are several ways of gathering and compiling statistics, such as using published data or employing various survey and sampling techniques. This book aims to give the student an overall perspective of these varied methods and some of the related problems of obtaining valid, accurate, and representative statistics. Major emphasis is given to the use of random sampling as a method of fact-finding.

While this book does not expect to make readers either expert survey or analytical statisticians, it offers them an opportunity to learn a few of the most commonly used methods of collecting, organizing and interpreting statistical data and knowing where they can be applied. Some of the statistical methods include the use of percentages, averages, and measures of stability. In addition, it explains the importance of the principle of probability in drawing conclusions from samples and in knowing the risk or confidence associated with those conclusions.

A clear and systematic presentation of data is another essential element of decision making. Very often the basic tendency of a set of data and, therefore, the solution to a problem may be readily seen from a properly constructed statistical table or chart. It is an objective of the book to show the reader some of the elements of clear presentation of data, with particular emphasis on the preparation of final statistical tables.

Quantifying

The primary objective of statistics is interpretation or analysis of the data collected to serve specific uses, such as to make decisions or to shed light on problems. A number of basic analytical tools are described and illustrated in this book. It is essential, however, to point out that use of these analytical tools requires that the process or operation be quantified. There are only two forms of quantifying processes, namely, by *attributes* or by *variables*.

When quantifying by **attributes**, the data collector determines *how many* or what percentage of the cases possess a specified attribute or characteristic. Examples of attributes include "satisfactory" or "not satisfactory" service quality; black, brown, or blue eye color; and so on. When the required data have been collected either by a complete count or a random sample, the analyst can determine how many do, and how many do not, possess each particular attribute of interest. This also provides a basis for computing the percentage of cases possessing each attribute, for example, the percentage of female employees in an organization or the percentage of males aged 70 and over.

When quantifying by *variables*, the data collector determines the magnitude or value of each case, for example, *how much* postage is affixed to each letter. Since these values differ or vary from case to case, data in this form are called variables.

Some Principles of Statistics

Earlier, in our definition of statistics, we included the element "principles." Webster defines a principle as a fundamental truth; a primary or basic law or doctrine. The science of statistics contains such principles as *probability, normal distribution, stability of large masses of data,* and others. This book demonstrates some of these principles so that the users of statistics will be aware of the pillar of strength which underlies them. Professor Deming once said: "The use of statistical methods is not mere 'application.' There can, in fact, be no application of theory (or indeed of any 'rule') without theory to apply. There can be no knowledge without theory." The truth of this statement has been proven many times. There is much more to statistics than just the statistical methods and formulas which may be routinely memorized and used. A variety of laws and principles underlie the science and give it power. Without an understanding of these laws and principles, an unbalanced view of statistics may be obtained and misapplication is likely to result. With that understanding, breadth and scope are added to the science of statistics. An additional purpose of this book, therefore, is to demonstrate some of the laws and principles that give statistics its firm foundation.

In our classes we often use a sentence which summarizes the role of principles by stating that *statistical applications without principles are baseless;* on the other hand, *principles without applications are useless.* Some of the principles that underlie the statistical sciences are summarized below.

Probability and risk

Whenever we use samples to estimate a characteristic of a process or a phenomenon, we run some risk of being wrong. It would be unfair to introduce statistics without mentioning this fact. A powerful technique for determining risk in quantitative terms is offered by the *law of probability.* With it we can determine the chance of an event occurring or not occurring, provided appropriate data are available and are used properly. For example, what are the chances of drawing an ace of spades from a 52-card poker deck? The answer is 1 in 52, because there is only one ace of spades in the deck of 52 cards. What are the chances of picking any ace from such a deck? The answer is 4 in 52 or 1 in 13, because there are four aces in the 52-card deck. By inference, it can be seen that probability is defined as the ratio of the number of possible successful outcomes of an event (however success is defined for that particular event) to the total number of possible outcomes of that event. It may be shown by the simple formula that follows:

$$\text{probability (p)} = \frac{\text{number of successful outcomes (s)}}{\text{total number of outcomes (T)}} \quad \text{or} \quad p = \frac{s}{T}.$$

With this formula, the chances of an event happening can be readily computed, provided the number of possible successful occurrences for the numerator and the total number of possible occurrences for the denominator (which must be equally likely) are known or can be approximated by a random sample of observations.

It should be pointed out that by knowing the chances that an event will occur is not predicting when it will occur, but that in the long run it will occur. Thus, any conclusion faces the risk that, *at any given time*, it may not be correct or the event may not occur. (Each of these points is discussed further in Chapter 6.)

Universal variation

The primary reason for the use of statistics is variation. Every process, every phenomenon, every individual, every operation displays variation. Temperatures vary, rainfall varies, salaries vary and so forth. Statistical methods for collecting data and analyzing quantitative data are essential to deal or cope with this fundamental truth of *universal variation* that all "things differ" or "things change" — nothing is constant. (See Chapter 5.)

Stability of mass data

In spite of the law of universal variation, there are many situations when statistical data display a certain amount of stability. This occurs most often when the phenomenon deals with large volumes of data. When the analyst discovers this stability, he or she is able to make accurate predictions into the future. For example, by analyzing the Census Bureau's published statistics on the population of the United States each year, it will be found that our population has been growing at a yearly rate of very nearly one percent. Similarly, by analyzing published data on the high school drop-out rate over the past 10 years, it will be noted that while the rate is decreasing, it is decreasing at a fairly constant rate. One of the main problems in making predictions is to find mass data over a sufficient time period and to determine if the data show stability in their patterns. (See problem 1 at the end of this chapter.) Experience has shown that large masses of data on a given process will, in many cases, show a stable pattern of behavior, which may be characterized as *the law of stability of mass data* or *statistical regularity*.

An example of the principle of stability of mass data or the law of statistical regularity is the widespread applicability of statistical methods in life insurance. Life insurance companies have found, from analyses of data on the number of deaths, that certain percentages of policyholders at certain ages die in the course of a year. Because these percentages are based on large numbers, often many thousands, they can be relied upon to permit reasonably accurate forecasts of the number of future deaths among policy holders at given ages. Life insurance premiums are set on the basis of these forecasts. However, while such forecasts are found to be accurate for the overall population from which the data were obtained, there is no statistical basis for predicting which *specific individual* policyholders will die in any given year. This illustrates the applicability of statistics to masses of data but not to individual cases. In other words, we can make a general prediction or *generalization* using statistical methods, but we can not generally predict a specific *individual* outcome. (See Chapters 6 and 9.)

Analytical Tools

Statistical tools for data analysis comprise the major part of this book. A few are mentioned here in this introductory chapter.

Percentages or rates

Many problems can be solved or enlightened by computing the percentage or rate of occurrence of a characteristic, as long as reliable data are available. A percentage reduces figures of different dimensions or different units of measurements to relative terms and it therefore facilitates comparisons. Yet, percentages sometimes are not used in interpreting statistics when they could be used or, if used, they sometimes are not used properly. A magazine article stated that statistics showed fewer accidents occurring among people crossing streets at the middle than at the intersection of streets. One may conclude from these facts that it is safer to cross streets in the middle of the block than at corners. If percentages or rates were used to interpret these figures, however, it would have been found that the percentage or rate of accidents (computed by dividing the number of accidents by the total number of pedestrians crossing at these respective places) was much higher at the middle of the street than at the corner.

Even when percentages or rates are used, they occasionally are not computed correctly. For example, because sales dropped from $3,000 a week to $1,000 a week, some would say that there was a 200 percent decrease in sales. Can there be a decrease greater than 100 percent, unless the resultant amount is negative? This is a case of using the wrong base or denominator for the percentage. The correct percentage is a 67 percent decrease in sales (i.e., 2,000/3,000). As another example, a newspaper item stated that figures showed homes to be more dangerous than highways because the accident rate at home is about 119.5 per 1,000 population, compared with 13.3 per 1,000 population for motor vehicle accidents. The fallacy of this conclusion lies in the fact that both rates were computed with the same denominator, the entire population. However, the population exposed to highway accidents is much smaller than that exposed to home accidents, resulting in a much higher motor vehicle accident rate. In addition, the total time spent at home is much greater than the time spent on the highways. Finally, the seriousness of the accidents are not likely to be equal (although this is actually a different dimension or measurement and therefore should be considered separately). Therefore, if the proper comparative computations are made, the most likely truth is that highways are more dangerous than homes, in terms of exposure to accidents.

Averages

Probably one of the most frequently used statistical measures for describing masses of data is the average, because it reduces many measurements to a single figure and makes it possible to generalize about the phenomenon being measured. Thus, we may hear that the average family income in 1992 was $44,483, a single figure. Yet this average is computed for a total of 68.1 million families. Also, while the average is used frequently, its real nature is often misunderstood.

Often the average is mistaken to represent each of the values used to compute it; thus the variation around the average is forgotten. For example, the average age of students in a sophomore class was 20 years. This is sometimes taken to mean that practically each of the students was 20 years old. In reality, however, the range of ages could be from 19 to 65, with a fair percentage of students above the average age of 20 years. As another example: The quartermaster of an army depot stated during a certain campaign that the average food consumption per soldier was ample. Later, however, it was found that some of the soldiers were underfed, while others received far more than the average as their share.

Another misuse of averages occurs when they are calculated and used to represent the central tendency of a process although in fact two or more processes are involved. For example, by calculating the average rate of production from measurements that include the production records of both men and women, skilled and unskilled workers, and old and young workers, we get an average that represents neither the skilled nor the unskilled, neither men nor women, neither young nor old workers. Thus, it is an average comprising heterogeneous or diverse groups, and an average of this kind (i.e., for a highly heterogeneous population) generally has limited analytical or practical meaning. Averages can also be misused if the kind of average that has been calculated is not specified, since there are several different types of averages, each with its own use. (See Chapter 4.)

Measures of variation

The law of universal variation previously mentioned assures us that every phenomenon, individual, commodity, product, etc., displays variation. Therefore, an average standing by itself can be, and often is, misused unless it is followed by a statistical measure of the extent of *variation* from it on both sides of it. For example, the average family income in 1992 was estimated by the U.S. Bureau of the Census to have been $44,483. However, the variation around this average is great. This is evident from the fact that about 9.6 percent of the 68.1 million families earned less than $10,000, while 6.2 percent of the families earned more than $100,000 in 1992.

Two useful measures of variation are available to the analyst. One is the *range* of the variable (the difference between the highest and lowest values) and the other is the *standard deviation* (a measure of the average difference of the individual values from their overall average value.) (See Chapter 5.)

Some Cautions in the Use of Statistics

Some years ago, the publication "How To Lie With Statistics"* gave many people the impression that statistics are not reliable because they can be distorted to serve any purpose. This gives statistics a bad reputation, for the analyst who knows the concepts and qualifications of the data at hand can make objective and correct interpretations, without lying. Some of the qualifications or cautions for the proper use and interpretation of statistics follow.

Generalizing or jumping to conclusions

A common misuse of statistics is to draw a general conclusion when the data refer only to a particular situation. The oft-argued question as to whether men or women are safer drivers, for example, was answered easily by a local city analyst who dug up statistics that showed that in his particular city many fewer fatal accidents were caused by women than by men and, therefore, that women were safer drivers. What wasn't realized by this analyst was that perhaps women in that particular city drove fewer miles than men; if true, then women would have been exposed less frequently to situations that are more likely to cause accidents. Furthermore, even if women were proven to be safer drivers in that city, can it be concluded that women in general are? This is an illustration of using specific statistics (i.e., city-specific data) to draw an *unwarranted generalization*.

Very often, mail surveys fail to get a complete or even a high response rate. Yet, some researchers draw general conclusions about the population sampled as though the nonrespondents have the same characteristics as the respondents. This illustrates drawing unwarranted conclusions from *incomplete data*.

A certain company advertises its product by saying that a survey found more persons in a socially prominent class used their product than anyone else's product. Many people will generalize from this that they, too, ought to use this product. Advertisements need to be studied with a critical attitude. Often they use to good advantage the fallacy of generalizing from a particular point to convince people to use their product. Unless the full story on the methods of the survey and the

---

*Darrell Huff, *How to Lie with Statistics*, 1954, W.W.Norton & Co. paperback reissue, 1993.

representativeness or *validity* of the results are considered, general conclusions without adequate support should not be readily accepted.

The Chamber of Commerce of a certain city claims that its city is the healthiest city in the United States because statistics show that it has the lowest mortality rate in the country. The people who want to believe this generalization will. But do the quoted statistics on mortality rates really measure the healthy condition of the city? Perhaps the city is occupied by a relatively young population so that the mortality rate is naturally lower than would be expected for an older population.

Bishop Fulton J. Sheen once illustrated how incomplete statistics are misused to draw general conclusions. In a certain television program he stated it might be concluded that working at Johns Hopkins Hospital is promising for young women since statistics show that 33 percent of those who were recently married, married doctors. Then he pointed out that actually this percentage was based on the fact that, out of the three women working at Johns Hopkins who were married in the past year, one married a doctor. The probability that the one-third ratio would prevail in the future would appear rather slim in view of the fact that the sample used to draw the conclusion was very small and also not a random sample from which generalizations could be made with validity. (See Chapters 8 and 9.)

False accuracy and rounding

One important characteristic of the science of statistics is that, unlike mathematics and accounting, it is a science of close approximations and not an exact science. Often the decision management needs to make can be made by getting a reasonably good approximation of the value of an inventory or of accounts receivable, etc. As a matter of fact, statistics, whether collected by sample or census surveys, are hardly ever 100 percent accurate. Dr. W. Edward Deming once stated that there are about 18 different causes of error in the compilation of statistics. Yet, some statistical results are presented in a way that implies or conveys the impression that they are practically 100 percent accurate when, in fact, they are not. For this reason spurious accuracy should be avoided in presenting figures of a statistical nature without proper qualifications. Examples of misunderstanding of this fact are available in many sources.

The population of Guam, as of April 1990, was quoted as 133,152; the 1990 population of Maryland was quoted at 4,908,322; the number of preschool age children in a given state was quoted as having increased from 76,782 in 1980 to 112,674 in 1990. In all these instances it would have been more realistic, and not affect management decisions, to present the figures rounded out to the nearest 1,000, since population figures are not 100 percent accurate. The extent of rounding should be judicious, guided by the extent of error we believe to exist in the figures.

Error and risk

All decisions involve some element of risk. "There is no certainty without some doubt," said one author. There is even some risk in walking the streets. A decision might result in overproduction or underproduction; in overstaffing or understaffing; investing or not investing. Similarly, when using statistics, particularly those based on samples, we deal with incomplete data and therefore we make decisions with some risk because we can never be certain that the sample data are completely representative of the population of concern. Much of this book, therefore, attempts to explain the concept of risk and chance variation, especially when statistics are based on samples.

Common sense and thinking

Even in this world of computers, powerful statistical methods, and technology, one of the most precious characteristic of humans is our ability to reason and use common sense. Numerical data, whether derived by sampling or accounting, cannot always be accepted without some thought and critical check against common sense. In fact, in spite of how unfamiliar people may be with statistical jargon, statistical concepts and techniques actually "make sense" once their underlying logic is brought to the fore. In general, use of statistics in decision-making should be preceded by a check of their reasonability.

Statistics is not boring

Finally, this book aims to alert readers to the vast and almost unlimited potential application of statistics to problems of government, business, industry, economics, social studies, and research in all fields of life. This book aims to give the reader both a philosophy of statistical reasoning and a relatively small kit of tools to use for improved management, decision-making, or scientific research. The kit consists of some of the simplest and most frequently used methods of collecting and analyzing data, complimented by some of their underlying principles. It attempts to convince students and management that in statistics lies a profession that, like any respected profession, requires a reasonable amount of training and discipline, that statistics is not "dry" or "boring" as many believe, and that it is a key to better management and political decisions, dealing with real-world problems both of large and small organizations of business, industry, and government. For example, one of the most important developments in recent years has been the adoption by industry of statistical methods to improve the quality of products and services. (see Chapter 11.)

Variety of Uses of Statistics

In the Private Sector

Any inquisitive person who undertakes the study of statistics should ask the questions: "Why should I devote time and energy to studying statistics? Of what practical value will it be to me now, or in the future?" As the foregoing sections of this chapter have suggested and other chapters will give proof, an answer to these questions is that an understanding of statistics and its use will afford a person a way of dealing effectively with the many problems of administration and decision-making, particularly in directing the resources for which managers are responsible. Because statistics involves basing decisions on quantified and objective facts, rather than on intuition, reasoning, or memory alone, it can lead to improved economy, efficiency, and effectiveness in decision-making. Furthermore, because statistically-based decisions rely on numeric data (a universal communication language), statistics can strengthen the bond of communication not only throughout an organization but also among nations. Finally, in the face of proliferating legal challenges, statistics, properly collected and analyzed can provide a sound basis for defending actions or decisions in courts of law, especially when they are used as a guide for decision-making, before final decisions have been made. Some specific illustrations of the large variety of statistical applications follow.

Quality improvement — There is no better proof of the value of statistics than its actual applications in various fields. Its foremost applications in recent years have been in the field of quality improvement and process control, as a result of the efforts of Dr. W. Edwards Deming, Dr. J. M Juran and other quality professionals throughout the United States and the world. A number of companies, both large and small, have been improving the quality of their products and services, and thereby competing more successfully in the global market place.*

While Statistical Process Control (Chapter 11), a major element of *Total Quality Management* (TQM), is revolutionizing the field of quality management, with associated improvements in productivity, many other fields of endeavor are also depending on statistics to improve management. Some of these are described below.

Mail order business — Mail order houses afford a good example of short-range planning. Some mail-order houses estimate the amount of business they will be required to handle the entire week on the basis of the weight of their mail on Monday. Techniques of correlation and regression analysis (Chapter 12) are used in this application.

Traffic management — Railroad, airline, and bus companies gather and analyze statistics on passenger traffic daily, weekly, and monthly to estimate in advance the service requirements at different locations, on different routes, and for different seasons of the year. They rely on a variety of statistical methods, such as averages, measures of variation, time series, and correlation and regression analyses for their guidance.

Advertising — Advertising departments of many large organizations gather statistics to compare the effectiveness of alternate methods and outlets of advertising. Sampling and probability principles are used in gathering essential data and other techniques are employed to measure response, costs, potential sales, and net return.

Life insurance — Life insurance companies exist on statistics, because their annual premiums or rates are fixed on the basis of statistical data that show the number of persons in a given group who are expected to survive at given ages. Use is made of simple ratios or percentages derived from life experience data and applied to the relevant population.

Consumer preferences — Some parts of the automobiles we own are a result of statistical surveys on consumers' preferences that guided the automobile manufacturers to meet general demand for these characteristics. What is involved in these analyses? Data are collected by sample surveys which are analyzed for customer preferences.

A large variety of other applications of statistical techniques are made in the private sector in such fields as medical research,

---

*Based on numerous articles of the American Society for Quality Control in their *Quality Progress* magazine and other sources.

management and labor relations, market planning, education, financial control, inventory control, and public opinion assessment.

In Government

The following are some examples of statistical applications in the government, with particular emphasis on management problems in the Federal Government.

Inventory valuation — The question before a former Commissioner of the Social Security Administration was whether or not to authorize the Internal Revenue Service to destroy a file of some seven million self-employment income tax reports prepared for a given year. Since these reports also provide the earnings and tax information needed under the Social Security record program, the question before the Commissioner really was: Has the Internal Revenue Service transmitted to the Social Security Administration all the social security tear-off sheets which contain the necessary earnings credits for self-employed persons? If not, these self-employed persons would lose social security credits.

To provide a basis for the Commissioner's decision, a random sample of 2,000 of the waiting-to-be-destroyed tax reports was examined. It indicated that nearly 0.6% (six tenths of one percent) of the returns processed for income tax purposes had not been transmitted to the Social Security Administration. This was such a small percentage of under-transmittal that at first it did not appear to be a significant problem to destroy the entire file and thereby provide IRS immediate filing space for other incoming reports. However, when the percentage is applied to the universe total of seven million returns, it meant that about 40,000 self-employed persons (i.e., 0.6% multiplied by 7 million returns) would suffer a loss of earnings credits. The appropriate decision was to screen the entire file to identify the unreported records.*

Estimating income tax liability — In Chicago some years ago, the Internal Revenue Service caught up with a gambling house which had not paid income tax for the 3 prior years. The operators claimed that they did not make a profit sufficient to pay taxes. However, confiscated stubs of betting tickets (such as those used for football pools) provided a basis, by use of the law of probability, for estimating the operators' gross profit based on the total amount of money placed in bets. A tax assessment of about $100,000 was made to which was added the appropriate amount of interest and penalty.

---

*Actual 100% screening located 38,900 self-employed reports.

Rate-making — Another type of rate-making application is typified by the U.S. Postal Service sampling systems. Two different random samples provide the basic data to guide the setting of postage rates. One random sampling system collects data on revenue earned by each class of mail processed by the postal establishment. Another random sample (random time sample) collects data on the cost of in-house processing of each class of mail. The ratio obtained by dividing estimated revenue by the estimated direct costs of processing each class of mail indicates whether or not a class of mail is breaking even (ratio of one), losing (ratio of less than one), or making a profit (ratio in excess of one). These findings provide a basis for recommended postal rate changes.

Billing for services rendered — The Federal Telecommunications System (FTS) for long distance calls is administered by the General Services Administration (GSA), but each agency was to be billed for its share of usage of the system. Since the total number of messages completed through the system exceeded 100 million a year, it would have been prohibitively expensive to maintain a record of each agency's share of this total. Therefore, a random sampling of circuits and time was designed which provided estimates of the number of long distance messages completed by each agency. Thus, with but a fraction of the would-be cost of maintaining a 100% message-count system, the sampling system provided a sound basis for billing each agency for its equitable share of the total FTS cost.

Voucher examination — An analysis was made by a number of government agencies to determine the cost of examining vouchers for monetary accuracy and the comparable monetary return for this investment. It was found that the cost of examining small vouchers (under $1,000) far exceeded the monetary return. Thus, a number of agencies, such as the Department of Health and Human Services, the Internal Revenue Service, the Department of Agriculture, and the U.S. Postal Service adopted random sampling to examine a sample of vouchers and pay the rest outright. The size of the sample used to examine these vouchers varies from agency to agency, but the fact remains that reductions in the total government cost for voucher examination have been achieved through the use of random sampling.

Productivity measurement — An application of random time sampling was made by the General Accounting Office (GAO) in auditing a multi-million dollar contract to determine the efficiency of the contractor's use of operational personnel charged to the contract. GAO auditors were permitted by plant management and labor to observe, at random moments of time, the activity of employees working on the contract. From this *random time sampling* study, it was determined that there was an inordinate amount of idle waiting time on the part of production assembly employees and also that a relatively large percentage of employees were absent from their work stations. Substantial improvements in productivity, as well as cost reductions, were achieved when the contractor adjusted for the use of personnel on the contract.

Auditing — Random sampling and other statistical techniques play an important role in many auditing activities conducted by such agencies as the Internal Revenue Service, Army Audit Division, Defense Contract Audit Agency, and Offices of Inspector Generals in various government agencies throughout the United States.

Quality of service — Since the days of Benjamin Franklin , when he served as the first Postmaster General, the U.S. Postal Service had no sound statistical information on the length of time used to deliver mail of various types. In 1970, the U.S. Postal Service designed, for the first time in postal service history, a comprehensive random sampling system which provides reliable data on the amount of time which elapses from the time of stamp cancellation of a piece of mail to its delivery. These data also are compiled by originating and destination city for large cities. Thus, for example, a recent quarterly report showed that first-class mail required an average of 1.6 days for delivery (exclusive of holidays and time for pickup from individual mail boxes) and that 97% of this class of mail was delivered within 3 days. Delivery of first class mail from New York to Chicago averaged 2.3 days, and from Washington to New York City 1.5 days.

Universal Application of Statistics

It is apparent from these examples and many other applications that statistics and statistical methods can be used with good results in practically every field of human endeavor. Uses abound in management, short-range forecasting, productivity measurement, quality improvement, marketing, advertising, medical research, labor-management negotiation, financial control, personnel classification, inventory control, and auditing.

In concluding this chapter, we quote a person who has experienced the benefits of statistical applications.*

"A very little consideration shows that there is scarcely a hole or corner of modern life which could not find some application, however simple, for statistical theory and show a profit as a result.

"It has something to offer the person who specializes in any of the branches of management. It offers assistance to the person responsible for purchasing and quality management. In the hands of the cost accountant or industrial engineer or management analyst, it acts as a hone to sharpen traditional tools and serves as a mechanism for generating additional information and insight. ...

"In the research laboratory it is a powerful adjunct, offering optimum criteria for the assessment of data, eliminating wishful thinking, and yielding principles of experimental design which face the fact of experimental error and make possible the highly desirable objective of experimenting with a great diversity of combinations of the factors under test. Perhaps most important of all, it enables research to leave the controlled conditions of the laboratory and proceed in the rough and tumble of the real world where, after all, the results of experimental work have finally to be turned into work processes reasonably immune from trouble."

Summary

This chapter introduces the field of statistics, its scope and widespread applicability to practically all fields of endeavor, with particular emphasis on management uses. Statistics deals with methods of collecting, summarizing, analyzing and presenting quantitative (numeric) data.

The validity and reliability of quantitative data for decision-making are supported by a body of principles. Among them are the law of *universal variation*, *normal distribution*, *probability*, and *statistical regularity or stability of mass data*. Analytical tools mentioned in this chapter include percentages, rates, averages, and measures of variation. In addition, some qualifications and cautions in the use of statistics are given as a guide to avoiding its misuse. Numerous examples are given to illustrate the large variety of its applications.

Overall, this chapter exhorts present and future managers, analysts, researchers, technicians, and professionals in all fields to

---

*M.J. Moroney, *Facts from Figures*, Penguin Ltd., 1951, pages 460-461 (edited slightly).

devote some time to the study and use of statistics and statistical reasoning. Statistics offers potential economies and management improvements in a wide variety of situations.

Problems

1. The XYZ University had compiled the following statistics on the number of students who withdrew from school during the fall term after having registered:

Year	Number registered	Number withdrawn
1987	2,208	46
1988	2,350	47
1989	2,180	48
1990	2,200	49
1991	2,340	50
1992	2,300	56
1993	2,450	53
1994	2,532	41

    (a) Would you be able to tell the registrar of that school which students would withdraw in the fall term of the next year, if the total registration for that year were 3,000?

    (b) Would you be able to estimate the number of withdrawals after registration for the above fall term?

    (c) On what principle of statistics presented in this chapter did you base your answer to (b)?

    (d) What is your estimate of the number of withdrawals? Explain how you made it.

    (e) What other elements of statistics described in this chapter does this problem illustrate?

2. The ABC Bank has found from its records for the past 3 years that about 1 percent of the personal checking accounts in the bank are charged with a service charge each month.

    (a) On what basis can they predict the number of the personal checking accounts that will be reduced by a service charge next month?

(b) Can they specify the individual accounts that will be charged with a service charge next month? Why?

(c) By what method might they achieve the objective in (b)?

3. On the average, it was found that 49 persons out of 50 survive a given type of operation. Since the last 49 patients operated on for this ailment lived, what is probability that the next person will not make it? Explain.

4. A study was made to determine the average mileage one can drive on a gallon of gas in a given make of car. The result was presented as 18.348 miles per gallon. Criticize this method of presentation.

5. "The airplane is a more dangerous mode of transportation than the train because more deaths result from this mode of travel." True or false? Explain.

6. What are the chances of throwing an "ace" in a single throw of an honest die? Assuming you have already thrown an ace, what are the chances of throwing an ace on the next throw?

7. What are the chances of winning on a given number on a perfect roulette wheel which has 50 different numbers?

8. Indicate in which of the following activities statistical methods may be used effectively:

(a) In grading different scientists in their work.

(b) In measuring the extent to which student grades differ in a college entrance examination.

(c) In determining which grade of chocolate bar is better.

(d) In ranking a group of computer data-entry operators by productivity.

9. Ms. Davidson, a recently hired salesperson in the company, was able to sell policies to 30 percent of her prospects in the first 6 months, while Mr. Johnson, an "old timer" with the company, sold policies to only 15 percent of his prospects during that period. This proves that:

(a) Ms. Davidson is a better salesperson than Mr. Johnson.

(b) That Mr. Johnson is a better salesperson because he has been with the company a longer time.

Criticize these conclusions.

10. Statistics have shown that in a given State a drought has occurred every seventh year in the past 27 years. Since the past 6 years did not experience a drought, preparations should be made for another drought. True or false? Explain.

11. The following tabulation shows, without specifying, the accident rates per 1,000 workers in the automobile manufacturing industry and in all other manufacturing industries in the United States combined during the past 10 years (hypothetical data):

Year	A	B
1993	4.2	3.6
1992	4.8	3.8
1991	4.0	3.9
1990	3.8	3.7
1989	2.7	3.6
1988	5.1	3.5
1987	4.9	3.4
1986	3.7	3.9
1985	3.2	3.7
1984	5.4	3.5

(a) Which column of accident rates probably represents the automobile industry and which all other manufacturing industries?

(b) What is the basic principle of statistics which guided your choice?

12. A given lot of 10,000 safety pins was inspected to determine its quality. Two out of a sample of five pins inspected were found to be defective.

(a) Can it be concluded that the lot is of poor quality? Why?

(b) Which of the limitations of statistics does this problem illustrate?

13. Give a specific illustration of quantifying by means of "variables" and one by means of "attributes."

14. Describe a fictitious or real application of one of the statistical methods described in this chapter.

Chapter 2

Conducting a Statistical Survey

"Scientific data are not taken for museum pieces; they are taken as a basis for doing something. If nothing is to be done with the data, then there is no use collecting any. The ultimate purpose of taking data is to provide a basis for action or a recommendation for action. The step intermediate between the collection of data and the action is prediction."[*]

To make the fullest possible use of the science of statistics for more informed decision-making, management must first be able to recognize if a problem is statistical in nature. If a problem can be reduced to quantitative terms, an objective decision can be made by an analysis of the data collected on it. Many managers recognize statistical problems, but without an appreciation of the technical elements of data collection and data analysis, they may assign the task of collecting the needed data to their immediate administrative staff or other office staff, whether or not that staff is skilled in collecting and analyzing statistics. The results often can be disappointing (or worse) for there is many a slip between the recognition of a statistical problem and the proper collection, processing, analysis, and use of the data.

One purpose of this chapter is to illustrate the importance of planning a statistical survey in a systematic, logical way that recognizes the technical problems that need to be resolved when compiling, analyzing, and interpreting statistical data. It is hoped that it will thus alert management that special skills and training are necessary to understand and deal with data collection and related statistical problems.

Another purpose of this chapter is to describe several possible ways of quantifying problems so that management will be in a better position to recognize that practically all problems can be dealt with

---

[*] W. Edwards Deming, "On a Classification of the Problems of Statistical Inference," *Journal of the American Statistical Association*, Vol.37, pages 173-185, June 1942.

statistically and thus be encouraged to evaluate problems objectively. In addition, the chapter describes some of the pitfalls in collecting accurate and representative data, and some of the ways to overcome these problems.

A Statistical Problem and How to Deal With It

A medical service agency under contract with the government was found by a government audit to have an unacceptable rate of errors in adjudicating Medicare claims. The medical service agency was told that they would lose their contract unless they improved the quality of their claims adjudication to an acceptable level within six months, at which time a new audit would be made of their performance.

How should the medical service agency deal with this problem? The manager of the Medicare department of that agency first thought of meeting with the 10 claims adjudicators to exhort them to do better, warning them that they stand to lose their jobs unless they improve. After thinking further, the manager decided that a fact-finding survey may be needed first to see what exactly is causing the problem. Finally, the manager decided to consult an experienced statistician about possible ways of solving the problem and avoiding the loss of the contract.

The statistician advised that this clearly was a statistical problem requiring a special fact-finding survey. The statistician further stated that no fact-finding survey should be undertaken unless the problem is first formulated, before any data collection effort is undertaken, referring to a significant statement once made by Professor Albert Einstein, namely, *to formulate the problem is often more than half its solution.*

The importance of clarifying the problem also is illustrated in Margaret L. Jones' article on "A New Science of Thinking," published some years ago (but still valid today) in *Dun's Review and Modern Industry,* as follows (with slight editorial changes):

"Irving J. Lee, noted general semanticist, author and lecturer, mentioned a small incident he recently witnessed.

"A vice-president gave some precisely worded instructions to one of his department heads. The department head listened attentively, nodded, and left the office. Lee caught up with the department head soon afterwards, and asked, 'Do you know clearly what the boss wants?' Hesitating a moment, the department head replied, 'No, to tell the truth, I don't.' 'Well then.' said Lee, 'Why not go back and clear the thing up?' 'Do you think I am crazy?' was the retort.

"As happens in many places, the instructions will be carried out as the department head understood [or interpreted] them, but not necessarily as the boss may have intended, and the job will be slightly bungled. Everyone will wonder later why things did not click as expected."

Steps in Conducting a Survey

Using the foregoing general statement of the Medicare claims adjudication problem we now proceed to describe the steps required to conduct a statistical survey.

First step — Clarify the problem

What are some specific pointers for clarifying the problem? First, we must be sure that we understand what the problem is. Here, the agency is threatened with losing an important contract unless the claims adjudication error-rate is reduced substantially.

Once the basic problem is understood, a number of possible explanations (hypotheses) for it should be formulated. These possible explanations then should be expressed in writing as a list of questions to be answered. This is an extremely important part of clarifying the problem because it gives direction to the succeeding steps, which are aimed at answering the questions in a way that should shed light on the problem and provide a basis for appropriate action. Successful framing of the questions relevant to the problem involves the collaborative efforts of management, the study team, and the statistical consultant if one is used.

Because some problems are relatively simple and others complex, some problems require less consultation and others more consultation with management. Even the simplest problems need to be discussed first, however, to assure a meeting of minds between management and the survey team. For, if a single important part of a problem is not understood, the final results can often be of limited use for decision-making. Even the meaning of words used in the listed questions must be clarified or defined.

In our example, the statistical consultant pointed out that unless the causes and the sources of the overall high error rate were determined, little progress could be possible in improving the quality of the claims adjudication process. The statistician, the manager, and the study team, working together, decided that quantitative data were needed (by use of sampling) on the number and percent of all the errors that were made by each claims adjudicator (source of error), categorized by each type (cause) of error. Ultimately, the potential solution to the problem lay in statistical analysis of relevant data based on the following table format:

Table 2.1 (Format Only)
Distribution of error cases, by source and cause of error

Source of error	Cause of error			
	Total	#1	#2	#3
Total				
Employee 1 Employee 2 Etc.				

When the figures for this basic table are filled in, as shown later, a relatively simple analysis can be made of the basic data by computing the percentage of all errors committed by each employee and for each possible type or cause of error. Types or causes of errors could include misinterpretation of the adjudication instructions, lack of care, arithmetical errors, use of the wrong formulas, etc. It would appear logical to attack the problem where it is worst and to take corrective action on the most numerous causes and sources of errors.

Another essential set of calculations would determine the error rate, or percentage of errors made, by each employee. This error-rate is obtainable for each adjudicator by simply dividing the number of errors made by the number of claims that person adjudicated. Still another type of data needed would be on the difficulty of the case-load assigned to each employee; that is, which, if any, of the employees were given more technically-involved claims and which were assigned simpler claims.

Second step — Plan the data collection methods

Various questions arise regarding the collection of data. For example, we need to know how important the basic problem is to the organization and how accurate the results need to be. We also need to know how long management can wait to get the final results, and how much it is able or willing to spend on the study. This information will help to determine the methods of data collection to be used and the amount of detailed data to be collected. It will also lead to decisions regarding the size of sample and the method of selecting the sample, if sampling rather than a complete-count method should be used.

Most of these decisions involve tradeoffs among the practical realities of deadlines and the availability of staff and funds balanced against the extent of detailed data desired as well as the accuracy and confidence required in the end results. Finally, based on these decisions, costs can be estimated and management's approval of funds and staff to allocate to the survey can be obtained or negotiated.

In the case of the medical service agency, for example, the method of quantifying the problem — that is, the method of collecting data relevant to the problem — was a *review by independent reviewers* of the accuracy of adjudicated claims completed by each of the 10 adjudicators. In consideration of the limited time for data collection, a decision was made to have the reviewers complete their reviews during the next four weeks based on a random sample of adjudicated claims. The size of the workload and time-table were unavoidably influenced by the mandate that substantial improvement in quality must be shown within six months.

The above method of quantifying the problem could be classified as a review of performance by agency employees. In general, there are several other ways of collecting data to quantify problems. These include the use of *mail questionnaires* or *personal interviewes,* taking *measurements,* making *observations* and recording what has been seen, and *assigning numeric weights* or rankings based on judgment (for example, rating the performance of ice skaters in the Olympics on a scale of one to ten). These are all *primary* methods of quantifying, i.e., they are all used for obtaining original quantitative data. Alternatively, *secondary* data, i.e., data already collected, may be used if appropriate for the problem at hand.

So far, we have addressed only indirectly the critical question of what kind of data to collect, that is, what characteristics to *measure* that are most useful for analyzing the problem at hand. A large variety of useful data range from measures of cost, quality, efficiency and productivity to measures of profitability, judgmental preferences, political opinions, etc. The choice of the characteristics to measure depends on the most relevant and useful data for the problem at hand. In complex problems, extensive communication and collaboration between management and the statistical survey team is necessary to define and agree on the approach and characteristics that are most important.

Other elements that need to be considered in conducting a statistical survey are:

(1) Method of selecting the sample and the size of the sample to be used — If time and cost constraints exist, use of sampling is dictated; therefore, the method of random selection needs to be chosen, as discussed in Chapter 7. In addition, the size of the sample (or the number of causes to be measured or observed) has to be determined. This determination must conform with management's desire for reasonable reliability of the results and confidence in using them. (See Chapter 9 for methods of determining sample size.)

(2) Designing the data collection instrument(s) — Mail questionaires, interview schedules, and recording forms are some of the choices. If it is decided to collect the data by mail, the questionnaire to be used for mailing has to be constructed. Similarly, if a personal interview is to be used, the appropriate interview schedule has to be developed. If data are to be recorded from agency records or from observation or measurement, an appropriate recording form or tally sheet needs to be set up. Experience has shown that errors made by data-collectors are often a more serious problem than the probable error caused by sampling. While some human errors are unavoidable, a major cause of such errors is a poorly designed data-collection or data-recording form. In planning and developing the recording form, therefore, due consideration must be given to such matters as adequate spacing, logical arrangement of the entry-items, precoding, etc. In addition, the reporting form usually should be accompanied by a set of clearly written instructions, definition of classifications and appropriate codes.

(3) Developing the mailing or contact list — If a mail questionnaire survey is to be conducted, the appropriate mailing list has to be obtained. If personal interviews have to be made, the contact list or the method of locating the persons or families to be interviewed has to be determined.

(4) Quality control of the basic data — Errors of omission or commission are always a threat to accuracy. Therefore, methods of assuring the accuracy and completeness of the incoming reports must be developed. The choice to use computers or individuals to edit the raw data depends on the volume of data. If data entry is done manually, plans for assuring the accuracy of the data input must be made. If data entry is done electronically, all components, from the survey instrument to the analysis program, must be checked for appropriateness and compatibility.

(5) Planning the project with respect to staffing, training, and scheduling — Appropriate staff has to be selected and trained for handling the various tasks in conducting the survey. Required time schedules have to be established and controlled to avoid slippage.

(6) Conducting a pilot study — An essential step before implementing a large-scale survey is conducting a small-scale test of the planned survey instruments and methodology. The *pilot sample* can uncover problems early and help to make necessary revisions and adjustments. For example, in a mail survey it can indicate the extent of the probable non-response rate and thus adjust the incentives for response or increase the preplanned size of the sample. It also can indicate in advance other bugs or problems to deal with; it is too late to correct them during the full scale survey.

Third step — Implement the plans

After the plans and necessary arrangements and adjustments in the survey design have been made, the work of collection may start. This usually involves a tangible operation, no matter which method of collection is used. In the foregoing adjudication error-rate problem, for example, it was decided to review the adjudicators' work on a random sample of the claims in the preceding four weeks in order to meet time constraints imposed by the government agency. This required selecting the cases to be reviewed, identifying the adjudicator, and independently reviewing each case for type or cause of error.

Fourth step — Process the data

As part of the collection and verification process, there usually accumulates in the office a mass of papers or raw data, such as returned questionnaires, filled-out schedules, or recording forms, which have to be arrayed, summarized, or organized, so that analytical tables or charts may be developed to reveal the required information. This process, known as summarization or tabulation of data, is possible in one of two ways or in combination — manually (hand tallying) or mechanically (machine tabulation). It should be noted that these tabulations (in the form of table shells) and summarizations should have been planned before the data were collected, during problem formulation. (See Table 2.1). In our claims adjudication problem the tabulations were made by hand because of the relatively small volume of records included in the sample.

Fifth step — Analyze the data

While some tentative analysis of the data may take place in earlier steps, usually the rigorous, more systematic analysis comes after the data have been tabulated and grouped in accordance with previously planned table formats. The grouping and tabulation should be so designed that they yield answers to the questions or hypotheses related to the objectives of the study. Methods of analysis may be of the simplest type, such as the computation of percentages, ratios, or averages. (These relatively simple statistical tools are helpful in solving many management problems, provided the data assembled are appropriate and sufficiently accurate for the purpose.) Several of the more commonly used statistical methods of analysis (frequency distributions, averages, measures of variation, and correlation and regression analysis) are described in subsequent chapters.

Suppose that in step 4 (data processing) we tabulated the data prespecified in Table 2.1 showing the information needed for our Medicare adjudication problem. With these data, we can readily determine the most frequent sources and types of errors by use of percentages. To illustrate this method of analyzing data, the numerical figures on source of the errors are converted into percentages relative to their total. In percentage form, the data tell a clear story of the main sources of the problem.

Table 2.1

Distribution of claims adjudication errors, by source (employee)
and type of errors, November 1 - November 26, 1993

Source of error	Cause of error				Percent of total
	Total	#1	#2	#3	
Total	82	22	26	34	100
Employee 1	4	1	1	2	4.9
Employee 2	9	1	3	5	11
Employee 3	7	3	1	3	8.5
Employee 4	19	5	7	7	23.2
Employee 5	11	3	3	5	13.4
Employee 6	10	2	3	5	12.2
Employee 7	6	1	1	4	7.3
Employee 8	5	2	2	1	6.1
Employee 9	1	0	1	0	1.2
Employee 10	10	4	4	2	12.2

Source: Hypothetical results of review of adjudicated claims by reviewers
of Medical Services Company

The percentages in the extreme right of Table 2.1 tell us that
employee #4 was the primary source of errors (23.2 %) and employees
#5, #6 and #10, collectively caused nearly 38% of the additional errors.
It seems clear that these employees need to be retrained or helped to
cut down their error rate. Furthermore, analyzing the reasons for their
high error rate (by running percentages horizontally) we would find
that error type #3 is the predominant reason for their poor performance. Effective remedial action directed at preventing this type or
cause of errors likely will improve future quality and thus help to
retain the contract.

Sixth step — Present the final results

At the conclusion of the analysis, the findings have to be presented
to management for its guidance in decision-making. There are several
ways of presenting findings (see Chapter 14). An informal personal
report on the findings from the survey may be made to management,

and this alone may be sufficient to provide the key facts or shed light on the problem. On the other hand, a formal presentation of the findings may be required. In formally reporting to management, the presentation may be either a written report describing the methods of the survey and giving an analysis of the results; or it may be a self explanatory, simple analytical table (or tables) systematically set up so that management can see the results clearly; or it may be several graphs or charts that present the major findings visually. Some reports to management may combine all three methods of presentation. Some may be brief and simply give a summary of the key findings; others may be quite detailed, describing the findings and all the administrative and technical aspects of the survey. The specific choice of reporting depends upon the relationship between management and the survey team, management's inclination or preference for one or another type of final report, the importance of the study and its intended uses, and even the volume of detailed data collected.

Quick Summary of Steps

From the foregoing, it is hoped that the major steps and technical skills in conducting a statistical survey or investigation are clear. Nevertheless, here is a quick summary:

Step 1. Clarify the problem with management or the responsible person or group, taking particular pains to set up several possible solutions or questions that are closely related to the problem and can be answered by relevant data to be collected in subsequent steps.

Step 2. Plan and organize the survey design and make the necessary arrangements for staffing, training, time schedules, and so forth. Do not overlook conducting a small scale pilot study first to shed light on any problems which may be rectified before they show up later in the full-scale survey.

Step 3. Collect the data by sampling or complete count, after problems disclosed by the pilot study are ironed out. Record data from agency records, or by other methods (such as direct measurements, observation, mail questionnaires, personal interviews, or ranking).

Step 4. Process the data to detect and correct errors, to assure their quality and to compile the basic pre-planned tables.

Step 5. Analyze the data for substantive information, using appropriate statistical methods.

Step 6. Present the results of the survey either orally, in writing, in tables, in charts, or in any combination of these.

Relationship Between the Steps in a Statistical Survey and the Scientific Method

The logical sequence of major steps followed in conducting a statistical investigation bears a close similarity to the scientific method of arriving at conclusions from actual facts and not from opinion or guesswork. Specifically, the scientific method starts out with a clearly stated problem and the construction of a set of plausible hypotheses that may shed light on the problem. An experiment then is designed to test the hypotheses for acceptability. Data are collected and verified as to accuracy, grouped, tabulated and analyzed. From an analysis of the data the hypotheses are accepted or rejected, and the results are presented for action or for the record and future use. Thus, any efficient problem-solving method, whether it is in business or government, is often referred to as the scientific method.

Methods of Quantifying a Process or Problem

In our hypothetical management problem we started out with the premise that management had recognized the problem as statistical in nature, that is, as a problem dealing with quality of adjudication that could be reduced to quantitative terms and analyzed objectively. Many a management problem goes unsolved or is dealt with by judgment, guess, or opinion simply because the problem is not recognized as statistical in nature. There may be a belief that the problem cannot be quantified. With a little imagination, and help based on the methods discussed in this section, *practically all* management problems can be reduced to quantitative or numerical terms, if worthwhile.

There are six ways to quantify a problem or a process, as described in the following few paragraphs.

1. Extracting data from the organization's records

Probably the easiest way of quantifying is by recording data from the available records of the organization. Thus, it is relatively simple for an organization to determine the age distribution of its personnel or the number of its skilled, semiskilled, and unskilled workers. This method of quantifying involves reference to accessible data files and records on individual cases or transactions. Such data can be recorded from an organization's records, summarized, tabulated, and analyzed, to keep management informed on the characteristics of the organization's employees, supplies, operations, productivity, sales, and so forth.

2. Recording measurements

Many management problems exist where the source for the data is either a person or a machine performing an operation such as producing a product or performing a service, or where a commodity or piece of material is purchased or rented by the organization. In these or related instances, quantifying is done by measurement. The application of statistics in the field of quality management depends heavily on measurement. Thus, for example, the length of metal strips for a given type of umbrella coming off a production process can be obtained by measurement; the thickness of bolts produced by a precision machine can be measured with a measuring gauge; the length of strips of cloth to be used for coat sleeves cut by persons in a clothing factory can be measured for both length and width; similarly the timeliness of providing a service to the public or internal management can be measured.

3. Recording observations

Data frequently can be collected without measurement simply by observing and recording what has been observed as being of one type or another or as possessing or not possessing a given attribute. Observations can be made, for example, on whether floor managers in a department store supervise activities for which they are responsible and how they otherwise spend their work day. Observations can be made of what particular types of work certain office employees perform, and how much time they spend on each activity can be estimated by use of random-time-observation sampling.

4. Using the mail questionnaire

In the mail survey, a questionnaire (see Figure 2.1 as an example) is distributed to the persons or organizations who are believed to have the needed information and a completed survey form, usually returned through the mail, is requested. When a questionnaire is mailed to an individual's home or office, the recipient becomes the most important cog in the wheel of obtaining statistical data, for the success of the survey depends upon receiving the required information from the respondent. Consequently, all possible effort (such as offering an incentive to reply) should be concentrated on getting the individual to cooperate and give the correct information. Since in a mail survey we are not there in person to obtain the information, to explain and observe, the questions have to be made clear and simple for the individual to reply correctly, objectively, and to the point. A more detailed guideline for constructing good mail questionnaires is given in the section, "Elements of Good Questionnaires."

5. Personal interviews

When data have to be collected by a personal interview, a schedule or guide is developed for use by the interviewer on which to record the required information during a personal meeting with the respondent. The schedule is similar in nature to a questionnaire, but it may contain many more, and more searching, questions than a mail questionnaire, because the risks of not getting valid responses are generally much smaller than by the questionairre method. See Figure 2.2 for a sample interview schedule.

There are many guidelines for collecting data by personal interviewing techniques. Enumerators or interviewers need to be trained in a uniform way; the schedule for data-entry has to be constructed with adequate coding and appropriate guiding instructions; the methods of selecting the individuals to be interviewed has to be designated in advance. These and other guidelines related to interviewing are beyond the scope of this book, but other publications deal with them in more detail.*

---

* Jahoda, Duetsch, and Cook, *Research Methods in Social Relations, Part I,* Dryden Press, Inc., 1951 or subsequent reprints. Also, Herbert H. Hyman, et al, *Interviewing in Social Research,* U. of Chicago Press, 1954.

Figure 2.1 — Sample Mail Questionnaire

U.S. Bureau of the Census User Questionnaire

Dear user:
In an effort to improve the quality of this report, the following questionnaire has been included for your comments so we may direct our efforts to providing the information most needed by you, the user. Please take a few moments to fill out this questionnaire. To mail the questionnaire, fold A to A and fold B to B, then tape and drop it in the mail, postage paid. Your comments can be faxed to us on 301-763-8531. Thank you for your suggestions and cooperation.

Current Population Reports, P60-188
Income, Poverty, and Valuation of Noncash Benefits: 1933

1. What is your organizational affiliation?

☐ **Federal Government**
☐ **State/Local Government**

☐ **Educational institution** Mark (X) one
    ☐ Student
    ☐ Faculty
    ☐ Administration

☐ **Private Organization** Mark (X) one
    ☐ Media/information service
    ☐ Trade Association
    ☐ Marketing research
    ☐ Other — Please specify

    ☐ Legal firm
    ☐ Professional Association

2. Are you a frequent user of reports issued in this series?
    ☐ First time user   ☐ Infrequent   ☐ Frequent/routine user

3. Are you a user of similar data from: *Mark (X) all that apply.*
    ☐ Other Census Bureau reports
    ☐ Reports issued by other government agencies
    Please specify organization and report title

    ☐ Reports issued by private, non government organizations
    Please specify organization and report title

4. *The following asks two questions about specific sections of the report.*

Was the section useful to you? *(Did it contain information you were looking for?)*

Was the section easy to understand and use?

Please answer each question using the scale provided. Four (4) indicates useful or easy to understand; one (1) indicates not useful or hard to understand. Check the box of the item was not used or is not applicable to you.

		Usefulness				Easy to understand				Not used or not applicable
		Low			High	Low			High	
Analytical:	Text — Introduction	1☐	2☐	3☐	4☐	1☐	2☐	3☐	4☐	☐
	Charts	1☐	2☐	3☐	4☐	1☐	2☐	3☐	4☐	☐
	Text tables	1☐	2☐	3☐	4☐	1☐	2☐	3☐	4☐	☐
Appendixes:	Definitions or Explanations	1☐	2☐	3☐	4☐	1☐	2☐	3☐	4☐	☐
	Sampling or Statistical Statements	1☐	2☐	3☐	4☐	1☐	2☐	3☐	4☐	☐
Detailed or reference tables		1☐	2☐	3☐	4☐	1☐	2☐	3☐	4☐	☐
Introductory sections: (e.g., content and use)		1☐	2☐	3☐	4☐	1☐	2☐	3☐	4☐	☐

Figure 2.2 — Sample Interview Schedule or Guide

SOUTH STREET INTERVIEW GUIDE

Hi! I'm a student at Drexel University and we are doing a survey for South Street area businesses and residents. Would you please take a few moments to answer our survey?

1. How did you get to South Street?
    ☐ Car   ☐ Bus   ☐ Bike   ☐ Subway   ☐ Train   ☐ Walk

2. How often do you visit South Street?
    ☐ Times/Wk.   ☐ Times/Mo.   ☐ Times/Yr.   ☐ Other _____

3. What days and at what times do you generally visit South Street? *(Check all that apply)*

	Mon	Tues	Wed	Thurs	Fri	Sat	Sun
Morning	☐	☐	☐	☐	☐	☐	☐
12-3P	☐	☐	☐	☐	☐	☐	☐
3-6P	☐	☐	☐	☐	☐	☐	☐
6-9P	☐	☐	☐	☐	☐	☐	☐
9-12P	☐	☐	☐	☐	☐	☐	☐

4. Average time spent in the South Street area per visit (hours) _____

5. How often have you come to South Street during the past six months for each of the following reasons? *(Check all that apply)*

	7 or more	4-6	1-3	0
a. Fast Food/Take Out	☐	☐	☐	☐
b. Restaurant/Dining	☐	☐	☐	☐
c. Clothes, gifts, & merch.	☐	☐	☐	☐
d. Groceries/Necessities	☐	☐	☐	☐
e. Clubs/Bars	☐	☐	☐	☐
f. Socialize/Meet people	☐	☐	☐	☐
g. Other	☐	☐	☐	☐

6. Please identify two aspects of South Street which appeal to you about coming here. *(Circle two items)*

    Convenient location   Liveliness   Prices   Security/Safety

    Transportation/accessibility   Variety of merchants   Sanitation   Other _____

7. Are you aware of the barricades which stop traffic along South Street from 8th to Front?
    ☐ Yes   ☐ No
    Do they   encourage you to come to South Street,   or   deter you?   *(circle one)*

8. What is your current age?
    ☐ Under 18   ☐ 18-21   ☐ 22-25   ☐ 26-29   ☐ 30-39   ☐ 40-49   ☐ 50 or over

9. What is your occupation? _____

10. What is your education level?
    ☐ Some High School   ☐ Some College   ☐ Post College
    ☐ High School Grad   ☐ College Grad   ☐ Other _____

11. What is your current Zip Code? _____   Gender of respondent: ☐ M   ☐ F

THANK YOU **FOR YOUR TIME.** DO YOU HAVE ANY OTHER COMMENTS?

_____
_____

• •

Interviewer _____   Survey No. _____

Day _____ Date _____ Time _____ Location _____

Weather _____   Miscellaneous _____

6. Assignment of weights or rankings

As a last resort, when none of the foregoing methods of quantifying are applicable, a special way of converting an activity to quantitative form is available by use of weights or ranking. Many applications of statistics to management problems are being made possible by judgmentally assigning a numeric rank to activities that are otherwise not measurable but can be subjectively or judgmentally assessed. For example, the winner in a prize-fight ending in a decision is determined by the cumulative numbers judgmentally assigned to each fighter at the end of each round by the three judges. The winner in a beauty contest is similarly chosen by the combined numerical ratings judgmentally assigned by the judges to each performance of the contestants; the medal winners in ice skating contests or dancing contests are determined by numeric weights assigned by the judges. While this method depends on the subjective assessments by the judges, nevertheless the final decisions are based on quantified data.

Elements of Good Questionnaires*

To achieve a reasonably successful mail survey, the sampler must aim for a high response rate and thus reduce expensive follow-up costs. Also, to minimize the cost of coding responses, the questionnaire should have pre-coded answers wherever possible. Finally, clarity and simplicity of the questions is more likely to yield usable results.

The achieve these and other objectives, the following are some guidelines to consider:

(1) Arouse interest — Why should the recipient of the questionnaire respond? Offer some incentive to respond. Sometimes offering a copy of the resulting statistics, a monetary award, or some other attractive item may lead to response cooperation. Figuring out the most appropriate way of arousing interest is a challenge to the imagination.**

(2) Provide return postage — Do not impose on the respondents to pay the return postage.

---

*These apply mostly to mail questionnaires.
**Arthur H. Dix, "Mail Questionnaires Won't Pull Unless You Tell and Sell and Flatter," *Industrial Marketing*, December 1951.

(3) **Keep questionnaire brief** — Many mail surveys are doomed to failure because too much information is requested. All efforts should be made to reduce the number of questions to a minimum. The value of marginal information should be weighed against the possible loss of respondents. Not only should there be few questions, but each question itself should be as brief as possible.

(4) **Give questionnaire eye appeal** — Construct a well-designed questionnaire, uncrowded, with ample space, neat and made of good quality material.

(5) **Avoid ambiguity** — Questions should not be phrased in such a way that the answer can be interpreted variously. For example, a questionnaire on personal care contained the following: "Do you shine your own shoes or do you have them shined? Yes or no."

(6) **Be concise** — Wherever possible the answer requested should be in specific terms, such as "yes" or "no", and preferably in numerical terms.

(7) **Define your terms** — If there is the slightest chance that a term may be interpreted in different ways by different respondents, give a definition or illustration of the term. For example, "How large is your house?" may be answered in several different ways, while "How many rooms, exclusive of bathrooms and storage or utility rooms, are there in your house?" is more likely to be answered uniformly.

(8) **Avoid personal questions** — Questionnaires should exclude, wherever possible, requests for personal information or information going far back in time and placing considerable reliance on the respondent's memory.

When personal information must be asked, proper planning can increase the likelihood of obtaining a response. For example, instead of asking the specific age of the individual, ask the respondent to merely check an age group. Similarly, instead of asking for income earned, ask in which income group such as $20,000 to $29,000, the persons falls into.

(9) **Assure confidentiality of information** — Many people do not wish to give information through the mail, especially personal information. Assure the respondent that the information will be kept confidential and that only summary statistics will be derived from the responses.

Problems of Accuracy in Collecting Data

The major objective in the collection of data by any of the above methods is to obtain accurate and representative data. Aside from sampling errors (discussed in Chapters 8, 9, and 10) there are potential errors of measurement, coding, data-entry, tabulation, calculations, etc. Some problems of accuracy are detailed below when the mail questionnaire technique is used to collect data.

1. Non-response — A mail survey almost always is subject to the problem of non-response or non-participation. The percentage of response will, or course, depend on the ability of the survey taker to deal effectively with the various problems listed earlier. It has been estimated that mail questionnaire surveys conducted by business organizations may be expected to achieve 10 percent to 30 percent response rates. Even if the percentage of response is considered good — say, 50 to 60 percent — how can one use the results of such a survey? A common mistake is to assume that the characteristics of the non-respondents are about the same as those of the respondents.

In a mail survey of members of the American Federation of Labor regarding housing, for example, 33 percent of those in the sample responded after one or two follow-ups. It was tempting to assume that the characteristics of the non-respondents were not much different than those who responded. However, telephone and personal contact with a small random sample of the non-respondents yielded data which proved the fallacy of such a simplifying assumption. Even without such evidence, logic would cast doubt on this assumption, since generally non-respondents are likely to be different in many respects than cooperating respondents.

In mail questionnaires, a suggested procedure for dealing with the problem of non-response is to follow up on a small random sample of the non-respondents, possibly by telephone or preferably by an interview, since a personal interview can overcome the problem of non-response by actual fact-finding rather than by assumption. Of course, in the most fortunate situations, where the non-response rate is very small (say, less than 5 percent of the total), the conclusions to be drawn from the survey can hardly be significantly affected.

2. Completeness of the mailing list — Mail surveys depend heavily on the availability and completeness of the mailing list from which to draw the sample. If the mailing list is incomplete or not up to date, the results of the survey may not be valid for the purposes it was intended.

3. **Miscellaneous problems** — In addition to the problems listed above, there are a number of miscellaneous problems of accuracy to contend with, including impossible and inconsistent answers, late responses, illegible answers, and partial or incomplete responses.

It is hoped that the foregoing discussion gives sufficient warning that the task of conducting a successful mail survey is fraught with many problems and obstacles. Even with the pointers provided, administrative or office staff unskilled in collecting data are hardly ideal candidates for this assignment without the guidance of experienced survey takers.

Comparative Advantages of Mail Questionnaire and Personal Interview

Most of our discussion of problems dealt with mail questionnaire surveys. This is not to say that personal interview surveys are relatively simple. They have their own problems. For example, the personal interview method encounters the problem of possible interviewer errors. Interviewers must be fully trained on the method of conducting the interviews, on properly obtaining and recording all responses, and on consistency from one interview to the next.

Table 2.2 compares some of the advantages of the personal interview and the mail questionnaire as methods of collecting data by surveys.

Table 2.2 — Comparative advantages
of two methods for collecting data

Personal Interview	**Mail Questionnaire**
1. Response rate is generally higher.	1. Cost per individual is generally lower unless many follow-ups are necessary.
2. More detailed data and data on more complex subjects can be obtained.	2. Training interviewers is not necessary, except for interviewing a small random sample of non-respondents.
3. A complete list of potential respondents is not needed in an area or block survey.	3. More time is given for answering; also respondent error may be reduced because the questionnaire can be filled out when the respondent has time.
4. More accuracy in response to questions can be obtained because on-the-spot explanations of unclear terms can be provided readily.	4. Is not subject to enumerator or interviewer errors.
5. Usually valid results are obtained more quickly, since the problems of non-response and late response are overcome more readily.	5. Time required to complete the overall study is generally shorter, provided the response rate is sufficiently high.
	6. The impersonal nature of the questionnaire may insure more uniformity of responses, especially where the questions are pre-tested, as they should always be.

Summary

Statistics may be available because someone else has collected them (secondary data), or they may have to be collected for the first time (primary data). Because of the many technical and related problems that have to be dealt with, primary data should be collected under the direction of experienced survey takers. The process of collecting and using primary data for the enlightenment of management problems and decision-making is not simple; it follows a specific pattern or discipline that is an application of the scientific method. To avoid waste and inefficiency in conducting a statistical survey, six major steps have to be taken in sequence: (1) clarifying the problem, (2) planning and organizing for the survey, (3) collecting and editing the raw data, (4) summarizing or tabulating the resulting data, (5) analyzing the data, and (6) presenting the results to management or the intended users.

An effective way of solving many management problems is to reduce them to quantitative or numeric form. Problems can then be analyzed by statistical methods that are objective and, therefore, do not rely entirely on memory, intuition, or subjective judgments.

There are three ways of collecting data: (1) complete count, (2) judgment sampling, and (3) random sampling. These are discussed in more detail in Chapters 7 and 8. There are six ways of converting problems to quantitative terms. The choice involves selecting one or a combination of the following methods: (1) extracting data from existing records, (2) measuring the magnitude (e.g., weight, time, etc.) of the products or services studied, (3) observing and recording activities seen, (4) conducting a mail survey, (5) conducting a personal interview survey, or (6) weight assignment or ranking based on judgment. Another method is to use secondary data wherein someone else previously has collected relevant data that is accessible to the survey team.

In all instances, the accuracy and validity of the data are of paramount importance to using the data for decision-making. Many problems are encountered in an effort to obtain accurate and reliable data. One problem deals with measuring sampling error when random samples are used in collecting data, as discussed in Chapters 8, 9, and 10. Others arise as the result of a high rate of non-response to mail questionnaires, biased answers, incomplete responses, incomplete or inaccurate mailing lists, enumerator errors, data-entry errors, tabulating or processing errors, and so forth. In particular, the planning of good mail questionnaires combines imagination, knowledge of the psychology of human beings, a great deal of judgment, and technical and operating skill in the art of data collection, so that cooperation of the respondents and clear and objective answers are obtained. We have presented some pointers intended to help in this process. However, management in need of statistical information should be aware that conducting a statistical survey requires staff trained and experienced in collecting valid and reliable data for decision-making.

Problems

1. A manufacturer of a well-known brand of soap wishes to know why the volume of sales of their product dropped in the past year. What are some possible ways of finding out the reasons for this condition?

Problems 2, 3, and 4 contain some of the steps in a statistical survey. For each problem, indicate the logical order in which these steps are usually taken in a comprehensive statistical survey.

2. (a) Interviewing the persons in the sample.
    (b) Determining the arrangement and content of the schedule.
    (c) Formulating the problem and purposes of the survey.
    (d) Determining the methods of selecting the sample.
    (e) Deciding whether to portray the data in a chart or a table.

3. (a) Choosing the method of sampling.
    (b) Preparing the questionnaire.
    (c) Preparing an analytical report of the data.
    (d) Calculating averages, percentages, and other statistical measures from the data.
    (e) Interviewing a small sample of the non-respondents.
    (f) Meeting with management to discuss the problem.

4. (a) Interpreting the tabulated data.
    (b) Setting up a time schedule for collecting and presenting the data.
    (c) Deciding the specific classifications by which to group the data.
    (d) Deciding on the specific purposes of the study.
    (e) Determining the size of the sample.
    (f) Preparing a tabulation of the data.

5. Indicate whether the following are good or bad questions for a mail questionnaire survey, and explain why.
    (a) Is this the brand of gasoline you generally buy, or do you buy a different brand most of the time? Yes_____ No_____
    (b) What brand of gasoline do you buy most often?
    _____

   (c) In which age group do you belong ? (Check one.)

_____ under 18	_____ 36-45
_____ 18-25	_____ 46-55
_____ 26-35	_____ 56 or over

6. In the following instances, which method of collecting primary data (observation, measurement, mail questionnaire, personal interview, extraction from organization records) would you use? Explain the basis for your choice.

   (a) Determine the income and size of families in your state.

   (b) Determine the types of electrical equipment owned by families in rural farm areas of the country.

   (c) Determine the average number of letters in the surnames of residents in your city.

   (d) Determine the average diameter of bolts produced by a machine.

   (e) Determine the average number of letters typed per work-day by a clerk during the past year.

7. List five causes of error in data collected either by mail questionnaires and/or personal interviews.

8. Indicate which of the following you would consider primary and which secondary data.

   (a) Statistics collected by you from your organization's records on weekly earnings of workers (assuming you can get permission to review such records).

   (b) Statistics published in a magazine on the number of motor vehicles registered in each state.

   (c) Data collected by your statistics class on the amount of rent paid monthly by families renting apartments in the city.

   (d) An index of industrial production in the *Federal Reserve Bulletin*.

   (e) Data published by the Census Bureau on the age distribution of persons in the United States.

9. List five ways in which an activity or process might be converted into quantitative terms, and give a specific example of each.

10. Two baseball players, each about equally skilled, are to act as captains of two baseball teams. Each captain is to choose 8 players

from a group of 16 who are generally known to vary gradually in baseball skill from best to poorest. They tossed a coin for first choice and then each captain chose alternate players thereafter.

(a) Would this method give balanced teams? Why?

(b) By using statistics, devise a better method?

(c) What is a qualification of the latter method?

11. If a mail questionnaire yields at least a 60 percent response, it is usually safe to use the results in making intelligent and important decisions. Do you agree? Explain.

12. In the following, explain how you would deal with the non-respondent cases in your sample in order to reach reasonably reliable conclusions from a mail questionnaire survey.

(a) The non-response rate is 30 percent of the total mailed.

(b) The non-response rate is 3 percent of the total mailed.

13. A large high school will decide to establish a lacrosse team if 50 percent or more of the students favor it. A sample survey is made of 1000 students and the following is obtained: 450 favor, 400 do not favor, and 150 did not answer. How would you deal with the problem of non-response?

Chapter 3

Organizing Data for Analysis— Frequency Distributions

"I have never yet seen an inspection problem which would not benefit from the point of view that the product inspected was a frequency distribution."*

Often an organization has on hand data that could prove valuable, but it has no one who can organize the data to learn what significant facts they contain. We will attempt here to describe how a large number of records, measurements or observations can be organized to facilitate their analysis by means of frequency distributions. In addition, we will illustrate how one particular type of frequency distribution, the "normal" distribution, can serve many important uses in management and research problems. The chapter also presents statistical terms commonly used in constructing frequency distributions and in analyzing data. All new terms are in bold italics.

Frequency Distribution Defined

When a statistical survey is conducted, numerous measurements or responses are obtained for each unit or line item. They usually form a complex volume of ungrouped or disorganized information that hardly tells anything about the characteristics of the universe under study. How can this mass of ungrouped data be organized and arranged to make sense and to begin to reveal the salient characteristics of the process or activity being studied? The *frequency distribution* is a method of condensing masses of disorganized data and organizing them for analysis.

---

* G.D. Edwards, "Quality Control of Munitions — The Modern Ounce of Prevention Applied to Ordinance," *Army Ordinance*, Volume 23, November-December, 1942, pages 482—485.

A frequency distribution shows how many of a large number of items or cases under study fall into pre-chosen *classes* or groups arranged from high to low or, conversely, from low to high. For example, the following is a frequency distribution of the 68 million families in the United States by their 1992 total money income.* Here, the classes are the money income categories or groups and the frequency is the number of families in each class.

Income Class (in thousands)	Number of Families	Income Class (in thousands)	Number of Families
Total Families	**68,437**	$25,000 to 34,999	10,139
Less than $5,000	2,398	$35,000 to 49,999	12,263
$5,000 to 9,999	4,179	$50,000 to 74,999	13,290
$10,000 to 14,999	4,932	$75,000 to 99,999	5,617
$15,000 to 24,999	10,618	$100,000 and over	5,001

Uses of Frequency Distributions: A Problem

A company that owns two restaurants located in different sections of the same town made a survey to determine which of the two serves customers who spend higher amounts for lunch. Both restaurants have the same variety of food, the same special luncheon plates, and the same service. The owners wanted to determine the differences in the lunch-spending habits of their customers by an analysis of the amounts spent for lunch. Restaurant A had 60 customers for lunch on Tuesday, and Restaurant B had 45 customers on the same day.** We will use the standard notation of the small letter n to represent the number of observations in a sample, or the *sample size*. Thus, n = 60 in the first instance and n = 45 in the second. The ungrouped data on the amounts spent for lunch in each restaurant are presented in Tables 3.1 and 3.2.

From the ungrouped data (amounts listed in customer order) for Restaurants A and B, it is practically impossible to determine the differences in the amount spent for lunch by customers in the two places. One observation, however, can be made readily — that is, the amounts

---

*Source: *Money Income of Households, Families and Persons in the United States*, U.S. Bureau of the Census, 1993.

**The inquisitive reader would ask at this point if data collected from a single day's luncheon sales could be used to generalize about luncheon sales throughout the year. The answer is "Not very likely." A representative sample would include sales from each restaurant over a longer and more dispersed period of time than a single day, in order to reflect differences due to holidays, seasonality factors, weather conditions, etc. Since the data are being used to illustrate frequency distributions, however, the discussion of sampling is deferred to Chapters 7, 8, 9 and 10.

spent vary for the different customers of each restaurant. We can scan the different amounts listed, but we can hardly form a conclusion about the major characteristics of the variable. A *variable* denoted by the symbol x is any specified measurement or observation that differs from item to item or from time to time. In this case, the variable is the amount spent for lunch at each restaurant.

Table 3.1 — Amounts spent on lunch in Restaurant A (in dollars)

Customer Number	Amount Spent	Customer Number	Amount Spent	Customer Number	Amount Spent	Customer Number	Amount Spent
1	5.51	16	6.02	31	5.79	46	5.54
2	6.24	17	4.06	32	5.23	47	4.55
3	7.71	18	7.57	33	7.05	48	6.58
4	6.57	19	9.05	34	3.75	49	4.26
5	4.58	20	5.57	35	7.02	50	7.53
6	5.09	21	4.52	36	3.04	51	4.03
7	4.52	22	5.05	37	5.50	52	6.50
8	7.04	23	7.53	38	8.27	53	7.07
9	6.54	24	5.09	39	4.74	54	4.52
10	6.01	25	6.53	40	6.05	55	5.58
11	4.06	26	5.50	41	6.06	56	6.57
12	7.00	27	6.06	42	5.09	57	5.22
13	6.24	28	7.04	43	8.02	58	9.06
14	8.56	29	7.03	44	4.07	59	5.57
15	6.09	30	6.57	45	7.02	60	6.06

Table 3.2 — Amounts spent on lunch in Restaurant B (in dollars)

Customer Number	Amount Spent	Customer Number	Amount Spent	Customer Number	Amount Spent	Customer Number	Amount Spent
1	8.00	13	4.22	24	7.07	35	7.55
2	5.50	14	6.55	25	6.73	36	8.52
3	8.79	15	4.55	26	5.03	37	7.51
4	7.72	16	6.51	27	5.57	38	8.51
5	7.55	17	7.25	28	7.02	39	6.03
6	6.59	18	6.77	29	4.51	40	5.56
7	5.04	19	5.57	30	6.07	41	6.53
8	7.55	20	6.59	31	7.51	42	7.29
9	7.04	21	6.73	32	7.01	43	7.55
10	7.07	22	5.55	33	5.08	44	7.02
11	6.59	23	7.54	34	6.02	45	7.50
12	7.04						

As indicated earlier, a frequency distribution organizes data and condenses a large number of individual measurements, or values, of a variable into a few systematically arranged groups or classes. The concentration of values in the different groups thus can be seen and the significant features about the data begin to stand out, thus facilitating their interpretation.

The luncheon expenditures listed in Tables 3.1 and 3.2 form the frequency distributions shown in Table 3.3.

Table 3.3 — Frequency distributions
of luncheon costs in two restaurants

Restaurant A		Restaurant B	
Amount spent (in dollars)	Frequency (f)	Amount spent (in dollars)	Frequency (f)
3.00-3.99	2	3.00-3.99	0
4.00-4.99	11	4.00-4.99	3
5.00-5.99	14	5.00-5.99	8
6.00-6.99	16	6.00-6.99	12
7.00-7.99	12	7.00-7.99	18
8.00-8.99	3	8.00-8.99	4
9.00-9.99	2	9.00-9.99	0
Total, n =	60	Total, n =	45

From these frequency distributions it can be seen that the 60 individual x-values for Restaurant A have been reduced to seven classes in ascending order of size, and the 45 values for Restaurant B have been grouped into five classes, although two more groups with zero frequency have been added to the latter for comparability. The size of each group, i.e., the *class interval,* and the number of groups can vary depending on a number of factors, as described later. Each frequency distribution now shows the information in a usable format. It is apparent, for example, that in Restaurant A the greatest concentration of sales is at $6.00-6.99, and that in Restaurant B, it is at $7.00-7.99. Other, but lesser, concentration points are at $5.00-5.99 in Restaurant A and at $6.00-6.99 in Restaurant B.

Can the two frequency distributions in this form, i.e., in absolute terms, be compared to determine which restaurant catered to persons who usually spend more for lunch? In other words, can the number of values in a group in one frequency distribution be readily compared with the number in the corresponding group in the other frequency distribution? The answer is: Not readily, because the total number of servings in each restaurant differed; this influences the numbers falling in each class. However, by use of a percentage frequency distribution. this problem is eliminated. When the frequencies in each group are converted into a percentage of the total number of values (n) in the set, a *percentage frequency distribution* is formed. A direct comparison of the percentages in each group is now possible since the frequency in each group or class is now based on the same total, 100 percent. In general, the percentage distribution eliminates the problem of noncomparability between the absolute numbers or frequencies in each group that results when the total number of values (n) is different for each set of data.

The percentage of the total number of values falling in each group can be computed for Restaurant A by dividing the number of customers in each class by 60, the total number of servings, and then multiplying the result by 100. For the first class ($3.00-3.99), this yields (2/60) 100 = 3.33 percent. Similarly, the second group gives (11/60) 100 = 18.34 percent, and so forth. The two percentage frequency distributions can now be compared, as shown in Table 3.4.

Table 3.4 — Percent distribution of luncheon
costs in two restaurants, by amount spent

Amount spent (in dollars)	Restaurant A Percent of total	Restaurant B Percent of total
3.00-3.99	3.33	0.00
4.00-4.99	18.34	6.67
5.00-5.99	23.34	17.78
6.00-6.99	26.67	26.66
7.00-7.99	20.00	40.00
8.00-8.99	5.00	8.89
9.00-9.99	3.33	0.00
Total percent (and n)	100.01* (n=60)	100.00 (n=45)

It now becomes apparent that Restaurant B served nearly 50 percent of its luncheons for $7.00 or more, as compared with about 28

---

* The percentages do not add exactly to 100 because of rounding. Statistical practice does not require forcing the percentages to add to 100 percent when the difference is due to rounding. When the difference from 100 percent is large, however, it is an indication that an error may have been made and the results should be checked.

percent served at that level by Restaurant A. On the low end of the scale, on the other hand, Restaurant B served approximately 24 percent of its luncheons for less than $6.00, as compared with about 45 percent for those amounts by Restaurant A. On the whole, it is fairly clear that customers of Restaurant B spent more for lunch than those of Restaurant A.

By grouping the values of a variable to form a frequency distribution in absolute units and then calculating a percentage frequency distribution, i.e., the percentage of the total number of units in each class, we get a good start in the analysis of many quantitatively expressed processes, because the large number of values are not only reduced to a few classes but also standardized into comparable terms by the percentage frequency distribution.

Organizing a Variable for Analysis

The foregoing is an illustration of an essential need for frequency distributions in the analysis of data. It illustrates the process of organizing a fairly large body of ungrouped data (which at first glance hardly tell anything about the activity or process) by condensing them, in an organized way, into a few classes in order to make it easier to analyze large masses of data. While this type of analysis may be all that is necessary for the simple restaurant problem, frequency distributions also can be used for other, more diversified problems, as described later in this and other chapters. Frequency distributions also are important because they form a basis for using other analytical tools, such as averages and standard deviations (Chapters 4 and 5).

Because of the need for frequency distributions in the analysis of statistical data, the analyst must know how to construct them. In the above problem, the 60 and 45 values were condensed to seven and five groups, respectively, by constructing *uniform classes* (classes of equal size) with class intervals of $1.00 each, starting with $3.00-3.99 for Restaurant A and $4.00-4.99 for Restaurant B. Why could these frequency distribution not be constructed with different class intervals, a different number of classes, or a different starting point? Actually, many acceptable frequency distributions could have been set up with the 45 and 60 values, or with any number of values in general. This is especially true and easy to accomplish with computer software. However, we are seeking the best or clearest portrayal of the data, and that may not be readily possible even when computers are used.

Computers easily generate frequency distributions and graphs, but user intervention often is required to achieve distributions or graphs that are suitable for their intended use.

What are the conditions to consider and steps to follow in constructing an acceptable frequency distribution? The conditions for a satisfactory frequency distribution generally can be determined by a five-step process:

1. Decide on the number of classes to use, based on the number of values in the universe or the sample (n) being analyzed, using the following general guidelines:*

    (1) When n < 50, use somewhere between 3 and 7 classes.

    (2) When n ≥ 50, use 8 to at most 15 classes.

    For example, we chose 5 classes for Restaurant B (n = 45) and 7 classes for Restaurant A (n = 60). In the latter case we chose one less class than the guideline recommended. Slight deviation from the above guidelines is not serious in the light of the original objective, a comparison of customer expenditures for lunch in the two restaurants.

2. Determine the class interval (or range) of each class, by dividing the *range* of the variable (the largest value minus the smallest value) by the number of classes determined in step 1. For Restaurant B, this step yields a class interval of 91¢:

$$\frac{\left(\text{maximum value}\right) - \left(\text{minimum value}\right)}{\text{number of classes}} = \frac{\$8.79 - \$4.22}{5} = \frac{\$4.57}{5} = \$0.91 = 91¢ \; ;$$

    Since this is an awkward interval it was adjusted to a more convenient class interval of $1 per step 3 below.

3. Round the class interval to integers, or better still, to accommodate multiples of 5 or 10 so that each interval represents a range of commonly used numbers (e.g., $1.00 - 1.99; $10 - 19.99; etc.). Here we chose $1.00 intervals, such as $3.00-3.99.

4. Set up the first class to insure that the smallest value is included in it. Since the smallest value for Restaurant A is $3.04, we chose $3.00-3.99 as the starting interval.

---

* The symbol N usually is used to represent the size of the universe. For simplicity, we do not make that distinction here.

5. Construct the remaining classes with the same uniform class interval in ascending order (usually) up to the class that contains the largest value. Thus, for Restaurant B, for which the largest value is $8.79, we have the classes $4.00-4.99, $5.00-5.99, $6.00-6.99, $7.00-7.99, and $8.00-8.99, each with the same (uniform) class interval.

Sometimes in constructing frequency distributions it may be necessary to consider other conditions as well. For example, special groupings may be needed to analyze specific segments of the variable, such as a distribution by single years of age of persons in the age group 60-64, to determine the number of persons expected to attain age 65 in the next 5 years. In some instances we may need an open-ended frequency distribution, as described in the section "Uniform versus nonuniform class intervals."

Each of the above steps or conditions is explained in more detail below, along with other definitions and considerations pertaining to frequency distributions.

Number of cases and number of classes

A primary consideration in deciding on the number of groups or classes to use is the number of cases in the universe (N) or the sample (n). The larger the number of values in the set, the larger the number of groups to use, and vice versa. Generally, fewer than eight groups should be used when the number of values is fewer than 50. A larger number of groups should be used when n is more than 50, but the maximum is usually about 15.* The basic idea is that too many groups create many classes with but a few values in each, stretched out in a way that would conceal the concentration points; conversely, there should not be too few groups, which might conceal the graphic pattern of the distribution.

Range and size of each class interval

Having decided on the number of groups to use in constructing the frequency distribution, we next need to decide on the size of each class, or the class interval. This process may be likened to the job of cutting a slab of wood into equal pieces, keeping in mind the desirability of

---

*A formula for determining the approximate number of desirable groups, usually referred to as Sturges' rule, is: number of groups = 1 + 3.3 logarithm of n. For example, where n = 100 and the log of 100 equal to 2, this formula advises using 8 groups.

having uniform-sized pieces (class intervals). Before cutting the slab, we need to know its length (range) and the number of pieces (groups) desired. By dividing the total length (range) by the number of slabs (groups), we determine the equal length of each slab (the uniform-sized class interval).

Thus, in constructing a frequency distribution, we determine the class interval by first finding the range, or span, of the variable. When the range of the variable is divided by the number of groups we previously chose in step 1, we obtain the class interval. Since this size often comes out as a fraction, it is generally rounded to a convenient whole number. If, as in Restaurant A, the highest value is $9.06, and the lowest $3.04, the range is $6.02. Since the desired number of groups is 7, the class interval would be $6.02 divided by 7. The result is 86¢, but the number $1.00 is used as the class interval to avoid working with cumbersome fractions. The most convenient whole numbers to use for class intervals are usually multiples of 5 or 10 (i.e., divisible by 5 or 10).

Position of the first class

After determining the class interval, we next need to establish the location of the first group. Obviously, the first group must be established to include the smallest or lowest value of the variable, but it need not necessarily start exactly with that value. If the lowest value is $4.22, for example, a good starting point would be $4.00.

What determines a good starting point? Generally, the starting point should be based on commonly used figures, not far removed from the lowest value. Starting with a fraction or decimal point would almost always be ruled out unless the values of the variable are expressed in decimals. Generally, the more commonly used figures are those ending with a zero (e.g., 10, 20, 100, etc.), or those that are divisible by 5 or 10. In our example, the smallest amount spent for lunch in Restaurant A was $3.04. Therefore, $3.00-3.99 was considered to be a good starting group.

Once the starting group is chosen, the remaining groups follow with uniform-sized classes. Thus, the next classes were chosen to be $4.00-4.99, $5.00-5.99, etc. The number of choices for the position of the first class can be fairly large. However, the guideline for using integers divisible by 5 or 10 generally should be followed. When the variable has a wide range and n or N is large, the preferred class interval usually is 100, 1000, or 5000. (The Census Bureau table at the beginning of the chapter at first used intervals of $5000, then began using wider intervals in order to avoid having too many classes.)

Uniform versus nonuniform class intervals

It should be noted that the foregoing frequency distributions analyzing the restaurant luncheon costs have uniform, or equal-sized class intervals. In other words, each class has the same range. For reasons of comparability, ease of interpretation, and plotting the frequency distribution to determine its graphic pattern, it is essential to use uniform-sized intervals.

While most data can be condensed to form a frequency distribution with equal-sized intervals, unequal classes may have to be used in some cases. This is especially true in cases where there is a wide range of values with only a relatively few values at either (or both) ends of the variable. This is the case, for example, for data on age of the population or on family income, both of which have a very wide range of values. In such cases, it usually is desirable to set up an *open-ended class* at the beginning or end (or at both extremes) of the frequency distribution in order to facilitate condensing the data into a reasonable number of classes. For example, the Bureau of the Census, in presenting frequency distributions on family incomes in 1992, used two open-ended classes — "Less than $5,000" and "$100,000 and over."

Midpoint of each class

It is also desirable in constructing a frequency distribution to choose class intervals that will yield appropriate *class midpoints*. A midpoint, denoted herein by the symbol m, is the point on the scale of the variable halfway between the two class limits of any particular class; it is the sum of the two class limits (the ends of the class interval) divided by 2. It is subsequently easier to make manual calculations if the frequency distribution is planned to yield midpoints ending in whole numbers, in order to avoid decimal numbers; midpoints ending in zero or five are easiest for manual computations. When computations are performed by computer, obviously, this is not an important consideration, except for ease of "visualizing" the data when the results are presented.

In a frequency distribution with an open-ended group, the midpoint for the open-ended group is not readily available because the class limits are unknown. In some cases, however, the approximate midpoints can be estimated by special research of the variable under study. Because of this difficulty, it is best to avoid open-ended frequency classes, if possible.

Continuous versus noncontinuous variables

Because of the need to use the midpoint of each class in plotting frequency distribution graphs, in computing averages, and in other statistical analyses, it is worthwhile to digress from the main objective of describing frequency distributions to discuss the methods of obtaining midpoints in relation to continuous and noncontinuous variables.

As noted earlier, the midpoint of a group is a point halfway between the upper and lower limit of the group; it is the sum of the two class-limits divided by 2. While this explanation sounds simple, there is a fine point to consider in computing midpoints. This comes about because the variable under study may be either continuous or noncontinuous. A variable is *continuous* if any value can occur within its range, no matter how refined or rough the actual measurement of the variable may be. For example, suppose we are measuring the length of wires that may be anywhere from 1/2 inch to 1 inch long. One particular wire may actually be exactly 0.520 inches long, another may actually be exactly 0.723760 inches long. In practice it may not be feasible to measure the exact length of any particular wire, but in theory its true length may be determined to whatever degree of precision we wish. Thus, regardless of the measures actually used, it is proper to think of a variable under study as a continuous variable if it theoretically could be measured to an infinite number of decimal places.

Let us suppose that we are grouping persons by height into 2-inch class intervals. What is the midpoint of each group for this continuous variable? If we have a group "62 - 63" inches, this group would have a midpoint of 63 inches. This seemingly strange result occurs because we are dealing with a continuous variable (heights), so the group 62 - 63 inches actually would include heights from 62.0000.... inches through 63.9999.... inches. The midpoint of 63 would be obtained as follows:

$$\frac{62.0000 + 63.9999...}{2} = \frac{125.9999...}{2} = 62.9999... = 63.$$

An alternative calculation of the midpoint for continuous variables is to add the lower limits of the two adjacent groups and then divide the sum by 2. Thus, in this case, we would add 62 (the lower limit of the group 62 - 63) to 64 (the lower limit for the next larger group, 64 - 65) and then divide by 2 to obtain the midpoint of 63 inches:

$$\frac{62 + 64}{2} = \frac{126}{2} = 63.$$

This method of calculating the midpoint is correct when the variable is continuous. This results from the fact that for continuous variables such as inches, age, height or weight, the value of the upper end of each class theoretically has a string of nines preceded by a decimal, .9999...ad infinitum.

In contrast, the midpoint of a class dealing with a *noncontinuous (or discrete) variable* — a variable which has gaps between successive values or whose successive values differ by relatively large amounts — such as shoe sizes 7, 7 1/2, and 8 — is computed as though a string of 0's follows the upper limit of the class. Thus, the midpoint for the class 7 - 8 size of shoe is 7.5 but not 8. It is derived as follows:

$$\frac{7 + 8.00...}{2} = \frac{15}{2} = 7.5.$$

In dealing with a noncontinuous variable, it is often preferable not to construct frequency distributions by groups but rather to obtain a count of the number of times each individual value occurs (e.g., size of family 2, 3, 4, etc.) In this way, the value itself is the midpoint. In some instances, however, grouping of a noncontinuous variable is a "must" in order to condense large masses of data to facilitate their analysis. Therefore, the foregoing method of computing the midpoint is used. Thus, a group of shoe sizes 7 - 7 1/2, yields 7 1/4 as a midpoint, a nonexistent size; on the other hand, a group consisting of shoe sizes 7 - 9, yields a midpoint of 8, a value that actually exists. Other examples of noncontinuous variables are size of house measured by number of rooms, hat sizes, and number of customers.

For practical reasons it may sometimes be desirable to consider a noncontinuous variable, such as annual salary, as a continuous variable, since the difference between successive values is very small relative to the magnitude of the variable under study. Thus, when dealing with income or amount of sales, where the difference between successive values may be as little as 1 cent, or a very small percentage of the variable amount, it may be assumed that there is no break in continuity and the variable may be treated as continuous.

Other Frequency Distributions

The problem of luncheon costs dealt with a variable that differed in size (amount spent for lunch), so that the resulting frequency distributions were "size distributions." Many size distributions are encountered in the analysis of data. However, three additional kinds of frequency distributions are encountered in statistical problems. They are generally identified as frequency distributions by "attribute," and include distributions of data by time, area, or kind. The construction of *attribute frequency distributions* is relatively simple and is illustrated below.

Time

If we had data on the number of company sales (units sold) in each of the 5 years 1989-93, the "time" frequency distribution could be in the following form:

Year	Number of sales
Total - - - - - - - - - - - - - -	**1,985**
1993 - - - - - - - - - - - - - -	460
1992 - - - - - - - - - - - - -	540
1991 - - - - - - - - - - - - -	400
1990 - - - - - - - - - - - - -	285
1989 - - - - - - - - - - - - -	300

Area

An "area" distribution is one that shows the frequency of occurrence of an event, or values of a variable, by geographic location. For example, the 460 company sales in 1993 were made in the following states:

State	Number of sales
Total - - - - - - - - -	**460**
California - - - - - - - - -	140
Minnesota - - - - - - - -	60
New York - - - - - - - - -	200
Oregon - - - - - - - -	20
Pennsylvania - - - - - - - -	40

Kind

A distribution of workers in an organization by their skill, or by gender, illustrates a "kind" frequency distribution. A company's manufacturing workers were distributed by skill as follows:

Skill		Number of workers
Total	- - - - - - - -	**950**
Highly skilled	- - - - - - - -	280
Medium skilled	- - - - - - -	410
Unskilled	- - - - - - - -	260

Other examples of classification of data by "kind" are color, brand name, and occupation.

Graphic Patterns of Frequency Distributions

An orderly, systematic grouping of the values of the variable is an essential part of constructing acceptable frequency distributions. Thus, the "size" distributions were in order of size and usually in uniform class intervals. The "time" distribution was in chronological sequence; the most recent period is listed first and the period furthest away is listed last. The "area" distribution shown was an alphabetic listing of the locations; other area distributions may be in terms of geographic proximity. The "kind" distribution also followed some system of ranking or logical grouping. We may choose from among many possible ways of constructing frequency distributions, but the predominant principle is an orderly and systematic grouping that portrays the data in a manner that facilitates understanding and interpretation.

Earlier in this chapter we observed that by constructing a frequency distribution we can condense a large mass of information into a few systematically arranged groups that facilitate the interpretation of the data. Furthermore, by constructing percentage frequency distributions, comparisons between several different sets of data can be made. These two uses (condensation and comparison) of frequency distributions are not, however, the whole story of their analytical value.

By presenting frequency distributions as a graph, another valuable field of applications of frequency distributions is opened. A *graph*, or *chart*, whether it is a line graph or bar graph, or any other type (see Chapter 14), is a useful analytical tool, for it not only shows the shape of the frequency distribution but also pictorially displays concentration points, direction of movement, and other "patterns" in the data. It also permits visual comparison of two or more frequency distributions, especially when they are in the form of percentage distributions.

How can a graph be drawn of a frequency distribution? To begin, the usual vertical and horizontal *scales* (or lines) are drawn, with the appropriate headings, as shown in Figure 3.1.

A number of points should be noted about techniques for constructing a line graph such as the one shown. First, the scale of the basic variable (x) is usually placed on the horizontal axis. Second, the scale for the frequency of occurrence (f) of the variable is placed on the vertical axis. Third, adequate space should be provided for the highest frequency in any given group. Fourth, adequate space should be provided for the largest midpoint of the class involved. For a *line graph*, where *each class midpoint is used to represent the entire class*, the midpoint for each class is marked as a single point on the horizontal scale. If a *bar graph* is to be drawn, however, the midpoints are not needed, since each bar fills the space of the class interval (See Figures 3.2 and 3.3).

Figure 3.1

Line graphs of the frequency distributions
of luncheon sales in two restaurants, by amount of sale

After all the points are plotted and connected by lines (or, as shown in Figure 3.1), we have a visual picture of the variable being studied. This picture enables us to classify the chart by any of the five types that generally exist (as explained later and illustrated in Figure 3.6). Knowledge of the type of frequency curve involved can serve as a guide for selecting the appropriate statistical methods of analysis and also for possible management action, as explained in the next section.

To identify which of the five graphic patterns is displayed by a line graph it may be necessary to smooth out the jagged edges of the lines. This is generally called *smoothing*. Examples of smoothing are shown in Figures 3.2 and 3.3. The smoothed lines on the bar chart for Restaurant A (Figure 3.2) form a fairly symmetrical pattern, with a concentration of values in the middle of the scale and about an equal number tapering off on both sides of the center.

Figure 3.2
Smoothed frequency distribution of luncheon sales,
Restaurant A

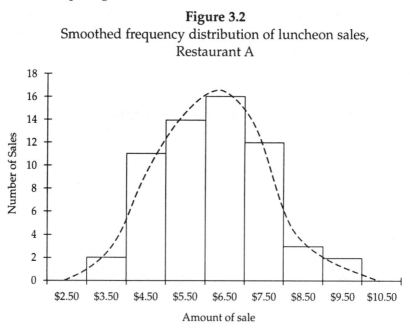

Frequency distributions that form a balanced pattern are called *symmetrical distributions,* while those that form an unbalanced pattern are called *skewed* or *asymmetrical distributions.* A special kind of symmetrical distribution is the *normal distribution,* in which the pattern formed is not only symmetrical but also is in the general shape of a bell, so often called the *bell curve.*

Figure 3.3
Smoothed frequency distribution of luncheon sales,
Restaurant B

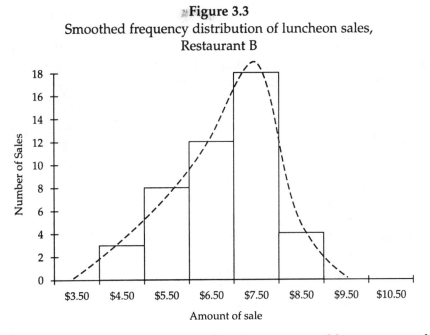

Figure 3.4 shows some of the many possible patterns of symmetrical distributions.

Figure 3.4
Some examples of different symmetrical distributions

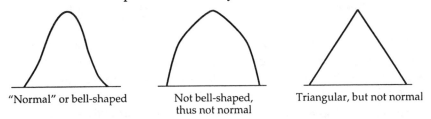

"Normal" or bell-shaped   Not bell-shaped,   Triangular, but not normal
                                 thus not normal

If we find that one frequency distribution forms a "normal" curve and another does not, what can we do with this knowledge? The answer lies in the fact that all normal distributions have certain known and fixed properties (described in Chapter 5 and in Appendix B), so that when a set of data representing a process forms, or is expected to form, a normal distribution, these fixed properties can be used with confidence to make estimates of a variety of characteristics of the process. Some of these are discussed in the section of this chapter, "The Normal Frequency Distribution and Some of Its Uses." In fact, normal distribution theory is basic to dealing with all kinds of estimates derived from random samples (Chapters 7, 8, 9, 10 and 11).

Many processes or operations directed by management, when quantified, generate data that follow the normal frequency distribution. This generally occurs when the process is operating under a constant-cause or stable system of influences. *Constant-cause systems* occur when a large number of factors combine to influence the magnitude of the variable being measured, but none of these factors alone exert a singularly outstanding influence on the resultant measure. Several other conditions which result in normal distributions are described in the section entitled "The Normal Frequency Distribution and Some of Its Uses".

Asymmetrical frequency distributions can form a variety of patterns, all off-center and skewed either to the right or left, as shown in Figure 3.5.

Figure 3.5
Some examples of asymmetrical distributions

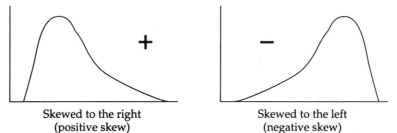

Skewed to the right   Skewed to the left
(positive skew)   (negative skew)

These patterns usually are the result of the fact that one factor, or several factors combined, bear a major influence on the final outcome of the values of the variable. Examples are workers by age groups in a particular industry requiring considerable skill, or the number of families in a geographic area distributed by their annual income.

There are three other patterns of frequency distributions, two of which are special types of asymmetrical distributions, and the third is a special type of symmetrical distribution called a *rectangular* or *uniform distribution*. Of the two asymmetrical distributions, one is called a *J-shaped curve*, the other a *U-shaped curve*.*

The five graphic patterns are illustrated in Figure 3.6 with data compiled by the National Institutes of Health, published in the Journal of the American Statistical Association some years ago. These charts

---

*U-shaped curves may be either symmetrical or asymmetrical.

show the index of fatalities in the United States by month of occurrence for several different affliction types.

Approximately Normal:	Certain diseases of early infancy
Rectangular:	Malignant neoplasms
Asymmetrical:	Suicides
J-shaped:	Motor-vehicle accidents
U-shaped:	Influenza and pneumonia

Figure 3.6

Five common graphic patterns or types of frequency distributions

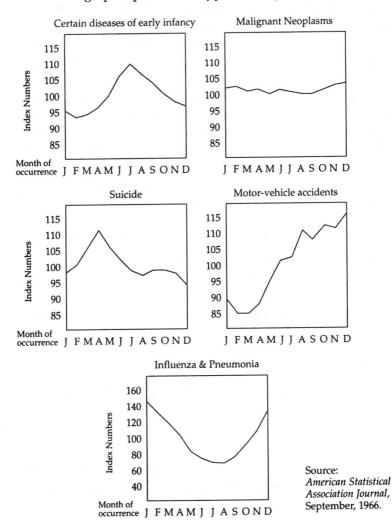

Source:
*American Statistical
Association Journal,*
September, 1966.

There are, of course, a multitude of variations of graphical patterns, but all generally fall, at least roughly, into one of the five different types.

The Normal Frequency Distribution and Some of Its Uses

Of the five types of distribution patterns, probably the most common and definitely the most useful in practical applications is the special type of symmetrical distribution called the "normal" or bell-shaped distribution. This frequency distribution is described by a complex mathematical formula and has fixed mathematical properties (Appendix B). Since many frequency distributions in management problems, and in life in general, approximate the normal curve, the known properties of this curve can be used to estimate the characteristics of many of life's variables and their distributions. One of the mathematical features of the normal curve, for example, is that its frequencies (on the vertical axis) approach zero at its two extremities (on the horizontal axis), but in theory never reach it. This feature and the other properties of the normal curve, as explained in later chapters, play an important role in estimating from samples and calculating the chances that estimates based on samples are correct within a given range. (See especially Chapters 5, 8, 9, 10, and 11).

A normal frequency distribution can generally be expected to occur when any of the following four conditions exist and when a reasonably large random sample of measurements (e.g., more than 100) are taken of the universe or process involved:

1. Hereditary or biological factors influence the variable under study, such as weight of infants at birth, height of adult females or adult males, length of adult human arms, circumference of heads, etc.

2. Nature's forces influence the variable, such as length of leaves which fall from a tree under natural conditions, weight of lima beans from the same crop, weight of olives grown under a fixed set of conditions, etc.

3. A variable influenced purely by chance, such as rolling a pair of honest dice, tossing 10 coins many times to derive a frequency distribution by number of heads, etc.

4. Measurements of a variable (such as a machine part) emanating from a process which operates under a set of stable conditions (i.e., a constant-cause system), such as the length of life of flashlight bulbs, the varying length of six-inch nails, etc.

Because of the exceptional importance of the normal distribution in research and particularly in Total Quality Management (TQM), which aims to improve the quality of products and services, we single out for further discussion the latter of the four conditions for normal frequency distributions. Many different factors, each of minor individual importance, influence the quality of a product or service emanating from a process. When measured, the varying results usually form a normal or approximately normal curve, and significant deviations from this frequency distribution pattern may be questioned with good reason. Here lies a basis for rational management action in many operations, particularly in quality and process control. This use is discussed in detail in Chapter 11, Statistical Process Control.

In practice, a perfect normal curve is hardly ever attained, although many frequency distributions closely approximate it, as illustrated in Figure 3.7.

Figure 3.7 — The bell-shaped curve

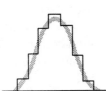

Length of life of light bulbs

Thickness of the wall of
a cartridge case

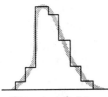

Diameter of pistons

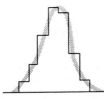

Deflection of compression ring

The specifications of this constant-cause condition for production and service operations seems reasonable when we consider an example in a manufacturing process. In manufacturing metal bolts of a specified dimension by a machine, there are many small chance factors which influence this dimension, such as the room temperature, dust particles in the air, humidity, slight differences in the width of the wire, slight differences in the hardness of the wire, and the "play" in the many machine gears and tools, all of which combine to affect the final product, a metal bolt. So long as each of the many chance factors influence the product to a small extent, influences in one direction will tend to cancel out influences in the other, with the result that the final product, when measured, will show a normal distribution pattern centered on the average (or peak point) such as that illustrated above.

Experience has shown that this condition exists not only for metal bolts but for every mass-produced product or service provided under a constant or stable set of conditions. It follows, therefore, that we can predict the distribution pattern to be formed of the product or service dimensions of many routine and repetitive processes. By having a rational basis for prediction we also have a basis for rational action. When the expected or predicted normal pattern does not materialize, there is a basis for management action to determine the cause for the unexpected. Usually, after a check on the process, it will be found that a new factor (or factors) that have great influence on the process have entered it. If, for example, the circumference of the heads of 1,000 copper hose nozzles selected at random from a process were measured and a frequency distribution were constructed of the 1,000 values, we would expect to obtain a normal, or approximately normal, distribution because very likely the same chance and common factors, none of which were outstanding in their influence on head-circumference, affected each nozzle.

Suppose, however, that in such a case, the expected normal distribution did not materialize and that, instead, a highly skewed distribution was obtained. Then the question becomes: What happened to yield this unexpected distribution? One plausible explanation is that one or more special factors other than those normally involved in the process entered to affect it significantly. One such factor could be that a sizable number of one-directional errors were made in measuring the circumference of the nozzle. Another factor could be that the machine fell off its required setting (or wasn't set properly), or that a machine gear had worn out. There may be many other causes for the situation, and, of course, they can only be determined by checking into the process operations; in other words, the statistics can only point out possible abnormalities, but management must act to find the causes and prevent them from recurring, if desirable. Chapter 11, Statistical Process Control, deals with this application of the normal distribution in detail.

Several examples of the normal distribution follow:

Example Number 1

Statistics were gathered by a mail questionnaire on the height of 456 male students in day-session freshmen classes in a given school. The frequency distribution and frequency chart in Figure 3.8 were obtained:

Figure 3.8
Frequency chart of students' heights

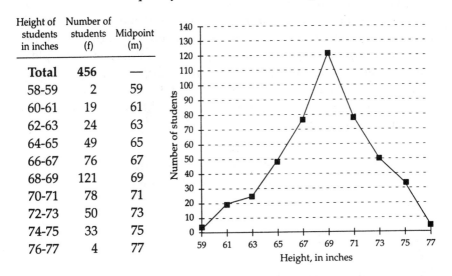

Height of students in inches	Number of students (f)	Midpoint (m)
Total	**456**	—
58-59	2	59
60-61	19	61
62-63	24	63
64-65	49	65
66-67	76	67
68-69	121	69
70-71	78	71
72-73	50	73
74-75	33	75
76-77	4	77

Does the frequency distribution shown in Figure 3.8 form a curve that could have been predicted? A symmetrical or an approximately bell-shaped curve could be expected for several reasons. First, the size of sample is sufficiently large for condensation into a reasonable frequency distribution. Second, the variable, height of adult persons, is influenced by heredity and should be expected to form a normal distribution. Third, the heights were taken from a fairly homogeneous or comparable universe — all male adult freshmen.

Since the factors that tend to cause a normal distribution existed, why was the frequency chart not smoother or closer to the shape of a bell? Possible answers include the following. The sample of 456 students may not represent a random sample since those who did not respond to the questionnaire were of different heights. Additionally, perhaps there were some women erroneously included in the sample survey, thus affecting the homogeneity of the sample. Possibly some of the freshmen were of different racial origins, so that there was more than one homogeneous universe in the distribution. Perhaps also there were some one-directional errors caused by overstatement or understatement of the true height by the responding students.

Example Number 2

In an evening Business Statistics class consisting of 34 students, the frequency distribution and frequency chart, by weight of student, were obtained as shown in Figure 3.9.

This frequency distribution is partially symmetrical or partially bell-shaped. Why shouldn't it be more nearly normal? A few reasonable explanations are: there are too few values in the sample to expect a smooth frequency distribution pattern; weight is not fully influenced by heredity and is not expected to form a bell-shaped distribution; there may have been some one-directional biases in the answers regarding the weight of the students.

Figure 3.9
Frequency chart of students' weights

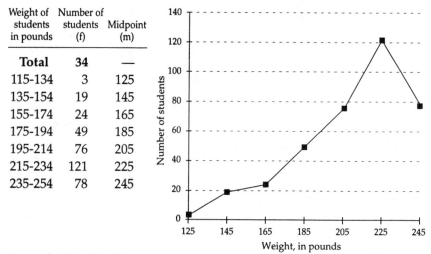

Weight of students in pounds	Number of students (f)	Midpoint (m)
Total	**34**	—
115-134	3	125
135-154	19	145
155-174	24	165
175-194	49	185
195-214	76	205
215-234	121	225
235-254	78	245

Example Number 3

Measurements were taken of the length of nails coming off several similar machines in a factory, each machine having been set to produce a 4-inch nail. The frequency distribution and frequency chart shown in Figure 3.10 were obtained for 1,730 nails inspected over a period of several days.

Figure 3.10
Frequency chart of nail lengths

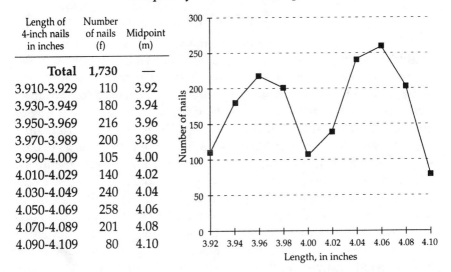

Length of 4-inch nails in inches	Number of nails (f)	Midpoint (m)
Total	**1,730**	—
3.910-3.929	110	3.92
3.930-3.949	180	3.94
3.950-3.969	216	3.96
3.970-3.989	200	3.98
3.990-4.009	105	4.00
4.010-4.029	140	4.02
4.030-4.049	240	4.04
4.050-4.069	258	4.06
4.070-4.089	201	4.08
4.090-4.109	80	4.10

Here we should expect a curve that is fairly symmetrical and close to normal, since the size of the sample was large, the machines were all set to produce a 4-inch nail, and the variations in dimension were supposedly caused by chance, or by a constant-cause system. By glancing at the frequency distribution, however, we see *two* concentration points — that is, a ***bimodal distribution***. Why did this unexpected distribution occur? There are several possible explanations.

(1) Two different grades of wire may have been mistakenly used for cutting the nails;

(2) By mistake, some of the machines may not have been set to cut at exactly 4 inches;

(3) Some of the inspectors may not have used the measuring gauge correctly.

A comparison of the actual shape of the curve with the expected pattern makes its clear that there was *something* wrong either with the product or the measurements, and that management should find the root of the trouble.

Because of the many uses of frequency distributions in problems of quality control, it is appropriate at this point to repeat the preamble to this chapter: "I have never yet seen an inspection problem which would not benefit from the point of view that the product inspected was a frequency distribution."

Summary

In this chapter, an attempt was made to bring out several main points about initial steps in the analysis of data. Foremost is the fact that a large number of ungrouped values of a variable cannot readily reveal their characteristics until they are condensed and grouped systematically to form a frequency distribution. The array, or listing of the values of the variable in order of size, often is useful in setting up a frequency distribution, but it is not essential. When large masses of data are involved, it is not practical to construct an array manually. However, computer software is available to organize the data and portray it in a frequency table and chart. In any case, it is essential to specify the number of classes in the frequency distribution, the class interval, the outer limit of the starting (and ending) class, and adhere to the requirements for uniformity of classes. The large variety of potential management analyses and uses of quantitative data can be greatly improved by understanding the basic ideas of frequency distributions and by use of good judgment. Data organized in the form of a frequency distribution are made manageable when the large mass of detail or records has been reduced to a relatively few groups or classes, thus showing concentration points, graphic patterns, and behavior tendencies not otherwise apparent from the raw and ungrouped data.

The art of constructing acceptable frequency distributions combines judgment and skill. It involves: (a) making wise decisions on the number of classes or groups into which the values of the variable should be condensed — an important consideration is the number of values being analyzed, since a large number requires more groups than a small number; (b) determining the appropriate class interval — the basic considerations are the range of the variable and the pre-determined number of groups; and (c) constructing uniform or equal-sized classes, except in special cases. These considerations are important whether the frequency distribution is constructed manually or by computer.

While the frequency distribution in absolute terms is useful in facilitating the analysis of masses of data, it cannot be used readily to compare one set of data with another. A percentage frequency distribution is essential for making comparisons, since it converts the number of values in each group into a percentage of the total number of values and thus reduces each frequency distribution into common, comparable terms.

Midpoints of each class are essential in drawing a line graph of the data and in computing averages and other statistical measures. The midpoint of a group is obtained by adding the values of the lower and upper extremes of the group and dividing the sum by 2. When dealing with a noncontinuous variable, the upper limit is considered to end with a string of zeros (.000...). In contrast, when dealing with a continuous variable, (when a value can occur at any point on a continuous scale of measurement), the upper limit is considered to end in a string of 9's (.999...). Consequently, the midpoint of a class for a continuous or noncontinuous variable can be obtained by adding its upper limit to the lower limit and dividing that sum by 2.

In addition to the frequency distributions by "size" of the variable, data also can be condensed into frequency distribution by time, area, and kind of item. The main consideration in constructing these distribution types is an orderly and logical arrangement of the groups. Frequency distributions, when plotted, generally form one of five well-defined patterns of frequency curves: the symmetrical or balanced curve, of which the normal or bell-shaped curve is a very special case; the asymmetrical curve showing skewness or a leaning either to the left or right; the J-shaped curve; the U-shaped curve; and the rectangular or constant frequency pattern. It is important that each of these types of frequency curves be identified in order to make the appropriate analysis of the data. The most important and most widely used of these is the special symmetrical curve known as the normal or bell-shaped curve. It plays a major role in such fields as quality control and a large variety of other management problems. Its importance derives from the fact that several conditions (hereditary factors, natural factors, chance variations, and constant-cause systems) tend to form bell-shaped distributions. Furthermore, the properties of the distribution are known and fixed, thus making it possible to analyze data statistically for a wide variety of characteristics. The resultant analyses provide rational guidance for management action or inaction. If the expected pattern of variation is not attained, the underlying reasons are sought. Often these reasons lead to the discovery of abnormal factors that have a major effect on the process, and this discovery in turn leads to remedial action, usually with quality or productivity improvement.

This chapter also presented many statistical terms. Some of them will recur in later chapters and are reviewed in some of the practical problems that follow. An understanding of these terms will enhance communication and more effective use of the statistical concepts and techniques that are presented here and later.

Problems

1. Define and illustrate each of the following:

    (a) Variable (x)
    (b) Range
    (c) Percentage frequency distribution
    (e) Bimodal distribution
    (f) Normal curve
    (g) Skewed distribution
    (h) Continuous variable
    (i) Uniform class intervals
    (j) Frequency of a group (f)
    (k) Chance variations
    (l) Ungrouped data
    (m) Noncontinuous variable
    (p) Bell-shaped distribution
    (q) Class interval
    (r) Homogeneous data
    (s) Grouped data
    (t) The symbol "n"
    (u) Open-end distribution
    (v) Rectangular distribution
    (w) Midpoint
    (x) Smoothing

2. Twenty students in a class received the following grades in a mid-term examination in statistics: 64, 78, 92, 69, 84, 94, 52, 81, 87, 58, 75, 76, 84, 82, 88, 91, 71, 72, 76, 75.

    (a) Set up an acceptable frequency distribution.

    (b) From (a) set up a percentage frequency distribution.

    (c) Which of the five patterns of frequency charts would you expect with this variable? Why?

3. Many hundreds or thousands of a specified part coming off a mass production process, when measured for a certain characteristic, are expected to form a frequency distribution of the bell-shaped type for that characteristic. Instead of a bell-shaped curve, however, the actual frequency distribution showed two concentration points, or a bimodal distribution. What are some possible explanations for this unexpected occurrence?

4. The following is the size of 40 retail food stores in a given city (size is measured by number of employees on the payroll of the store in the middle of February 1994): 3, 6, 11, 14, 15, 7, 8, 9, 5, 6, 7, 6, 22, 54, 27, 8, 8, 9, 18, 19, 32, 68, 45, 5, 7, 8, 9, 17, 12, 22, 48, 37, 34, 23, 25, 15, 8, 6, 7, 3.

    (a) Set up an acceptable frequency distribution, but read question (b) first.

    (b) What percentage of the stores have 30 or more employees?

    (c) Plot the frequency chart.

    (d) Tell which of the five types of frequency curves the chart shows.

5. Determine the midpoints for the following groups;

    (a) Amount the weekly wages: $300 - 399.

    (b) Height of school children: 40 - 44 inches.

    (c) Size of shoes: 7 - 8.

    (d) Size of men's shirts: 14-1/2 - 15-1/2.

    (e) Age of workers: 30 - 35 years.

    (f) Tearing weight of thick paper: 135 - 144 pounds

6. Define and illustrate each of the following frequency distributions:

    (a) by kind   (c) by time

    (b) by size   (d) by area

7. The following data were obtained from a dairy farm: milk yield, in pounds, of a herd of 14 Guernsey cows on a given day (fractional pounds dropped):

    Morning milking: 20, 10, 14, 2, 19, 12, 25, 16, 17, 20, 17, 5, 9, 18.
    Evening milking: 17, 12, 18, 24, 19, 21, 20, 16, 15, 19, 15, 6, 9, 16.

    (a) Would you expect the values of this variable to form a bell-shaped distribution? Explain.

    (b) Construct a frequency distribution for each milking.

    (c) Compare the milk yield in the morning with the evening milking by use of the percentage frequency distribution, and interpret the results.

    (d) Which of the five frequency curves did this variable actually form?

   (e) Give a few reasonable explanations for the difference between, or similarity with, the pattern you predicted in (a).

8.   Statistical data may be classified by "variables" and "attributes" Which of the following classifications are variables and which attributes? Which are continuous?

   (a) A distribution of employees by gender.

   (b) Age distribution of children in school.

   (c) Size of school, size classified by number of classrooms.

   (d) Amount of family income.

   (e) Distribution of pages in a book, by number of words per page..

   (f) Circumference of different automobile wheels.

   (g) Distribution of employees by skill level.

9.   List at least one use of the normal frequency distributions in business or government.

Chapter 4

Averages and Their Uses

*"The average has its limitations, but provided they are recognized, there is no single statistical quantity more valuable than the average."**

In the preceding chapter we have seen how large masses of data are organized into a few groups, by means of a frequency distribution, to facilitate their analysis. In this chapter another effective way of summarizing data, averaging, is introduced. The chapter shows the different meanings of the term "average," how these different averages are computed, how they are used in analyzing various problems or processes, and how they can guide management decisions. The limitations of averages are emphasized so that some common misuses of averages may be avoided.

What is an Average?

A newspaper heading featured this statement: "Average American Family Spending $400 More Than Its Income." A reader remarked: "No wonder I can't save — nobody else can either." This type of comment is typical of how averages can be misinterpreted.

Many adults and many school children know that an average is a single value derived from a number of values and that it is used to represent the general character of all the values of the group. It is condensation of data to its ultimate, a single figure. Some persons forget this fact and think that each of the values of a set is, or should be, the same as the average. Knowing the average annual temperature in a given city, for example, will not necessarily help you to determine the extent of real hot or very cold days. The temperature will differ from day to day and hour to hour. As an example, the top weather reading for any March 5 may be quoted normally at 60 degrees, but since

---

* L.H.C. Tippett, *Statistics*, Oxford University Press, London.

"normal" is an average of peak weather readings for many March 5's, the top weather reading for next year's March 5 is very likely not going to be 60 degrees. On that day the Weather Bureau will show both the "normal" temperature reading, representing the average of many March 5's in the past, and the actual peak reading for the particular March 5 being reported; there may be a substantial difference between the two readings. It is well to remember that an average, being a single figure, conceals the differences among the individual values used to compute it and that it is incorrect to assume that each value is the same as the average of all the values.* Some examples are: the batting average of a baseball player is a single figure derived by adding in the batter's good and bad experiences in hundreds of times at bat; a worker's efficiency rating may be based on his or her average daily production — a single figure calculated from production records over a long period of time; a bowler's ranking is determined by his or her average varying score per game based on scores made in many games.

While many of us know that an average is a single figure used to represent a set of values, not all of us may realize that there are several different kinds of averages, each with a different meaning and uses. Actually, unless we know the type of average being used, we can be led to a wrong conclusion. In calculating the average family income, we can arrive at a high figure by using the *arithmetic mean*, a low figure by using the *mode* as the average, and a figure between these two by using the *median*. There is also an average known as the *harmonic mean*, and still another as the *geometric mean*. Actually there may be an unlimited number of averages, as long as the set of data under study is converted by some method of calculation or counting into a single figure representing the entire set. An example is the *average of extremes* which is obtained by adding the lowest value of a set of numbers to its highest value and dividing the sum by 2.

With this introduction, the main objectives of this chapter may be restated briefly:

1. To become acquainted with the specific concept of 3 major averages as a method of analyzing data.

2. To learn how to calculate these averages.

3. To show how averages can be used to shed light on many different problems and how to chose from among the

---

* Chapter 5 describes methods of determining the extent of the differences.

several averages the one that is most appropriate in dealing with a specific problem.

Several Concepts of an Average

As indicated earlier, an average is used to represent the general character of a mass of data. While there are many ways of converting masses of data into single figures representing "typical" values, the most frequently used method is the *arithmetic mean* or, more briefly, the *mean*. Two other useful averages are the median and the mode. Often, when averages are quoted, the kind of average used is not stated, thus leading to misunderstandings. For example, it is unlikely that all of the following are based on the same definition of "average." "The average family income in the United States was estimated at $44,500 in 1992." "The average size of household was 4.9 persons in 1990." "The average height of students in a given class was 68 inches." "The average length of nails produced by a given machine was 4.3 inches." "The average hat size sold in a given store was 7-1/2." "The average income of persons with 5 or more years of college education was $65,000 in 1992."

To avoid misuse of averages, the specific kind of average should be stated. For example, the mean family income in 1992 was $44,483, or $7,671 higher than the average of $36,812 quoted in the newspapers at the same time. Why should there be such a large difference? Because the $36,812 average is a median and the $44,483 average is a mean.

The mean family income is derived by adding all the family incomes and then dividing the resulting total by the number of families. Thus the families with incomes of one million or more dollars constitute quite a big part of the total of all the income amounts used to derive the mean.

The median income is derived differently. A *median* of a set of values is defined as the value in the middle of the array of values.* In the family income example, half the families (34.1 million) had incomes above the median and the other half had incomes below the median. Thus, the median locates the middle value after all the values are arranged in order by size. If, for example, a sample of 541 families were arranged in order by the amount of their income, the income of the 271-st family would represent the median family income. Thus, 270 (or half) of the families would have received a lower income and the same number (or half) a higher income than the middle-income family.

---

* The median value may also be considered to be the value of the 50th percentile.

A statement that the average family income in 1992 was about $25,000 could also be correct, although that figure represents a different average from either of the two averages given earlier. The $25,000 average is the *mode*. This average is defined as the most frequently occurring value of the variable. The family income that occurred most frequently in 1992 was quoted to be $25,000, so that by definition it becomes the modal family income. The size of mens' hats sold most frequently can be called the average, or modal, hat size; the size of shirt sold most often becomes the modal shirt size; etc.

From the above definitions it may have been noted that the median and mode averages are averages of counting or of location, while the mean is an average of arithmetic calculation. To obtain the median, we have to arrange the values of the set in an array and count until we reach the middle case and determine its value. For the mode, we count to see which value occurs most frequently. To obtain the mean, we need to add all the values and divide the sum by the number of cases; hence its identity as the "arithmetic" mean. These conceptual distinctions are of practical importance when averages are used to analyze data.

As indicated earlier, there are other averages, such as the geometric mean, the harmonic mean, and the quadratic mean, that are valuable when properly used.

How to Derive the Mean, Median, and Mode

Averages from ungrouped data

In the preceding paragraphs we attempted to describe the meaning of averages in general and of the mean, median, and mode in particular. To illustrate how these three averages are derived, we assume that a salesperson in a department store made the following sales of mens' shirts in each of the 13 weeks of the last calendar quarter.

Amount of sales

First week	$1,468	Seventh week	1,140
Second week	1,020	Eighth week	750
Third week	1,234	Ninth week	850
Fourth week	1,333	Tenth week	1,155
Fifth week	850	Eleventh week	1,360
Sixth week	1,085	Twelfth week	685

The mean — How do we determine the (arithmetic) mean weekly sales? The mean is an average obtained by arithmetic calculation —

by adding all the values of the variable and dividing the resulting sum by the number of values. In this example, we first find the sum of the 13 sales figures, as follows:

$1,468 + 1,020 + 1,234 + 1,333 + 850 + 1,085 + 1,140
+ 750 + 850 + 1,155 + 1,360 + 685 + 850 = $113,780.

By dividing this sum by 13 (the number of values), we calculate the mean to be $1,060.

In statistics, to save space and time, symbols and formulas are frequently used to denote a particular calculation or set of steps. While symbols may give the impression that higher mathematics and complicated operations are necessary, actually they are nothing but statistical language for performing simple arithmetic calculations.

Thus, the arithmetic mean is calculated by the formula: $\overline{X} = \dfrac{\Sigma x}{n}$.

The capital X with a line over it ($\overline{X}$) represents, in standard statistical terminology, the arithmetic mean and is referred to as "X bar." The Greek letter Σ, which is the capital "S" in the Greek alphabet, is referred to as "sigma." The symbol Σ indicates "obtain the sum of" whatever follows it. Since the letter x stands for the variable involved in the calculation, the combined symbols Σx represent the process of calculating the sum of the x-values. The n stands for the number of values in the sample set of data.* The entire formula calls for obtaining the sum of the values of the variable and dividing their sum by the number of values to derive the arithmetic mean, as follows:

$$\overline{X} = \frac{\Sigma x}{n} = \frac{\$13,780}{13} = \$1,060.$$

The median — How do we determine the median weekly sales? Since the median is the value of the middle item in the array, it can be exactly identified only when the number of values, n, is odd. Thus, if n =13 and the items are arranged in order of size, the seventh item will represent the median value, since six items are below it and six are above it. The middle term is determined by the formula n/2; in this

---

* We are assuming that the 13 weeks represent a sample of the salesperson's weekly sales. In contrast, if the 13 weeks were the total population of interest, i.e., we were interested in these particular 13 weeks only, then the symbol N would be used in the formula. Capital N represents the total number of x-values in the universe or the entire field of study. The small n represents the number of x-values sampled from the universe. Generally, we work with sample data, so the symbol n is used here. Chapters 7, 8, and 9 discuss sampling methods.

case, 13/2 = 6.5, rounded up to 7. It will not matter if we count seven items from the top or seven from the bottom of the array — in either case we will arrive at the same value for the median, as long as the values are in size order.

When n is even, say 14, strictly speaking there is no middle item; two items share midplace. This problem is overcome by computing the median half way between the two middle items, i.e., by averaging the values of the two items on either side of the halfway point. If n = 14, the two middle items are the seventh and eighth. The median would be the average of the seventh and eighth values in the array, thus the resulting value leaves us with seven items above and seven below it.

The derivation of the median may be illustrated with our 13 sales values in three steps:

(1) Determine the middle item — in this case: 13/2 = 6.5 = 7.

(2) Arrange the values in an array. Thus we get:

$685; $750; $850; $850; $850; $1,020; $1,085; $1,140; $1,155; $1,234; $1,333; $1,360; $1,468.

(3) Count down (or up) in the array to locate the middle item in the array; its value is the median. In this problem the seventh value in the array has the value of $1,085, which is the median weekly sales. Thus, the median is an "average" of position, or counting, because it is the value of the item located in the middle of the array.

The mode — How do we determine the modal weekly sales? The mode is the value of the variable that occurs most frequently. To determine which value occurs most frequently the usual procedure is to arrange the values in an array or frequency array (unless we have but a few values to work with and can detect the mode by inspection). The array constructed for determining the median is equally useful for determining the mode. It is now a matter of counting the number of times each value occurs to determine the value that occurs most frequently. Obviously, the weekly sales value of $850 occurs most frequently; therefore, the mode is $850. Like the median, the mode is an average of position, location, or counting.

Averages from frequency distributions (grouped data)

The foregoing illustrations were made with a complete listing of the values of the variable, i.e., from *ungrouped data,* where each value of the variable was known. When dealing with a large number of values, however, the data usually are organized into groups or classes. When the x-values are distributed to their appropriate group the frequency distribution makes the analysis more manageable. If each salesperson's record extended over the 52 weeks of the year and records for ten salespeople had to be analyzed, there would be 520 sales values (52 times 10) to deal with. When faced with that many values, the analysis generally would be confined to the frequency distribution. It is, therefore, essential that we know how to calculate the averages not only from the ungrouped data but also from the frequency distribution, or the *grouped data,* as well.

Assume that the 13 weekly sales figures (given in the preceding section) are organized into the frequency distribution shown below. (Actually a frequency distribution would not be necessary to analyze so few values.)

Amount of weekly sales	Number of sales (f)
$ 600 – 799	2
800 – 999	3
1,000 – 1,199	4
1,200 – 1,399	3
1,400 – 1,599	1
Total	13

The mean — How do we determine the mean sales from the distribution? The concept of the mean is the same whether it is computed from the complete listing or from the frequency distribution: it is the sum of all the values divided by the total number of values. In the frequency distribution, however, the items are placed in the various groups, so there is no way of telling the precise amount of each individual value. Therefore, the exact amounts of each of the two values in the first class, $600-$799, would not be known (unless the complete listing were available and could be examined). Neither would we know the exact amounts of each of the three items in the class $800-$999, or in the remaining classes.

Faced only with a frequency distribution we are stymied in trying to arrive at the sum of all x-values. Statisticians, however, have worked out a way of computing the mean by assuming that the midpoint (m) of each class represents the value of each case in that class. Then, by multiplying the number of cases or frequency of cases (f) in each class by its midpoint (m), we arrive at an appropriate subtotal (fm) of the x-values in that class. By adding these class subtotals, $\Sigma(fm)$, we obtain the grand total needed to compute the mean by the standard method as will be explained momentarily.

Statistical experience has demonstrated that by assuming each of the values in a group to be equal to the midpoint of the group and by multiplying the number of items in the group (f) by its midpoint (m), we usually get a reasonably close approximation of the sum of the items in the group. The product (fm) for a given group may in some cases be larger and in others smaller than the actual sum of that group of items. However, in the long run (i.e., in large samples), the differences offset each other and thus tend to make the sum of all the group subtotals (Σfm) a reasonably accurate approximation of the actual sum of all the values.

Once a good approximation for Σx is available, i.e., by $\Sigma(fm)$, the mean of the data can be estimated from the frequency distribution by dividing $\Sigma(fm)$ by n, the total number of values in the set of data. The standard formula for the mean from the frequency distribution, therefore,

becomes $\overline{X} = \dfrac{\Sigma(fm)}{n}$, where f is the frequency of the class or the number

of values in it, m is the midpoint of the class, and fm is the product of the two for any group; $\Sigma(fm)$ represents the sum of the individual group-products of f times m — it is an estimate of the total of all the x-values; and n is the sum of all the class frequency counts, i.e., $\Sigma f = n$. In mathematical symbols, these calculations are portrayed in the

formula: $\overline{X} = \dfrac{\Sigma(fm)}{\Sigma f}$ or $\dfrac{\Sigma(fm)}{n}$.

The method and the calculations are illustrated in the accompanying table.

Amount of weekly sales (hundreds)	Frequency (f)	Midpoint (m)	Frequency times midpoint (fm)
$ 600 - 799	2	$ 700*	$ 1400
800 - 999	3	900	2700
1000 - 1199	4	1100	4400
1200 - 1399	3	1300	3900
1400 - 1599	1	1500	1500

Total count = $\Sigma f = n = 13$ Total of all values = $\Sigma fm = \$13,900$

$$\overline{X} = \frac{\Sigma(fm)}{n} = \$13,900 / 13 = \$1,069$$

The mean computed from the frequency distribution, $1,069, is slightly different from the actual mean of $1,060, determined from the ungrouped data. The reason for the difference can be ascribed mostly to the fact that we are dealing with a small number of cases (n=13) and also that the midpoints are assumed to represent each of the individual values in the class.

It should be observed again that the formula for the mean computed from a frequency distribution is $\overline{X} = \Sigma(fm) / n$, that is, the sum of the products of the midpoints (m) of each group and the respective number of values (f) in the group, divided by the total number of values (n).

The median — The concept of the median is basically the same whether it is derived from an array or from a frequency distribution: it is a counting or a position-located item; it is a value above and below which lies an equal number of values (or items). In the frequency distribution, however, the resulting median may differ from the one obtained from the array because of the need to make certain assumptions (although the difference is usually insignificant when the set of data contains a large number of values). In dealing with an array we attempt to have a median value represented by a specific item, one that actually occurs. In a frequency distribution we do not know the actual value of each item in a group, so that the value of the median item must be estimated. The method of estimation assumes that the values in each group are evenly spread over the class-interval, i.e., they are in size-place order and each item in the

---

* The midpoint is $700 because the variable is considered to be continuous and the upper limit of the group $600-$799 actually ends in $799.99. The midpoint is the point midway between $600 and $800, or $700.

group differs from its adjacent one by an equal amount over the range of the class. It also assumes that the variable under study is continuous even though in fact it may be noncontinuous. This latter assumption could result in an estimated median value that does not actually exist.

Since the frequency distribution is itself an orderly size-place arrangement of values in groups either in ascending or descending order, it lends itself readily to the derivation of the median. The first step is to determine which is the middle case (n/2), since this would be the point where half the values are assumed to lie on one side and half on the other side. The next step is to count accumulatively the number of items, starting with the first group, to determine in which group the median item lies. The final step is to determine the value of the (n/2)-th item in that group. This is done by assuming (as indicated above) that the items in the group that contains the median differ from each other by equal amounts within the class-interval; we then count to reach the middle item in that class.

In our illustrative problem the median would be the value of the n/2-th item, or the value of item number 6.5 (13/2). This happens to be located in the interval $1000-$1199, counting cumulatively from the top towards the bottom (or vica versa). To find the value of the median item in this group, we must interpolate in it. Thus, the following four steps are taken to determine the median:

1. Determine which is the middle case by dividing n by 2 (e.g., 13/2 = 6.5-th case).

2. Determine the group that contains the middle item. Thus, the 6.5-th item in our frequency distribution of weekly sales is located in the group $1000 - $1199. This was determined by counting cumulatively the number of items starting with the first group, as follows: 2 in the first group; 3 more in the next, which makes cumulatively 5 items; and 4 more in the next group ($1000 - 1199), which makes 9 items. It is obvious that the 6.5-th item is somewhere in the group $1000 - $1199 and that its value is at least $1000, because it is an item past the beginning of the group.

3. Determine how many items we need to count or to go in this group to reach the 6.5-th or median item. Since we need the value of the 6.5-th item and we have already counted 5 items

through the group $800 - $900, we obviously need 1.5 more items (i.e., 6.5 – 5) to reach the median item.

4. Estimate the value of the median item by interpolation, i.e., by assuming that the items in the group containing the median are spaced an equal distance apart from each other over the interval of the group. In other words, the class-interval (i) of the group and the number of items (f) within it will determine the equal size of the difference between successive items in the group, i.e., i / f. Thus, since in our problem the middle item lies in the group $1000 - $1199, the spotlight is cast on this group. It has four items (f) that have to be spaced an equal distance apart over an interval (i) of $200. This means that each item is assumed to differ from its adjacent one by $50, i.e., by $200 / 4 or (i / f). Thus, the first of the four items in the spot-light class will be at $1050. If we needed to go one more item to reach the median item, we would be at $1100. However, we need only go one-half an item, or $25 more, to reach the middle item. This would mean that the median is $1075 (i.e., $1050 + $25).

This procedure is compacted into the following formula after steps 1, 2 and 3 are taken:

Median (n/2-th) value $= L + \dfrac{g\,i}{f}$, where each term is defined as follows:

L stands for the lower limit of the class containing the middle (n/2-th) item;

g stands for the number of items in that class we need to go (or count) to reach the middle case;

i stands for the size of the interval of that class; and

f stands for the frequency (or number of items) in that class.

The above formula is repeated in words below:

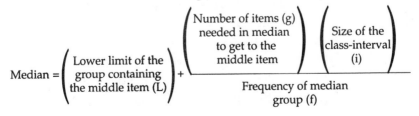

By substituting the appropriate figures into this formula we obtain the median value as $1,075:

$$\text{Median} = \$1000 + \frac{(1.5)(\$200)}{4} = \$1000 + \frac{\$300}{4} = \$1,075 \ .$$

Note that this median value differs but slightly from the median value of $1,085 obtained earlier from the array of ungrouped values.

Graphic determination of the median — For those who find it easier to use a graph, a graphic method of determining the median is available. This method involves plotting two separate cumulative frequency distributions on a graph, the *"more-than"* and the *"less-than" cumulative distributions.* The point of intersection of the two frequency curves is the estimated median value. In the sales problem, the following two cumulative distributions are used to illustrate the graphic method of estimating the median.

The "less-than" cumulative distribution		The "more-than" cumulative distribution	
Less than $800	2	$600 or more	13
Less than $1000	5	$800 or more	11
Less than $1200	9	$1000 or more	8
Less than 1400	12	$1200 or more	4
Less than $1600	13	$1400 or more	1

A graph of the two cumulative frequency distributions is shown below.

Figure 4.1
Cumulative distribution of sales, by amount of sale

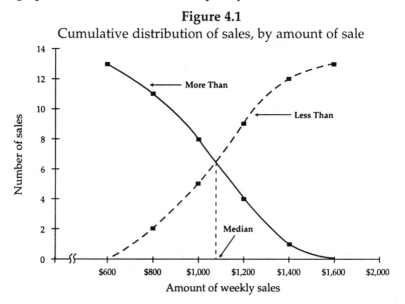

The point of intersection of the two curves, when read on the horizontal scale, is about $1,080. If coordinate paper is used, so that the scales are fairly precise, this intersection gives an accurate estimate of the median.

The mode — Since the mode is the value of the item that occurs most frequently, the first step in determining the mode is to locate the class with the greatest number of values. (Note: Uniform class intervals are essential.) There are two ways of estimating the modal value of the variable. The simplest method is to assume that the midpoint of the modal class is the modal value. Therefore, by this method, the modal sales in our demonstration problem (see frequency distribution) would be $1,100. This method is generally satisfactory when the frequency distribution is symmetrical and has uniform class intervals. In highly asymmetrical or skewed distributions, a more refined method must be used.*

Uses of Averages in Management Problems

Now that the methods of determining the three principal averages have been demonstrated, the practical-minded reader might raise a few relevant questions, such as: Why do we need to know how to calculate these averages? Of what use is this statistical tool in business, industry, government, management, or research problems? Also, why do we need to know three different averages (or more)?

Averages are used in summarizing and analyzing large masses of data. Therefore they can aid management in many different situations — decision-making, planning, forecasting, etc. Some of the uses may be illustrated by the following:

(1) Generalizing

An average helps us to reduce a mass of data into a single "typical" figure, so that we can draw a general conclusion about the phenomenon or problem being measured. Thus, if there are 1,000 workers in a given manufacturing company and we wish to generalize about the age composition of the work force, a mean age of 31, for example, would indicate a relatively young work force.

---

* This method takes into account the number of values in the groups immediately adjoining the modal group. The formula is: $Mo = L + \frac{f_h}{(f_h + f_l)}(i)$, where Mo is the mode, L is the value of the lower limit of the group containing the modal item, f_h is the number of items in the next higher group, f_l is the number of items in the next lower group, and i is the class interval.

(2) Comparison of different groups

An average is useful in comparing one set of data with others, since general conclusions can then be drawn about the comparative characteristics of the separate sets of data.

As an example, the average tearing weight of one grade of paper may be compared with that of another grade to determine which is stronger. The one with a higher mean tearing weight would be considered the more durable paper. Another example is a comparative study of heights of students in several classes. The average height of students in one class may be compared with the averages for other classes, to determine which class has the tallest students, on average.

(3) Setting standards

The Weather Bureau regularly uses averages in reporting temperature and rainfall readings. Thus, by calculating the mean peak temperature of a city on a given day based on many temperature readings for that day in previous years, a standard for comparison or "normal" is established. Daily peak readings can then be determined as being a specific number of degrees above or below "normal" for that day.

In a certain company, 100 fully trained operators produce manufactured assemblies. Some operators prepare 5,000 assemblies a workday, others 6,000, others fewer, and others more. What is a reasonable standard of production for an operator in this company? An average can be used effectively to calculate the standard of performance actually attained for each type of assembly.

(4) Estimating totals and planning

The payroll manager of a company knows from a previous study the mean weekly wages of the company's 350 workers. How much money would be needed on Friday to meet the next payroll? An answer to that question can be obtained quickly by multiplying the mean wage by 350.

A quality control system was adopted in a given organization to determine, on a sample basis, the extent of monetary errors in a billing process. A random sample of n=100 invoices out of a total of N=400 invoices was audited and the total value of the monetary errors in the sample was found to be $750. The mean error per invoice therefore was estimated as $7.50 (i.e., $750/100). It may be inferred from the random sample that if all the invoices were checked, the same mean error would be obtained. Therefore, the estimated total amount of errors on all invoices would be $3000 (i.e., $N\overline{X}$ or 400 times $7.50).

As an additional example of this very important use of the mean (but not the median or mode), let us assume that a manufacturer has received an order to produce 3,500,000 "giant" size paper clips. An earlier study has indicated that an operator produces on the average (mean) 10,000 clips an hour on a standard machine with its related packaging line in good working order. How many machine operator hours will be needed to meet the order? The answer is 350 hours (i.e., 3,500,000/10,000). With this estimate of the resources needed, the company can estimate how many days it would require to fill the order depending upon the number of machines and operators that it can assign to the job.

Without the mean it would have been difficult to make this type of estimate, which is necessary for proper scheduling of the job. The mean, thus, can aid in production planning and scheduling, establishing standards, controlling billing errors, etc. In general, if we know or can estimate the arithmetic mean ($\overline{X}$) by a sample (n) and also the total number of items in the universe (N), then we can estimate the grand total of the values by multiplying the mean value by the number of items, i.e., the grand total = $N\overline{X}$.

Other uses

The mean is also used in constructing index numbers, in correlation analysis (Chapter 12), and in other analytical problems, particularly in a large number of situations when dealing with normal frequency distributions or the bell-curve (Chapter 5).

Which Average to Use

From these examples, it is clear that the arithmetic mean is a useful statistical tool for research, business, and management, but we have not yet answered the question: Why do we need to know three *different* averages? Couldn't one average be used to serve all purposes? The answer is: No. While the mean is the most useful of the averages, there are situations where only the median or mode is needed or appropriate. Furthermore, in some cases, the form or nature of the available data does not permit the determination of the mean but it does the median or mode. Two main criteria determine which average to use in dealing with a problem. One is the use to be made of the average and the other is the nature or form of the available data.

Following are a few guidelines for selecting the average to use under different conditions.

The problem at hand

(1) To determine the most stylish or most frequently occurring item we would use the mode. Thus, when we need to determine the "typical" size of family, or the typical family income, or the typical mortgage amount we would need to use the mode, which deals with the most frequently occurring item.

(2) If the problem were to determine an average that would indicate its position or ranking in relation to all the values, we would use the median. For example, what is the average population of cities in the United States? It would be the population of that city which would be larger than half of all cities and smaller than the other half (in population).*

(3) To determine a standard, or norm, for comparison we generally would want to use the mean. For example, what is the normal peak temperature for May 5 in your city? It would be the arithmetic mean of all May 5 peak temperatures over a long period of time. In quality control, the mean dimension of a product or service is often established as the bulls-eye or goal to achieve.

(4) To estimate the aggregate or total amount of all outstanding accounts, we would use the mean, since only this average, when computed from a random sample can be used to estimate the total value of all items by using $N\overline{X}$.

(5) The mean is the average that takes into account all the values of the variable, giving each one a weight according to its magnitude. The resultant average is a *point of balance* or an *equilibrium point*. In fact, the mean is often identified as the *moment-of-force* or center of gravity in engineering uses. It is the point at which the stresses and strains in the various directions are balanced (or where the sum of the differences of the individual values from their mean is equal to zero, as shown in Chapter 5). Thus, it is useful in construction engineering and related problems where precise balance points are essential.

---

* The concept of the median as the 50-th percentile (the value of the $n/2$-th case for sample data, or the $N/2$-th case for the universe) can be extended to determine other locational values, such as the value of the first quartile ($n/4$ or $N/4$-th case) or the first percentile ($n/100$ or $N/100$-th case).

(6)   The mean is the most commonly used average. Because it is most widely known, the mean may be selected for simplicity in presenting and quoting averages to persons with no statistical background.

The nature or form of the basic data

Even though one or another average may be needed to serve a specific use, technical difficulties created by the form of the data being analyzed often preclude the determination of the required average.

(1)   Generally the mean cannot be computed accurately when the frequency distribution has an open-ended class at either extreme. For example, when a frequency distribution of families by amount of their income is analyzed, the last class interval is usually open-ended (e.g., "$100,000 or more").   Calculation of the mean from a frequency distribution requires the use of the midpoint for each class, and an open-ended distribution does not readily provide a midpoint for the open-ended classes.   When it is not possible to make a reasonably accurate estimate of the midpoint of the open-ended class, we are forced to use either the median or the mode as the average.   The Bureau of the Census publications on annual family income in the United States use the median as the average family income in most of their tables, although in some instances they present mean family income by estimating a midpoint for the open-ended classes by special research methods.

(2)   When a closed frequency distribution of *unequal class intervals* is used, it may be impossible to determine the mode accurately.   The largest number of values may, for example, fall in the class with the widest interval, and yet the most frequently occurring actual value may be located in a narrower class interval. Either the mean or median is used in such a situation.

(3)   When an average must be determined quickly from a set of ungrouped data, the mean can be computed by adding the values without grouping. Both the median and mode require that the data be arranged in order of size before they can be determined accurately. Therefore, when an average is needed quickly, a mean computed from the ungrouped data may be used.   (Another quick method is to compute the *average of the extremes*, by adding the highest and lowest values and dividing the sum by two, although using just the two extreme values can often lead to very misleading results.)

(4) When the variable is of a noncontinuous type (e.g., rented apartments distributed by number of rooms, pairs of shoes by size), it is generally preferred to determine the median or mode as actual existing values, since in ungrouped sets of data they generally will yield an average value that actually exists and not an impossible value, such as 3.7 rooms per apartment or hat size of 7.2. Of course, other considerations, such as the need to estimate the aggregate of the values, might make it preferable to use the mean even though the variable is noncontinuous.

(5) In some sets of data there are a few extremely large or extremely small values at either end of the array (or the frequency distribution), and yet the great majority of the values concentrate around a narrow band. In such instances the median (or mode) may be the preferred average because it is not affected by the extreme values while the mean is influenced by extreme values, which tend to draw the mean toward them.

(6) When there are only a few values, say fewer than 15, it may not be possible to determine the mode, since there may be no more than one value of any given amount. In such instances either the mean or median is the preferred average to use.

It can be seen from the foregoing that the mean is usually the most useful of the three averages. However, it is not necessarily the most "accurate." None of the averages is "more accurate" than any other; each is a description of the central tendency of a set of data, with its own special characteristics.

Averages and the Normal Distribution

In Chapter 3, a description was given of the normal frequency distribution and it was stated that it was important in many practical applications. It will be recalled that a normal distribution may be expected when any of the four conditions listed in Chapter 3 is involved. Since the normal distribution is a symmetrical distribution, its three averages — the mean, median, and mode — are equal. When the mode is estimated as the midpoint of the class with the greatest frequency, it is easy to determine the mean and median values too, since they are all the same.

An illustration that the three averages of a symmetrical frequency distribution are equal is given by the following:

Height of students in a school (in inches)	Number of students in sample (f)
64-65	1
66-67	6
68-69	18
70-71	36
72-73	18
74-75	6
76-77	1
Total	86

What are the mean, median, and mode in this frequency distribution? When actually calculated from the frequency distribution, by the methods described earlier, the mean is 71.00 inches; the mode is 71.00 inches, and the median is 71.00 inches. (The reader should actually calculate the mean, mode, and median to check these results.) It seems logical to expect the averages to be equal when we think of the concept of each of the averages: the mean being a balance point, the median a middle value, and the mode a concentration point. In a symmetrical distribution all these points are located at the peak point on the scale of the variable.

Another significant fact about the averages in relation to the normal distribution is that the mean, together with another statistical measure, the standard deviation, can be used to construct the complete frequency distribution from which the data originated. This fact provides a basis for accurately estimating many characteristics of the general population when the frequency distribution forms a bell-shaped curve. (See Chapter 5 for illustrations.)

Special Sections

Short-Cut Methods of Computing the Mean

The task of computing the mean without the aid of computers or calculators becomes laborious when the values are large in magnitude and especially when the number of values in the set is large. To facilitate and expedite computing the mean in such situations, short-cut methods have been developed. In this section, we present two such methods, one dealing with ungrouped data and the other when the data are in the form of a frequency distribution.

Later in this section we illustrate the concept of a *weighted mean*, to enhance our understanding of averages and the correct technique for calculating the arithmetic mean.

From ungrouped data

The main basis for computing the mean by short-cut methods is the fact that, in all cases, the sum of the differences of the individual values from their mean is equal to zero. This fact was mentioned but not proven earlier in the chapter when reference was made to the mean as a point of balance or an equilibrium point. This fact is demonstrated in Chapter 5 in the section on "Methods of Measuring Variation."

Taking this fact for granted, the short-cut method of computing the mean from a set of ungrouped values may be illustrated by using three simple numbers: 1, 6, and 2. If we guess correctly that the mean of this set of numbers is 3, the sum of the differences of the individual values from the guessed mean should be equal to zero. Thus, $(1 - 3) + (6 - 3) + (2 - 3) = (-2 + 3 - 1) = 0$. Since the sum of the differences is zero, we are sure that the mean actually is 3, as we guessed.

On the other hand, if our guess was incorrect, the sum of the differences of the individual values from the incorrectly-guessed mean would not equal zero; it would either be a minus or a plus number, depending on whether we over-guessed or under-guessed the mean.

Assume that we guessed the mean of the above three values to be 4. The differences of the individual values from it would then be $(1 - 4) + (6 - 4) + (2 - 4) = (-3 + 2 - 2) = -3$. The correct mean could then be obtained by adjusting the guessed mean, so that the sum of the differences from the correct mean would be zero. This is done by the following equation:

$$\text{Correct mean } (\overline{X}) = \text{Guessed mean } (\overline{X}_g) + \frac{\text{Sum of the differences from the guessed mean } (\Sigma d)}{\text{number of values (n)}}.$$

In symbols, the formula becomes: $\overline{X} = \overline{X}_g + \Sigma d/n$.

An example follows (where the guessed mean is 2, but the correct mean is actually 3):

Value (x)	$(x - \overline{X}_g) = d$
2	0
4	+2
3	+1
Total..... 9	+3

So, the correct mean $(\overline{X}) = \overline{X}_g + \Sigma d/n = 2 + 3/3 = 3$

Thus, given any set of ungrouped values, we can use the short-cut method to compute its mean by: (1) guessing the mean by observation or judgment; (2) obtaining the difference between each individual value and the guessed mean; (3) obtaining the algebraic sum of these differences; (4) dividing the resulting sum by the number of values in the set (to get an average difference per value); and (5) adding, or subtracting, the resulting average difference (as the case may be) from the guessed mean.

This is considered a short-cut method because it reduces the addition of large-magnitude figures (i.e., the original x-values) to figures of smaller magnitude — i.e., differences from a guessed mean — and can sometimes save time when not using a computer. Its main advantage, though, comes about when, in addition to computing the mean manually, we also need to compute the standard deviation. (See Chapter 5.) When a computer is used, there is little advantage to this short-cut method.

From a frequency distribution

When a frequency distribution is involved, the short-cut method of computing the mean continues to be based on the concept that the sum of the differences from the mean must equal zero (i.e., $\Sigma fd = 0$). However, because we are dealing with class intervals and midpoints which represent the values in each class, the method of computing the adjustment factor to apply to the guessed mean is different.

Suppose we have the following frequency distribution of 50 supervisory employees in an office, by their hourly wages, showing also the mid-points for each class.

Hourly wages	Number of employees f	Midpoint m
$40 - 45.99	1	43
46 - 51.99	3	49
52 - 57.99	6	55
58 - 63.99	8	61
64 - 69.99	11	67
70 - 75.99	7	73
76 - 81.99	5	79
82 - 87.99	4	85
88 - 93.99	3	91
94 - 99.99	2	97

$$\text{Total} = \Sigma f = n = 50$$

By the method illustrated earlier in this chapter, the mean would be computed by multiplying the class-frequencies by their corresponding midpoints (to get a column of fm values), adding the separate products (Σfm), and dividing the resulting sum by the number of values in the set, i.e., $\overline{X} = \Sigma(fm) / n$.

Here, the main idea in the short-cut method is to guess a mean and then adjust it by determining how far off from zero is the sum of the differences from the guessed mean. If the guessed mean is a value equal to one of the class midpoints, a considerable amount of computing work can be saved, particularly when the frequency distribution has uniform class intervals. The procedure is as follows:

(1) Assume that the midpoint of one of the classes is the guessed mean. For example, $67 in hourly wages, the midpoint of $64-$69.99, is the guessed mean.

(2) In the difference column, place a zero for the group whose midpoint was chosen as the guessed mean.

(3) Determine, in terms of number of classes, the difference between the class containing the guessed mean and adjacent classes. Thus, the class-interval just above the one representing the guessed mean is –1 class off the guessed mean; the next one is –2 classes off; etc. The classes below

the guessed mean are +1, +2, etc. The column of difference-figures is identified as the "d" column (see example).

(4) Multiply the frequency in each class by the number in the d column, the product (fd) being either a negative or positive value. This multiplication process yields a column of fd figures.

(5) The sum of the negative products (Σfd's) is obtained separately and the sum (Σfd's) of the positive products is obtained separately.

(6) The net difference which results from adding the two sums (either a minus or plus amount) is used as a basis for adjusting the guessed mean.

(7) The guessed mean ($\overline{X}_g$) is then adjusted by the net sum (Σfd) obtained above, divided by the total number of items in the distribution (n), and then multiplied by the size of the class-interval (i).

The formula is: $\overline{X} = \overline{X}_g + \dfrac{(\Sigma fd)i}{n}$.

Turning to our hypothetical frequency distribution of 50 employees by their hourly wages, we illustrate each of the above seven steps, as follows:

Hourly wages	f	m	d	fd (step 4)	
$40 - $45	1	43	−4	−4	
46 - 51	3	49	−3	−9	
52 - 57	6	55	−2	(step 3)	−12	(step 5) Σfd = −33
58 - 63	8	61	−1	−8	
64 - 69	11	$\overline{X}_g$: 67 (step 1)	0 (step 2)	0	
70 - 75	7	73	1	+7	
76 - 81	5	79	2	+10	
82 - 87	4	85	3	(step 3)	+12	(step 5) Σfd = +51
88 - 93	3	91	4	+12	
94 - 99	2	97	5	+10	

(step 6) Net Σfd = +18

(step 7)

$$\overline{X} = \overline{X}_g + \left(\frac{\Sigma fd}{n}\right)i = 67 + \left(\frac{+18}{50}\right)6 = 67 + \left(\frac{108}{50}\right) = 67 + 2.16 = \$69.16 \text{ per hour}$$

Two points of caution should be noted in using this short-cut method:

(1) It applies *only* to a frequency distribution with uniform class intervals. Specialized methods are needed for non-uniform or open-ended frequency distributions. Therefore, to use the above method, a uniform frequency distribution should be constructed, if feasible.

(2) The column of differences (d) is obtained by determining the *number of classes* each specific class is removed from the class containing the guessed mean (the d=0 class). Therefore, if the frequency distribution is in ascending order, the d's above d=0 will be negative and those below it will be positive integers. Conversely, if the frequency distribution is in descending order, the d's above d=0 will be positive and those below it will be negative integers. It is important to show the correct sign for d, since the sign determines if the adjustment is negative or positive.

How to Compute a Weighted Mean

Weighted means are particularly important in problems involving the mean of two or more sets of data, when each set differs in relative importance or frequency (e.g., average food prices which combines several different food prices into a mean). An illustration of the weighted mean follows:

Suppose that the two divisions of a department store report their average amount per sale for last week as follows:

Division No. 1	$75.00 per sale
Division No. 2	$25.00 per sale

What is the average sale for the entire department store? The answer is not $50.00 per sale. The latter average is commonly thought to be correctly obtained by adding the two separate averages and dividing the sum by 2. However, this method represents an unweighted average and would be correct only in the exceptional situation when both divisions made exactly the same number of sales.

To compute the correct average, it is essential to know the number and total amount of sales made in each division. These numbers represent the weights (or multipliers) for each division. Suppose that division No.1 made 1,000 sales and division No.2 made 500 sales; the correct average would then be $58.33. It is obtained by multiplying each division's average by the known number of sales $(N\overline{X})$ to get the total amount of the sales in each division. This sum is then divided by the total number of sales $(N_1 + N_2)$ to get the overall and correctly weighted mean. The procedure is shown in the following table.

Division	Mean Sale $(\overline{X})$	Total Number of Sales (N)	Total amount = Product of mean and total number of sales $(N\overline{X})$
1	$75.00	1,000	$75,000
2	25.00	500	12,500
	Totals	1,500	$ 87,500

$$\text{Correct (weighted) mean} = \frac{\$87,500}{1,500} = \$58.33.$$

The general formula for obtaining a weighted mean is similar to the formula used in computing a mean from a frequency distribution, i.e., $\overline{X} = \Sigma fm / n$, where m is the midpoint or mean value for a group, f is the frequency of the group or weight, and n is the total of the weights (or the sample size, Σf), and Σfm is the sum of the products which result from multiplying the weights by their respective midvalues.

Summary

Perhaps the most important feature of this chapter is the illustration of the varied and widespread usefulness of averages in dealing with practical problems, once the problem has been reduced to measurable terms. What more objective method of setting a standard of actual performance is there than by the mean computed from homogeneous data obtained on the varying performance of individual processes or people?   The standard provides a basis for making comparisons and for making informed decisions.   In setting specifications for the quality of a product to be manufactured, a useful way to determine the "natural" capabilities of the process under its normal operating conditions is to randomly select a sufficient number of measurable items from the machine and calculate the mean and then allow for normal variation around it.   Similarly, measures of service time and customer satisfaction can be presented by the mean quality of service.   The mean is also a useful statistical tool for management in scheduling, in incentive programs, in estimating totals when the average is derived from a random sample, and in statistical process control (Chapter 11).

Of the several averages that are useful for analysis of measurable processes, the most useful is the mean. The median is useful in problems dealing with rank comparisons, and the mode is useful in determining typical or most fashionable values. In frequency distributions that are approximately symmetrical and bell-shaped, the three averages will be about the same in value, and the easiest way to calculate them may be to estimate the mode by the midpoint value of the class with the greatest frequency.

There are a number of misuses of averages to guard against. One results from the misconception that each value of the variable is the same as the average. Another results from not knowing that there is more than one type of average and that each type has a different meaning and use. Another misuse of an average occurs when it is used to draw a general conclusion from data that are not homogeneous or represent two or more universes where the average represents neither one nor the other universe.

Problems

1. There are three principal averages. Demonstrate your comprehension of each by determining the mode, median, and mean from the following data on the age of 15 workers in a plant (where age is as of last birthday):

    Age in years: 25, 36, 23, 41, 33, 30, 24, 25,
                          30, 54, 50, 30, 21,20, 55.

2. What do we mean by "an average of position" and "an average of calculation"? Of the averages in problem 1, which are position averages and which is called an average of calculation?

3. If experience has shown that the average child begins to take first steps at 12 months, then the child who doesn't walk at 12 months is abnormal and the parents should consult a doctor. Analyze this statement in the light of your knowledge of averages.

4. Two statistical analysts came up with different averages from the same set of data on the earnings of workers in an industry. Did one or the other or both make a mistake in arithmetic? Explain.

5. Set up a grouped frequency distribution of the 15 values (age in years) listed in problem 1 above, and

   (a) Determine the mean, median, and mode from it.

   (b) Because the respective averages in this problem differ from those derived in problem 1 above, there is something wrong. (True or false?)

   (c) Give one reason why the respective averages here may differ from those derived in problem 1.

   (d) Which of the three averages discussed in this chapter is the most accurate? Why?

6. Two different brands of washing machines were tested for length of service by use of a very large sample of each brand, with the following results:

Brand of machine	Median life	Mean life
A	3,000 hours	3,500 hours
B	3,500 hours	3,000 hours

   You are preparing to purchase 20 machines for your company. Which of these two brands would you say is likely to last longer, that is, give a higher aggregate number of hours of use? Explain.

7. Suppose you are the payroll manager of a business organization with 150 wage earners, and from last year's data on the average weekly wages of these workers for the first week of October you knew the following: Median weekly wages, $1,448; mean weekly wages, $1,465; modal weekly wages, $1,440. Approximately how much money would you need to pay the 150 wage earners of the company for the first week of October in the current year if the wage level has increased 10 percent?

8. In 20 seconds, make your best estimate of the mean length of steel nail produced by a single machine, if the following data were

obtained by measuring the length of a representative sample of 723 nails.

Length of nail (in inches)	Number of nails (f)
3.40-3.41	42
3.42-3.43	70
3.44-3.45	145
3.46-3.47	216
3.48-3.49	140
3.50-3.51	75
3.52-3.53	35
Total =	723

(a) Explain your method of estimating the mean and the reason for having confidence in it.

(b) How does your estimate compare with the mean computed from the actual data in the frequency distribution shown?

9. Specify which of the three averages you would use in making the following estimates. In each case, justify (explain) your choice.

(a) Estimate the average income of physicians from data on annual incomes of doctors collected from a special survey.

(b) Estimate the average age of the United States population from census data showing a frequency distribution of people by age.

(c) Estimate the aggregate national income of families in a given year when only one of the three averages of family income and the total number of families in the United States are known.

(d) Estimate the average size of straw hats sold to men in the Spring and Summer.

(e) Estimate the predominant color of bathing suits sold in the United States.

(f) Estimate the average daily amount of rainfall in a given city in the course of a year.

10. Through the use of statistics, how can you tell which Winter was colder, the one just past or the one in the preceding year?

Problems — Special Sections

11. Compute the mean age of the students in problem 1 by use of the short-cut method for computing the mean from ungrouped data.

12. Following are the weights (in pounds) of 20 students in a class.

170	120	185	178	112
145	147	198	168	135
125	157	206	145	160
110	138	145	150	129

Compute the mean weight by the long and short method, keeping track of the time required to complete each computation. Which required more time and how much more?

13. The following is a frequency distribution of 60 families in a given low-cost apartment house, by the amount of weekly rental. Compute the mean weekly rental per family by use of the short method for frequency distributions.

Weekly rental	Number of families	Weekly rental	Number of families
$ 80 - 89.99	3	$ 120 - 129.99	15
90 - 99.99	7	130 - 139.99	10
100 - 109.99	8	140 - 149.99	4
110 - 119.99	10	150 - 159.99	3
		Total =	60

14. The following are the tearing weights for two grades of paper, based on a test conducted with a sample of n=100 strips of each grade. Determine which is probably a stronger grade of paper.

Paper A Tearing weight in pounds	f	Paper B Tearing weight in pounds	f
3 - 4	5	3 - 4	12
5 - 6	20	5 - 6	16
7 - 8	40	7 - 8	46
9 - 10	35	9 - 10	26
Total =	100	Total =	100

15. Two agencies pay different monthly salaries to their clerical, data-entry, and secretarial staff, as shown below. Agency A has 30 such employees and Agency B has 50 such employees. Determine the overall average monthly salary paid by each agency.

Job Classification	Monthly Salary	Number of employees Agency A	Agency B
Secretarial Staff	$4,500	5	4
Data-entry Staff	4,000	7	28
Clerical Staff	3,500	18	18
		Total = 30	Total = 50

16. The hourly wage rate paid by a given retail specialty store in 1990 was $8 for inexperienced help and $12.00 for experienced help. In 1995, the wage rate for inexperienced help rose to $9.25 an hour and for experienced help to $14.50 an hour. Determine the overall average hourly wage rate paid by the company in each of the two years if it employed the number of persons shown below.

Type of Employee	Calendar Year 1990	1995
Inexperienced	18	22
Experienced	30	28
	Total = 48	Total = 50

Chapter 5

Variation —
Its Measurement and Analysis

"Variation seems inevitable in nature... Whether one is attempting to control a dimension of a part which is to go into a precision assembly, the resistance of a relay, the acidity of a solution used for dyeing textiles, the weight of the contents of a container, or any other quality of a manufactured product, it is certain that the quality will vary."*

This chapter tries to make us more aware of the universal existence of variation in the world we live in and in all the problems of managing organizations. It will show that management processes or activities cannot be fully understood or interpreted unless the extent to which they differ or vary is known in quantitative terms. The chapter therefore presents methods of measuring variation and illustrates ways of applying this knowledge to specific types of business, government, and management activities. It particularly stresses the fixed pattern of variation characteristic of the normal or bell-shaped frequency distribution, which provides a guide for many management decisions.

Universal Existence of Variation

When we look around us we see people with different characteristics — some have black hair, others have gray hair; some are tall, others are short; some are heavy, some are light. In general, no two human beings are exactly alike.

Similarly, when we look at activities in the business world and government we also note the ever-presence of variability. Employment in a company or industry varies from month to month and sometimes from day to day; production volume and production

---

* E. L. Grant, *Statistical Quality Control*, McGraw-Hill, 1964.

rates vary; company sales differ from day to day; a person's productivity or quality of work performed on the job will differ from time to time; a machine in a production process will produce items that differ in dimension or weight; a given grade of material will differ in thickness or hardness from point to point. The list of variations can continue indefinitely; no single aspect of our universe is static.

Not only is variation universal, but different activities vary to different extents. In other words, even variation varies. Thus, some persons are more consistent in their performance than others; some machines are more precise in their productivity than others; some products are more uniform in quality than others. It is clear from these truisms that we live in a world of differences and that we would be better able to understand this world if we could measure the extent of variability in its differing activities and phenomena. Since variability is also present in every aspect of management's functions, it follows that better and more informed management actions and decisions can result from an appreciation of the existence of variation and a knowledge of the extent of variability in different processes.

Quantitative Concept of Variation

The preceding chapter pointed out that one misuse of averages results from the fact that each of the values of a variable is sometimes considered to be the same as the average. The truth is that an average, being just a single figure representing a mass of values and thus serving an important use, conceals the variation around it. Knowledge about an activity or process can be extended beyond knowledge of its average by measuring its variability, for an average with great variability around it can often be meaningless or misused.

What is the basis for measuring variability in a set of data, regardless of whether they refer to jobs, workers, people, machines, material, or methods? The first prerequisite is the selection of a norm or standard against which the individual values may be compared to determine the amount of their differences. Without a norm we can well ask the question "Difference from what?" One value must be compared with another value or with a standard to determine the difference or variation between them. A useful method of setting a standard for comparison was illustrated in the preceding chapter, namely, the arithmetic mean. There, we were referring to the difference between a single value and the mean of all values.

However, in measuring variability of a set of values from their mean we will get as many differences as there are values or numbers in the set. The question then arises: How do we combine these differences to draw a general conclusion? The usual way is to average these many differences into a single figure. Thereby is created the concept of variation. *Variation is the average difference of the individual x-values from their mean value* $\overline{X}$.

The concept of variability may be illustrated by the following hypothetical data on the number of acceptable units of work produced by a worker in N=9 successive full days:*

Day	Units of Work
1	40
2	38
3	45
4	28
5	35
6	42
7	47
8	40
9	45
Total.....	360
Mean ($\overline{X}$).....	40

If we knew that the worker produced an average (mean) of 40 work units per day we could see from glancing at the data that the worker varied in productivity from day to day. Thus, on the first day average productivity was achieved; on the second it was two units short; on the third day average productivity was exceeded by five units; and so forth.

It can be seen that while this method of comparing the individual daily values with their average value shows the amount of variation for each day, it does not provide a basis for generalizing about the extent of variability or inconsistency in the worker's daily production. In other words, the data do not tell us whether daily production varied little, moderately, or greatly. If the number of values in the set of data were larger than nine, it would be even more difficult to generalize about the

---

* In the demonstration we are assuming, that we are dealing with a universe (not a sample) whose size is N=9.

extent of variation from looking at the individual differences from the average. What is needed is a single quantitative measure of variation that would provide a basis for generalizing. We now know that we can obtain a single figure from a set of figures by calculating an average. In fact, a commonly used method of measuring variation involves determining an average difference of the individual values from their average. With but slight modification, described in the next section, this is the basic definition of variability. Without the original average there would be no standard against which to compare the individual values. Without an average of the *differences* between the values and their overall average, there would be no basis for generalizing about the extent of variability.

This concept of variability may be further illustrated by the following example: Suppose we wish to find the height of the table in our dining room. If we take many measurements of the table's height, the various measures will differ one from another, even though slightly. The most accurate estimate of the true height of the table would be the mean of all the measurements. To what extent did the individual measurements differ from the true height (or the best estimate of the true height)? The best way of obtaining an answer is through a comparison of the individual measurements with the mean of all the measurements. The mean becomes the standard against which each of the individual measurements are compared. To generalize about the variability or error of measurement, however, we need an average of the individual differences from the average of all the original measurements.

We have purposely repeated the concept of variation several times because we believe that the measurement and analysis of variation, which exists in practically every field of human endeavor, is a must.

Methods of Measuring Variation

In light of the above concept of variation, let us see how we can actually measure the extent of variation in the worker's daily production, so that we can generalize about his or her consistency in production. First, we need an average of the nine daily production figures to use as a standard against which to compare each of the daily production figures. Any one of the three averages — the mean, the median, or the mode — can be used as a standard for comparison. However, as indicated in Chapter 4, the most useful average is the mean, and we will use it as a standard for comparison with the individual values. In some special cases, however, the median or mode may be used as the standard.

The average deviation

When we calculate the mean daily production for the worker we obtain a productivity rate of 40 units per day by the formula: $\overline{X} = \dfrac{\Sigma x}{N} = \dfrac{360}{9} = 40$. Since the main objective in measuring variation is to obtain an average variation of the individual values from their overall average value, we first calculate the differences between the individual values and the mean. To illustrate this step, let us look again at the daily production figures for the worker given earlier. The difference between the mean and each of the individual x-values, calculated by $d = x - \overline{X}$, are as follows:

Day	Units of work (x)	Difference from mean $(d = x - \overline{X})$		
1	40	40–40	=	0
2	38	38–40	=	–2
3	45	45–40	=	+5
4	28	28–40	=	–12
5	35	35–40	=	–5
6	42	42–40	=	+2
7	47	47–40	=	+7
8	40	40–40	=	0
9	45	45–40	=	+5

To obtain an average of the differences of the individual values from their overall average, that is, an average of the d's, it would seem that all we need to do is add the individual differences and divide the resulting sum by the number of values. When the column that represents the differences is added, however, we get the subtotals of +19 and –19, where the algebraic sum of these two subtotals is zero. When the sum of all the differences, zero, is divided by 9 (the number of values), the average difference is also zero. Does this result mean that the worker is completely consistent in his or her work? The actual production figures make it clear that this conclusion is not correct.

Why should the sum of the differences from the mean equal zero? Will it always be zero, or is this an exceptional case? The answer is that a definite and fixed characteristic of the arithmetic mean is that *the sum of the differences of individual values from their mean will always be zero.** (The reader should try a few more problems, and see if this is true. For example, given the following five numbers, 6, 4, 3, 2, and 10, the mean is 25/5 = 5, and the respective sum of the differences is 6–6 = 0.) Because of this property of the mean, as indicated in Chapter 4, engineers may use this average (but not the median or mode) in construction projects involving a point of equilibrium where the stresses and strains in all directions offset each other.

Since the algebraic sum of the differences from the mean is always zero, how can we get an average difference as a measure of variation? There are two ways. One way is to ignore the plus and minus signs and add the differences as if they were all plus differences. The other way is to square each difference, thus making all the differences plus values. By ignoring the signs, the average difference in the illustrative problem becomes $\dfrac{19 + 19}{9} = \dfrac{38}{9} = 4.2$ units. This average difference is defined as the *average deviation.*

Ignoring the sign of the differences is referred to as taking the *absolute values* of the differences. An *absolute value* is the value of a number (in this case, the difference) regardless of its sign, either positive or negative. While the average deviation can be used as a measure of variation, its utility is very limited in analyzing diverse statistical problems. On the other hand, the *standard deviation*, as described below, is useful in practically every analysis of variation problem because of its special mathematical properties, as will be seen throughout this book. In fact, some analysts consider the standard deviations as the most important analytical tool in statistical analysis.

The standard deviation

The other way of overcoming the problem of offsetting differences is done by squaring each difference. Squaring any number, i.e., multiplying it by itself, always results in a positive number; for example, –2 times –2, represented as $(-2)^2$, is 4. Thus, all squared differences are positive numbers. When these squared differences are added and divided by the number of measurements in the set, it yields an average

---

* Unless the mean is rounded.

difference but it is in squared units. To return this result to the original units of measurement, we take the square root of the squared average of the differences. The result is called the standard deviation.

A more complete definition of the standard deviation is thereby offered. *The **standard deviation** is a measure of the average difference of the individual x-values from their overall mean, using the technique of squares and square roots.*

Unlike the average deviation, which may be calculated around any average, the standard deviation *always* is computed around the mean in order to serve the large variety of its yet to be demonstrated uses. Calculation of the standard deviation is illustrated by use of the previous data on the daily production of a worker, as reproduced below. First, the differences (d-values) of the individual values from the mean are obtained, as before. In attempting to obtain an average of the differences, instead of ignoring the signs, we square the individual differences. An additional column of squared differences, symbolized by d^2 or $(x - \overline{X})^2$, is obtained, as follows:

Day	Units of work x	Difference from mean $d = (x - \overline{X})$	Squared difference $d^2 = (x - \overline{X})^2$
1	40	0	0
2	38	−2	4
3	45	+5	25
4	28	−12	144
5	35	−5	25
6	42	+2	4
7	47	+7	49
8	40	0	0
9	45	+5	25

It now becomes possible to add the column of squared differences (d^2) without encountering the problem of offsetting differences that yield a sum of zero. In the above problem, the sum of the squared differences (Σd^2) is 276. The average of the squared differences is

$$\frac{\Sigma d^2}{N} \text{ or } \frac{\Sigma(x - \overline{X})^2}{N} = \frac{276}{9} = 30.67 \text{ squared work units.}$$

The resulting average of the squared differences (30.67) is an inflated measure of the average variation of the values from their mean because the original differences were squared rather than left in their original measurement units. To correct this condition the square root is taken of the above average of the squared differences. In algebra we learn that the square root operation is the counter-operation to squaring a number. Thus, the square root of 30.67 is ±5.54 units. The resulting average of 5.54 units is called the *standard deviation*.

To assure that the method of computing this most important analytical tool is understood, we list the sequence of six steps taken in obtaining the standard deviation, as follows:

(1) Obtain the mean, $\overline{X}$, of all the values. This average is essential as a base from which to measure variation or differences.

(2) Calculate the difference between each value of the variable and the mean: $d = (x - \overline{X})$. The result is a column of differences (d's) containing as many numbers as there are values. (At this point, arithmetic errors in calculating the mean and the individual differences can be detected by checking to see whether the algebraic sum of the individual differences is equal to zero (provided the mean is not rounded).

(3) Square each difference, obtaining a column of positive numbers denoted by $(x - \overline{X})^2$ or d^2. With this step, the problem of offsetting plus and minus differences (whose sum would otherwise be zero) is avoided. However, we recognize that we are now dealing with inflated (squared) figures.

(4) Add the column of squared differences (d^2) to obtain the sum of squared differences: $\Sigma(x - \overline{X})^2$, or Σd^2. This sum is needed to calculate the average (mean) squared difference from the original average $(\overline{X})$.

(5) Divide the sum of the squared differences, $\Sigma(x - \overline{X})^2$, or Σd^2, by the number of values N.* The method is the same as that used in calculating any mean. At this stage, however, the resulting mean variation is in squared units, requiring step 6 as the final operation.

6) Take the square root of the mean of the squared differences. This step is necessary to counteract the inflation of the differences caused by squaring them in step 3. It also

---

* When data for the entire population is used, the divisor is N. However, when a random sample is used, the divisor is n-1 and the technically correct formula for σ_x is $\sqrt{\dfrac{\Sigma(x - \overline{X})^2}{n-1}}$.

converts the squared units into their original units. The resulting standard deviation is the square root of the mean of the squared differences.

These six steps are compactly summarized by using the following statistical symbols and formulas:

$$\sigma'_x = \sqrt{\frac{\Sigma(x-\bar{X}')^2}{N}} \; .$$

When computed from a sample,
$$\sigma_x = \sqrt{\frac{\Sigma(x-\bar{X})^2}{n-1}} \; .$$

Much of the language of statistics is in symbols and it is essential to learn their meaning so that the meaning of the resulting formulas be understood. In statistical symbols the standard deviation is assigned the Greek lower case letter σ. The symbol σ stands for "variation in ...."; the subscript x on σ (i.e., σ_x) means variation in the variable x. (Later we will see that $\sigma_{\bar{x}}$ stands for variation in a sample-derived mean, or variation due to sampling error). The meaning of the above symbols is given below.

x   is the varying characteristic being measured;

Σx means obtain the sum of the x-values in the set;

$\bar{X}'$ stands for the mean obtained for the *universe* by $\Sigma x / N$ (where N is the total number of values in the universe);

σ'_x stands for the universe standard deviation of x computed from the universe data by
$$\sigma'_x = \sqrt{\frac{\Sigma(x-\bar{X}')^2}{N}} \; ;$$

When sample data are used,

$\bar{X}$ stands for the mean obtained from the *sample* by $\Sigma x / n$ (where n is the total number of values in the sample);

σ_x stands for the sample standard deviation of x computed from a sample of n values by
$$\sigma_x = \sqrt{\frac{\Sigma(x-\bar{X})^2}{n-1}} \; .$$

The range

There is still another way of measuring variation. If we subtract the lowest value from the highest value of a set of values, the resulting difference is called the *range*. This is a concept which was previously introduced in Chapter 3. In our example, the range in daily production for the worker is 47 units minus 28 units, or 19 units. The figure of 19 units is one of the measures of variation in the worker's daily production; it shows the span or spread of the variable.

While the range is a measure of variation (or spread) it has an obvious weakness as a general method of measuring variability. Its limitation lies in the nature of the range, which is obtained by subtracting the lowest value of the variable from its highest value. If, in any one set of data, either one of the extreme points is exceptionally large or small, despite the fact that most of the other values may concentrate closely around the average, a false impression of variability may be derived. If, for example, the worker in the above problem produced 85 units in the seventh day instead of 47 units, the range would have been 85 minus 28 = 57, a very wide span in relation to the worker's average daily production. Yet, the worker's production in the remaining 8 days was fairly consistent. Using the range method, therefore, might have classified the worker as "highly inconsistent," when in fact the production was fairly consistent.

The range is useful to approximate σ_x in statistical quality control problems when a large number of small samples are used, i.e., when n is as small as 3 or 4 on up to about 20, and when a substantial number of independent random samples is accumulated (as in Chapter 11). The average of the ranges ($\overline{R}$) obtained from the many small random samples of a process provides a good basis for estimating σ_x by $\overline{R}/d_2$, where d_2 is a constant determined by the number of items in each random sample. For example, when $n = 4$, $d_2 = 2.059$; when $n = 5$, $d_2 = 2.326$; and when $n = 6$, $d_2 = 2.534$. Chapter 11 gives more detail on this method of computing the standard deviation.

Uses of the Standard Deviation

Consistency or dependability of a worker's performance

Earlier, we found by using the standard deviation formula that the standard deviation of the worker's production over the 9 days was 5.54 units. How can this figure be interpreted? What does it tell us about the worker's consistency in productivity?

When the standard deviation is quoted in this fashion — that is, in absolute units, there is no straight-forward way of judging whether the values of the variable differ greatly or not from their mean. Therefore, it is difficult to establish standards for judging if variability is large or small. The standard deviation may be a large dimension or a small dimension solely because the magnitude of the variable being studied is large or small; for example, daily deposits in a bank are large as compared with runs scored in a baseball game. Since the magnitude of the standard deviation is dependent largely upon the magnitude of the variable under study, it is difficult to use it directly to determine the extent of variation or consistency of a variable. However, when the standard deviation is divided by the mean from which it differs, in the same measurement units, it is converted into a percentage of the average called the *coefficient of variation,* or *C.V.*, the problem of the magnitude of the variable is solved. In the form of a percentage, it is easier to establish standards for judging if variability is large or small. In addition, as a percentage of the mean, the coefficient of variation can be compared with similar measures of variation in other processes regardless of the magnitude of the original measurement units. In our demonstration problem, for example, the standard deviation of 5.54 units around the worker's mean daily production of 40 units represents a variability of nearly 14 percent (5.54/40). We can judge the consistency in the worker's production in relation to some rule or standard measure of stability, also expressed in percentages. Below we have established a "variability ruler," based on the coefficient of variation (C.V.), with suggested possible interpretations of the extent of stability or consistency it indicates.

A Variability Ruler
Coefficient of Variation (C.V.), Percent

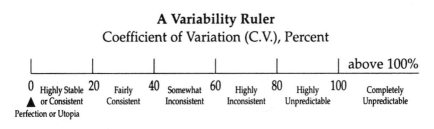

This grouping of the coefficients of variation, of course, need not be universally adopted as a measure of stability. The measure may be quite different depending upon the type of activity, process, or product being studied. For example, when analyzing a precision instrument, a 20 percent coefficient of variation would indicate a product of very poor quality; in this case, it might take a C.V. of one-half of one percent to indicate a product of great precision.

In the form of a percentage relative to its average, the standard deviation can be used not only to differentiate between large and small variations of a single product or service, but also to make comparisons between the variation in different sets of data or products. It does not necessarily follow, for example, that a worker with a standard deviation of 5.54 units is more consistent in production than another worker with a higher standard deviation, say 6.5 units. It is possible that the average daily production of the second worker may be 65 units compared with 40 units for the first worker. Thus, the second worker, with a coefficient of variation of 10 percent, could be considered more dependable than the worker with a 14 percent coefficient of variation.

Reliability of a product or service

It has been shown above that the standard deviation converted to a coefficient of variation can be used to measure the dependability of workers in their field of production or service. In the same way, the coefficient of variation can tell us about the reliability of any measurable product produced by a machine or service provided by employees. Generally, the lower the coefficient of variation, the more reliance can be placed on the product or service quality.

As an example, three grades of paper were tested for their tearing strength with the following coefficients of variation:

Grade No.1	Grade No.2	Grade No.3
2.8 percent	4.5 percent	1.3 percent

Which grade is most consistent in withstanding weights? Obviously, Grade No. 3 appears to be the most consistent, because it shows relatively less variation from its mean tearing weight than the other two grades show from their respective means. However, a word of caution is necessary. The coefficient of variation aids us only in answering the question with respect to consistency. It does not tell us which product to choose if the criterion for choice is productivity, regardless of consistency. To answer such a question we would use the arithmetic mean, as explained in Chapter 4. Thus, it is important to use the correct statistical measure for each decision: the mean for general *magnitude* and the coefficient of variation for consistency or *reliability*.

Homogeneity of a set of data

An average is a popular statistic. Some persons like to compute an average for any set of data. Yet the average may be meaningless when the values used in computing it differ so widely that there is no real central tendency. In such instances, the coefficient of variation can be used to judge whether the average is a valid general description of a set of data. For example, in a given year the coefficient of variation for the annual earnings of construction workers was nearly 90 percent. What does this figure indicate about the comparative annual earnings of construction workers? It may be an accurate reflection of the high variability in construction workers' earnings. On the other hand, it may indicate that the frequency distribution included persons with greatly varying characteristics, such as skilled and unskilled workers, part-time and full-time workers, and so forth. If the original data lack homogeneity, the average used to represent the central tendency of that set of data is not a useful measure of central tendency. The high coefficient of variation would indicate that such data should be broken down into more appropriate or more homogeneous sub-groups before the average is used to draw general conclusions.

Determining size of sample to select from different universes

In Chapter 9 we will see how the coefficient of variation, as a measure of the extent of variability of a characteristic of a given universe, is used to determine the appropriate size of sample needed to obtain a specified level of reliability of estimates to be derived from the sample.

Summary of uses of the coefficient of variation

The foregoing uses of the coefficient of variation, which depends on the mean and standard deviation, indicate its importance in: (1) analyses of many management problems that deal with determining the consistency of a process and the comparative consistency in two or more processes, or even individuals; (2) judging whether a set of data represents a population with dissimilar characteristics, i.e., one that may consist of more than one homogeneous sub-group; and (3) determining the appropriate size of sample to select from a universe.

In each of the above types of applications of measures of variation it was necessary to convert the standard deviation into a coefficient of variation. In many types of situations, however, only the standard deviation expressed in the measurement units of the process (e.g., inches, dollars, pounds, etc.) is used. Because of its wider utility, we should appreciate why so much emphasis is placed on the standard deviation rather than the other two measures of variation mentioned in this chapter (range and average deviation). Some of the additional uses of the standard deviation are described in the following paragraphs.

Guide for management action in quality control and other situations where normal distributions occur

It will be recalled from Chapter 3 that variations in the dimension of a product produced under a constant set of conditions tend to form a normal frequency distribution, and in Chapter 4 we learned that the value of the mean, median, and mode are equal in a normal distribution. The standard deviation, too, behaves in a known way when we deal with a normal distribution. However, the standard deviation has a partner and cannot readily behave in this known manner without it; that partner is the mean. The partnership "mean-standard deviation" when a normal curve is available for analysis provides, as a minimum, the following known characteristics:*

(1) Invariably, when the value of the standard deviation is added to the value of the mean, about a third (34.134 percent) of all the items will fall within the interval between the mean and the mean plus one standard deviation.

(2) Invariably, also, when the value of the mean is diminished by the value of the standard deviation, about a third (34.134 percent) of all the items will fall within the interval between the mean and the mean minus one standard deviation.

(3) The interval formed by the mean and the mean plus two standard deviations includes 47.725 percent of all the items.

(4) The interval formed by the mean and the mean minus two standard deviations includes 47.725 percent of all the items.

(5) The interval formed by the mean and the mean plus three standard deviations includes 49.865 percent of all the items.

(6) The interval formed by the mean and the mean minus three standard deviations includes 49.865 percent of all the items.

---

* Note that these characteristics hold exactly only for a perfectly bell-shaped distribution.

These fixed and known characteristics of the bell-shaped distribution, as well as numerous other characteristics, are provided in Appendix B. A graphic presentation of the Normal Curve is shown in Figure 5.1 (with the percentages rounded). Note that the tails of the distribution technically extend to plus and minus infinity.

Figure 5.1
The Normal Curve and Some of Its Properties —
Percent of all values or items included within
various ranges of $\overline{X}$ and σ_x

Numerical Presentation

(1) Mean ± 1 standard deviation includes 68.268 percent of the x-values

(2) Mean ± 2 standard deviations includes 95.450 percent of the x-values

(3) Mean ± 3 standard deviations includes 99.730 percent of the x-values

Graphical Presentation

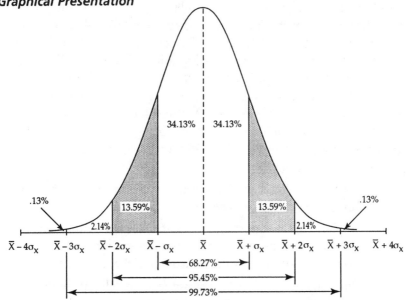

It is emphasized that all properties of the normal distribution involve measurements from the center (or mean) of the distribution

moving outward both to the left and to the right of the mean. These properties hold well even if the distribution is approximately normal, as illustrated by the following data, which show a frequency distribution of 100 strips of paper by their length. The data presumably were derived from a random sample of 100 strips taken from a given paper-production process (hypothetical data).

Length of paper (inches)	Number of strips (f)
3.45-3.49	5
3.50-3.54	11
3.55-3.59	20
3.60-3.64	28
3.65-3.69	21
3.70-3.74	12
3.75-3.79	3
Total	100

It is apparent from inspection that this frequency distribution is symmetrical and approximately bell-shaped. The mean length of a strip estimated from the frequency distribution is 3.63 inches, and the standard deviation is .07 inches.* Therefore, it should be expected from the properties of normal distributions that one standard deviation (.07 inches) of the variable, when added to and subtracted from the mean (3.63 inches), should yield a range within which about 68 percent of the items (strips of paper) would fall.

The following calculations are made to show how closely the actual percentage of items falling within a given interval is to the corresponding expected percentage.

(1) Mean ± 1 standard deviation is 3.63 ± .07, which gives a range of 3.56 – 3.70 inches.

(2) By glancing at the frequency distribution it can be seen that about 69 percent of all the items in the sample (20 + 28 + 21) would fall within the interval from 3.55 through 3.69 inches.

(3) Thus, it is seen that the percentage of all the items falling within the mean ± 1 standard deviation is nearly the same as the 68.3 percent expected for a perfect normal distribution.

---

* The method of calculating the standard deviation from a frequency distribution is presented later in this chapter.

It is known from the fixed properties of the normal distribution that the "mean ± 2 standard deviations" includes 95.5 percent of the items in a normal curve. This property, too, can be illustrated by calculations based on the above frequency distribution:

(1) Mean ± 2 standard deviations = 3.63 ± 2(.07) = 3.63 ± .14 = 3.49 to 3.77 inches.

(2) Within this range we find the following number of items:

    (a) In the interval 3.45-3.49 inches   1 *
    (b) In the interval 3.50-3.54 inches   11
    (c) In the interval 3.55-3.59 inches   20
    (d) In the interval 3.60-3.64 inches   28
    (e) In the interval 3.65-3.69 inches   21
    (f) In the interval 3.70-3.74 inches   12
    (g) In the interval 3.75-3.79 inches   2 *

                          Total   95

(3) Again, it is apparent that the percentage of all the items included within the mean and two standard deviations on both sides of it is about 95 percent, which is very close to the 95.5 percent expected in the normal distribution.

Similarly, the mean (3.63) ± 3 standard deviations (± .21) can be shown to include all the items, compared with 99.7 percent expected in the normal curve, as follows:

(1) Mean ± 3 standard deviations = 3.63 ± .21 = 3.42 to 3.84 inches.

(2) The range 3.42 – 3.84 inches includes all the values in the distribution.

(3) This 100 percent compares well with the expected 99.7 percent in the normal distribution.

It would not be correct to assume that a given frequency distribution forms a bell-shaped pattern only because observation indicates that $\overline{X} \pm 3\sigma_x$ contains all the values in a set of data. In some frequency distributions $\overline{X} \pm 1\sigma_x$ may include, say, 80 percent of the values, and $\overline{X} \pm 2\sigma_x$ may also include all the values. In such a case, the frequency distribution would not be shaped like a normal curve even though $\overline{X} \pm 3\sigma_x$ would include all the items. In studying normal

---

* Estimated by assuming equal spacing of the items in each group.

distributions, therefore, it is best to compare the actual proportion of values with the theoretically expected proportion for $\overline{X} \pm 1\sigma_x$, $\overline{X} \pm 2\sigma_x$, and $\overline{X} \pm 3\sigma_x$.*

This known pattern of variation of normal distributions is extremely important in the analysis of many industrial and management problems. A Special Section to this chapter describes some more practical uses of the principle of normal distributions, and Chapter 11, Statistical Process Control, covers its uses in process control, and quality, and productivity improvement.

An example of the use of the standard deviation in estimating from a sample

When random samples are taken from a universe, the mean and standard deviation of the values in the sample may be used as estimates of the true mean and true standard deviation of the universe. Following is an example of the use of a sample-derived mean and standard deviation to estimate a specified characteristic of the universe.

A random sample (see Chapter 7 for a definition of random sample) of 1,000 electric bulbs of a given power was tested to determine their length of service. It was found that the average (mean) service of these bulbs was 900 hours. Furthermore, the standard deviation around this average was found to be 20 hours. With these results, how many bulbs out of a shipment of 1 million may be expected to last 920 hours or more?

This is a problem involving the use of normal distribution theory. It is reasonable to assume that if the 1 million bulbs were all tested for length of service, a normal frequency distribution would have been obtained, because in a mass-production process of this type it is reasonable to assume that they were all manufactured under a stable and constant set of conditions. Therefore, the main reason for differences in length of service is chance. Thus, with the reasonable assumption that bulb-life is normally distributed, the fixed properties of the mean and standard deviation of the universe (which are estimated from the sample) can be relied on to provide reasonably accurate estimates of the number of items (bulbs) falling within specified ranges of the mean and a given number of the standard deviations. A graph of the normal curve (Figure 5.2), enables us again to observe the indicated relationships and make the required estimates.

---

*In Chapter 10 we present a more refined method of testing for normality by using the Chi-Square test.

Figure 5.2
Normal distribution of electric bulbs by length of service

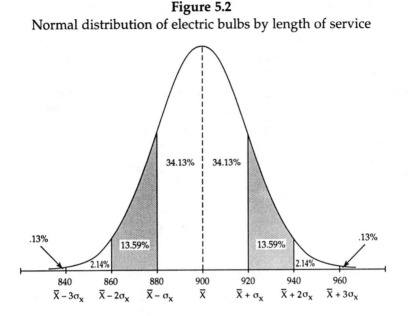

From this graph we can see that 13.59 percent plus 2.14 percent plus 0.13 percent of the bulbs in the sample fall on the scale with 920 or more hours of service. Consequently, 15.83 percent (13.59 + 2.14 + 0.13) of the bulbs may be *estimated* to last at least 920 hours. When this percentage is multiplied by the total shipment of 1 million bulbs, it may be estimated that 158,300 bulbs (1,000,000 times 15.83 percent) will last 920 or more hours. (As Chapter 9 indicates, this estimate is subject to *sampling error* that can be measured by appropriate formulas.)

The same method can be used to estimate the number of bulbs that will last less than 900 hours (less than $\overline{X}$), or less than 880 hours (less than $\overline{X} - 1\sigma_x$), and so forth. In fact, it can be applied in making a large variety of estimates of universe characteristics based on random samples taken from universes whose items are normally or nearly normally distributed — in setting product warranties, in estimating, for example, the length of life of automobile batteries, automobile tires, etc.

Guide for management action in non-normal distributions

Another significant point about the standard deviation is that it can be used to estimate the *minimum* percentage of cases that will fall within given ranges of the mean and σ_x in any frequency distribution, whether it is bell-shaped or not. Even if we know nothing of the pattern of the frequency distribution formed by a given variable, or if its pattern is highly skewed, the standard deviation together with the mean of that distribution still will provide a basis for estimating. Mathematical theory* has determined that, regardless of the shape of the frequency distribution, $\overline{X} \pm 2\sigma_x$ will include *at least* 75 percent of the values of a given set of data and $\overline{X} \pm 3\sigma_x$ will include at least 88.9 percent of all the values of that set. This application of the standard deviation takes on importance in many government, business, or economic studies, where skewed distributions occur frequently. A further exploration of these properties of the standard deviation, however, is beyond the scope of this book; it is sufficient to note that σ_x is useful even beyond normal distributions.

Some Additional Applications of $\overline{X}$ and σ_x to Normal Distributions

In the foregoing sections, it was indicated that in a normal distribution about two-thirds of all the values are included within the interval formed by the mean value and the value of one standard deviation on both sides of it ($\overline{X} \pm 1\sigma_x$); about 95.5 percent of all values are included within the interval $\overline{X} \pm 2\sigma_x$; and 99.7 percent within the interval $\overline{X} \pm 3\sigma_x$.

These properties were expressed in terms of integers of σ_x and may have created the impression that no other properties exist except those which are in whole numbers of σ_x. This is not correct, for the normal curve is a continuous curve, patterned in the shape of a bell, whose properties can be determined in terms of *any* number of σ_x units around the mean of the distribution. In fact, the normal curve can be completely plotted by reference to a mathematical equation which is expressed in terms of the given values (x), the mean ($\overline{X}$) and standard deviation (σ_x) of the distribution.** It is possible, therefore, to determine what proportion of the values in the distribution fall within any interval formed by $\overline{X}$ and some multiple of σ_x, even when

---

* Developed by a Russian mathematician, P.L. Tchebycheff (1821-1895),

the general formula is: $\overline{X} \pm$ number of σ_x's includes at least $\left(1 - \dfrac{1}{Z^2}\right)$ 100% of all values, where Z is the number of σ_x's larger than one.

** For those who are interested, the equation for the normal curve is: $y = \dfrac{e^{-\frac{1}{2}\left(\frac{x - \overline{X}'}{\sigma_x'}\right)^2}}{\sqrt{2\pi}}$,

where y is the value of the ordinate (or frequency) on the y-axis for any given value of x on the x-axis; $\overline{X}'$ and σ_x' are the population mean and standard deviation, respectively, of the distribution, and e and π are mathematical symbols representing special constants.

the multiplier is expressed in fractions or decimals. The normal distribution curve in Appendix B is defined for as many as 400 $\overline{X} \pm Z\sigma_x$ intervals, where Z is any number (integer or not) of standard deviations.

For example, what proportion of the values in a normal distribution fall within $\overline{X} \pm .5\sigma_x$? By referring to Appendix B, we note that $.5\sigma_x$ units is shown in the first column as .5 and under column 2 as .00; this means $.50\sigma_x$ units. We then find a figure of 19.15 percent. Since the Appendix B table gives only the percentage of values included on one side of the mean within the interval formed by the mean plus (*or* minus) the specified number of standard deviation units, and since the normal curve is a symmetrical curve, the proportion of all values included in the interval formed on *both* sides of the mean, $\overline{X} \pm .5\sigma_x$, is twice that shown in the table, i.e., 38.30 percent. Thus, we should be able to determine the proportion of all values that fall within any interval about the mean; however, we must be careful of the plus *and* minus and the plus *or* minus situations.

As another example, what proportion of the values in the normal curve fall within $\overline{X} \pm 2.0\sigma_x$? The percentage in the table in Appendix B is 47.72 percent. When this percent is multiplied by 2 the answer is that $\overline{X} \pm 2.0\sigma_x$ includes 95.44 % of all values in the distribution.

What proportion of the values fall within $\overline{X} \pm 2.5\sigma_x$? The answer is 49.38 percent times 2 = 98.76%.

An example of an application — With these examples, we may illustrate a further useful application of the principle of normal distributions to a type of management problem which occurs quite frequently, as follows.

The accounting department of a knitwear manufacturing company determined from a study of past sales records that orders (in hundreds of dollars) of less than $100 were usually filled at a loss to the company. Past data on orders taken by the company showed that the mean amount per order ($\overline{X}$) was $200 with a standard deviation (σ_x) of $80. If it is assumed that the distribution of sales, by amount, approximates the normal curve, what proportion of the orders may be expected to be filled at a loss this year (orders for less than $100), if the mean and standard deviation have not changed materially?

In attempting to solve this problem it is desirable to sketch the normal curve and set off on it the values that are critical, as shown by Figure 5.3.

Figure 5.3
Sketch of normal curve to help locate a critical value
of knitware sales (in hundreds of dollars)

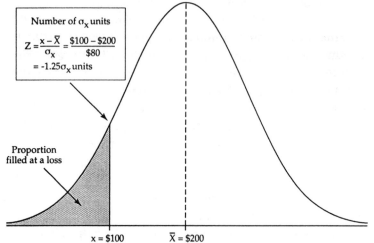

As indicated earlier, unlike a ruler, all measurements in normal distributions are in terms of number of standard deviations away from the center (mean) of the distribution rather than its ends. Since 50 percent of all values are on either side of the mean in a normal curve, we need to find what percentage of all the values are within the mean and $100 (the critical point) on its left and then subtract this percentage from 50 percent, to yield the percentage of values which are less than $100. Generally, this type of problem can be solved by a simple formula called the *standard normal variate*, or the *Z-score*, where Z = number of σ_x units separating a critical point (x) from the mean ($\overline{X}$).

In formula form, $Z = \dfrac{\text{critical point (x)} - \text{mean }(\overline{X})}{\text{one standard deviation } (\sigma_x)}$; in symbols, $Z = \dfrac{(x - \overline{X})}{\sigma_x}$.

In our case, $Z = \dfrac{(\$100 - \$200)}{\$80} = -1.25$ standard deviations.*

By referring to the normal curve table in Appendix B, we find that 39.44 percent of the values are included within the mean and 1.25 σ_x units. Therefore, by subtraction (50 – 39.44), 10.56 percent of the values lie *below* $100. Thus, it may be estimated that about 10 to 11 percent of the orders of the knitwear manufacturing company would be

---

* The minus sign indicates that we are on the left side of the normal curve.

filled at a loss, if the company continues to fill such orders. Alternative ways of filling small-valued orders are, of course, a management determination. Normal distribution theory provides a method of estimating the proportion that would be filled at a loss under existing conditions.

Another management application — In a given department store it was found that the frequency distribution of accounts receivable at the end of each quarter generally approximated a normal curve. The mean amount per account receivable at the end of the last quarter (in thousands of dollars) was $485 and the standard deviation was $150. If it is believed that at the end of the following quarter the mean will have risen to $500 and the standard deviation will have remained at $150, what proportion of the accounts will amount to $900 or more? Also, what proportion will be between $750 and $900?

Following a systematic procedure, we first sketch the normal curve and enter the appropriate critical values, as shown in Figure 5.4.

Figure 5.4

Sketch of normal curve to help locate a critical value
of accounts receivable (in thousands of dollars)

$$Z = \frac{x - \bar{X}}{\sigma_x} = \frac{\$750 - \$500}{\$150}$$
$$= 1.67\sigma_x \text{ units}$$

$$Z = \frac{x - \bar{X}}{\sigma_x} = \frac{\$900 - \$500}{\$150}$$
$$= 2.67\sigma_x \text{ units}$$

$\bar{X} = \$500$ $x = \$750$ $x = \$900$

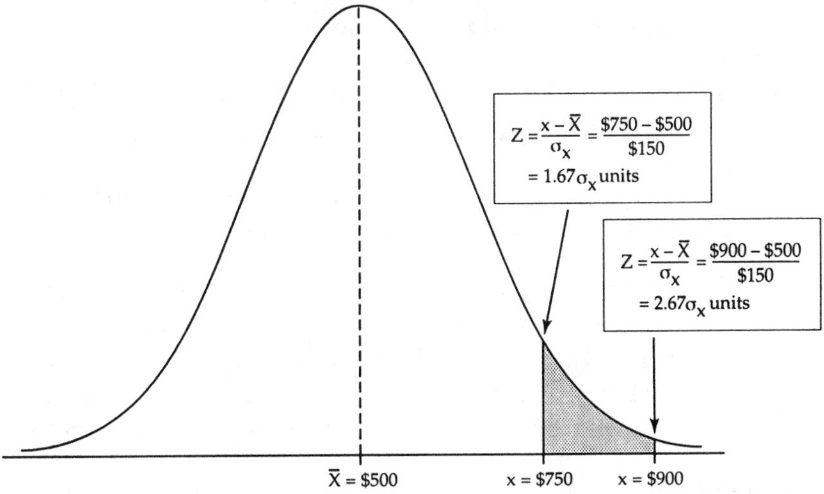

One critical value lies at the far right hand of the distribution, that is, $900 or more. Since 50 percent of the values are on either side of the mean in the normal curve, we first need to determine what percentage of the values lie between the mean of $500 and $900. Then we can subtract this percentage from 50 percent to estimate the percentage beyond $900. Since the Z-variate shows that 2.67 standard deviations separate x from $\overline{X}$, the normal curve table shows that 49.62 percent of the accounts are valued between $500 and $900. Therefore, 0.38 of one percent (50.00 − 49.62) of the values lie beyond $900. Thus, if the department store has as many as 20,000 accounts receivable at the end of the quarter, it may be estimated that 76 accounts (0.0038 of 20,000) would be in amounts of $900 or more.

The solution to the second question requires a slightly different approach. It deals with two critical points — one at $750 and the other at $900. Therefore, the solution requires that we first determine the proportion of accounts which lies between the mean of $500 and $900 (which we have determined already) and then the proportion that lies between the mean of $500 and $750; then we subtract the smaller percentage from the larger to get the percentage within the critical interval of $750 to $900. The computations are:

(1) For the interval $500 to $900, the number of σ_x units are
$$\frac{(\$900 - \$500)}{\$150} = 2.67.$$ The normal curve table shows that 49.62 percent of all the values lie between the mean and 2.67 σ_x units on either side of the mean.

(2) For the interval $500 to $750, the number of σ_x units are
$$\frac{\$750 - \$500}{\$150} = 1.67.$$ The normal curve table shows that 45.25 percent of all the values lie between the mean and 1.67 σ_x units on either side of the mean.

(3) For the interval $750 to $900, we find, by subtraction, that 4.37 percent (49.62 − 45.25) of the accounts are included within it. Thus, if the department store had 20,000 accounts receivable, it may be estimated that about 874 accounts (.0437 times 20,000) would be in amounts between $750 and $900.

Guidelines

This, and many similar types of management applications (e.g., establishing product warranties) are possible through use of the normal distribution principle. The problems at the end of this section provide additional exercises and further illustrations. The following serve as a guide in the solution of this type of normal curve problem:

(1) It is essential to compute or estimate the mean and standard deviation of the universe of concern.

(2) It is essential to be reasonably sure that the distribution approximates a normal curve. (In Chapter 3, we pointed out that four conditions can be expected to yield normal distributions.)   This can be done by visual examination of previous distributions to note if a general bell-shape exists; or by considering the nature of the variable under study (e.g., naturally caused variations or not); or by more sophisticated mathematical methods of fitting a normal curve to a given distribution by use of its mean and standard deviation and then making a Chi-Square test of normality (Chapter 10).

(3) It is essential to recognize the fact that all measurement in normal curve applications start from the mean value and move in one or both directions, i.e., either to the right or left or to both sides of the mean. In other words, the mean is the base point of the distribution and the standard deviation measures the extent of variation from it.

(4) It is also essential to recognize that the distance (or difference) from a particular critical point (x) to the mean ($\overline{X}$) must be converted from the original units of measurement (e.g., age, miles, tons, etc.) to a distance in terms of *number of standard deviations*.   This distance is commonly obtained by the standard normal variate, or Z-score, and is determined by:

$Z = \dfrac{(x - \overline{X})}{\sigma_x}$. Once the distance in terms of σ_x units between the critical point and the mean is determined, we find the percentage of cases included within that interval by reference to the normal curve table (Appendix B). Thus this table and the Z-variate formula can aid in the solution of all normal curve problems, regardless of the magnitude of the measurement units involved.

(5) It is essential to sketch a normal curve and set off on it the particular critical x-values to assure clarity of the problem. It then becomes a matter of figuring out which segments of the curve must be subtracted, or added, to arrive at the percentage of cases falling in the critical interval of interest.

Calculating the Standard Deviation from Frequency Distributions

More often than not, data with a large number of values are condensed into frequency distributions to facilitate their analysis, and the standard deviation has to be computed from a frequency distribution. Even when the data are grouped in this form the standard deviation still is defined as before: it is the average of the differences of the values from their mean value, using the technique of squares and square roots. Since, however, in a grouped frequency distribution we do not know the exact value of the individual items in each group, we assume that the value of *each* item in the group is equal to the midpoint (m) of the group. After calculating the mean, $\overline{X} = \dfrac{\Sigma fm}{n}$, the following steps are taken to calculate σ_x:

Step #1 — Obtain the difference of each value in the class from the mean; it is $d = m - \overline{X}$, where m is the midpoint of each class.

Step #2 — Since the sum of these differences will be zero when properly weighted by each class frequency (f), we square each difference to convert all the differences to positive numbers. Thus, $d^2 = (m - \overline{X})^2$.

Step #3 — Since each squared difference represents only *one item* in the class, we multiply it by its respective frequency. Thus, we obtain a total squared difference of $fd^2 = f(m - \overline{X})^2$ for each class.

Step #4 — Obtain the sum of all the squared class differences, obtaining $\Sigma fd^2 = \Sigma f(m - \overline{X})^2$.

Step #5 — Calculate a mean difference squared by dividing $\Sigma f(m - \overline{X})^2$ by $n-1$ (assuming a sample is involved).

Step #6 — Calculate the standard deviation (σ_x) by taking the square root of the resulting mean of the squared differences. This yields the following compact formula for the standard deviation from a frequency distribution:

$$\sigma_x = \sqrt{\frac{\Sigma fd^2}{n-1}} = \sqrt{\frac{\Sigma f(m - \overline{X})^2}{n-1}}.$$

These six steps are illustrated with the following data after the mean ($\Sigma fm \div n$) is computed:*

Length of paper (in inches)	Midpoint	Frequency	Step #1: Product of frequency and midpoint	Step #2: Difference	Squared difference	Step #3: Frequency times squared difference
	m	f	fm	$(m - \overline{X})^*$	$(m - \overline{X})^2$	$f(m - \overline{X})^2$
3.45-3.49	3.475	5	17.375	.15	.0225	.1125
3.50-3.54	3.525	11	38.775	.10	.0100	.1100
3.55-3.59	3.575	20	71.500	.05	.0025	.0500
3.60-3.64	3.625	28	101.500	.00	.0000	.0000
3.65-3.69	3.675	21	77.175	.05	.0025	.0525
3.70-3.74	3.725	12	44.700	.10	.0100	.1200
3.75-3.79	3.775	3	11.325	.15	.0225	.0675
Totals		100	362.350			

Step #4: $\Sigma f(m - \overline{X})^2 = .5125$

Step #5: $\dfrac{\Sigma f(m - \overline{X})^2}{n - 1} = \dfrac{.5125}{99} = .00518$

Step #6: $\sqrt{\dfrac{\Sigma f(m - \overline{X})^2}{n - 1}} = \sqrt{.00518} = .07$

Special Section
Short-Cut Method of Computing the Standard Deviation
(For those who are interested in these short-cut methods)

Ungrouped data

By algebraic expansion of the numerator, $\Sigma(x - \overline{X})^2$, of the standard deviation formula, we arrive at the following short-cut formula for computing the standard deviation from ungrouped data: $\sigma_x = \sqrt{\dfrac{\Sigma x^2}{n} - \overline{X}^2}$.**

---

* By rounding the mean from 3.6235 to 3.625, a number that ends in the same digits as the midpoints, we facilitate our calculations of differences from the mean, i.e., working with simpler numbers, without significantly affecting the accuracy of the results.

**When a small sample, e.g., n < 31, is used, this formula is $\sigma_x = \sqrt{\dfrac{\Sigma x^2 - n\overline{X}^2}{n - 1}}$; that is, the

above formula is adjusted for small sample size by multiplying it by $\sqrt{\dfrac{n}{n - 1}}$.

This is considered a short-cut formula because it reduces manual computations. It requires only that the original x-values be squared and summed instead of first calculating all the differences $(x - \overline{X})$, then squaring and summing them, as shown by the following example:

Item number	Value x	Value squared x^2
1	$2	$4
2	4	16
3	3	9
Total 3	$9	$29

Since the mean of the set is 3 and the sum of the squared values is 29,

$$\sigma_x = \sqrt{\frac{\Sigma x^2}{n} - \overline{X}^2} = \sqrt{\frac{29}{3} - 3^2} = \sqrt{9.67 - 9} = \sqrt{.67} = \$0.82.$$

If the long method were used for the above set of data, we would perform the following computations:

Item number	Value x	Value minus $\overline{X}$ $d = (x - \overline{X})$	Squared difference $d^2 = (x - \overline{X})^2$
1	$2	−1	1
2	4	+1	1
3	3	0	0
Total 3	$9	0	$2

Here, $\sigma_x = \sqrt{\dfrac{\Sigma d^2}{n}} = \sqrt{\dfrac{2}{3}} = \sqrt{.67} = \$0.82$, the same result as above.

The computational savings from using the short-cut formula result from replacing the calculation of differences $(x - \overline{X})$ and then squaring of all the differences, a two-step process, as compared with simply squaring the individual x-values. When a large number of values is involved, and especially when their magnitudes are large, considerable savings in computations can be realized by using the short-cut method. It is to be recognized, however, that the practical value of this method is mitigated by computers, statistical calculators, and even standard electronic calculators.

Grouped data

The short-cut formula for computing σ_x from a frequency distribution deals with the number of classes separating the one whose midpoint we assume is an approximation of the mean.

It is: $\sigma_x = i \sqrt{\dfrac{\sum f d^2}{n} - \left(\dfrac{\sum f d}{n}\right)^2}$,

where:

i = the size of the class interval (must use uniform class intervals);

f = frequency of the class;

d = number of classes separating the specific class from the one whose midpoint we assume is the mean (for this class d = 0);

n = number of items in the sample.

An example follows:

Age	f	d	fd	fd^2
20-29	3	–1	–3	3
30-39	7	0	0	0
40-49	9	1	9	9
50-59	1	2	2	4
	n = 20		$\sum fd = 8$	$\sum fd^2 = 16$

Substituting in the formula above, we get:

$$\sigma_x = 10 \sqrt{\frac{16}{20} - \left(\frac{8}{20}\right)^2} = .8 - .16 = .64 = 10(.8) = 8 \text{ years.}$$

The reader may wish to check this result by using the long formula given earlier:

$$\sigma_x = \sqrt{\frac{\sum f (m - \overline{X})^2}{n}}.$$

Summary

Everyone must appreciate the existence of variation in all aspects of governmental, business, industrial, economic, social, and natural life. It follows from the existence of universal variation that we must have a basis for measuring and distinguishing large from small, and normal from abnormal, variation. Among the three measures of variation presented in this chapter (range, average deviation, and standard deviation), the standard deviation is the most useful because of the large variety of its applications. The standard deviation (σ_x) for ungrouped data, is computed by the formula $\sigma_x = \sqrt{\dfrac{\sum\left(x - \overline{X}\right)^2}{n-1}}$. In this formula, $(x - \overline{X})$, is the difference between each x-value and the mean of all the values; $\sum(x - \overline{X})^2$ = the sum of the individual squared differences between the x-values and the mean; and n is the number of values in the sample.

When the standard deviation needs to be computed from a frequency distribution, its concept is the same as when computing it from ungrouped data, namely, it is a measure of the average difference of the individual measurements from their mean. Because the value of each item in a group is unknown, we use the midpoint (m) of each group to represent each individual item in that group. The formula for the standard deviation computed from a frequency distribution is:

$\sigma_x = \sqrt{\dfrac{\sum f\left(m - \overline{X}\right)^2}{n-1}}$, where f is the number of items in the class, m is the midpoint of that class, and the other terms are defined as before.

Short-cut methods for computing the standard deviation were given in this chapter which can save a great deal of computational time. However, the shortest short-cut may be through use of a computer.

The standard deviation computed by these formulas always comes out in the same units as the variable. It is difficult to determine whether variation is large or small when the standard deviation is in absolute units. However, when the standard deviation is related to the mean around which it is calculated by dividing it by the mean, the percentage variation is determined, regardless of the magnitude of the absolute units. This percentage, which is computed by the formula $\sigma_x \big/ \overline{X}$ (times 100 to get a percentage), is called the coefficient of variation.

It is easier to establish standards of large and small variability when the standard deviation is expressed in percentage form. The coefficient of variation is a guide in answering questions on the extent of steadiness, constancy, uniformity of performance, reliability, and dependability of individuals, machines, or material. The standard deviation, when converted into the coefficient of variation, also can be used to compare the relative stability of, or variability in, two or more different processes or operations; it also can be used to judge whether a set of data is non-homogeneous or whether the average can be used to predict individual x-values with reasonable accuracy.

The standard deviation plays an especially important role in analyzing industrial, business, and governmental problems when the frequency distribution of the variable approximates a normal distribution. In a normal distribution, fixed percentages of all the measurements of a given process fall within given ranges of the mean and standard deviation units on either side of the mean. Thus, the interval formed by the mean ± 1 standard deviation includes about two-thirds of all data values. Similarly, the mean ± 2 standard deviations includes about 95.5 percent of the values, and the mean ± 3 standard deviations includes 99.7 percent of all the values. These known properties of the normal distribution based on the standard deviation and the mean serve to guide management in judging if processes are behaving normally or not. The standard deviation can also be used to estimate the *minimum* percentage of cases that will be included within specific ranges of the mean in *any* frequency distribution, whether normal or not.

Other uses of the standard deviation are in measuring the sampling error in estimates derived from random samples; in determining the size of sample to select from given universes; in statistical process control; in correlation studies; and in numerous other statistical applications to management problems, as presented in this and subsequent chapters.

Problems

1. Suppose you had four coins of the same denomination in your hand and were to toss them on the floor.

   (a) How many would you expect to fall with heads up?

   (b) Now actually toss four coins and note how many fall with heads up. Repeat this tossing 20 times and show the frequency distribution by number of heads, i.e., where m = 0, 1, 2, 3, 4 heads. (These are the midpoints of each class.)

   (c) Compute the mean number of heads from your frequency distribution.

(d) From the frequency distribution in (b), calculate the standard deviation.

(e) What is the coefficient of variation based on the data in (c) and (d)?

2. Two cable car operators in San Francisco were assigned to the same route; they showed the following (hypothetical) results over a long period of time:

	Operator A	Operator B
Mean length of time per round trip (minutes)	78	70
Standard deviation (minutes)	6	7

(a) Which operator appears to be more consistent in the time taken to make a round trip? Why?

(b) Which operator appears to be faster in completing the round trips? Why?

3. (a) The average (mean) size of men's hats was 7-1/4 as determined from a survey of 1,000 men who wear hats. The standard deviation was 1/4. Would you expect the frequency distribution of the 1,000 men by hat-size to be bell-shaped? Why?

(b) On the assumption that a normal distribution exists by hat size, what percentage of the men wearing hats wear sizes between:

(1) 7 and 7-1/2?,   (2) 6-3/4 and 7-3/4?,   (3) 6-1/2 and 8?

4. Here are the ages of 20 students in a business statistics class (age last birthday):

Student	Age	Student	Age
1	21	11	23
2	20	12	24
3	23	13	19
4	20	14	21
5	25	15	27
6	19	16	22
7	18	17	20
8	20	18	21
9	21	19	25
10	22	20	20

(a) What is the average age (mean) of the class?

(b) Calculate the standard deviation in the students' ages.

(c) In terms of the "C.V. Ruler" given in Chapter 5, what is the extent of variability in age among the students, measured as a percentage of the mean (the coefficient of variation)?

5. A survey was made of the earnings of workers in three different plants of a company, with the following results:

	Mean hourly wage	Standard deviation
Plant A	$15.88	$1.98
Plant B	21.04	1.51
Plant C	12.65	1.26

(a) Which plant paid the highest wage rates? What is the basis for your conclusion?

(b) Which plant had the most uniform wage rates?

(c) Which plant had the greatest wage differentials?

6. From a skewed frequency distribution of families in a given community by amount of annual income, we obtained $54,500 as the mean income and $18,700 as the standard deviation. This distribution seems to indicate that about two-thirds of the families received between $35,800 and $73,200. Discuss this estimate, explaining whether you believe it to be a good estimate and why.

7. A random sample of 100 flashlight batteries was tested for length of life with the following results: $\overline{X}$ = 500 hours, σ_x = 10 hours. Estimate the percentage of batteries that will last:

(a) 490 hours or less; (b) 510 hours or more;

(c) 480 hours or less; (d) 530 hours or more.

8. Two different employees in a plant assigned to performing a similar task showed the following production over a 9-day period:

Units of work completed

Day	Employee A	Employee B
1	7	7
2	6	9
3	11	8
4	12	7
5	6	6
6	10	11
7	9	8
8	12	7
9	8	9

(a) If the above data on production is typical of each employee's performance, which employee is probably a better producer?

(b) Which employee is probably more predictable, or consistent in productivity?

(c) Why is it necessary to qualify the answers with the word "probably"?

9. From a wage rate study, it was determined that the 850 non-salaried clerical employees of a given company were distributed by their hourly wage rates as follows:

Hourly Wages	Number of Employees
$10.00 - 10.99	3
11.00 - 11.99	20
12.00 - 12.99	42
13.00 - 13.99	51
14.00 - 14.99	73
15.00 - 15.99	80
16.00 - 16.99	100
17.00 - 17.99	121
18.00 - 18.99	160
19.00 - 19.99	200
Total =	850

Using the long method of computations, provide answers to a, b and c:

(a) Determine the mean hourly rate paid by the company.

(b) Determine the standard deviation.

(c) Compute the coefficient of variation and indicate your opinion regarding the equality among the employees in their wage rates.

10. Using the appropriate short-cut methods, compute the mean, standard deviation, and coefficient of variation for the 850 non-salaried employees whose wage rate distribution is given in problem 9.

11. Two grades of wrapping paper were tested for resistance to tearing. A sample of 80 equal-sized strips of each grade was selected and subjected to a standard tearing-weight test. The results are shown in the following distributions:

	Number of strips of	
Tearing Weight (pounds)	Grade A paper (f)	Grade B paper (f)
20-29	6	4
30-39	40	36
40-49	16	21
50-59	14	10
60-69	4	9
	Total = 80	Total = 80

(a) Which grade of paper is probably more resistant to tearing?

(b) Which grade of paper is probably more consistent or uniform in tearing quality?

(c) Why are these questions put in terms of "probably?" Is it possible for the reverse answers to be true? Why?

12. Some years ago, a sample study was made of monthly rentals paid by families renting one-bedroom apartments in Washington, DC, and Baltimore, Maryland, with the following results (hypothetical data):

Amount of monthly rental	Washington families (f)	Baltimore families (f)
$400 - 499	2	5
500 - 599	12	12
600 - 699	21	19
700 - 799	30	27
800 - 899	20	31
900 - 999	12	8
1,000 - 1,099	8	10
1,100 - 1,199	8	5
1,20 0- 1,299	7	3
	Total = 120	Total = 120

(a) In which city is the monthly rental probably higher?

(b) In which city is the monthly rental probably more uniform?

13. The following is a list of frequency distributions which provide statistics for some of our economic, industrial and social phenomena. Indicate which are likely to form a normal or approximately normal distribution, and give the reason for your choice.

(a) Distribution of families in the United States, by number of persons.

(b) Distribution, by length of leaf, of a random sample of 500 green leaves taken at random from a given tree.

(c) Distribution of families in the United States, by amount of annual income tax paid.

(d) Distribution, by length, of a run of 1,000 small nails of a specific dimension taken from the production line.

(e) Distribution of the number of clerical errors made by a data-entry clerk each day over a period of 15 days; 100 days; 300 days.

(f) Distribution of private automobiles in the United States, by age in years.

14. In problem 11 above, assume that the 25,000 strips of grade A and grade B wrapping paper from which the sample of 80 was selected, were distributed in the form of a normal curve, by tearing weight.

    (a) Using the mean and standard deviation computed from each sample, estimate what proportion and how many strips of the total lot of 25,000 each would have torn at a weight of less than 30 pounds.

    (b) What percentage and number of strips of each grade would have torn at 50 pounds or less?

    (c) What percentage and number of strips of each grade would have torn at 70 and over pounds?

    (d) Suppose the company of Grade B paper advertised a guaranteed tearing weight of at least 25 pounds, what percent of that grade would fail to meet the guarantee?

15. A large truck-renting agency has found from previous experience that its trucks have an average service life of 4.2 years, with a standard deviation of 1.3 years.

    (a) Assuming that the above experience is applicable to a new fleet of trucks and that their distribution by years of service life is approximately normal, about how many of a new fleet of 250 trucks will have to be replaced during the first year (i.e., year 0-.999)?

    (b) How many will have to be replaced during the third year (i.e., year 2 - 2.999)?

    (c) How many will last 6 or more years?

16. A sample of 100 television picture tubes of a given size and make was tested for length of life. It was found that the mean life was 1875 hours, with a standard deviation of 25 hours. Why is this estimate subject to some error?

Chapter 6

Probability —
The Foundation of Statistics
and Guided Decisions

*"Probability is, for men, the guide of life."**

Everything we do involves some risk, whether we know it or not. When we cross the street there is a chance of being hit by a car; when we ride a train, a bus, a plane, or a ship, we run a risk. When we decide to cut a class, we take a chance on missing some useful information presented by the instructor. When we decide to vacation in a northern or southern climate we run some risk of unusual weather that will interfere with the vacation. Similarly, in making a management decision, for example to adopt a certain procedure in the office, we run a risk that the decision will adversely affect some employees or will decrease company profits.

To decide on a certain action without knowledge of the likelihood of success, or failure, is equivalent to "blind" decision-making, or decision without guidance. With probability theory we can assess the chances we take with a knowledge of the probable success.

This chapter introduces the concept of probability; it also shows how probability can be computed and its application in many different situations.

The General Concept of Probability

Chances can be expressed qualitatively, e.g., "high," "low," "medium," "good," "bad," or "excellent"; they can also be expressed quantitatively or mathematically, e.g., "95 in 100," "5 in 100," "10 to 1,"

---

* Joseph Butler's *Analogy*.

etc. It is, or course, better to make important decisions for action or inaction on the basis of quantitative rather than qualitative information; then, there is more specificity as to what chances are really being taken. A chance of making a wrong decision in "5 out of 100" cases has the same meaning everywhere, whereas a "good" chance of being correct can be variously interpreted. "Good" might be taken by some to be better than 50-50, or better than 60 percent, and so forth. Therefore, by expressing risks (or confidence) in quantitative terms, a common language is used, like simple arithmetic which is uniformly understood.

Some types of decisions involve trivial consequences and it is therefore not worth the effort to collect data or to work out a quantitative expression of the risks. However, when the consequences are important, it is characteristic of scientific management and prudent human behavior to gauge the mathematical probability (chances) of failure. Action or decision-making with a knowledge of the risks involved is guided decision-making.

Fields of Application of the Theory of Probabilty

Aside from the use of probability in making informed management decisions, it is applicable to many fields of business, industry and government. It is the cornerstone, or an indispensable element, of politics, modern physics, genetics, business ventures, quality control, all kinds of research, and almost all fields of human endeavor. Probability plays a very important role in the field of insurance (life, weather, accident, etc.). Premiums are established on the basis of rates of occurrence based on past experience.

One broad field of application is in the lotteries and all games of chance where the operators figure out their expected returns by the law of probability and on the assumption that a large number of players will participate. Generally, the operators' take is much larger than their fair share would be according to the theory of probability.*

Other gambling applications are baseball pools, football pools, dice, bingo, "numbers" games, election pools, slot machines, carnival games, etc. Some problems on the odds actually offered and the fair odds in games are given in the problem section of this chapter.

---

* The Theory of probability may be traced to seventeeth century France, when gambling was a favorite sport of the aristocracy. Chevalier de Mere, a noble, once brought to the mathematician Blaise Pascal some of his gambling problems. From the solution of these problems, in 1654, Pascal developed the basic ideas of a new branch of mathematics, now knows as the theory of probability.

In the field of statistical quality control, for example in using control charts to locate a major cause of poor quality, the odds of wastefully stopping the production process to investigate a significant cause of variation generally can be determined (Chapter 11). Also, in inspecting a product by means of a sample, the risk of passing a poor lot of goods when the sample looks good can be determined.

In fields related to statistical sampling, such as determining confidence in estimates derived from samples (Chapter 9) and in significance testing (Chapter 10), the chances of making a correct inference are determined by the law of probability.

In military decision-making, prominent examples are missile research, ballistics, and logistics. Numerous other fields of human endeavor rely on the law of probability.

The Measurement of Probability

Probability is a measure of the likelihood of the occurrence of a random event. * It is the ratio of the number of successful possible outcomes (s) to the total possible outcomes (T), each outcome being equally likely to occur in the "long run," that is, in a very large number of repeated trials made under the same conditions. There is a simple formula for computing the probability of success in any given venture. It is the probability formula of $p = s / T$ given earlier in Chapter 1. Here, p represents the probability that the event called "success" (s) will happen. It is computed by dividing the number of possible successful outcomes (s) in an event by the total number of possible outcomes (T). Some examples of computed probabilities follow.

In the long run, the probability of drawing an ace of spades from a conventional deck of 52 bridge cards is $\frac{1}{52}$, since there is only 1 ace of spades in the deck; the probability of rolling an ace (one) with a normal die is $\frac{1}{6}$; the probability of winning on any one number of a 10-numbered roulette wheel is $\frac{1}{10}$; the chance of coming up with a head in tossing a coin many times is $\frac{1}{2}$; the chance of drawing an ace from a deck is $\frac{4}{52}$, since there are 4 aces in a 52-card deck.

These are mathematical expressions of the probability of success, where the number of "successful" outcomes (s) and the total number of possible outcomes (T) are both known in advance (**a-*priori*** proba-

---

* Due to the element of chance, a random event may result in any one of a number of possible outcomes, so that it is impossible to foretell exactly a specific outcome in any one particular trial.

bility) and each outcome is equally likely. In these instances, it is also easy to compute the chance of failure. It is similarly computed by a simple formula: $q = f / T$, where q represents the probability of failure, f represents the number of "failure" outcomes, and T the total number of possible outcomes. Thus, the chance of not drawing an ace of spades in a conventional 52-card deck is $^{51}/_{52}$, since there are 51 cards in the deck which are not an ace of spades; the chance of not getting an ace in rolling a die is $^{5}/_{6}$; the chance of missing on any one specified number on a 10 numbered roulette wheel is $^{9}/_{10}$; the chance of not getting a head in tossing an unbiased coin is $^{1}/_{2}$.

It is to be observed that the probability of failure may also be obtained by subtracting the probability of a success from 1. Thus, the above probabilities of failing to achieve the specified objective are:

$$q = 1 - \frac{1}{52} = \frac{51}{52} \quad \text{(cards)}$$

$$q = 1 - \frac{1}{6} = \frac{5}{6} \quad \text{(die)}$$

$$q = 1 - \frac{1}{10} = \frac{9}{10} \quad \text{(roulette wheel)}$$

$$q = 1 - \frac{1}{2} = \frac{1}{2} \quad \text{(coin)}$$

In symbolic language, the probability of success is usually given by the letter p and the probability of failure by the letter q. Therefore, we can state that $p + q = 1$; in other words, the chance of either a success or a failure is 1, or certainty. By subtraction we also find that $p = 1 - q$ and $q = 1 - p$. Another way of saying this is that the sum of the probabilities over *all* possible outcomes (in this case, success or failure) must add to 1.0, which is considered certainty; in other words, *some* outcome *must* happen in every chance situation.

Deeper Meaning of Probability

The foregoing discussion of the main ideas involved in quantitatively measuring probability and risk was purposely simplified to introduce the essential elements of the subject. However, there are two important qualifications regarding a computed probability which must be considered. First, the above probabilities were readily computed because both the number of successful outcomes and the total number of possible outcomes were known in advance. While this a-priori knowledge applies in many situations, particularly in the field of games, there are many situations when s and T are not known beforehand. Consequently, in such instances, the number of successful outcomes (numerator) and the total number of possible outcomes (denominator) have to be estimated by means of random sampling, or other experiments.

A second main consideration in computing a probability is the correctness of the tacit but underlying assumption that each of the outcomes in the randomly selected sample in the numerator (s) and the denominator (T) are *equally likely* to occur. Thus, in the 52-card illustration it was subconsciously assumed that each card had an equal chance of being selected. Of course, this would be as nearly true as possible only if all cards were face down, of equal size, the same age and wear, made of the same material, etc., and if the deck were "thoroughly" shuffled on each drawing.

In the case of the die, it was assumed that it was perfectly symmetrical both in size and weight distribution, and that it was "thoroughly shook-up" before rolling, thus making it equally likely for each face to turn up.

In the roulette wheel illustration, it was assumed that each number was allotted the same sized arc on the circumference of the circle, that the wheel was fully balanced, and that the turns of the wheel were of varying strength.

In the coin example, it was assumed that one side was a "head" and one a "tail," that the coin was symmetrical, that the weight was evenly distributed, and so forth.

Of course, the assumption of equal chance, or that each outcome is "equally likely" to occur, is not always correct.* Therefore, this assumption must first be evaluated for acceptability before computing the probability of success or failure on an *a-priori* basis. If the assumption is validated, the simple formula can be used. When the "equally likely" situation is not validated, a more complex situation exists and estimation techniques such as repeated experiments or random sampling are necessary. The following are some not-equally-likely-to-occur events:

---

* In fact, in some games of chance, e.g., the roulette wheel, the odds can be beaten because some of the outcomes are more likely to occur than others due to uneven manufacture, wear and tear, etc. What one needs to do is determine the more-likely-to-occur outcomes by repeated experiments and then to bet on these outcomes over a sufficient number of spins.

(1) The selection of a package from a large bin of unequal sized packages, using a fixed sized scoop to make the selection. Packages which are larger than the diameter of the scoop will hardly have the same chance of being scooped up as the smaller packages.

(2) A die which is not uniform in its weight distribution will not yield an equal chance of 1/6 for obtaining a 1, 2, 3, 4, 5, or 6 on a roll. The face with the heavier weight concentration will obviously have a better chance of turning down and, therefore, a lesser chance of coming up.

(3) A random sample of families in a small city is selected by use of random digits from a register of the names and addresses of all persons living in the city. Because of the varying number of persons per family, the random sample of names will not give each family an equal chance of selection. The families with a larger number of persons will have a better chance of selection than the smaller families.

In determining probabilities, care must be exercised not to assume automatically that events are "equally likely" to occur.

Different Ways of Determining Probability

Due to the many different conditions which exist in problems dealing with management, games, and life in general, methods appropriate to the situation need to be used to determine the probability of success. The following are some of the more common situations and the appropriate method of determining the required probability.

(1) When s and T are known in advance

To use the simple formula $p = s / T$ requires knowing, counting, or estimating the values of s and T. In the foregoing illustrations of games, s and T were known in advance and were assumed to be equally probable. When the number of successful outcomes (s) and the total number of possible outcomes (T) are known in advance, and each outcome is equally likely to occur, the probability of success (p), or failure (q), is readily computed. When s and T are not known, or each outcome is not equiprobable, they must be determined. There are several ways of making such determinations.

(2) Actual complete count

Once the definition of a "successful" outcome is established for any fixed process, it is possible in many cases to determine s and T by making a complete count of the total number of outcomes and the corresponding number of successful outcomes. Thus, suppose two different decks of cards are combined (for instance, a pinochle deck of 48 cards and a bridge deck of 52 cards) and we wish to know the probability of selecting an ace from the combined deck. It is possible here to count the total number of cards (in this case 100 cards) and the number of "successful" outcomes (for instance, 8 aces in the pinochle deck and 4 in the bridge deck equals 12 aces in the combined deck). From these counts, the required probabilities of "success" for any one card may be computed by p = s / T. The probability of drawing an ace in the above example would be $^{12}\!/_{100} = 0.12$.

(3) Estimation of s and T by random sampling or experiments

There are numerous situations when, for practical reasons, s and T cannot be counted completely because of the high cost. These situations occur when the universe consists of a very large (or inexhaustible) number of items. For example, when a large shipment of incandescent bulbs is made and we wish to determine the probability of selecting a defective one, it is not feasible to test each bulb. In such a case, the probability of picking a defective bulb must be *estimated* by an experiment or a random sample. This makes the ratio $\frac{s}{T}$ a *random variable*, since it is computed from independent *random samples* selected from the same universe and will vary due to chance from sample to sample.*

Similarly, to estimate the percentage of time that a machine (or person) is working (or idle), the population of "trials" consists of an inexhaustible or infinite number of split-second instant look-sees [instances] in the course of a month, or year, when the machine may be working or idle. To avoid the burden of continuous clock-watching and recording, it is usually feasible to estimate p = s / T by sampling the stream of time at random instants to determine whether or not work is being performed (by a technique called *random time sampling* or *work sampling*). If it is found, for example, that in 30%

---

* The concept of a random variable is basic to the entire field of probability, since the pattern of behavior of random variables can be described mathematically.

of the sampled instances the machine is idle, its proportion of idle time, p, would be estimated as 0.3.

Thus, there are many management decision situations where it is not feasible or economical to count completely the number of successful and total possible outcomes, and random sampling or random experiments are used to estimate the required probabilities. The true probability of success, which is estimated from the sample, would be the "relative frequency" of occurrence of the successful event in an infinite number of trials, or in the "long run." In fact, another good definition of probability is the *relative frequency of success obtained when the trial is repeated indefinitely under the same set of circumstances.*

(4) Estimating s and T by combination and permutation formulas

Combinations — As indicated above, s and T can often be determined by counting. This method, however, can be very time consuming. Another way of determining the total number of different events (T) and the number of successful events (s) is through the use of algebraic "combination" and "permutation" formulas. The following are illustrations of counting which lead to adoption of combinatorial formulas. These formulas are actually short-cuts to counting.

If a group consists of 4 persons, Art (A), Bob (B), Carol (C), and Debbie (D), what is the probability that Art and Carol (A and C) will be paired off as a bridge team, if pairs are randomly selected? *Answer:* 1 in 6. In this case, where any pair is equally likely, T is 6; it is determined by finding all possible combinations of 2 persons out of 4, as follows:

AB, AC, AD, BC, BD, and CD; s is 1, namely AC; then, $p = \dfrac{s}{T} = \dfrac{1}{6}$.

The approach is no different, conceptually, if the number of persons, objects, or letters is larger or smaller. What is the probability of drawing the letters AB out of the six letters ABCDEF? *Answer:* 1 in 15. What is the probability of drawing ABC out of ABCDEF? *Answer:* 1 in 20. These probabilities can be determined by listing all possible combinations to obtain T and then all possible combinations representing s. (The reader is advised to do so for the above two examples, to check their accuracy.)

These determinations become more complex with larger numbers of objects or persons. In drawing two cards out of an ordinary 52 card deck, what is the probability of drawing a pair of aces? *Answer:* 1 in 221. When taken two at a time, there is a total (T) of 1,326 combinations. To be successful, we must draw 2 aces. This means that the 4 aces in the deck "taken 2 at a time" would give 6 possible combinations of 2 each. Therefore, $p = \dfrac{s}{T} = \dfrac{6}{1326} = \dfrac{1}{221}$.

In solving probability problems of this type, it is of course possible to determine T and s by listing all possible combinations and counting the numbers thus listed. This "brute-force" approach will yield the correct probabilities, but at a high cost in time. A much more efficient method of determining T and s is through the use of a well known algebraic formula for *combinations*: $_nC_r = \dfrac{n!}{r!(n-r)!}$

Here, n! means the product of (n) (n-1) (n-2) ... (1). The row of dots indicates the omission of intermediate numbers to save space, each being one unit less than the prior one. In other words, n! (called "n *factorial*") means the sequential product of a given integer n by all positive integers smaller than it. Thus,

$$2! = (2)\,(1) = 2$$

$$3! = (3)\,(2)\,(1) = 6$$

$$4! = (4)\,(3)\,(2)\,(1) = 24$$

$$5! = (5)\,(4)\,(3)\,(2)\,(1) = 120, \text{ etc.}$$

The above combination formula, $_nC_r$ involves n objects, taking them r at a time. Thus, if there are 4 persons and we wish to take 2 at a time, we have a total of $_4C_2 = \dfrac{4!}{2! \times 2!} = \dfrac{(4 \times 3 \times 2 \times 1)}{(2 \times 1 \times 2 \times 1)} = 6$ combinations. This represents T, the total number of possible outcomes. The number of successful outcomes, s, is similarly determined.

The probability of drawing a pair of aces from a 52-card deck can be readily determined by computing T and s. In this case, there are a total of $_{52}C_2$ possible ways of drawing 2 cards. This is equivalent to

$$T = {}_{52}C_2 = \frac{52!}{2! \times 50!} = \frac{52 \times 51 \times 50 \times 49 \times \ldots \times 2 \times 1}{(2 \times 1) \times (50 \times 49 \ldots \times 2 \times 1)} = \frac{52 \times 51}{2 \times 1} = 1326.$$

On the other hand, the number of successful outcomes consists of the number of combinations of 2 aces out of the 4 in the deck, i.e., the number of combinations of 4 aces, taking 2 at a time. Therefore,

$$s = {}_4C_2 = \frac{4!}{2! \times 2!} = \frac{4 \times 3 \times 2 \times 1}{(2 \times 1) \times (2 \times 1)} = 6, \text{ so } p = \frac{6}{1326} = \frac{1}{221} \ .$$

It can, therefore, be observed that the formula for combinations provides an efficient way of solving probability problems where s and T would otherwise have to be determined by developing extensive and time-consuming listings of all possible combinations of a set of objects (or persons).

Permutations — In the prior examples our concern was with determining the number of different ways we could group n objects taking r at a time. In these examples, it did not matter in which order a group was drawn, that is, whether A was taken first and B second, or B first and A second. There are situations, however, when *the order of drawing, or the arrangement of the objects within the group, is important* and represents additional ways of determining s and T. For example, what is the probability of selecting the 2 persons AB in that specific order (and no other order) out of all possible orders of two persons from the four persons A,B,C, and D? *Answer*: 1 in 12. Here, T is 12: AB, BA, AC, CA, AD, DA, BC, CB, BD, DB, CD, and DC. Note that for each combination there are two permutations, since the orders are reversed. In this instance, s is 1 and p = $\frac{1}{12}$.

Another example of permutations: What is the number of permutations of the four letters A, B, C, and D taken three at a time? By listing all permutations, we obtain the following 24 permutations or arrangements (remember, order matters in permutations):

ABC	BAC	CAB	DAB
ABD	BAD	CAD	DAC
ACB	BCA	CBA	DBA
ACD	BCD	CBD	DBC
ADB	BDA	CDA	DCA
ADC	BDC	CDB	DCB

Again, as in the case of combinations, the number of different permutations can be determined by brute force, namely, listing all possible combinations and for each combination listing all its possible internal arrangements. Of course, this could become an enormous, time-consuming task, especially when there is a large number of objects.

Using the following formula for *permutations*, $_nP_r = \dfrac{n!}{(n-r)!}$, we can quickly determine the number of permutations as follows:

$$_4P_3 = \frac{4!}{(4-3)!} = \frac{4 \times 3 \times 2 \times 1}{1} = 24 \ .$$

Once we determine the total number of possible permutation outcomes (T) and the number of successful permuted outcomes (s), the probability of success can easily be determined by $p = s / T$.

The formula for permutations, $_nP_r$, provides a powerful way of simplifying the task of counting all permutations. This formula derives from the combination formula, by permuting the number of combinations as follows:

$$_nP_r = (r!)(_nC_r) = \frac{r!n!}{r!(n-r)!} = \frac{n!}{(n-r)!} = {_nP_r} \; .$$

Let us try an example: In how many different ways can we arrange the first ten letters of the alphabet by taking two letters at a time, counting each order of arrangement as an extra grouping (permutation)? The answer is:

$$_nP_r = \frac{n!}{(n-r)!} = {_{10}P_2} = \frac{10!}{8!} = (10)(9) = 90 \; .$$

(5) Probabilities for normal distributions

In previous chapters, reference was made to the fixed graphic pattern formed by a normal distribution of x-values. In this special frequency distribution, specific percentages of all units, items, or observations fall within specific ranges formed by the mean of the distribution ($\overline{X}$) and its standard deviation (σ_x). From these pre-established percentages, it is possible (by use of the formula $p = s / T$) to determine the probability that any given unit, item, or observation will fall in any specified range of $\overline{X} \pm Z\sigma_x$, where Z represents the number of standard deviations of the variable being measured. Thus, for example, the probability that any randomly chosen unit of a given normally distributed population will fall within plus or minus one standard deviation ($Z = 1$) around the mean of all units is 0.68. Here, s = 68% (since 68% of all units in a normal distribution are included within one standard deviation around the mean) and T = 100% (i.e., all units).

Therefore, $p = {}^{68}\!/_{100} = 0.68$.

In sampling problems (Chapters 9 and 10), it is often essential to determine the probability that a specified range, or interval constructed from the sample data, includes the true parameter; normal-distribution theory is applied effectively to determine this probability. Similarly, normal-distribution theory is used in determining the probability that a certain specified magnitude of sampling error of an estimate derived from a random sample will, or will not, be exceeded. These concepts, related to confidence-interval estimation, are discussed in greater detail in Chapters 8 and 9 on sampling.

Basic Rules of Probability

Often the computation of the probability of success or failure in a given situation is not as simple as indicated by the formula $p = s / T$, for *simple probability* or a single outcome. Many applications involve probabilities for several related outcomes. Consequently, a set of rules has been developed for determining probabilities under more complex situations. These rules may be classified under two main headings: (1) *rules of addition*, and (2) *rules of multiplication*. Each of these is in turn discussed under two subheadings: (a) *mutually exclusive* and *not mutually exclusive*, and (b) *independence* and *dependence*. These are explained and illustrated below.

Rules of addition — Mutually exclusive

If we were asked to determine the probability of rolling *either* an ace (1) *or* a deuce (2) on an honest die, we could easily obtain this probability by adding the separate probabilities of obtaining an ace ($\frac{1}{6}$) and a deuce ($\frac{1}{6}$). The correct answer is therefore $\frac{1}{6} + \frac{1}{6} = \frac{1}{3}$.

Similarly, the probability of obtaining *either* a head *or* tail in tossing a coin is 1, or certainty. This is obtained by adding $\frac{1}{2}$, the probability of obtaining a head, to $\frac{1}{2}$, the probability of obtaining a tail, since one *or* the other *must* occur with *certainty*.

What is the probability of drawing either an ace or a king in a single selection from a complete 52-card casino deck? The answer is $\frac{2}{13}$: $\frac{4}{52} + \frac{4}{52} = \frac{8}{52} = \frac{2}{13}$.

The above rule of addition is valid for computing "either ... or" probabilities *only* under a specified condition, namely, that the two (or more) probabilities involved are **mutually exclusive**, i.e., if one event occurs the other(s) cannot. For example, in rolling a die it is impossible to obtain both an ace *and* a deuce on a single roll; in tossing a coin it is impossible to obtain *both* a head and a tail at the same time. Thus, in determining probabilities of the "either-or" or "at least one or the other" type, the separate probabilities may be added only if the separate events are mutually exclusive.

Rules of addition — Not mutually exclusive

When the two (or more) different events are not mutually exclusive, that is, part of one event overlaps the other(s), or vice versa, the above addition rule must be modified by introducing a subtraction adjustment for the overlap. For example, if we compute the probability of drawing either an ace or a spade in a single selection from a 52-card bridge deck, we can no longer add the two separate probabilities of $\frac{4}{52}$ (ace) and $\frac{13}{52}$ (spade), yielding $\frac{17}{52}$, since the outcome of the first influences the outcome of the second trial (draw). The solution can be obtained by adding the two separate probabilities (under the mutually exclusive rule) and adjusting the sum by subtracting from it the overlap probability, i.e., by drawing both an ace and a spade (i.e., the ace of spades, $p = \frac{1}{52}$). (See Figure 6.1.) Thus, the either-or probability may be obtained by $(\frac{4}{52} + \frac{13}{52} - \frac{1}{52}) = \frac{16}{52} = \frac{4}{13}$.

Figure 6.1
A graphic illustration of events that are
not mutually exclusive — i.e., an illustration of dependence

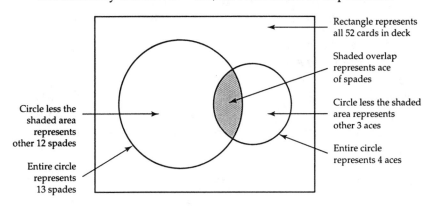

Rules of multiplication — Independence

If we wish to determine the probability of tossing two aces in a row (a "1" and then another "1") on an honest die, we may multiply the probability of obtaining an ace ($\frac{1}{6}$) on the first roll by the probability of also obtaining an ace ($\frac{1}{6}$) on the second roll. Since both events are *independent* of each other, that is, *the first event is not at all influenced by the occurrence or non-occurrence of the second*, the two independent probabilities may be multiplied without adjustment for overlap. Thus, the probability of rolling two aces in a row is $(\frac{1}{6})$ $(\frac{1}{6})$ = $\frac{1}{32}$.

This may be proved by reference to the general formula p = s / T. There is only one way of obtaining an ace on a die on both the first roll and on the second roll, i.e., s=1. However, on two consecutive rolls there are a total of 36 possible outcomes, i.e., T = 36, as follows: 1 and 1; 1 and 2; 1 and 3; 1 and 4; 1 and 5; 1 and 6; 2 and 1; 2 and 2; and so on, through 6 and 6, for a total of 36 pairs. Therefore, p = $\frac{1}{36}$, i.e., the single outcome "1 and 1" combination out of the 36 possible outcomes.

Some additional examples of the simultaneous or successive occurrence of two (or more) independent conditions are:

- The probability of tossing two heads in succession is $(\frac{1}{2})(\frac{1}{2})$ = $\frac{1}{4}$.

- The probability of drawing two aces in succession from a 52-card bridge deck after replacing the first drawn card is $(\frac{4}{52})(\frac{4}{52})$ = $\frac{1}{169}$.

- The probability of winning twice in succession on the same number on a 10-numbered roulette wheel is $(\frac{1}{10})(\frac{1}{10})$ = $\frac{1}{100}$.

Thus, we see that the general rule for determining the probability of the occurrence of successive or simultaneous events, so long as the separate occurrences are independent of each other, is: multiply the two (or more) separate probabilities by each other. This application is necessary in determining the risk of taking management action when 6 or 7 successive points in quality control fall on the same side (+ or –) of the mean (Chapter 11).

Rules of multiplication — Dependence

As in the case of the addition rule, the multiplication principle must also be modified when the two (or more) events are not independent. For example, what is the probability of drawing two aces in succession if we do not replace the first card drawn? *Answer*: $(\frac{4}{52})(\frac{3}{51})$ = $\frac{1}{221}$.

It can be observed by this example that the outcome of the second drawing is influenced by (or depends upon) the outcome of the first drawing. At the first drawing there are 4 aces (s = 4) and a total of 52 cards (T = 52). Therefore, the probability of drawing an ace at first is $\frac{4}{52}$ = $\frac{1}{13}$. Since the first successful draw is an ace and it is kept out of the deck (generally called "without replacement"), there are only 3 aces left in the remaining 51 cards so the probability of drawing an ace on the second draw is $3/52 = 1/17$. Therefore, the probability of drawing two aces in succession if the first card is held out is $(1/13)(1/17) = 1/221$.

The probability situation when two (or more) events are interdependent is called *conditional probability*, since the outcome of the second (or later) event(s) is conditioned by (or dependent on) the outcome of the first event. There are other elements of conditional probability to describe,* but discussion of these is beyond the intended scope of this book.

Special Section
Probability and the Bionomial Distribution

Suppose we wanted to determine the probability of obtaining exactly two sixes in three rolls of an honest die, how would the required probability be computed. As will be seen in this section, this is not just an academic question, its solution has many practical decision-making applications, utilizing the *binomial distribution theory*.

Here we have a situation where the probability of success in a single trial is known in advance ($p = 1/6$) and the size of the experiment, or sample size, is fixed at n=3 rolls. In any problem, p may be any fraction between 0 and 1, x may be any desired number of successes, and n as large a sample as necessary.

One of the many possible ways a given number (x) of successes (e.g., sixes on a die) can occur in n trials is: rolling x successes consecutively and then failing to do so in the remaining n–x rolls. If we denote p as the probability of a success (rolling a six) and q as the probability of a failure, this sequence may be presented as:

$\underline{\begin{matrix} x \\ \text{successes:} \end{matrix}}$	and	$\underline{\begin{matrix} n-x \\ \text{failures:} \end{matrix}}$	
p p p p ⋯ p	⋯	q q q q ⋯ q	$= p^x q^{n-x}$

Since each trial is independent, the probability of obtaining x successes in this particular sequence is the product of the individual probabilities or $p^x q^{n-x}$.

---

*Such as Baysian theory as described in Andrew F. Siegel, *Practical Business Statistics*, Richard D. Irwin, Inc., 1990.

Another way of achieving x successes is: rolling the n–x non-sixes consecutively followed by x sixes. This sequence may be presented in reverse of the one above as:

$$
\underset{\text{failures:}}{\underbrace{\quad n-x \quad}} \quad \text{and} \quad \underset{\text{successes:}}{\underbrace{\quad x \quad}}
$$

$$
\underbrace{q\ q\ q\ q \cdots q} \quad \cdots \quad \underbrace{p\ p\ p\ p \cdots p} \ = \ p^x q^{n-x}
$$

Again, the probability of achieving n–x failures in a row followed by x success is $p^x q^{n-x}$. Therefore, in order to answer the question at the beginning of this section, it is necessary to determine the number of different orders or sequences of obtaining x successes and n–x failures (i.e., the number of ways of arranging n things of which x are alike and n–x things which are not alike). This has been determined algebraically to be the same as the combination formula previously presented:

$$
{}_nC_x = \frac{n!}{x!(n-x)!}.
$$

Therefore, the probability (p_x) of obtaining exactly x successes and n–x failures of a given event in n trials is:

$$
P_x = {}_nC_x p^x q^{n-x} = \frac{n!}{x!(n-x)!}\ p^x q^{n-x}.
$$

This is the general formula for the binomial distribution. It provides the probability (p_x) of achieving exactly x successes under the following specified conditions:

(a) the probability of success in a single trial (p) is known and the probability of failure, of course, would be q = 1 – p;

(b) the sample size or number of trials n, is known, and

(c) the trials are independent and mutually exclusive (e.g., the die is shaken before each roll).

To illustrate the use of the general formula, let us compute the probability of rolling 3 sixes in 5 rolls of an honest die. Here p = ⅙, q = ⅚, x = 3, and n = 5. Therefore, the required probability is:

$$
P_x = {}_nC_x\, p^x\, q^{n-x} = \frac{5!}{3!\,2!}\left(\frac{1}{6}\right)^3\left(\frac{5}{6}\right)^2 = \left(\frac{5\times4\times3\times2}{3\times2\times2}\right)\left(\frac{1}{216}\right)\left(\frac{25}{36}\right)
$$

$$
= (10)\left(\frac{1}{216}\right)\left(\frac{25}{36}\right) = 0.03215.
$$

By the general binomial formula, we can determine the probability of obtaining exactly 0, 1, 2, 3, 4, and 5 successes in 5 trials (n=5); in other words, x = 0, x = 1, x = 2, x = 3, x = 4, and x = 5. The correct probabilities in our illustrative problem are:

Number of Sixes (x)	Probability (p_x)
0	$p_0 = {}_5C_0\, p^0\, q^5 = \dfrac{5!}{0!\ 5!}\left(\dfrac{1}{6}\right)^0\left(\dfrac{5}{6}\right)^5 = 0.40188*$
1	$p_1 = {}_5C_1\, p^1\, q^4 = \dfrac{5!}{1!\ 4!}\left(\dfrac{1}{6}\right)^1\left(\dfrac{5}{6}\right)^4 = 0.40188$
2	$p_2 = {}_5C_2\, p^2\, q^3 = \dfrac{5!}{2!\ 3!}\left(\dfrac{1}{6}\right)^2\left(\dfrac{5}{6}\right)^3 = 0.16075$
3	$p_3 = {}_5C_3\, p^3\, q^2 = \dfrac{5!}{3!\ 2!}\left(\dfrac{1}{6}\right)^3\left(\dfrac{5}{6}\right)^2 = 0.03215$
4	$p_4 = {}_5C_4\, p^4\, q^1 = \dfrac{5!}{4!\ 1!}\left(\dfrac{1}{6}\right)^4\left(\dfrac{5}{6}\right)^1 = 0.00322$
5	$p_5 = {}_5C_5\, p^5\, q^0 = \dfrac{5!}{5!\ 0!}\left(\dfrac{1}{6}\right)^5\left(\dfrac{5}{6}\right)^0 = 0.00013$

It can be seen from the addition rule that the probability of obtaining *either* 0, 1, 2, 3, 4, *or* 5 sixes in 5 rolls of the die is the sum of the separate probabilities, or 1, which is certainty. This outcome is obvious, since the die *must* fall on any one of its faces. The resulting probability for any number of successful outcomes could also be obtained by expanding the binomial and adding all the appropriate

---

* Note that 0! is equal to 1.

terms.* The sum must be equal to 1; therefore, since p + q = 1, so the sum of $(p + q)^n$ expanded must equal 1.

In the same way, the probability of obtaining either 0 or 1 success; 0, 1, or 2 successes, etc., is determinable by adding the separate probabilities for the appropriate terms. When all the possible terms of the binomial are developed, the resulting expansion is:

$$(p + q)^n = p^n + n\,p^{n-1}\,q + \frac{n(n-1)p^{n-2}q^2}{2} + \dots + q^n.$$

Thus, the various terms of the binomial distribution give the separate probabilities of the various possible successful outcomes in a systematic order. This provides the basis for computing the probability of any one, two, or more successful specified types of outcome. In the above example, the probability of obtaining *either* no sixes or one six on five rolls of a die is 0.80376, i.e., the sum of the first two terms in the preceding expansion of the binomial distribution. The probability of obtaining *either* 0, 1, *or* 2 successes is 0.96451, the sum of the first three terms.

---

* In algebra, the binomial expansion is illustrated by the following:

Given: A constant a and another constant b.
Find: Their sum raised, separately, to the power of 1, 2, ... , n.

$(a + b)^1 = a^1 + b^1$
$(a + b)^2 = a^2 + 2ab + b^2$
$(a + b)^3 = a^3 + 3a^2b + 3ab^2 + b^3$
$(a + b)^4 = a^4 + 4a^3b + 6a^2b^2 + 3ab^3 + b^4$
etc., to:

$$(a + b)^n = a^n + n\,a^{n-1}\,b^1 + \frac{n(n-1)a^{n-2}b^2}{2} + \frac{n(n-1)(n-2)a^{n-3}b^3}{(3)(2)}$$

$$+ \frac{n(n-1)(n-2)(n-3)a^{n-4}b^4}{(4)(3)(2)} + \dots + b^n.$$

This is the general expression of the binomial expansion. If we substitute p for a and q for b, it will be seen that the general formula for the binomial expansion is $_nC_x\,p^x\,q^{n-x}$. For example, if we wish to know the term representing 4 successes, it will be:

$$_nC_4\,p^4\,q^{n-4} = \frac{n!\,p^4q^{n-4}}{4!\,(n-4)!} = \frac{n(n-1)(n-2)(n-3)(n-4)!\,p^4q^{n-4}}{4!\,(n-4)!}$$

$$= \frac{n(n-1)(n-2)(n-3)\,p^4q^{n-4}}{(4)(3)(2)(1)}$$

Thus, we link the general algebraic expansion with the binomial distribution used in determining the probability of x successes in n trials of an event with a probability p of success occurring on a single trial.

Practical uses of the binomial distribution

The general term of the binomial distribution provides a model for determining probabilities in many practical problems involving percentages or rates (i.e., attributes). Since the inspection of products for their quality or auditing of vouchers for accuracy concern themselves with the percentage of defectives or error-rates, some of the main applications of binomial theory are in the fields of inspection and auditing for attributes, through the use of random samples of the product or work performed. In this and related situations, it is essential to know, or to approximate the percentage (p) of "defective" items (or the error-rate) in the entire population or in a specific lot. After p is estimated from a random sample, the p and q can be entered in the binomial expansion for any specified size of sample, n. Thus, the probability of occurrence of any stated number of successes (or failures, as the case may be) can be determined. This probability provides a basis for accepting or rejecting a given lot or a universe of items of a given size with a known risk of being wrong (generally called *acceptance sampling*).

An illustration — A manufacturing process produces darning needles with a specified eye-width; it was determined by previous experience that one-percent of the needles are defective in meeting the width-of-the-eye specification. A carton (lot) of 5,000 such needles is to be purchased by a clothing manufacturer with the understanding that the incoming product must be at least 99 percent acceptable. To check the acceptability of the shipment, the purchaser selects a random sample of, say, 10 needles and inspects them for width of the eye. Assuming that the 99 percent (or better) quality claimed by the needle manufacturer is true, what is the probability of finding zero "defectives" in the sample?

To answer this question, we set up the essential figures for entry into the general binomial formula. Here, n, the size of sample (or number of trials) is 10. The expected percentage of non-defectives is $p = .99$, and the percentage of defectives is $q = .01$. We seek to estimate the probability of zero defectives or 10 non-defectives ($x=10$) in the lot.* To repeat, $n = 10$; $p = .99$; $q = .01$; $x = 10$. Using the general formula for the probability of obtaining x successes (or failures), we have:

---

* Care must be taken in these problems to correctly define p, q, and x, and to fill them into the general binomial formula correctly. Note that in this problem, for example, to achieve zero defectives means achieving 10 non-defectives; therefore, $x = 10$, not zero.

$$P_x = {}_nC_x \, p^x \, q^{n-x} = P_{10} = {}_{10}C_{10} \, (.99)^{10} \, (.01)^0$$

$$= \frac{10!}{10! \ 0!} \, (.99)^{10} \, (.01)^0 = (1) \, (.99) \, (1) \, * = 0.903.$$

This means that the chances are 90% that a random sample of 10 from a lot consisting of a product with 99 percent or better quality will contain no defectives. Similarly, the general binomial term provides the probability of finding 1, 2, 3, ..., 10 defectives in a random sample of 10 under the stated conditions.

By using the rules of addition, the binomial can also determine the probability of finding any specified range or number of defectives. Thus, a typical approach to making a decision whether to accept or reject a given lot of items being purchased or released on the market is provided by the binomial distribution. If management states in advance the risk it is willing to take in accepting (or rejecting) a given lot originating from a population with a known quality level, the decision can be based on the number of defectives found in the sample. A part of the field of quality control commonly called acceptance sampling uses binomial distribution theory. Tables are available for the general term of this distribution for various values of n, p, and x, as well as for cumulative sums of these terms.**

The mean and standard deviation of the binomial distribution

Because of its mathematical properties, it is possible to determine the mean number of successes and the standard deviation of successes very quickly for binomial distributions. The mean (or expected number) is the product of sample size (n) and the proportion of successes (p). Thus $\overline{X} = np$. The standard deviation for the distribution is $\sigma_x = \sqrt{npq}$.

An illustration of the correctness of these quick computations may be given by a simple binomial distribution. Assume we are tossing an honest coin 4 times. Here, $n = 4$, $p = \frac{1}{2}$ for heads and $q = \frac{1}{2}$ for tails. The separate probabilities of obtaining 0, 1, 2, 3, and 4 heads, thereby establishing the entire distribution, are shown in Table 6.1.

---

* $0! = 1$ and $(.01)^0 = 1$.

** In practical sampling problems of this type, the binomial does not provide the exact probabilities because when an item is drawn and not replaced, the conditions of independence and a fixed probability (p) at each trial no longer hold. However, this inexactness is of no practical concern so long as the size of sample is small relative to the size of the universe, or expressed differently, so long as the size of the population approaches infinity.

Table 6.1

Illustration of the long way of computing
$\overline{X}$ and σ_x for a binomial distribution.

Number of heads (x)	Frequency Probability (p_x)	Midpoint (m)	in 16th's (f)	fm	d	d^2	fd^2
0	$\left(\frac{1}{16}\right)$	0	1	0	2	4	4
1	$\left(\frac{4}{16}\right)$	1	4	4	1	1	4
2	$\left(\frac{6}{16}\right)$	2	6	12	0	0	0
3	$\left(\frac{4}{16}\right)$	3	4	12	1	1	4
4	$\left(\frac{1}{16}\right)$	4	1	4	2	4	4
			$n = 16$	$\Sigma fm = 32$		$\Sigma fd^2 = 16$	

The computation procedure for $\overline{X}$ and σ_x is the same as given in Chapters 4 and 5 for any frequency distribution. Here, $\overline{X} = \sum \frac{fm}{n} = \frac{32}{16} = 2$. This means that the average number of heads which may be expected in tossing a coin four times is 2. The standard deviation is $\sigma_x = \sqrt{\sum \frac{fd^2}{n}} = \sqrt{\frac{16}{16}} = 1$.

By using the mathematically-derived formulas for the mean and standard deviation of binomial distributions we obtain exactly the same results:

$$\overline{X} = np = 4\left(\frac{1}{2}\right) = 2, \text{ and}$$

$$\sigma_x = \sqrt{npq} = \sqrt{4\left(\frac{1}{2}\right)\left(\frac{1}{2}\right)} = 1.$$

Consequently, considerable time may be saved by using the above mathematical formulas for computing the mean and standard deviation of frequency distributions which can be developed from the binomial expansion $(p + q)^n = $ sum of $_nC_x\, p^x\, q^{n-x}$ for all possible values of x.

Other specialized distributions and probability

In the more complex applications of the theory of probability still more specialized distributions than the binomial and normal distributions become essential. Some of these are: the t-distribution and Chi-Square distribution, each covered in Chapter 10. Other distributions, such as the Poisson distribution, the Hypergeometric distribution, and the F-distribution, are beyond the scope of this book.

Summary

Gene Fawcette, in a Washington Post article, stated: "Probability is the basis of life insurance, telephone traffic, business, politics, war, modern physics, genetics, and life on other planets. ... The whole Universe obeys only laws of chance." However, probability carries little meaning by such qualitative statements as "good," "bad," "high," or "low." When quantitatively determined by the formula p = s / T, where s represents the number of possible successful outcomes for a given event, and T represents the total number of possible outcomes, a common language of expressing risks is used. *Probability is defined as a measure of the likelihood, or relative frequency, of occurrence of a random event (such as the roll of a die) in the long run.* In many situations, both s and T are known (such as dice, roulette wheel, etc.) and computations of the probability of success (p) is simple. In other situations, s and T have to be either counted, estimated by reliance on sampling or randomly-based experiments, or computed by use of combination and permutation formulas. The latter formulas are particularly essential when large numbers of outcomes are involved, to save the enormous work and time of listing and counting all possible combinations of n things taken r at a time.

The formula for combinations, where the different order or arrangement of things does not matter is: $_nC_r = \dfrac{n!}{r!(n-r)!}$. The formula for permutations, or number of different *orders or arrangements* is: $_nP_r = \dfrac{n!}{(n-r)!}$. These symbols are explained in the text.

Probability must consider the correctness of the oft-made assumption that each event is equally likely to occur, mutually exclusive, or independent. Rules for computing the correct probability differ, depending on whether the events are equiprobable, mutually exclusive, or independent.

There are situations which require determining the probability of either one or the other event occurring, and of *both* or several events occurring *simultaneously.* In "either-or" situations, the separate probabilities are additive without adjustment if the events are mutually exclusive. Thus, the probability of A or B = probability of A + probability of B. However, adjustment of the sum for "overlap" is necessary when the events are not mutually exclusive. Thus, probability of A or B = probability of A + probability of B – joint probability of A and B.

To determine the probability of simultaneous occurrences, we must also distinguish between independence and dependence. When the two (or more) events are independent, the probability of simultaneous occurrence is the product of the two separate probabilities, i.e., the probability of *both A and B* equals the probability of A multiplied by the probability of B.

When the two (or more) events are dependent, i.e., one is conditioned by the other, the use of a conditional probability formula becomes necessary. In such a case, the probability of *both A and B* occurring is obtained by: (Probability of A) (Probability of B assuming A has happened).

The normal distribution (described in several chapters) and the binomial distribution (described in Special Sections of this chapter) play an important role in determining probabilities involved in various sampling, medical research, and general research problems. Both also provide a basis for determining the probability of success in a very large variety of management problems. A background in the theory of probability is essential in the following chapters of this book: 7, 8, 9, 10, 11, and 12.

Problems

1. A large retail sales store, to attract customers, ran a weekly raffle whereby a prize was to be given to the winners. One thousand (1,000) customers were given a pre-numbered slip on which they entered their name and address. These slips were placed in a large bowl and mixed thoroughly.

    (a) What would be your chances of being selected for a prize at one of the weekly drawings, if you had entered one entry-slip and only one winner were drawn?

    (b) Before drawing, what would be your chances of being selected if the number of winners were 2?

(c) If your friend was among the 1000 eligible customers, what would be the *a-priori* chance of both of you being selected, if two winners were selected?

(d) In the above, what would be the chances of both of you being drawn as winners if the number of winners were 3?

(e) Indicate which probability situation the above items (a) through (e) represent simple, addition, multiplication, or conditional probability.

2. In one numbers betting game, a person picking the correct three-digit number (000-999) wins $500 for every dollar bet. Explain with specific probability computations why this amount of payoff in the long run will lead one to lose $500 for every $1,000 wagered; or show that the "operator's take" is 50 percent.

3. In some football pools, the operator pays off $40 for $1 if you correctly pick 7 out of 7 winning teams. What should be fair odds in this case and what is the operator's take?

4. In pursuing problem 3 further, compute the operator's take when the following prizes are offered

(a) 3 out of 3 ($5 for $1);   (b) 4 out of 4 ($10 for $1);

(c) 5 out of 5 ($16 for $1);   and (d) 6 out of 6 ($30 for $1).

5. In preparing to issue license numbers to private car owners, a State Motor Vehicle Department wishes to determine how many different licenses they could issue altogether by placing two different letters of the alphabet before a 3-digit number (for example, AB-107; AB-108; BA-107; BA-108; etc.).

(a) How many un-duplicated sets of licenses can they issue? (Note: this is a permutations rather than a combinations problem.)

(a) How many plates can be issued for any 3 different letters followed by any 3 digits?

6. In seeing the many names of motion pictures, one begins to wonder whether the movie colony will run out of names in a given generation.

(a) Given: 10,000 different words in a vocabulary, how many one-word movies can be produced without duplication?

(b) How many two-word movies?

(c) How many three-word movies?

7. Social Security account numbers consist of 9 digits, as follows:

area		block	sequence number
000	–	00	– 0000

Serial (sequence) numbers are issued consecutively 10,000 in each block (consisting of the four digits from 0000 to 9999) in a maximum of 1,000 areas (consisting of the three digits from 000 to 999). In other words, there are a maximum of 1,000 areas, 100 blocks to each area, and 10,000 numbers for each given area-block. For example, the account number 001-02-9999 represents area 001, block 02, and serial number 9999.

(a) Determine how many unduplicated numbers the social security system was able to accommodate at the start of the social security program.

(b) If at the end of 1994, the system already had issued 377 million numbers, and an average of about 7 million is needed every subsequent year, how many more years past 1994 can the system last before "old" numbers will need to be reused?

8. We have a normal frequency distribution consisting of a group of 1,000 male college seniors classified by height The mean height was computed to be 68 inches with a standard deviation of 4 inches. What is the probability that any of the 1,000 students selected at random will:

(a) Have a height somewhere between 64 inches and 72 inches?

(b) How many will be at least 6 feet tall?

(c) Have a height between the group's mean and one-half standard deviation on either side of the mean?

(d) Have a height between the mean and 0.675 standard deviations on either side of it?

9. The mean length of life of a certain type of flashlight battery is 300 hours with a standard deviation of 15 hours.

(a) What is the probability that a given battery will expire before 255 hours of service?

(b) What is the probability that a given battery will last 255 hours or more?

(c) What condition must hold for the above probabilities to be approximately correct?

Special Section — The Binomial Distribution

10. Medical records covering a period of 10 years show that the "success" rate for a given type of operation is 0.9. In a given week, 3 persons in a given hospital are scheduled for this operation.

(a) What are the chances that all 3 persons will have a successful operation?

(b) What are the chances that at least 2 of the 3 persons will have a successful operation?

(c) What are the chances that none of them will have a successful operation?

(d) What are the chances that at least one of the three will have a successful operation?

11. A shipment was made of 10,000 ballpoint pen fillers of a specified dimension, with a guarantee that no more than 2 percent "deviate but slightly" from this dimension (defective). A random sample of 5 fillers was selected for testing from the shipment.

(a) Indicate the general formula (or expression) by which probabilities may be computed for any number of detectives by any sample size.

(b) What is the probability that the sample of 5 would contain no defective fillers?

(c) All defectives?

12. A company files payroll and other records about its employees in folders, one for each employee. The 1,000 folders are arranged alphabetically based on the employee's surname. Past inventory checking of these files has turned up a 10% misfiling rate. Currently, a random sample of 6 folders, together with their adjacent folders on both sides (to determine whether a folder was misfiled), was drawn to check on the misfiling rate. What is the probability of finding:

    (a) No misfiled folders in the sample?   (b) One?

    (c) Less than two?

13. A given process is said to produce 3% defective pieces. If a random sample of 4 pieces is selected, what is the probability of finding:

    (a) No defective? (b) At least one defective? (c) All defective?

Chapter 7

Random Sampling —
A Short-Cut to Fact-Finding

*"Our knowledge, our attitudes, and our actions are based
to a very large extent upon samples."**

In the preceding chapters we discussed methods of analyzing data
by means of frequency distributions, averages, and standard deviations.
In those chapters hardly any emphasis had been placed on the need for
first collecting reliable data before making a statistical analysis of the
subject of interest. Yet, it is obvious that no matter how suitable the
methods of analysis may be, the results can be almost worthless if the
data at hand are not appropriate or are subject to serious inaccuracies.
Earlier, in Chapter 2, methods of collecting data were introduced in a
general way, and it was noted that statistics can be collected either by
making a complete enumeration (census) or by sampling the universe
of inquiry, preferably by random sampling, as the most economical way
of gathering information. Methods of random (probability) sampling
were distinguished from judgment sampling methods. Furthermore,
because the size of the sample has a substantial bearing on the precision
of the final results and on the costs of collecting data, Chapter 2 also
mentioned some factors that need to be considered in deciding on the
size of sample to use in statistical surveys.

In this chapter, two of the six major elements of sampling are
discussed: (1) problem formulation and (2) methods of selecting
random samples.

The Meaning of Random Selection

Because of its widespread use in government, business, industry,
social life and, in fact, in every field of human endeavor, everyone now

* William G. Cochran, *Sampling Techniques,* John Wiley & Sons, New York, 1977.

seems to know what sampling is. When participants in our introductory statistics classes were asked to define *sampling*, many said, correctly, that sampling is the selection of a part of a whole field (the *"universe"* or *"population"*) for the purpose of drawing conclusions about the entire universe from a study of this part (the sample). In their definitions, however, the participants in practically all cases neglected to use the words "random selection". Unless the sample is selected *randomly*, that is, by reliance on the law of probability, the many advantages of using sampling as a method of collecting data are dissipated, and the risk is increased when making inferences about the characteristics of the universe of concern.

The basic requirement is that a sample be *representative* or serve as an off-spring from the parent or the entire universe from which it is selected. The best way of meeting this requirement is to use a *random* sample that also is *large enough* to provide a reasonably accurate picture of the universe.*

Sampling may be likened to taste-testing, where the taster tastes a small part (or piece) of the item and thereby draws a conclusion regarding its quality or other characteristics. Unless the taster gets a *representative* piece (or part) of the whole item, the conclusions may be misleading and reliance on that piece may be risky. The expert taster, therefore, will try to taste a representative sample, of sufficient size, to avoid an erroneous conclusion. Similarly, the researcher or manager should make use of the principles of probability, as described in this chapter, in order to avoid getting misleading information about the universe under study.

*The basic criterion in selecting a **random** sample from a given population is that each item (or unit), either in the entire universe or in each sub-universe (stratum) we may wish to construct, is given an equal chance of being selected into the sample.* Therefore, the selection must be guided to assure the free operation of chance. Unless each item in the sample is chosen by truly random selection techniques there will be no way of assessing how accurately the sample reflects the characteristics of the universe from which it is selected; consequently, two of the many advantages of sampling (validity of the inferences and measurement of the precision of the results) are lost unless random selection is used.

---

* Random selection methods are presented in this chapter. Chapter 9 presents factors that influence sample size which need to be considered and provides formulas for determining the appropriate sample size.

Confidence in Results

Amazing as this may seem, even in this modern age of science and technology, there are still some skeptical business people, managers, and legislators who mistrust evidence about a population unless the information is collected from its entirety.* Such mistrust is primarily due to a lack of knowledge of the ability of randomly selected samples to reproduce the characteristics of universes with reasonable accuracy. Sometimes it is due also to a false impression that samples are generally wrong because of occasional failures of samples. In this and the following three chapters we attempt to demonstrate the general dependability as well as the specific qualifications of random sampling. Professor Robert R. Sears, speaking to a graduating class at the Harvard University Graduate School of Education, once said, "The man who does not understand the laws of sampling and probability is intellectually crippled in today's world." Perhaps this assertion is a bit too strong and needs a little tempering, but after reading the sampling chapters, it is hoped that readers will understand why a manager or researcher who does not know what random sampling is, how it works, and what it can do to make administration and management more informed and efficient, is lacking a basic tool of management and decision-making.

Practical Value of Sampling

In Chapter 1 we cite many cases where random sampling has served the purpose better than a complete enumeration — better in terms of cost and time invested and better in terms of accuracy. In some instances there is no choice other than to use sampling. One might think of the advantages of sampling as encompassed by the word SAFE. When spelled out, SAFE sampling can mean:

S – Savings: in money to collect the required information.

A – Accuracy: often the accuracy of random sample result is greater than that of complete enumeration.

---

* This statement should not be misconstrued to mean that many managers, legislators, researchers, attorneys, and judges are not relying on the results of random samples. Evidence from food and drug inspections is based on samples; estimates of the nation's unemployment rate are based on random samples; and many, many other aspects of government and, of course, business administration depend on random samples for much of their information.

F – Feasibility: in some instances, sampling is the only feasible method of getting information.

E – Expediency: it takes fewer work-hours to collect data by sampling; hence, results can be obtained sooner for decision-making.

Savings of money — Suppose it costs an average of about $50 to interview an adult in a given community for the purpose of learning the preference among several brands of a given product. If there are 100,000 adults in the community, the interviewing cost of collecting the required information from all of them would be approximately $5,000,000. Since the same information may usually be obtained with a sufficient degree of accuracy from a randomly selected sample of relatively small size, imagine what the money savings in this case would be! There are many illustrations of actual economies in data collection resulting from the use of samples,* and in many future statistical surveys a great deal of money will be saved, provided management encourages the adoption of random sampling, where appropriate, as a device to collect their required statistics.

Accuracy — While no one can deny the money saving advantage of sampling, very few will recognize that as a method of obtaining data about a population, random sampling is frequently more nearly accurate than a complete enumeration. It is a fact that in many large-scale surveys sampling has yielded more nearly accurate information than that obtained from complete counts. For example, both in the 1980 and 1990 U.S. Censuses of the Population, random samples found under-enumeration of the population by as much as 5 million persons each time. How is this possible? It is a result primarily of the fact that so-called complete counts have a great propensity for non-sampling errors. These causes of error are more easily controlled in small samples than in massive enumerations. Some of the main causes of *non-sampling errors* are: interviewer error, response error, incomplete enumeration of the survey area, data-entry errors, and many other causes. Of course, when these and other causes of error are controlled

---

* The Consumer Price Index of the Bureau of Labor Statistics is based on a sample of stores and households. The index of factory employment, the monthly estimates of unemployment in the United States, estimates of savings and spending in the United States, estimates of crop yield, estimates of accident rates, and other important social and economic statistics are all compiled from samples. Sampling also is used in statistical process quality control and in receiving inspection, in order to decide on the basis of samples whether or not to accept a complete lot of a given material or product. (See Chapter 11.)

and corrected in a complete enumeration, greater accuracy can be expected from a complete enumeration — but at what cost? Therefore, a major advantage of sampling is that it frees funds which would otherwise be used for complete enumerations for more complete control of the causes of non-sampling errors, thus often leading to greater over-all accuracy as a result of sampling.

An important decision that management is often obliged to make is whether to use random sampling in its auditing or inspection programs. The alternative choices are limited: (1) either use 100 percent surveys (which involve large costs and often give no assurance of perfect accuracy), (2) use judgment sampling with selection of a hopefully representative sample by good judgment, or (3) use random sampling by reliance on chance in a knowledgeable way.

As compared with judgment sampling, random sampling also has the advantage that it provides a sound basis for measuring the *precision* and *confidence* in the sample results. (See Chapters 8, 9, and 10.) This measurement of precision and confidence, when relying on random samples, gives management knowledge of the risks involved when making decisions based on the resulting statistical data. Measurements of precision and confidence (or risk) generally are not acceptable when judgment samples are used, because no sound principles support them.

Feasibility — Suppose it was vitally important to test the effectiveness of a new drug to cure a given malady. Sampling is the only feasible way of testing its ability to do so. Suppose we were to measure the tearing weight of a certain grade of paper by subjecting each and every piece to destructive testing. There is the threat that no usable paper might be left. Similarly, imagine 100 percent crush-testing of a grade of brick to determine its hardness, or crush-testing glass, or fire-testing bullets. In certain research, industrial, and managerial studies, particularly those involving destructive testing, sampling is the only feasible method of fact-finding to determine quality.

Expediency — Suppose it takes one-half hour to interview a person in a market-research survey. It is obvious that it will take less time to complete the survey by interviewing a small random sample of the population than it would to interview the whole population. Does it not also follow that the results would be obtained sooner, given the same staff resources? Not only would the results be available sooner but further savings might be realized from quicker remedial action taken on the basis of the more timely information. One practical illustration of this point is sampling a product in the course of its mass production to determine its quality (process control). Based on timely sampling results obtained during production, almost immediate corrective action can be taken, when necessary, to prevent the manufacture of defective items, rather than later rejecting an accumulation of defectives during the final inspection of the manufactured product.

Six Elements of a Sampling System

Six main elements are invloved when designing a sampling system, as follows:

Element #1 — Formulate the problem, which includes defining the population of interest and the objectives of the study (Chapters 2 and 7).

Element #2 — Decide on the appropriate method of selecting the sample (Chapter 7).

Element #3 — Determine the appropriate size of sample (Chapter 9).

Element #4 — Choose the best way of extending the results of the sample to the universe level, i.e., the estimation procedure (Chapter 9).

Element #5 — Choose the appropriate formulas for calculating the extent of sampling error in the estimates (Chapters 9 and 10).

Element #6 — Establish procedures for controlling the entry of non-sampling errors in the estimates, i.e., control the quality of the basic data (Chapters 2 and 11).

Element #1 — Problem Formulation

Before sampling a universe, it is essential to formulate the problems to be enlightened, in order to avoid collecting data irrelevant to the problem, to economize as much as possible in sample selection, and to develop an efficient sample design.

First, there must be a clear definition of the population to be surveyed or audited. (See "Defining the population to be sampled" hereafter.)

Second, the general as well as the specific goals of the survey must be spelled out and clarified so that we know precisely what information is wanted and how it will be used to serve the objectives (see Chapter 2). There must be advance specification in the form of table shells of the classifications and cross-classifications for which data are required, as well as specific frequency distributions and statistical measures that will be needed, such as the percentage of people with income above $100,000, the median family income, the distribution by amount of income classes, and so forth.

Finally, the desired degree of accuracy and confidence needed in the end-results should be decided on before sampling. These decisions have a direct influence on the size of sample to use and the credibility of the subsequent findings. A fact not often recognized is that management, not the statistician, should specify the range of sampling error it can tolerate in the end-results, so that this, plus the desired level of confidence and other factors can form the basis for choosing the appropriate size of sample. In some situations, the statistician can advise management of the possible effect on costs of alternative choices of tolerable error and desired confidence.

Defining the population to be sampled — Two examples will demonstrate the importance of clearly defining the universe to be sampled.

In an interview survey to predict which candidate likely will win in a Senatorial election in a given state, a sample was to be selected to estimate the candidates' popularity. What is the source of the information? The universe most relevant to this problem would be citizens of voting age who will actually vote in the coming election. To include in the sample young persons who would not be eligible to vote, or eligible voters who would not vote, would be a waste of interviewing time as well as a departure from the original purpose of the survey. Consequently, for maximum efficiency the universe to be sampled needs to be carefully defined.

As another illustration, the Baltimore Chapter of the American Cancer Society some time ago obtained the cooperation of the U.S. Postal Service to deliver a cancer-education pamphlet to all households in the City of Baltimore. In order to determine the impact of such a mass mailing, it was decided to interview by telephone a random sample of the recipients of the pamphlet. Households without telephones or with unlisted numbers were to be surveyed later by a small sample of city blocks. The sample to be contacted by telephone was selected from the local telephone directory. However, the telephone directory listed the names and telephones of many business, government, and industrial organizations, as well as private households and even some addresses beyond the city limits. Deliveries of the pamphlets were made only to private homes within the city. Therefore, rules of selection had to be devised to exclude from the telephone book, in an unbiased manner, business firms, government agencies, and non-city addresses, in order to get information about the universe of interest directly from the source and to save time and money by avoiding irrelevant contacts.

Other essential points regarding the universe to be sampled are: Know its size (N*), its geographic location, and the time-period to be covered by the survey. It also is necessary to distinguish between the *universe of elementary units* from the *universe of sampling units*. In the first example they were the same, namely, persons; while in the second example the universe of sampling units was households. Furthermore, it is essential to have access to the *sampling frame*, or a listing of the sampling units which comprise the universe of interest from which to select the sample.

Specifying the goals of the survey and the resources available — From the above, it would appear clear that defining the universe in advance of sampling is an essential step. However, some sample surveys have turned out to be partial failures because the required statistical measures and objectives, or basic questions to be answered, were not clearly thought through or specified in advance. These specifications have a direct bearing on the type of data to be gathered, the size of the sample (n) to be used, and the cost and methods of the survey. For example, in a market-research survey to determine the public acceptance of a certain toothpaste, it makes a difference whether management wants to know the over-all rate of acceptance or whether it wants to know this rate by age groups, gender, region, or any other classifications. The size of sample would have to be larger in order to obtain the more detailed data, and other requirements of random sampling would have to be considered depending on the specific end-results sought.

---

* N represents the total number of units in the universe, or the population size; if it is not known, an attempt should be made to approximate its size. The small letter n represents the size of the sample.

Another part of formulating the problem is having management's agreement on the amount of time and funds being allocated to conduct the survey; agreement is needed also on whether to conduct a small scale *pilot study* to test the plans, the reporting form, the expected non-response rate, etc.

Specification of reliability and confidence — Management has still another important obligation to its sample-design staff and that is to state the *maximum amount of error due to sampling* it can tolerate in the most important estimate to be derived from the sample, as well as the *confidence* it seeks that the tolerable error will not be exceeded. If management does not state the degree of reliability it requires in quantitative terms, it should at least state the relative importance of the decision which will be made from the main results of the survey. The sample designer will then have to use his or her own judgment in deciding on both of these specifications. Often management needs assistance in expressing numerically the precision and confidence required in the end-results; this assistance can be provided in discussion with the statistician.

Element #2 — Sample selection procedures

This chapter deals mostly with sample-selection methods. Persons not trained in the art of sampling might conceive of many ways of selecting a random sample from a given population. The most usual misconception is randomly to take any part of the universe that happens to come along, or is conveniently obtainable, and to consider it a sample representative of the universe. This procedure, however, is not random sampling.

We repeat an earlier definition of *random selection*: The basic criterion in selecting a random sample from a given population is that each item (or unit), either in the entire universe or in each sub-universe (stratum) which we may wish to construct, is given an *equal* chance in being selected into the sample. Therefore, the sample selection must be guided to assure the free operation of equal chance. Unless each item in the sample is selected by truly random techniques there is no acceptable way of measuring later how accurately the sample reflects the characteristics of the universe from which it was selected. Consequently, some of the major advantages of sampling, such as the measurement of precision and confidence of the estimates of the population characteristics are lost.

The concept of random selection may be new or rather vague to some readers, and therefore it needs some illustration. When we have a universe, let us say, of 1,000 invoices, each of which we consider to be of equal importance, our method of sample selection should ordinarily be such that each invoice would be given an equal chance of being included in the sample — in other words, 1 in 1,000. In contrast, if within this universe of 1,000 invoices some are substantially more important than others (e.g., the ones with very large dollar amounts), our sample selection should ordinarily be such that the more important units are given a better chance of selection than the less important ones (although *every* unit in the universe of interest must be given *some* chance of getting into the sample). How much more, or how much less, of a chance of selection should be given to some units depends upon the relative importance we assign to the respective units and on the cost of including them. There are many different ways of assigning probabilities of selection to various items in the universe, and elaborate probability sample designs have been developed by sampling experts for such purposes.* For simplicity, we shall first confine our discussion primarily to sampling from universes where each item is of equal importance. In order to select a probability sample from such a universe, *each item must be given an equal chance of selection at each drawing.*

There are five basic, but different, ways of selecting random samples from universes giving each item an equal chance of selection. The basic methods, described in subsequent sections, are: (1) simple random, (2) systematic random, (3) digital random, (4) systematic random cluster, and (5) simple random cluster sampling. Additional, more specialized methods, such as stratified sampling, are described later in this chapter.

Each of these methods is described and then demonstrated by reference to a hypothetical universe of luncheon costs incurred by 500 students in a university cafeteria on a given day. This universe is listed on the following page. It is also used in Chapters 8 and 9 to illustrate important concepts and calculations related to the analysis of sample-derived results.

---

*See: *Sampling Survey Methods and Theory,* by Hansen, Hurwitz, and Madow, Volume I, Wiley Classics, 1993; *Sampling Techniques* by Cochran, 1977; and *Sampling Design in Business Research,* by Deming, 1960; all are published by John Wiley and Sons, New York.

Hypothetical Universe of 500 Luncheon Costs

Amount spent for lunch in a given day by students in the cafeteria of ABC University

$2.52	$3.09	$5.27	$4.27	$4.41	$4.41	$3.62	$3.97	$2.80	$4.30	F
4.14	4.99	2.33	2.95	3.38	3.04	3.48	2.91	4.15	3.73	R
5.33	4.77	2.35	3.57	3.16	3.32	5.16	4.46	1.74	1.77	E
6.00	3.65	2.86	3.06	3.99	4.15	4.06	4.75	4.44	2.08	S
2.87	5.23	5.23	4.18	3.00	5.37	4.18	3.77	4.50	3.82	H
3.48	4.66	2.88	3.16	3.55	4.91	2.90	3.74	3.37	3.78	M
3.80	3.02	2.83	2.33	2.55	3.04	3.66	5.38	4.88	3.75	E
5.18	6.03	4.70	4.33	4.55	5.35	3.55	5.31	5.72	5.53	N
4.01	3.19	4.43	2.37	2.93	5.72	3.40	5.08	3.58	4.72	
3.50	3.91	5.41	5.73	4.73	3.76	3.82	4.53	5.00	4.48	
$3.59	$3.36	$4.94	$5.72	$4.02	$4.00	$3.32	$2.45	$3.53	$3.15	S
4.78	3.32	5.78	4.85	5.29	4.61	5.22	3.53	3.07	3.56	O
2.86	5.95	2.88	5.78	3.99	6.21	4.60	3.65	3.45	3.79	P
3.24	3.80	5.42	5.51	3.21	4.94	3.94	2.66	2.54	3.42	H
4.35	4.46	4.27	6.09	3.42	5.62	4.07	4.10	3.01	4.35	O
1.49	4.80	4.62	5.52	3.56	3.41	3.18	5.24	5.09	5.01	M
4.63	6.52	4.52	4.39	3.84	3.24	5.59	4.71	2.39	4.74	O
5.25	4.93	4.75	4.36	4.72	3.61	3.72	4.21	6.27	2.70	R
5.74	5.15	2.85	3.35	2.72	3.84	2.20	3.75	4.32	2.80	E
3.63	3.30	2.23	3.89	3.35	4.99	4.63	5.73	1.84	4.21	S
$3.42	$5.33	$2.72	$5.15	$5.39	$4.46	$4.42	$2.43	$4.04	$6.76	J
4.84	4.35	5.22	3.19	2.61	5.12	3.26	3.43	4.21	3.86	U
3.03	4.44	3.04	4.93	5.42	5.97	4.52	6.42	6.55	3.21	N
3.92	4.72	5.26	4.74	3.91	4.62	3.74	3.20	3.00	3.75	I
4.43	4.94	4.79	5.04	6.30	3.81	3.48	3.83	3.69	5.42	O
3.26	5.05	3.50	3.70	3.81	4.26	5.88	5.72	5.53	4.01	R
5.86	6.28	3.35	4.20	5.97	2.44	3.36	5.09	3.97	5.97	S
4.12	4.23	4.10	4.95	4.69	4.92	3.64	4.69	2.84	4.23	
5.71	4.55	3.54	6.56	4.53	5.23	3.12	3.50	3.82	3.82	
3.20	5.10	4.40	3.65	3.95	4.96	5.44	5.32	4.92	3.34	
$3.85	$5.03	$4.56	$3.42	$4.02	$5.56	$4.85	$4.12	$5.46	$6.01	S
4.45	4.56	6.14	5.13	5.37	6.21	5.96	5.80	7.03	6.81	E
4.24	5.43	5.46	6.37	3.94	4.30	5.21	4.86	2.65	4.56	N
4.74	4.40	5.54	3.46	3.47	5.17	4.53	6.18	4.53	3.53	I
5.01	4.68	5.52	4.68	4.61	4.93	6.08	5.96	3.50	5.15	O
5.24	5.26	6.24	5.62	5.73	6.45	3.56	5.12	4.44	3.64	R
4.97	5.82	5.41	6.66	4.30	4.13	4.89	4.54	6.61	6.17	S
4.28	5.86	2.72	5.21	8.04	5.27	6.67	5.96	2.83	2.81	
5.37	6.62	5.28	4.42	5.02	5.05	5.01	3.98	4.56	4.79	
4.47	5.75	7.43	3.66	7.67	4.43	6.41	5.04	5.68	3.43	
$3.00	$2.92	$3.84	$6.06	$6.63	$5.83	$3.94	$2.93	$3.45	$4.98	F
4.39	3.98	4.95	5.92	6.48	6.40	5.43	2.98	3.44	5.03	R
4.34	5.92	2.89	3.94	4.48	6.41	5.40	4.92	2.96	4.40	E
3.94	3.47	3.67	4.14	4.91	5.12	5.88	5.62	5.43	4.82	S
3.29	3.44	4.81	3.93	4.41	4.92	3.82	2.25	2.62	2.40	H
4.94	2.23	4.87	2.39	2.46	1.43	2.90	4.97	4.43	1.92	M
3.78	2.89	2.75	2.27	2.19	2.97	3.56	4.28	3.73	3.45	E
3.66	3.69	2.91	4.83	4.79	4.64	5.14	4.10	4.10	1.90	N
3.46	4.25	4.70	4.22	4.23	4.16	3.20	2.76	2.56	3.28	
4.94	1.62	4.72	3.59	3.64	3.50	2.34	3.31	5.23	5.12	

Five Basic Methods of Random Selection

Simple random selection

Simple random sampling, also identified as purely random or unrestricted random selection, is the most basic method of the five methods listed earlier. This method must be used at one stage or another regardless of the complexity or simplicity of the sample design used. Therefore, it behooves every would-be sampler to learn both its preparatory and operational steps.

How should we select a simple random sample of ten luncheon costs from the universe of 500 luncheon costs to assure that each student expenditure is given an equal chance of selection? A little imagination will show that there are several possible ways of doing it. For example, one way would be to cut out the amounts separately and place each in an identical round capsule; place the 500 capsules in a bowl; mix them well, and then select one; record its value and do not replace it (i.e., keep it out);* mix again and select a second capsule; and so forth, until ten capsules have been selected and the luncheon values inside them recorded.

Another way is to mix the capsules in the bowl and grab a handful of ten capsules in one scoop (a cluster sample). In either instance, if the mixing is thorough, each capsule theoretically would have as good a chance of being chosen at any one drawing as any other, namely, 1 in 500; 1 in 499; 1 in 498; etc. Unfortunately, in practice it is almost impossible to know when we have achieved "thorough" mixing. Consequently, these two methods do *not assure* truly random selection; neither are they practical in terms of time and effort.

The method of simple random selection generally used in this type of problem (and in many other problems) is to rely on *tables of random digits* to choose the sample items with equal chance assured. An example of a random-number table is given on the following two pages, borrowed from "A Million Random Digits".** This book contains many such pages, and has been developed specifically for use in random selection. These pages list the digits 0 to 9 in a purely random manner, each digit occurring practically the same number of times as any other. The random digits in a random number table often are grouped into groups of two to five digits for ease of visualization and use.

---

* This is called sampling without replacement.

**A Million Random Digits with 100,000 Normal Deviates, Rand Corporation, The Free Press, Glencoe, Illinois, 1956. See also *Table of 105,000 Random Decimal Digits*, Interstate Commerce Commission, Washington, DC, 1949.

A Page of Random Digits

05128	59866	51281	68124	75064
86746	89698	56020	37810	88684
87513	17690	61427	72914	48563
02622	41026	80875	41293	21529
64981	28180	38629	76962	93285
57888	13938	38554	86836	02195
56316	37723	00234	21424	26664
98849	72762	59767	52497	24227
51632	54799	27973	68568	68465
12874	82160	67202	85199	27908
57580	77884	07032	01671	53362
51875	64611	19736	25589	46569
39133	30393	58319	85098	66519
24541	61477	89731	18421	29861
50859	84746	28302	13264	07595
28119	24200	09110	28485	30326
45206	53300	38688	39968	32604
57571	65919	56405	17839	92073
52829	01172	08915	11467	14793
00134	36233	89434	38669	91592
99826	64005	94325	73553	78280
11694	46262	55067	64603	59762
57622	93328	98885	07783	04351
82691	51238	14106	43983	33356
88799	65621	59809	37850	66128
69125	95591	81168	99246	66416
74698	44233	67602	21615	72336
77451	47350	21234	67672	80567
61715	96485	22121	98844	59289
92735	45064	50924	00865	19690
72353	45775	68590	85685	99975
12979	05720	92754	76911	55240
44365	70254	50864	36619	30094
49076	18439	29522	42541	79327
78143	65919	13699	91844	10676
03474	76025	97043	33834	44638
35870	89158	55864	98078	50563
73887	67928	60045	70782	11937
45968	73667	65062	73306	76045
67622	54579	17279	67440	56441
66913	60664	67547	39528	02043
74859	62155	09234	47367	13047
90879	44969	11129	17139	79630
95909	82459	96218	60768	76417
29212	40873	41590	67255	30757

Source: *A Million Random Digits with 100,000 Normal Deviates*, Rand Corporation, The Free Press, Glencoe, Illinois, 1956.

Another Page of Random Digits

79419	22359	65206	54941	95992
59914	04146	01419	48575	77822
43374	25473	60982	27119	16060
22199	11865	26201	18570	72803
13786	27475	31254	36050	73736
45445	41059	55142	55585	39829
21067	57238	35352	67741	98761
30302	95327	12849	15795	97479
70040	91385	96436	58982	91281
13351	48321	28357	88526	74396
15564	04716	14594	22363	85700
30987	57657	33398	63053	46792
79172	72764	66446	78864	96004
57875	45228	49211	69755	27896
58146	64665	31159	06980	68709
42826	06974	61063	97640	13433
93929	01836	36590	75052	89475
83585	00414	62851	48787	28447
27548	37516	24343	63046	02081
32982	56455	53129	77693	25022
30104	67126	76656	29347	28492
35240	00818	09136	01952	48442
94031	62209	43740	54102	76895
99321	11331	06838	03818	77063
78236	71732	04704	61384	57343
43108	56592	42467	88801	91280
91058	60958	20706	31929	57422
98172	44346	60430	59627	26471
12523	57345	41246	98416	08669
66682	82517	33150	27368	53375
01056	27534	23085	49602	74391
18730	96197	64483	40364	90913
07794	60475	49666	17578	12830
48883	77154	74973	42096	34934
70171	59431	76033	40076	20292
48830	55029	10371	09963	85857
73151	64463	50058	11468	93553
06571	95934	09132	13746	82514
76609	52553	47508	25775	91309
32138	61197	95476	69442	54574
04855	27029	01542	72443	72302
65434	12124	91087	87800	34870
86800	16781	65977	65946	65728
51233	81409	46773	69135	36170
92933	77341	20839	36126	18311

Random numbers can be developed by any random process where equal chance prevails. In more recent years, they can be generated by computers, using mathematical formulas which assure the appearance of numbers with equal frequencies. Alternatively, they can be generated by any random physical phenomenon, such as electrical "noise" in electronic circuits, sun-spot activity (explosions on the surface of the sun), etc. An example of physically generating random digits is twirling many times the dial of a ten-digit roulette wheel (Figure 7.1) and recording each resulting numeric outcome in the order in which it occurs. Since this roulette wheel has only the ten digits 0 through 9 on its circumference and each is spaced an equal distance from the next one, each of these digits 0 through 9 has an equal chance (i.e., 1/10th) of coming up simply because of the law of chance. In the long run (i.e., after thousands of twirls of the wheel), the digit 0 occurs just about 10 percent of the time; the same is true for the digits 1 through 9 and any combination of these digits. The key characteristic of a random number table is that each digit has been randomly generated, meaning it has the same chance as any other digit of being selected (recorded) at any position in the table. For demonstration purposes, the two pages of random numbers will be used to select random samples.

Figure 7.1
A Roulette Wheel System for Generating Random Digits

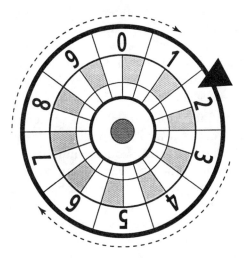

Illustrating Equal Chance of Selection of the Digits 0 through 9

Selection of a simple random sample of ten luncheon costs is illustrated below by use of the random number table. The very first step involves assigning each luncheon cost an identification number, in sequence, starting with 001 (or 000) and ending with 500 (or 499), i.e., until all costs have been assigned a distinct number in succession. (The work of assigning each unit a number may be laborious, especially in large universes. Therefore, in a fixed file or list it is not really necessary to actually assign each unit a number, but to assume that each unit has an identification number already determined by its order or sequence of occurrence in the file or list.)

Specifically, selection of a simple random sample by reference to a table of random digits involves the following four steps in the designated order:

1. As indicated above, assign a number in sequence to each unit in the universe up to N. In the universe of 500 luncheon costs we could assign the number 001 to the first, upper left, luncheon cost of $2.52; then assign the number 002 to the next luncheon cost ($4.14) right below it, going down the first column, and so forth, until all luncheon costs have been assigned an identification number. In this way, the identification number 500 would be assigned to the $5.12 luncheon in the lower right-hand corner of the universe listing of luncheon costs.

2. Count the number of digits in the largest assigned identification number. Since the largest assigned identification number is 500, it tells us that we must use a random number consisting of 3 digits, or a 3-digit column in the table of random digits, to assure that each unit in the universe has an equal chance of selection, i.e., 1 in 500.

3. Enter the Table of Random Digits at some randomly chosen location,* covering a column of digits equivalent to the number representing the largest sequence number (in our case, a three-digit column). For example, if we randomly started with the last three digits at the extreme right-hand corner and at the top of the first page of random digits, the first such three-digit number is 064. Since 064 has previously been assigned to a specific luncheon cost, that luncheon cost is included in the sample.

---

* To avoid criticism of subjective choice of the startup point, it is preferable to choose the start by some random process. For example, if we open a telephone book to, say, page 497, this could mean to start on page 4, column 9, and row 7 in the book of random digits.

4. From this starting point, follow a predetermined path on the table of random digits and select into the sample those cases in the universe whose previously assigned identification number appears on that path.

Any random number that exceeds the largest identification number assigned to the units of the population is skipped. Duplicates or reoccurring random numbers are also skipped and excluded. For example, proceeding from the starting number 064 down the chosen column of random numbers, the next random number is 684; since this is larger than the largest preassigned identification number in the universe (500), this number is ignored. The next usable random number lower than 501 is 285. Recalling that we are numbering luncheons from the top down each column, this results in the selection of item number 285 in the population, or the luncheon cost of $4.93. The next random number is 195, which identifies the cost of $3.93 as being in the sample. This process is repeated until all ten sample items are selected. The ten luncheon costs in the resulting sample are shown in the accompanying table. The reader should verify that this is the correct random sample of luncheons.

Results of a Simple Random Sample of Ten (n=10)
Luncheon Costs
(in dollars)

$3.80	4.93	3.93	5.97	4.35
3.53	5.88	4.44	4.96	3.97

It should be noted at this point that any objective scheme used to select the simple random sample can be used. This includes the random starting point and the pre-determined path to follow in the table. The random order of the digits listed in the table and their.guaranteed equal occurrence assures that a truly simple random (equal chance) sample has been selected by following the foregoing four steps.

The random digits shown in the accompanying two pages are organized into five-digit columns only to facilitate reading within the mass of numbers. If in a given sampling problem we need to select a sample from a very large universe, for example one that has a half-million units, and which therefore requires following a path of six digits, the random sample may be selected by taking the 5 digits of a column and one digit from an adjacent column either to the left or right;

or by taking 3 digits from one five-digit column; and 3 digits from the next five-digit column; etc. With some imagination, practically an unlimited number of choices exists for using a random number table to select equal-chance samples.

In problems where the results of the sample may be challenged (e.g., by the auditee, management, or an attorney), it is essential to select the sample by reference to tables of random numbers or computer-generated random digits. Thus, in developing legal evidence by a random sample, the results derived from it will be more easily defended on grounds of validity and objectivity than those based on judgment sampling or any sampling process which does not strictly observe the foregoing selection procedures. A sample selected by reference to random number tables cannot be challenged successfully on the ground of subjectivity of the sampler or on the ground that it is a sample "fixed" to prove the sampler's case. However, no matter what sample selection method is used, it should be fully documented, so that the detailed methods can be reviewed by persons who wish to do so.

In light of the above discussion, can we accept as valid the findings of the old Kinsey sample of women in the United States who were interviewed to provide information on their sexual behavior? Here is a universe where each adult woman was considered of equal importance, so that each should have been given an equal chance of selection for the sample. The sample, however, consisted only of women who *volunteered* to provide the required information on the Kinsey questionnaire.* Since not all women in the universe were equally likely to be "selected" for the sample by volunteering, it cannot be considered a random sample, and the resulting data cannot validly represent *all* adult women in the United States.

Systematic random selection

A method of sampling which is generally more expedient than simple random sampling, especially for large universes, is called *systematic random sampling*. The main objective of this method is to overcome the practical difficulties of assigning sequence numbers, especially to very large universes, and selecting random samples from them. Systematic sampling selects items from all parts of the universe in a controlled, systematic manner, and requires use of random

---

*For a discussion of the statistical problems of the Kinsey study, see Chochran, Mosteler, and Tukey, "Statistical Problems of the Kinsey Report," *Journal of the American Statistical Association*, December, 1953.

numbers only once, namely, in making a random start. In other words, instead of picking all items by reference to random digits, we pick them systematically, but still make sure that each item has been given an equal chance of selection by means of the random starting point. For example, in the universe of 500 luncheon costs we could pick a systematic random sample of ten luncheon costs by choosing every 50th one systematically, *after selecting the first one by the simple random method.* Three steps are involved in systematic random sampling, as follows:

1. Determine the *skip-interval* (k) between successive selections from the universe, by dividing the number of units in the universe by the number to be included in the sample (N / n). In the luncheon-cost universe, this would yield a skip-interval of 50 (500 / 10).*

2. Select a unit randomly from among those which are in the first skip-interval group. This "random start" is essential in order to assure that each item in the universe and in subsequent skip-intervals will have an equal chance of being selected for the sample. Thus, in the universe of 500 luncheons with a skip-interval of 50, we would choose one of the first 50 items by using the simple-random selection method described earlier. Assume that the starting point is number 13.

3. After having chosen the first unit by a random start, we need to select the remaining units systematically, i.e., every k-th unit thereafter. In our example, the 63rd, then the 113th, etc., luncheon would be selected. This systematic selection with a random start assures selection of the desired sample size (n) and, is usually considered a sample approximately equivalent to a simple random sample. However, one caution must be observed; it is explained in the later section "Caution in systematic sampling."

The requirement of systematic selection can be met by simply being systematic in whatever direction or pattern of directions we choose to follow in counting the subsequent items to reach the one to be selected. A balanced geometric design usually results from a systematic traversing of the universe. For example, in the luncheon universe, two possible systematic ways of counting is shown by Figure 7.2. Actually,

---

*If the skip-interval is not an integer, one possible procedure is to round it to the next higher integer and then the next lower integer and select the sample by these alternating intervals.

there is a large number of systematic ways of traversing the universe to select a systematic sample. The choice depends on practicality.

Figure 7.2
Counting Systems for Systematic Sampling

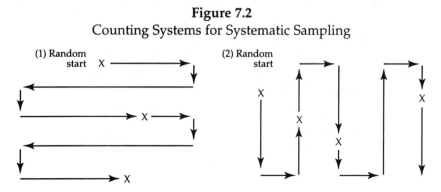

Situations for systematic sampling — It may be rare to have the complete universe listing of items from which to draw a sample as is the case with our luncheon-costs illustration. Often, the records for the universe may be in folders in filing cabinets; it may be a file of records in a data base or a computer print-out listing; it may be a succession of objects on an assembly line; it may be homes in a town; and so forth. Once the idea of systematic sampling is understood, it becomes a simple matter to adapt it to any practical situation. For example, in selecting a sample of folders from folders filed in many drawers, a random drawer and a random folder in that drawer may be selected by reference to a table of random digits. From this random start, every k-th folder (using the appropriate skip-interval) is selected by a continuous count of folders in successive drawers. An important precaution here is to make sure that we continue the count of folders from one drawer to the next even if only a few folders remain in a drawer after the last sample folder has been selected from it.

Often the skip-interval is a large number, making the task of counting units from one skip-interval to the next laborious and time-consuming. In such situations, the skip-interval may be converted to a measurement, i.e., we can calculate the average distance represented by the skip-interval and use that distance to select the next successive sample item. For example, if the folders are approximately of uniform width, and 6 inches represents the average distance of the skip-interval in terms of number of folders, a 6-inch cardboard strip may be used to measure off the distance from one sample item to the next, and thus avoid counting to reach the next skip-interval item. The cardboard strip, in fact, becomes the skip-interval.*

Caution in systematic sampling — While systematic sampling is used fairly frequently in statistical surveys because of its simplicity and general expediency when dealing with large universes, we should be aware of a pitfall to guard against in this method of sampling. This can occur if the items in the sampling frame (universe) are ordered, i.e., are arranged in some kind of repetitive or cyclical pattern. In such an orderly universe, the skip-interval might sometimes (but rarely) be the same as the length of the cycle and thus it could yield a sample of items with similar characteristics which may be far from typical of the universe. For example, hourly temperature readings or hourly traffic counts show a definite periodicity each day. If the skip-interval were 24 hours, it would always yield a sample of about equal temperatures, or traffic volumes, over the period of study. The sample thus would fail to include items with varying characteristics typical of the universe. By being on guard to recognize universe files with such periodicity, it is possible to overcome this pitfall of systematic sampling. One procedure is to split the universe into segments, or strata, and then choose independent random starting points for each segment. (This method would be roughly equivalent to stratified sampling, a method discussed in a later section.) Such a procedure will minimize the chance of repeating for long any specific cycle which might accidentally match the skip-interval.

Digital random selection

Since persons covered by the social security program or those who file an income tax return are identified by name as well as their social security account number, another way of selecting a random sample of persons or employees is by *digital random sampling,* i.e., by selecting a sample of persons based on randomly chosen terminal (last place) digits in their account number. This method of selection is confined to the last four digits of the social security account number, since these digits are issued sequentially to applicants for account numbers. Thus, for example, by randomly selecting a single digit (i.e., from 0 to 9) in the

---

*In the early years of the 5-digit zip code, the U.S. Postal Service needed to estimate by a systematic sample of letter mail, the extent to which inhabitants in major post office cities were using the zip code. The skip-interval of every 2000th letter was converted to inches and a string of equivalent length was used to select every 2000th letter moving on the conveyer in trays on the way to the delivery route point.

very last place of the account number, we can readily obtain a random sample of 10-percent of the persons in the universe of interest if it is reasonably large (e.g., N>500). This selection method therefore is similar to simple random or systematic sampling. Similarly, random selection of any two last-place digits (between 00 and 99) will yield a one-percent random sample. Different combinations of such two-digit selections will yield multiples of one-percent samples, as needed for a given sample survey.

There are some advantages to using digital random sampling when dealing with a universe of people. Since the account numbers are generally issued sequentially in all geographic sections of the United States, this type of sample automatically gives representation of persons in each geographic area where the account number was originally issued, roughly equivalent to area-stratified sampling described later. Some other advantages of this type of sampling are: ease in computer selection of the sample; easy way of checking for erroneously selected items by scanning the selected terminal digits to assure that unchosen digits were not included in the sample; and automatic replacement of those who have dropped out by new entrants into the population. A number of agencies use this method of random sampling because of its advantages and simplicity. In fact, public opinion survey takers have begun to use telephone numbers to select random samples of persons to be interviewed — a method called the *random-digit dial* method.

Two types of cluster sampling

Suppose that individual income tax returns, numbering several million, are filed in metal cabinets and that each cabinet contains batches (master blocks) of tax returns each consisting of 100 individual tax returns, bundled and bound by a metal clamp. In this condition, it would be time-consuming and difficult to select either a simple random or systematic random sample of a individual tax returns, since this would require unclamping and unbinding numerous master-blocks in order to select a sample of individual tax returns from within each block. On the other hand, it would be quite easy, in this instance, to select either a simple random or systematic random sample of master-blocks, each consisting of 100 individual returns. Thus, when the items in the universe are arranged in such a way as to make other types of sampling difficult and expensive, random selection of batches or blocks, called *cluster sampling*, becomes a convenient alternative.

There are then two choices of cluster sampling: selection of clusters systematically or by simple random selection. If all the items in the cluster are included in the sample, the method is called *single-stage cluster sampling*. If a sample of items is selected from within each of the sampled clusters, the method is called *two-stage cluster sampling*. Our coverage deals only with the former, i.e., single-stage cluster sampling. In this discussion of cluster sampling it is presumed that *all* items in the clusters randomly selected are included in the sample. There are many situations when it is more efficient to select a sample of items from the cluster rather than include all of them.

Examples of single-stage cluster sampling —

(1) In order to estimate the proportion of persons in the labor force and measure the rate of unemployment in a large city, we could theoretically do well to select a systematic random sample of households in the city and interview an adult in each such household. It can be readily seen that simple random or systematic random selection of individual households would require a considerable amount of time to travel throughout the city to reach an adult in the households randomly selected in the sample. One of the main reasons for using a cluster, in this case a city block, of households is to economize on travel costs in gathering the required data.

(2) In order to estimate the total number of printed words in a large encyclopedia volume we could select a random sample of pages (clusters). By calculating the average number of words per page included in the sample we would have an efficient way of estimating the total number of words, namely, by multiplying the average by the total number of pages in the volume.

(3) In order to compile information about the years of experience, salary, etc., of school teachers in a given school district, we would do well to select a random sample of schools (clusters) and obtain the information from all teachers in the schools included in the sample.

While these are illustrations of single-stage cluster sampling, two-stage cluster sampling may be more appropriate in many sample surveys.*

For emphasis, we repeat that single-stage clusters may be selected either by the simple random or systematic random method. Thus, we include them in the five basic random selection procedures.

---

*For a more detailed discussion of cluster sampling, see *Sample Survey Methods and Theory*, Hansen, Hurwitz, and Madow, Volume I, John Wiley and Sons, Inc., Wiley Classics, 1993; also, *Sampling Techniques*, William G. Cochran, John Wiley and Sons, Inc., 1977.

Stratified Random Sampling

Earlier it was pointed out that when the items of the universe are considered to be of about equal importance, the sample selection procedure needs to assure that each item is given an equal chance of selection. Therefore any one of the five basic random selection methods thus far discussed may be used, considering which one is most appropriate to the existing conditions. However, if we know that some items are more important with respect to the survey objectives (e.g., very large-valued accounts or invoices), it would be more efficient to give the more important items a better chance of selection than the less important items. This can be accomplished only if we can separate the more important from the less important items, and form separate *sub-universes*, commonly called *strata*. Selection of a larger sample from the more important stratum and a smaller sample from the less important stratum then becomes more desirable to achieve more reliable results. Thus we enter the realm of *stratified random sampling*.

It has been found that for a fixed size of sample, greater precision of estimates can most often be obtained by a properly stratified random sample than by any of the five basic sampling methods described earlier. The extent of gain in precision depends on the appropriateness of the criterion chosen for stratification and the size of sample used for each stratum. If strata of units are constructed on the basis of some characteristics (for example, size of shoe) that have no bearing on the specific characteristic we are trying to estimate (for example, income), no gain in precision can be expected from stratified sampling. Conversely, if the strata are constructed on a characteristic (such as occupation) that has a direct relationship to the characteristic under study (for example, earnings), greater precision will be achieved from stratified than from simple random sampling or its equivalent. Selecting items from each such stratum by simple random or systematic random sampling will greatly increase the chance of obtaining a representative sample with much smaller sampling error than by using any of the five basic methods.

A specific illustration

In our universe of 500 luncheon costs, we have listed the students into four supposedly homogeneous groups, each representing an academic class-year. It becomes apparent, once we have been able to separate the universe into the academic classes (strata) and have sampled independently from each stratum, that we can get a more nearly correct representation of student characteristics (such as age) in our stratified sample than by relying on chance alone to do that. If we have reason to believe that the amount spent for lunch is related to academic year, e.g., that seniors spend more than juniors, then stratification on the basis of class-year would give us a more precise estimate of the mean cost of lunch than would a simple random sample. Each stratum can now be treated as an independent sub-universe and either a simple random sample or a systematic random sample of luncheon costs can be selected from it.

Proportional stratified sampling

There are two broad categories of stratified sampling — one is proportional stratified, the other is nonproportional stratified. Either a constant percentage size of sample may be picked from each stratum (*proportional stratified sample*) or the percentage size of sample may vary from stratum to stratum (*nonproportional stratified sample*). See the illustration below.

Given: $N = 1000$; $f = .1$; $n = 100$			
Stratified Proportional	$N_1 = 50$ $f_1 = .1$ $n_1 = 5$	$N_2 = 250$ $f_2 = .1$ $n_2 = 25$	$N_3 = 700$ $f_3 = .1$ $n_3 = 70$
Stratified Nonproportional	$f_1 = 1$ $n_1 = 50$	$f_2 = .1$ $n_2 = 25$	$f_3 = .035$ $n_3 = 25$

The proportional percentage size of sample is simpler to deal with since, in the final analysis, the units from all strata may be combined into one sample and estimates about the population as a whole can be derived directly from the combined sample, as in the case of a simple random sample selected from a given universe. However, the nonproportional sample, while somewhat more complex, can yield more reliable estimates of the same characteristics, and is generally preferred over the proportional method.

A factor to emphasize at this point is that a random sample drawn with different sampling rates from several strata clarifies our previous definition of random selection as giving an "equal chance" of selection *either* to each item in the universe *or* each item in the sub-universe we wish to construct.

Another important requirement in stratified sampling is that, to consider the sample as random, sample selection within each stratum must be by any of the five basic random selection methods described earlier. In other words, stratified sampling where the items within the strata are not selected by a random method cannot claim the advantages of random sampling, such as measuring the reliability of the results as can be done in the stratified *random* type of sample.

Nonproportional stratified sampling

Probably the most widely used and most efficient method of stratified sampling is the *nonproportional stratified random sample,* i.e., where the proportion of units selected from each stratum is not the same (i.e. unequal chance of selection). For a fixed sample size and large universes with a high coefficient of variation (great diversity in the x-values), this method is more *efficient* (has the smallest sampling error for a given sample size) than those we have covered. Therefore, it is desirable to group the units in the universe so that they are as nearly alike as possible within their strata but vary greatly among the strata. Thus, a real opportunity for getting very precise estimates is available to the sampler with good skill and judgment in constructing the strata. Since the coefficient of variation can differ greatly from stratum to stratum, it would be wise to select a larger proportion of the items from the strata whose units vary more than from strata whose units vary less. A method for guiding the sampler to select the appropriate sample size from each stratum is described later as an optimum allocation of the total sample to the strata.

In the nonproportional stratified sample, the items selected from each stratum can no longer be combined into one sample. Each stratum-estimate must first be multiplied by a weighting factor which takes into account the size of each stratum. These strata-weighted estimates can then be combined and analyzed for the population as a whole. Only after each stratum-derived estimate has been multiplied by its respective weight can the results be combined to yield an unbiased estimate of the population characteristics as a whole. (See Chapter 9.)

As indicated above, an important factor in designing effective strata is the skill and judgment of the sample-designer. For example, if an estimate is needed of the average annual salary paid by an agency, it would be good judgment to group the employees by occupation and rank in the organization and select a random sample separately from each such stratum.

Another important requirement is skill in determining the optimum, or best, sample size to select from each stratum. This may be achieved by judgment or by an *optimum allocation* formula for allocating the overall sample to the various strata, as illustrated in the section "Optimum allocation of sample to the strata."

An illustration — The importance of the above factors in designing a good stratified sampling application is illustrated with a hypothetical universe of eight invoices, the purpose being to estimate their total monetary value.

Hypothetical Universe of N=8 Invoices
Amount of Invoice (thousands)

Invoice #1	$ 3		Invoice #5	4
Invoice #2	25		Invoice #6	3
Invoice #3	5		Invoice #7	6
Invoice #4	30		Invoice #8	2
			Universe total	$ 78

A simple random sample of four invoices could, by chance, select invoices 1, 3, 5, and 6. This sample would yield a substantially understated estimate of the true total value of the invoices ($78,000). The estimated total using simple random selection is $30 thousand, obtained by the formula $N\overline{X}$, where $N = 8$ and $\overline{X} = \$3.75$ thousand. On the other hand, a systematic random sample of invoices 2, 4, 6, and 8 would yield a greatly overstated estimate of the total amount, namely, $120 thousand.

To illustrate the greater accuracy achieved by nonproportional stratified sampling, let us, by using good judgment, construct the following two strata of the universe of eight invoices:

Stratum No. 1 ($N_1 = 2$)		**Stratum No. 2 ($N_2 = 6$)**	
Invoice #2	$ 25	Invoice #1	$ 3
Invoice #4	30	Invoice #3	5
		Invoice #5	4
		Invoice #6	3
		Invoice #7	6
		Invoice #8	2

By selecting a stratified nonproportional sample of four invoices as follows, we could get the estimated total shown below:

From Stratum No. 1, select both Invoice #2 ($ 25) and Invoice #4 ($ 30), and

From Stratum No. 2, select two invoices by simple random sampling; assume they are Invoice #1 ($3) and Invoice #5 ($4).

It can be shown that any one of the 15 possible stratified nonproportional samples of two invoices from each stratum would yield estimates of the total amount of the eight invoices very close to the actual total amount of $78,000.* Below we show the results for four possible such non-proportional stratified samples. The reader can find the same closeness by picking any combination of two random samples from Stratum #2.

Estimate 1: $25 + $30 + 6 x ($3.5) = $ 76,000
Estimate 2: $25 + $30 + 6 x ($5)   = $ 85,000
Estimate 3: $25 + $30 + 6 x ($4)   = $ 79,000
Estimate 4: $25 + $30 + 6 x ($3)   = $ 67,000

We realize that a universe of eight invoices is not a candidate for sampling applications; nor is a sample of two units from a stratum very appropriate. This example was chosen merely to demonstrate how nonproportional stratified sampling can yield estimates closer to the true value of the universe than simple random or systematic random sampling or even proportional stratified sampling.

Optimum allocation of sample to the strata

As indicated earlier, an important question when using stratified sampling is: How many or what proportion of the n units we decided to sample should we select from each stratum to get the best estimates? The answer can be partly derived from the judgment used in constructing the strata. In particular, we attempt to construct strata of units which are as similar as possible (as measured by the standard deviation) within each stratum and as different as possible between or among the strata. Since the standard deviation (σ_x) measures the variability of the items in each stratum, it can be seen that the magnitude of σ_x plays a major role in deciding what proportion of the n units to allocate to each stratum. Another major factor is the size of each stratum as measured by the total number of units (N) it contains.

---

* The general formula for estimating a total from a stratified sample is: $N_1 \bar{X}_1 + N_2 \bar{X}_2$ + etc., where N_1 is the size of stratum no. 1, etc.; and $\bar{X}_1$, etc., is the mean per item as estimated by the sample of n_1 items from stratum no. 1, etc.

Thus, to achieve the best reliability of the estimated total value or mean value of a universe, an optimum allocation of the overall sample (n) to the various strata would lead us to use the following formula:*

$$n_1 = \begin{pmatrix} \text{Number of units} \\ \text{to select from} \\ \text{Stratum No.1} \end{pmatrix} = \frac{(\text{Size of Stratum \#1})(\text{Standard deviation of Stratum \#1})}{(\text{Sum of the above products for all strata combined})}(n).$$

Similarly, when the product (Size of Stratum #2)(Standard deviation of Stratum #2) is divided by the sum of these products over all strata combined, and then multiplied by n, we obtain the optimum n_2; and so forth for the sample sizes of the other strata.

A logical question can be raised about the optimum allocation formula: Since its use requires knowing the value of σ_x for each stratum, how can we determine its value? One way to approximate σ_x is to select a small-scale random sample from each stratum and compute σ_x from it. The use of such a *pilot sample* was mentioned earlier in the section on formulating the problem.

It is emphasized that the above optimum allocation formula deals with estimating a variable characteristic of the universe. The footnote provides the optimum allocation formula in symbols for both variables and attributes sampling. In fact, situations for attributes sampling where stratification may be desirable occur quite frequently in the real world, as exemplified by the mnemonic TASK:

T   stands for stratification by Time (an attribute or variable)

A   stands for stratification by Area (an attribute)

S   stands for stratification by Size (a variable measure), and

K   stands for stratification by Kind (an attribute, such as occupation, gender, etc.)

Essential points regarding stratified sampling

1.   **When to stratify**

  (a) In variables sampling — when the coefficient of variation is high (e.g., > 75%).

  (b) When estimates of strata characteristics are needed.

  (c) In attributes sampling — When certain items in the universe are believed to be most prone to error or non-compliance.

---

* For variables sampling, this formula, expressed in symbols, is: $n_1 = \dfrac{N_1\sigma_1}{N_1\sigma_1 + N_2\sigma_2 + \text{etc.}}(n).$

For attribute sampling, the formula is: $n_1 = \dfrac{N_1\sqrt{p_1(1-p_1)}}{N_1\sqrt{p_1(1-p_1)} + N_2\sqrt{p_2(1-p_2)} + \text{etc.}}(n).$

(d) When the cost of special research to construct the best strata will be recouped in the long run by the advantages of stratified sampling.

2. **Advantages of stratified sampling**
   (a) The standard error of estimate generally will be smaller than that of any of the basic sample selection procedures for the same size of sample.
   (b) It can yield information regarding some important characteristics of the strata.
   (c) If desired, a smaller sample can be used than the basic selection methods to achieve equal reliability.

3. **How to construct the strata**
   (a) By use of good judgment.
   (b) By use of the array technique to seek out large breaking points between adjacent variable values.
   (c) For large universes, by use of a frequency distribution to detect the vital few cases or items which contain a large proportion of the variable.
   (d) By detecting obvious exceptional items or cases.

4. **How to allocate the sample size to the strata**
   (a) Proportional allocation — by good judgment.
   (b) Non-proportional allocation — by good judgement.
   (c) By use of the optimum allocation formulas for variables and attributes sampling. (See formulas presented earlier.)

Other Methods of Selection

Samples selected not in compliance with the principle of chance usually are called *judgment samples*. In this type of sample the sampler's best judgment based on past experience is used in selecting those items for the sample which are believed to give a representative picture of the universe. In some instances, where good judgment is used, or by good luck, such a sample *may* give a fairly accurate representation of the universe. The main disadvantage of a sample which does not rely on random selection is that when the estimate is made there is no way of measuring its reliability, since there are no principles which provide a sound basis for computing the sampling error of non-random samples. Furthermore, the results of judgment samples are difficult to defend on grounds of objectivity.

In some instances, samplers select items by the ***spot-check sampling*** method. This is neither a judgment nor a probability sample. It differs from probability sampling in that the items usually included in the sample are "grab" items. This type of sample rests on the illusion that no rule is the best rule for obtaining a representative sample. There is neither a control to assure a known chance of selection nor a system of considered judgment. Consequently, it does not have the advantages of either a simple random sample or a judgment sample, but it retains the disadvantages of a judgment sample.

There are other methods of random sampling such as sampling proportional to size, multi-stage sampling, and sequential sampling. These methods are beyond the scope of this book.

Summary

This chapter concentrated on two of the six major elements of a random sampling system: *problem formulation* and *methods of selecting random samples*, and, in the case of stratified sampling, how to allocate the overall sample to the strata. It described five basic methods of random selection. They are simple random, systematic random, digital random, and single-stage cluster sampling whereby clusters can be selected either systematically or by simple random selection.

Random sampling is a method of selecting a part of the universe by reliance on the principles of probability. The purpose of random sampling is to provide representative data for drawing conclusions about the characteristics (parameters) of the entire universe from which they are selected. Because only a part rather than the whole of the universe is used, an obvious advantage of random sampling is savings in the cost of collecting data; for the same reason, the results can be obtained faster than from a complete accounting of records or a complete enumeration. In addition, random samples often yield results which are more nearly accurate than those obtained from complete enumerations. Although this sounds implausible, the limited number of cases included in the sample can permit tighter control over possible non-sampling errors of data-collection and data-processing than would be possible under complete, massive enumerations. It has been found that non-sampling errors are often a more serious threat to accuracy than sampling error. By using random sampling to collect data, the extent of sampling error can be measured and controlled, but special efforts are always needed to control non-sampling errors.

To realize the advantages of random sampling, we must first formulate the problem to be enlightened. This includes, in the main, clearly defining the universe of interest and clarifying the objectives and conditions under which the survey will be conducted. Then, the sample must be selected *randomly* to obtain a *representative* sample of the universe.

Random sampling involves placing reliance on chance (or probability) for selecting the items to be included in the sample. *Simple* random sampling relies entirely on chance; by this method *every* item in the universe is given an *equal* chance of being included in the sample, using random digits (such as the random number pages in this chapter) to select the sample. Systematic random sampling also relies on chance to give a representative sample, except that a system is followed for selecting every k-th item where the skip-interval k equals N/n. *Digital sampling*, using the social security number is a very practical method of sampling since it contains elements of systematic, random, and stratified random sampling. *Cluster sampling* randomly selects batches, or clusters, of units primarily to reduce the cost of sample selection and data collection. Cluster samples can be selected either by *simple* random or *systematic* random sampling. The five single-stage random selection methods covered in this chapter are called "basic" selection methods, since one or another of them *must* be used in selecting random samples of any type.

When some items in the universe are considered to be more important to the study objectives than others, it is desirable to subdivide the universe of items into distinct strata or sub-universes. Selection of random samples from each stratum assures that both the more important and other items are included in the total sample, thus not depending on chance to do so.

Stratified random sampling breaks up the universe of items into separate strata using judgment and selects random samples from each stratum by any of the five basic random selection methods. Of the various methods of sampling covered, stratified random sampling, if the strata are properly constructed and the overall sample size (n) is optimally allocated to the strata, generally yields results with smaller sampling error than any of the basic random selection methods.

A major advantage of random selection over judgment selection methods is that random samples permit objective measurement of the reliability of the results, as will be seen in Chapter 9. Methods of sampling which do not rely on chance to select the sample are called *judgment* or non-random samples. Judgment samples often have the advantage of being relatively easy and inexpensive to select, and many of them may give good results. Their major disadvantage is that one never knows how reliable the results are; in other words, there is no way of measuring the magnitude of error due to sampling in the results. There is also no basis for expressing a level of confidence in presenting the results; therefore, the results are difficult to defend against challenges regarding their validity and reliability. Consequently, the preferred method of selecting a sample is by means of random selection, whichever of the fifteen methods covered in this chapter is most appropriate.

Problems

1. Select a random sample of thirty items from the universe of the 500 luncheon costs shown in the chapter (recording how you selected each sample for problem #2), by each of the following methods of selection:

   (a) Simple random sampling.

   (b) Systematic random sampling.

   (c) Stratified proportional random sampling.

   NOTE: Retain your three sample data sets for use in the problems in Chapters 8 and 9.

2. Explain exactly how you selected your sample in each of the above instances.

3. Estimate the mean cost of lunch from each of the above three types of random samples.

4. Compare each of the above estimated averages with the true average of the universe of luncheon costs, and indicate which sample average came closest to the true average. (True mean = $4.31.)

5. Which of the three methods of sampling stated in problem 1 would normally yield the most reliable results? Why?

6. Explain a possible advantage of a random sample over a complete enumeration with reference to accuracy in the final results.

7. Using either of the two pages of random digits in this chapter, select a systematic random sample of 25 family listings in your

city telephone directory and calculate from the sample the average (mean) number of letters in the last name (surname) of families residing in your city (exclude business names).

8. Define the following in planning a sample survey, and give an example of each:

   (a) Universe of ultimate interest
   (b) Universe of sampling units
   (c) Judgment sample
   (d) Skip-interval
   (e) Stratum
   (f) Cluster sample
   (g) Multi-stage sample
   (h) Stratified nonpropor-
       tional sampling
   (i) Random selection
   (j) Digital random sample
   (k) Optimum allocation
   (l) Systematic sample
   (m) Random digits
   (n) Sub-universe
   (o) Stratified proportional
       sample
   (p) Sampling frame

9. (a) How would you select a simple random sample of 50 workers from a universe of 1,000 workers of a given company, where the name and address of each worker is listed on a 3" x 5" card and where the cards are filed alphabetically?

   (b) In the same universe, how would you select a systematic random sample of 50 workers?

   (c) A digital random sample?

10. In a given local sample survey, one sampler selected a sample of twenty city blocks by using a table of random digits and another selected a sample of twenty blocks by using judgment. In both instances the objective was to interview an adult member of each household on the selected block in order to estimate family size and the number attending school.

    (a) Explain the difference in the two methods of sampling.

    (b) Which method would you favor and why?

11. The data on the following page represent a hypothetical universe of 160 travel vouchers by amounts and other characteristics.

    (a) Select a simple random sample and then a systematic random sample, each of size 30, from this universe.

    (b) For each sample, estimate the mean voucher-value and the total value of all 160 vouchers.

An inventory list of 160 travel vouchers

(processed in order of receipt by the travel unit of ABC agency; special codes below)

Voucher Number	Amount	Voucher Number	Amount	Voucher Number	Amount	Voucher Number	Amount
1025*	$183	1065*	$191	1105	$145	1145	$174
1026	(318)	1066	251	1106	201	1146	133
1027	211	1067	205	1107*	248	1147	201
1028	276	1068	196	1108	158	1148	199
1029	208	1069	192	1109	186	1149	221
1030	(327)	1070	176	1110	167	1150	182
1031	106	1071	269	1111	165	1151	(315)
1032	294	1072	(497)F	1112	185	1152	278
1033	250	1073	180	1113	(301)	1153	224
1034	150	1074	(399)	1114*	92	1154*	165
1035	241	1075	257	1115	146	1155	167
1036*	283	1076	121	1116	162	1156	267
1037	187	1077	166	1117	191	1157	192
1038	195	1078	252	1118	293	1158	160
1039	175	1079*	210	1119	263	1159*	65
1040	199	1080	178	1120	136	1160	131
1041	234	1081	220	1121	70	1161	(367)
1042	237	1082	148	1122	204	1162	117
1043	261	1083	177	1123	171	1163	144
1044	(443)F	1084	212	1124	88	1164	(307)
1045	(379)	1085	195	1125	174	1165	124
1046	173	1086	297	1126	174	1166*	273
1047	290	1087	171	1127	262	1167	143
1048	223	1088*	126	1128	267	1168	151
1049	(301)	1089	255	1129	167	1169	173
1050	183	1090	224	1130	196	1170	(311)
1051	242	1091	239	1131*	(317)	1171	(344)
1052	194	1092	142	1132	156	1172	(361)
1053	181	1093	213	1133	218	1173	173
1054	135	1094	(403)	1134	128	1174	182
1055	214	1095	211	1135	266	1175	217
1056	179	1096	200	1136	255	1176	260
1057*	172	1097*	165	1137	144	1177	(359)F
1058	164	1098	182	1138	158	1178	(310)
1059	174	1099	133	1139	265	1179	276
1060	240	1100	180	1140	232	1180*	(301)
1061	279	1101	278	1141	(354)	1181*	168
1062	194	1102	222	1142	(374)	1182	168
1063	183	1103	272	1143	225	1183	182
1064	168	1104	264	1144*	160	1184	195

Codes for special characteristics of travel vouchers:

    *   Voucher required some minor adjustment.

    F   Voucher involved misapplication of travel regulations.

    ( ) Indicates voucher of $300 or more (for possible stratification)

Chapter 8

Some Principles and Concepts of Sampling

"Sampling theory and methods are the proper concern of practical business managers, public officials, and social scientists because they all do now, and will increasingly henceforth, depend upon the results of sampling for much of their factual information."*

....

The main purpose of this chapter is to offer readers of sampling an appreciation and understanding of some of the major principles and concepts which underlie this field of fact-finding The principles, such as probability and normal distributions, serve as a sound defense for the validity and reliability of the inferences drawn about population characteristics from random samples. By covering some of the basic concepts of sampling, such as the concepts of variation, error, confidence, and risk, the chapter aims to provide a deeper understanding of the field of sampling than merely its techniques and applications. These principles and concepts are illustrated with a controlled experiment later in this chapter.

Management and Knowledge of Sampling Principles

From time to time we hear an executive, a manager, or an auditor question their need to devote some of their precious time to learning statistical principles and concepts. Their feeling is that this learning effort is essential for professional statisticians or analysts, but as managers, they claim, all they need are the final results.

---

* Howard C. Grieves, Assistant Director, Bureau of Census, in his Forward to *Sampling Survey Methods and Theory,* by Hansen, Hurwitz, and Madow, Volume I, Wiley Classics, 1993.

To counter this position is not simple; it involves the viewpoint or the philosophy we often adopt about seeking knowledge in general. Some people are content just to exist in their environment and learn about it by events as they occur — and that often can be very little. Others thirst for knowledge about the world we live in and strive to acquire as much of it as possible. Knowledge, Professor Edward Deming once said, is power. Knowledge makes us more informed and tolerant human beings and makes us better able to serve society and the world we live in. Specifically, knowledge of sampling and its ability to help us find objective facts makes us better fitted both to fulfill our responsibilities in business, industry, or government and to manage efficiently our day-to-day private lives.

Knowledge of sampling principles and concepts is particularly important in the management field because sampling is a key to finding meaningful facts relevant to handling the resources for which management is responsible. Although managers need not become sampling experts, a comprehension of the basic principles and concepts of sampling can lead to better communication between managers and statisticians, both in the initial discussion and clarification of problems and in the final acceptance and use of the sample results.

The Concept of Error in Data

Three main types of error are encountered in fact-finding surveys. One type results from *unsystematic mistakes,* another arises from *systematic mistakes,* called non-sampling errors, and the third is *sampling error.* The ultimate accuracy of a sample-derived estimate depends on the combined net effect of these three types of error.

When a random sample is selected from a universe in order to estimate the value of a given characteristic of that universe, *sampling error can be defined as the difference between the value of that characteristic as estimated from the sample and the true universe value of that characteristic.* Estimates derived from samples are always subject to error by some amount, either on the high or low side of the true figure, simply because they are based on cases in the universe that have been drawn into the sample purely by chance. This type of error is also called *sampling variation* of the estimate derived from sample data. Sampling error on the plus or minus side can be estimated by appropriate formulas for computing its magnitude along with a specified confidence that it is not larger.

Of the two *non-sampling error* types, one is caused by unsystematic occasional human mistakes, such as an erroneous measurement or code. Such *unsystematic mistakes* may creep into large-scale surveys. However, because these are honest human errors of a plus and minus nature, they often tend to offset each other and, in the long run, are not likely to seriously affect the final results.

Systematic mistakes are repeated over and over again, and usually are in one direction. For this reason this type of error results in biased estimates which overstate or understate the true universe value. This is generally called *bias*. Bias in data may be caused by any number of factors, for example, by use of a judgment sample which includes either an over-representation or an under-representation of a characteristic; or it may result from responses in a survey (or even in a complete census) by people who purposely overstate or understate a characteristic such as age or weight. Bias in data also can result from systematic erroneous data-entries into the computer; or from tabulating errors which consistently misclassify a large number of items; or from use of a procedure which incorrectly inflates the sample data to the universe level (i.e., if estimates of a certain characteristic based on a 10-percent sample are extended to the universe level by a multiplier of 9 instead of 10). Thus, it can be seen that systematic non-sampling error can seriously distort sample-derived estimates; they must be pursued and eliminated from the final results.

The Nature of Sampling Error

There is a fundamental difference between sampling error on the one hand, and non-sampling errors (i.e., unsystematic mistakes and systematic biases) on the other. Theoretically, non-sampling errors can be totally eliminated if sufficient time and funds are put into the effort. In practice it is often difficult, expensive, or impossible to control sources of error such as, for example, memory failure on the part of a respondent in a mail questionnaire survey or purposeful understatement of age or income. Sampling error, on the other hand, is an inherent part of all sampling systems; it cannot be eliminated as long as the estimate is based on a sample. Random sampling error, however, is subject to the law of probability which is well-known; as a result, sampling error can be measured and, moreover, made as small as we wish to make it (other than zero) by properly designed and large enough samples. Consequently, we have the seemingly paradoxical situation: while in theory non-sampling errors can be eliminated and sampling error can not, in practice sampling error can often be made to be a much smaller part of the total error in an estimate than the non-sampling errors. Furthermore, sampling error can be readily measured, but non-sampling errors cannot without substantial effort. A thorough discussion of systematic and unsystematic mistakes is beyond the scope of this book. However, it should be recognized that special effort must be made in all surveys or audits to set up some methods to minimize the problem of non-sampling errors. This problem was listed in Chapter 7 as Element #6 of all sampling systems.

Sampling error and variability in the universe

Sampling error is influenced by several factors. One of these is the standard deviation (or coefficient of variation) of the items in the universe of interest. If every item in a universe being sampled had the same value it would make no difference which items fell into the sample, for any sample from that universe, regardless of size or method of selection, would yield the same result. Therefore, there is no sampling error in estimates derived from samples of universes without variability (or with a coefficient of variation of zero).

However, in reality there are hardly any universes without variability. Universes have a range of values, and therefore, they have variability of differing amounts. In earlier chapters we called this truism *The Law of Universal Variation*. For example, the amount of income tax paid by different workers varies considerably from worker to worker; the number of children of school age in the different households in a city varies from household to household; and so forth. In manufacturing processes it is well known that parts which are produced to meet a previously specified standard of measurement tend to vary around that standard in a random manner. Such variations are an inherent characteristic of universes. Discovery and measurement of the magnitude of these variations (measured by the standard deviation, σ_x) and utilization of this knowledge in guiding management actions to improve quality, are part of the applied science of Statistical Process Quality Control (covered in Chapter 11). In Chapter 5 we demonstrated the universal existence of variation and, therefore, the essential need for methods of measuring and analyzing variation, particularly by calculating the standard deviation and coefficient of variation of the universe of values and the standard error of sample-derived estimates.

Since practically every universe has variability, an estimate of a universe characteristic, for example the U.S. unemployment rate, which is based on a random sample is subject to sampling error; in other words, the estimated value may be different from the true universe value. For a given sample size (n), the magnitude of sampling error varies *directly* with the extent of variability among the items in the universe as measured by its standard deviation or coefficient of variation. In other words, the larger the coefficient of variation in the population, the larger the sampling error for a fixed sample of n units.

Sampling error and size of sample (n)

Conversely, sample size (n) influences sampling error. This influence is *inversely* proportional to sampling error; that is, the larger the sample size, the smaller the sampling error. However, mathematics has shown that this inverse relationship is with the *square root* of n, i.e., Sampling Error $\approx \dfrac{1}{\sqrt{n}}$. Thus, for example, to cut the sampling error in half would require using a sample four times larger than the original size. This relationship leads us to a principle generally called the *Law of Decreasing Variation*, i.e., the larger the sample, the smaller the sampling error, but inversely to $\sqrt{n}$.

Sampling error and the sampling fraction (f = n/N)

Sampling error also is influenced by the percentage of the universe of items (N) included in the sample, generally called the sampling fraction, f = n/N. The fraction of the universe items not sampled, 1-f, under the square root sign, i.e., $\sqrt{1-f}$, influences sampling error directly. Thus, by combining the three influencing factors into a single formula, we get: Standard error of $\overline{X} = \dfrac{\sigma_x \sqrt{1-f}}{\sqrt{n}}$.

Sampling error and confidence

Sampling error varies directly with the desired confidence. One standard error tolerance yields 68% confidence. By tolerating twice as much error we can increase the confidence from 68% to 95.5% that the calculated amount of error would not be exceeded. This relationship is explained more fully by the controlled experiment to follow.

Sampling error and other factors

Sampling error also is influenced by the size of the universe (N) and by the methods of sampling and estimation used.

Sampling principles

Random sampling operates under a set of fixed principles. These make it possible to measure the magnitude of error caused by random sampling and to state the confidence that the indicated error is not larger. What are these principles? They are truths, laws, and fixed patterns on which we can depend with full confidence. Once we understand the main principles of sampling, we are able to depend on them. We also have a better understanding of errors associated with estimates derived from samples and the corresponding risks taken in using those estimates. The basic principles which underlie sampling are those which Professor Robert R. Sears of Harvard University once emphasized must be understood by people in today's world, particularly decision-makers and managers, if intelligent decisions are to be made from incomplete (sample) but measurable data. Among the important principles are the *laws of decreasing variation, probability,* and *normal distributions* to which the reader previously has been introduced (Chapters 3, 5, and 6). These principles as well as basic concepts are now illustrated with the controlled experiment which follows.

A Controlled Experiment in Sampling

Participants in our sampling courses continue to ask questions about, or seek explanations of, various concepts in the field of sampling, such as:

> What is the difference between a standard error and a standard deviation?

> What is the meaning of confidence, or risk?

> Why is the confidence 68% with one standard error and 95.5% with two standard errors?

Verbal answers and/or written explanations of these and other concepts, while communicative to some, do not always "hit the nail on the head." Experience has shown that a demonstration of the principles and concepts with a set of simple numbers can greatly enhance understanding. Therefore, explanations of some of the concepts and principles given earlier in this chapter are now demonstrated with simple numbers — in this case, with a controlled experiment in sampling.

One such a controlled experiment is regularly conducted in our statistical sampling courses. In many cases, the universe of 500 luncheon costs listed in Chapter 7 is used in the experiment. Each student is asked to independently select a simple random sample of 30 luncheon costs (by reference to a table of random digits) and to estimate the mean amount $(\overline{X})$ spent for lunch by the 500 students in the university cafeteria on the given day. In these classes, students also are requested to compute the standard deviation (σ_x) and the standard error of their estimated mean by the formula $\sigma_{\overline{X}} = \dfrac{\sigma_x \sqrt{(1-f)}}{\sqrt{n}}$.*

The small sample size of 30 luncheon costs was judgmentally chosen to avoid lengthy computations in class using pocket calculators; but it still provides a reasonable sample size for the experiment. Chapter 9 describes various methods for determining the sample size appropriate to a particular fact-finding situation.

By recording the students' estimated means from several classes, we obtained 50 independent random sample estimates (replicates), each derived from the same size of sample (30), the same population (N=500), and the same simple random method of selection. The resultant set of 50 sample means provides a reasonably large experiment to illustrate the concepts and principles mentioned earlier. These 50 different and independently derived sample means are shown in Table 8.1.

Two types of error in sampling

By examining the 50 different estimated averages, we note that they differ from each other, some by small, and others by large, amounts. We ask the question: Why do they differ? Perhaps in view of the fact that each sample contained the same number of luncheon costs and was selected from the same universe and by the same method of random selection, we might expect each mean to be the same. The answer can be readily deduced; the variations are a result of two factors: (1) sampling error, due to chance variations in selecting the random sample — and (2) possible non-sampling errors, such as computational errors, transposition errors, non-random selection, or other non-sampling error-causes.

In this experiment, non-sampling errors were virtually eliminated when the participants rechecked their work and corrected their original estimated means, where necessary. Thus, with non-sampling errors presumably fully removed, we are dealing with 50 replicated

---

* Where f is the sampling fraction, n/N, or in our experiment f = 30/500 = 0.06; and $\sigma_x = \sqrt{\dfrac{\Sigma(x-\overline{x})^2}{n-1}}$.

means, subject only to sampling variations.* In this way, our study of the behavior of the estimated means was confined to estimates whose only cause of variation is chance or random sampling error.

**Table 8.1 — Mean luncheon costs
estimated from simple random samples of 30 costs each
(The 30 individual cost items in each sample are not shown.)**

Sample number	Mean cost	Sample number	Mean cost	Sample number	Mean cost	Sample number	Mean cost
1	$4.63	14	$4.07	27	$4.32	40	$4.33
2	4.06	15	3.63	28	4.06	41	3.94
3	4.71	16	4.36	29	4.41	42	4.58
4	4.02	17	4.19	30	4.46	43	4.29
5	3.73	18	4.36	31	4.09	44	4.41
6	4.27	19	4.22	32	4.01	45	4.48
7	4.28	20	4.39	33	4.11	46	4.32
8	4.34	21	4.55	34	4.23	47	4.41
9	4.18	22	4.60	35	4.29	48	4.39
10	4.44	23	4.43	36	4.41	49	4.25
11	4.63	24	4.27	37	4.09	50	4.43
12	4.06	25	4.42	38	4.31		
13	4.71	26	4.12	39	4.38	Sum $(\Sigma \overline{X})$ = 214.67	

$$\overline{\overline{X}} = \frac{\Sigma \overline{X}}{50} = \$4.29 \qquad \sigma_{\overline{x}} = \sqrt{\frac{\Sigma(\overline{X} - \overline{\overline{X}})^2}{50-1=49}} = \$0.225$$

The Central Limit Theorem —
or the normal distribution of replicated random sample estimates

Now that we have made these preliminary observations, how can we best proceed to analyze the behavior of the 50 chance-caused varying means estimated from simple random samples of 30 items? Our procedure is the same as that used to analyze any set of varying figures, as demonstrated in Chapters 3, 4, and 5. Therefore, we use the method of organizing data for analysis by frequency distributions. By constructing a frequency distribution of the sample-derived $\overline{X}$'s,

---

* This does not mean that picking 50 samples, each with 30 luncheons, has in essence included all 500 luncheons of the universe. In this experiment the universe is infinite, since each sample was in effect replaced; *sampling with replacement* makes the universe inexhaustible or infinite.

usually called a *sampling distribution,* we condense the 50 values into a smaller number of groups to facilitate their analysis. The frequency distribution can reveal concentration points and also show the graphic pattern of the distribution.

To construct a frequency distribution of 50 values we first determine the "right" number of groups based on the guidelines in Chapter 3. With 50 or fewer values we decide to use seven groups in this case. Based on the range of the variable and the desirability of using class-intervals which are multiples of 10 we decide to use a class-interval of 20 cents each. The resulting frequency distribution is shown in Table 8.2, consisting of 7 groups.

Table 8.2
Frequency distribution of 50 estimated mean
luncheon costs, by amount

Mean Amount	Number of estimates f	Midpoint m
$3.60-3.799	2	$3.70
3.80-3.999	1	3.90
4.00-4.199	12	4.10
4.20-4.399	18	4.30
4.40-4.599	12	4.50
4.60-4.799	5	4.70
4.80-4.999	0	4.90
Total	50	

When plotted, as shown in Figure 8.1, this frequency distribution shows clearly the pattern of the distribution of the estimated means; it shows a marked concentration of estimates in the "$4.20-4.399" class and successively lower concentrations in the adjacent classes.

Figure 8.1

Frequency distribution of the 50 sample means in the experiment

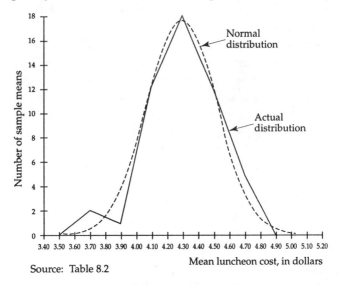

Source: Table 8.2

We also note that this frequency distribution resembles the symmetrical and approximately normal distribution demonstrated in Chapters 3 and 5. This resemblance to the bell-shaped curve would become closer if we had included in the experiment many more replicates than 50 and used sample sizes in excess of 30 items.

What general conclusions are we inclined to make from seeing the graphic pattern formed by the distribution of sample estimates? We may be tempted to say: It appears that estimates of means derived from simple random samples are arranged in a roughly bell-shaped or normal distribution. This is indeed so. It has been proven mathematically that the distribution of a large number of replicated sample-derived means will form a normal distribution. This result also can be verified empirically by repeating our experiment additional times or by adding many more replicated estimated means beyond those we have accumulated for this experiment.

In fact, statisticians can save us the time necessary to increase the size of our experiment. *The curve of random sample estimates, i.e., the sampling distribution of means, is nearly the same as the normal curve.* The only reason there are differences between the various individual sample means is chance (sampling variation), since each of the means has been derived from a simple random (chance) sample. As indicated in

Chapters 3 and 5, values of a variable influenced solely by chance, or a random variable, tend to form a normal curve.

The bell-shaped distribution of estimated sample means also could have been predicted before the frequency distribution of means was constructed, from our knowledge of the pattern of variations obtained from a random variable and a constant-cause system.* Since each estimate was made under the same set of conditions, i.e., each was based on the same size of sample, selected by the same method, and from the same universe, a constant-cause system was in operation. It has been found that when many common influences, none of which are outstanding, combine to cause the variations, the values of the characteristic being measured will vary and tend toward a bell-shaped frequency distribution.

Thus, in the preceding few pages we have illustrated with a simple experiment the *normal distribution principle of replicated random sample estimates*, commonly known as the *Central Limit Theorem*.

The Law of Decreasing Variation

In Chapter 1 we listed several principles which underlie the field of statistics. Among them was the Law of Stability of Mass Data, meaning the larger the universe the greater its stability. The leads us to a corollary principle in the field of sampling called the Law of Decreasing Variation, meaning, the larger the sample the smaller the sampling variation. Since our experiment included 50 independent random samples of 30 items each, namely, a total random sample of 1500, the most reliable estimate of the universe mean luncheon cost is derivable from the combined 50 samples.

By calculating the *grand mean*, or the mean of the means ($\overline{\overline{X}}$) of the 50 estimates — $\overline{\overline{X}} = \dfrac{\sum \overline{X}}{m}$, where m=50 replicated mean-values — we can claim it to be the best estimate of the universe mean. In fact, the mean actually computed of all sample means combined is $4.29; it differs by only 2 cents (or about 0.5 percent) from the true mean of $4.31 which was computed by $\overline{X}' = \dfrac{\sum x}{500}$. This difference is small enough that, for the purposes of our experiment, we can consider it to be the true universe mean.

The above illustrates the principle of sampling called the Law of Decreasing Variation. It is presented by the following:

---

* In Chapter 3 we pointed out that variations in a chance-influenced variable and in a process operating under a constant-cause system tend to form a bell-shaped distribution.

Sampling Error $\approx \dfrac{1}{\sqrt{n}}$, i.e., sampling error (S.E.) varies inversely with the size of sample (n) under the square root sign.

This principle is informative from a stronger viewpoint — from the viewpoint of determining the appropriate size of sample. Assume that an auditor or sampler used a judgmentally-determined random sample of 100 invoices to estimate a specified universe characteristic and later found out that the estimate was subject to a sampling error of as much as 60%. How can this embarrassing finding be rectified? To cut the sampling error in half would require a sample four times larger than 100 invoices — i.e., $\dfrac{\text{S.E.}}{2} \approx \dfrac{1}{2\sqrt{n}} \approx \dfrac{1}{\sqrt{4n}}$. Similarly, to cut the sampling error to a third of the 60% would require a sample nine times larger (i.e., $\dfrac{\text{S.E.}}{3} \approx \dfrac{1}{3\sqrt{n}} \approx \dfrac{1}{\sqrt{9n}}$). Methods for determining the "appropriate" size of sample are given in Chapter 9. However, the point can be made here that determining the appropriate sample size in advance can save a lot of embarrassment and questionable results.

The standard error concept

When we looked at the 50 sample means we recognized that they differed from each other and from their grand average ($\overline{\overline{X}}$). These differences were due to chance or sampling variation. Since the grand mean is very close to the true mean of the universe $\overline{X}'$ it is possible to compute fairly accurately the actual sampling error of any single sample mean by subtraction, i.e., $\overline{X} - \overline{\overline{X}}$. For example, the sample #1 mean of $4.63 was in error by $.34 (i.e., $4.63 – $4.29 = $.34). Similarly, the sampling error of other individual sample averages could be computed. However, to obtain such single measures of sampling error does not provide a general measure of the average error of the 50 estimates. What is needed is a measure of the average error to draw a general conclusion, just like the standard deviation of x-values, $\sigma_x = \sqrt{\dfrac{\sum (x - \overline{X})^2}{n-1}}$, provides a measure of the average difference of the x-values from their mean value ($\overline{X}$). It follows that the average sampling error of a mean of many replicated estimated means can be computed by $\sigma_{\overline{X}} = \sqrt{\dfrac{\sum (\overline{X} - \overline{\overline{X}})^2}{m-1}}$, where m is the number of replicated sample means. Table 8.1 shows this average measure of variation to be $.225. This measure of variation is not of the individual luncheon costs (x's) in the universe, but that of estimated means based on n=30 items. Since the individual means vary because of sampling error, their sampling variation is generally called the *standard error of the estimated mean.*

In reality it is not feasible (or necessary) to conduct an experiment such as ours to generate a sampling distribution in order to compute the standard error, as was done in our controlled experiment. Instead, the sampling error of an estimated mean can be approximated by use of a single random sample. The formula for computing it is: $\sigma_{\overline{X}} = \dfrac{\sigma_x \sqrt{(1-f)}}{\sqrt{n}}$. In other words, the standard error of $\overline{X}$ equals the standard deviation of the x-values divided by $\sqrt{n}$, multiplied by the finite correction factor, $\sqrt{(1-f)}$, where f is the sampling fraction, n/N.

Concepts of standard deviation and standard error — It should be emphasized that there is a similarity and yet a difference between a standard deviation of x-values (σ_x) and a standard error of estimated $\overline{X}$'s ($\sigma_{\overline{X}}$). In general, the standard deviation (σ_x) measures the extent to which the individual x–values in the sample, which represent the universe, differ on the average from the estimated mean ($\overline{X}$) of all those measurements. On the other hand, the standard error ($\sigma_{\overline{X}}$) is a special standard deviation which measures the sampling variation of estimated means (not only of means but also percentages or other estimates) derived from random samples.

It should be noted further that the term "standard deviation" or "standard error," standing alone has no complete meaning. Thus, if we say standard error of the estimated mean (or percentage), our statement is complete because it signifies that we are quoting a measure of sampling error of a mean (or percentage) estimated from a random sample. On the other hand, the symbol σ_x makes it clear that we are not measuring variation due to sampling but that due to the inherent variability of universe x-values.

The concept of confidence

Having demonstrated that the sampling distribution of many sample-derived means approaches the shape of the normal distribution, we can now harness the known properties of normal distributions (shown in Appendix B) to estimate the percentage of sample-derived means that lie within specified intervals or ranges from the population mean ($\overline{X}'$), estimated by the mean of means, $\overline{\overline{X}}$. Thus, when one standard error of an estimated mean is added to, and subtracted from, the true mean, we can justifiably conclude that about 68% of the many sample means will be included within the interval $\overline{X} \pm 1\sigma_{\overline{X}}$; that 95.5% of the sample means will be included within the interval $\overline{X} \pm 2\sigma_{\overline{X}}$; and that 99.73% of the sample means will be included within the interval $\overline{X} \pm 3\sigma_{\overline{X}}$.

To see how closely the results of our experiment confirm these basic characteristics of normal distributions we used the $\overline{X}$ of our experiment ($\overline{\overline{X}} = \$4.29$) which closely corresponds to the true mean of $4.31 and the experiment's standard error of the estimated mean ($\sigma_{\overline{X}} = \$0.225$) to construct the above intervals and determine the percentage of sample means which were actually included within these intervals. Thus the following intervals were constructed:

$\overline{X} \pm$ one $\sigma_{\overline{X}} = \$4.29 \pm \$0.23$, or $4.06 - $4.52

$\overline{X} \pm$ two $\sigma_{\overline{X}} = \$4.29 \pm 2(\$0.23)$, or $3.83 - $4.75

$\overline{X} \pm$ three $\sigma_{\overline{X}} = \$4.29 \pm 3(\$0.23)$, or $3.60 - $4.98

To determine the number of estimated means that were actually included within these intervals we constructed the following array of the 50 estimated means, to facilitate the counting process:

Array of the 50 sample means
(From Table 8.1)

$3.63	$4.09	$4.28	$4.38	$4.44
3.73	4.11	4.29	4.39	4.46
3.94	4.12	4.29	4.39	4.48
4.01	4.18	4.31	4.41	4.55
4.02	4.19	4.32	4.41	4.58
4.06	4.22	4.32	4.41	4.60
4.06	4.23	4.33	4.41	4.63
4.06	4.25	4.34	4.42	4.63
4.07	4.27	4.36	4.43	4.71
4.09	4.27	4.36	4.43	4.71

The expected and actual percentages are shown in the following table:

| | Percentage of sample estimates | |
Range of true mean plus or minus specified number of standard errors	Expected within specified limits (per normal distribution properties)	Actually included within specified limits (per results in array of 50 means)
One ($4.06–4.52)	68.3	70.0
Two ($3.83–4.75)	95.5	96.0
Three ($3.60–4.98)	99.7	100.0

It can be observed from the comparison that the actual percentages of estimated means falling within the various ranges of true mean ± the indicated number of standard error units agree fairly well with the normally expected percentages. In fact, the comparison would show an even closer agreement if the number of sample means in the experiment were much larger than 50 or the sample size used were larger than 30 items.

Origin of confidence — By relying on the combined principles of probability and the fixed normal distribution properties embodied in the Central Limit Theorem, we can demonstrate readily the basis for and source of confidence. The law of probability provides us with the formula: $p = s/T$, the probability of success p in any given venture is equal to the number of possible successful outcomes (s) divided by the total possible outcomes (T). On the other hand, the Central Limit Theorem provides us with the s and T figures we need to enter in the probability formula. When any given number of standard errors (Z) of an estimated mean is set off on both sides of that mean, the resulting *confidence*, or chance, that the interval of $\overline{X} \pm Z\sigma_{\overline{X}}$ will embrace the true mean, depends on the number of standard errors (Z) that is tolerated. Thus,

(1) 68 percent of the time any given sample mean ± one standard error will include the true mean (with 68% confidence);

(2) 95.5 percent of the time any given sample mean ± two standard errors will include the true mean (with 95.5% confidence)

(3) 99.73 percent of the time any given sample mean ± three standard errors will include the true mean (with 99.73% confidence).

These confidence-interval statements, alternatively, can be expressed in the form of *risk* that the conclusion may be *wrong*; e.g., the probability that our sample mean $\pm 1\sigma_{\overline{x}}$ will *not* include the true mean is 32 percent (100% - 68%); etc.

In actual practice, or course, we do not know the true mean or the population's true standard error. Therefore, we must estimate both of them from the sample. However, our experiment demonstrated that the two principles, namely, the law of probability and the Central Limit Theorem combine to form the basis for determining the confidence we have in making a correct inference about the true mean from the sample mean ± a given number of standard errors. The correct manner in which we present this inference is discussed in Chapter 9.

Sampling and the Three Fundamental Frequency Distributions

To better grasp the concepts and principles presented in this chapter it is appropriate to point out that all sampling problems involving variables deal with three different but related frequency distributions. The first frequency distribution is the one formed by all of the original x-values in the universe, for example, the universe of 500 luncheon costs classified by the variable "cost in dollars." When plotted, this frequency distribution formed the pattern shown in Figure 8.2, with a true mean of $\overline{X}' = \$4.31$ and a true standard deviation of $\sigma'_x = \$1.15$. These are the actual parameters of the universe of 500 luncheon costs.

While this universe frequency distribution of x-values looks like it is close to normal, the Central Limit Theorem applies to skewed distributions, even to J-shaped distributions which are highly skewed, so long as n is sufficiently large, e.g., more than 30 items.

The second frequency distribution is formed by the values included in a single random sample selected from the universe. For example, the frequency distribution of the first sample of 30 luncheon costs selected from the above universe of 500 luncheon costs forms the pattern shown in Figure 8.3.

It can be noted that the frequency distribution of the 30 luncheon costs in the sample tends to reflect the pattern of the universe frequency distribution, but being based on a small sample it does not show the exact shape of its parent distribution. Also, its mean and standard deviation are approximations of the universe mean and standard deviation.

Figure 8.2
Universe frequency distribution of 500 luncheon costs

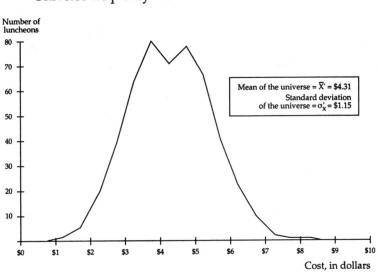

Source: The 500 luncheon costs listed in Chapter 7.

Figure 8.3
Frequency distribution of 30 luncheon costs in a random sample

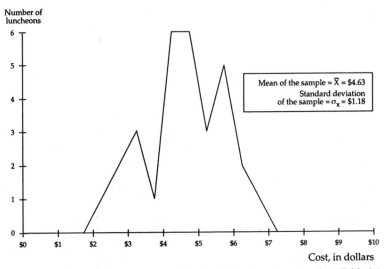

Source: The 30 luncheon costs included in the first random sample in Table 8.1.

225

The third frequency distribution is the sampling distribution. It is the nearly bell-shaped distribution formed by estimates derived from many random samples, each of the same size, randomly and independently selected from the same universe. An illustration of this theoretical normal distribution is shown in Figure 8.4, the distribution of the 50 estimated sample means of our experiment.

Figure 8.4
Frequency distribution of the 50 sample mean costs

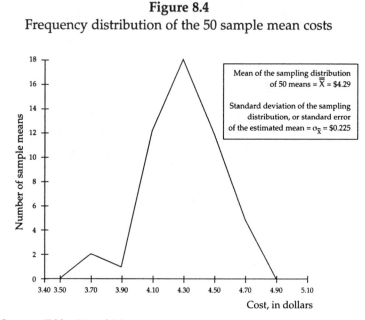

Sources: Tables 8.1 and 8.2.

To emphasize, any distribution of sample means (with n > 30) tends to form a normal distribution, regardless of the frequency distribution pattern of the universe. Furthermore, the mean of the many individual means in this sampling distribution ($\overline{\overline{X}}$ = $4.29) approaches the universe mean ($\overline{X}'$ = $4.31) as the number of replicates increases. However, the standard deviation of the sampling distribution, which is defined as the standard error of the sample mean $\sigma_{\overline{x}}$, is considerably smaller than either the standard deviation of the universe (σ'_x) or the standard deviation of any single random sample (σ_x) selected from the universe. The reason for this difference is that the standard error of the mean ($\sigma_{\overline{x}}$) is based on the number of items in the sample, while the standard deviation measures the variability of individual x-values in the sample or universe. Figure 8.5 shows the universe and sample distributions together. In contrast, Figure 8.6 shows the distribution of sample means (the sampling distribution) compared to the distribution of individual x-values in the universe. Here, it can be seen that the individual x-values in the universe (or in the sample) are more widely dispersed than the distribution of sample means.

Figure 8.5

Two of three fundamental frequency distributions —
the universe and a random sample

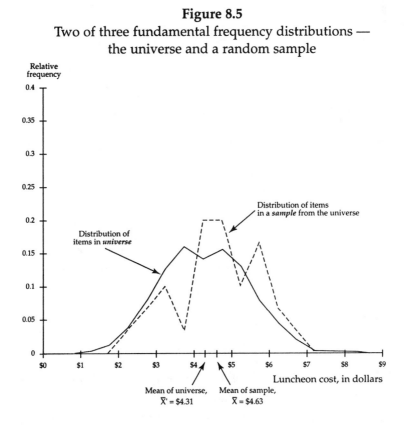

Sources: Figures 8.2 and 8.3.

Each of these three related but different frequency distributions has its own distinctive features. Thus, we have the true standard deviation of the universe (σ'_x), of the random sample (σ_x), and of the sampling distribution of means ($\sigma_{\bar{x}}$). When dealing with sampling problems, it is well to keep these distinct distributions in mind.

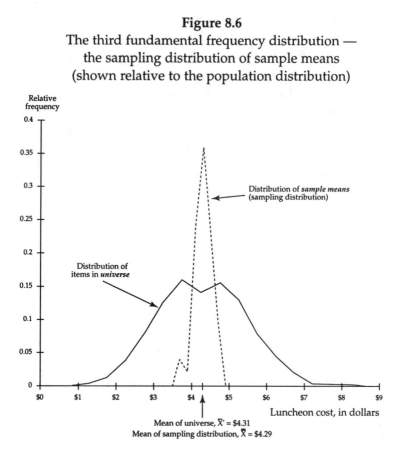

Figure 8.6
The third fundamental frequency distribution —
the sampling distribution of sample means
(shown relative to the population distribution)

Sources: Figures 8.2 and 8.4.

Summary

This chapter described several basic principles and concepts which underlie random sampling. These are:

(1) *the Law of Universal Variation*, which states that every process, phenomenon, or measurable characteristic displays variation, thus causing variation, or sampling error, in sample-derived estimates;

(2) *the Law of Decreasing Variation*, which states that the larger the sample (n) the smaller the sampling error. Here, the square root of n inversely influences the magnitude of sampling error, that is: Sampling Error $\approx 1/\sqrt{n}$;

(3) *the Central Limit Theorem*, which states that many independent sample-derived estimates, i.e., replicates, when organized into a frequency distribution will tend to form a graphic pattern shaped like the bell or normal curve, regardless of the shape of the original universe values. An experiment conducted with 50 replicated averages gave empirical proof of the Central Limit Theorem, although it has been proven mathematically;

(4) *the Law of Probability*, which provides the basis for determining the chances of success in any given venture. Together with the Central Limit Theorem, these two principles provide the basis for determining the different levels of confidence that the estimated sampling error will not be exceeded when tolerating a given number of standard errors;

(5) the concept of variation in x-values inherent in a universe of such values (σ_x); the concept of variation due to chance in sample-derived estimates ($\sigma_{\bar{x}}$); and the concepts of confidence and risk, both expressed in percentages or as odds.

In gathering data with random samples we contend with three main types of error. One arises from unsystematic mistakes made in processing the material associated with the survey, such as human errors in recording data, in coding the answers, and other types of human and related mistakes. These errors are often compensating and therefore, in the long run, tend to offset each other, with the net result that the final data may not be significantly biased.

A second type of error is caused by one-sided systematic mistakes, and leads to biased estimates. These errors can result from many sources, such as non-response to a specific question, use of convenient rather than probability samples, purposely biased responses, and use of biased methods of extending sample-derived estimates to the universe level. If the results of surveys are to be useful, these systematic errors must be kept within reasonable control.

A third type of error in sample data, which is unavoidable, arises from chance variations which are caused by the law of probability on which we depend to select representative items for the sample. These are errors due to sampling and are called sampling error or sampling variation.

The first two types of error — unsystematic mistakes and systematic mistakes — may sometimes be more serious than sampling errors; they must be avoided or kept under control, although in practice some of them may be extremely difficult to control. Chance errors due to sampling cannot be avoided (except by not sampling), but fortunately they can be measured and controlled by the appropriate sample size and by efficient sample designs and estimation procedures. In particular, the risk of making incorrect inferences solely due to sampling error can be calculated; this, however, can be done only when the sample is selected by probability (random) methods.

The principles and concepts underlying sampling can be better understood if the three different frequency distributions involved in practical sampling are understood. The first frequency distribution is that of all the original values in the universe. The second is the frequency distribution of original values or items that have been included in the random sample. If the sample is sufficiently large and randomly drawn, this frequency distribution tends to form the pattern of the universe frequency distribution, with a mean and standard deviation fairly close to the universe mean and standard deviation. Finally, there is the theoretical frequency distribution of many sample-derived estimates of a universe characteristic based on many independently selected random samples of equal size from that universe. The graphic pattern of this sampling distribution generally is very close to the normal or bell-shaped curve, even though the distribution of original values in the universe might depart widely from normality. The mean of this sampling distribution will be the same or very close to the universe mean, but its standard deviation, which is actually the standard error of any one of its replicates ($\sigma_{\bar{x}}$), will be much smaller than the universe standard deviation (σ'_x). The universe standard deviation is a measure of variability of the original universe values around the universe mean, while the standard error is a measure of chance error in, or variation of, an estimate derived from a random sample.

It is important that management understands the principles and concepts presented in this chapter because they deal with some of the fundamental elements of sampling. Management often depends, and will increasingly depend in the future, on sampling techniques as a short-cut to fact-finding. With a knowledge of the main sampling concepts and principles, of the existence of chance and non-chance variations, as well as confidence and risk, managers can be a more successful planners and users of random sampling techniques for obtaining objective information and for making decisions.

It is appropriate at the conclusion of this chapter to recall the powerful statement about statistical sampling once made by Dr. Deming: *"Theory without practice is useless; practice without theory is baseless."*

Problems

1. Explain and illustrate the difference between the three major types of error in statistical data.

2. Explain and give an illustration of the following: (a) sampling distribution, (b) probability sample, (c) chance variations of sampling, and (d) a constant-cause system.

3. If you computed the means from many independent random samples of equal size taken from the same universe and then formed a frequency distribution of these sample means, you would expect to obtain a normal or approximately normal distribution. Explain the conditions under which this would occur.

4. (a) What is the chance that, if a single sample of size n is randomly selected from the universe, its mean ± one standard error will include the true mean of the universe?

    (b) ± two standard errors?

    (c) ± two and a half standard errors?

    What are these chances when expressed as "odds"?

5. (a) Give a property of the sampling distribution and

    (b) of a frequency distribution of sample x-values.

6. Explain the difference between the standard deviation of sample data and the standard deviation of replicated sample means (the sampling distribution).

7. Distinguish between the three frequency distributions encountered in sampling problems and give the symbols of the mean and standard deviation in each.

8. State at least two of the basic principles of sampling you have learned from this chapter.

9. In order to achieve a specified precision in an estimate based on a random sample we need to be concerned with the extent of variability among the units in the universe and the size of sample used. Explain the direction of the influence of these two factors on the magnitude of the sampling error.

10. Show the formula for computing the standard error of the estimated mean $(\overline{X})$.

11. (a) Determine the number of standard errors that needs to be tolerated in the estimated mean to achieve the following levels of confidence: 68%, 95.5%, 99.73%, 90%, and 99%.

    (b) Using the simple random sample data you identified in problem #1 of Chapter 7, compute the amount of sampling error that results for each of these confidence levels.

Chapter 9

Estimation and Sample-Size Determination

"Precision is expressed by an international standard, viz., the standard error. It measures the average of the differences between a complete coverage and a long series of estimates formed from samples drawn from this complete coverage by a particular procedure of drawing, and processed by a particular estimating formula." *

Sampling is an economical and expeditious way of collecting quantitative data about the characteristics of universes. However, certain skills plus knowledge of sampling principles are necessary to use sampling effectively. The objectives of this chapter are many-fold. Thus far we have described several different ways of selecting random samples (Chapter 7) and some basic principles and concepts which underlie random sampling (Chapter 8). This chapter aims to describe the remaining elements of a data-collection system outlined in Chapter 7, as follows:

(1) How to derive unbiased estimates *(inferences)* of universe characteristics *(parameters)* from random samples.

(2) How to measure quantitatively the *reliability* (sampling error or sampling variation) of such estimates with reasonable assurance (high *confidence*) that the tolerable sampling error is not larger than specified. Also covered is how to present the estimates in forms readily understood by management or the recipient of the estimates.

(3) How to determine the size of sample (n) appropriate to a given fact-finding situation.

(4) How to use stratified random sampling when it is appropriate.

---

* W. Edwards Deming, "On the Presentation of the Results of Sample Surveys As Legal Evidence," *Journal of the American Statistical Association*, December 1954.

Estimation Procedures

Four main estimates, two for variables and two for attributes, often are sought from sample surveys, as follows: $\overline{X}$; $N\overline{X}$; p; and Np. These symbols and their formulas were presented previously, but are redefined below for review.

When dealing with variables

When dealing with any particular characteristic that varies in some measurable way, we encounter the symbol x which is used to denote a single measured value of that characteristic. This is referred to as the *variable* of interest. Often, we wish to estimate the average (usually the arithmetic mean) value of the characteristic in a specified universe. In this case, the mean value generally is referred to as a parameter of that universe. For example, we may wish to estimate the mean or total earnings of a particular group of workers, or the average age of accounts receivable, or average rentals paid, or average elapsed time in paying an invoice, etc.

The estimated mean, $\overline{X}$, is derived from the sample by the standard formula: $\overline{X} = \dfrac{\sum x}{n}$, where x represents the variable, $\sum$ represents the sum of the varying values, and n is the number of items in the sample. This sample mean is an estimate of the population mean. This average is used for different purposes, such as establishing a norm, or for comparison with similar averages over a period of time, or among different groups, regions, etc.

One of the most important uses of the mean is to estimate the universe total of all x-values, such as the *total value* of an inventory of property, or of all accounts receivable, or total revenue earned, etc. The estimated total is derived by multiplying the arithmetic mean ($\overline{X}$) derived from the sample by the total number of items in the universe, namely by $N\overline{X}$. This estimate relies on the premise that the sample average is a close approximation, plus or minus sampling error, of the universe mean and therefore its total ($N\overline{X}$).

When dealing with attributes

In many sample surveys, estimates are needed of the *percentage* of cases in a universe possessing a given *attribute* or characteristic, such as an error-rate, a non-compliance rate, the percentage of houses with fireplaces, the percentage of invoices not paid on time, etc. The estimated percentage, or the estimated *proportion*, p, computed from the sample data is a good reflection of the true universe percentage. It is computed by $p = \Sigma x / n$, where $x = 1$ if the case possesses the attribute and $x = 0$ if it doesn't possess the attribute.

Often management needs to estimate the *total number* of cases in the universe which possess a specified attribute, such as the total number of accounts past-due, the number of items which are rejected because of unacceptable quality, the number of persons possessing a given characteristic, etc. This estimated total is readily obtained by the formula Np, where p is expressed in decimals. Again, it is necessary to recognize that this estimate is subject to + or − a certain amount of sampling error.

Making the estimate − illustrations

If the first random sample of 30 luncheon costs selected from the universe of 500 luncheon costs in Chapter 8 was the only sample we had with which to estimate the true mean amount students spent for lunch, the estimated mean would be obtained by simply adding the 30 cost figures and dividing the sum by 30: $\overline{X} = \Sigma x / n$. The sampled luncheon costs are shown in the accompanying table.

Simple random sample of 30 hypothetical luncheon costs
(taken from Chapter 8 experiment)

$4.26	$3.55	$4.35
6.21	3.45	4.02
4.93	4.10	5.52
5.72	2.52	4.95
4.55	5.21	6.45
5.96	6.66	4.94
4.07	5.43	2.35
4.94	5.62	4.72
3.06	2.65	5.43
3.15	4.24	5.95

First, we calculate the mean of the sample as:

$$\overline{X} = \Sigma x / n = \$138.96 / 30 = \$4.63.$$

The resulting mean of $4.63 is an unbiased estimate of the universe mean ($\overline{X}'$). Furthermore, if we wanted to estimate the total amount taken in by the cafeteria on the given date we would estimate it by $N\overline{X}$, which is (500) ($4.63) = $2,315 ± sampling error.

To illustrate attributes estimation, let us assume that we needed to estimate the percentage of luncheon expenditures amounting to $5.00 or more. The above sample would yield: p = 11 / 30 = 0.37, or 37% ± sampling error. Furthermore, if we needed to estimate the total number of students who spent $5.00 or more for lunch on the specified day, the estimated total would be obtained by:

Np = (500) (0.37) = 185 students ± sampling error.
(The reader should verify these calculations.)

Measuring the Precision of Estimates

When dealing with variables

Merely estimating a population parameter from the sample data is not enough. When a randomly drawn sample is used to estimate a universe characteristic, three elements comprise the estimating process: (1) the value of the characteristic being estimated (such as the mean or percentage) calculated from the sample; (2) a measure of the error in the estimate due to sampling (also called the sampling variation); and (3) a clear presentation of the estimate which states, with a specified confidence, that the true value of the characteristic in the population lies within a particular interval or range of values, or that the specified sampling error will not be exceeded.

In the sampling experiment conducted in Chapter 8 we defined and illustrated that one *standard-error-of-the-estimated-mean* (or the standard-error of any other sample-derived estimate) is the benchmark for measuring sampling error; it states, with a confidence of 68%, that the indicated error (plus or minus) is not larger. In the experiment, the standard error of the estimated mean was derived by computing the standard deviation of the *sampling distribution* of the many replicated sample means by the following formula:

$$\sigma_{\overline{X}} = \sqrt{\frac{\sum\left(\overline{X} - \overline{\overline{X}}\right)^2}{m-1}},$$

where m was the number of sample replicates used, which in this case was m = 50.

In the real world, such experiments with replication are not generally feasible due to time and cost limitations. In sample surveys or audits we rely on a single sample both to derive the required estimates and to compute the standard error of each estimate.

Sampling theory provides the following formula for approximating the standard error of the estimated mean:

$$\sigma_{\overline{x}} = \frac{\sigma_x \sqrt{(1-f)}}{\sqrt{n}}$$

where σ_x is the standard deviation of the sampled x-values,

i.e., $\sigma_x = \sqrt{\dfrac{\Sigma(x-\overline{X})^2}{n-1}}$;

f is the sampling fraction, i.e., $f = n\,/\,N$;

n is the number of items in the sample; and

N is the number of items in the universe.

It should be noted that the number "one" while not shown precedes the formula for $\sigma_{\overline{x}}$. Thus, one standard error corresponds to 68% confidence that the indicated error is not larger.

Simple logic supports this formula for measuring the sampling error of the estimated mean, as follows:

(1) The larger the variation of the x-values (σ_x), the larger the sampling error; i.e., sampling error varies directly with σ_x;

(2) The larger the sample size (n), the smaller the sampling error; i.e., sampling error varies inversely with n (or $\sqrt{n}$); and

(3) The larger the sampling fraction not sampled (1–f), the larger the sampling error; i.e., sampling error varies directly with the fraction not sampled under the square root sign.

The preceding formula for the standard error of the estimated mean is generally applicable to estimated means derived from a simple random, systematic random, or digital random sample.

Illustration — To illustrate how the standard error of the estimated mean and the estimated total are computed, we use the random sample of 30 luncheon costs shown earlier. The data and appropriate calculations are shown in Table 9.1.

Table 9.1 — Calculation of the sample mean and standard deviation
needed to compute the standard error of the estimated mean and
estimated total, where n = 30 luncheon costs

x-values Sample luncheon costs	$d = (x - \overline{X})$ Difference from mean	$d^2 = (x - \overline{X})^2$ Difference squared
$ 4.26	$ –0.37	$ 0.14
6.21	1.58	2.50
4.93	0.30	0.09
5.72	1.09	1.19
4.55	–0.08	0.01
5.96	1.33	1.77
4.07	–0.56	0.31
4.94	0.31	0.10
3.06	–1.57	2.46
3.15	–1.48	2.19
3.55	–1.08	1.17
3.45	–1.18	1.39
4.10	–0.53	0.28
2.52	–2.11	4.45
5.21	0.58	0.34
6.66	2.03	4.12
5.43	0.80	0.64
5.62	0.99	0.98
2.65	–1.98	3.92
4.24	–0.39	0.15
4.35	–0.28	0.08
4.02	–0.61	0.37
5.52	0.89	0.79
4.95	0.32	0.10
6.45	1.82	3.31
4.94	0.31	0.10
2.35	–2.28	5.20
4.72	0.09	0.01
5.43	0.80	0.64
5.95	1.32	1.74
Σx = $138.96	$\Sigma(x - \overline{X})$ = 0.06*	$\Sigma(x - \overline{X})^2$ = 40.54

* The $\Sigma(x - \overline{X})$ always equals zero when the mean is not rounded.

When the component totals from Table 9.1 are entered into the appropriate formulas, we obtain the following results.

$$\text{Mean} = \overline{X} = \frac{\Sigma x}{n} = \frac{\$138.96}{29} = \$4.63$$

$$\text{Standard deviation} = \sigma_x = \sqrt{\frac{\Sigma(x-\overline{X})^2}{n-1}} = \sqrt{\frac{40.54}{29}} = \sqrt{1.40} = \$1.18$$

Sampling fraction = $f = n/N = 30/500 = .06$.

When we enter these three values into the standard-error-of-the-mean formula, we find its value to be ± $0.21, as computed below.

$$\text{Standard error of estimated mean} = \sigma_{\overline{X}} = \frac{\sigma_x \sqrt{(1-f)}}{\sqrt{n}}$$

$$= \left(\frac{1.18\sqrt{1-.06}}{\sqrt{30}}\right) = \left(\frac{1.18\sqrt{.94}}{5.48}\right) = \left(\frac{1.18(.97)}{5.48}\right) = \pm\$0.21.$$

It is worthwhile emphasizing the fact that the formula for the exact standard error of the mean would have as its numerator σ'_x which denotes the actual universe standard deviation. Since we do not know σ'_x we estimate it from the sample and use the symbol σ_x to represent it in the formula. Because σ_x is based on a random sample, its value will vary from sample to sample because of sampling error. In practice, however, the sampling error of a standard deviation estimated from the sample is much smaller than the sampling error of the sample mean ($\overline{X}$). Consequently, it is generally assumed that the sample standard deviation (σ_x) is a reasonably good approximation of the true standard deviation (σ'_x), especially when n is large. As defined earlier, the standard error measures the sampling error (+ or −) of the estimate, with 68% confidence that it is not greater. Better confidence can be achieved by increasing the number of standard errors. Thus, for example, by doubling the standard error (thereby increasing the tolerable sampling error) we increase the confidence to 95.4% (as shown in Chapter 8).

The *standard error of an estimated total* ($N\overline{X}$) is a simple extension of the formula for the standard error of the estimated mean, namely, it is $N\sigma_{\overline{X}}$. In other words, the only cause for sampling error of the estimated total is that caused by the estimated mean. For example, if a sample study were made to estimate the total annual earnings of

10,000 employees (N = 10,000) and, from a random sample of 100 workers (n=100 and f=.01), the estimated mean ($\overline{X}$) was \$45,000 and the standard deviation in individual earnings estimated from the sample (σ_x) was \$28,400, the standard error of the estimated total (N$\overline{X}$ = \$450 million) would be obtained by the following:

$$\sigma_{N\overline{X}} = N\sigma_{\overline{X}} = N\left(\frac{\sigma_x\sqrt{(1-f)}}{\sqrt{n}}\right) = (10,000)\left(\frac{28,400\sqrt{(1-.01)}}{\sqrt{100}}\right) = \pm\$28.4 \text{ million.}$$

Thus, the estimated total annual earnings of \$450 million is subject to a sampling error of ±\$28.4 million with a confidence of 68 percent that the indicated sampling error is not larger. When the standard error is multiplied by "2", the confidence is increased to 95.4 percent that the \$56.8 million (twice the standard error) will not be exceeded. The basis for these confidence levels was demonstrated in Chapter 8. (The reader also may check this by looking up 1.0 and 2.0 standard deviation units in the normal distribution table in Appendix B.)

Another illustration — We wish to measure the sampling error of the average number of years of work-experience of a group of 5,000 employees in a given company. A simple random sample of 50 employees showed the estimated mean years of work experience to be 13.9 years with a standard deviation of 10 years. How reliable is the estimated average of 13.9 years?

Here, n = 50 employees, σ_x = 10 years and f = 0.01.

The standard error of $\overline{X}$ is:

$$\sigma_{\overline{X}} = \frac{\sigma_x\sqrt{(1-f)}}{\sqrt{n}} = \left(\frac{10\sqrt{(1-.01)}}{\sqrt{50}}\right) = \left(\frac{10(.995)}{7.07}\right) = \pm1.41 \text{ years.}$$

Thus, we are 68 percent sure that the sampling error of the estimated mean of 13.9 years is no larger than ±1.41 years.

When dealing with attributes

Earlier, we indicated that the random sample of 30 luncheon costs (selected from the universe of 500 luncheons) showed that 37 percent of the luncheon expenditures were in amounts of \$5.00 or more ± sampling error.* As in the case of variables, formulas are available to compute the

---

* In the case of attributes there also is the requirement that np or n(1-p) exceeds 5 in order to use normal distribution theory.

standard error of an estimated percentage or total by use of the sample data. The formula for the *standard error of a proportion*, p, is

$$\sigma_p = \sqrt{\frac{p(1-p)(1-f)}{n-1}},$$

where σ_p is the standard error of p expressed in percentage points (decimals); p is the percent (expressed in decimals) of items possessing the attribute; n is the number of items sampled from the N items in the universe; and f is the sampling fraction, f = n/N.

In our example, using p = 0.37, $\sigma_p = \sqrt{\frac{(.37)(.63)(.97)}{29}} = \pm 0.088$.

To compute the *standard error of the estimated total number of items* **(Np)** *possessing the attribute*, where, for example, Np = (500)(.37) = 185, we multiply the standard error of p by N, namely,

$$\sigma_{Np} = N\sigma_p = N\sqrt{\frac{p(1-p)(1-f)}{(n-1)}} = \pm 45 \text{ luncheons.}$$

Illustrations — The following examples illustrate how a percentage (and a total) estimated from a sample may be evaluated with respect to error due to sampling.

An example — Assume that a simple random sample of 100 darning needles was selected from a lot containing 10,000 needles (f = .01) in order to estimate the proportion of needles in the lot that was defective (for example, without an eye). Let us further suppose that 6 needles out of the 100 in the sample, or p = .06 (or 6%), were defective. How can an appropriate inference be made from the sample regarding the quality of the entire lot (the population)?

First of all, we measure the sampling error of the estimated percentage. This is done by using the standard-error-of-a-percentage formula using decimals, as follows:

$$\sigma_p = \sqrt{\frac{p(1-p)(1-f)}{(n-1)}} = \sqrt{\frac{(.06)(.94)(.99)}{99}} = \pm 0.0237.$$

Since .024 (rounded) represents one standard error of the estimated percentage of defective needles, the chances are 68% that the true percentage is within ±.024 of the estimated percentage (p = .06). Thus, we may present the sample estimate in the form of a 68% *confidence interval*: "The true percentage of defective needles is somewhere between 3.6 and 8.4 percent (i.e., 6% ± 2.4%). We are 68% confident that this assertion is correct."

Should we need to estimate the number of defective needles in the lot of 10,000, we use the formula Np. Thus, Np = (10,000) (.06) = 600. The standard error of the estimated total is: $N\sigma_p$ = (10,000) (.0237) = ±237 needles. Thus, with a confidence level of 68%, we can say that the sampling error of the estimated total of 600 defective needles is no larger than ±237 needles.

Another example — The data-entry work of a computer operator was reviewed for accuracy. A total of 25,000 items were entered into the office computer during the past week. A systematic random sample of 900 entries was selected and checked for accuracy. As a result, 54 entries were found to be in error. What conclusion can be drawn regarding the quality (error rate) of this work?

In this problem, N = 25,000; n = 900; p = 54 / 900 = 0.06; and f = 900 / 25,000 = 0.036. Therefore, the standard error of the estimated percentage, using decimals, is computed by:

$$\sigma_p = \sqrt{\frac{p(1-p)(1-f)}{(n-1)}} = \sqrt{\frac{(.06)(.94)(.964)}{899}} = \pm 0.0078.$$

It may be stated, with a confidence of 68% of being correct, that: "The true percentage of erroneous entries is somewhere within 6 percent ± 0.78 percentage points, or between 5.2 and 6.8 percent (rounded)." It may also be stated with 95.4% confidence of being correct, that: "The true percentage is somewhere within 6 percent ± 2 (0.78 percent), or between 4.4 and 7.6 percent." It may also be stated with 99.73% confidence of being correct, that: "The true percentage is somewhere within 6 percent ± 3(0.78 percent), or between 3.7 percent and 8.3 percent."

Presenting Sample-Derived Estimates

In the foregoing sections we have demonstrated the derivation of four types of estimates from random samples (i.e., $\overline{X}$, $N\overline{X}$, p, and Np) and the corresponding formulas for measuring the sampling error of each of these estimates. In measuring the latter we have come up with the previously mentioned concept of "standard error" of the estimate. In each case the standard error represented the maximum sampling error of the estimate with a confidence of 68% that the indicated error is not larger. We have also presented some of these estimates in the form of a "confidence interval," using a 68% confidence level. Later examples (data-entry errors) dealt with 95.4% and 99.7% confidence.

In this section we aim to clarify the basis for the different levels of confidence and to demonstrate several different ways of presenting sample-derived estimates which contain the three required elements: the estimate, sampling error, and confidence.

The basis for confidence levels

In Chapter 8 we described an experiment with many replicated random sample means. This experiment was designed to help us understand the behavior of a random variable (e.g., the random sample mean which varies due to chance). We demonstrated empirically that the frequency distribution of the many independently derived estimated means, called a sampling distribution, approached the shape of the normal (bell-shaped) distribution. It was also demonstrated that the standard deviation of this distribution of means closely approximated the true standard error of the estimated mean.

Because the sampling distribution of many random sample means displays the pattern of the normal distribution, its properties are known and fixed by its overall mean (a very close approximation of the universe mean) and its standard deviation (called the standard error of the sample mean). Thus, it is expected that 68% of the many means will be included within the overall mean and ± one standard error; that 95.4% of the means will be included within the overall mean ± two standard errors; and 99.7% will be included within the overall mean ± three standard errors. These percentages are not the only ones which make up the normal distribution properties. The properties of the normal distribution are given in the table in Appendix B, which gives as many as 400 such percentages on half of the curve, each depending on the number of standard deviation units away from the overall mean.

From these properties, it follows that the probability (confidence) that an interval formed by estimated mean ± one standard error will include the true mean of the normal distribution 68 times out of 100 trials or 68% of the time. In the same way, the probability is 95.4% that the interval $\overline{X} \pm 2\sigma_{\overline{X}}$ will include the true mean, and so forth. A rereading of Chapter 8 can provide a fuller grasp of the basis for confidence. This basis is equally applicable to the remaining three estimates: $N\overline{X}$, p, and Np, each of which can be considered to be random variables.

Different ways of presenting the estimates

There are five different ways of presenting sample-derived estimates which are appropriate and correct in the light of sampling theory. They are: (1) confidence interval; (2) absolute error; (3) relative error; (4) at least; and (5) at most. Each is explained below.

(1) Confidence interval method — In the luncheon-cost problem in Chapter 7, we would be in a precarious position if, after we calculated the mean cost of all lunches at $4.63 from the first-listed random sample of 30 items, we used it without further qualification to make a decision about the true universe mean. We can appropriately ask ourselves the question, "What risk will management run in using this estimate, or what are the chances that this estimate is exactly equal, or close to, the true mean?"

Since there are millions of possible combinations of replicated random samples of 30 items each that can be drawn from this universe, the chances are practically nil that this *particular* sample mean ($\overline{X}$) is exactly the same as or even close to the universe mean ($\overline{X}'$). When the chances of being exactly right are so slim, management must recognize that every estimate derived from a random sample is subject to some error due to chance. Therefore, it must *tolerate some sampling error.* The amount of error to tolerate in the estimate, and the desired confidence that it will not be larger, are usually management decisions, often made in consultation with the sample designer. The decision-makers are most familiar with the original goals of the survey, and it is their responsibility to choose the tolerable sampling error and confidence level.

This line of reasoning leads us to observe that we cannot utilize the full advantages of random sampling by simply presenting an estimate from a sample as a single unqualified figure, called a ***point estimate***. It is not possible to associate a reasonable probability of being right or wrong with a point estimate; therefore, a given amount of sampling error (+ or −) must be tolerated in it. One way of presenting the estimate is in terms of a range or interval with reasonable assurance (e.g., 95%) of making a correct decision. This interval estimate is called a *confidence interval,* since we attach a specific confidence that the interval will include the true universe parameter we are trying to estimate.

Harry G. Romig, noted statistician, once said:*

"In the management area it may be very desirable to carry the notion of confidence intervals. In predicting a market, provide minimum and maximum values as well as the expected or nominal value. When analyzing and listing estimates of costs, building requirements, inspection and testing needs, as well as production schedules, make charts that are simple but present with a probability sense the range of variation of the estimates. In discussing this matter with various prominent consulting firms in management and engineering, they believe that such bands, rather than expected values only, would prevent disastrous decisions. The risks would be appreciated and would properly be evaluated before selecting a final course of action."

A concrete illustration of the confidence interval method of presentation can be given with the luncheon-cost problem. Earlier, we estimated the mean to be $4.63 and the standard error of the mean to be $0.21. By subtracting the standard error from the estimated mean we obtain the lower-limit estimate of $4.42 ($4.63 minus $0.21). Similarly, by adding the standard error to the estimated mean we obtain the upper-limit estimate of $4.84. The 68% confidence-interval presentation follows: *The true mean cost of lunch on the day the sample was taken was between $4.42 and $4.84. We are 68% confident that this conclusion is correct.* In other words, our assertion will be true 68% of the times we tolerate just one standard error in a sample-derived estimate.

Being aware of the chance of being right, management can now accept the estimate or express concern over it. Management generally should express concern at a confidence of only 68 %. This level of confidence is not very high or cannot generally be considered to give "reasonable assurance". How can we present an estimate from a sample with confidence of greater than a 68% chance of being correct? The answer is: Allow, or tolerate, more sampling error. For example, if management were willing to tolerate twice one standard error (in this case plus or minus 2 times $0.21), we would have 95.4% confidence, and thus considerably increase the chances that our resulting estimate-interval will include the true mean. Any desired confidence other than 100% may be converted to the corresponding number of standard errors to tolerate by reference to the fixed properties of the normal curve table given in Appendix B. That table shows that 2.0 standard deviation

---

* Harry G. Romig, "The role of Quality Control in Industry," *Industrial Quality Control,* July 1954.

units or two standard errors on one side of the mean of a normal curve includes 47.72% of the items. Therefore, if we tolerate as much as ± two times one standard error or $0.42, we can validly claim, with 95.4% confidence (two times the 47.72%), that the resulting interval of $4.21 to $5.05 includes the true universe mean.

As compared with a 68% chance of being correct, a confidence of 95.4% of being correct is usually considered satisfactory for management decisions. Of course, to be that confident we need to tolerate greater sampling error. It should be emphasized that the actual error may be much smaller since the tolerable error refers to the outer limits of the confidence interval.

In some extremely critical management decisions, it may be risky to a chance a decision with 95.4% confidence, in which case there are ways of presenting estimates with still greater confidence. For example, if we tolerate ± three standard errors of the mean, which in our illustrative problem is ± three times $0.21, or ±$0.63, we would expect to be correct 99.73% of the times with an assertion that the true mean is included within $4.00 and $5.26.

It seems hardly worthwhile going beyond a confidence level of 99.73 percent. At this level, the odds are 369 to 1,* *practically certain,* that we will not miss the mark.

The main point to be emphasized in connection with our use of estimates derived from random samples is that beyond stating the estimate itself, two additional criteria must be met before the method presentation of the estimate is acceptable. They are: (1) a tolerance for a specified range of sampling error and (2) a confidence that this tolerable error will not be exceeded.

(2) Maximum absolute error method — The standard error formula measures sampling error in the same units as the variable (or attribute) in *absolute units.* Therefore, a second way of presenting sample-derived estimates is in the same units, as illustrated with the luncheon cost problem:

> "The mean cost of lunch in the cafeteria of the ABC University on the specified day is estimated at $4.63; however, this estimate is subject to an error due to sampling of as much as ±$0.21, with a confidence of 68% that it is not larger."

---

*Obtained by dividing the confidence-percent by the corresponding risk-percent, in this case 99.73 / 0.27 = 369 to 1.

This method of presentation shows the maximum absolute size of the error, i.e., in terms of the original units of measurement (dollars).

When dealing with an estimated percentage, i.e., attributes, the presentation language would be as follows:

"We estimate that 37% of student luncheons cost $5 or more; this estimate may be in error due to sampling by as much as ± 9 *percentage points* with a confidence of 68% that the error is not larger."

A point of emphasis: In presenting findings in the same units as the standard error, the size of the sampling error of an estimated percent must be expressed in ± *percentage points* (which are additive) and not in percent of the estimate. This will become more apparent when we present findings in relative error terms, as shown below.

(3) Maximum relative error method — Another way by which we might wish to present the estimate is:

"The mean cost of lunch is estimated at $4.63, subject to an error no larger than ±4.5 percent, with 68% confidence that the indicated sampling error is not higher."

In this method of presentation, the absolute amount of the standard error of the mean was converted to a percentage of the estimated mean as follows: ±$0.21 / $4.63 = ±0.045 = ±4.5 percent. A specific way of arriving at the *relative error* is: Relative error of the estimate = the sampling error of the estimate (at whatever chosen confidence) divided by the estimate.

An example: The relative error of the estimated mean cost of a luncheon (in our luncheon universe) is: $\frac{\sigma_{\overline{X}}}{\overline{X}}(100) = \pm 4.5\%$, with 68% confidence that it is not higher.

In the same way, the relative sampling error of a percentage at a given level of confidence is the sampling error of the percentage, expressed in percentage points, divided by the estimated percentage. Thus, the relative error of $p = \frac{\sigma_p}{p}(100)$.

Another illustration: Using the previous example in which 6 percent of a sample of 100 darning needles (from a universe of 10,000 needles) was defective, the absolute error was ±0.024, or 2.4 percentage points. Thus, relative error is (0.024 / 0.06) (100) = ± 40%.

Another example: In the luncheon-cost problem, it was estimated that 37 percent (0.37) of the luncheons were for $5 or more with a standard error of ±.09. In relative terms this would be a standard error of ± 24.3% (i.e., .09 / .37 = ± 24.3 percent).

Caution — In situations where p is a small percentage, such as .01, .02, or .03, the relative error is bound to be very high, such as 50% or more. This is due to the smallness of the estimated percentage which is the denominator of the relative error formula. In such situations it is better to use the confidence interval method of presentation.

Presentation methods (4) and (5): The at-most and at-least methods — When an estimate is not needed in the form of a confidence interval or relative error, but in the form of "at most" or "at least," it is possible to do so with a higher confidence than either of the other three methods of presentation. This is made possible by the fact that we are using only one tail of the normal distribution in either of these two methods.

An example:

Given: A universe of 10,000 pieces of property (computer record).

Objective: To establish the accountability of this universe of property.

A random sample 400 pieces (f=.04) was selected from the Central Office computer listing of 10,000 pieces of property. When the audit was completed, 28 pieces, or 7%, were not located. What is the reliability of this estimate with 90% confidence?

Solution:

$$\text{Standard error of p} = \sigma_p = \sqrt{\frac{p(1-p)(1-f)}{(n-1)}} = \sqrt{\frac{(.07)(.93)(1-.04)}{399}} = 0.0125$$

For 90% confidence we tolerate 1.65 standard errors or (1.65)(.0125) = ±0.0206. Therefore, the 90% confidence interval is 0.07 ± 0.0206, or a low of 0.0494 and a high of 0.0906.

By drawing a picture of the normal distribution of sample-derived percentages, we can see how the "at most" or the "at least" presentation method increases the confidence from 90% to 95%. See Figure 9.1. These two results are presented as follows:

> "We are 95% confident that the proportion of property missing is at most 0.09."

> "We are 95% confident that the proportion of missing property is at least 0.05."

Figure 9.1
Sampling distribution of estimated percentages

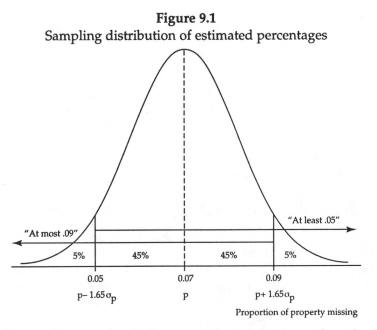

Proportion of property missing

From this graph of the normal distribution of replicated percentages of unaccountable property pieces, it is apparent that while the interval estimate has a confidence of 90%, the "at most" and the "at least" estimates add in another 5% confidence at each tail (left or right, respectively) of the distribution and thereby each method yields a 95% chance of being correct.

"Odds" – another way of communicating confidence

We don't often consider the fact that sampling is really a game of chance. Experience with presenting sample-derived estimates with a given confidence by any of the five modes of presentation has shown that confidence expressed in percent often does not readily convey the notion that sampling is a game of chance. For example, what does 90% sure of being correct mean? Is it a good level of confidence? When converted to odds of being correct , the usual form of expressing confidence in games of chance, it becomes clear that 90% confidence is equivalent of 9 to 1 odds of being correct (i.e., 90/10), which are pretty good odds in any game of chance. Not only does this form of expressing confidence convey the notion that in sampling we are playing games of chance, but more importantly it provides another way of communicating the strength of a given confidence level.

Some Examples:

68% confidence means 32% risk (100% − 68%); by dividing 68% by 32%, we have odds of 2 to 1;

80% confidence means 20% risk; the odds have now doubled to 4 to 1, even though it doesn't seem like a big increase in confidence from 68% to 80%.

In the same way, 95% confidence means odds of 19 to 1;

99% confidence means nearly 100 to 1 odds; and

99.73% confidence means 369 to 1 odds, or practical certainty.

Determining the Appropriate Size of Sample

One government sampler decided to use a sample of 100,000 Social Security records to check the accuracy of the earnings credited to the universe of over 100 million employee records. When asked what was the basis for auditing so many records, the sampler explained that management decided on this sample size. After all, it was pointed out to the auditors that 100,000 isn't a large sample compared with the universe of over 100 million employee records, namely, it is but one-tenth of one percent of the universe.

Another sampler decided on using a 10% sample of a universe of 15,000 records, explaining that this is a nice round figure that makes it simple to select every tenth record by systematic random selection.

The first sampler was unaware of a misconception that a large universe requires a large sample, i.e., the larger the universe, the larger the sample. *This is not true.*

The second sampler used judgment which often can be *bad judgment* in deciding on the appropriate size of sample.

In trying to estimate universe characteristics from a random sample, a great deal of time and money can be wasted if the size of sample used is too large; on the other hand, if it is too small, it may fail to meet the precision and confidence required in important decision-making situations. In other words, more items sampled than are required could waste funds, while fewer items than necessary could give results with less than the required reliability.

Different ways of determining sample size

This section presents four methods of determining the appropriate size of sample, assuming that a simple random selection method, or its equivalent, is used. Management or researchers can choose any one of the following methods to decide on the size of sample:

1) Judgment
2) Time and cost constraints
3) Formulas based on factors influencing sample size
4) Tables for attribute sample size

Judgment

One of the dangers in using judgment to decide on sample size is the misconception that a large universe requires a correspondingly large sample. Another example, in addition to those given above, is the instance where a researcher decided to use a random sample of 21,000 persons to conduct a survey by a mail questionnaire because the universe consisted of 14 million persons. Experience showed that a much smaller sample size could have achieved better results because the non-response rate remained at 67% after two follow-up mailings. The large funds spent on follow-ups could otherwise have been used more effectively to reduce the non-respondent percentage below 67%, if a sample such as 5000 persons were used.

Time and cost constraints

When data are needed quickly, a small sample size may be the fastest way of obtaining the results. However, a small sample size may sacrifice reliability and confidence in the results. Similarly, with a limited budget for the survey, the sample size must be kept in control to avoid exceeding the available funds, but again with a possible sacrifice of reliability and confidence. In this case, the average cost of collecting and processing the data per 100 units could be estimated from a small pilot sample. When the available fund is divided by the average cost per 100 units, the appropriate sample size is determined.

Factors influencing sample size for variables

In variables sampling, at least five distinct factors must be considered in a disciplined way in order to determine the appropriate size of sample. These are: (1) size of universe; (2) tolerable sampling error expressed in percent; (3) confidence desired that the tolerable error will not be exceeded; (4) variability of the universe, measured by its coefficient of variation; and (5) time and cost constraints. Other factors to consider may be use of stratified sampling or ratio estimation and the amount of detailed data required for analysis.

Before developing the sample-size formula for variables, we expand on the meaning of these five factors in the following paragraphs.

Size of universe — Sample size may be considered from two viewpoints: (1) the actual number of units in the sample (n) and (2) the number of units in the sample as a percentage of the total number of units in the universe, or the sampling fraction, $f = n/N$. Contrary to the lay person's usual conception, the actual numerical size (n) rather than the percentage size is usually more important when considering desired reliability of the results. In fact, if the sampling fraction is less than 5 percent of the universe ($f < .05$), N plays no significant role in determining reliability. In general, "small samples" and "large samples" are defined in terms of the number of units (n) in the sample. A good example is the 1-percent sample of workers comprising the Continuous Work History Sample of the Social Security Administration. A one-percent sample sounds like a small sample; yet, in this case the sample included over one million workers, which is a very large sample in absolute terms. Therefore, we shall think of sample size in terms of the *number* of observations (items) in the sample rather than the percentage of units from the universe.

Even if sample size is thought of in terms of number of units rather than a percentage of the universe, it is often believed that a large sample in absolute size should be taken from a large universe and a small sample from a small universe; in other words, the larger the universe the larger the sample should be. In random sampling where large universes are involved, this is not generally the case. Much more important than universe size (in sample-size determination) are: the extent of variability in the universe (or the coefficient of variation), amount of sampling error tolerable in the yet-to-be estimated parameter, and confidence sought in decision-making. Of course, consideration must always be given to the extent of detailed data required for analysis, and the amount of money and time one is willing to spend to collect the data.

Variability (coefficient of variation) — Suppose we wish to determine the average age (in whole years at last birthday) of school children in kindergarten classes of a large city. If we know that there are about 40,000 kindergarten children in the city, how large a sample should be drawn to estimate the average age of these children using age at last birthday?

Forty thousand is a fairly large universe. Consequently, it would appear to the lay person that a reasonably large sample should be drawn from it. This, however, is an incorrect assumption, because a random sample of about a half-dozen children from this universe will answer the question almost as well as a sample of 600. Why? Because this universe of preschool children has very little variability in age, i.e., it has a small coefficient of variation (or C.V.). Kindergarten children are usually about the same age because of the prescribed admittance age of the school systems. For example, if practically all the children were 5 years old (age at last birthday), a sample of only one child would give the true average, 5 years, since the coefficient of variation is just about zero.

On the other hand, suppose we wish to determine the average age of children in all public schools in the city. Since the ages of public school children range from approximately 5 years to 18 years, it should be obvious that a simple random sample of half a dozen students would not yield a reliable estimate. In general, the more varied the universe the larger is the sample necessary to obtain a reliable estimate. This automatically means that sample size is influenced by the standard deviation or the coefficient of variation of the universe under study. Unless consideration is given to this important factor in sample size, we can miss the mark and either greatly over-sample or under-sample in an effort to get the desired information.

Tolerable error — Ordinarily the larger the sample (in terms of number of units taken from a given universe), the smaller will be the sampling error in the end results. As the sample is increased until it is the size of the whole universe, the error in the final results will continually decrease until there is no error due to sampling. From this we infer that error due to sampling will vary inversely in some way with size of the sample — that is, the smaller the sample the larger the sampling error, and the larger the sample the smaller the sampling error. In fact, there is a simple expression for this relationship, which indicates that sampling error varies inversely with the square root of the size of sample, as follows: Sampling Error $(E) \approx 1/\sqrt{n}$, where sampling error (E) denotes the relative error, or percentage tolerable error, in the main estimate to be derived from the sample, $\approx$ denotes proportionality, and n denotes the number of items in the sample. It follows, therefore, that before we can decide on the size of sample to use in a given survey we must give due consideration to the tolerable error in the end results.

Without this essential consideration we may arbitrarily decide on a sample which is either too large or too small for the intended purpose.

Desired confidence — A further consideration is the confidence that management or the user wishes to have that the maximum tolerable error (E) would not be exceeded. Since random sampling can never give 100 percent assurance that the tolerated sampling error would not be exceeded, a confidence less that 100 percent must be accepted. Whatever confidence is decided upon (for example, 95% assurance), sampling theory offers a corresponding number of equivalent standard errors to achieve that level of confidence.

This discussion is given not for the purpose of confusing readers with the variety of factors involved in determining the size of sample, but to emphasize the fact that the appropriate size of sample (n) is not arrived at by judgment alone, nor haphazardly, nor by instinct, but that a specific amount of tolerable error, level of confidence, and universe variability are basic factors in this determination. A formula for determining size of sample is available that takes into account these sample-size influencing factors, as will be shown later.

The second and main purpose at this point, however, is to emphasize that at least two *management decisions* are required in determining the appropriate sample size. Management must (1) decide the maximum percentage of sampling error (E) that can be tolerated in using the resulting and *most important** estimate to be derived from the sample and (2) the degree of confidence that this tolerable error will not be exceeded. These decisions are fundamentally management decisions, based on the managerial requirements or the purposes of the study. The statistician, where appropriate, may be helpful or consulted in making these decisions.

Extent of detailed data — A simple random sample of 300 families, if it is randomly selected, may be large enough to give a reasonably reliable estimate of the average family income. A sample of this size, however, may not be large enough to yield estimates of the average income of families in each of 40 communities in a State, separately for urban and rural areas. If a total sample of 300 families was used, the number of families in each of the 80 groups or cells (40 community groups times the two area groups) for which a reliable estimate is needed would be so small as to yield estimates subject to large sampling error.

---

*A third decision of management is necessary. When more than one estimate is needed, management must decide which of the several estimates is the most important, since the sample-size formula applies only to one of the several estimates that may be needed.

Consequently, in deciding on the size of sample to use in a given survey, consideration also must be given to the extent to which detailed data will be required. The more detailed data to be analyzed, the larger the overall sample size needs to be. Here, the cost and time factors enter.

Time and cost factors — A final decision with respect to size of sample must also take into consideration cost and time constraints. There are occasions when an estimate of a universe characteristic is needed quickly, even though it may be a rough estimate. This factor alone may determine the size of sample. Generally, the sample size would be small in order to shed quick light on an urgent problem.

On other occasions, the funds allotted for a sample survey are specified. Again, the size of sample would be dictated by the cost constraints and an estimate would be needed of the average cost per case of collecting and processing the required data. The sample size would then be determined by dividing the available funds by the average cost per case.

The factors of cost and time should, in any event, be considered when the size of sample is determined by the basic sample-size formula to follow. The advantage of determining sample size by a precise formula is that it allows management to see the tradeoffs between time and cost on one hand and the resultant reliability and/or confidence in the results on the other hand. If, after the sample size is calculated, it appears that adequate funds are available for the survey, the size of sample should be increased somewhat, judgmentally, to give extra assurance that management's requirements of confidence and tolerance will be met. Why should the size of sample be increased beyond the size indicated by the formula? Answer: Because the variability in the universe (i.e., the population coefficient of variation) usually is not known and, therefore, has to be estimated by a pilot sample, and it may be underestimated. Furthermore, experience has shown that in any survey some units selected in the sample may not be available, others must later be discarded for various reasons and, in mail surveys, we must allow for non-response losses from the sample. Thus, the augmented sample will give greater assurance that the results will fall within the required bounds of reliability and confidence.

Formula for sample size for variables

A formula for sample size for variables can be derived logically based on the foregoing influencing factors, with two modifications based on experience in the field. What is logically necessary to know is the direction of the influence of each factor on the size of sample (n), i.e., as the factor increases, n increases (direct relationship) or as the factor increases, n decreases (inverse relationship). These relationships are outlined for each factor in the following table.

Influencing factor	Symbol for the factor	Direction of influence
1. Size of the universe	N	direct
2. Tolerable sampling error (percent, expressed in decimals)	E	inverse
3. Desired confidence (expressed in number of standard errors)	Z	direct
4. Variability of items in the universe (expressed by the coefficient of variation)	V	direct
5. Time and funds allotted	$	direct

In any formula for determining sample size (n), directly-influencing factors are entered in the numerator and inversely-influencing factors are entered in the denominator. Holding off consideration of the time and cost factors until after n is computed, a building-block formula for size of sample for variables sampling can be presented as follows:

$$n \approx \frac{N\,Z\,V}{E}, \text{ where, as indicated above,}$$

N is the size of the population, Z is the number of standard errors required to provide the desired level of confidence, V is the coefficient of variation of the universe for the main characteristic being estimated, and E is the tolerable error in percent of the estimated mean or total (expressed in decimals).

This building-block formula needs two modifications to reflect the relative sensitivity of each of its factors. First, it is a fact that N has but a minor influence on n. For example, when the sample size is less than 5% of N (i.e., $f = n / N < 0.05$), any increase in the universe size will hardly cause an increase in the required size of sample. In contrast, sample size is highly sensitive to a change in any of the remaining three factors E, Z, and V. For example, increasing the tolerable error (E) from 5% to 10% can sometimes cut the size of sample in half or more. The same is true for Z and V.

To reflect the relative insensitivity of N, we minimize its effect by dividing the building-block formula by N, but to avoid its complete elimination we also add the factors Z and V to the denominator. To reflect the relatively high sensitivity to sample-size of changes in E, Z, and V, we square each of these factors in the numerator and the denominator. As a result, the sample size formula for variables becomes:

$$n = \frac{N\ Z^2\ V^2}{N\ E^2 + Z^2\ V^2}.^*$$

When the universe size is large, i.e., the sampling fraction, f, is expected to be less than 5%, this sample-size formula is simplified to the following:

$$n = \frac{Z^2\ V^2}{E^2}.$$

Since two of the essential requirements in sampling are the tolerable error (E) in the main estimate and the desired confidence (Z), these two are generally determined after discussion between the statistician and the users of the data. Therefore, only an estimate of the universe coefficient of variation (V) is needed in order to use this formula to solve for size of sample, n. The coefficient of variation of the universe may be estimated in three ways: (1) on the basis of the known coefficient of variation of the universe or a related universe based on a past survey; (2) on the basis of a judgment estimate concerning the variability in the universe under study; or (3) on the basis of a V-value derived from a small pilot sample of about 50 items randomly selected from the universe before the regular, larger sample is selected. Note that this pilot sample may later be added to the larger sample if randomly selected.

An example — We wish to know the size of sample to use in order to estimate the mean and total earnings of individuals in a large company of 10,000 employees (i.e., N = 10,000 employees). We are willing to tolerate an error in the mean (or total) of as much as 5% or .05 in either direction, with 95% confidence (i.e., Z = 1.96) that this error will not be exceeded. Using a small pilot sample, we estimate

---

*Algebraic proof of the correctness of this formula can be derived by solving for n in the formula for the relative sampling error (E) of an estimated mean when it is converted to any desired confidence, indicated by Z (number of standard errors).

Thus, $E = \dfrac{Z\ \sigma_x\ \sqrt{1 - \dfrac{n}{N}}}{\overline{X}\ \sqrt{n}}$. When V is substituted for $\dfrac{\sigma_x}{\overline{X}}$ we get: $E = \dfrac{Z\ V\ \sqrt{1 - \dfrac{n}{N}}}{\sqrt{n}}$.

When solved for n algebraically, the resulting formula for n is exactly the one shown above.

the coefficient of variation for individual earnings in the company to be 70% or 0.7. The desired size of sample would be:

$$n = \frac{N\ Z^2\ V^2}{N\ E^2 + Z^2\ V^2} = \frac{(10,000)\ (1.96)^2\ (0.7)^2}{(10,000)\ (.05)^2 + (1.96)^2\ (0.7)^2} = 700 \text{ individuals.}$$

This computation would guide us to use a simple random sample of 700 individuals aimed at meeting the specified precision (± 5 percent) with the desired confidence (95 percent). In this case, with 700 individuals in the sample, the chances would be about 95% (or odds of 19 to 1) that the estimated mean will be within ±5% of the true mean (or true total).

As indicated earlier, it is good practice to increase the sample size somewhat to protect against possible underestimation of V, and to allow for non-response and other loss of units in the sample. If the non-response rate is large, for example, the reliability of the resulting estimates may be seriously impaired by having to rely on a smaller sample size than required. In this kind of situation, it may be well to increase the sample to, say, 1000. This is a judgment decision, or it can be based on an estimate of the response rate obtained from a pilot sample or from previous studies of a similar sort.

If management were willing to make a decision with a confidence of 90% (or odds of 9 to 1) and still tolerate a sampling error no larger than 5%, the formula would point to a sample of 507 employees, as shown below:

$$n = \frac{N\ Z^2\ V^2}{N\ E^2 + Z^2\ V^2} = \frac{(10,000)\ (1.65)^2\ (0.7)^2}{(10,000)\ (.05)^2 + (1.65)^2\ (0.7)^2} = 507 \text{ individuals.}$$

It is to be noted that a reduction in the desired level of confidence from 95% to 90% results in a 28% reduction in the size of sample.

Formula for attribute sampling, based on influencing factors

When management decides that the most important characteristic to be estimated is an attribute, such as the percentage (p) or total number (Np) of cases which are not in compliance with regulations or are in error, a sample size formula can be derived by logic based on the factors which influence sample size (n). As in the case of variables sampling, we list the influencing factors and their direction of influence as follows.

Influencing factor	Symbol for the factor	Direction of influence
1. Size of the universe	N	direct
2. Tolerable sampling error (in percentage points)*	E	inverse
3. Desired confidence (expressed in number of standard errors)	Z	direct
4. Magnitude of the percentage sought	p	direct
5. Time and funds allotted	$	direct

As in the case of variables, we establish the building block formula by placing the direct-influencing factors in the numerator and the inverse-influencing factors in the denominator. Then, the same two adjustments required in the variables sampling building block formula are made — one for the relatively small influence of N and the other for the very large influences of Z and E on the resulting sample size. The following sample size formula for attributes results after these adjustments are made:**

$$n = \frac{N \ Z^2 \ p \ (1-p)}{N \ E^2 \ + \ Z^2 \ p \ (1-p)}.$$

It is important to be aware of the meaning of E. In the variables formula for n, E is expressed as a relative error (percent). In the attributes formula above, E is expressed in percentage points or absolute error of p. This distinction is based on the fact that in attribute sampling we need to make a reasonable guess of p which is in absolute units. Thus, it is simple to express the tolerable error (E) in the same units, which is percentage points.

Regarding a reasonable estimate of p — The non-compliance (or other attribute) rate, p in the above formula, can be estimated on the basis of prior experience with the particular universe involved, or by a pilot sample made in advance of the main survey. As a last resort, p can be assumed to be .5 (i.e., 50%), the extreme case which will result

---

* Note that contrary to variables sampling, the authors recommend that tolerable error (E) in attributes sampling be expressed in absolute units (percentage points) rather than in percent.

** An algebraic solution for n can be obtained by solving the following sampling error

formula for n: S.E. or $E = Z \sqrt{\dfrac{\left[p(1-p)\left(1 - \dfrac{n}{N}\right) \right]}{(n-1)}}$.

in the largest possible sample. If the resulting size of sample is beyond the time and cost constraints of the survey, n might be adjusted downward by judgment.

An example — What size of sample (n) should the Housing Authority use in making a sample survey to estimate the percentage (p) of vacant apartments in a given city with 25,000 apartments (N=25,000). Management is willing to tolerate a maximum sampling error of 5 percentage points (E=.05) but wishes to have 90% confidence (Z=1.65) that the indicated tolerable error will not be exceeded.

Here, we have all the required factors for the above sample-size formula except p, the expected percentage of vacancies. However, a vacancy survey made last year yielded a 10% vacancy rate. By assuming that this percentage has not changed much from last year, we can now solve for n:

$$n = \frac{N\ Z^2\ p\ (1-p)}{N\ E^2\ +\ Z^2\ p\ (1-p)} = \frac{(25,000)\ (1.65)^2(.1)\ (.9)}{(25,000)\ (.05)^2\ +\ (1.65)^2(.1)\ (.9)} = 98 \text{ apartments.}$$

To play it safe, and for the reasons given earlier, we can increase this sample size by about 20%, thus making n=120 apartments, if the time and cost constraints permit it.

It is to be noted that an assumption of p=.5 will yield the largest possible size of 269 apartments, or nearly three times the above size. This sample size might be preferable if it is acceptable under the time and cost constraints and a good estimate of p is not available from a previous survey of this universe.

A special note regarding the sampling fraction — The forgoing sample size formula becomes less complex-looking if we can assume that the sampling fraction is almost surely turn out to be less than 5%. The short formula for n is:

$$n = \frac{Z^2\ p\ (1-p)}{E^2}\ .$$

As an illustration, if p is assumed to be 0.5 (i.e., 50%),

$$n = \frac{(1.65)^2\ (.5)\ (.5)}{(.05)^2} = \frac{0.681}{0.0025} = 272 \text{ apartments.}$$

This sample size is practically the same (272 versus 269) when computed by the more general formula and assuming p=.5.

Tables for attributes sample size

A large number of tables have been developed from which the sample size for attributes can be determined.* When using these tables it is necessary to determine the size of universe (N) under study, the desired confidence (Z), the tolerable sampling error (E) expressed in percentage points, and the expected percentage of cases with the attribute (p).

The tables on the next two pages illustrate the many tables available for the different factors influencing sample-size. The tables, however, are limited to certain specific values of p, E, and Z, while the formulas for sample size are not so limited. For example, the formula can use any p, any E, and any Z, depending on management's determinations, while the tables generally are limited to a few such values.

---

*Such tables have been compiled by staff members of the U.S. Air Force and Herbert Arkin in *Handbook for Auditing and Accounting*, Third Edition, 1984, McGraw-Hill Book Company.

Table 9.2

Sample size for attributes, for specified degree of assurance, maximum tolerable error, and indicated universe size

For random samples only, where guessed percentage does not exceed 5%

SAMPLE SIZE

	Based on 95% assurance				Based on 99% assurance			
	that the percent in the sample will **not differ** from that in the universe by more than:							
Number in Universe	±1%	±2%	±3%	±4%	±1%	±2%	±3%	±4%
150				65				
200				73				99
250			112	79				110
300			121	83				119
350			129	86				126
400			135	89			187	132
450			140	91			197	137
500		239	144	93			206	142
600		259	152	96			221	148
700		276	157	98			234	154
800		291	162	100		397	244	158
900		303	166	101		420	252	162
1,000		314	169	102		441	260	165
1,500		350	179	106		517	284	174
2,000	954	372	184	108		565	298	179
2,500	1,055	386	188	109		599	307	183
3,000	1,135	396	190	110		624	314	185
3,500	1,200	404	192	110	1,659	643	318	187
4,000	1,253	410	193	111	1,763	658	322	188
4,500	1,299	414	194	111	1,854	671	325	189
5,000	1,337	418	195	112	1,934	681	327	190
6,000	1,400	424	196	112	2,067	697	331	191
7,000	1,448	428	197	112	2,174	708	334	192
8,000	1,486	432	198	112	2,261	717	336	192
9,000	1,517	434	198	113	2,335	725	337	193
10,000	1,543	436	199	113	2,397	731	338	193
15,000	1,627	443	200	113	2,605	749	342	194
20,000	1,672	446	201	113	2,723	758	344	195
25,000	1,701	448	201	114	2,799	764	345	195
30,000	1,720	449	201	114	2,852	768	346	196
40,000	1,745	451	202	114	2,922	773	347	196
50,000	1,761	452	202	114	2,965	776	348	196
75,000	1,782	453	202	114	3,025	780	349	196
100,000	1,792	454	202	114	3,056	782	349	197
200,000	1,809	455	203	114	3,103	785	350	197
500,000	1,818	456	203	114	3,132	787	350	197
Over 500,000	1,825	456	203	114	3,152	788	350	197

Source: U.S. Department of the Air Force

Table 9.3
Sample size for attributes, for specified degree of assurance, maximum tolerable error, and indicated universe size

For random samples only, where guessed percentage does not exceed 10%

SAMPLE SIZE

	Based on 95% assurance					Based on 99% assurance				
Number in Universe	±1%	±2%	±3%	±4%	±5%	±1%	±2%	±3%	±4%	±5%
150					72					
200					82					
250				116	89					122
300				126	95					133
350				134	99					142
400			196	141	103				193	150
450			207	146	106				204	156
500			217	151	108				214	162
600			234	159	113				230	171
700			248	165	116			341	244	178
800			260	170	118			363	255	184
900		441	269	174	120			382	264	189
1,000		464	278	178	122			399	272	193
1,500		549	306	189	127		748	460	299	206
2,000		604	322	195	129		855	498	315	213
2,500		642	333	199	131		935	525	325	218
3,000		671	341	202	132		997	544	332	221
3,500	1,739	693	346	204	133		1,047	558	337	224
4,000	1,855	711	351	205	134		1,087	569	341	225
4,500	1,955	725	354	206	134		1,121	578	345	227
5,000	2,044	737	357	207	135		1,150	586	347	228
6,000	2,194	756	361	209	135	2,993	1,196	598	351	230
7,000	2,314	769	364	210	136	3,223	1,231	606	354	231
8,000	2,414	780	367	210	136	3,420	1,258	613	357	232
9,000	2,498	789	368	211	136	3,590	1,281	618	358	233
10,000	2,569	796	370	212	136	3,739	1,299	622	360	233
15,000	2,810	817	375	213	137	4,272	1,358	635	364	235
20,000	2,948	828	377	214	137	4,599	1,389	642	366	236
25,000	3,037	835	378	214	138	4,821	1,409	646	368	237
30,000	3,100	840	379	215	138	4,981	1,422	649	369	237
40,000	3,182	846	380	215	138	5,196	1,439	653	370	237
50,000	3,234	850	381	215	138	5,335	1,450	655	370	238
75,000	3,305	854	382	215	138	5,532	1,464	658	371	238
100,000	3,342	857	383	216	138	5,636	1,471	659	372	238
200,000	3,398	861	383	216	138	5,799	1,482	661	373	239
500,000	3,433	863	384	216	138	5,902	1,489	663	373	239
Over 500,000	3,457	864	384	216	138	5,972	1,493	664	373	239

that the percent in the sample will not differ from that in the universe by more than:

Source: U.S. Department of the Air Force

Stratified Random Sampling

Estimation

Variables — In Chapter 7 we demonstrated the improved precision achieved in estimates derived from stratified random samples. The general method of estimating a total from a stratified random sample involves first estimating each stratum total by $N\overline{X}$ and then adding the separate strata totals, i.e., by $N_1\overline{X}_1 + N_2\overline{X}_2 + \dots$. Here, the size of each stratum is identified by N_1 units, N_2 units, etc., and each stratum mean is $\overline{X}_1$, $\overline{X}_2$, etc. In more compact form, the estimated total is $\sum_{h=1}^{L} N_h\overline{X}_h$, where h identifies the stratum number which goes from 1 to L, the number of strata in the universe.

From this estimated total we derive the estimated mean for the universe by:

$$\overline{X} = \frac{N_1\overline{X}_1 + N_2\overline{X}_2 + \dots}{N}.$$

Attributes — It is fairly simple to extend to attributes the method of estimation presented for variables. The estimated total possessing the attribute is: $\sum_{h=1}^{L} N_h p_h = N_1 p_1 + N_2 p_2 + N_3 p_3 + $ etc., where N_1, N_2, etc., are the strata sizes and p_1, p_2, etc., are the estimated strata percentages with the attribute (expressed in decimals).

The overall estimated universe percentage with the attribute is:

$$p = \frac{\sum N_h p_h}{N}.$$

Measuring sampling error

Variables — The previous formulas for measuring the standard error of estimated means and percentages (and corresponding totals) are directly applicable to each stratum. However, they need modification when they are combined to yield the standard error for the entire universe.

In stratified sampling, each stratum is treated as a separate universe (called a sub-universe) which is part of the overall universe of interest. Therefore, if a simple random sample is used to derive a mean for each stratum, the standard error of the stratum mean may be computed by the simple random sampling formulas previously presented. However, the question is: How can we combine the separate sub-universe standard errors to compute the standard error of the universe mean or total?

The answer to this problem is based on a principle of sampling called the **Variance Principle**, which states that *the sampling variance of a sum is the sum of the separate component variances*. The term *sampling variance* means the square of the standard error of the specified estimate. Therefore, we present the essence of the above principle, as follows:

$$\left(\begin{smallmatrix} \text{Standard error of} \\ \text{the estimated universe mean} \end{smallmatrix}\right)^2 = \left(\begin{smallmatrix} \text{Standard error of} \\ \text{stratum \#1 mean} \end{smallmatrix}\right)^2 + \left(\begin{smallmatrix} \text{Standard error of} \\ \text{stratum \#2 mean} \end{smallmatrix}\right)^2 + \text{ etc. } \dots$$

In symbols, this formula translates to:

$$\left(\sigma_{\overline{X}}\right)^2 = \left(\sigma_{\overline{X}_1}\right)^2 + \left(\sigma_{\overline{X}_2}\right)^2 + \text{ etc. } \dots.$$

It would now be easy to obtain the standard error of the universe mean by taking the square root of both sides of the equation. However, another statistical requirements, namely, obtaining a weighted average needs to be taken into consideration. By assigning each stratum a weight (w) equivalent to its size as a percent of the total universe size, the weight for stratum #1 is $w_1 = N_1 / N$; $w_2 = N_2 / N$, and so forth. When these weights are squared and multiplied by their respective standard errors squared, we obtain the following:

$$\text{Variance of universe mean} = \left(\sigma_{\overline{X}}\right)^2 = \left(w_1\right)^2\left(\sigma_{\overline{X}_1}\right)^2 + \left(w_2\right)^2\left(\sigma_{\overline{X}_2}\right)^2 + \text{ etc. } \dots,$$

and when the square root of each side is taken, the formula for the standard error of the estimated universe mean becomes:

$$\sigma_{\overline{X} \text{ stratified}} = \sqrt{\left(w_1\right)^2\left(\sigma_{\overline{X}_1}\right)^2 + \left(w_2\right)^2\left(\sigma_{\overline{X}_2}\right)^2 + \dots}\ .$$

Using the same Variance Principle, the formula for the standard error of the estimated *total value* of the universe characteristic (e.g., dollars) derived from a stratified random sample, is:

$$\sigma_{\sum N_i \overline{X}_i} = \sqrt{\left(N_1\right)^2\left(\sigma_{\overline{X}_1}\right)^2 + \left(N_2\right)^2\left(\sigma_{\overline{X}_2}\right)^2 + \dots}\ .$$

When dealing with an estimated total, the weights are automatically taken care of by the strata sizes (N_1, N_2, etc.).

Attributes — Using the same Variance Principle for attributes, the standard error formula of the overall estimated percentage, p, derived from a stratified random sample is:

$$\sigma_p = \sqrt{(w_1)^2(\sigma_{p_1})^2 + (w_2)^2(\sigma_{p_2})^2 + \ldots}\;.$$

Again, using the Variance Principle, the standard error of the estimated total number of cases possessing a given attribute in the universe derived from a stratified random sample, is given by the formula:

$$\sigma_{\Sigma N_i P_i} = \sqrt{(N_1)^2(\sigma_{p_1})^2 + (N_2)^2(\sigma_{p_2})^2 + \ldots}\;.$$

Strata sample sizes

By using stratified sampling, where appropriate, we can generally expect a smaller standard error than would result from a simple random sample or its equivalent. Therefore, the question arises: Should we use the sample size (n) determined by the foregoing simple random sampling formulas, or reduce the sample size to some extent and take advantage of the greater efficiency of stratified sampling and still achieve the original management requirements of tolerable error and confidence?

The answer to this question should be provided by management, depending primarily on cost constraints. If funds are not a problem, it would seem preferable to stick with the size of sample (n) determined by the simple random sampling formulas and thereby derive estimates which very likely will yield a more reliable estimate than that specified originally by management. Conversely, if fund limitations are an obstacle, it would seem desirable to reduce the sample size determined by the formulas consistent with available funds.

If the decision is to use the sample size determined by the simple random-sample formula, another question arises: How can we allocate n to the strata in order to achieve the most reliable estimate or the smallest standard error?

The following three choices are available:

(1) Allocate n to the strata proportionally. This means that the sampling fraction, f = n/N, will be applied to each stratum as follows:

Stratum 1 — $f N_1 = n_1$,

Stratum 2 — $f N_2 = n_2$, and so forth.

(2) Allocate n to the strata non-proportionally, using judgment guided by stratum size or relative importance of each stratum.

(3) Allocate n to the strata non-proportionally, using the *optimum-allocation* formula referred to in Chapter 7. This method generally will yield the smallest possible standard error for the most important estimate.

The optimum allocation formula uses the following symbols:

N_1, N_2, etc. represent strata sizes,

n_1, n_2, etc. represent strata sample sizes,

σ_1, σ_2, etc. represent strata standard deviations,

p_1, p_2, etc. represent strata attribute percentages (as decimals), and

n is the overall or total sample size computed by the formulas given earlier.

Optimum Allocation for variables —

$$n_1 = \frac{N_1\sigma_1\ (n)}{N_1\sigma_1 + N_2\sigma_2 + \text{etc. ...}}$$

$$n_2 = \frac{N_2\sigma_2\ (n)}{N_1\sigma_1 + N_2\sigma_2 + ...}$$

$$n_3 = \text{etc. ... .}$$

Optimum Allocation for attributes —

$$n_1 = \frac{N_1\sqrt{p_1(1-p_1)}\ (n)}{N_1\sqrt{p_1(1-p_1)} + N_2\sqrt{p_2(1-p_2)} + \text{etc. ...}}$$

$$n_2 = \frac{N_2\sqrt{p_2(1-p_2)}\ (n)}{N_1\sqrt{p_1(1-p_1)} + N_2\sqrt{p_2(1-p_2)} + ...}$$

$$n_3 = \text{etc. ... .}$$

If it is decided to use the optimum allocation method, the question now arises: How can we determine the strata standard deviations (σ_1, σ_2, etc.) for variables sampling or the strata percentages (p_1, p_2, etc.) for attribute sampling? The answer is: Either use small pilot samples from each stratum to approximate them or use the best judgment based on past studies of the universe of interest.

An illustration of proportional and judgmental non-proportional allocation of n to the strata is given below for a hypothetical universe (N) of 1000 vouchers and a sample (n) of 100 vouchers. Here, f = 100 / 1000 = 0.10.

Allocation Method	Stratum Size			Universe
	$N_1 = 50$	$N_2 = 200$	$N_3 = 750$	$N = 1000$
Proportional	$f_1 = .1$ $n_1 = 5$	$f_2 = .1$ $n_2 = 20$	$f_3 = .1$ $n_3 = 75$	$f = .1$ $n = 100$
Non-proportional	$f_1 = 1$ $n_1 = 50$	$f_2 = .1$ $n_2 = 20$	$f_3 = .04$ $n_3 = 30$	$f = .1$ $n = 100$

Summary

This chapter covered three main elements of a sampling system, namely, estimation procedures, sample-size determination, and measurement of sampling error. The other three elements — problem formulation, methods of selecting random samples, and the importance of controlling non-sampling errors were covered in Chapters 7 and 8. Thus, all six major elements of a sampling system were covered in the last three chapters.

Four types of estimates frequently derived from random samples were covered and demonstrated. These estimates are: $\bar{X}$, $N\bar{X}$, p, and Np.

In addition, the chapter covered five different ways of presenting estimates and also a way of expressing confidence not only in the form of percentages but also in the form of odds. Thus, 90 percent confidence can be expressed as odds of 9 to 1; 80 percent as 4 to 1; etc. In this form, recipients of sample-derived estimates are made aware of the real meaning of confidence and also that there is an element of chance in sampling.

Considerable attention was given to stratified sampling, including how to allocate the overall sample size to the strata in order to achieve the smallest standard error, how to derive unbiased estimates, and the how to correctly compute the standard error for all strata combined.

Four formulas for determining appropriate sample-size were derived by logical inference — two for variables and two for attributes. In variables sampling, a logical way of determining the appropriate size of sample (n) is by reference to the factors which influence the size of sample, namely: the size of universe (N); the maximum tolerable error (E) in the required estimate, expressed in decimals; the desired confidence that this maximum error will not be exceeded, expressed in terms of the number of standard errors (Z) which will yield this confidence; and the coefficient of variation, V, also expressed in decimals. When these factors are considered in terms of the direction of their influence on n, the following formula for variables results:

$$n = \frac{N\ Z^2\ V^2}{N\ E^2 + Z^2\ V^2}\ .$$

When it is known that the universe is so large as to yield a sampling fraction (f = n/N) of less than .05 (i.e., f < 5%), N can be eliminated and the following simpler formula is available for sample-size determination: $n = \dfrac{Z^2\ V^2}{E^2}\ .$

For attributes sampling, the following sample size formula was presented:

$$n = \frac{N\ Z^2\ p\ (1-p)}{N\ E^2 + Z^2\ p\ (1-p)}\ .$$

Again, as in variables sampling, if the sampling fraction is expected to be less than 5%, the following simpler formula can be used: $n = \dfrac{Z^2\ p\ (1-p)}{E^2}$. In the attribute sampling formulas, E, the tolerable error of the estimated p, is expressed in percentage points, i.e., in decimals, rather than as a percentage (of p) as in variables sampling.

Problems

1. Here is an example of practical statistical sampling:

   An estimate was needed of the average and total number of miles driven last year by the 50,000 owners of a given type of passenger automobile. A systematic random sample of 1,600 persons who own this type of automobile was selected for a mail survey. The resulting estimates were: $\overline{X}$ = 8,000 miles, σ_x = 6,000 miles, and $N\overline{X}$ = 400,000,000 miles.

Question: How reliable is the estimated mean mileage per year and the estimated total miles driven by the 50,000 automobile owners?

(a) Assuming no significant non-response problem, the standard error of the estimated mean is:

$$\sigma_{\overline{X}} = \frac{\sigma_x\sqrt{(1-f)}}{\sqrt{n}} = \frac{6{,}000\sqrt{1-\dfrac{1{,}600}{50{,}000}}}{\sqrt{1{,}600}} = \pm147.6 \text{ miles.}$$

(b) Since the standard error of an estimated total is $N\sigma_{\overline{X}}$, the resulting standard error of the estimated total miles driven is $(50{,}000)(147.6) = \pm7{,}380{,}000$ miles.

(c) In percentage form, the estimated mean is subject to a sampling error no larger than $\dfrac{\sigma_{\overline{X}}}{\overline{X}} = \dfrac{147.6}{8{,}000} = \pm1.84\%$. The same relative sampling error is applicable to the estimated total mileage.

(d) Presentation: Our confidence would be 68 percent (or odds of 2 to 1) that the sampling error of the estimated mean mileage is not greater than 147.6 miles, or 1.84%. In the form of a confidence interval, this presentation would be: The true mean is between 7,852 and 8,148 miles, with 68% confidence (i.e., the odds are 2 to 1) that this conclusion is correct.

2. In a given fact-finding survey to determine the average retail price charged per ton of hard coal by retail coal dealers, the mean price calculated from the random sample was $60 a ton.

(a) If the sample contained 225 respondents ($n = 225$) out of a total of 2000 coal dealers in the universe and the standard deviation of the various prices quoted by the respondents was $25, what was the standard error of the estimated mean?

(b) If you wanted to be practically certain (369 to 1 odds) that the interval would include the true mean, what would be the range within which you can state the true mean lies? Express the answer in the appropriate statistical symbols.

(c) Present your estimate in (b) in terms of maximum absolute error and then maximum relative error.

3. A certain publishing company made a sample survey to estimate the number of persons who read one of its magazines in a given

month. A systematic random sample of 1,600 was selected from the list of 40,000 regular subscribers. They found the following: Mean number of readers per subscription in the month, 2.4 persons and standard deviation of the number of readers, 0.4 persons.

Question:

(a) How many persons read this particular magazine in the given month?

(b) Present the estimate in terms of relative error with 99% confidence.

(c) Would this estimate represent all readers of this magazine?

(d) Why?

4. At a given point of time, a simple random sample of 25 gas meter readings was selected from a universe of 1500 meters in a given district, with the following readings in cubic feet: 32; 40; 16; 29; 60; 20; 25; 30; 35; 42; 55; 38; 14; 25; 70; 45; 47; 49; 22; 18; 35; 32; 30; 24; 62.

With the results of the above sample, do the following:

(a) Estimate the total cubic feet of gas used in the entire district at the time of the survey.

(b) State the standard error of the estimated total: (1) in absolute terms (i.e., cubic feet), and (2) as a percent of the estimated total.

(c) Indicate the maximum amount of error you would have to tolerate in the estimated total cubic feet of gas used if you wanted to have confidence of about 100 to 1 that the sampling error would not be greater.

5. The percentage of automobiles carrying two or more passengers to work on a given morning in your city was 20 percent. If this percentage was estimated from a systematic random sample of 400 cars out of 40,000 driven to work in the city on that morning, what was the standard error of the estimated percentage? Present the finding with a 90% confidence interval.

6. Here is an example of sample size determination: Suppose a company employing 2,500 workers wanted to estimate their workers' average and total annual earnings from outside sources. Management was willing to tolerate a maximum error of 5% in the estimated total outside earnings (E = .05). In addition, management wanted to be practically certain that the error would

not be greater than 5%; hence, the confidence factor, Z, had to be 3 standard errors. Not knowing the coefficient of variation of annual outside earnings, the company management analyst used data from a prior survey of outside earnings and guessed that it be 190% (V = 1.9). The size of sample (n) was then computed as follows:

$$n = \frac{N\ Z^2\ V^2}{N\ E^2 + Z^2\ V^2} = \frac{(2500)(3)^2(1.9)^2}{(2500)(.05)^2 + (3)^2(1.9)^2} = \frac{81,225}{38.74} = 2,097 \text{ employees.}$$

Question for the reader: Assuming this is too large a sample in terms of costs, what alternatives are open to reduce the sample size?

7. We wish to determine by an audit the extent to which student loans have been fully paid by graduates from a given school. All together, 500 loans were made during the period studied. How large a sample should be selected when management believes that about a third have been fully paid. They are seeking an estimate with a tolerable error no larger than four percentage points with 90% confidence. What sample size should they use?

8. We wish to estimate the mean wages of workers in a given week in an organization employing 10,000 workers. From past experience we know that the coefficient of variation of weekly wages in this company is about 100% (V = 1). Assuming we can tolerate an error of as much as 15 percent in the estimated mean, but we wish to have a confidence of 95% that the error will not be greater than that, how many workers should be included in a digital random sample (based on social security number) to make this estimate?

9. The Census of Population indicated that in a given large city 12.6 percent of the population were persons aged 65 and over. An estimate of the current proportion of people aged 65 and over in the city was needed by a life insurance company. Assume that a register of the population of that city was available from which to select a random sample.

   (a) How would you select the sample?

   (b) If you were aiming to achieve an estimate with no larger a sampling error than 5 percentage points with 95.4 percent confidence, how many persons would you include in the sample?

(c) If the data were to be obtained by a mail questionnaire, how many additional persons would you include to allow for non-response?

10. Show how a 95.4 percent confidence is equivalent to 21 to 1 odds and 99.73 percent confidence is equivalent 369 to 1 odds of not exceeding the tolerated sampling error.

11. Management wishes to determine the total amount of outstanding credit at the end of a given month on their 12,000 charge accounts. They want to be 95% certain that the error of the estimate will not exceed 2%. Past experience indicated a coefficient of variation of 50% for this universe. Determine the required sample size.

12. In an audit to determine the percentage of ineligible recipients of Food Stamps in a given county, a government agency wanted to be 90% certain that the ineligibility rate estimated from the sample would be within one percentage point of the true ineligibility rate for that county. What size of sample should they use to make the audit, if the total number of families receiving such assistance was 25,000 and the Administrator thought that the ineligibility rate was probably about 5%?

13. What are the possible trade-offs when sample size must be made smaller to save data collection costs, i.e., what can (or will) be given up when the sample size is reduced?

14. The 12 divisions of a certain agency contributed the amounts (in thousands of dollars) shown below to the annual March of Dimes drive.

Division	Amount	Division	Amount
1	$ 3	7	$ 4
2	16	8	4
3	5	9	2
4	20	10	21
5	2	11	1
6	15	12	3
		Total	$96

(a) With a random sample of six (n=6) divisions, estimate the total amount contributed by the agency, using the following three sampling methods:

(1) Simple random sampling

(2) Systematic random sampling

(3) Stratified random sampling

(b) Compute the actual error of your estimated total and rank the three sampling methods on their accuracy percent.

(c) Compute the standard error of each estimated total using your sample data.

(d) Present your estimated total in the form of a 95% confidence interval.

(e) Why is the systematic sample result so poor?

15. A universe of 5,000 payment vouchers of a given agency was audited as of a given date to determine the extent of compliance with internal control requirements. A systematic random sample of 400 vouchers was selected. Six percent of the vouchers in the sample were determined to be in non-compliance status.

(a) Calculate the standard error of this percentage.

(b) Present your finding with a 90% confidence interval.

(c) Estimate the total number of vouchers which did not meet the compliance requirements.

16. To estimate the average monthly rent of apartment dwellers, the size of sample (number of apartment renters) for New York City should be about twice as large as for Chicago, since the population of apartment dwellers in New York City is about twice as large even though the variability in rentals is about the same. Is this true of false? Explain your answer.

17. Suppose you wish to obtain about equal reliability in the results of the four surveys specified below. Indicate from which population you would select the largest sample, the next largest, and so forth, and explain the basis for you choice.

(a) Average age of all students in the first year of high school in the United States.

(b) Average age of all students attending evening college classes in the United States.

(c) Average age of all male workers in the United States.

(d) Average age of all male persons in the United States.

18. If the coefficient of variation in two universes is the same and their size is not much different, it is fairly safe to conclude that a 10-percent sample from the first universe will give more reliable results than a one-percent sample from the second universe. True or false? Explain.

19. A 0.1 percent sample taken from a universe containing 10 million items may be considered a large sample. True or false? Explain.

Chapter 10

Significant and Insignificant Differences

*"We use Reason for improving the Sciences: whereas we ought to use the Sciences for improving our Reason."**

....

A local newspaper article decries the rising juvenile delinquency and backs its conclusion with "facts and figures" which show that the number of juvenile arrests this year is 5 percent higher than last year.

In another part of the country, a newspaper headlines the need for better state highways, claiming that automobile fatalities in the State are 4 percent higher than last year and 12 percent higher than the national average.

In yet another publication, a claim is made that drug user arrests by local law enforcement authorities have increased significantly in the past year.

Inferences of this nature abound, not only in public documents but in the internal management of business and government organizations and in personal decisions made by many individuals. To the executives and administrators concerned with such matters, these can be inferences of great import.

Do the quoted "facts" support such assertions? How likely are they to be correct? Is it not a fact that some differences from one date to another or from one place to another are mostly due to chance or based on incomplete data and are, therefore, not real changes in level or trend?

In this chapter, we are concerned specifically with finding a way to judge whether claims of so-called "statistical facts" or claims based on hearsay or even on random samples can be accepted as facts by scientific tests of their significance. The danger of automatically

---

*Antoine Arnauld, *The Port-Royal Logic*, 1662.

accepting findings from so-called fact-finding surveys are often far-reaching. The fundamental problem is how to avoid the pitfalls of making wrong decisions or of accepting figures as significant when they are not.

In reality, numerous decisions are continually being based on researchers' experiments and tests. The conclusions based on these studies affect every one of us, as indicated by a sampling of newspaper headlines:

"Heart Patients Prosper on Mediterranean Diet"

"Study Calls Polyp Removal Effective Method to
　　Prevent Colon Cancer"

"Moderate Alcohol Intake Decreases Risk of Heart Attack"

"Study Links Level of Lead in Blood to IQ"

"Aspirin Lessens Men's Risk of Stroke"

"Study Links Genes, Risk of Divorce"

"Drugs May Top Alcohol as Highway Hazard"

"Plunger Device No Better Than CPR"

A basic law of statistics, illustrated in earlier chapters, is the *principle of universal variation.* Under this principle, some amount of normal variation is to be expected in every phenomenon, process, or activity, since it is caused by the many unavoidable natural or chance factors inherent in life's phenomena. The basic question in drawing inferences of this type is: *How much variation is due to normal conditions and chance (and therefore a result of the usual or non-identifiable causes) and how much variation may be ascribed to significant or identifiable causes, usually called assignable causes?* Statistical theory and methodology provide a basis for distinguishing between significant and insignificant variations with great confidence or slight risk. This chapter shows how sound inferences may be made by reliance on sampling theory, the principle of probability, and the standard characteristics of normal distributions.

Decisions with Known Risk

Previous chapters have indicated that, under specified conditions, the *sampling distribution* of a random variable (such as many independent equal-sized random sample estimates of a population mean or percentage) tends to form a normal frequency distribution. In this and other normal distributions, the percentage of items or cases falling within the mean plus or minus a specified number of standard deviations can be determined readily. It is known that, for example, in the sampling distribution of means, about half of the estimated means will be above the average of the distribution and about half below it; that about 95 percent of the estimates will fall within two standard deviations around the average; that about 99 percent will fall within 2.58 standard deviations around it; and so forth. These and other percentages are shown more precisely in the normal curve table, Appendix B.

The principles of normal distributions and probability are the major principles which in many situations can be relied on to determine whether a difference is significant, with a known chance of being wrong.* A *significant difference* is one which *has a high likelihood of being caused by some factor or factors other than chance,* i.e., a difference that is not due to chance variations. On the other hand, an *insignificant difference* is one which *has a high probability of being caused by chance.* Importantly, in making the determination of whether or not a difference is significant, it is the responsibility of management or the researcher to choose the risk level of being wrong, called the *level of significance,* it is willing to accept. The level of significance is *the risk of making a wrong inference when the statistics indicate the likelihood of a significant difference* (identified as the probability of a *Type I error*). It is the maximum risk the decision maker is willing to take that a difference will be (incorrectly) declared to be significant, when in fact it very well may be due to sampling error or chance variation. This choice of the maximum acceptable level of significance should be made *before* the data are analyzed. In selecting a level of significance, management has an unlimited number of choices between almost 0 and 100 percent, although levels such as 1 through 5 percent are most often used.

The concepts involved in significance testing may seem to be more complex than they really are. Perhaps an illustration with a real-world statistic of great import to the nation will help to clarify the concepts.

---

*Besides the normal distribution, several other theoretical distributions can be used, where appropriate, to make inferences with known probabilities of being wrong. These include the binomial distribution, introduced in Chapter 6, and the t-distribution and the Chi-Square distribution introduced later in this chapter.

In 1994, the U.S. unemployment rate released by the U.S. Department of Labor rose from 6.1 percent in June to 6.2 percent in July. These are estimates of the unemployment rate based on a random sample of the labor force and therefore both monthly estimates are subject to sampling variation. Some would claim that the country's unemployment situation worsened from June to July, 1994. However, a significance test, using the standard normal variate explained later, would show that the difference is more likely caused by sampling variation of the estimated percentages than by a real increase in the unemployment rate.

Those who believed that unemployment really worsened would have committed a Type I error, since the likelihood that the difference was significant (that it was caused by non-chance factors) is very slim, (approximately 2.5% as determined by the aforementioned significance test). Therefore, the increase (or difference) is not significant since it is not big enough to be due to non-sampling errors or non-chance variations in both estimates.

If the situation were such that the unemployment rate rose from 6.1 percent to 6.4 percent, the increase of 0.3 of a percentage point would have yielded a test result that could be declared significant since that difference could not be accounted for by chance variation at a 5 percent risk level (level of significance).

In contrast, a *Type II error* would occur if one erroneously called this latter difference insignificant when the difference, in fact, was due to some assignable cause other than chance variation or sampling error. The Type II error is at the opposite extreme from the Type I error (of declaring a difference to be significant, or real, when it is not). A Type II error occurs when a difference in fact does exist, but is not identified and is incorrectly declared to be insignificant; in such a case the statistical test does not detect the fact that the difference actually exceeds what should be expected as a result of sampling error or chance variation alone.

Of these two types of erroneous inferences, Type I and Type II, management usually is more concerned with avoiding a Type I error, that is, avoiding investigating a variation or difference which appears to be significant when in fact no identifiable cause exists. Consequently, the level of significance, or the probability of a Type I error, usually is preferred to be low, e.g., 5 percent or less (although a level of significance as high as 10 percent is sometimes used).

Nine Ways of Determining Significant Differences

In the complexities of the modern world, numerous decisions for action or inaction are made. Sometimes these decisions are based on judgment or personal recollection of past experiences; sometimes on accounting or other data for the entire universe (complete counts); sometimes on data derived from a random sample; and sometimes on various combinations of these sources. In fact, taking all possible combinations either one or two at a time, yields nine possible decision-situations:* (1) judgment alone without the backing of quantitative data, (2) complete count or census, (3) random sample estimate, (4) two different judgments, (5) judgment versus a complete count, (6) judgment versus random sample estimate, (7) complete count versus random sample estimate, (8) two complete counts or censuses, and (9) two random sample estimates. Each of these combinations is now considered for soundness and methodology.

1. Judgment alone

An expert in supplies visually inspected the firm's inventory on hand and claimed that the company's inventory at the end of the year was worth $150,000. Should the company's management accept this figure as a basis for planning next year's inventory investment?

Here, the basis for decision is judgment, without either a sample-based estimate or a 100-percent inventory valuation. What should management do when faced with the expert's judgment? Without going to another source, management can either accept or reject the judgment estimate, depending on the confidence it has in the expert's ability. However, the level of significance or risk involved in making either decision is not determinable, since even an expert's judgment supported by past experience does not provide a quantitative measure of the risk level of a particular decision.

2. Complete count (census)

In the above situation, if the accounting records of the firm's stock on hand showed its value to be $200,000, this can be the most precise basis for a decision. There is one major proviso, however, namely, that the accounting records have been maintained so as to assure their completeness and accuracy.

---

*Of course, there may be many more possible combinations in actual decision situations. However, this limited number will serve to illustrate several important points that apply to most decision situations.

3. Random sample estimate

If a random sample estimate of the inventory showed that the value of the stock on hand was, let us say, $125,000, a sound basis would exist for making a decision with a known chance of being wrong. A random sample estimate can always be evaluated in terms of the magnitude of its error due to chance variation and the confidence that this error will not be exceeded (or, conversely, the risk that this error will be exceeded). This evaluation can be conducted by constructing a confidence interval around the estimate, as discussed in Chapter 9.

4. Two judgments

Suppose that management claims, on the basis of its judgment and recollected experience, that the prevailing average wage in its industry is $18.75 an hour. Suppose, in addition, that a labor representative claims that the true average wage is currently $17.00, based on this person's vast knowledge of union members' wages. Which judgment claim is more nearly correct and should be accepted as a basis for wage arbitration and settlement?

The answer is: Probably neither can be accepted and the argument can go on indefinitely, since neither claim is supported by objective statistical evidence. In a situation such as this, with no supporting evidence, the difference of $1.75 between the two claimed rates is neither statistically significant nor insignificant, and no basis exists for a sound decision with a known probability of being wrong. The only available sound alternatives are: (a) collection of wage data from a random sample of employee records from which to derive an estimate, or (b) determination of the true wage rate from an analysis of the complete and verified accounting records.

Alternatively, if estimates from two or more independent sources tend to differ only slightly (i.e., the two or more sources are in general concordance), then there is some likelihood that they are correct. Nevertheless, the probability in quantitative terms of the significance of their difference, however slight, still is indeterminable.

5. Judgment versus complete count (census)

Occasionally, a universe characteristic is "judged" to be of a certain magnitude and a complete accounting shows a different figure. Should the accounting figure be preferred over the judgment estimate? Not automatically. Consideration first must be given to the errors or biases that can creep into all so-called 100% enumerations. All data, whether compiled from accounting records (complete census) or by a sample, are subject to various types of error, such as errors of coding, editing, posting, calculating, and other kinds of non-sampling errors. It cannot be assumed that these types of non-sampling errors will not occur or that they will offset each other. If a large disparity exists between an expert's judgment estimate and a complete-count figure, it is safer to assume that an audit based on a random sample is necessary to validate the complete count. This could be a post-audit random sample of cases or records drawn from the universe file.

6.   Judgment versus random sample estimate

Another decision situation exists when an estimate based on a random sample is challenged by a judgment estimate. Suppose that the labor union estimates on the basis of a random sample that the average wage of the employees in a given industry to be $16.25 an hour. In contrast, management claims on the basis of judgment that the average wage is higher, let us say, at least $18.75 an hour. Is the difference of $2.50 an hour significant?

In this situation, probability and normal distribution theory (or other appropriate statistical theory) provide the basis for a decision with a known risk of being wrong. The following four requirements must be met: (1) the risk level expressed in quantitative terms of making a wrong decision must be specified in advance, (2) the size of the random sample must be known, (3) an estimate of the standard deviation of the universe must be available, and (4) serious non-sampling errors must be eliminated. In this case, the sample estimate can be compared with the judgment estimate and a determination made if they are significantly different at the pre-specified level of significance.   How can this determination be made?

The confidence interval test of significance — The confidence interval technique is one way of making the determination. Suppose that in the above wage-rate disagreement both parties, under a wage rate mediator, agreed on using a statistical significance test to settle their dispute, keeping in mind that management claimed that the true average wage is higher than the sample wage rate. Both parties agreed to use a 95% confidence interval test and to use the union's sample of n=100 employee wage records selected randomly from the universe of N=5000 hourly wage employees as the basis for establishing the confidence interval.

Suppose that the results of the random sample were available and verified as to accuracy, and the sample mean ($\overline{X}$) was $16.25 and the sample standard deviation (σ_x) was $7.50. Using these statistics, how can we determine if credence should be placed in management's judgment claim that the mean hourly wage rate was $18.75 an hour?

Any sample-derived estimate is, admittedly, subject to sampling variation (measured by its standard error). In this case, based on the sample results, the standard error of the estimated mean of $16.25 is $0.75, i.e., $\sigma_{\overline{X}} = \frac{\sigma_x}{\sqrt{n}} = \frac{\$7.50}{\sqrt{100}} = \pm\$0.75$. Therefore, allowing ±1.96 standard errors of the sample mean to comply with the specified 95% confidence level, we have a maximum variation *on either side* of the sample mean of ±1.96 times $0.75, or $\pm\$1.47$. When this $\pm\$1.47$ is subtracted and then added to the sample mean, the 95 percent confidence interval for the estimated mean would be between $14.78 and $17.72.

Since this confidence interval does not include management's judgment estimate of $18.75, it is quite unlikely that the claimed mean came from the same population as the sample mean of $16.25. Management's claim cannot be accepted.

The Z-test of significance — In Chapter 5 we introduced the Z-variate, called the *standard normal variate*, to determine the percentage of cases in a normal distribution of x-values that lie between a critical point (x) and the mean ($\overline{X}$) of that distribution. In that chapter, Z was computed by $Z = \frac{x - \overline{X}}{\sigma_x}$.

Similarly, the Z-variate can be used when we are dealing with a normal distribution of many replicated means (Central Limit Theorem, Chapter 8) and an assumed true mean of that distribution. Here, the critical point is the sample mean ($\overline{X}$) derived from a random sample from the population of concern and the Z-variate in testing for significance is:

$$Z = \frac{\overline{X} \text{ (critical point)} - \overline{X}' \text{ (assumed true mean)}}{\sigma_{\overline{X}}}, \text{ i.e., } Z = \frac{(\overline{X} - \overline{X}')}{\sigma_{\overline{X}}},$$

where $\sigma_{\overline{X}}$ (computed earlier) is the standard error of $\overline{X}$ (which also happens to be the standard deviation of the theoretical normal distribution of estimated $\overline{X}$-values).

The Z-variate with the appropriate values is:

$$Z = \frac{(\overline{X} - \overline{X}')}{\sigma_{\overline{X}}} = \frac{(\$16.25 - \$18.75)}{\$0.75} = \frac{\$ - 2.50}{\$0.75} = -3.33.$$

This Z-value is called the *actual Z-ratio* because it is computed from the actual sample results. From this result, we find that the sample mean is separated by 3.33 standard errors from the claimed mean on the left side of the sampling distribution (as indicated by the minus sign). This compares to the *critical ratio* of Z=–1.645$\sigma_{\overline{X}}$, which is found from the normal curve table in Appendix B for a 5% risk level. This ratio and its associated rejection area are shown in Figure 10.1. It is evident from the figure that the actual sample result of $16.25 is unlikely to have come from a universe whose mean is $18.75. Therefore, management's claim that the hourly wage rate is at least $18.75 is rejected.

Figure 10.1
Theoretical sampling distribution of replicated means
based on n = 100 employee wage records

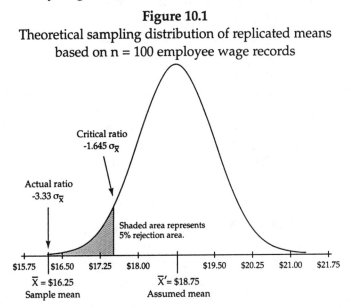

The actual Z-ratio of –3.33$\sigma_{\overline{X}}$ indicates that the difference can hardly be explained by chance. In fact, in normal distributions, the percentage of cases falling beyond –3.33 standard errors from the mean on one side is infinitesimally small, with a risk of about .04 of 1% (or odds of about 2,500 to one) that the difference between the two means is not due to chance. This probability is determined by looking up the Z-value of 3.33 in the normal curve table in Appendix B; the corresponding probability of .4996 (49.96% in the table) represents a probability of .5000–.4996=.0004 or .04%; expressed as odds, it would be .9996 / .0004 = 2,499 to one. The resultant decision is that management's claim (that the average hourly wage is at least $18.75) must be rejected.

From this finding it also can be seen that the Z-test method is superior to the confidence interval method because, in addition to forming a basis for rejecting (or accepting) a judgment claim, the Z-test also provides a basis for computing the probability that a difference as large as or larger than the one observed can occur by chance.

7. Complete count versus random sample estimate

When an accounting figure is compared with an estimate based on a random sample, and their difference exceeds the number of standard errors representing the chosen level of significance, one may be inclined to accept the "complete-count" figure as correct. In other words, the sample figure may be rejected on grounds that it is, after all, subject to sampling variations, and therefore, cannot possibly be as accurate as the figure based on a complete count. However, as indicated previously, this decision should not be made hastily without considering the possibility that the complete count may be subject to serious non-sampling errors. In fact, there have been a number of situations when the sample estimate was more accurate than the complete count. For example, a post-enumeration random sample of the 1990 Census of the United States Population found the population to have been under-enumerated by approximately 4 to 5 million persons. Similar situations have occurred in the past and will likely occur in the future.

8. Two complete counts

Does it ever happen that two figures representing the same population, each based allegedly on a 100% census, differ substantially enough to warrant an evaluation before either one or the other, or neither, is accepted as a basis for decision? Yes, but rarely. We say "rarely" because there are not many recorded situations when duplicate complete counts were made of supposedly the same universe. In the few instances when this does occur (e.g., recounts of election votes), a small difference can be accepted when it does not affect the decision. On the other hand, if the decision depends on the extent of the difference, an analytical investigation of the extent of the difference might be measured by a random sample of sufficient size.

9. Two random sample estimates

Much of the medical research to improve health involves comparison of findings from two independent samples. For example, a study conducted at Memorial Sloan-Kettering Cancer Center in New York found, from a sample of 1,418 men and women, that the incidence of colon cancer was only 5 out of 1,418 persons (p=.0035) when polyps were removed early. Another, earlier study, with a sample of 1,618 patients in St. Mark's Hospital in London showed 55 cases (p=.0339) of colon cancer when their polyps had not been removed.* A Z-test (assuming random sampling) indicated, with a risk level of less than 1 percent, that a highly significant difference existed between the two findings. (For the method of making this test, see the section "Significance Tests for Percentages.")

As another example in continuing our illustrative problem on average hourly wages, recall that labor had estimated the mean hourly wage rate to be $16.25 based on their random sample of 100 employee pay records. Suppose that management wanted to refute this finding, i.e., to test whether the actual wage rate might be different from the union result. As a basis for this test suppose that management independently selected a different random sample of 100 employee records from the same universe and determined the mean hourly rate from their sample to be $18.75. Let us call management's estimated mean $\overline{Y}$ = $18.75, to differentiate it from labor's estimated mean of $\overline{X}$ = $16.25. Is the difference between the two sample means significant, i.e., real, or (conversely) probably due to sampling variation?

Confidence interval test — Since each estimated mean is based on a random sample, each is subject to sampling variation. Provided that non-sampling errors are inconsequential, one way of determining whether the means differ significantly is to construct their respective confidence intervals at a chosen significance level and then observe whether these intervals overlap. To apply the *overlapping-confidence-interval method* of testing, one must compute the standard error of each mean. Since the universe standard deviations from which each sample was drawn are not known, the standard deviations derived from their respective sample data are used, as follows:

$$\sigma_x = \sqrt{\frac{\Sigma(x-\overline{X})^2}{(n_x-1)}} \text{ and } \sigma_y = \sqrt{\frac{\Sigma(y-\overline{Y})^2}{(n_y-1)}}.$$

---

* *New England Journal of Medicine*, December 23, 1993.

Suppose that the sample standard deviations were $\sigma_x = \$7.50$ based on the labor union sample of 100 records and $\sigma_y = \$8.25$ based on management's sample of 100 records. The respective standard errors of the means are then computed:

Union: $\sigma_{\overline{X}} = \dfrac{\$7.50}{\sqrt{100}} = \$0.75$ (one standard error of $\overline{X}$), and

Management: $\sigma_{\overline{Y}} = \dfrac{\$8.25}{\sqrt{100}} = \$0.83$ (one standard error of $\overline{Y}$).

Allowing a range of 1.96 standard errors in each estimated mean to establish two 95% confidence intervals, we obtain:

Union:

$\overline{X} \pm Z\sigma_{\overline{X}} = \$16.25 \pm (1.96)(\$.75) = \$16.25 \pm \$1.47 = \$14.78$ to $\$17.72$;

Management:

$\overline{Y} \pm Z\sigma_{\overline{Y}} = \$18.75 \pm (1.96)(\$.83) = \$18.75 \pm 1.63 = \$17.12$ to $\$20.38$.

Since the two 95% confidence intervals overlap, even though barely, it may be concluded that the two estimated mean wage rates do not differ significantly, i.e., that the two sample means could have been drawn from the same universe. In this case, the best estimate of the true mean wage rate would be obtained from the combined (pooled) sample of 200 employees. Similarly, a better confidence interval test would be made by using the standard deviation from the combined sample of 200 cases.

The Z-test — The overlapping-confidence-intervals method of testing is a weak test primarily because it does not provide for determining the specific probability that the indicated difference between the two estimates may be due to causes other than chance. With the Z-test method, on the other hand, we determine the difference between the two figures in terms of the number of standard errors separating them. From this Z-value, the probability that such a difference (or a larger one) could be due to non-chance causes may be determined from the normal curve table (Appendix B). To use the more powerful Z-test, however, we face the new situation, namely, computing the *standard error of the difference between two sample means*, symbolically expressed by $\sigma_{\overline{X}-\overline{Y}}$, and explained in the next few paragraphs. We also encounter a choice of using the pooled or the unpooled method for computing the standard deviation.

The unpooled method of computing the standard error of a difference — The above confidence interval test used the two separate sample-derived standard deviations, not from the combined or pooled sample; instead, they were left *unpooled,* assuming that they came from different universes with different degrees of variation. The *pooled* method of computing the standard deviation and then the standard error of the difference between the two means, on the other hand, assumes that the two samples came from the same population with the same mean and the same standard deviation.

To illustrate the unpooled method of estimating the standard error of a difference between two sample means, let us imagine drawing two separate random samples from a single population. We compute the mean of each sample and then the difference between the two means. If this process of drawing pairs of random samples (with replacement) is repeated many times, some of the differences between the means will be large and others small, and some of the differences will be plus and others minus. Based on the Central Limit Theorem, the frequency distribution of these many differences $(d = \overline{X} - \overline{Y})$ will approach a normal distribution centered around a mean difference of zero, provided each of the samples is sufficiently large $(n \geq 31)$. The standard deviation of such a sampling distribution of differences is called the standard error of the difference between two sample means, $\sigma_{\overline{X}-\overline{Y}}$.

The Variance Principle (Chapter 9) provides the following formula for estimating the standard error of the difference between two random sample means (or percentages). *The standard error of the difference between two sample means is the square root of the sum of the squares of the two separate standard errors.* In symbols, the standard error of the difference formula is $\sigma_{\overline{X}-\overline{Y}} = \sqrt{\sigma_{\overline{X}}^2 + \sigma_{\overline{Y}}^2}$.

In our illustrative problem, we test the hypothesis with a 5% risk level that the two population means are equal (or that the sampling distribution of differences is centered on zero). For a two-tailed test, the critical Z-ratio (generally called the critical ratio) for a 5% risk level is 1.96 standard errors. Since we have previously computed the standard error of each mean, each based on a random sample of 100 employees, these values are now substituted in the standard error of the difference formula. Thus, the unpooled standard error of the difference between the two means is:

$$\sigma_{\overline{X}-\overline{Y}} = \sqrt{\sigma_{\overline{X}}^2 + \sigma_{\overline{Y}}^2} = \sqrt{\$.75^2 + \$.83^2} = \sqrt{1.2514} = \pm\$1.1187.$$

Once the standard error of the difference between the two means has been computed, the number of standard errors separating the observed difference between the two sample averages ($16.25 and $18.75) from the claimed difference of zero can be determined by the Z-variate (generally called the actual ratio), which expresses the actual difference (or ratio) in terms of number of standard errors. Thus, the actual ratio is:

$$Z = \frac{(\overline{X} - \overline{Y})}{\sigma_{\overline{X} - \overline{Y}}} = \frac{(\$16.25 - \$18.75)}{\$1.1187} = \frac{\$-2.50}{\$1.1187} = -2.235.$$

The minus Z-value results from subtracting the larger of the two sample means from the smaller; if the smaller sample mean had been subtracted from the larger (a permissible alternative), the Z-value would have been a plus. Since there is no *a priori* basis for the direction of the difference, the plus or minus is inconsequential; it is the relative magnitude of the *difference* that matters, in either tail of the distribution.* See Figure 10.2.

Figure 10.2
Theoretical sampling distribution of differences between two sample means, for pairs of random sample means, with $n_x = 100$ and $n_y = 100$

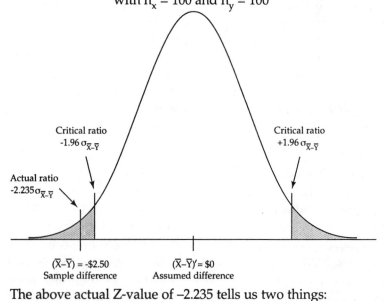

The above actual Z-value of –2.235 tells us two things:

(1) Since the actual ratio associated with the difference between

---

* This generally is called a two-tailed test, as discussed more fully in the later section "One-Sided and Two-Sided Tests."

the two means ($2.50) exceeds the critical ratio of 1.96 standard errors, the difference between the two means is considered significant at the 5% level of significance.

(2) The difference of $2.50, representing 2.235 standard errors, is so large that it (or an amount larger than it) could occur due to chance only about 1.3% of the time in repeated pairs of samples drawn from the respective populations.

Expressed differently, it is highly unlikely that both means come from the same universe, so that something else (other than sampling error) must be causing this difference. One possible explanation for the difference may be the inclusion by management in its sample of some non-union employees, such as low to middle or higher-level management personnel, whose wage rates generally are higher than those of union employees; this, of course, would make the two universes different.

This result, namely, that the difference between the means is significant, contradicts the result from the overlapping-confidence-intervals test, which showed that the confidence intervals of the separate means overlapped and therefore were not significantly different. Why does this contradiction occur? The answer is that the Z-test method of testing the difference between the means is more powerful than the overlapping-confidence-intervals method. A test is said to increase in *power* as its ability to detect significant differences increases.

The pooled method of computing the standard error of a difference — In the foregoing Z-test it was assumed that the two universe means were the same (i.e., their difference was zero), but that the two standard deviations represented different universes. Therefore, the two sample standard deviations were not combined into a single pooled standard deviation.

It is sometimes appropriate to assume that the standard deviations as well as the means come from the same universe. If this is a valid assumption, a still more powerful test can be made by pooling the data from the two samples and computing a single standard deviation from the enlarged sample. The idea of pooling is appealing from the standpoint of precision for we derive the best estimate of the universe standard deviation by using the largest possible sample. The following demonstrates the pooled standard deviation method.

The *pooled standard deviation* (σ_{pooled}) is obtained from the combined sample by adding the squared differences from each separate sample, as follows:

$$\sigma_{pooled} = \sqrt{\frac{\sum(x-\overline{X})^2 + \sum(y-\overline{Y})^2}{n_x + n_y - 2}}$$

The denominator of this formula allows for a loss of two *degrees of freedom*, one for each sample size. A loss of one degree of freedom results from using an estimated mean to compute each standard deviation. This is reflected by subtracting one from each n, or two from the sum of the two n's.

In cases where the sum of the squared differences is not readily available, but σ_x and σ_y have already been computed, algebraic manipulation is required to obtain sums of squared differences. This is done by squaring both sides of $\sigma_x = \sqrt{\frac{\sum(x-\overline{X})^2}{(n_x-1)}}$ and $\sigma_y = \sqrt{\frac{\sum(y-\overline{Y})^2}{(n_y-1)}}$,

which yields $\sum(x-\overline{X})^2 = (n_x-1)\sigma_x^2$ and $\sum(y-\overline{Y})^2 = (n_y-1)\sigma_y^2$.

As a result, an alternative to the above σ_{pooled} formula becomes:

$$\sigma_{pooled} = \sqrt{\frac{(n_x-1)\sigma_x^2 + (n_y-1)\sigma_y^2}{n_x + n_y - 2}}.$$

Once a pooled standard deviation for the combined sample has been computed, it can be entered in the formula for computing the standard error of the difference between two means, as follows:

$$\sigma_{\overline{X}-\overline{Y}} = \sigma_{pooled}\sqrt{\frac{1}{n_x} + \frac{1}{n_y}}^{*}.$$

---

* For the mathematically inclined, this formula is obtained as follows, starting with the general formula that $\sigma_{\overline{X}-\overline{Y}} = \sqrt{\sigma_{\overline{X}}^2 + \sigma_{\overline{Y}}^2}$. Since both σ_x and σ_y become σ_{pooled}, then $\sigma_{\overline{X}} = \frac{\sigma_{pooled}}{\sqrt{n_x}}$ and $\sigma_{\overline{Y}} = \frac{\sigma_{pooled}}{\sqrt{n_y}}$. Thus, by substitution into the formula for the standard error of a difference, $\sigma_{\overline{X}-\overline{Y}} = \sqrt{\frac{\sigma_{pooled}^2}{n_x} + \frac{\sigma_{pooled}^2}{n_y}} = \sqrt{\sigma_{pooled}^2\left(\frac{1}{n_x} + \frac{1}{n_y}\right)} = \sigma_{pooled}\sqrt{\frac{1}{n_x} + \frac{1}{n_y}}$.

Choice between pooled and unpooled methods — The choice between the pooled and the unpooled methods of significance testing depends on our prior knowledge about the universes from which the samples were drawn. If we know from past studies that the same universe is involved in the two groups being compared (i.e., the same union employees in our example), the pooled method will provide a more powerful test than the unpooled method. On the other hand, if the assumption of equality of standard deviations cannot be made, the unpooled test is more appropriate.

A numeric illustration of the pooled method — To derive the pooled standard deviation in our hypothetical hourly-rate problem we recast the basic figures as follows.

Type of Statistic	Labor Union (x)	Management (y)
Sample size (employee pay records)	n_x = 100	n_y = 100
Sample standard deviation	σ_x = \$ 7.50	σ_y = \$ 8.25
Sample mean	$\overline{X}$ = \$16.25	$\overline{Y}$ = \$18.75
Standard error of the sample mean	$\sigma_{\overline{X}}$ = \$ 0.75	$\sigma_{\overline{Y}}$ = \$ 0.83

Since the original sums of squares are not given (although they could well be on the original work sheets), they are derived by the formula:

$$\Sigma(x-\overline{X})^2 = (n_x-1)\sigma_x^2 = (99)(\$7.50)^2 = \$5568.75 \text{ and}$$

$$\Sigma(y-\overline{Y})^2 = (n_y-1)\sigma_y^2 = (99)(\$8.25)^2 = \$6738.19.$$

The pooled standard deviation is:

$$\sigma_{pooled} = \sqrt{\frac{\Sigma(x-\overline{X})^2 + \Sigma(y-\overline{Y})^2}{n_x+n_y-2}} = \sqrt{\frac{5,568.75+6,738.19}{100+100-2}} = \sqrt{62.156} = \$7.88.$$

Having computed the pooled standard deviation, we next compute the standard error of the difference between the two means using the same pooled standard deviation. The standard error of the difference between the two means is:

$$\sigma_{\overline{X}-\overline{Y}} = \sigma_{pooled}\sqrt{\frac{1}{n_x}+\frac{1}{n_y}} = \$7.88\sqrt{\frac{1}{100}+\frac{1}{100}} = \$7.88\sqrt{.02} = \$7.88(.1414) = \$1.114.$$

The resulting actual ratio is:

$$Z = \frac{(\overline{X} - \overline{Y})}{\sigma_{\overline{X} - \overline{Y}}} = \frac{(\$16.25 - \$18.75)}{\$1.114} = \frac{\$-2.50}{\$1.114} = -2.24 \ .$$

Since the calculated Z-value exceeds the two-tailed critical Z-value of 1.96, the difference is considered to be significant at the 5% level of significance. In fact, the chances are about 2.5% (or about 40 to 1) that a difference as large as ±2.24 standard errors between the two means could have occurred by chance alone. In other words, they are significantly different, and something other than chance must explain the difference between them.

Assumptions Underlying Significance Tests

The statistical tests of significance discussed thus far (and later) are based on certain assumptions which must be carefully evaluated for validity, particularly in medical research and other important "controlled" experiments. These assumptions are presented below.

Method of sampling

It is assumed that samples are independently (randomly) selected from their respective universes by simple random sampling or equivalent methods. Thus, the formulas for the standard error of the sample mean, $\sigma_{\overline{X}} = \frac{\sigma_x}{\sqrt{n}}$, and for the standard error of the estimated percentage, $\sigma_p = \sqrt{\frac{p(1-p)}{n-1}}$, are applicable, based on these methods of sample selection. If a stratified method of sampling is used, a different standard error formula is required.

Non-sampling errors

Every data collection process is susceptible to systematic non-sampling errors which may be large and biased in one direction. In making the tests, it is assumed that such non-sampling errors are inconsequential and therefore will not affect the test. If the validity of this assumption is not verified, wrong decisions are likely to result.

Method of estimation

The standard error of the sample mean formula also depends on the way by which the estimate is prepared. When, for example, the mean is computed as the weighted average of the separate means (as in stratified sampling, Chapter 9), the standard error of the estimated mean also must be computed by a weighted method:

$$\sigma_{\overline{X}} = \sqrt{\sum w_i^2 \sigma_{\overline{X}_i}^2} \text{ , where } w_i = \frac{N_i}{N} .$$

Frequency distribution of the population

The Z-test assumes that the universe frequency distribution from which the sample is drawn forms a bell-shaped or an approximate normal curve. In cases where the underlying population is not normally distributed, it assumes that replicated sample *means* (each based on at least 31 cases) are used as the data for the analysis. The Central Limit Theorem (Chapter 8) has shown that these sample means will be normally distributed regardless of the graphic pattern of the universe frequency distribution.

Size of sample

When samples of 30 or fewer cases are used but the universe frequency distribution is still bell-shaped, another testing procedure, called the *t-test of significance,* must be applied. This procedure is presented in a later section of this chapter.

The standard deviation

When a test is made of the significance of a difference between two sample means, we usually hypothesize that the means of the populations are the same, and that therefore their difference is zero. The test we presented earlier was designed to disprove this hypothesis. However, with respect to the standard deviations of the populations, there are two possible assumptions. In the unpooled method, it is assumed that the standard deviations originate from two different universes whose standard deviations are not necessarily equal. Thus, each random sample yields an independent estimate of the standard deviation of the specific universe from which it was drawn. In this case, the unpooled standard error of the difference would be used, as explained earlier.

Alternatively, if there is reason to believe that the standard deviations are equal, in that they originate from the same universe, a more appropriate way of computing the standard error of the difference is provided by the pooled method. Pooling increases the reliability of the resulting estimated standard deviation since it is computed from the enlarged combined sample.

Significance Tests for Percentages
(Large Samples)

The foregoing significance tests involved arithmetic means, estimated from one and two random samples. There are many decision-situations when the more appropriate test involves the significance of a difference between two percentages. Thus, for example, a question may arise whether the percentage of aged persons in a given community has changed significantly over the past ten years; whether a one-percent decrease in mortality from one year to another due to use of a certain drug is significant; or whether there has been a significant drop in the percentage of persons receiving public welfare as a result of a new policy adopted by the government.

In general, similar techniques and the same theory of normal distributions for sample means may be applied to sample percentages, provided the percentages are estimated from sufficiently large random samples. Experience has shown that the sampling distribution of proportions will be sufficiently close to normal for practical purposes if the product of np and nq (q=1–p) exceeds 5 cases. For example, we can expect the sampling distribution of p in the following cases to be approximately normal:

(a) $p = .10$ for samples of at least 50 units;
(b) $p = .05$ for samples of at least 100 units;
(c) $p = .005$ for samples of at least 1,000 units;
(d) $p = .80$ for samples of at least 25 units.

If these conditions are not met, other statistical tests, such as those based on the binomial distribution, beyond the scope of this book, should be used to make significance tests for percentages.

The following discussion illustrates how the previously-presented methods of significance testing (confidence interval and Z-test) may be applied when percentages are estimated from one or two large random samples.

Judgment versus sample estimate of a proportion

A systems engineer claims that the company's mainframe computer is idle an average of no more than 12 percent of the time each calendar quarter ($p \leq 0.12$). A random-time sampling study, on the other hand, based on 1,000 random observations made in the last calendar quarter, yielded 160 observations of down-time, or an estimate of 16 percent idle time (p=0.16). Can we place credence in the engineer's claim, using a 5% significance level?

The engineer's claim can be tested in either of two ways, namely, by the confidence interval technique or the Z-test method. A confidence interval can be constructed around the sample percentage to see whether the claimed percentage falls within it. Alternatively, the Z-test can be made at a specified risk level, where the test attempts to disprove the primary claim on the right tail of the normal curve. Below, we demonstrate both these tests.

Confidence interval technique for percentages — In our idle-time problem, the random sample estimated the percentage of idle machine-time to be 16% (p=0.16). The standard error of this percentage is:

$\sigma_p = \sqrt{\dfrac{p(1-p)}{n-1}} = \sqrt{\dfrac{.16(.84)}{999}} = 0.0116$. This yields a 95% confidence interval

between 13.7 and 18.3 percent, i.e., $0.16 \pm 1.96(0.0116)$. Since the engineer's claim of 12 percent computer idle time does not lie within this interval, the engineer's claim is rejected; it is very unlikely that idle time is 12 percent.

The Z-test of significance for percentages — If we assume (or hypothesize) that the engineer's claim of 12 percent idle computer time is correct we can test this assumption (hypothesis) by a Z-test, e.g., using a 5% risk level. To do this, we first need an estimate of the standard error of the percentage. In this case, since we are assuming that the engineer's claim of .12 is correct, the formula for the standard error of p uses $p' = .12$. Therefore,

$$\sigma_p = \sqrt{\dfrac{p'(1-p')}{n-1}} = \sqrt{\dfrac{(.12)(.88)}{999}} = 0.0103 .$$

Thus, in standard error units, the difference between the judgment claim and sample estimate of 16 percent is:

$$Z = \dfrac{p-p'}{\sigma_p} = \dfrac{0.16-0.12}{0.0103} = \dfrac{0.04}{0.0103} = 3.88 \text{ standard errors.}$$

Since the number of standard errors separating the sample percentage of 16 percent from the claimed percentage of 12 percent is greater than 1.645 (the one-tailed 5% critical Z-value), the engineer's claim is rejected at the 5 percent significance level. In fact, the probability that such a difference or larger is due to chance, is about 0.01%, i.e., odds of 10,000 to 1. Figure 10.3 graphically displays this test.

Figure 10.3 — A right-tail Z-test
Theoretical sampling distribution of an assumed percentage (p=.12)
with a 5 percent significance level

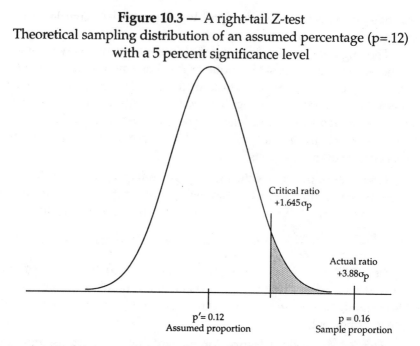

Critical ratio
$+1.645\sigma_p$

Actual ratio
$+3.88\sigma_p$

p'= 0.12
Assumed proportion

p = 0.16
Sample proportion

As another example of the Z-test and its strength, a Federal agency audited a State agency, by use of a random sample of 115 cases, for compliance with a Federal standard which required the State to investigate at least 75 percent of its case load each year. (The stated risk level was 5% and the critical ratio or Z-value was 1.645.) The resulting sample showed that 63 percent of the case load was investigated during the year. In this case, the consulting statistician had recommended that a one-tailed Z-test to the left should be used, as indicated below. Here, we are assuming that the State did have a 75% compliance rate; therefore, the standard error of p was $\sqrt{\dfrac{(.75)(.25)}{114}} = 0.0406$. Thus, the actual Z-ratio was:

$$Z = \frac{p - p'}{\sigma_p} = \frac{0.63 - 0.75}{0.0406} = \frac{-0.12}{0.0406} = -2.96 \text{ standard errors.}$$

This is a one-tailed test, since the competing claim was that action was taken on at least 75% of the case load. Therefore, the critical ratio was –1.645. The Z-value of –2.96 indicates that this difference of –12 percentage points is likely to occur due to chance only .15 of 1% of the time; in other words, the odds are about 666 to 1 that the 75 percent government standard was not met. When the random sample-derived percentage (p = .63) was proven to be a valid estimate of the universe characteristic, the Federal Government decision was ruled acceptable in a court of law when it was challenged by the State.

Two random sample estimates of a proportion

Suppose that in the earlier situation regarding computer idle-time, an independent random-time sampling study, this time based on 600 random observations during the most recent calendar quarter, showed that the computer equipment was idle 18 percent of the time. Is the difference between the two sample-derived percentages (16 and 18 percent) significant at the 5 percent significance level?

In dealing with this particular problem, we have at our disposal three test methods, namely: (1) the overlapping-confidence-intervals method, (2) the unpooled Z-test method, and (3) the pooled Z-test method.

Confidence interval test of two percentages — This is typically a two-tailed test, since the sample percentages can be reversed, i.e., either sample could have the larger percentage. Therefore, when the significance level is 5%, this test requires a 95% confidence interval. The standard error of each percentage is first determined; to identify the two samples, we use symbols with subscripts 1 and 2:

$$\sigma_{p_1} = \sqrt{\frac{p_1 q_1}{n_1 - 1}} = \sqrt{\frac{(.16)(.84)}{999}} = 0.0116 \text{ and}$$

$$\sigma_{p_2} = \sqrt{\frac{p_2 q_2}{n_2 - 1}} = \sqrt{\frac{(.18)(.82)}{599}} = 0.0157 .$$

Thus, the 95% confidence interval for p_1 is
$$0.16 \pm (1.96)(0.0116) = 0.16 \pm 0.023$$
$$= 0.137 \text{ to } 0.183;$$

the 95% confidence interval for p_2 is
$$0.18 \pm (1.96)(0.0157) = 0.18 \pm 0.031$$
$$= 0.149 \text{ to } 0.211.$$

Since the two 95 percent confidence intervals overlap, the difference between the two percentages is not considered to be significant. It cannot be concluded from the overlapping-confidence-intervals test that a significant change has occurred in the proportion of computer idle time from the first to the second period of study.

Z-test of two percentages, unpooled method — In dealing with the above problem, it would be valid to assume that the two percentages come from two different universes and use the unpooled method of computing the standard error of their difference. After all, the percentages represent different periods of time. Therefore, with this hypothesis and a risk level of 5% (or $Z = \pm 1.96$), we use the unpooled method to obtain the standard error of the difference between the two percentages, as follows:

$$\sigma_{p_1 - p_2} = \sqrt{\sigma_{p_1}^2 + \sigma_{p_2}^2} = \sqrt{(.0116)^2 + (.0157)^2} = \sqrt{.0001345 + .0002464}$$
$$= \sqrt{.0003809} = 0.0195 .$$

Thus, $Z = \dfrac{p_1 - p_2}{\sigma_{p_1 - p_2}} = \dfrac{0.16 - 0.18}{0.0195} = \dfrac{-0.02}{0.0195} = -1.03$. This Z-value is less than the critical value of ± 1.96 for a two-tailed test, so we conclude, as we did with the confidence interval test, that the difference between the two percentages is not significant, i.e., the difference very well could be due to chance.

Z-test of two proportions, pooled method — In this particular problem, we cannot validly assume that the two estimated percentages originated from the same universe. Therefore, the pooled test would not be appropriate. Nevertheless, we can demonstrate the use of the pooled two-tailed Z-test of proportions for use in situations where it is appropriate. In this case,

$$p_{pooled} = \frac{n_1 p_1 + n_2 p_2}{n_1 + n_2} = \frac{(1,000)(.16) + (600)(.18)}{1,000 + 600} = \frac{268}{1,600} = 0.1675 .$$

Therefore, the best (or pooled) estimate of the universe proportion of idle time would be 16.75%.

Using the pooled percentage (p_{pooled}), it is possible to compute the standard error of the difference between the two percentages, as follows, where $p = p_{pooled}$ and $q = 1 - p_{pooled}$: *

---

* The testing formula above, $\sigma_{p_1 - p_2} = \sqrt{\sigma_{p_1}^2 + \sigma_{p_2}^2}$, is the same when using the pooled p, where

$$\sigma_{p_1}^2 = \left(\sqrt{\frac{p_1 q_1}{n_1 - 1}}\right)^2 = \frac{p_1 q_1}{n_1 - 1} \text{ and } \sigma_{p_2}^2 = \left(\sqrt{\frac{p_2 q_2}{n_2 - 1}}\right)^2 = \frac{p_2 q_2}{n_2 - 1} , \text{ so } \sigma_{p_1 - p_2} = \sqrt{\frac{p_1 q_1}{n_1 - 1} + \frac{p_2 q_2}{n_2 - 1}} .$$

But, since p_{pooled} is used for both p_1 and p_2, and if we let $p = p_{pooled}$, then

$$\sigma_{p_1 - p_2} = \sqrt{p q \left(\frac{1}{n_1 - 1} + \frac{1}{n_2 - 1}\right)} .$$

$$\sigma_{p_1-p_2} = \sqrt{p\,q\left(\frac{1}{n_1-1}+\frac{1}{n_2-1}\right)} = \sqrt{(0.1675)(0.8325)\left(\frac{1}{999}+\frac{1}{599}\right)}$$

$$= \sqrt{(.13944)(.00100+.00167)} = \sqrt{(.13944)(.00267)} = \sqrt{(.0003723)} = \pm0.0193 \ .$$

Once the pooled standard error of a difference is obtained, the actual ratio computed by the Z-variate is –1.04:

$$Z = \frac{p_1-p_2}{\sigma_{p_1-p_2}} = \frac{0.16-0.18}{0.0193} = \frac{-0.02}{0.0193} = -1.04 \ .$$

Since the observed difference is less than ±1.96 standard errors, we decide, at a 5 percent significance level, that the difference between the two proportions is not significant, i.e., that the idle machine time has not changed significantly from the first to the second period of random-time sampling. By examining the normal distribution table, we find that a difference of this magnitude (or larger), might occur due to sampling error or chance about 30 percent of the time.

In this problem, it is observed that the Z-test by the pooled method led to the same decision as that reached by the unpooled Z-test. This single-case illustration should not lead us to conclude that the same result will always be obtained by the two methods. The magnitude of the differences between the two sample sizes and the two percentages influence the result. In our case, the percentages did not differ much (16 versus 18 percent); neither did the sample sizes differ greatly. Since the best estimate of the universe mean or percentage is obtained from the largest possible sample, the pooled method is generally preferred over the unpooled method, if it is appropriate to use it.

One-Sided and Two-Sided Tests

Significance tests can be either one-tailed or two-tailed. Since the choice between these two is critical to making the correct decision, this section provides guidelines for choosing which one of the two tests is appropriate.

When a judgment claim is made that a specified universe characteristic (mean or percentage) is a certain magnitude, it is the primary claim and is placed at the center of the theoretical sampling distribution. Generally, the nature of the claim determines whether the test is one-sided or two-sided. If the claim is that a specified mean (or proportion) is larger than another mean (or proportion), the test is one-tailed to the left; if the claim is that the mean (or proportion) is smaller than a specified or comparable mean (or proportion), the test is one-sided to the right.   These two one-tailed choices are displayed graphically by Figures 10.4 and 10.5.

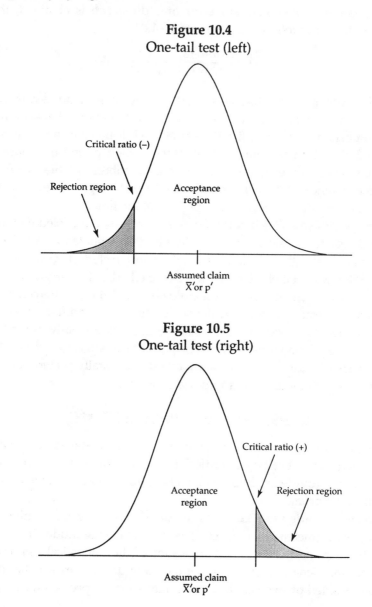

Figure 10.4
One-tail test (left)

Critical ratio (–)

Rejection region

Acceptance
region

Assumed claim
$\bar{X}'$ or p'

Figure 10.5
One-tail test (right)

Critical ratio (+)

Acceptance
region

Rejection region

Assumed claim
$\bar{X}'$ or p'

In both one-tailed tests, the claimed value is treated as the population value and placed at the center of the sampling distribution. The critical ratio is determined from the appropriate statistical table, e.g., the normal curve table in Appendix B, based on the level of significance chosen for the test. The actual Z-ratio based on the sample is then compared with the critical ratio to determine whether the claim has credibility or should be rejected. In particular, if the actual ratio exceeds the critical ratio, the claim is rejected, meaning that the sample result is unlikely to lie in the same sampling distribution assumed by the primary (judgment) claim. If the actual Z-value is less than the critical Z-value, the claim is accepted, meaning that the difference between the claimed result and the sample result could be due to chance variation or sampling error alone.

For situations involving two sample means (or proportions), the claim or hypothesis usually is that the two values simply are not different; in other words, if there is no *a priori* reason to believe one is larger (or smaller) than the other, then the test is two-sided. In this case, it is usually simplest to work with the difference between the two sample estimates and to test whether their difference is significantly different from zero. What we are really testing here is the hypothesis, called the *null hypothesis*, that there is *no difference* between the two population means (or proportions). Figure 10.6 displays this situation. In general, when the null hypothesis involves an assumption of "no difference," there are two critical regions (or limits), and such tests are two-tailed.

Figure 10.6 — Two-tailed test

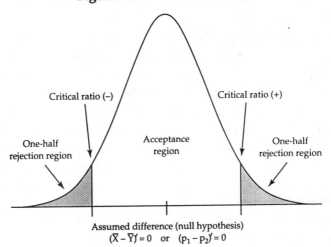

Critical ratio (–)   Critical ratio (+)

One-half rejection region   Acceptance region   One-half rejection region

Assumed difference (null hypothesis)
$(\bar{X} - \bar{Y}) = 0$ or $(p_1 - p_2) = 0$

Logical Steps in Tests of Significance

Because there are many decision-making situations in research and management when significance tests are necessary, we provide the following step-by-step guidelines in logical order to aid in making the kinds of tests covered in this chapter:

(1) Decide if the test is one or two-tailed.

(2) Decide on the significance (or risk) level.

(3) Translate the chosen risk level into the number of standard errors (called the critical ratio), from the appropriate standard table (e.g., Appendix B).

(4) Compute the appropriate standard error(s).

(5) Compute the actual number of standard errors (called the actual ratio) from the sample data.

(6) Make the appropriate decision from a comparison of the actual ratio with the critical ratio; if the actual ratio exceeds the critical ratio, the difference is significant, and vice-versa, insignificant.

(7) Check on the validity of the assumptions.

Guidelines for applying these steps

As suggested earlier, to answer the above questions it is advisable to sketch the normal curve and enter on it the appropriate points, such as the judgment claimed mean $(\overline{X}')$, the rejection region(s), and the acceptance region. (See Figures 10.4 through 10.6.)

(1) The decision regarding whether the test should be one-tailed or two-tailed is up to the researcher or management, guided by the competing claim. If the competing claim is that the mean or percentage is larger (or smaller) than the primary claim, the test is one-sided. If no such direction is specified, but the assumption is made that the two means (or percentages) are equal (null hypothesis), except that they may differ by chance in either direction, then the test is two-sided.

(2) Also decided by management or the researcher is the risk (in percent) they are willing to tolerate for making a wrong decision or concluding that there is a significant difference when, in fact, there is no difference. While our examples often used the 5% risk level, critical decisions may well use stricter risk levels, such as 1%.

(3) The critical ratio converts the chosen risk level into the corresponding number of standard errors to be tolerated, guided by whether a one-tailed or two-tailed test is involved. For a two-tailed Z-test, first divide the risk level percent by two and subtract the result from 50 percent; then look up the resulting percentage in Appendix B, to determine the number of standard errors involved, i.e., the critical ratio. For a one-tailed Z-test, subtract the risk level percent from 50 percent; then look up the result in Appendix B to determine the critical ratio (minus for a left-tailed test or plus for a right-tailed test).

(4) Based on the particular situation, calculate the appropriate standard error of the difference. For two-sample tests, determine whether the pooled or unpooled method is more appropriate.

(5) Compute the actual ratio from the sample data to determine the number of standard errors which actually separate the primary from the competing value, using the appropriate formula, as summarized below.

Formulas for steps (4) and (5), involving both averages and percentages are:

(a) Judgment or claimed mean $(\overline{X}')$ compared to a sample mean $(\overline{X})$:

$$Z = \frac{\overline{X} - \overline{X}'}{\sigma_{\overline{X}}} = \text{actual ratio, where } \sigma_{\overline{X}} = \frac{\sigma_x}{\sqrt{n}}$$

(b) Two sample means $(\overline{X} \text{ and } \overline{Y})$ compared to one another:

$$Z = \frac{(\overline{X} - \overline{Y})}{\sigma_{\overline{X} - \overline{Y}}} = \text{actual ratio, where:}$$

(unpooled) $\qquad \sigma_{\overline{X} - \overline{Y}} = \sqrt{\sigma_{\overline{X}}^2 + \sigma_{\overline{Y}}^2}$

or (pooled) $\qquad \sigma_{\overline{X} - \overline{Y}} = \sigma_{pooled} \sqrt{\frac{1}{n_x} + \frac{1}{n_y}}$,

where $\qquad \sigma_{pooled} = \sqrt{\frac{(n_x - 1)\sigma_x^2 + (n_y - 1)\sigma_y^2}{n_x + n_y - 2}}$,

or $\qquad \sigma_{pooled} = \sqrt{\frac{\sum(x - \overline{X})^2 + \sum(y - \overline{Y})^2}{n_x + n_y - 2}}$

(c) Judgment or claimed proportion (p') compared to a sample proportion (p), provided np and nq > 5:

$$Z = \frac{p - p'}{\sigma_p} = \text{actual ratio, where } \sigma_p = \sqrt{\frac{p'(1-p')}{n-1}}$$

(d) Two sample proportions (p_1 and p_2) compared to one another, provided np_1 and $nq_1 > 5$, and np_2 and $nq_2 > 5$:

$$Z = \frac{p_1 - p_2}{\sigma_{p_1 - p_2}} = \text{actual ratio, where:}$$

$$\text{(unpooled)} \quad \sigma_{p_1 - p_2} = \sqrt{\sigma_{p_1}^2 + \sigma_{p_2}^2}$$

$$\text{or (pooled)} \quad \sigma_{p_1 - p_2} = \sqrt{p\,q\left(\frac{1}{n_1 - 1} + \frac{1}{n_2 - 1}\right)},$$

$$\text{where } p = p_{pooled} = \frac{n_1 p_1 + n_2 p_2}{n_1 + n_2} \text{ and } q = 1 - p_{pooled}$$

(6) The appropriate decision as to significance of the difference between the two values depends on a comparison of the results in (4) and (5) above. If the actual ratio exceeds the critical ratio, the primary claim (null hypothesis) is rejected and the difference is declared *significant*, meaning the difference is probably real and is not likely to be due to sampling error or chance variation alone; if the actual value is less than the critical value, the primary claim is not rejected and the difference in the population is considered *not significant*, meaning the observed difference well may be caused by sampling error or chance variations rather than a real difference in the groups being compared.

(7) The assumptions required to make valid significance tests were summarized earlier in the section on "Assumptions Underlying Significance Tests." The assumptions include: sample data were obtained by random selection methods; serious non-sampling errors have been guarded against or removed; the appropriate method of computing the standard error of the sample mean or the sample percentage was used; the underlying universe of data-values follows, at least approximately, a normal or bell shaped curve; the sample size should be more than 30 for Z-tests; and, for Z-tests dealing with percentages, there is the additional requirement that np > 5 and nq > 5.

Three examples:

Example #1 — The monthly rate of unemployment, a figure of national importance, for November of a recent year dropped to 5.9 percent (0.059) from 6.1 percent (0.061) in October. Both estimates were derived from a random sample of about 60,000 respondents. Some people claimed this to be a significant improvement in the employment situation. Can this be considered a significant decline in the unemployment rate?

Since there is no reason to believe that the unemployment rate had to go down (it could have gone up), this is reasonably a two-tailed test.* Since the Census Bureau computed the standard error of the diffencence between the two monthly percentages to be .13 of one percent, the following is a solution to the question:

1. This is a two-tailed test for the reasons stated above. (See figure below.)

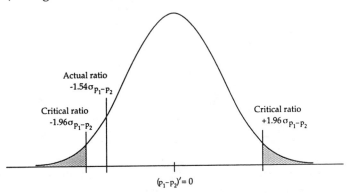

2. The significance level was chosen to be 5%.

3. The critical Z-ratio, therefore, is ±1.96.

4. The actual ratio is:
   $$Z = (0.059 - 0.061) / 0.0013 = -1.54 \; \sigma_{p_1-p_2}.$$

5. Decision: Since the actual ratio does not exceed the critical ratio, the change in the rate is not significant; it is probably caused by sampling variation in both estimated percentages.

---

* Alternatively, since this change was claimed to be a decrease, we could apply a one-tailed test and consider only the right side of the sampling distribution as a basis for *rejecting* the claim that it *decreased*.

A month later, in December, the unemployment rate dropped to 5.8 percent (0.058). Was this a real drop in the unemployment rate from 6.1 percent in October?

> *Answer:* Yes, because the actual ratio, obtained by
> $Z = (0.058 - 0.061) / 0.0013 = -2.31$, is in excess of ±1.96 standard errors, the critical ratio at the 5% level of significance.

Example #2 — The entertainers of a local television program claimed that at least 20 percent of the households in the area watched their program. Representing the competing claim, management made a random sample survey by telephone and found from 60 respondents that only 10 percent watched that program.

1. Is this a two-tailed or one-tailed test?

    Answer: One-tailed on the left side, since the claim was that 20 percent or more watched the program. (See figure.)

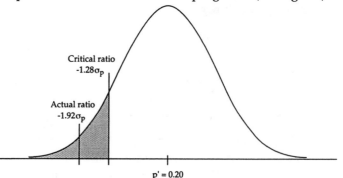

2. What is the critical ratio if the one-tailed test was based on a 10 percent level of significance?

    Answer: Critical ratio = -1.28 standard errors (minus because it is left-tailed).

3. What would be the standard error of the claimed percentage?

    Answer: $\sigma_p = \sqrt{\dfrac{(.20)(.80)}{59}} = 0.052$.

4. What is the actual ratio as determined by the Z-test?

    Answer: $Z = (0.1 - 0.2) / (0.052) = -1.92 \ \sigma_p$.

5. Is the difference significant?

    Answer: Yes, since the actual ratio exceeds the critical ratio, the evidence is strong enough to allow management to reject the entertainers' claim.

Example #3 — Company A tested a random sample of 100 sheets of wrapping paper and found a tearing weight of 4 pounds and a standard deviation of 0.1 pound. A competitor's paper (Company B) was found to have a tearing weight of 3.8 pounds with a standard deviation of 0.15 pounds based on a random sample of 120 sheets.

1. Is this to be a one-tailed or two-tailed test?

   Answer: A two-tailed test, because there is no statement that one paper is expected to have a stronger tearing weight than the other, i.e., the direction of any difference does not matter. Therefore, the null hypothesis is that the difference is zero.* (See figure.)

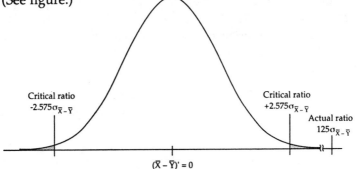

Critical ratio $-2.575\sigma_{\bar{X}-\bar{Y}}$

Critical ratio $+2.575\sigma_{\bar{X}-\bar{Y}}$

Actual ratio $125\sigma_{\bar{X}-\bar{Y}}$

$(\bar{X}-\bar{Y})'=0$

2. At a 1 percent level of significance, what is the critical ratio?

   Answer: 2.575 standard errors.

3. What is the standard error of the difference between the two sample means?

   Answer: Using the unpooled estimate because the two samples supposedly represent two different grades of paper,

$$\sigma_{\bar{X}-\bar{Y}}=\sqrt{\left(\frac{0.1}{100}\right)^2+\left(\frac{0.15}{120}\right)^2}=0.0016.$$

4. What is the actual ratio?

   Answer: $Z = (4 - 3.8) / 0.0016 = 125\sigma_{\bar{X}-\bar{Y}}$.

5. Are the two tearing weights different?

   Answer: Yes, because the actual ratio of 125 standard errors far exceeds the critical ratio of 2.575.

---

*The problem could be re-stated as a one-sided test: Is Company A's paper stronger than that of Company B's? This test would more appropriately support an advertising claim Company A's paper is stronger.

The t-Test of Significance (Small Samples)

Reference was made previously to the fact that the Z-test is valid when large samples are used (n>30) and the universe is approximated by a normal distribution. In such situations, the known normal distribution properties (Appendix B) can be used to determine the critical ratio and compare it with the actual ratio, using the Z-variate. However, when samples with 30 or fewer units are used and the universe standard deviation is not known, i.e., it must be estimated from a sample (as is usually the case), we need a testing method other than the Z-test, mainly because the sampling distribution of means (or percentages) based on small samples differs from the normal distribution. In such situations, sampling theory provides a different symmetrical distribution, called the *t-distribution*, to make significance tests, called *t-tests*. See Figure 10.7.

Figure 10.7
Comparison of the normal distribution and the t-distribution
for random samples of 4 units (n=4)

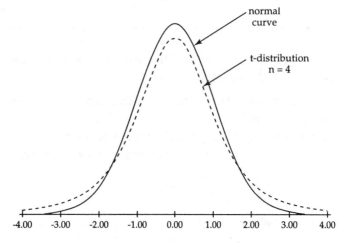

It can be seen from Figure 10.7 that the range of the t-distribution is wider than that of the normal distribution. Therefore, the percentages of sample estimates which fall within various standard errors around its mean differ from the corresponding percentages in the normal distribution. These differences become smaller as the samples become larger and conversely, become larger as the sample decreases. For example, while the normal sampling distribution includes 95% of all values within ±1.96 standard errors around the mean, it would require ±2.26 standard errors around the mean of the t-distribution when random samples of 10 units are involved. The required standard-error values can be readily determined from the table of t-values in Appendix C, recognizing that the term *degrees of freedom* (identified as d.f.) in the table means (in this case) that the sample size is reduced by 1. For samples of 5 units, ±2.78 standard errors would be required to include 95% of the estimates. In some cases, these characteristics of the t-distribution can seriously affect the results required to detect a significant difference.

A distinguishing feature of the t-distribution is that the critical t-value (in the table in Appendix C) depends on the number of *degrees of freedom*, that is, the size of sample (n) reduced by the number of statistics previously estimated from the sample data. For example, the sample mean has already been computed and is used to derive the sample standard deviation, so the effective sample size is reduced to (n–1) degrees of freedom whenever the standard deviation must be used; this is the case, for example, when an actual t-value is calculated. When a single sample mean is involved, n is reduced by 1; when two sample means are pooled (as in the case of the pooled method), the combined sample size $n_1 + n_2$ is reduced by 2.

Two additional conditions underlie use of the t-distribution: (1) the population about which inferences are to be made must be approximately normally distributed, and (2) the population standard deviations of the two random samples must be assumed to be equal if they are used in a t-test.

Two examples

The following examples illustrate applications of the t-test, where t, the number of standard errors separating a sample mean from a claimed mean is $t = \dfrac{\overline{X} - \overline{X}'}{\sigma_{\overline{X}}}$ or, for comparing two means, $t = \dfrac{\overline{X} - \overline{Y}}{\sigma_{\overline{X} - \overline{Y}}}$. Other than determining the critical ratio, the similarities between the application of t-tests and Z-test become readily apparent by the following two examples:

Example #1 — In a test of life-span, 20 electric bulbs (randomly selected) were burned until they failed, giving a mean failure time of 400 hours ($\overline{X}$ = 400 hours) and a sample standard deviation of 10 hours. At a 5 percent level of significance, decide whether credence can be given to a judgment claim that the mean life of these bulbs is at least 430 hours.

First, note that this is a one-tailed test on the left side, since the competing claim based on the sample must be that the life of the bulbs is less than 430 hours. (See figure.)

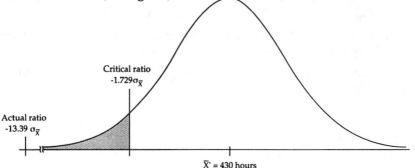

Critical ratio
$-1.729 \sigma_{\bar{X}}$

Actual ratio
$-13.39 \, \sigma_{\bar{X}}$

$\bar{X}' = 430$ hours

We also observe that the life-span frequency distribution of these electric bulbs is likely to be normally distributed (due to chance variations in the manufacturing process, as discussed in Chapter 3). Also, since n is less than 31, a t-test is appropriate. The universe standard deviation is estimated from the sample and, as a result, one degree of freedom is lost; therefore, the critical t-value must be located alongside d.f. = 19 in the t-table, Appendix C. With a 5 percent significance level on one tail, we would look for the critical t-value under the column $t_{.050}$. Thus, the critical t-value is −1.729 standard errors. Note that if this were a two-sided test, we would look under $t_{.025}$; since this table deals with one-half of the distribution, like Appendix B for the normal curve, the total of 5% for a two-sided test would be split equally into .025 in each tail, shown in the table under $t_{.025}$.

From the sample data we estimate the standard error of the sample mean to be:

$$\sigma_{\bar{X}} = \frac{\sigma_x}{\sqrt{n}} = \frac{10}{\sqrt{20}} = \frac{10}{4.47} = 2.24 \text{ hours.}$$

Next, we compute the actual t-value (or actual ratio) for the difference between the two means by

$$t = \frac{\bar{X} - \bar{X}'}{\sigma_{\bar{X}}} = \frac{400 - 430}{2.24} = \frac{-30}{2.24} = -13.39 \, \sigma_{\bar{X}}.$$

This leads to our *decision:* The actual t-value exceeds by far the critical t-value of 1.729 at the 5 percent significance level. The claim of a mean life of at least 430 hours is strongly rejected.

Example #2 — Extending the above problem, suppose that a second random sample, this time of 10 electric bulbs, drawn later from the same process, gave a mean life of 375 hours (say, $\overline{Y}$ = 375 hours) and a standard deviation of 5 hours. Is the difference between the two sample means (400 versus 375 hours) significant at the 5 percent significance level?

First, we decide that this is a two-tailed test, since there is no reason to suppose that one mean must be larger (or smaller) than the other. In other words, the difference of ±25 hours is to be tested to determine whether it is significantly different from zero. Thus, we have a null hypothesis that the difference is zero, which is to be tested by the appropriate significance test. (See figure.)

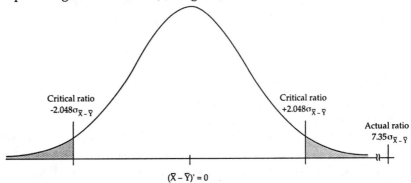

Critical ratio $-2.048\sigma_{\overline{X}-\overline{Y}}$

Critical ratio $+2.048\sigma_{\overline{X}-\overline{Y}}$

Actual ratio $7.35\sigma_{\overline{X}-\overline{Y}}$

$(\overline{X}-\overline{Y})' = 0$

We also observe that a t-test is required, since the number of observations in the combined sample is 30, resulting in $n_x + n_y - 2$ = 20+10–2 = 28 degrees of freedom. The critical value of t at the 5 percent significance level, with 28 degrees of freedom, is 2.048 standard errors. This value is located in the column for 28 degrees of freedom under the column $t_{.025}$. (Remember, for a .05 two-tailed level of significance, divide the .05 by 2, which gives .025 in each tail of the t-distribution).

Since our problem states that the samples were drawn from the same population, though at different times, it is valid to assume equality of the standard deviations; therefore, the two sample standard deviations can be pooled. The standard deviation from the combined samples may be obtained by the pooling formula:

$$\sigma_{pooled} = \sqrt{\frac{\Sigma(x-\overline{X})^2 + \Sigma(y-\overline{Y})^2}{n_x + n_y - 2}} \text{ , or, equivalently, } \sigma_{pooled} = \sqrt{\frac{(n_x-1)\sigma_x^2 + (n_y-1)\sigma_y^2}{n_x + n_y - 2}} \text{ .}$$

Substituting into the second pooling formula, we get:

$$\sigma_{pooled} = \sqrt{\frac{(20-1)(10)^2 + (10-1)(5)^2}{(20+10-2)}} = \sqrt{\frac{2125}{28}} = 8.71 \text{ hours.}$$

Next we compute the standard error of the difference between the two sample means by:

$$\sigma_{\overline{X}-\overline{Y}} = \left(\sigma_{pooled}\right)\sqrt{\frac{1}{n_x} + \frac{1}{n_y}} = (8.71)\sqrt{\frac{1}{20} + \frac{1}{10}} = (8.71)(0.39) = 3.40 \text{ hours.}$$

Finally, we compute the actual t-value by:

$$t = \frac{\overline{X}-\overline{Y}}{\sigma_{\overline{X}-\overline{Y}}} = \frac{400-375}{3.40} = \frac{25}{3.40} = 7.35 \, \sigma_{\overline{X}-\overline{Y}}.$$

Decision: Since the actual t-value exceeds the critical t-value of 2.048, we reject the claim that the two means could well represent the same population, i.e., we conclude that they are almost surely significantly different due to causes other than chance.

Importance of significance testing

It should be apparent from the discussion of both the t-test and Z-test of significance that each has widespread real-world applicability in many fields of human endeavor. Significance testing plays a particularly vital role in medical research to improve health and the quality of life, as exemplified by its use in the testing of drugs and other interventions for treating AIDS, heart disease, cancer, polio, tuberculosis, etc. Significance testing also plays a very important role in many other fields, including quality and productivity improvement. In general, when small samples are involved and the actual standard deviation of the population is not known, as is the case in many medical, biological, chemical, engineering and agricultural research situations, the t-test must be used. The Z-test, on the other hand, may be used to make decisions in research and management problems involving the use of large samples, such as inventory valuation, auditing, and inspection.

The Chi-Square Test of Significance

The significance tests discussed previously in this chapter were confined to arithmetic means and percentages, utilizing normal-distribution or t-distribution theory. However, there are other decision-making situations to which these theories do not apply. One such situation which arises quite often in statistical analyses deals with determining if a given frequency distribution differs significantly or not from another frequency distribution. A few examples of this type of problem are:

(1) Is the frequency distribution of the diameter of a bicycle wheel as derived from a random sample of wheels reflective of a normally distributed universe of such wheel diameters?

(2) Is the distribution of apartment renters by the amount of their annual income significantly different from that of home owners by their amount of annual income?

(3) Is the age distribution of the non-respondents to a mail questionnaire survey, as shown by a random sub-sample of such non-respondents, significantly different from the corresponding age distribution of the respondents?

To deal effectively with such decision-making situations, mathematicians have developed another powerful sampling distribution, called the Chi-Square distribution. When applied to testing hypotheses about frequency distributions, the Chi-Square distribution is a theoretical frequency distribution of replicated random sample-derived frequency distributions, somewhat similar conceptually to the normal distribution expected from replicated sample-derived means, except that these are estimated frequency distributions obtained from equal-sized random samples drawn from a specific population frequency distribution. The Chi-Square distribution provides a sound basis for testing the assumption (or hypothesis) that the frequency distribution derived from a given random sample does not differ significantly from its expected parent distribution or any distribution that is specified, regardless of its shape or pattern.

To measure the likelihood to which the frequency distribution derived from the sample (the observed frequency distribution) deviates by chance from the specified or expected frequency distribution, it is necessary to compute a sort of Z-value or actual ratio, namely, a Chi-Square value. The actual Chi-Square ratio is obtained by the formula:

$$\text{Chi} - \text{Square} = \sum \frac{(\text{Observed frequency} - \text{Expected frequency})^2}{\text{Expected frequency}}.$$

315

In symbols, this is: $\chi^2 = \sum_{i=1}^{k} \dfrac{(O_i - E_i)^2}{E_i}$,

where O_i represents the observed number of items, or the observed frequency, of the i-th class of the k classes in the frequency distribution, based on the sample; E_i represents the expected number of items or the expected frequency of the i-th class; and Σ represents the summation of the terms $(O_i - E_i)^2 / E_i$ over the separate k cells or classes of the distribution.

The Chi-Square test, when applied to frequency distributions or differences in *cell counts*, deals with noncontinuous or discrete data. Contrary to the case of normal distributions, the Chi-Square distribution has fixed probabilities of occurring due to chance that are completely dependent on the number of cells (classes) in the distribution reduced by 1, i.e., k–1 cells. Thus, for example, if the sample-derived distribution, which is being tested for significance from the expected distribution, has seven (7) classes or cells, 2.5% of the many theoretically possible Chi-Square values will equal or exceed a Chi-Square value of 14.45 due to chance. This property is readily found by examining Appendix D. In the row marked 6 degrees of freedom (7–1 = 6) and in the column showing the probability of occurrence due to chance of 0.025, the corresponding critical Chi-Square value is 14.45. In essence, the Chi-Square variate is a one-tailed test. It looks like the distribution shown in Figure 10.8 (for a seven-cell frequency distribution).

Figure 10.8

Chi-Square distribution for a seven cell frequency distribution

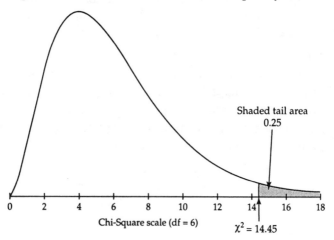

Shaded tail area 0.25

Chi-Square scale (df = 6)

$\chi^2 = 14.45$

There are three major differences between the Chi-Square distribution and the normal distribution. First, Chi-Square is a skewed distribution, although it approaches a normal distribution as the number of cells or classes of the frequency distributions increases. Second, whereas there is only one normal distribution with one set of fixed properties (determined by the mean and standard deviation), there is a separate and distinct Chi-Square distribution for each separate number of cells involved in the frequency distribution being tested. Therefore, the Chi-Square table in Appendix D summarizes its properties for numerous cell sizes as reflected by the corresponding degrees of freedom (k–1). For example, for a test dealing with five cells (k=5) we will find that for a significance level of 2.5% the critical Chi-Square value will be 11.14 (for 4 degrees of freedom), as compared with 14.45 for a seven-cell test (degrees of freedom = 6) at the same significance level.

Procedural guidelines for χ^2 tests

The following guidelines can be used to make tests of significance of the difference between an observed and an expected frequency distribution.

1. Note that these tests are always one-tailed tests on the right-hand side of the Chi-Square distribution.

2. Determine, with the decision-maker, the significance level that will be used to make the decision whether the two distributions differ significantly or not.

3. Locate in the Chi-Square table the critical Chi-Square value consistent with the significance level and the appropriate number of degrees of freedom, i.e., the number of cells (k) in the frequency distribution reduced by one (k – 1).

4. Using the data for the observed and expected cell frequencies, compute the actual Chi-Square value by the Chi-Square formula given earlier. Note that the observed and expected distributions must have the same number of cells and the same *total* number of cell frequencies (i.e., $\Sigma f = n$).

5. Compare the actual Chi-Square value thus computed with the critical Chi-Square value determined in step 3. If the actual value exceeds the critical value, the difference between the

two frequency distributions is considered to be significant; otherwise, accept the hypothesis that they may be the same and that any difference probably is due to chance.

Two examples

To illustrate the procedure for this type of Chi-Square test we present the following two decision-making situations.

Decision-situation #1 — In a past housing survey conducted by mail with a national random sample of households, a substantial number of those contacted did not respond. However, a random sample of 58 non-respondents was successfully re-contacted in a follow-up survey, and selected information was obtained from them. One of the important characteristics was the "number of rooms in homes owned by the home owners." The question to be answered was: Are the non-respondent home owners (represented by the follow-up random sample) different from the respondent home owners (treated as the true or expected population) with respect to the number of rooms in their homes?

The distribution of number of rooms in the homes of the 58 households in the non-respondent (observed) sample is compared, as shown below, with the corresponding expected distribution of the respondent households. The latter distribution was obtained by applying to the number 58 the percentage distribution actually shown by the original respondent households. This was done because the Chi-Square test requires, as explained previously, that the total cell counts be the same for both the observed and expected distributions. The sample of original respondents, which numbered in the thousands, thus was appropriately reduced to equal the number of home owners in the special follow-up sample.

Number of rooms in home	Non-Respondents (Observed)	Respondents (Expected)
under 5	6	8
5	11	17
6	17	17
7	15	8
8	9	8
Total	58	58

Thus, treating the distribution of original respondents as the true or expected (E) distribution, and the distribution of follow-up non-respondents as the observed (O) distribution, we obtain the numbers shown in the table above.

The guidelines then were followed to decide whether these two distributions differed significantly:

1. This is a right-hand tail test (as is always the case in χ^2 tests).

2. The risk level acceptable to the research director was 5% (.05 level of significance).

3. For this risk level the critical Chi-Square value for four degrees of freedom is 9.49. This was determined by entering the Chi-Square table (Appendix D) in the column marked .05 and then moving down to the row corresponding to four degrees of freedom (i.e., five cells less one).

4. The actual Chi-Square value was then computed, as follows:

$$\chi^2 = \sum_{i=1}^{5} \frac{(O_i - E_i)^2}{E_i} = \frac{(6-8)^2}{8} + \frac{(11-17)^2}{17} + \frac{(17-17)^2}{17} + \frac{(15-8)^2}{8} + \frac{(9-8)^2}{8}$$

$$= \frac{4}{8} + \frac{36}{17} + \frac{0}{17} + \frac{49}{8} + \frac{1}{8} = 0.5000 + 2.1176 + 0 + 6.1250 + 0.1250 = 8.8676.$$

5. *Decision* — Since the computed Chi-Square value is less than its critical value (8.87 compared to 9.49), we conclude that the difference between the non-respondent and respondent home-owning households, on the characteristic "number of rooms in the house," is not significant at the 5% level. In other words, it is probably valid to use the percentage distribution by number of rooms of the respondents to represent the entire universe under study.

Decision-situation #2 — Chapter 7 presented two pages of random digits. Altogether there are 2250 digits between 0 and 9 on both pages. Because these were generated by a random process, each digit is expected to occur 10 percent of the time, or 225 times over the two pages.

Question: Is there a significant difference between the actual and expected frequency of the 10 digits 0 through 9? This is a typical candidate for a Chi-Square *goodness-of-fit* test. We follow the guidelines given earlier.

1. This is a right-hand-tail test.
2. The level of significance chosen is 5%.
3. For this level of significance (in the 0.050 probability column), the critical Chi-Square value is 16.92 for (10 – 1) = 9 degrees of freedom.
4. The actual Chi-Square value, computed by reference to the data shown in the accompanying table, is 8.52.

Digit (k=10)	Observed frequency (O)	Expected frequency (E)	Difference (O–E)	Difference squared $(O-E)^2$	Ratio to expected $(O-E)^2/E$
0	201	225	−24	576	2.56
1	216	225	−9	81	0.36
2	224	225	−1	1	0.00
3	220	225	−5	25	0.11
4	233	225	8	64	0.28
5	239	225	14	196	0.87
6	250	225	25	625	2.78
7	233	225	8	64	0.28
8	208	225	−17	289	1.28
9	226	225	1	1	0.00

Total ... 8.52

5. *Decision* — The actual Chi-Square value is 8.52. Since this is well below the critical Chi-Square value of 16.92, we conclude that the actual distribution of the single digits is not significantly different from their expected random distribution. Since we have no reason to believe that the distribution is not random, we can reasonably use the two pages to select simple random (equal-chance) samples, at least on a one-digit basis. In other words, the two pages may be accepted as usable random digits for universes no larger than 10 items. Similar tests would be required for universes with as many as 100 items (double digits), 1000 items (3 digits), etc.

Caution

An important caution to be observed in using the Chi-Square test is to assure that each cell in the frequency distribution of the sample contains at least 5 items. Experience has shown that the foregoing Chi-Square formula yields a close approximation to the theoretical Chi-Square distribution provided the above condition is met. To comply with this requirement when a sample cell with less than 5 items occurs, it should be combined with the number of items in an adjacent cell. This, of course, reduces the number of classes or cells in the distribution and thus reduces the degrees of freedom too.

Summary

This chapter presented many different ways of making decisions, so many that it can make one wonder which is the most appropriate method for a given decision situation. Often decisions are made entirely on the basis of judgment, without knowing the chances in quantitative terms of being wrong. In important decision situations, it is best to know quantitatively the risk of an erroneous conclusion. Statistical theory provides a sound basis for making decisions with a quantitative knowledge of the risks involved. Using random sampling and the theory of normal distributions in combination with the law of probability, insignificant differences (probably caused by chance variations) can be distinguished from significant differences (probably due to causes other than chance variations). Several different methods for accomplishing this differentiation are available. As described in this chapter, they are: the confidence interval, the Z-test, and the t-test techniques.

By deciding in advance on the acceptable level of confidence (the probability of making a correct decision), it is possible by use of a random sample to construct a confidence interval around the competing sample mean (or proportion) corresponding to that confidence level and to determine if the assumed or claimed mean (or percentage) falls within the interval. If it does, the claim is accepted. When the difference under study is between two sample means or percentages, two independent confidence intervals can be constructed, and if they overlap, the claim that the means (or percentages) of the populations under study are the same can be accepted; otherwise, the claim or assumption of equality is rejected, i.e., it is concluded that each mean (or percentage) probably comes from a different universe.

More powerful tests of significance than the confidence interval method are the Z-test and the t-test. Under these methods, the risk level we are willing to tolerate is converted to the corresponding number of standard errors by referring to the appropriate Appendix table (B, C, or D) for the critical ratio (Z, t for samples of n<31, or χ^2, respectively). Based on the sample data, the actual ratio is then computed. When the actual ratio is larger than the critical ratio, the difference is considered to be significant; otherwise, the difference is considered to be not significant.

In applying significance tests, a distinction between one-sided and two-sided tests is essential, since the critical ratios for Z or t will differ when one tail or both tails of the theoretical sampling distribution are involved. The basic criterion for determining on which side the test falls is the competing (or alternate) claim, which must be determined in advance by management or the researcher. Thus, if the competing claim is that the true mean is smaller, a one-sided test on the left tail of the sampling distribution is involved. On the other hand, if the competing claim is that the true mean is larger, the test is on the right tail of the sampling distribution. When the competing claim or hypothesis is simply that the two means are really not different (i.e., the sample means differ because of sampling error or chance variation), then the difference may be either positive or negative and a two-sided test is involved; in other words, the test is two-tailed if the claimed difference (null hypothesis) is zero between the two estimates. It is suggested that a graphic sketch be drawn to display the claimed or hypothesized value as the central value, and the rejection region(s), in order to clarify the "direction" of the test.

In addition, the analyst should consider whether the assumptions underlying the various significance tests are valid. Among the primary considerations are: the use of random selection methods, the elimination of serious non-sampling errors, if any, in the estimates, the size of sample used, the use of the pooled or unpooled method for computing the standard error of the estimates, and the underlying distribution of the population x-values; furthermore, when tests on proportions are involved, it should be assured that the products np and nq exceed 5, in order to validate the assumption that we are dealing with normal distributions.

Because many different significance tests are available, the stronger ones are summarized below.

Large sample theory Z-tests, used for:

1. Claimed mean (or percentage) versus sample mean (or percentage)
2. Sample mean (or percentage) versus sample mean (or percentage), unpooled method
3. Sample mean (or percentage) versus sample mean (or percentage), pooled method

Small sample (n<31) theory t-tests, used for:

1. Claimed mean (or percentage) versus sample mean (or percentage)
2. Sample mean (or percentage) versus sample mean (or percentage), unpooled method
3. Sample mean (or percentage) versus sample mean (or percentage), pooled method

In addition to these 12 tests (6 for mean-values, 6 for proportions), the less direct and less powerful confidence interval tests may be used.

Chi-Square tests:

Another important significance test is the Chi-Square test. It deals with determining if a frequency distribution derived from a random sample differs from another (or expected) frequency distribution. Some actual examples are described in detail in "The Chi-Square Test of Significance" section. Important cautions to be observed in using this test are to assure that each cell in the frequency distribution of the sample contains at least 5 items and that the total number of items in each frequency distribution (n) is the same.

Problems

Suggestion: Use the guidelines given in the text.

1. After visually inspecting a wooden bridge for pedestrians over a small brook, a consulting engineer advised management that the bridge could hold a maximum weight of 4,500 pounds.

    (a) Which of the nine decision-situations does this illustrate?

    (b) What are its limitations?

2. A complete inventory was made of the value of rubber tires in stock by an automobile tire distributing company. The result showed a total value of $450,000. This result was challenged by the supplies manager, who claimed its value as being "no more than $350,000".

    (a) Which of the nine decision situations does this problem illustrate?

    (b) Which figure would you advise management to accept, and why?

    (c) What step or steps would you advise be taken before accepting either one or the other figure?

    (d) What are the advantages and disadvantages of a complete count as a basis for decision?

3. A special population enumeration in a small town made by the local government yielded the following figures: population = 34,508; employed = 13,875; unemployed = 565. At about the same time, a random sample block survey, made by a market research organization to obtain more detailed information, yielded estimates which were about 5% higher for each of the three categories above.

    (a) Which of the nine decision-situations does this problem illustrate?

    (b) Which of the two sets of figures would you accept as a benchmark? Why?

    (c) What other alternatives are open to accepting either set of figures?

4. For the following specified levels of significance, determine the critical value of Z in making significance tests involving large random samples.

   (a) One-sided: .10; .05; .02; .01; .005

   (b) Two-sided: .10; .05; .02; .01; .005

5. A team of radio entertainers claimed that at least half ($p' \geq .50$) of the local radio audience listened to their program. Before contracting for their services, a consulting firm ran a random sample survey and found that out of a sample of 100 radio listeners, 40% listened to the team's program. Does the sample result provide enough evidence to reject the entertainers' claim at the 5% level of significance?

   (a) Would this involve a one-tailed or two-tailed or test?
   What determines a one-sided and a two-sided test?

   (b) What is the critical Z-value in this case, at a 5 percent significance level?

   (c) Can the team's claim of at least 50% be accepted at the 5 percent significance level?

   (d) What is the probability that the difference, or larger, is due to an assignable cause, such as a subjective inclination in the team's claim?

6. In testing a roulette wheel for "bias," an experimenter found that the number "7" out of 19 other numbers on the wheel turned up 540 times in a run of 10,000 trials.

   (a) Would this test of bias toward "lucky 7" involve a one-tailed or two-tailed test?

   (b) At a 1 percent significance level, what would be the critical Z-value?

   (c) At a 1 percent level of significance, would you conclude that the wheel is biased toward the "lucky" number 7?

7. The engineering aimed-at thickness of 10-ounce copper sheets is .0212 inches. A firm manufacturing these sheets tested a random sample of 100 sheets and found that the average thickness was .0214. The standard deviation as determined from the sample was .00033 inches. Analyze the problem that seems to be indicated by the test data.

8. A group of students, using a judgment sample survey of 625 cars on the parking lots in the city of their school, found that 25 percent were Fords. About three months later, the Department of Motor Vehicles showed that 20 percent of the cars in the city were registered as Fords. Is the sample proportion significantly different from the true (registration) percentage? Give possible explanations for your findings.

9. Two grades of paper (high grade and medium grade) were tested for tearing strength by use of random samples of 100 and 60 sheets, respectively. The following are the results:

	High Grade	Medium Grade
Sample size	$n_x = 100$	$n_y = 60$
Sample mean	$\bar{X} = 5$ pounds	$\bar{Y} = 3$ pounds
Sample standard deviation	$\sigma_x = .03$ pounds	$\sigma_y = .02$ pounds

Management wished to determine at a .05 significance level whether there was a real difference in the strength of the two grades of paper.

(a) Would this be a one-tailed or two-tailed test?

(b) Make this determination by the unpooled method of computing $\sigma_{\bar{X}-\bar{Y}}$.

(c) Make this determination by the pooled method of computing $\sigma_{\bar{X}-\bar{Y}}$.

(d) Would the latter be valid?

10. Two persons applied for a file clerk job in a Veterans Administration hospital. After a day's training on the filing codes, the following test results were obtained:

	Clerk A	Clerk B
Number of items filed (per hour)	1400	1400
Number filed with some error	84	112
Error rate (p)	.06	.08

Using the appropriate methods, determine which of the two clerks to choose for the job, based on quality; assume all other skill factors are about equal for each clerk.

11. Ten randomly selected company tires were tested for average wear-out mileage. The mean mileage was 21,000 and the sample standard deviation was 630 miles.

    At a 1 percent level of significance, determine if a management claim of an average mileage of 22,000 can be given credence? *(Note: Use t-distribution table and appropriate degrees of freedom.)*

12. The breaking strength, in pounds, of eight specimens of a given type of manila rope, randomly selected, were: 570, 540, 490, 530, 550, 560, 480, and 520.

    (a) Using a 5 percent significance level, determine if a claimed average strength of 550 pounds can be given credence.

    (b) If the true standard deviation of the population of this type of manila rope is 25 pounds, what affect would this information have on your conclusion in (a) above? (Note: It is possible to use the Z-test, since σ'_x is known and the sample is drawn from a normally distributed population.)

13. Two grades of transistor radio batteries were tested for length of life (with a random sample of 8 each) to determine if one is better than the other, with the following results:

    Numbers of hours of life:
    _____

    Grade A — 217; 219; 220; 218; 242; 220; 220; 229
    Grade B — 191; 222; 241; 252; 209; 199; 199; 225

    Using the appropriate methods and assumptions, test the equality of the two means.

14. Two different samples of circular discs were taken from a production process, one in the morning and one in the night, with the following summary data:

Time	Sample Size	Sample mean diameter (inches)	Sample standard deviation (inches)
Morning (x)	16	3.8	0.24
Night (y)	10	4.1	0.36

    At a 5% significance level, is there reason to believe that the mean diameter in the evening shift is different from that in the morning production process?

15. A coin was tossed 100 times with the following outcomes. Can we conclude that it is a fair coin at the 1 percent level?

Outcome	Frequency
Heads	30
Tails	70
Total	100

Chi-Square Test Problems

16. A roulette wheel consisting of ten digits 0 to 9 yielded the following results after 100 spins of the wheel.

Digit:	0	1	2	3	4	5	6	7	8	9	Total
Frequency:	6	11	12	8	7	13	10	15	8	10	100

Can we conclude at the 5 percent level of significance that the wheel is behaving as expected?

17. A single die with six facets was rolled 120 times to test it for "bias" with the following results:

Outcome:	1	2	3	4	5	6	Total
Frequency:	25	30	15	22	9	19	120

What is the decision with respect to bias of the die, on a 2.5 percent significance level?

Chapter 11

Statistical Process Control

*"Quality Is Job 1"**

Total Quality Management and Statistics

In the past decade, considerable publicity in magazines, newspapers, and television has been given to three letters in our alphabet, namely, TQM, meaning Total Quality Management. Because of this extensive publicity, few people in the work force have not heard or seen these three letters or some variant of them, but how many know what TQM really means? It means total management commitment to achieve, and continually maintain and improve, high levels of quality of product and service; and it means that satisfying consumer quality requirements is the prime goal of management. It also means that statistical theory and methods must play a key role in achieving these goals, for without measurement and objective analysis of relevant data there is no way of knowing present levels of quality, where the quality problems are, how to overcome them, and how to measure improvement and maintain satisfactory levels of quality.

Statistics alone cannot improve quality. It takes management commitment, participation, support, and leadership; it also takes employee participation; it takes employee empowerment, a team approach, and above all, training.** An essential part of training is knowing how to harness the power of statistics — its principles, concepts and methods to measure, analyze, and act to improve quality.

The primary objective of this chapter is to describe and illustrate some of the main principles, concepts, terms, and methods of statistics that play a major role in TQM and its variants through what is known as *statistical process control*, or *SPC*. SPC is a body of principles,

---

*Slogan of Ford Motor Company.

** Quality professionals are convinced that without fundamental changes in the organization's culture along these lines, TQM is unlikely to succeed in its objectives.

concepts, and statistical methods for periodically measuring and analyzing variations in process quality or performance, and for establishing clear-cut signals for management to investigate the causes of "significant" variations or error-rates. Thus, readers will not only appreciate the essential contributions of statistics to quality improvement, but also, when the opportunity arises, will understand and know how to use these methods. The chapter's objective, however, assumes that a reasonable background in statistics has been, or will be, acquired from studying earlier chapters of this book, particularly Chapters 3, 4, 5, 7, 8, 9, and 10. With an understanding of the statistical tools covered in these chapters, it should become relatively simple to apply them in that part of TQM generally identified as statistical process control, which is the primary subject of this chapter.

Statistical Tools and Key Words

As a refresher, some of the basic statistical tools and terms related to quality management are reviewed briefly here.

Statistical tools

Array — A listing of measured items arranged in order of size. (Chapter 3)

Percentage — A percentage is obtained by dividing the number of items representing a specific attribute (e.g., those with an error), by the total number of items examined. (Chapters 1 and 3). This percentage is also called the *fraction defective,* generally expressed in decimals.

Frequency distribution — The number of items in a sample or universe that fall into each class or grouping of the variable chosen by the analyst. (Chapter 3)

Arithmetic mean — The average computed by adding the x-values of a set of data and dividing the sum by the total number of items in the set: $\overline{X} = \dfrac{\sum x}{n}$. (Chapter 4)

Standard deviation — A standard measure of the extent of variation of a process characteristic. It is a measure of the average difference of the individual x-values from their mean value by:

$$\sigma_x = \sqrt{\frac{\sum (x - \overline{X})^2}{n-1}} \ . \ \text{(Chapter 5)}$$

Coefficient of variation — The standard measure of variation from the mean expressed as a percent of the mean by: $\frac{\sigma_x}{\overline{X}}(100)$. (Chapter 5)

Range — The difference between the highest and lowest x-values of a set of values. (Chapters 3 and 5)

Standard error of the sample mean — A measure of the extent of variation due to chance in a sample-derived mean, with 68% confidence that this variation is not larger: $\sigma_{\overline{X}} = \frac{\sigma_x}{\sqrt{n}}$. (Chapters 8, 9, and 10)

Standard error of the sample percentage — A measure of the extent of chance variation in a sample-derived percentage, with 68% confidence that this variation is not larger: $\sigma_p = \sqrt{\frac{p(1-p)}{(n-1)}}$. (Chapters 8, 9, and 10)

Key words

Process — An operation producing a product or service with a beginning and an end, generally operating continually. Some processes are divided into sub-processes each with a beginning and an end. To understand the complete make-up of a process, a flow-chart is necessary to identify each sub-process and its place and direction in the overall stream of production or service delivery from beginning to end.

Quality — A product or service which can be satisfactory or unsatisfactory to its consumers, whether internal or external to the organization. When measured quantitatively, quality can be expressed in the form of variables (e.g., varying dimensions) or attributes (e.g., in conformance or not in conformance with a specific quality requirement).

Control — Periodic and continuous monitoring of variations in product or service quality designed to control excessive variation and thus improve quality or avoid deterioration of satisfactory quality levels.

Subgroup — A random sample of a number of measurements or observations used to quantify and analyze quality.

Statistical process control (SPC) — A body of principles, concepts, and statistical methods for periodically measuring and analyzing variations in process quality or performance, and for establishing clear-cut signals for management to investigate the causes of "significant" variations or error-rates. Such signals must be acted upon to determine if they are due to "assignable causes;" if so, further action must be taken to prevent the recurrence of "bad causes" and encourage the adoption of "good causes" of variation. (This definition generally applies to "control charts," since other methods are available to improve process quality).

Assignable causes — Quality variations which are found to have been caused by a factor (or factors) other than chance (e.g., a machine breakdown).

Constant-cause system — A process operating under its usual (normal) conditions which cause it to produce items or services which vary in quality. The factors causing variation are numerous (such as humidity, temperature, machinery used, facilities, etc.), but none is outstanding in its impact on the process. Under constant-cause systems, process variations generally exhibit an important feature, namely, the variations approach a normal frequency distribution or a bell-shaped curve.

Significant variations — Quality variations which have a very low probability of having been caused by chance, that is, variations which are very likely due to special or assignable causes.

Insignificant variations — Quality variations which have a very high probability of having been caused by common causes or chance, and therefore, are very unlikely to be due to assignable or special causes.

Risk — The numeric chance (e.g., 5%) that a signal for investigating a significant variation may not be due to an assignable cause and, therefore, the investigation may result in an unfruitful effort (called a *Type I error*).

Confidence — The numeric chance (e.g., 95%) that a variation is caused by chance and, therefore, is not worthy of investigation.

Type II error — The numeric chance that an insignificant variation may be due to an assignable cause but is not acted upon.

Control chart — A graphic method of displaying process variations over time with upper and lower control limits; it is used to identify significant variations as distinct from insignificant variations in the process. It emits signals for investigation when significant variations occur.

Statistical control — A process whose variations are insignificant, said to be operating "in statistical control" or (simply) "in control," indicating that the process is operating under a constant-cause system and its natural capability.

Specifications — Management or engineering quality objectives which aim at a specified quality dimension for individual parts or items, but with some (specified) tolerable plus and minus (±) variation from the standard dimension.

Natural process capability — The general maximum and minimum variations in the dimensions of a product or service produced by a process that is in a state of statistical control. These limits are usually set at ± 3 standard deviations from the mean dimension produced by the process.

Measurement of Quality

Quality must be measured to reduce variation in product or service quality. One way to measure quality is through the use of *variables*; the other is through the use of *attributes*.

In the case of variables, the x-values differ in dimension from item to item, such as the length of wire strands used in making umbrellas, length of time to deliver mail, number of days (time) elapsed in paying invoices, etc. Practically an unlimited number of products or services are quantifiable in the form of variables. In all these instances, an average of the variables being measured (x-values), excluding outliers, can be computed to represent the process norm.

In the simplest case of attributes, the items produced or services rendered differ only in two ways — either they have the attribute (e.g., they are acceptable) in which case x=0, or do not possess the attribute (e.g., they are not acceptable) in which case x=1. Thus, for example, when a payment-voucher has no errors, it is given an x-value of zero; when it has one or more errors, x=1. When the sum of these x-values is obtained it yields a count of the number of items which possess the attribute. When this number is divided by n, the sample size, it yields a percentage (p) of items possessing the attribute. This percentage is generally identified as the fraction defective, an error rate, a non-compliance rate, a non-conformance rate, a reject rate, etc.

How to collect appropriate data

To measure and control the quality of a process in either quantitative form (i.e., variables or attributes), it is necessary to collect data over a reasonable period of time in order to get a representative sample of the process variations. There are three different ways of collecting such data: complete accounting, judgment sampling, and random sampling. To assure a valid reflection of process variations and also to economize in data collection, the preferred method is periodic random selections of produced items or services, using the smallest possible size of sample.

Two ways are available to obtain a random sample large enough to reflect the behavior of a process. One is by using a one-time large sample. This method would be reasonable and acceptable for a survey or audit of a fixed universe at a given point of time; however, it would not be adequate for a process that continually produces items or services over a long period of time. For SPC purposes, the appropriate way to measure process variation is to select small, random samples periodically. When cumulated over a reasonably long period of time these periodic small samples produce a large sample. A question, however, arises: What is a "small periodic random sample" and what is a "reasonably long period of time"? When the quality characteristic being measured is a variable, samples as small as 4 to 10 items taken periodically are generally considered adequate. In attribute sampling (e.g., error rates), samples of 50 or more items are generally considered necessary. Choices for a "reasonably long period of time" remain to be demonstrated in the sections "How to Construct and Use a Control Chart" and "Control Chart for Fraction Defectives (p Chart)."

Selecting a process to control

When we think of starting a statistical quality improvement effort, which requires management commitment and leadership as well as skilled staff and the allocation of funds, we need to decide where our resources will most likely yield the best returns. This means selecting a fairly costly process which is believed to be causing quality problems. In addition, it means knowing which person (or machine) or persons (or machines) are actually doing the work (input). Persons and machines are considered to be the origin or source of good or poor quality. A flow chart is an essential way of identifying the sub-processes of a process and work-flow from person to person or machine to machine. A simple example of a flow chart is shown below. This is followed by another, more complex, flow chart shown in Figure 11.1.

Adjudicating a Claim for Reimbursement

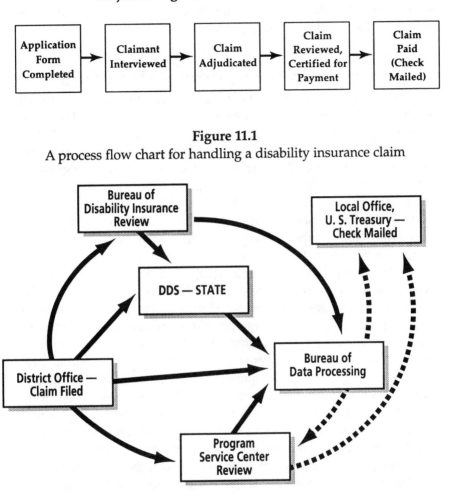

| Application Form Completed | → | Claimant Interviewed | → | Claim Adjudicated | → | Claim Reviewed, Certified for Payment | → | Claim Paid (Check Mailed) |

Figure 11.1
A process flow chart for handling a disability insurance claim

Source: Social Security Administration, OASIS (November, 1978)

Some causes of poor quality or errors

The causes of poor quality depend on the particular product or service involved in the chosen process. The following are examples of causes of quality problems:

Product — Failing to meet a quality standard of weight, length, fluid content, diameter, life span, strength, time lapse, etc.

335

Service — Misfiling, mishandling, misclassification, computer-entry errors, complaints, missing signatures, typos, failure to meet time-schedule, damaged or lost luggage, etc.

The Pareto Method of Quality Improvement

There are a number of statistical methods for detecting quality problems and taking action to prevent their recurrence. A primary requirement is to measure or quantify the process or operation in order to identify the source and/or cause of the problem. Among the available techniques of statistical analysis are the array technique, frequency distributions, graphic displays, and control charts. One method that can pay good dividends is called the *Pareto method,* named after the person who first formalized it. Because it is a logical and reasonable method, many statistical analysts have used this method long before it was credited to Pareto.

The objective of the Pareto method is to determine, by the collection of appropriate quantitative data on performance, which source or sources and which cause or causes create a major part of the quality problem, such as a large percentage of defective or erroneous items. Experience has shown that, in many instances, a relatively few persons or machines or *sources* (e.g., 20%) account for a large percentage (e.g., 80%) of the quality problem. The same condition of "concentration" often occurs when the analysis is of the *causes* of the problem, such as operator error, power surge, defective material, incorrect coding, etc. Professor Joseph Juran, in his many writings, calls this analysis "sorting out *the vital few and the trivial many.*"

This phenomenon occurs so frequently that the Pareto method of analysis is a good investment of resources, especially in the initial effort to improve quality. To apply this analytical method, we first need to determine if this vital few and trivial many condition actually exists in a process or activity. Once found by proper statistical analysis, usually by computing the percentage of all errors or defects by source or cause, management action can be concentrated on the main problem areas to correct the quality problem at its source. Actions on the source, such as giving proper training, clarification of instructions, improving communication, improving the quality of raw materials, etc., can result in reduced errors or defectives. Some illustrations of the "vital few and trivial many" condition are shown in the next four tables.

It can be readily observed from Table 11.1 that nearly 63 percent of the visitors to the United States entered through only 1.3 percent of the ports (vital few) and that less than 0.25 of one percent entered through nearly 63 percent of the ports of entry (trivial many). Furthermore, 98 percent of non-immigrants entered through fewer than 20 percent of the ports, whereas the other 2 percent entered through the remaining 80 percent of the ports.

Table 11.1

Distribution of ports of entry and non-immigrants admitted to the U.S.A., by size of port, in a given year

Size of Port (Entrants)	Number of Ports	Number of Visitors (000)	Percent of total Ports	Percent of total Visitors
Total	296	6,704	100.00	100.00
500,000 or more	4	4,212	1.34	62.83
90,000-499,999	8	1,256	2.70	18.73
15,000-89,999	25	968	8.45	14.44
5,000-14,999	14	136	4.73	2.04
1,000-4,999	41	101	13.85	1.51
500-999	18	13	6.08	0.20
under 500	186	17	62.84	0.25

Source: Immigration and Naturalization Service, U.S.A.

Table 11.2

Distribution of vouchers and amounts requested for payment, by size of voucher, October, 19XX

Amount requested	Number (000)	Amount (millions)	Percent of total Vouchers	Percent of total Dollars
Total	61.0	$25.30	100.0	100.0
Under $25	19.9	$0.30	32.5	1.1
25 - 49	9.9	$0.40	16.3	1.6
50 - 99	10.2	$0.90	16.7	3.6
100 - 199	8.2	$1.20	13.4	4.8
200 - 499	6.9	$2.00	11.4	7.9
$500 and over	5.9	$20.50	9.7	81.0

Source: Special study by U.S. Department of Health and Human Services.

Table 11.2 shows a similar condition of concentration, namely, nearly 10 percent of the vouchers, those amounting to $500 or more, covered 81 percent of the total amount requested for payment. Conversely, vouchers of less than $100 (nearly two-thirds of all the vouchers) accounted for only about 6% of all the money.

Listed in Table 11.3 are various causes of filing errors and the frequency of each cause as determined by a random-sample study for a given organization. This table shows that over 55 percent of the filing errors were caused by an incorrect data transmission code and by computer failure.

Table 11.3

Number and percent of record-filing errors,
by cause of error, Agency ABC

Cause of error	Number	Percent of total
Total	370	100.00
1. Keying error	40	10.81
2. Lack of signature	34	9.19
3. Data transmission code	107	28.92
4. Incorrect Social Security number	20	5.41
5. Name spelled incorrectly	15	4.05
6. Computer failure	98	26.49
7. Lost or misplaced	15	4.05
8. Illegible entry	28	7.57
9. Procedural error (untrained employee)	13	3.51

Table 11.4

Distribution of errors made by local postal employees
in a sample study

Code	Cause of error	Number	Percent of total
	Total	286	100.0
1	Wrong identification	41	14.34
2	Arithmetic error	127	43.01
3	Misclassification of mail	82	28.67
4	Data in wrong column	14	4.90
5	Wrong weight	6	2.10
6	Miscellaneous errors	20	6.99

Source: U.S. Postal Service special study

Table 11.4 shows that out of 26,000 pieces of mail analyzed, the overall error rate of 1.1 percent (286/26,000) was very low. However, of these relatively few errors, the major causes were arithmetical computation errors (43%) and misclassification (of the class) of mail (28.67%). Management action to prevent recurrence of these primary causes of error led to further quality improvement.

Pareto analysts often prefer to present this type of data graphically, presumably because of its simplicity and clarity. The data in Figure 11.2 illustrate this mode of presentation.

Figure 11.2
Graphic presentation of error rates, by cause,
from data in Table 11.4

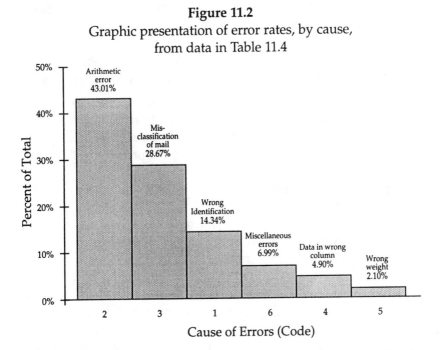

A final illustration of the "vital few and trivial many" condition is given by the following news items which appeared in the Washington Post (1/11/87):

"The medical establishment has argued that it's the current litigious nature of society, not bad medicine, that is driving up the cost of malpractice insurance. The doctor's lobby contends that physicians in high-risk fields such as obstetrics or surgery should consider themselves lucky if they have never been threatened with lawsuits. There is evidence from insurance company data, however, that a relatively small number of doctors is responsible for a large share of

339

claims payouts. Figures from the medical Mutual Society of Maryland, which insures about 85 percent of the doctors in the State, show that 6.6 percent of the doctors have been responsible for 93.7 percent of the company's payouts and defense costs during the 10-year period from 1976 to 1986."

These illustrations are enough to convince management and quality analysts that a promising start to improve quality is to use the Pareto method. A basic requirement, of course, is to collect quantitative data by source and cause of the quality problem. Then, the relatively simple Pareto method of analysis can contribute much to quality improvement at a given point in time.

The General Concept of a Control Chart

Another powerful technique, not only in quality improvement at a given point of time but also in maintaining satisfactory levels of quality on a continuous basis is the *control chart*. There are several types of control charts, each designed to reduce variation in the selected process and maintain quality at an acceptable level. Probably the most frequently used control charts are the $\overline{X}$ chart (for averages) and the R chart (for ranges).

As previously defined, a control chart is a graphical display of variations in a given measurable characteristic of a product or service. By using appropriate statistical methods, it provides signals for management action when variations are significant and worthy of investigation. When significant variations are found to be due to assignable causes, rather than chance, and management acts to prevent the recurrence of bad quality causes, quality improvement will result; likewise, when assignable causes are due to exceptionally good quality practices and management adopts these practices, improved quality also will result.

The ability of the control chart to emit signals for management action rests, in many respects, on several major principles. Among them are: the law of probability (Chapter 6), Central Limit Theorem (Chapter 8) and the law of normal distributions (Chapters 3, 4, 5, and 8). In Chapters 3 and 5 it was pointed out that variations due to chance tend to form a frequency distribution shaped like a bell.*

---

*As a refresher, the reader is advised to read the section of Chapter 5 entitled "Some Further Applications of $\overline{X}$ and σ_x to Normal Distributions."

Chance causes of variation generally result from processes operating under a constant-cause system. They are also the result of a sampling distribution, i.e., the frequency distribution of many replicated sample-derived means (or percentages) of a given process characteristic, as demonstrated in Chapter 8. It was also demonstrated in Chapter 8 that all the properties of a normal distribution are known and fixed by its mean and standard deviation. Thus, for example, one standard deviation set off on both sides of the mean includes 68% of all x-values in a normal distribution of original measurements. Similarly, replicated $\overline{X}$-values form a normal distribution when they are estimated from many random samples of a given size and by the same method of sample selection from a given process.

The effective use of control charts requires adherence to the following basic rules:

(1) The same measurement unit (e.g., time-lapse, length, weight, height, etc.) must be used throughout to determine the extent of variation;

(2) Sample size (number of items selected from each sub-group) must be known in order to measure the magnitude of sampling variation due to chance of each $\overline{X}$ or percentage (p), since that magnitude is influenced by the size of sample;

(3) The time-sequence order of the sub-groups (when the samples are taken) must be preserved to track quality problems at the time of their occurrence.

(4) The same measurement device must be used consistently under the existing constant-cause system.

When these rules are observed and periodic random samples of the process characteristic are analyzed over a reasonable period of time, the resulting data will be representative of the operation or the process under its usual (normal) conditions. The process mean and upper and lower variation *control limits* will serve their purpose of signaling management to take action at the appropriate time. Thus, management will be guided to concentrate attention on statistically-determined significant variations (the vital few), and to avoid undue concern with the numerous insignificant (chance) variations which occur in processes operating under a constant-cause system (the trivial many).

Constructing and Using a Control Chart for Averages ($\overline{X}$ Chart)

General Procedure

The following **six general steps** must be taken in logical order to construct and use any control chart:

1. Organizing
2. Planning
3. Data collection
4. Analysis for possible outliers
5. Revision of preliminary control chart
6. Operating the revised control chart.

These steps are demonstrated below with a chosen process and a control chart for averages ($\overline{X}$ chart).

1. Organizing — Cognizant of the fact that a successful SPC program follows TQM principles which require total management commitment to quality improvement, certain organizational steps must be taken before the collection of data and construction and use of control charts. At least the following five steps are considered essential:

(1) A top level manager (a quality facilitator) is selected to provide leadership and coordination across all divisions of the organization.

(2) A team (or teams) of staff members representing each subdivision of the organization is formed to conduct the study on a selected process or sub-process.

(3) The team, together with the quality facilitator, selects the process to be analyzed; preferably, the initial effort should be directed toward a reasonably simple quality problem to build confidence and expertise. The team flow-charts the process and decides on the type of control chart to use for the particular process characteristics of concern.

(4) A practical, down-to-earth training program in SPC is essential for management as well as professional and technical staff. Included in this program should be SPC techniques, concepts, and principles, without getting too complex.

(5) A training program is also required for supervisors and employees who will be involved in the process chosen for analysis.

2. Planning — Decide on the size of sample (sub-group size) and the history period (length of time) necessary to collect data typical of the process variations. Experience has shown that for an $\overline{X}$ chart, samples of 4, 5, or 6 items are generally sufficient, if the samples are selected regularly over a period of at least 40 days. To demonstrate the $\overline{X}$ and R charts, however, we deem it acceptable in this chapter to use data for 5 or 10 days with at least 10 sub-groups. The resulting control charts are **provisional** (just to get started).

A decision is needed on how often samples of process variations should be taken during each work day. In mass production processes, it may be quite often, such as hourly or every two hours. In service activities, the time-interval may be longer, such as twice a day, once a day, or every other day.

A decision is also needed on the "management level" of control and action. Generally, this would be at the first-line supervisory level and should include the employees of that unit. Also, the form of quantifying the product or service needs to be determined. It may be attributes, such as a go/no-go test. It may be variables, such as measurement of the length of an automobile part or length of elapsed time in providing a service. The demonstration to follow is based on variables (hours elapsed) and therefore is an $\overline{X}$ chart.

Table 11.5

A typical data entry sheet for an $\overline{X}$ chart and R chart

Process — Interoffice Mail Delivery, July, 1994

| Period of reading | Number of Hours to Deliver Internal Mail | | | | | | Mean | Range |
	x_1	x_2	x_3	x_4	x_5	Total	$\overline{X}$	R
Day 1	10	12	9	14	15	60	12	6
Day 2	12	14	8	16	10	60	12	8
Day 3	17	23	19	15	21	95	19	8
Day 4	14	16	12	15	13	70	14	4
Day 5	16	15	14	17	13	75	15	4
Day 6	20	18	15	10	17	80	16	10
Day 7	10	14	19	18	19	80	16	9
Day 8	14	17	12	15	17	75	15	5
Day 9	10	13	10	15	12	60	12	5
Day 10	21	14	10	20	15	80	16	11
Total	144	156	128	155	152	735	147	70

$\overline{\overline{X}}$ = Grand mean = 14.7 hours; Mean range = $\overline{R}$ = 7.0 hours

3. Data collection — Collect data over the chosen history-period typical of the process whose characteristic is being measured. The history-period should usually cover a reasonable period of time to allow for seasonal variations (if any) or other causes of variation that influence the characteristic being measured. However, the period need not necessarily cover a full year, recognizing that the initial operation of the control chart, even during a test-period, can yield good results as long as the chart is considered provisional, subject to change as more data and experience are accumulated over the year. Table 11.5 is a typical data entry sheet for an $\overline{X}$ chart and an R chart (to follow later).

4. Analysis for possible *outliers* — Since the history-period data may contain abnormal or unusual variations, they need to be detected, investigated, and eliminated if they are due to assignable causes. This is done later when, for example, the mean for day #3 ($\overline{X}$ = 19 hours) is found to represent an assignable cause. This would leave the remaining data reflective of a constant-cause system (or a process "under statistical control"). One way by which outliers can be found is by plotting the data and observing their movement and their pattern of variation. On occasion, an extremely out-of-line point can be thus identified as an outlier. Another way is to compute the average of averages, $\overline{\overline{X}}$, with preliminary upper and lower control limits. Some persons recommend using tight control initially, such as ±two sigma limits, and investigate all points outside of the control limits.* Most organizations use three sigma units for the control limits. Figure 11.3 illustrates a *preliminary* control chart, using 3 sigma limits to detect significant variations, i.e., outliers.

5. Revision of preliminary control chart — If inspection of the preliminary control chart reveals that an outlier point (or points) falls outside of the control limits, or that a series of successive points show a *trend* or a *run* of points (see the later section on "Signals for action"), such points must be investigated to determine whether they are due to assignable (bad) causes. If they are, they must be deleted from the history-period data and a revised, *provisional* control chart constructed.

6. Operating the revised, provisional control chart — When statistical control has been achieved (i.e., no points fall outside the control limits and no runs or trends are shown), the revised provisional

---

* See article by Raymond R. Mayer, "Selecting Control Chart Limits," *Quality Progress Magazine*, September, 1983.

control chart can be used as a starting point for continuous statistical process control.

Figure 11.3

Preliminary $\overline{X}$ control chart to investigate outliers

Average Number of Small Parcels per Cart, XYZ Post Office

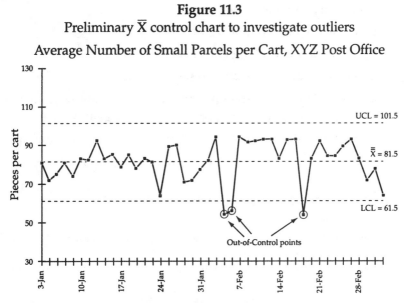

Demonstration with numbers and formulas

Using the hypothetical data shown in the data entry sheet of Table 11.5, we demonstrate the logical sequence of **eight technical steps** we use to construct and operate a provisional control chart for averages.

1. Consult with management (quality facilitator) and team members to determine the risk level for operating the preliminary control chart. The conventional control limits are generally three-sigma limits (with an associated risk of .26 of 1%), but there sometimes is reason to use tighter control limits initially, aimed at obtaining data reflecting a stable process by being more sensitive to the detection of possible outliers. "Risk" in this context means the chances that a signal for investigating a significant variation will fail to uncover an assignable cause and, therefore, the time spent investigating it will be wasted. After assignable-cause outliers are excluded, the revised, provisional control chart becomes the one to adopt.

    Assume that management has initially decided on a .26 of 1% risk level, with the primary objective of detecting assignable causes. This actually means a .13% risk on either side of the center line ($\overline{X}$), since action-signals are given on both sides of the control chart.

2. Translate the risk level chosen by management into the equivalent number of standard errors to tolerate. This can be done by reference to Appendix B, as follows:

   (a) Divide the risk-percentage by 2;

   (b) Subtract the resulting percentage from 50%;

   (c) Look up that percentage inside Appendix B;

   (d) Read off the corresponding number of sigma units in the first column (which is with one decimal point) and at the top row (which adds a second decimal point). In our example, $50\% - \left(\dfrac{.26\%}{2}\right) = 49.87\%$. This yields 3 sigma units.

3. Compute the mean for each sub-group by $\overline{X} = \dfrac{\Sigma x}{n}$.

4. Compute the average of these sub-group means, called the **grand mean**, or the mean of the means, by $\overline{\overline{X}} = \dfrac{\Sigma \overline{X}}{m}$, where m represents the number of sub-groups. Here, $\overline{\overline{X}} = \dfrac{147}{10} = 14.7$ hours. This $\overline{\overline{X}}$ is now established as the preliminary *norm* of the process.

5. Compute the standard deviation (σ_x) of the *process*, which is needed to compute the standard error of each sample mean. This can be computed by the method given in Chapter 5, by $\sigma_x = \sqrt{\dfrac{\Sigma\left(x - \overline{\overline{X}}\right)^2}{(nm)-1}}$.

   This method would be quite laborious, since it would involve making nm separate computations (in our example, nm = 50 computations, i.e., 5 daily measurements times 10 days). A short-cut method referred to in Chapter 5 has been developed by quality specialists which utilizes the average of the sub-group ranges, $\overline{R} = \dfrac{\Sigma R}{m}$. The standard deviation is then computed by

   $\sigma_x = \dfrac{\overline{R}}{d_2}$, where d_2 is a constant determined by the size of sample, n. Table 11.6 gives values of d_2 for various sample sizes. Since n=5 in our demonstration problem, $d_2 = 2.326$. Then, since $\overline{R} = \dfrac{70}{10} = 7.0$

(see Table 11.5), it follows that $\sigma_x = \dfrac{\overline{R}}{d_2} = \dfrac{7.0}{2.326} = \pm 3.01$ hours.

Table 11.6
Values of d_2 for computing σ_x by $\left(\dfrac{\overline{R}}{d_2} \right)$*

Sample Size		Sample Size	
n	d_2	n	d_2
1	none	11	3.173
2	1.128	12	3.258
3	1.693	13	3.336
4	2.059	14	3.407
5	2.326	15	3.472
6	2.534	16	3.532
7	2.704	17	3.588
8	2.847	18	3.640
9	2.970	19	3.689
10	3.078	20	3.735

6. Since each sample-derived mean is subject to sampling variation, compute the standard error of the sample mean based on n=5 measurements by $\sigma_{\overline{X}} = \dfrac{\sigma_x}{\sqrt{n}} = \dfrac{3.01}{\sqrt{5}} = \pm 1.346$ hours.

7. Construct the preliminary control chart and use it to detect outliers. To better understand how this control chart comes about, we demonstrate its origin step by step, as follows:

(a) The $\overline{X}$ chart requires a process mean or norm which is represented by $\overline{\overline{X}}$; in our case, $\overline{\overline{X}} = 14.7$ hours (see Table 11.5).

(b) It requires an upper control limit (UCL) namely, $\overline{\overline{X}} + Z\sigma_{\overline{X}}$, where Z is the number of standard errors previously decided on by the management risk level (step 1). In our case, Z = 3, so that

UCL = 14.7 + 3 (1.346) = 14.7 + 4.04 = 18.74 hours.

---

* Assumes that samples are selected from a normal distribution of x-values. Table 11.7 provides additional factors used in SPC.

(c) It requires a lower control limit (LCL), namely, $\overline{\overline{X}} - Z\sigma_{\overline{X}}$. In our case, the LCL = 14.7 – 4.04 = 10.66 hours.

(d) It requires an $\overline{X}$-vertical scale to plot the sample averages.

(e) It requires a horizontal date scale to identify the time period when each sample was selected.

The concepts underlying the construction of the preliminary control chart are shown pictorially in Figures 11.4 and 11.5. Since each $\overline{X}$ reflects the process average derived from a random sample, it is correct (based on the Central Limit Theorem) to assume that their frequency distribution will form a normal curve as shown in Figure 11.4. On it is shown $\overline{\overline{X}}$ and the UCL and LCL lines.

Figure 11.4
The theoretical distribution of $\overline{X}$'s, a normal curve

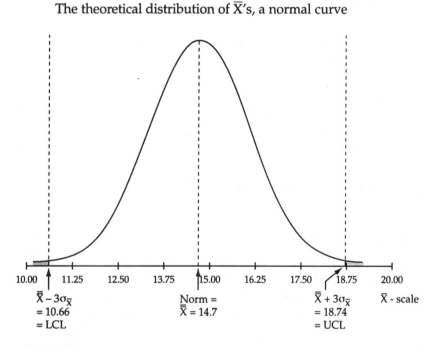

| 10.00 | 11.25 | 12.50 | 13.75 | 15.00 | 16.25 | 17.50 | 18.75 | 20.00 |

$\overline{\overline{X}} - 3\sigma_{\overline{X}}$
= 10.66
= LCL

Norm =
$\overline{\overline{X}}$ = 14.7

$\overline{\overline{X}} + 3\sigma_{\overline{X}}$
= 18.74
= UCL

$\overline{X}$ - scale

Source: Table 11.5.

Now imagine that this curve is turned 90 degrees counter clockwise. The line representing the norm and the upper and lower control lines are now parallel horizontal lines on the page. The resulting normal curve would look something like Figure 11.5.

Figure 11.5
Control chart format for the theoretical distribution of $\overline{X}$'s

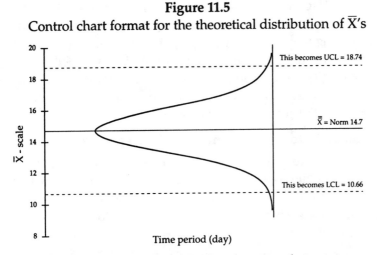

When the curved lines representing the normal curve are removed from the chart in Figure 11.5, and we show the individual $\overline{X}$-values by time period, we end up with an $\overline{X}$ control chart, as shown in Figure 11.6.

Figure 11.6
Preliminary $\overline{X}$ chart for average hours to deliver inter-office mail

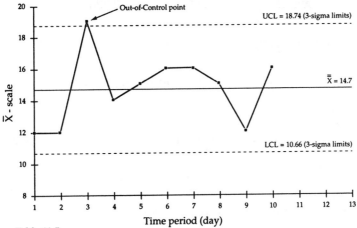

Source: Table 11.5.

8. Are there any outliers? — Now that the preliminary control chart has been constructed, it would usually be ready for use on a continuing basis if it did not have points representing assignable causes. When the original 10 points are plotted on the $\overline{X}$ chart, as

shown in Figure 11.6, the average for day #3 (19 hours) falls outside of the upper control limit. Assume that an investigation found it to be an assignable cause (e.g., the regular, trained mail clerk was on sick leave and an untrained employee was substituting). Therefore, the whole sub-group of five x-values for day #3 needs to be deleted and a revised, provisional $\overline{X}$ chart constructed excluding the entire outlier sub-group.

How to adjust history-period data for assignable causes

The data for day #3, representing an assignable cause, must be deleted. To use the control chart, even on a provisional basis, it must reflect a "state of statistical control," that is, a process operating under a constant-cause system. The steps for deleting the data for day #3 are as follows:

(a) Delete the assignable-cause data from the totals. The sum of the averages becomes 128, i.e., 147 – 19.

(b) The sum of the ranges becomes 62, i.e., 70 – 8.

(c) The revised norm, $\overline{\overline{X}}$, becomes 14.22, i.e., 128 / 9.

(d) The revised average of the ranges, $\overline{R}$, becomes 6.89, i.e., 62 / 9.

(e) The revised $\sigma_x = \dfrac{\overline{R}}{d_2} = 2.96$, i.e., 6.89 / 2.326.

(f) The revised $\sigma_{\overline{X}} = \dfrac{\sigma_x}{\sqrt{5}} = 1.32$, i.e., 2.96 / $\sqrt{5}$.

(g) The revised UCL $= \overline{\overline{X}} + 3\sigma_{\overline{X}} = 18.18$, i.e., 14.22 + 3 (1.32).*

(h) The revised LCL $=$ UCL $= \overline{\overline{X}} + 3\sigma_{\overline{X}} = 10.26$, i.e., 14.22 – 3 (1.32).*

The revised *provisional* $\overline{X}$ chart, called provisional because it may still be revised as more samples are taken over time, is shown in Figure 11.7. This chart is now in statistical control (all points are inside the control limits and no run or trend of points is displayed), so it can be used to monitor the process on a continuing basis.

---

* The 3 sigma control limits for the $\overline{X}$ chart also may be derived by the short-cut formula $\overline{\overline{X}} \pm A_2\overline{R}$, where the value of A_2 is obtained from Table 11.7 based on the size of sample. For our problem, the control limits become:

UCL $= \overline{\overline{X}} + A_2\overline{R} = 14.22 + 0.58(6.89) = 18.22$ and LCL $= \overline{\overline{X}} - A_2\overline{R} = 14.22 - 0.58(6.89) = 10.22$. These differ but very slightly from those derived above.

Operating the control chart

Assume that over the next 10 days, average mail delivery times, based on random samples of 5 deliveries a day, yielded the following hourly averages: 13; 14; 15; 15; 16; 16; 14; 9; 13; 16. Day by day these points are plotted on the provisional control chart and adjacent points are connected with straight lines, as shown in Figure 11.7.

Figure 11.7

Revised provisional $\overline{X}$ chart for interoffice mail delivery

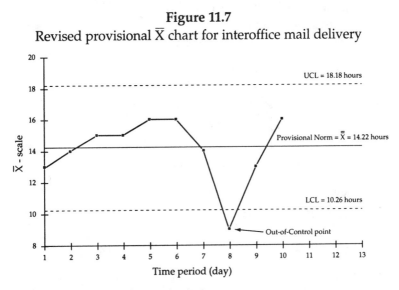

Source: Table 11.5, exclusive of day #3 (outlier).

Based on the 10 sample averages plotted on the provisional control chart (Figure 11.7), we see only one signal for investigation, namely, the 8th day's average of 9 hours, which falls outside of the lower control limit. When this point was investigated it was found to be a result of an innovative method of sorting and mail delivery developed by the supervisor of the unit. Management adopted this method and commended the supervisor.

Signals for action

The above example illustrated that an effective signal for management action is an out-of-control point on either side of the control limits. Actually (as mentioned casually earlier), at least two other signals for action exist. These are: (1) a *run* of points (about 7 or 8 points in a row on either side, above or below, the center line) and (2) a *trend* of points (about 7 or 8 points in succession, all moving in the same direction and crossing the center line). The four signals can be likened to the signals emitted by a traffic light, as follows:

> Green (all points are within the control limits, with no trend or run) = GO (chart A)
>
> Red (an out of control point) = ACTION (chart B)
>
> Yellow (7 or 8 points in a trend or run) = CAUTION (charts C and D)

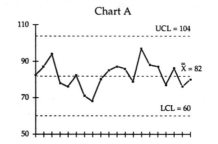

Chart A

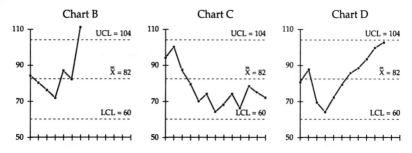

Management action

Management action involves four steps, taken whenever there is a "signal for action:"

(a) Investigate the cause of the signal.

(b) If it is determined to be due to an assignable bad cause, take steps to prevent its recurrence. Make a record of the cause and time

(c) If it is determined to be due to an assignable good cause, take steps to issue a commendation and/or adopt the improved procedure.

(d) If no assignable cause is found, take no further action but continue periodic sampling and monitoring of the process.

Review the status of the control chart

After a reasonable period of operation of the provisional control chart (perhaps 3 to 6 months), the norm and the control limits should be reviewed to determine if a significant improvement has occurred. For example, in our demonstration problem, if the average delivery time, exclusive of points representing bad assignable causes, decreased from 14.7 to 13 hours, we would determine whether the earlier mean has been significantly reduced. A Z-test of significance of the difference between the two means ($\overline{\overline{X}}_1 = 14.7$ hours and $\overline{\overline{X}}_2 = 13$ hours) would be appropriate, as demonstrated in Chapter 10. If the process mean has improved significantly, the control chart should be adjusted to the new norm and control limits.

The Range Chart (R Chart)

A Range chart (R chart) *must* always accompany the $\overline{X}$ chart. This is necessary because the $\overline{X}$ chart controls only the process norm but not the individual x-variations from the norm. The following are examples of different possible ways of obtaining the same $\overline{X}$ from a sample of two (or more) items but not the same standard deviation or range (R). They illustrate the necessity of tracking the variation as well as the average of any process being monitored.

$x_1 = 1$	$x_1 = 2$	$x_1 = 0.5$
$x_2 = 5$	$x_2 = 4$	$x_2 = 5.5$
$\overline{X} = 3$	$\overline{X} = 3$	$\overline{X} = 3$
$\sigma_x = 2.83$	$\sigma_x = 1.41$	$\sigma_x = 3.54$
$R = 4$	$R = 2$	$R = 5$

The ideal control chart for this purpose is the standard deviation (σ_x) chart. However, because of the numerous computations involved, the R chart was found to be a satisfactory substitute for the σ_x chart. It requires a bare minimum of computations by the short-cut methods developed by quality control specialists, as shown below.

The procedure for constructing an R chart is practically the same as that for constructing an $\overline{X}$ chart. We need a center line ($\overline{R}$) and upper and lower control limits based on a management-determined risk level for the initial trouble-shooting period to detect outlier points. In the $\overline{X}$ chart, it is simple to convert any risk level into the corresponding number of standard errors to tolerate by reference to the normal curve table in Appendix B. Based on the Central Limit Theorem, the sampling distribution of $\overline{X}$-replicates derived from a stable process approaches a normal distribution. In the control chart for ranges, however, the frequency distribution of replicated sample-derived ranges is not expected to closely approach the shape of a normal curve. Therefore, the control limits for the Range chart may not be exactly symmetrical around the norm ($\overline{R}$). To overcome this problem, the generally accepted 3 sigma control limits for the R chart are based on two factors whose values are determined by the size of the sample (n). These two factors are labeled D_3 and D_4 in Table 11.7. The D_4 factor when multiplied by $\overline{R}$ gives the UCL and the D_3 factor when multiplied by $\overline{R}$ gives the LCL for the R chart.

Table 11.7
Factors A_2, D_3 and D_4 for determining
three sigma control limits for $\overline{X}$ and R charts

Number of observations in sub-group	Factor for $\overline{X}$ chart	Factors for R chart	
		Lower control limit factor	Upper control limit factor
n	A_2	D_3	D_4
2	1.88	0	3.27
3	1.02	0	2.57
4	0.73	0	2.28
5	0.58	0	2.11
6	0.48	0	2.00
7	0.42	0.08	1.92
8	0.37	0.14	1.86
9	0.34	0.18	1.82
10	0.31	0.22	1.78
11	0.29	0.26	1.74
12	0.27	0.28	1.72
13	0.25	0.31	1.69
14	0.24	0.33	1.67
15	0.22	0.35	1.65
16	0.21	0.36	1.64
17	0.20	0.38	1.62
18	0.19	0.39	1.61
19	0.19	0.40	1.60
20	0.18	0.41	1.59

Upper Control Limit for $\overline{X} = \overline{\overline{X}} + A_2\overline{R}$ | Upper Control Limit for $R = D_4\overline{R}$
Lower Control Limit for $\overline{X} = \overline{\overline{X}} - A_2\overline{R}$ | Lower Control Limit for $R = D_3\overline{R}$
All factors in the table are based on the normal distribution.

Construction of the R chart is demonstrated by using the mail delivery data in Table 11.5, after removal of the outlier data for day #3. In the section "How to adjust history-period data for assignable causes," we found $\bar{R}$ = 6.89 hours. By the short-cut method, the UCL and LCL for ranges are as follows:

$$UCL = D_4 \bar{R} = (2.11)(6.89) = 14.54 \text{ hours, and}$$
$$LCL = D_3 \bar{R} = (0)(6.89) = 0 \text{ hours.}$$

Figure 11.8 is the appropriate R chart based on these data.

Figure 11.8
Provisional Range chart for hours to deliver interoffice mail

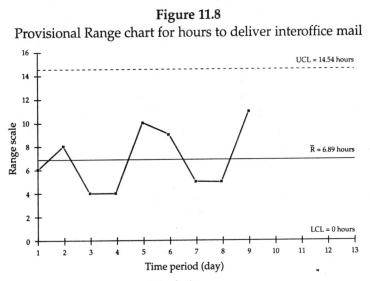

Source: Table 11.5, exclusive of day #3 (outlier).

Since none of the nine daily ranges in this problem fall out of the control limits and no runs or trends are displayed, the process (internal mail delivery) is in statistical control with respect to its variation (ranges) over time.

In general, before using the provisional R chart to monitor the variations in the process, outliers must be identified and, if attributable to assignable cause(s), eliminated from the history-period. This is the same procedure used in identifying outliers in the preliminary $\bar{X}$ chart, except that now we are concerned with exceptional ranges. After eliminating assignable causes, the resulting R chart is used provisionally to monitor variations in subsequent ranges.

Since both the $\bar{X}$ and R charts are essential to establish a sound system to improve quality and maintain a high and satisfactory level of quality, both charts should be displayed on the same posting sheet. Then, when each new sample of x-values is obtained, both $\overline{X}$ and R of each sub-group can be posted on the respective control chart.

By-Product Uses of the $\overline{X}$ and R Charts

The steps in constructing and using the $\overline{X}$ and R control charts were illustrated by using a service-type variable (time-lapse). This section uses a product-type variable to again demonstrate the construction of these two control charts. In addition, it describes some important by-product uses that can be made of the data collected for these charts.

Demonstration problem

Given: A random sample of 6 bolts (n=6) was taken by a defense contractor from a mass-production process geared to produce a 3-inch bolt. Over a period of 5 days, once in the morning and once in the afternoon, measurements of bolt length, in inches, were obtained, as shown in Table 11.8.

Table 11.8 — Data entry sheet for $\overline{X}$ and R control charts

Product: Three-inch bolt; Characteristic: Length; Measurement Unit: Inches

Contractor XYZ, Division #4

Period of measurement		x_1	x_2	x_3	x_4	x_5	x_6	Σx	$\overline{X}$	R
Day #1	Morning	3.0	3.1	2.9	3.0	2.9	3.0	17.90	2.98	0.2
	Afternoon	2.9	3.1	3.0	3.1	3.1	3.2	18.40	3.07	0.3
Day #2	Morning	3.1	2.8	2.9	3.0	2.8	3.1	17.70	2.95	0.3
	Afternoon	3.0	3.1	2.8	2.9	2.9	2.8	17.50	2.92	0.3
Day #3	Morning	2.9	3.0	3.1	3.1	2.9	3.2	18.20	3.03	0.3
	Afternoon	3.6	3.4	3.5	3.6	3.7	3.3	21.10	3.52	0.4
Day #4	Morning	3.0	3.1	2.9	3.0	3.1	3.0	18.10	3.02	0.2
	Afternoon	2.9	2.8	2.9	3.2	3.1	3.0	17.90	2.98	0.4
Day #5	Morning	2.9	2.9	2.9	3.0	3.0	3.1	17.80	2.97	0.2
	Afternoon	2.8	2.9	3.2	3.1	3.0	3.0	18.00	3.00	0.4
	TOTAL	30.1	30.2	30.1	31.0	30.5	30.7	182.6	30.43	3.0

$$\overline{\overline{X}} = 3.04; \quad \overline{R} = 0.3$$

We note that the data in Table 11.8 show $\overline{\overline{X}} = 3.04$ inches and $\overline{R} = 0.3$ inches for m=10 samples of n=6 bolts each. However, the first question, before proceeding further, is: Are there any outlier averages or outlier ranges? In this example, we demonstrate the array technique of detecting outlier points judgmentally, without first constructing a preliminary control chart. The history-period data may sometimes show an average or range that is clearly questionable by the array technique, although it is often worthwhile to use both methods, as indicated below. When the $\overline{X}$'s are arrayed in size-order, as shown in Table 11.9, the mean of 3.52 inches for the afternoon sample of day #3 seems way out of line when scanning the differences between adjacent averages. When investigated, that sub-group mean was found to be due to an assignable cause. A provisional $\overline{X}$ chart based on the conventional 3 sigma control limits confirms this finding, since $\overline{X}$ = 3.52 inches (the average for day #3, afternoon) is out of the upper control limit. Investigation found that the assignable cause was due to a faulty machine setting.

Table 11.9 — Array of $\overline{X}$'s

$\overline{X}$ (inches)	Difference from adjacent $\overline{X}$ (inches)	
2.92	–	
2.95	0.03	
2.97	0.02	
2.98	0.01	
2.98	0.00	
3.00	0.02	
3.02	0.02	
3.03	0.01	
3.07	0.04	
3.52	0.45	(day #3, afternoon)

When the ranges are analyzed using the array technique, none of the ranges are found questionable. Likewise, a check on the ranges using a Range chart found no outliers, since the control limits were:

$$UCL = D_4 \overline{R} = 2(.03) = .06 \text{ of an inch and } LCL = D_3 \overline{R} = (0)(.03) = 0.$$

By excluding the day #3, afternoon sub-group, the provisional $\overline{X}$ chart indicates that the process is in "statistical control." The revised $\overline{\overline{X}}$ becomes 2.99 inches and the revised $\overline{R}$ becomes .289 inches, resulting in the provisional $\overline{X}$ chart shown in Figure 11.9.

Figure 11.9
Provisional $\overline{X}$ chart for 3-inch bolts,
after eliminating the assignable-cause outlier sample

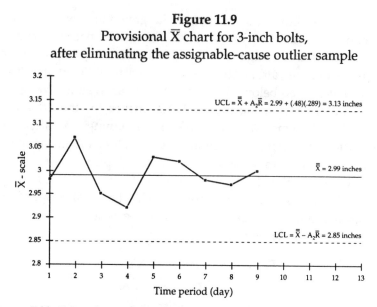

Source: Table 11.8, exclusive of day #3 afternoon (outlier).

Now to the by-product uses of the $\overline{X}$ chart and R chart data

The above provisional $\overline{X}$ chart, now based on 9 sub-groups, generally cannot yet be considered ready for final adoption. As a general guide, something in the neighborhood of data for 40 sub-groups should be used. However, as a learning device, we will use the limited data to demonstrate three other important uses of the $\overline{X}$ and R charts for a process which is in "statistical control."

Use #1 — Process capability — It is common practice for management to set *specifications* or objectives for its product or service quality before full-scale operation of the process. These specifications, whether set by engineering or management, generally deal with the dimensions of *individual items* (products or services). Thus, for example, the length of a wire strand for an umbrella may be set at 10 inches ± .01 of an inch. In our demonstration problem, these specifications would be based on the goal of producing a 3 inch bolt ± some reasonable allowance for variation in individual bolts. Since a process in a state of statistical control is expected to form a normal distribution of its individually produced items (i.e., its x-values), its *natural process capability* can be set at $\overline{\overline{X}} \pm 3\sigma_x$. Since management's specifications are also for individual items, it is appropriate to compare their specifications with the process capability. This analysis is always essential in the real world, because if the process is incapable of producing what the consumers want (as reflected in the specifications), many items would be rejected — at great cost and an impression that this is a poor quality producer.

For demonstration purposes, let us assume that management specifications for the individual bolt dimensions were stated in advance as 3 inches ± 0.2 of an inch* (perhaps overly liberal in the light of a competitive market). This means that a bolt larger than 3.2 inches or smaller than 2.8 inches would not be acceptable and, for that matter, would be rejected. These specifications can now be compared with the natural capability of the process ($\overline{\overline{X}} \pm 3\sigma_x$) determined from the control chart data, as follows:

(1) $\overline{\overline{X}}$ = 2.99 inches

(2) $\sigma_x = \dfrac{\overline{R}}{d_2}$ (where d_2 is obtained from Table 11.6) $= \dfrac{0.289}{2.534}$

  = 0.114 inches

(3) $3\sigma_x = 3(0.114) = 0.342$ inches

(4) $\overline{\overline{X}} \pm 3\sigma_x = 2.99$ inches ± 0.342, or the natural range
  of 2.648 inches to 3.332 inches

The comparison is made graphically below.

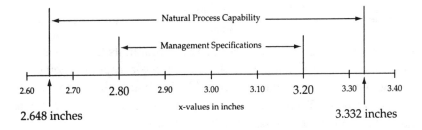

It can be seen that the process is unable to meet the management specifications. By drawing the normal curve of individual items produced by the normally operating process showing the rejection zones, this condition becomes readily apparent, as shown in Figure 11.10.

---

*The symmetrical tolerances implied here are not necessarily used in practice.

Figure 11.10
Management specifications compared with natural process capability

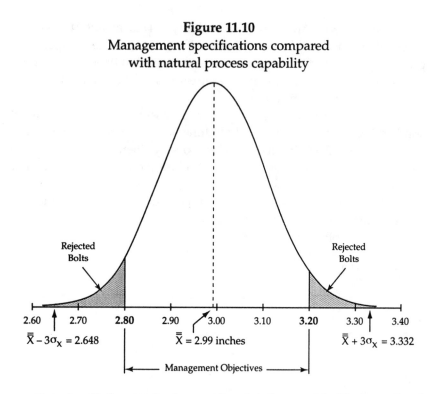

By using Z, the standard normal variate (covered in Chapters 5 and 10), we can determine quantitatively the extent of the problem facing management, namely, that about 8% of the bolts would be rejected. This 8% reject-rate is determined as shown below.

On the left-tail, $Z = \dfrac{2.8 \text{ inches} - 2.99 \text{ inches}}{1\sigma_x = 0.114 \text{ inches}} = -1.67$ standard deviations.

Appendix B shows that a distance of 1.67 sigma units from the mean of a normal distribution includes 45.25% of the acceptable items. By subtracting this percentage from 50% (the left half of the normal curve), it follows that 4.75% of the bolts would be rejected by the engineered standard of no-smaller a bolt than 2.8 inches.

On the right tail, $Z = \dfrac{3.2 \text{ inches} - 2.99 \text{ inches}}{0.114 \text{ inches}} = 1.84$ standard deviations.

Since 46.71% of the bolts between 2.99 and 3.2 inches would be acceptable (based on 1.84 sigma units), 3.29% would be rejected (50% − 46.71%).

Thus, all together, 8% of the bolts (4.75% + 3.29% = 8.04%) would be rejected by the process if management stays with the present specifications.

What are the management alternatives? —

(1) Accept the cost of 100% inspection to locate these poor-quality bolts and reject them from the production output. The customer would thereby get an acceptable product.

(2) Ignore these rejects and leave an undesirable impression on the customer that this is a poor-quality producer.

(3) By mutual agreement with the customer, perhaps with some price reduction, change the engineered specifications to meet the "normal" process capability of 2.648 – 3.332 inches.

(4) Improve the present process by developing innovative techniques or more refined tools or machines to meet the standards.

Importance of accuracy of the standard deviation — It can be readily seen that accuracy of the standard deviation σ_x is critical to this analysis and the resulting decisions. One way to assure its substantial accuracy is to compute σ_x by the more time-consuming, but more precise, standard deviation formula:

$$\sigma_x = \sqrt{\frac{\Sigma\left(x - \bar{\bar{X}}\right)^2}{nm - 1}}.$$

For example, the initial sample of 9 sub-groups (m=9), each with 6 bolts (n=6), represents a total sample of (9)(6) = 54 bolts. When σ_x was computed by the more precise formula, $\sqrt{\frac{.68517}{54 - 1}}$, it turns out to be substantially close — 0.1137 inches, as compared with 0.1140 inches computed by the short-cut formula $\sigma_x = \dfrac{\bar{R}}{d_2}$. While this comparison of the value of σ_x turns out to be good, it may in some cases be not as good. Therefore, a check on the accuracy of σ_x should always be made.

Use #2 — Product reliability — As indicated in Chapter 5, the coefficient of variation can be used to assess the overall reliability of a product or service. In our example, the coefficient of variation is

$\dfrac{\sigma_{\overline{X}}}{\overline{X}} = \dfrac{0.114 \text{ inches}}{2.99 \text{ inches}} = 0.038$ or 3.8%. A coefficient of variation this low, or lower, may reflect a high quality product with respect to its mean (2.99 inches). However, to interpret this 3.8% coefficient of variation as "good" or "bad" quality, we would need to compare it with other 3-inch bolt manufacturers in the competitive market to see if we are producing a more, or less, reliable product than others. It can be seen that an important objective of management in the competitive market can be to reduce the coefficient of variation of its product to its lowest possible percentage.

Use #3 — Discovering recurring problems — It is desirable, in the course of operating the control charts, to maintain a log of the assignable causes of excessive variation, when they are discovered. After a while, this log can provide valuable management information on the relative frequency of the different causes of quality problems and thus provide a guide for special efforts to prevent recurrence of the most critical causes of quality problems (*a la* Pareto method).

Control Chart for Fraction Defectives (p Chart)

Earlier we pointed out that quality of product or service can be quantified either by variables or attributes and sometimes by both. In the preceding sections we demonstrated the $\overline{X}$ and R charts, both of which deal with varying dimensions (x-values). This section introduces an attributes control chart, whereby the number and/or the percentage of items (or parts) in a process producing many items on a continuing basis are examined for conformance with a specific requirement. The *non-conformance* percentage is computed as a fraction (p) of all items produced. The control chart based on these non-conforming proportions is called a p chart, or a *fraction-defectives chart*. Thus, $p = \dfrac{\sum x}{n}$, where x is either 0 (in conformance) or 1 (not in conformance). We are using the word non-conformance, but in some applications non-conforming items are called "rejects," "defectives," "errors," or "non-compliance" cases. The variety of words used in connection with the p chart is indicative of the wide variety of fields of activity where this chart is applicable and, therefore, worthy of consideration for use in quality improvement and quality control.

To construct a p chart, it is appropriate to follow the logical sequence of steps described in the section "Constructing and Using a Control Chart for Averages." Suffice it to say, clear-cut management objectives or goals must be set for the p chart; definitions of the process and of a defective item are essential; a reasonably long period of time needs to be set aside to collect history-period data; the appropriate sample size (n) needs to be determined; and outlier points need to be detected and deleted from the history-period data if they are found to be due to bad assignable causes. To avoid repeating the details of the earlier guidelines, this section will cover only those elements of a p chart which need special treatment, namely, sample size, standard error of an estimated percentage, control limits, constructing the control chart, and determining process capability.

Size of sample

The $\overline{X}$ and R charts could be effectively constructed and used with about 40 subgroups, each based on as few as 3, 4, or 5 items. These sample sizes were adequate because of the Central Limit Theorem, whereby the sampling distribution of $\overline{X}$-values derived from a stable process will form a normal distribution. The symmetry of this sampling distribution made it simple to compute the control limits by tolerating a specified number of standard errors from the norm ($\overline{\overline{X}}$) on both sides of it based on the risk level chosen. Normality of the sampling distribution of p's, however, cannot readily be counted on unless the average number of defective (as well as non-defective) items of the process is more than 5, i.e., np and nq > 5.

This qualification results from the fact that when the average number of defective items of the process is not more than 5, the frequency distribution of replicated percentages is a binomial (asymmetrical) distribution. This distribution only approaches the normal distribution when the number of defective items averages more than 5. (See Chapter 10.) When the number is 5 or fewer, the control limits must be separately computed for the lower and upper limits of the p-chart by use of the binomial distribution properties. These computations, based on an expansion of the binomial distribution (shown in Chapter 6), are generally considered to be too complex. Thus, in the discussion that follows, the assumption is made that the average number of defective items in the process is more than 5.

In determining the size of sample (n) for a p chart, we need a good estimate of p, the process non-conformance rate, so that the average error rate ($\bar{p}$) can be determined. For example, if $\bar{p}$ for a given process is very low (e.g., 2.5%), n must be at least 200 items; when $\bar{p}$ is 5%, n must be more than 100 items. In general, the smaller the defective rate of the process the larger must n be, and conversely. (As with control charts for variables, in the course of assembling the history-period data, it is desirable, if feasible, to make a Pareto analysis to determine the major sources and causes of the defectives and act to reduce the non-conformance rate.) The foregoing considerations lead us to conclude that the sample size (n) for a p chart should be much larger than for $\bar{X}$ and R charts.

Standard error of an estimated percentage

As indicated in Chapters 9 and 10, the standard error of p depends on the percentage itself and on n. In large-scale sample surveys and large universes the standard error of p is $\sigma_p = \sqrt{\dfrac{p(1-p)}{n-1}}$, where p is determined by the reasonably large sample size (n) actually used in the survey. In process control, the best estimate of the process percentage, p, is available not from just the single small sample, but much more accurately from the largest possible sample, namely, all sub-groups combined. This percentage can be obtained from the periodic samples accumulated over the history-period (exclusive of those sub-groups whose p's are found to be caused by assignable causes). When using a constant sample size over the history-period, the overall process percentage, p, should be computed as $\bar{p} = \dfrac{\Sigma p}{m}$, where m is the number of sub-groups. Therefore, the standard error of an estimated percentage based on n items in each sample is computed by $\sqrt{\dfrac{\bar{p}(1-\bar{p})}{n-1}}$. When n varies from sub-group to sub-group, $\bar{p} = \dfrac{\Sigma(\text{defectives})}{\Sigma n}$, where the numerator and denominator are cumulated over the history-period of sampling.

Sensitivity of n

Once the appropriate sample size for each sub-group is determined, consideration should be given to its sensitivity in detecting significant variations. For example, assume that n=20 and $\bar{p}$ = 0.30. Since n$\bar{p}$ equals 6, the control limits for p can be validly constructed on the assumption of normality. However, it is clear that n=20 would be insensitive to the occurrence of defective rates within the range of 6 to 9 percent, 11 to 14 percent, etc., since an additional single defective would add a full 5 percentage points to p. Therefore, if the actual p= 6%, 7%, 8%, 9%, etc. the sample size of 20 would not be able to detect these non-conformance rates. The importance of detecting these in-between defective rates can, therefore, be a guide for determining n. For example, when n=100, the control chart will detect defective rates of 1%, 2%, 3%, etc. but nothing in between. If this insensitivity of n=100 to in-between one-percentage points is critical, samples larger than 100 may be necessary. It can now be noted that if the cost of inspecting large samples is prohibitive, the sample sizes can be kept low at the expense of insensitivity of the resulting defective rates. Thus, the choice of sample size becomes a trade-off, namely, lower cost versus greater sensitivity.

With the appropriate sub-group size determined, it is now possible to establish the control limits for the p chart. Because of the need to detect assignable causes in the history-period data, consideration should be given initially to using less than 3 sigma limits for the control chart. The upper control limit would be $\bar{p} + Z\sigma_p$; Z is the number of standard errors to tolerate and $\sigma_p = \sqrt{\dfrac{\bar{p}(1-\bar{p})}{n-1}}$. The lower control limit would be $\bar{p} - Z\sigma_p$. Here $\bar{p}$, the average of the defective rates determined from the accumulated samples of size n used for each sub-group is chosen as the provisional norm because it is more reliable than any p based on n items for a single sub-group.

If, for some good reason, varying sample sizes are necessary, the above formula for the standard error of p may still be used without serious loss of accuracy if sub-group sample sizes are within 15 to 20 percent of $\bar{n}$, the average size of sample, namely, $\dfrac{\Sigma n}{m}$. This tolerance for varying sample sizes is considered by quality practitioners to be worth the loss of sensitivity to avoid the task of computing varying control limits each time n is different. Thus, if varying sample sizes are used and are within 15 to 20 percent of $\bar{n}$, the standard error of p may be computed by the following formula:

$$\sigma_p = \sqrt{\frac{\bar{p}(1-\bar{p})}{\bar{n}-1}}, \text{ where } \bar{p} = \frac{\Sigma(\text{defectives})}{\Sigma n}.$$

Constructing and operating the provisional p chart

By using less than 3 sigma limits initially, the likelihood of detecting assignable causes in the history-period data is greater (at a greater risk level) than otherwise. After operating the preliminary p chart with, for example, a risk level of 1%, (i.e., $\pm 2.58\sigma_p$), and after a state of statistical control is attained, the tolerances can then be loosened to ± 3 sigma limits.

An Example — A company manufacturing ball-point pens decided to experiment with a p chart for the thousands of pen covers it is continually manufacturing for a standard ball-point pen. The judgment of the work-team assigned to this project was to inspect a random sample of 100 covers (n=100) each day for 20 days, thus yielding data for 20 sub-groups, as shown in Table 11.10.

Table 11.10
Number of ball-point pen covers found to be defective
by 20 samples of 100 inspected pens, Company XRT, August 1-26, 199X

Date August	Number of defectives	Fraction defectives (p)	Date August	Number of defectives	Fraction defectives (p)
1	8	.08	15	12	.12
2	0	.00	16	0	.00
3	16	.16	17	12	.12
4	40	.40	18	8	.08
5	4	.04	19	0	.00
8	0	.00	22	4	.04
9	20	.20	23	28	.28
10	12	.12	24	12	.12
11	4	.04	25	4	.04
12	8	.08	26	0	.00
			Total	192	1.92

Computations:

(1) $\bar{p} = \dfrac{\Sigma p}{m} = \dfrac{1.92}{20} = 0.096$ (the preliminary norm)

(2) $\sigma_p = \sqrt{\dfrac{\bar{p}(1-\bar{p})}{n-1}} = \sqrt{\dfrac{(.096)(.094)}{99}} = .0296$

(3) Team decision: risk level = 1%

(4) Equivalent number of standard errors
(from Appendix B) = 2.575

(5) Control limits = $\bar{p} \pm 2.575(0.0296)$
   (a) Upper control limit = $0.096 + 0.076 = 0.172$
   (b) Lower control limit = $.096 - 0.076 = 0.020$

Figure 11.11
Preliminary control limits for fraction
defective ball-point pen covers

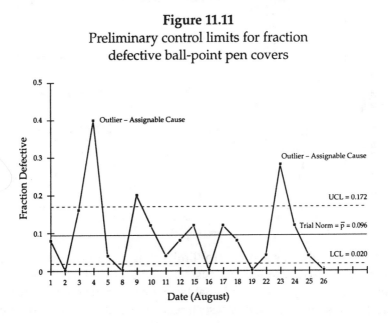

The p chart shows possible assignable causes on August 4 (.4), August 9 (.2), and August 23 (.28). Assume that investigation of these three questionable defective rates found no assignable cause for the August 9 sub-group (p=.20), but that the August 4 and August 23 percentages were the result of inaccurate machine settings. Thus, the data points for these dates are deleted and a revised control chart is constructed as follows:

1) Revised $\bar{p} = \dfrac{1.92 - 0.68}{18} = 0.0689$ (provisional norm)

2) Revised $\sigma_p = \sqrt{\dfrac{(0.0689)(0.9311)}{99}} = 0.0255$

3) The team now decided to construct the provisional p chart with ±3 sigma limits

4) Revised upper control limit = $\bar{p}$ + 3(0.0255)
   = 0.0689 + 0.0765 = 0.1454

5) Revised lower control limit = 0.0689 – 0.0765 = 0.00

Figure 11.12
Provisional control chart for fraction
defective ball-point pen covers

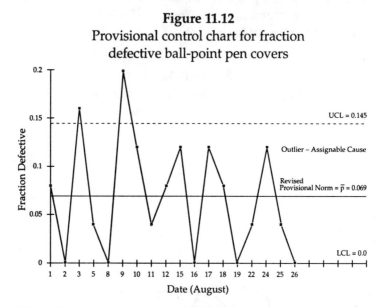

Note that the revised control limits now put in question the 16 percent defective rate for August 3. This would signal further investigation for possible assignable causes and deletion from the basic data if so found. In this case, let us assume that an investigation found no assignable cause for the August 3 defective rate.

Process Capability and Management Specifications

With the above preliminary data, it appears that the process is in statistical control. The available machinery, machine operators, and raw material all currently constitute the process constant-cause system. If management is satisfied with an average defective rate of 6.9% ± 7.6 percentage points, they can construct a control chart using the revised norm of .0689, UCL of .1454, and LCL of .000. By continually monitoring the process, further reduction of the defective rate may yet be achieved.

On the other hand, if management and the consumers are not fully satisfied with the current quality of the pen covers, better machinery, better raw material, and more fully trained machine operators can be considered as an option.

Control Chart for Number of Defectives (np Chart)

A control chart which accomplishes the same objectives as the p chart is known as the np chart. This control chart deals with the *number* of defective cases rather than the percentage of defective ones. A relatively small advantage of the np chart is that it eliminates the need to compute the percentage of defectives for each subgroup. A disadvantage is that it does not allow for use of varying sample sizes as indicated for the p chart. If a varying n is used, it requires that the control limits be recomputed each time changes are made in the subgroup size. The formulas for an np chart are:

(1) The norm (or center line) = $n\bar{p}$.

(2) The standard error of $np = \sigma_{np} = \sqrt{n\bar{p}(1-\bar{p})}$

(3) The UCL is $n\bar{p} + 3\sigma_{np}$

(4) The LCL is $n\bar{p} - 3\sigma_{np}$

To illustrate the computations for the np chart, we use the data on the ball-point pen covers (Table 11.10), as follows:

(1) The norm (or center line) = $n\bar{p}$ = (100)(0.096) = 10 defectives

(2) The standard error of np = $\sigma_{np} = \sqrt{(100)(.096)(.904)}$ = 3 defectives

(3) The UCL is 10 + 3(3.0) = 10 + 9 = 19 defectives

(4) The LCL is 10 – 9 = 1 defective

It should be noted that even by using 3 sigma limits to establish the control limits with very little risk, August 4 (40 defectives), August 9 (20 defectives), and August 23 (28 defectives) would be considered significant variations and would need to be checked for assignable causes. This indicates that precisely the same signals that are emitted by the p chart would be emitted by the np chart, had we used 3 sigma limits in both instances. This is an illustration of the similar effectiveness of the p chart and np chart, except for the need to round the figures on number of defectives to integers. With a knowledge of the pro's and con's of the p chart and the np chart, it becomes a management choice of the preferred chart to adopt in an attempt to reduce the non-conformance rate of a process.

Control Chart for Number of Defects Per Unit (c Chart)

Another useful control chart in the attributes class is the c chart, where c represents the total number of defects in an entity. It is a chart designed to improve the quality of whole units, such as airplane wings or automobile motors; reduce the number of accidents; reduce computer-entry errors, coding errors, etc. To use the c chart requires the existence of three special conditions, as follows:

(1) The "whole unit" selected for this chart must potentially have, but not actually have, a very large number of defects (e.g., an airline handling thousands of sacks of U.S. mail in a given day).

(2) The actual number of defects occurring in the chosen unit is "very small" relative to the total potential number of defects (e.g., less than one percent).

(3) The actual number of defects from unit to unit is fairly constant.

The above conditions satisfy an important principle called the *Poisson Distribution Theory*. There are many "units" in the real world which display this distribution, and the c chart can be widely used. A few of these whole units are:

1. Number of highway accidents on a large State highway.

2. Number of typing errors per page in a book being prepared for publication.

3. Number of welding defects in an airplane wing.

4. Number of payroll check errors in a large payroll department, the unit inspected being a weekly or bi-weekly payroll.

5. Number of service complaints per week received by a large customer-servicing company (e.g., the U.S. Postal Service).

6. Number of adjudication errors made in a week or month by fully trained Medicare adjudicators in a given medical service agency.

7. Crime control in selected areas or neighborhoods.

To use the c chart, it is essential not only to assure that the three basic conditions listed earlier exist, but also to clearly define the "unit" and a "defect" (as distinct from a p chart, where a defective item which may have many defects is counted as a single "defective" item). For example, a "unit" can be a day, a motor vehicle, an airplane wing, a sweater, a large post office, etc.

The primary advantage of the c chart over the p chart or the np chart is the simplicity of computing the center line and the standard deviation needed to establish the control limits, once a sufficient number of units is included in the history-period. Here is an example, using hypothetical data on the number of minor accidents per week in a large mail order delivery organization over a period of 6 weeks. The unit involved is the "company week."

Week	Number of accidents (c)
1	0
2	3
3	2
4	2
5	1
6	0
Total	8

Here, the center line or norm is $\bar{c} = \dfrac{\Sigma c}{n} = \dfrac{8}{6}$ = 1.33; and the standard deviation is

$$\sigma_c = \sqrt{\bar{c}} = 1.15 *$$

The c chart would then be:

Center line = $\bar{c}$ = 1.33 accidents per week

$$UCL = \bar{c} + 3\sqrt{\bar{c}} = 1.33 + 3.45 = 4.78$$

$$UCL = \bar{c} - 3\sqrt{\bar{c}} = 1.33 - 3.45 = 0$$

Since the three conditions required to use the c chart are fulfilled in this example, the simplicity of the calculations is apparent, particularly in computing the standard deviation of c (σ_c). As indicated, there are many possible applications of the c chart in industry and government.[**]

Other Control Charts

Thus far, we have presented five types of control charts. These include the $\bar{X}$ chart and R chart, which are widely applicable wherever the quality characteristic is measurable and varies from item to item.

---

[*] When the above σ_c is computed by the standard method, $\sigma_c = \sqrt{\dfrac{\Sigma(c-\bar{c})^2}{n-1}}$ = 1.21 accidents.

This figure is close to $\sigma_c = \sqrt{\bar{c}} = \sqrt{1.33} = 1.15$ derived by the c chart method.

[**] See, for example, the application described in the article "C Chart Sets Mail Fines," B.J. Mandel, *Quality Progress*, October, 1975.

Other charts are the p chart and the np chart, which involve controlling the quality of such characteristics as error-rates, non-compliance rates, and non-conformance rates. The c chart helps to control the number of defects in a large standard unit. This chart and the p and np charts deal with attributes, since the number of defects is counted, not measured from unit to unit.

At least three other control charts are worthy of mention, as follows:

(1) The *u-chart* deals with the average number of defects per large unit, where two or more standard units (e.g., 3 shifts in a work-day) are included in the sample. The center line of the u chart is $\bar{u}$, the average number of defects per unit, obtained by $\Sigma c / n$, where n is the number of standard large units in the sample, assuming approximately the same sample size each time period.* The control limits for the $\bar{u}$ chart are:

$$\text{UCL} = \bar{u} + 3\sqrt{\frac{\bar{u}}{(n-1)}} \text{ and LCL} = \bar{u} - 3\sqrt{\frac{\bar{u}}{(n-1)}}.$$

(2) The *x chart* deals with individually measured items. Here, $\bar{X}$ is the center line with an upper tolerance limit of $\bar{X} + 3\sigma_x$ and a lower tolerance limit of $\bar{X} - 3\sigma_x$. Some of the potential applications of the x chart are:

a) Waiting time for elevator service (outlier = a breakdown);

b) Length of time to get to work, or home, by a given mode of transportation (outlier = an accident blocking traffic);

c) Shipments of mail orders made each day (outlier = failure to ship an order on scheduled date);

d) Number of absent employees each day in a large agency (outlier = a circulating virus causing an inordinate number of absences due to illness);

e) Weight control, by taking daily or weekly weight readings by a person (outlier = overeating at a buffet dinner).

(3) The *regression control chart* — This is an effective control chart, where two variables are involved, one determined to be the independent variable, x, and the other the dependent variable, y, where y is logically dependent on, or influenced by, x. For example, the

---

*If the size of the sample varies, $\bar{n}$ would be used, provided no single n is more than ±25% beyond $\bar{n}$.

number of sales (x) influences the number of customer complaints (y). Thus, this chart makes it possible to identify excessive customer complaints while accounting for the influence of the volume of sales on the number of complaints. Another example is the number of work units completed per day (x) and its influence on the corresponding number of work hours used (y).*

Summary

The primary objective of this chapter is to describe the role of statistics in a Total Quality Management (TQM) program designed to improve the quality of product and/or services which organizations provide to users (or customers) both within and outside the organization. This chapter is thereby identified as Statistical Process Control (SPC).

The chapter presents and describes two methods of quality assessment and improvement. One is generally identified as the Pareto method. This method quantifies performance by source and/or cause of poor quality and identifies the sources and/or causes which account for a large percentage of the errors or excessive variation. Once it determines where and why this condition exists it enables management to concentrate its effort to reduce major quality problems. This method requires no sophisticated statistical tools. It depends on being able to quantify processes or activities and using random sampling to collect the data. Once the appropriate data are collected they are analyzed by the array (ranking) method or by the percentage frequency distribution. The method is enhanced by presenting the data graphically which in many cases aids in dramatically presenting and communicating the findings to management. Some quality analysts have referred to the Pareto method as "sorting out the vital few and the trivial many." This means finding the few situations which are very important (vital) to the quality problem so that efforts to minimize the recurrence of the problem at the source (and its main cause) can be made with success. On the other hand, unfruitful effort can be avoided by spending very little time on the many trivial sources and causes of variation or of poor quality. Examples of the way the Pareto method is used are given early in the chapter.

The second, and somewhat more sophisticated method of quality improvement as well as good quality maintenance, is generally

*A description of the regression control chart is given by the article "The Regression Control Chart," in *Journal of Quality Technology*, Vol. 1, No. 1, January 1969.

identified as the field of statistical process control (SPC). There are two main types of control charts used in SPC applications. One deals with variables or measurements, such as dimension, capacity, time-lapse. The other deals with attributes which identify an item as possessing or not possessing a certain attribute, such as being a defective, non-conforming, or non-complying item.

Either type of control chart requires the collection of data on the quality of product or service over a reasonable period of time (the history-period) and analysis of the results to establish a realistic norm or average performance of the process as well as upper and lower control limits of variation. Furthermore, each method analyzes the history-period data to determine if any of data points contain outliers, or cases which are unusual and not caused by chance variations but by assignable causes. These are deleted from the history-period data and a revised norm and upper and lower control limits are computed.

When the resulting control chart shows no further assignable causes over a reasonable period of time, the process is considered to be in statistical control. In this state, the chart can be used as a quality-monitoring tool if continuous and periodic data are collected and plotted on the control chart. Thus, the process is constantly watched for probable assignable causes. When the latter are detected and prevented from recurring in the future, quality improvement is generally achieved, and satisfactory quality levels are maintained by continuous monitoring of process variations.

When dealing with variables, there are usually two control chart types. One keeps a watch on the average dimension of items produced or services rendered, i.e., the norm. This chart is called the control chart for averages, or the $\overline{X}$ chart. The other chart keeps an eye on the variation of items (x-values) from their mean, using the range as a measure of variation. Ideally, a standard deviation chart or a σ_x chart would provide a more precise measure of variation. However, because the computations involved are too time consuming, quality specialists have found a way of tracking process variations with reasonable accuracy by use of the easy-to-compute range of the items in each sample. This chart, therefore, is called the R chart. It must accompany the $\overline{X}$ chart time-point by time-point to control process variations. In the chapter we demonstrated that the same average may have different standard deviations or ranges; hence, the $\overline{X}$ chart must be supplemented by the R chart, as is illustrated in the chapter.

There are as many as four control chart types for attributes. Probably the most popular is the p chart which aims to reduce the error rate (p) or non-conformance rate of items produced by a process or by services rendered. Here too, the history-period data are used to compute a norm ($\bar{p}$) as well as upper and lower control limits, which are used to detect significant variations in the error rates over time.

Another attribute-type chart is the np chart, which controls the number of defective items produced by the process. This chart serves the same purpose as the p chart. Its advantage is avoidance of the need to compute a percentage defective rate from each sample; it only requires counting the number of defective items found in the sample.

A third attribute control chart, called a c chart, deals with the number of defects (c) or non-conformities per unit. Some places where it has been or can be applied are: tracking the number of highway accidents, reducing the number of service complaints, and controlling the number of defects in a clothing article, such as a knitted sweater. A condition required for applying the c chart is that there be a very large possible number of non-conformities in the unit but that the actual number of non-conformities is very small (e.g., less than one percent).

A fourth attribute chart is an extension of the c chart whereby two or more standard units are monitored on their combined non-conformities (e.g., sick leave users per shift), which becomes an average number of non-conformities per standard unit. The symbol $\bar{u}$ is generally used to represent this average and the control chart is generally called a u chart, where $\bar{u} = \dfrac{\Sigma c}{n}$ and UCL = $\bar{u} + 3\sqrt{\dfrac{\bar{u}}{n-1}}$ and LCL = $\bar{u} - 3\sqrt{\dfrac{\bar{u}}{n-1}}$.

In addition to these variables and attributes control charts, the chapter mentioned several other types of control charts and also covered a number of statistical principles and a large number of words and symbols associated with SPC.

In conclusion, the chapter provides evidence that statistics plays an essential role in TQM which aims to improve the quality of both products and services. It also logically points to the fact that management at all levels, engineers, first line supervisors, and employees concerned with process quality improvement must undertake training courses in the SPC tools, and then use them to reap the advantages they offer.

Problems

1. Two of the following 5 formulas are equivalent. Which are they?

   (a) $A_2\bar{R}$;   (b) $3\sqrt{\Sigma(x-\bar{X})^2}$;   (c) $3\sigma_x$;   (d) $\dfrac{3\sigma_x}{\sqrt{n}}$;   (e) $\dfrac{3\sigma_x}{d_2}$.

2. Two of the following 5 formulas are equivalent. Which are they?

   (a) $\bar{p} + 3\sqrt{\dfrac{\bar{p}(1-\bar{p})}{n}}$;   (b) $\bar{p} + 3\sqrt{\dfrac{p(1-p)}{\bar{n}}}$;   (c) $\bar{p} + 3\sqrt{\dfrac{\bar{p}(1-\bar{p})}{\bar{n}}}$;

   (d) $n\bar{p} + 3n\sqrt{\dfrac{\bar{p}(1-\bar{p})}{\bar{n}}}$;   (e) $p + 3\sqrt{\dfrac{\bar{p}(1-\bar{p})}{n}}$.

3. Distinguish between $\dfrac{\bar{R}}{d_2}$ and $\dfrac{\bar{R}/d_2}{\sqrt{n}}$.

4. Given the following management risk levels, indicate how many standard errors should be tolerated for each of the risk levels.

   (a) 5%;   (b) 2%;   (c) 1%;   (d) .27%

5. What is the main reason for accompanying a control chart for averages with a control chart for ranges?

6. Given the following six symbols, when do you use each?

   (a) A_2;   (b) d_2;   (c) D_3;   (d) D_4;   (e) σ_p;   (f) $\bar{c}$

7. Five pieces of a certain wire strand were taken from a manufacturing process at regular two-hour intervals. The length of each piece is measured by x, and $\bar{X}$ and R values are calculated for each sub-group of 5. After 30 such sub-groups were obtained, the sum of the sub-group averages ($\Sigma\bar{X}$) was 429.0 inches. The sum of the 30 sub-group ranges (ΣR) was 11.88 inches.

Perform the following:

   (a) Compute the center line and upper and lower control limits for an $\bar{X}$ chart.

   (b) Do the same for an R chart.

   (c) If none of the 30 points fall out of control or show a trend or run of points, it may be assumed that the process was in "statistical control." Compute the apparent "natural tolerances" of the process by two different formulas.

(d) If the company specifications of a strand were 14.40 inches ± 0.15 inches, what conclusion can you draw regarding the ability of the process to produce pieces of wire strand within these specifications?

(e) What is the probable reject rate of the wire strands in light of the above data?

(f) Suggest possible alternative steps the company management may take as a result of these findings.

8. What is the reason for preserving the order of sub-group averages and ranges derived from process measurements?

9. The frequency distribution of individual measurements (x) of a part, as well as the averages of samples of 3 such parts, will generally approach the shape of the normal frequency distribution. Explain why this is so.

10. Each day over a period of 14 days, a sample of 200 computer data-entries were checked for errors with the results shown below.

(a) Using this history-period data, construct a provisional p chart using 3 sigma limits, analyze the history-period data for probable assignable causes, and construct a revised control chart for percent defectives if revision is necessary.

Date	No. Rejected	Percent Rejected
April 27	4	.020
28	9	.045
29	10	.050
30	11	.055
May 1	13	.065
2	30	.150
3	26	.130
4	13	.065
5	8	.040
6	23	.115
7	34	.170
8	25	.125
9	18	.090
10	12	.060

(b) When your analysis is completed, what other method of quality improvement can you use, and how would you use it?

11. Each day, over a period of five days, an agency selected a random sample of 50 current filings of medical records by each employee, and reviewed them for the correct filing code. A total of six file clerks were involved in this special study, with the results indicated below.

Employee and number miscoded

A	B	C	D	E	F
4	13	5	16	3	2
6	14	7	4	4	4
3	5	0	19	2	3
1	8	1	12	5	0
2	19	3	7	1	1
Total 16	59	16	58	15	10

Analyze the results of this special study to determine:

(a) The estimated percentage of miscoded cases;

(b) The best way of reducing the agency's errors in filing medical records.

12. The company specifications for a special walking cane were set by its engineers at:

Nominal dimension: 48 inches

Tolerance: ±.125 inches

A control chart for averages was constructed by the quality control manager with the following results, using a sample of 8 canes with 20 sub-groups:

Average of the 20 sub-group averages, $\overline{\overline{X}} = 48$ inches

Average of the ranges, $\overline{R} = .35$ inches

Since all 20 averages and ranges were in statistical control, what are your recommendations to the company regarding their specifications?

13. The U.S. Postal Service found that many airlines mishandled mail shipments* and sought a way of reducing the mishandling rate. Over a period of 21 days they collected the following data for one airline on the number of their mishandled shipments out of the thousands shipped:

*A shipment is mishandled for any of the following reasons: failure to pick it up on a scheduled flight; failure to drop it off in the correct city; failure to drop it at all and return it to its original pick-up airport.

Day	Mishandled per 1000 shipped	Day	Mishandled per 1000 shipped	Day	Mishandled per 1000 shipped
1	7.96	8	9.06	15	8.03
2	9.40	9	9.98	16	16.84
3	4.59	10	10.69	17	15.59
4	5.54	11	11.99	18	14.00
5	13.56	12	14.28	19	9.79
6	26.54	13	12.20	20	8.63
7	33.69	14	7.59	21	5.76

(a) Since the mishandling rates were generally running less than one percent, which is the appropriate type of control chart to use here?

(b) Does the chart show any possible outliers to remove from the basic data shown?

(c) If so, what would be the corrected control limits and norm?

14. In a typical week, the TQM team reviewed the work of 15 employees who were responsible for sorting mail by office of destination. Each employee handled about the same volume and mix. The number of incorrectly sorted pieces was recorded as shown below. Use the Pareto method to determine the appropriate action to be taken in order to improve the quality of sorting the mail.

Employee number	Errors detected	Employee number	Errors detected
1	4	9	2
2	11	10	2
3	4	11	0
4	0	12	16
5	16	13	0
6	3	14	2
7	7	15	1
8	9		

15. The following data were available from a large sample of items coming off a production line: Estimated population $\overline{X}' = 106$; Estimated population $\sigma'_x = 12$.

(a) Construct a control chart for averages when samples of 9 items each are drawn on a recurring basis.

(b) Of the following 6 sample averages obtained after the $\overline{X}$ chart was constructed, which indicate a probable assignable cause?

Sample No.:	1	2	3	4	5	6
$\overline{X}$:	102	117	95	93	112	114

16. (a) What are the control limits for a p chart when n is constant?

   (b) What are the control limits for a p chart when n varies but by relatively small amounts?

   (c) What are the control limits for an np chart?

   (d) When and why is an np chart preferred over the p chart?

17. Indicate which control chart is most appropriate in each of the following situations:

   (a) When the dimension of the item can be measured accurately;

   (b) When the items are each given a go or no-go test for acceptance;

   (c) When athletic socks are inspected for flaws.

Chapter 12

Introduction to Correlation and Regression Analysis

"One of the most popular current avocations is the attempt to look in the future of economic developments. The popularity of efforts to predict arises not only from the potential large gains to be made from successful performance in this endeavor but also from the challenge to man's ingenuity and his desire to shape his environment more to his liking."*

Correlation and regression analysis is a vast and intriguing field of study. It offers management a large variety of practical uses beyond forecasting and budgeting. It provides a way of improving productivity, constructing an index of productivity, establishing performance standards, detecting possible fraud or abuse, performing break-even analysis, forecasting, and preparing budgets.

This chapter introduces some of the basic concepts, terms and techniques of correlation and regression analysis, explains how it works, and describes some useful applications that have been made and can be made with these techniques. A primary purpose is to facilitate the reader's ability to conduct simple correlation-regression analyses in specific fields of interest. While the vast utility of correlation and regression analysis techniques is emphasized, the basic qualifications or requirements for the proper use of these techniques also are stressed. In short, the chapter introduces the major elements involved in this field of statistical applications.

Correlation and regression analysis is often thought of as one set of statistical methods. Actually this field of study consists of two separate techniques (*correlation* and *regression*) which are generally used in tandem, to address different aspects of problems in management.

---

* *Studies in Business and Economics*, Volume VIII, Number 3, December 1954, Bureau of Business and Economic Research, University of Maryland, College Park, Maryland.

Definitions

Correlation analysis

We look at the sky in the night. We see that it is full of stars, and we conclude that tomorrow will be a nice day. Some mornings when we are getting ready to leave the house, we see a cloudy sky, and — expecting rain — we decide to take our umbrella or raincoat. These are examples of correlation analysis and forecasting based on experience and judgment.

Perhaps no other method of statistics lives with us day in and day out as much as the method of correlation. With this method we subconsciously or knowingly decide practically every action we take. When we start our day's work or leisure we have many ways to go or actions to take. Many of us ordinarily act instinctively, according to some pattern that we have discovered from previous experience which is most likely to yield the desired result. On the other hand, many of our actions are a result of deliberate calculations, using statistics, which have indicated that a change in one specific activity or process is likely to cause, by way of a reaction, a corresponding change in some other variable that is dependent upon it.

The dictionary defines the word *correlate* as: "to connect systematically; *to establish a mutual or reciprocal relation of or between two related things so connected that one directly implies the other."* The dictionary definition is a good introduction to the meaning of the study of correlation. From it we gather that before we can use correlation to our advantage we must first establish if a systematic relationship exists between the two (or more) related variables in which we are interested.

A dictionary, or course, can give only a brief explanation of a term. The dictionary definition is incomplete in several respects when we use *statistical correlation.* It does not state the fact that correlation may be direct or inverse — *direct* if both variables move in the same direction, *inverse* if the variables move in opposite directions. Nor does the dictionary indicate that a single variable may be correlated with more than one other variable, i.e., *multiple correlation,* as opposed to being correlated with only one other variable, in which case it is called *simple correlation.* In addition, correlation may be *linear* (a constant relationship) or *curvilinear* (a varying relationship). The full meaning of these and other terms related to correlation analysis are developed later in the chapter.

In essence, the study of correlation may be briefly defined as *the study to determine the **extent** to which one variable (or more than one), designated by x, and called the **independent** variable, influences the magnitude of another variable, designated by y, and called the **dependent** variable because its value appears to be dependent on the value or magnitude of the independent variable(s).* By statistical correlation, for example, we may find that a student's final grade in statistics (y) is substantially influenced (maybe about 90 percent) by his or her midterm grade (x or x_1) and also by the amount of time spent studying the subject (another x, generally designated as x_2). Another example would determine whether a factor such as the amount of employee training (x) influences productivity or quality of work (y). One of the classic uses of correlation and regression analysis is crop forecasting and short-range weather forecasting. In general, correlation is used to determine the extent (in percent, from zero to 100 percent) to which one or more variables explain the magnitude of another variable logically dependent on them.

Regression analysis

There is a definite distinction between correlation analysis and regression analysis. A good way of distinguishing between them is to consider correlation as that phase of the study of variables to determine the *extent* of influence that one variable (the independent variable) seems to bear on another variable (the dependent variable). If the influence is sufficiently strong, we enter into regression analysis, in which the objective is to develop a formula or an equation with which we can *predict* the *magnitude* of the dependent variable based on a known magnitude of the independent variable(s). Logically, correlation should precede regression, for if the influence is not sufficiently strong (such as only 10 or 20 percent) there would be no sound basis for developing a correspondingly weak predicting or regression equation.

Applications of Correlation and Regression Analysis*

Would it not be profitable for an organization to be able to predict with reasonable accuracy the amount of business or the workload it could expect next week, next month, or next year? By being able to forecast with reasonable accuracy its sales or volume of business, an entity can be prepared to meet the demand for its products or services

---

* Also see section on "Some Additional Practical Uses of Correlation and Regression Analysis."

more efficiently than otherwise. With such knowledge, management could budget or plan in advance to meet service needs or to have enough of its product on hand to meet demand, enough material, machinery, and operating staff to produce it, and sufficient staff and equipment to distribute it on time to satisfy its customers.

Many events in business, industry, government, and life in general are "led" by other related events. If the events that lead the variable of interest could be discovered, we would be able to predict the event (the dependent variable) by watching those that precede it. *Correlation and regression analysis derives its value primarily as an instrument of prediction.*

However, we must not overlook many other valuable uses which have been made of these techniques not only in business and industry but also in government, education, medicine, chemistry, and other fields. For example, Sears, Roebuck and Company once stated that it estimates, by correlation analysis, daily mail-order receipts from the weight of its mail. In the operation of a mail order service it is profitable to know as early as possible the volume of each day's orders. Sears, Roebuck and Company weighed its mail early in the morning, and by 8:30 a.m. it had predicted the number of mail-orders for the entire day and accordingly made plans for handling them. The predictions were found to be very accurate, and, as a result, the decisions based on them led to more efficient operations than would otherwise have been possible.*

At Eli Lilly, it has been stated that sales volume could be predicted by correlation analysis techniques.** After much researching, the company found that the total sales volume of the industry bore a definite and measurable relationship to consumers' personal disposable income — figures estimated by the U.S. Department of Commerce. On the basis of the Department's estimates of disposable income, Eli Lilly claimed that it could estimate sales volume several months in advance.

The U.S. Department of Agriculture predicts annually the volume of crops that American farms will produce. It bases its predictions on a correlation involving several variables (a *multiple correlation*), such as expected seeding area, technological applications, and climate.

---

* C.W. Smally, "Estimating Daily Order Receipts from Weight of Mail," *American Statistician*, February, 1954.

** Kenneth F. Griffith, "Sales Forecasting at Eli Lilly," *Practical Techniques of Forecasting, Planning and Control, Manufacturing Series*, No. 216, 1954.

Numerous other applications of correlation analysis exist. They include the prediction of the effectiveness of advertising to increase sales, estimating the reliability of personnel testing for determining the suitability of employees for various jobs requiring varying types of skills, predicting financial returns from investments of various types, and assessing the strength (quality) of materials subjected to varying loads or stresses. The U.S. Postal Service uses regression analysis to prepare its annual budget. It estimates the mail volume it will be required to process during the budgeting years based on Census Bureau population projections. It found that U.S. population at mid-year correlates highly with its annual mail volume.

Probably the most frequent applications of correlation and regression analysis techniques are in forecasting sales. Gasoline sales and sales of automobile parts and supplies are estimated from data on automobile registrations and miles of highway construction; sales of building supplies correlate highly with the value of building contracts awarded; the volume of furniture sales can be predicted from data on the number of new home purchases; department store sales correlate highly with disposable national income.

There are many other actual and potential applications of correlation and regression analysis, too numerous to mention in their entirety.* Correlation and regression analysis techniques can be potentially useful whenever there is a need to predict the value of some important variable and there is reason to believe that it is logically related to, or influenced by, some other variable(s) which precedes it. For example, the consumer price index is influenced by the producer price index which precedes it.

Elements of Correlation Analysis

It takes some effort to learn the techniques of correlation and regression analysis but the valuable potential applications they offer should make that investment worthwhile. Some of the methods of correlation and regression analysis and the main concepts underlying them are illustrated by the following hypothetical problem.

Suppose an employment manager was requested by the company's management to add a dozen people to the sales force and

---

* For example, an article in the Washington Post (January 16, 1995) refers to the authors of *The Bell Curve* as using regression analysis to determine the relative impact of intelligence and environment on a person's chances of being imprisoned, living in poverty, divorcing, bearing a child out of wedlock, and dozens of other social outcomes.

to set an equitable starting wage for them. Suppose also that the manager thought of basing the entrance pay of the newly selected salespeople on the length of their selling experience in the particular line handled by the company. A number of questions are raised about this plan: (1) Can the manager's general policy be supported without further study? In other words, is there a substantial dependence of sales volume on years of selling experience in the same industry or product? (2) What factors other than experience might cause one salesperson to be worth more than another? (3) How can the volume of sales be estimated for a newly hired salesperson with, say, four years experience? (4) How much error may be expected in this and other estimates? (5) Can this information also be used to evaluate on-the-job performance after the person is hired? (6) How much confidence should be placed in the estimates?

These questions can be answered by use of correlation and regression analysis techniques.

Logical correlation analysis

One way of answering some of these questions is, naturally, through common sense and judgment. It would be reasonable to support the manager's policy on the basis of experience, if in the past it was found that salespeople with more "know-how" in this or a related line of sales generally have brought in more sales than those with limited experience. It would therefore be logical to assume that the same relationship also would hold true in connection with the current problem.

Selling power is not dependent solely on length of experience, however; such factors as the territory assigned, personality, and past connections also play a role in determining the amount of sales brought in. When two or more such independent variables affect the dependent variable, we are dealing with *multiple* correlation analysis. When some of the factors are held constant and we consider only a few of them, we are dealing with *partial* correlation analysis. When only two variables, are involved, such as experience and sales, we are dealing with *simple* correlation analysis. "Simple" correlation and regression analysis derives its name from the fact that any dependent variable that is influenced by the variation of only one independent variable is somewhat simple, i.e., not very complex. While this may be true, many real-life situations exist where more than two influencing variables are necessary to get accurate results from correlation and regression analysis.

When statistics are not used, but decisions or estimates are based on reasoning or common sense, *logical correlation analysis* is used. This technique is relied on so frequently in life that few of us are conscious that it is a method of correlation analysis. Its main weakness lies in the fact that it relies on the memory of experiences and doesn't provide a basis for measuring statistically the extent of influence of x on y. Memory is known to be fallible, and it is not unusual for a person to recall only part of the past, especially when many factors affect the outcome of a given event. Therefore, when a decision is important and more accurate estimates are needed, gathering and analyzing quantitative data rather than depending on memory or judgment alone is the more promising approach. Quantitative methods also are required when it is essential to know the probable error or risk involved in using the results to make decisions. Statistical methods are also important when it is necessary to substantiate or support the basis for an important policy or decision. More rigorous approaches than the logical analysis method are described in the following sections.

Graphic correlation analysis

As just indicated, when quantitative data relevant to a problem are collected, a basis exists for making more precise and objective estimates and thereby more successful decisions. Nevertheless, whenever quantitative correlation and regression analysis techniques are used, graphic analysis is essential for preliminary assessment of the problem.

Suppose that the employment manager in our problem obtained the data shown in Table 12.1, giving the years of experience of the company's 20 salespeople and the amount of their sales during the immediately preceding year. First of all, these data can and should be analyzed graphically to answer some preliminary questions, as described below.

Table 12.1
Hypothetical data on years of experience and corresponding sales volume (in thousands)

Salesperson	Variable #1 (x) Years of Experience	Variable #2 (y) Annual Sales Volume	Salesperson	Variable #1 (x) Years of Experience	Variable #2 (y) Annual Sales Volume
a	7	$ 90	k	1	$25
b	5	100	l	1	10
c	3	80	m	3	40
d	1	20	n	2	20
e	3	20	o	6	70
f	4	30	p	4	80
g	5	60	q	1	15
h	4	40	r	2	50
i	1	30	s	2	40
j	2	10	t	3	30
			Total	60	$ 860
			N=20*	$\bar{X} = 3$	$\bar{Y} = \$43$

Scatter diagram — A useful graphic method of correlation analysis is the *scatter diagram*, or, for short, the *scattergram*. By this method, corresponding pairs of values of the two variables being correlated are plotted on a graph at their point of intersection to observe the dispersion or scatter of the resulting points.**

It should be noted that the scatter diagram is limited to a correlation of two variables, known as simple correlation analysis. The scattergram method involves setting the scale for the independent variable on the horizontal (or x) axis, and the scale for the dependent

---

* For simplicity in presenting the basic concepts and techniques of correlation and regression analysis, we are assuming that the data represent the universe, with size N=20 here, and not a random sample of the universe of size n=20. Since all sample estimates are subject to sampling variation, tests of significance would be required for sample-derived estimates if sample data were used. Some cautions to observe when using sample data are given in item #4 of the section "Cautions in the Use of Correlation and Regression Analysis."

** Cautionary note regarding the use of graphing — The scales used on the graph can dramatically affect the perception of how well the data points in a scatter diagram conform to a straight line or which point or points are probably outliers. Consequently, different scales should be tried when performing graphical analysis.

variable on the vertical (or y) axis. The dependent variable (y) is the one to be estimated or predicted; in our case, the dependent variable is "sales." The independent variable (x) is the one which we use to improve our estimate of the magnitude of the dependent variable; in our case, the independent variable is "years of sales experience." To plot the scattergram, each pair of corresponding values of the two variables is then entered as a single point at their point of intersection. When all the corresponding pairs are thus plotted, a "scatter" of points is obtained, as shown in Figure 12.1.

Figure 12.1 — Scattergram representation of data in Table 12.1

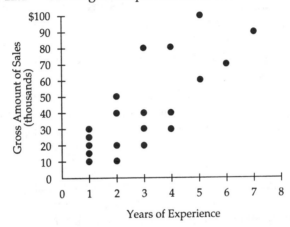

Points deduced from the scattergram — Looking at this scattering of points we begin to wonder how such a graph can possibly tell us anything about the extent of association between years of experience and amount of sales, or how it can aid in making estimates. The truth is that, unless we have had some previous experience in interpreting and using scattergrams, the diagram gives us limited but some essential information. With experience, the chart usually can give us the following useful information about the variables being correlated:

(1) It tells us how closely the two variables are associated, guided by the extent of scattering of the points. The degree of this scatter (and the associated *strength of correlation*) indicates how accurately we can estimate values of the dependent variable on the basis of given values of the independent variable. The less the scatter, the better the

predictive power; the more the points are scattered, the lower the correlation and the lower the predictive power.

(2) It tells us the direction of the correlation; i.e., whether the variables move in the same direction (*direct correlation*) or in opposite directions (*inverse correlation*). In our case, the correlation is direct, i.e., when x increases, y also increases.

(3) If the scattering of points seems to follow a straight path it indicates that the correlation is *linear*, i.e., with a constant proportional relationship between the variables.* A non-linear path or a curving path indicates a non-proportional relationship exists between the variables. This is useful information because the pattern of association between the variables (i.e., linear or curvilinear) determines the appropriate statistical methods of correlation and regression analysis to use.

(4) If the scatter diagram generally shows a linear path, as in our case, we can judgmentally draw a *"line of best fit"* by free-hand through the scatter of points to represent this general path and then use it to derive rough estimates of y for given values of x.

(5) Perhaps the most valuable contribution of the scatter diagram is that it offers a way of detecting abnormal or *"outlier"* points of data. When, for example, a point or points are far off the general path displayed by the rest of the points, there is good reason for investigating the causes for these outlier points. Often outliers may be caused by exceptional conditions not really part of the normal behavior of the process, or they may simply represent erroneous data. Outlier points should always be investigated.

Coefficient of correlation (r)

In linear correlation, the statistical measure of the *extent* or *strength* of the relationship between the two variables is called the *coefficient of correlation*. It is denoted by the symbol r. The value of r is fixed so that it can never exceed +1 or be less than –1. Values of r = +1 or r = –1 indicate a perfect association between the two related

---

* A constant proportional relationship may be illustrated by: as x increases by 5 units, y goes up 4 units. Thus, the constant proportion is 4/5, or 0.8; so, if x increases by 10 units, y increases by 8 units. An example of inverse correlation is: when x increases by 2 units, y decreases by 3 units. Thus, the constant proportion is –3/2, or –1.5; consequently, if x increases by 4 units, y decreases by 6 units.

variables, or complete "dependence" of one variable on the value of the other.

Two factors must be taken into consideration in estimating r from a linear scattergram. The first is the amount of dispersion or scatter, and the second is the steepness of the slope (or the angle) shown by the line of best fit. Following are illustrations of different scattergrams and a judgmental estimate of the extent of association or correlation (r) that exists between the variables. These illustrations can serve as a guide in approximating the coefficient of correlation when different scatterings of points occur.

Perfect correlation, when r = +1 (or r = –1) — When *all* the points in the scatter diagram fall exactly on a straight line (except a horizontal line*), the correlation between the two variables is perfect. See Figure 12.2. When such a rare situation occurs the coefficient of correlation is unity, i.e., r = +1, or r = –1 if the relationship is perfect but inverse.

No correlation, when r = 0 (or close to zero) — A scatter diagram where the points are widely dispersed and show no particular tendency to form a straight-line path, as in Figure 12.3, means that there is *no* apparent relationship between the two variables. In this case, r=0 or is close to zero.

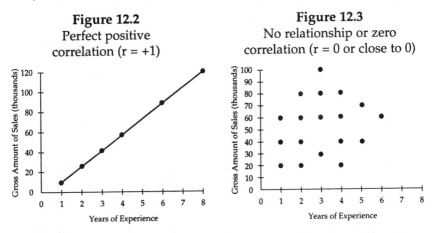

Figure 12.2	Figure 12.3
Perfect positive correlation (r = +1)	No relationship or zero correlation (r = 0 or close to 0)

High coefficient of correlation, when r is close to +1 (or –1) — When the points tend to hover closely around a straight-line path and when the path rises (positive correlation) or falls (negative correlation) steeply, Figure 12.4, the coefficient of correlation is high.

---

* When all the points fall on a perfectly horizontal line, r=0 because x has no influence on y, since y stays constant for all values of x.

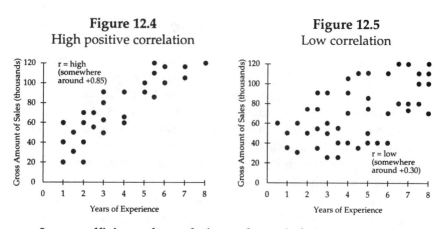

Figure 12.4
High positive correlation

Figure 12.5
Low correlation

Low coefficient of correlation, when r is between .2 and .4 — When the points are widely scattered but still show some tendency for concentration around a straight line, or if the line has only a slight slope (either positive or negative), the coefficient of correlation is generally low, as in Figure 12.5.

Using these rough guidelines for approximating r from the scattergram, we can estimate the coefficient of correlation between the two variables, years of experience and amount of annual sales, to be about +.8. The scatter diagram (Figure 12.1) looks something like the one in Figure 12.4.

While graphic analysis of the data is essential, the best way to determine the numerical value of the correlation coefficient is to calculate it, as illustrated in the sections "Correlation and Regression Analysis, Method #1" or "Method #2."

The coefficient of determination

The importance of an accurate calculation of r lies in its subsequent analytical use. Since the coefficient of correlation (r) measures the degree of linear association between two variables, it is appropriate to ask: "What do different values of r really tell us?" The real meaning of r can best be gleaned from the value of r-squared (r^2), called the *coefficient of determination*. When multiplied by 100, r^2 measures the extent, in percent, to which the independent variable (x) influences the variations in (y) the dependent variable. This determination is the ultimate objective of correlation analysis, to measure the influence (in percent) of x on y, consistent with our earlier definition of correlation analysis.

Thus, a value of r = 1, when squared and multiplied by 100, indicates that all the variations in y are influenced, or accounted for, by the independent variable x. This means that, all other conditions remaining the same as in the past, we can make predictions with *perfect accuracy* of the magnitude of y, given a value of x. On the other hand, when the correlation coefficient is zero or close to zero (which makes r^2 zero or very small) we can conclude that: (1) the influence of x on y is so slight that there is hardly any basis for estimating values of the dependent variable (y) from values of the independent variable (x), or (2) that the relationship between y and x may not be simple or may not be linear (although proper interpretation of the scattergram can detect cases where the relationship is non-linear).

The words "coefficient of determination" seem to be well chosen, for they indicate that some determinations must be made from its value when a practical application is being made, as follows:

(1) If we believe that the explained variation in y is sufficiently high (e.g., 85 percent), we may decide to move on to regression analysis and develop a forecasting equation for use in forecasting y on the basis of given values of x.

(2) If the explained variation is considered to be too low we may undertake any of the following:

(a) Postpone further computations with the single variable x and seek out other independent variables which also logically influence the variations in y, so that a sufficiently high *coefficient of multiple determination* is obtained. Thus, we may move from simple to multiple correlation and regression analysis.

(b) If appropriate, we can attempt to determine if the primary cause for the low coefficient of determination is a lag between the period of occurrence of x and its respective influence on y. If lag is found to be the cause, adjustment for lag may sometimes substantially increase r and r^2.

(c) We may find that we failed to detect, and therefore to exclude, an outlier point or two from the basic data.

(d) For simplicity, we are introducing the main elements of correlation and regression analysis by use of 100% (universe) data. However, if r is based on a small random sample, r^2 may be low because of sampling error. It will be recalled from Chapters 7 through 10 that values derived from samples are subject to sampling error which may be large when the size of sample is small. Consequently, if a small sample is used in calculating r, a low correlation coefficient may be caused by sampling variation, thus pointing to a need to increase n.

More on direction of the correlation

It will be noted that reference to r has been made in terms of plus or minus values. The implication is that some variables are correlated directly (where r is a plus value) and others are inversely correlated (where r is a minus value). When the scattering of points indicates that there is a linear association between two variables, it simultaneously indicates whether the relationship is direct or inverse. Direct correlation exists when the scattergram points from lower left to upper right in an upward slope, as shown in Figure 12.6. Inverse correlation exists when the scattergram points from upper left to lower right, in a downward slope, as shown in Figure 12.7.

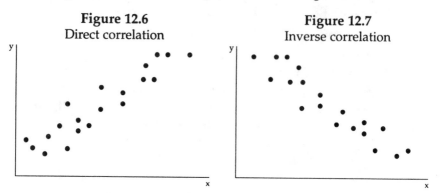

Figure 12.6
Direct correlation

Figure 12.7
Inverse correlation

It should be noted that a direct or inverse correlation of the same magnitude indicates the same degree of association (r), or the same extent of influence (r^2). Thus, a correlation coefficient of +1 and –1, or +0.8 and –0.8, indicate the same degree of association between two variables and therefore the same influence of x on y. The difference is that when r is positive the two variables move in the same general direction, such as sales volume and population. When the correlation coefficient is negative the two variables move in opposite directions, such as volume produced and cost per unit produced.

More on linear and curvilinear correlation

Our illustrations have dealt with straight-line (i.e., linear) relationships in which the scattering of points generally form a straight line path. While most applications have been found to be linear, it cannot be assumed, however, that every scatter diagram will tend to form a linear path. Linearity is present only when the two variables show a constant proportional relationship over the full range of values of the variables. When the relationship between two variables is not uniformly proportional, the scatter diagram may show some kind of curving or other complex pattern. The correlation between income and age of medical doctors is often curvilinear. Generally, average annual earnings increase from the beginning of medical practice, in early life, to middle age; in later life, when other factors become more prevalent (such as reduced physical activity or increased participation in other activities), average earnings may start to decline. The scattergram in this case might look something like Figure 12.8. When the relationship between two non-linearly related variables is perfect, the scattergram might look like Figure 12.9, with all points falling exactly on the curve, i.e., forming a perfect curve. Note, however, that this scattergram would not produce a high linear correlation coefficient, r, since a linear regression line would (because of its linearity) "miss" most points on the curve.

Figure 12.8
Curvilinear correlation

Figure 12.9 — Nearly perfect curvilinear correlation (but zero linear correlation)

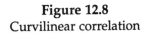
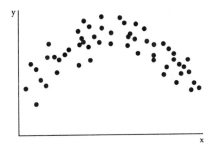
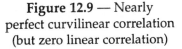
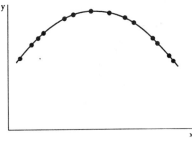

Elements of Linear Regression Analysis

When the influence (r^2) of x on y is found to be sufficiently strong, we may to enter into regression analysis, whose primary objective is to develop a *forecasting equation* which will yield forecasts of y with the least possible error of prediction, or the smallest possible standard error of estimate. This forecasting equation, or line, is referred to by various names, including the *regression line, line of least squares, line of average relationships*, and *line of best fit*.

The line of best fit

When the path of the scattergram is linear, the appropriate forecasting equation is that of a straight line fitted to the scattering of points. In algebra, we learn that the equation for a straight line is: y = a + mx, where y and x are the basic variables of the study, "*m*" is the *slope* (or angle) of the line, and "*a*" is its *intercept*, meaning the value of y where the value of x on the extended line is zero. In regression analysis, standard symbolism substitutes b for m so that the regression line is expressed as y = a + bx. The constants a and b are referred to as the *coefficients of the regression line*, or the *regression constants*. See Figure 12.10.

Figure 12.10 — The linear forecasting equation
expressed mathematically

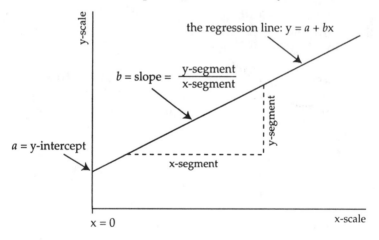

Standard error of estimate — To construct the regression line, it is necessary to compute the values of the constants *b* and *a* from the basic data. This line is fixed so that it cuts through the scattering of points to yield forecasts of y, for any given value of x, with the least (smallest) average error of estimate. The reason that the forecasting line is also called the line of "least squares" is that when the forecast errors are averaged by using the techniques of squares and square roots (similar to the technique of computing the standard deviation in Chapter 5), we arrive at the *standard error of estimate* (σ_e) with the lowest average estimation error. The technique of computing σ_e is demonstrated in the next section.

More on the correlation coefficient

There are two ways of computing r. One is based on statistical tools covered earlier (e.g., $\overline{X}$ and σ_x) in Chapters 4 and 5. The other method is based on solving algebraic equations. From a pedagogical viewpoint, the former is preferred because it deals with methods and concepts already covered earlier. It is presented here as Method #1. Method #2, the algebraic method, is demonstrated afterwords.

Correlation and Regression Analysis, Method #1

The coefficient of correlation (r) and coefficient of determination (r^2)

By Method #1, we use the well-known formula for r in linear correlation analysis called the product-moment technique or the Pearsonian formula (named after Karl Pearson who developed it), as follows:

$$r = \frac{\sum(x - \overline{X})(y - \overline{Y})}{N\sigma_x \sigma_y}.$$

The computations required to derive r and r^2 are shown in detail by the twelve steps that follow, and in Table 12.2, which provides the basic data. (Table 12.2 follows the description of the steps.)

(1) The mean of x: $\overline{X} = \dfrac{60}{20}$ = 3 years;

(2) The mean of y: $\overline{Y} = \dfrac{\$860}{20}$ = \$43 (thousand);

(3) $(x - \overline{X})$ is the difference between an individual x-value and the mean value, $\overline{X}$, showing + and – differences;

(4) $(y - \overline{Y})$ is the difference between an individual y-value and the mean y-value, $\overline{Y}$, showing + and – differences;

(5) $(x - \overline{X})(y - \overline{Y})$ is the algebraic product of each corresponding $(x - \overline{X})$ and $(y - \overline{Y})$;

(6) $\Sigma(x - \overline{X})(y - \overline{Y})$ is the net algebraic sum of the column of the $(x - \overline{X})(y - \overline{Y})$, where the sum of minus products is subtracted from the sum of plus products (dealing with + and − values separately) = 720;

(7) N is the number of pairs of values in the universe being correlated = 20;

(8) σ_x is the standard deviation of the x-values around their mean, namely, $\sigma_x = \sqrt{\dfrac{\Sigma(x-\overline{X})^2}{N}} = \sqrt{\dfrac{60}{20}} = 1.73$ (years);

(9) σ_y is the standard deviation of the y-values around their mean, namely, $\sigma_y = \sqrt{\dfrac{\Sigma(y-\overline{Y})^2}{N}} = \sqrt{\dfrac{14,670}{20}} = \sqrt{733.5} = \$27.1$ (thousand); and

(10) N $\sigma_x \sigma_y$ is the product of N, σ_x, and $\sigma_y = (20)(1.73)(27.1) = 937.66$.

(11) Thus, the coefficient of correlation, $r = \dfrac{\Sigma(x-\overline{X})(y-\overline{Y})}{N\sigma_x \sigma_y} = \dfrac{720}{937.66}$ = +0.768; and

(12) The coefficient of determination, $r^2 = (.768)^2 = 0.59$.

A correlation coefficient of +.77, such as the one computed above, indicates that a fairly good direct association exists between the two variables. However, the more meaningful measure is the coefficient of determination, r^2, which in this case tells us that 59 percent ($r^2 = 0.77^2 = 0.59$) of the variation in sales (y) is accounted for, or "explained" by, years of sales experience (x). If this extent of influence of x on y is acceptable to the analyst and management, we can proceed to develop the forecasting equation. Because the pattern of the scatter diagram (Figure 12.1) indicated a linear path, the forecasting equation will be a straight line, called the regression line or the line of best fit.

Table 12.2 — Computing the correlation coefficient
using data from Table 12.1, sales and years of experience

Sales person	Variable #1, years of experience	Variable #2, amount of sales ($1,000)	Difference from mean		Product of these two differences	Difference squared	
			Variable#1	Variable#2		Variable#1	Variable#2
	x	y	$(x - \overline{X})$	$(y - \overline{Y})$	$(x - \overline{X})(y - \overline{Y})$	$(x - \overline{X})^2$	$(y - \overline{Y})^2$
a	7	$ 90	+4	$+47	+188	16	2,209
b	5	100	+2	+57	+114	4	3,249
c	3	80	0	+37	0	0	1,369
d	1	20	−2	−23	+46	4	529
e	3	20	0	−23	0	0	529
f	4	30	+1	−13	−13	1	169
g	5	60	+2	+17	+34	4	289
h	4	40	+1	−3	−3	1	9
i	1	30	−2	−13	+26	4	169
j	2	10	−1	−33	+33	1	1,089
k	1	25	−2	−18	+36	4	324
l	1	10	−2	−33	+66	4	1,089
m	3	40	0	−3	0	0	9
n	2	20	−1	−23	+23	1	529
o	6	70	+3	+27	+81	9	729
p	4	80	+1	+37	+37	1	1,369
q	1	15	−2	−28	+56	4	784
r	2	50	−1	+7	−7	1	49
s	2	40	−1	−3	+3	1	9
t	3	30	0	−13	0	0	169
Totals	60	$860	0	0	720*	60	14,670

* Obtained by subtracting sum of − values from sum of + values.

The regression line

Many possible straight lines can be drawn by free-hand through the scattergram, all generally following the path outlined by the points. The best line, or the one that yields the least estimation error, on average, is the *regression line*. There is only one such line, and it is often referred to as the *line of least squares*. As indicated earlier, the regression line is expressed by the following equation using the symbol y_e to represent the estimated value of y for any given x-value:

y_e (estimated value of dependent variable) = a (the value of y when x = 0) + b (the slope of the line) multiplied by x (value of independent variable),

or, more succinctly,

$y_e = a + bx$.

After computing r and r^2, our task, of course, is to find the constant values of a and b that will yield the line of least squares. Continuing to use Method #1, the following additional steps are taken:

(13) The standard error of estimate (or average error),

$$\sigma_e = \sigma_y \sqrt{1-r^2} = (\$27.10)\sqrt{1-0.59} = (\$27.10)(.64) = \pm\$17.35 \text{ (thousand)}.$$

(14) The slope of the line, $b = \dfrac{r\ \sigma_y}{\sigma_x} = \dfrac{(.77)(27.10)}{1.73} = +12.06$. (This is the ratio of an increase in y triggered by a change in x.)

(15) The intercept, $a = \overline{Y} - b\overline{X} = \$43 - 12.06(3) = +\$6.82$ (thousand).

(16) The regression line, y_e = 6.82 + 12.06x. (This also is the forecasting equation.)

Since a line can be drawn by connecting any two points on it, the best line can now be fitted to the scattergram (see Figure 12.11) by locating any two points on it; for example, as follows:

When x = 0, y_e = 6.82 + 12.06 (0) = \$6.82 or \$7 (i.e., \$7,000).

When x = 4, y_e = 6.82 + 12.06 (4) = \$55.06 or \$55 (i.e., \$55,000).

Figure 12.11 — Regression line or line of least squares — sales based on years of experience (from Figure 12.1)

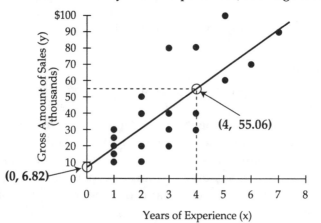

Further elucidation of the concept of standard error of estimate

The regression line is really a line of averages, since in theory, for each x-value there could be many y-values. These theoretical y-values are represented by a single figure (their average) on the regression line. Thus, connecting the points for these averages ($\bar{y}$'s), a straight line would be formed, and it would be the regression line: $y_e = a + bx$. If, as in Chapter 5, the coefficient of variation around the mean is very small, the mean may be used to estimate with a high degree of accuracy any of the values around it. Similarly, the line of averages will yield accurate estimates if its standard error (or scatter around it) is small. The formula for computing the standard error of estimate, denoted by σ_e, was presented previously in step 13 of the 16 steps used to establish the regression line.

A better understanding of the standard error of estimate concept can be gotten by testing (or simulating) the forecasting equation using the available data and measuring the actual error of prediction it yields for each x-value substituted into the line of best fit. In a sense, what we are saying is: Had we had the presently available forecasting equation, how accurately would we have estimated the sales of each of the 20 salespersons as well as the average error of these estimates?

Expected sales (y_e's) can be predicted by entering each actual x-value into the regression equation. The error of each estimate then can be determined by computing the difference between the actual y-value and the estimated y-value, i.e., by $y_a - y_e$. The *simulation method* for calculating the standard error of estimate is illustrated in the following steps.

(1) By entering each actual x-value into the regression equation, ($y_e = 7 + 12x$), we obtain an estimate of the dependent variable y_e. Thus, for example, for a salesperson with seven years of experience ($x = 7$), we would estimate an annual sales amount of $91(thousand), as follows: $y_e = 7 + (12)(7) = 7 + 84 = \$91$. When we compare the estimated value (y_e) with the actual value (y_a), the difference ($y_a - y_e = d = 90{-}91 = -\$1$) represents the error of the estimate for this salesperson.

(2) By entering the years of experience (x) for each of the 20 salespersons into the regression equation, a series of 20 different estimates of y_e and estimate errors is obtained, as shown in Table 12.3.

Table 12.3 — Calculation of standard error of estimate (in thousand dollars) by the simulation method

Years of experience	Actual sales	Estimated Sales	Difference (Error)	Squared difference (Error Squared)
x	y_a	y_e	$d = (y_a - y_e)$	$d^2 = (y_a - y_e)^2$
7	90	91	−1	1
5	100	67	+33	1,089
3	80	43	+37	1,369
1	20	19	+1	1
3	20	43	−23	529
4	30	55	−25	625
5	60	67	−7	49
4	40	55	−15	225
1	30	19	+11	121
2	10	31	−21	441
1	25	19	+6	36
1	10	19	−9	81
3	40	43	−3	9
2	20	31	−11	121
6	70	79	−9	81
4	80	55	+25	625
1	15	19	−4	16
2	50	31	+19	361
2	40	31	+9	81
3	30	43	−13	169
Totals	860	860	0	6,030

Standard error of estimate = $\sigma_e = \sqrt{\dfrac{\sum d^2}{N}} = \sqrt{\dfrac{6030}{20}} = \sqrt{301.5} = \pm\$17.4$ (thousand).

In more complete symbols, $\sqrt{\dfrac{\sum (y_a - y_e)^2}{N}} = \pm\$17.4$ (thousands).

Source: Table 12.1.

(3) We note that the average error, computed by dividing the net sum of the differences by N, is zero (this is the same condition found in computing the standard deviation of x). Therefore, to overcome this problem, the differences, $d = (y_a - y_e)$, are squared to convert all the errors to positive terms. When

added, $\Sigma(y_a - y_e)^2 = \$6030$. This is the total of all the squared errors with which we can readily compute the average of the squared errors of estimate ($\frac{\$6030}{20} = \$301.5$).

(4) The standard error of estimate then is calculated by "unsquaring" this average. Thus, the standard error of estimate is ±$17,4000, as follows:

$$\sigma_e = \sqrt{\frac{\Sigma(y_a - y_e)^2}{N}} = \sqrt{\frac{6030}{20}} = \sqrt{301.5} = \pm\$17.4 \text{ (thousand)}.$$

This average error, except for minor differences due to rounding, is precisely the standard error of estimate computed earlier by the formula in step 13. In fact, the standard error of estimate computed by the original formula and by simulation will always be exactly the same, except for insignificant differences due to rounding.

Use of the standard error, σ_e — Now that we have calculated the standard error of estimate to be about $17,400, what does it tell us? It tells us many things, among which are the following:

(1) *Accuracy check* — If σ_e computed by simulation agrees with σ_e computed by Method #1, step 13, it is a check on the accuracy of all the preceding computations.

(2) *Standard error as a standard deviation* — It enhances our understanding of the standard-error concept. It is not a measure of the standard error of an estimate derived from a random sample; it measures the average error (or one standard error) of y-values predicted by the regression line. In a sense, it is a standard deviation around the forecasting line.

(3) *Efficiency of estimating equation* — It can be used to measure the relative efficiency of the forecasting equation by computing the *relative error* of estimate $\left(\frac{\sigma_e}{\overline{Y}}\right)$ which elimi-nates the absolute units of measurement and converts the standard error to a percentage. Thus, for example, in our problem $\frac{\sigma_e}{\overline{Y}} = \frac{\pm\$17.4}{\$43} = \pm40.5\%$, indicating that we do not have an efficient forecasting equation, with such a high relative error.

(4) *Confidence in predictions* — The standard error of estimate can be used to determine the confidence that an estimate based

on the line of best fit will not exceed a given number of standard errors. This is because normal distribution theory underlies regression analysis; that is, the frequency distribution of the many possible y-values for each x-value (or the $y_a - y_e$ figures) will tend to form a normal curve. Thus, for example, we can conclude with 68 percent confidence that any predicted y-value will not be in error by more than one standard error of estimate. In our simulation demonstration (Table 12.3, using the $d = y_a - y_e$ column), 13 of the 20 errors or 65% of the errors are actually within one standard error (± 17.4).

By reference to the properties of normal distributions, it also can be stated with 95.5 and 99.7 percent confidence that the error of estimate will not exceed two and three standard errors, respectively. This application of the standard error is akin to the use of the standard error of the mean in establishing confidence intervals when using random samples.

(5) **Outliers** — The standard error of estimate can be used to detect and investigate outlier points. For example, for x=3 (point #3 in Table 12.3), how many standard errors separate the actual y-value of $80 from the expected y-value of $43? Using the Z-test, (appropriate for large samples or universe data), we find that $Z = \dfrac{\$80 - \$43}{17.4} = \dfrac{\$37}{17.4} = 2.13$ standard errors. The normal curve table in Appendix B shows that the probability that this difference ($y_a - y_e = \$37$) is due to chance is but 1.7 percent. Thus, under a significance level of 5%, this apparent outlier point would deserve an investigation to determine why it is so far "off" the expected value (y_e). (An actual application of this method to detect possible fraud or abuse is given later by item #5 in the section on "Some Additional Practical Uses of Correlation and Regression Analysis.")

(6) **Use in Method #2** — When Method #2 is used in determining the regression equation, it will be seen that it is essential to use the simulation method to compute not only σ_e but also r and r^2.

Correlation and Regression Analysis, Method #2

Establishing the regression equation

Another method of simple linear correlation and regression analysis involves creating two "normal" equations from the standard forecasting equation $y_e=a+bx$, and solving two simultaneous equations for the two constants a and b of the regression line. Subsequent steps then determine the values of r and r^2. This method is generally identified as the *backward solution method* because it constructs the regression line first without knowing r^2 — the extent of influence of x on y — and without analyzing for possible outliers, except by examination of the scattergram. Method #1, conversely, is called *forward solution method.*

Without going into the theory underlying the conversion of the general regression equation, $y_e = a + bx$, into the two so-called *normal equations,* we offer the following two steps by which they are derived:

(1) Sum the basic regression equation over all points: $\Sigma y = \Sigma a\ (= Na) + b\Sigma x$. This forms the first normal equation.

(2) Multiply the basic regression equation by x and then sum over all points: $\Sigma xy = a\Sigma x = b\Sigma x2$. This forms the second normal equation.

Thus, the two normal equations used to solve for a and b are:

(1) $\Sigma y = Na + b\Sigma x$

(2) $\Sigma xy = a\Sigma x + b\Sigma x^2$

Here, y is a value of the dependent variable and Σy is their sum; x is a value of the independent variable and Σx is their sum; xy is the product of the corresponding x and y values in each pair and Σxy is the sum of these products; x^2 is the square of each value of the independent variable and Σx^2 is the sum of these squared values; and N is the number of pairs of x and y values.

Again, using the basic data in Table 12.1 for the 20 salespeople as an illustration, first make the appropriate calculations shown in Table 12.4; then substitute the appropriate figures in the two normal equations.

Table 12.4 — Computations to solve for the regression coefficients, *a* and *b*

Salesperson	Years of experience	Sales (thousands)	Product of experience and sales	Square of years of experience
	(x)	(y)	(xy)	(x^2)
a	7	$90	630	49
b	5	100	500	25
c	3	80	240	9
d	1	20	20	1
e	3	20	60	9
f	4	30	120	16
g	5	60	300	25
h	4	40	160	16
i	1	30	30	1
j	2	10	20	4
k	1	25	25	1
l	1	10	10	1
m	3	40	120	9
n	2	20	40	4
o	6	70	420	36
p	4	80	320	16
q	1	15	15	1
r	2	50	100	4
s	2	40	80	4
t	3	30	90	9
Totals	$\Sigma x = 60$	$\Sigma y = \$860$	$\Sigma xy = 3{,}300$	$\Sigma x^2 = 240$

Source: Table 12.1.

The four sums from Table 12.4, when entered into the two normal equations, yield the following:

(1) $860 = 20a + 60b$

(2) $3{,}300 = 60a + 240b$

By algebra, we solve the equations for *a* and *b*, as follows. First, the two equations presented above, each with two unknowns, are reduced to a single equation with one unknown by constructing a third equation: by multiplying equation (1) by 3, and then subtracting the resulting equation from equation (2), as follows, to yield equation (4). Since this equation is limited to one unknown, we can readily solve it for b. These steps are summarized below.

(1) $860 = 20a + 60b$

(2) $3{,}300 = 60a + 240b$

(3) $2{,}580 = 60a + 180b$, results from the multiplication of equation (1) by 3.

(4) $720 = 60b$, results from subtracting equation (3) from (2).

(5) $b = 12$, results from solving equation (4) for b.

(6) $a = 7$, results from substituting $b = 12$ in the original equation (1), $860 = 20a + (60)(12)$, and solving it for a.

Since a is 7 and b is 12 the regression line is $y_e = 7 + 12x$. This is exactly the same forecasting equation derived earlier by Method #1.

Computing the other parameters

By using Method #2, we establish the regression line directly from the basic data. However, this method does not derive the coefficient of correlation (r), the coefficient of determination (r^2), and the standard error of estimate (σ_e). Since these are essential for determining the extent to which x influences y and the efficiency of the forecasting equation, additional independent steps are needed to compute these parameters, as follows:

(1) Compute the standard error of estimate (σ_e) by simulating the forecasting equation, as was demonstrated in Method #1. There, σ_e was determined to be $17.4 (thousand).

(2) To compute r^2, we use the Method #1 formula for σ_e:
$\sigma_e = \sigma_y \sqrt{1 - r^2}$. The equation for r^2 becomes: $r^2 = 1 - \dfrac{\sigma_e^2}{\sigma_y^2}$.

(3) Since simulation determined the value of σ_e as $17.4, we need only compute the value of σ_y by the standard deviation formula, $\sigma_y = \sqrt{\dfrac{\Sigma(y - \overline{Y})^2}{N}}$.

We previously found σ_y by Method #1 to be $27.1.

(4) Now we substitute the values of σ_e and σ_y in step (2) above and solve for r^2:

$$r^2 = 1 - \frac{\sigma_e^2}{\sigma_y^2} = 1 - \frac{17.4^2}{27.1^2} = 1 - 0.41 = 0.59 \text{ (or 59\%)}.$$

(5) The correlation coefficient is the square root of r^2:
$$r = \sqrt{0.59} = 0.77.$$

These parameters are precisely the same as those obtained by Method #1.

Some Additional Practical Uses of Correlation and Regression Analysis

Thus far, main emphasis on the practical aspects of correlation and regression analysis has been on prediction, e.g., sales forecasting. However, there are several other useful applications of these techniques, particularly when y is the variable representing workload or work output and x is the variable representing work hours input (or cost). Examples follow.

Analysis of Overhead

The ratio $a/\overline{Y}$, which may be used to represent the percentage of hours expended when the workload (x) is zero, can stimulate an analysis of the overhead of an operating unit, especially by analyzing this ratio for the different organizational units of an entity. It can also measure the extent of idle time or wait-for-work time.

Operating Efficiency

The slope, or b-value of the regression line, may be used to compare the relative efficiency of the different operating units. In positive correlation, b represents the ratio of the additional work hours required to produce a specific additional number of work units. The smaller the rate (or b-value), the more efficient is the operating unit.

Productivity Control

The regression line, $y_e = a + bx$, may be used to establish a *productivity control chart* on such variables as work-units completed (x) correlated with work-hours expended (y). The regression line may be considered as the norm or line of y-averages. A given number of standard errors (σ_e's) around the regression line may be used to establish control limits above and below the norm. Thus, points falling beyond these control limits (that is, more or less than acceptably normal hours used) may be considered significant management action-signals to investigate the causes and take appropriate preventative action.

An Index of Productivity

As a by-product of the productivity control chart, the data on work-load completed (x) and hours used (y) can be cumulated over time (e.g., a year) to determine the extent of gain (or loss) in productivity. This determination can be made by the formula: $1 - \dfrac{\Sigma y_a}{\Sigma y_e}$.

Here, Σy_a is the total number of hours actually used to perform the work cumulated over the 12 months of the year, and Σy_e is the total number of hours that should have been used (or expected by the regression line). When the above formula results in a plus, it represents the percentage gain in productivity. Conversely, when the formula results in a minus, the index represents a loss. For example, if $\Sigma y_a = 900$ hours and $\Sigma y_e = 1,000$, the index will be $1 - (900 / 1,000) = +.1$, or a 10% gain in productivity.

Detection of Possible Fraud or Abuse

A Blue Cross/Blue Shield agency compiled data from medical-provider records on the number of patients (x) they treated during a given year and the corresponding number of patient-visits (y). Z-tests of significance of the difference $y_a - y_e$ by $z = \dfrac{y_a - y_e}{\sigma_e}$, showed good reasons to investigate some probable outliers. Figure 12.12 displays such a probable outlier.

Figure 12.12 — Scatter diagram showing number of patients (x) and corresponding number of visits (y)

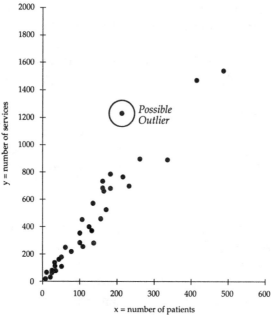

Source: Data recorded for 40 medical providers by the Blue Cross/Blue Shield Agency; data adjusted for illustration purposes.

Cautions in Use of Correlation and Regression Analysis

Correlation and regression analysis provides an understanding of the interrelationship between varying activities or processes in government, business, industry, psychology, and other diverse fields of endeavor, and it is therefore a valuable aid in interpreting data and guiding management decisions. However, an introduction to the power of these techniques without an evaluation of their qualifications can lead to inappropriate applications. The following lists some of the cautions that the user of correlation and regression analysis techniques should consider in order to avoid misapplications.

Caution #1 — *Simple* correlation and regression analysis

This chapter is restricted primarily to illustrations of methods of analysis when one variable influences one other variable. Rarely will one variable be the sole cause of variations in the other, i.e., rarely will r^2 be 100%. Therefore, in simple correlation analysis, we must know how much of the variation in the dependent variable is explained by the independent variable, so that we may decide whether there is a need for bringing in other influencing variables and using multiple correlation analysis.

Application of the explained-variation formula ($100r^2$) can be illustrated with our salesperson problem. We found a coefficient of correlation of r=+.77 between years of experience and sales. Therefore, the coefficient of determination is $100r^2 = (100)(.77)^2 = 59$ percent . Thus we note that 59 percent of the variation in sales is "explained" by years of experience. Conversely, we can state that years of experience *failed* to explain (100–59) = 41 percent of the variation in sales. Obviously, with such a large percentage of *unexplained* variation, other factors (such as personality, territory assigned, etc.) must also influence the amount of sales, and they must be brought into the analysis in order to obtain improved forecasts. This type of expanded analysis involves the use of *multiple* correlation and regression analysis, which, however, is beyond the intended scope of this book.*

Caution #2 — Use of *linear* correlation

The linear coefficient of determination, r^2, may turn out to be very small. Perhaps it is due to the fact that there is a strong curvilinear relationship. To avoid a wrong conclusion that there is no significant correlation (in general), it is essential to be guided by the scattergram to determine from it the general path or pattern of the relationship.

---

* For those interested, , it is possible to get an idea of how to conduct multiple correlation and regression analysis by following the steps covered in Method #2. This procedure deals with the solution of normal equations to obtain the constants of the regression equation. For example, in the case of two independent variables, x_1 and x_2, the derivation of the constants a, b_1, and b_2 of the multiple regression equation $y_e = a + b_1 x_1 + b_2 x_2$, involves the solution of the following three normal equations:

(1) $\sum y = Na + b_1 \sum x_1 + b_2 \sum x_2$

(2) $\sum x_1 y = a \sum x_1 + b_1 \sum x_1^2 + b_2 \sum x_1 x_2$

(3) $\sum x_2 y = a \sum x_2 + b_1 \sum x_1 x_2 + b_2 \sum x_2^2$.

For further information on multiple correlation-regression (and other advanced topics), the reader should consult a book such as David Kleinbaum and Lawrence Kupper, *Applied Regression Analysis and Other Multivariable Methods*, Duxbury Press, Wadsworth Publishing Co., 1978.

Caution #3 — Causal relationship

It is not difficult by associating many different pairs of variables to find a high correlation among some of them. In such a situation it is particularly tempting to conclude that one (or more than one) variable influences another, i.e., to automatically assume that a cause-and-effect relationship exists. In all correlation-regression analyses, however, it must be determined whether a strong correlation is not just a coincidence, called a *spurious correlation*, or whether the two variables are both associated with a third variable that influences both of them, or whether they represent only part of a "causal chain." For example, population in a community may influence both school enrollment and its labor force; yet, it would be risky to attempt to estimate the labor force from figures on school enrollment, two variables that would probably show a high coefficient of correlation. *In general, in order to avoid "spurious correlation," it is good practice not to assume without further thought and additional evidence that a high value of r is proof of causality.*

Caution #4 — When using *sample data*

The salesperson-sales data used to demonstrate the various elements of correlation and regression analysis were assumed to be universe data for simplicity, since the basic concepts, words, and principles could readily be illustrated without getting involved with sampling variation. However, random sample data often are used in the real world, and certain steps need to be taken to account for sampling variation and to provide acceptable estimates. The following illustrates three modifications required when sample data are used.

(1) The first consideration is to determine whether the correlation coefficient computed from sample data is significantly different from zero at a given level of risk or significance. A direct way of determining the significance of the correlation coefficient is by reference to the table of critical r-values constructed by R.A. Fischer and Frank Yates, shown in Appendix E. For example, if n is 20, then n–2 = 18 degrees of freedom, and r must be at least .44 to differ significantly from zero at a significance level of 5 percent.

(2) Another consideration is the unbiased estimation of r and σ_e when computed from a random sample. The following formulas would be used and computations made if we

assumed that our salesperson-sales data were based on a random sample of 20 persons. These are based on steps 8, 9, and 11 of Method #1, but using n–1 in place of N.

(8) $\quad \sigma_x = \sqrt{\dfrac{\Sigma(x-\overline{X})^2}{n-1}} = \sqrt{\dfrac{60}{19}} = 1.777$;

(9) $\quad \sigma_y = \sqrt{\dfrac{\Sigma(y-\overline{Y})^2}{n-1}} = \sqrt{\dfrac{14,670}{19}} = 27.787$;

(11) $\quad r = \dfrac{\Sigma(x-\overline{X})(y-\overline{Y})}{(n-1)(\sigma_x)(\sigma_y)} = \dfrac{720}{(19)(1.777)(27.787)}$

$\qquad = \dfrac{720}{938.172} = 0.767$.

Also, the standard error of estimate, derived by the simulation method in Table 12.3, would be modified by replacing N with n–2 (degrees of freedom):

$\sigma_e = \sqrt{\dfrac{\Sigma(y_a - y_e)^2}{n-2}} = \sqrt{\dfrac{6,030}{18}} = \pm\$18.30$.

It should be noted that the results obtained by assuming that the 20 points are sample data do not differ much from those obtained by assuming that the 20 points are universe data. Substantial differences between the results from these two methods of computation may be expected mostly when using small samples (e.g., much less than 30 cases).

When the sample size exceeds 30 and when r is not very high, a formula for approximating the standard error of r is: $\sigma_r = \sqrt{\dfrac{1-r^2}{n-2}}$. On this basis, if the r-value of .77 in our example had been based on a sample of size n=31 salespersons, then we would have obtained a standard error of $\sigma_r = \sqrt{\dfrac{1-.59}{29}} = \pm 0.119$.

(3) Finally, when using sample data, we should be aware that estimates derived from the regression line are subject to sampling variation. Therefore, for technically strict applications, confidence intervals should be established on the estimated values of the dependent variable (y_e) as well as the estimated values of *a* and *b*. The computational aspects of

establishing confidence intervals around the estimated values are beyond the scope of this book.

Caution #5 — Forecasting beyond the *range of the data*

A student term paper based on the relationship of age (x) of young children in a playground and their height (y) developed the following forecasting equation: y_e (expected height in inches) = 38 + (2.1)(age). When projected to age 30, one would expect these children to be over 8 feet tall. This is a clear demonstration of a caution to avoid forecasting much beyond or below the range of the basic data used to develop the forecasting equation.

Caution #6 — Estimating *the independent variable x*

The utility of correlation analysis as a tool for forecasting values of a dependent variable (y) rests primarily on our knowledge of the value of the independent variable (x). Can we always obtain a reasonably accurate figure for the independent variable? In many cases we can, because the independent variable usually precedes or "leads" the dependent variable. Thus, final grades in a statistics course may be predicted with reasonable accuracy from midterm grades; the number of telephone orders may be predicted from population or housing permit figures; etc.

Sometimes, however, the value of the independent variable is not readily known. For example, in estimating sales for a given future year on the basis of national disposable income, it is necessary to have an estimate of the disposable income for that year. Yet, there is no readily available figure on the actual amount of disposable income before it is earned. This brings up another caution point.

While the standard error of estimate allows for probable errors of prediction, it does not readily provide a basis for measuring the error which can result from possible inaccuracies in the independent variable (x) used to make the prediction.

Caution #7 — Failure to account for *time lag*

On occasion, the independent variable occurs in advance of the dependent variable, as in production which comes first and freight-car loadings, which come afterwards. If there is a lag between x and y, the lag factor must be properly dealt with. To deal with this problem it is advisable to calculate r with different time lags. The lag that yields the highest coefficient of correlation then can be used to develop the regression line.

Caution #8 — Change in the *constant-cause system*

The U.S. Postal Service, in developing its annual budget, had been using a regression equation to forecast its annual mail volume. The regression line was based on a very high association between annual mail volume and population growth over a period of 10 years. One year, its actual annual mail volume was significantly higher than the forecasted volume, requiring a request to Congress for a special supplemental appropriation of millions of dollars to handle the additional, unbudgeted mail volume. It was subsequently found that this embarrassing situation was not caused by an error in the forecasting equation but by a major change in the constant-cause system which did not exist in the previous years. The Mail Order Advertising Association had passed a resolution advising its members to advertise through the mail. With an annual increase of over a billion pieces of mail, this created a major change in the previous constant-cause system.

Caution #9 — Failure to detect *outliers*

The U.S. Forest Service once experimented with the use of regression analysis to forecast the sales price of given volumes of forest trees up for sale at auctions. The extent of influence (r^2) of volume (x) on sales price (y) turned out to be very low, contrary to a logical expectation of a high r^2. Upon further analysis, it was found that the basic data covering previous auctions included both healthy trees and trees that were partially charred due to forest fires. When sales of the latter trees, which auctioned off at a much lower price than healthy trees, were excluded, r^2 increased immensely.

We must always analyze the basic data for possible outliers either by the scattergram or simulation method and by significance tests to detect and eliminate outliers. Their elimination, however, must be documented and explained, i.e., *why* they are exceptional. Often, valuable information can be uncovered by such investigation.

Summary

Correlation and regression analysis are two distinct parts of this field of study. With correlation analysis we first attempt to determine the extent (in percent) to which one (or more than one) independent variable (x) influences the magnitude of the dependent variable (y). Regression analysis generally follows correlation analysis. If the influence of x on y is "sufficiently great" (based on a judgmental decision by the analyst and/or management), computations can be made to develop a regression equation with which we can forecast values of y for specific x-values.

When the appropriate data are collected and analyzed to develop the best forecasting equation, the power of correlation and regression analysis can be harnessed to yield valuable information which can be applied to a large variety of practical problems of management. While the primary use of the regression equation may be forecasting, e.g., in budgeting and short-range planning, it can serve other useful purposes of management and researchers. Among them are: determining if a new drug can help cure certain ailments or if certain human behaviors are detrimental to personal health; improving the scheduling of staff to more efficiently handle anticipated workloads or service demands; adopting a control-chart approach on the utilization of resources (people) and costs; establishing an index of productivity; assisting in the detection of possible fraud or abuse; and serving a variety of other practical uses.

Correlation and regression analysis can be linear (when a constant relationship exists between x and y), or non-linear (when the relationship varies for given values of x). This book only covers linear correlation analysis, which is considered to be the more prevalent of the two.

There are two basic methods of linear correlation and regression analysis. Method #1, generally identified as the forward method, is simpler for many persons because it utilizes the statistical tools already covered in Chapter 4 (averages) and Chapter 5 (standard deviations). Method #2, generally called the backward solution method, utilizes algebra. In simple correlation and regression analysis, it involves establishing two "normal equations," derived from the standard forecasting equation $y_e = a + bx$. Solution for the intercept (a) and the slope (b) of the regression line establishes the forecasting equation. Use of sample data requires certain modifications to the procedures, as well as an appreciation of the fact that the results are subject to sampling error.

Analysts attempting to adopt correlation and regression analysis to serve chosen purposes of the organization must be alerted to certain pitfalls in using the technique. Among these are: avoid including outliers in the data; investigate outliers to determine their cause, such as possible fraud or abuse, so that proper action may be taken to prevent their recurrence; consider whether multiple correlation will improve the accuracy of forecasts; be alert to a change in the constant-cause system subsequent to the history-period when the basic data were compiled; avoid forecasting much beyond or below the range of the basic data; and assure that there actually is a logical cause-and-effect relationship between x and y.

Problems

1. In the study of correlation and regression analysis we have encountered a large number of new terms. How many of the following do you understand? Give an illustration of each:

dependent variable	independent variable
multiple correlation	simple correlation
inverse and direct correlation	linear and curvilinear correlation
logical correlation analysis	coefficient of correlation
scatter diagram	horizontal and vertical scale
line of best fit	line of average relationship
standard error of estimate	standard deviation of the dependent variable
lag	reliability of the coefficient of correlation
explained variation	unexplained variation
method of least squares	"normal equations"
line of least squares	regression line
simple linear correlation	relative error of estimate
coefficient of determination	outlier points

2. What two computational methods of correlation and regression analysis were demonstrated in this chapter? Explain the difference in their approach.

3. Following are the respective grades of 20 students in their midterm and final examination in a Business Statistics class:

Student	Midterm	Final	Student	Midterm	Final
A	79	80	K	79	83
B	83	90	L	52	57
C	56	54	M	82	84
D	84	88	N	87	73
E	73	84	O	83	77
F	85	89	P	85	70
G	89	95	Q	85	89
H	53	54	R	68	69
I	78	72	S	85	88
J	69	72	T	86	90

(a) Using the scattergram method, estimate the coefficient of correlation, r, between midterm and final grades.

(b) Specify whether the correlation is linear or curvilinear, direct or inverse.

(c) By free-hand, draw what you believe to be the line that best fits the scattergram.

(d) One student who withdrew from class after the midterm examination had received a grade of 68 on the midterm, and he was given a final grade of I (incomplete). Estimate by reference to the free-hand line of best fit what his final examination grade would have been had he been able to complete the term.

4. Using the data in problem 3:

(a) Calculate the coefficient of correlation, r, by the Pearsonian (product-moment) formula and note the difference between your calculated value and the value estimated in problem 3 (a).

(b) Determine the line of best fit by use of the appropriate formulas.

(c) Estimate the final examination grade of the student with a midterm grade of 68 who was given an incomplete grade in problem 3(d), using the computed line of best fit.

(d) What percent of the variation in the final grades is influenced by the variation in the midterm grades? What percent of the variation in the final grades is unexplained by the regression line?

(e) What factors in addition to the midterm grade are likely to influence the final grade?

(f) If these factors could be measured and brought into the calculation of r, what type of correlation analysis would it be called?

5. This chapter emphasized the importance of the simulation method, whereby the forecasting equation is used to predict the y_e-values by inserting the basic data x-values into the forecasting equation and measuring the individual errors of prediction by $y_a - y_e$. Also, it provides for deriving an independent standard error of estimate by

$$\sigma_e = \sqrt{\frac{\Sigma\left(y_a - y_e\right)^2}{N}} \text{ and}$$

comparing it with the previously computed σ_e by $\sigma_e = \sigma_y \sqrt{1 - r^2}$.

(a) Simulate the forecasting equation of problem 4, $y_e = 6.937 + .921x$, and compute the standard error of estimate.

(b) Compare the resulting σ_e with the one obtained in problem 4. What do you find?

(c) The chapter also illustrated other uses of simulation, such as detecting outlier points by the Z-variate method and showing the approach of the individual errors of estimate $(y_a - y_e)$ to normality.

(1) Apply the Z-test to the two largest errors.

(2) What percentage of the errors are within one σ_e?

6. The following data show the total annual sales made by the ABC Co., a large retail chain with stores throughout the United States; also given are the figures on total disposable personal income in the United States for the same years. (See problem 7 to minimize computational effort and errors.)

Year	Disposable Income (billions of dollars)	Total store sales (millions of dollars)
1980	1,918.0	16,887.9
1981	2,127.6	18,303.6
1982	2,261.6	18,804.8
1983	2,428.1	18,519.3
1984	2,668.6	19,644.7
1985	2,838.7	20,469.9
1986	3,013.3	20,986.9
1987	3,205.9	20,774.6
1988	3,548.2	22,272.2
1989	3,787.0	23,595.1
1990	4,050.5	23,436.7
1991	4,230.5	23,068.1
1992	4,500.2	24,400.0
1993	4,706.7	23,636.7
1994	5,101.9	24,640.0

Sources: Disposable personal income: U.S. Department of Commerce, *Survey of Current Business,* various months; or U.S. Bureau of the Census, *Statistical Abstract of the United States,* various years.

Store sales: Securities and Exchange Commission, *Form 10-K* for selected corporation, available from several library sources, various years; data have been partially adjusted for this problem.

(a) Based on the information given above, is it logical to assume a cause-and-effect relationship between the two variables? Why?

(b) Which is the dependent and which the independent variable? Why?

(c) Draw a scatter diagram for the above data.

(d) From inspection of the scatter, specify whether you believe the relationship between the two variables to be linear or curvilinear. Justify your answer.

(e) Is the relationship direct or inverse? Justify your answer.

(f) By a freehand method, draw a regression line through the scattergram that you believe best fits the data.

(g) From the scattergram, what would be your rough estimate of the coefficient of correlation between the two variables?

(h) Estimate the company's total sales for a year with a disposable income of:

(1) $4.5 trillion, and (2) $6.0 trillion.

7. Problems 4, 5, and 8 may involve a lot of arithmetic (or data entry). How can you minimize it in these problems?

8. (a) In problem 6 above, using the appropriate statistical formulas, compute r and r^2 and determine the line of best fit , as well as its standard error of estimate.

(b) Estimate total sales when disposable income is:

(1) $4.5 trillion, and (2) $6.0 trillion.

9. (a) In the above problem, what percentage of the estimates based on the line of best fit will be subject to less than one standard error of estimate? Less than 2 standard errors of estimate?

(b) What percent of the variation in sales is accounted for by disposable income and what percent is unexplained or accounted for by other factors?

(c) Determine the relative error of estimate, or the coefficient of error.

10. (a) When the coefficient of correlation is –1, the standard error of estimate is always equal to ……. (Complete the sentence.) Explain your answer.

(b) When r is .9, what percentage of the variations in y is accounted for by variation in x?

11. If r is –1.2 when computed by the Pearsonian (product-moment) formula, it is a sign that ……. (Complete the sentence.)

12. When a high coefficient of correlation exists between two variables, it is valid to make linear regression estimates of one variable on the basis of value(s) of the other. Explain to what extent this statement is true or false.

13. A coefficient of correlation of +.90 indicates that 90 percent of the variations in the dependent variable is accounted for by variation in the independent variable. Explain to what extent this statement is true or false.

14. A coefficient of correlation of +.90 indicates a relationship between two variables that is twice as strong as a coefficient of

correlation of +.45 between two different variables. True or false? Explain.

15. Describe in your own words at least three pitfalls to guard against in simple linear correlation analysis.

16. Describe at least three practical uses or applications of correlation and regression analysis.

17. Fourteen empolyees in the Federal Government who attended a graduate level course in statistics gave their age (last birthday) and years of completed government service as follows:

Age	Years of service	Age	Years of service
34	13	44	7
46	23	33	9
39	10	45	26
57	29	47	28
27	5	24	2
46	21	38	16
46	5	43	5

(a) Plot a scattergram and detect possible outliers.

(b) Include the possible outliers and compute the correlation coefficient and coefficient of determination.

(c) Continue with the remaining steps and determine the forecasting equation (preliminary).

(d) Using this forecasting equation, use simulation to determine which student data seem pretty sure to reflect outliers, and state why.

(e) Exclude the outliers and develop a revised forecasting equation.

(f) To what extent does age influence the number of government service years?

18. A large word-processing unit kept records over a period of five weeks on the number of different letters it produced and the corresponding number of hours used to do this work, as follows:

Week	Letters produced	Hours used
1	308	40
2	605	82
3	412	73
4	510	80
5	240	35

(a) Assume that this is universe data (not a sample). Develop the regression line to be used in scheduling weekly person-hours in light of the expected weekly workload.

(b) Check out the accuracy of the resulting forecasting equation by use of simulation.

(c) How much error of estimation do you expect on the average?

Chapter 13

Time Series and Forecasting

"For the economist in his effort to learn more and more about how the economic system works, the study of time series is perhaps the most important source of information."[*]

A friend of ours entered the word-processing business and had just completed three years of operation. We recently asked her: "How is business"? She quickly responded: "Pretty good." What does "pretty good" really mean? Has the number of customers gone up 5 percent since the first year? Have net profits increased 10 percent in the past year? How good are the prospects for continuous growth? Which are the most active months? Which are the least active?

Our friend is operating a small business and may not need to collect and analyze time series data, but would it not be fun and possibly informative to record the data on the number and amount of sales and plot the monthly and annual receipts figures on a chart to keep in touch with business progress?

It has been repeatedly emphasized in previous chapters that we live in a world of change, where practically every phenomenon or process in business, government, and in life itself is subject to variation or irregularities. To avoid losing touch with changes in activities of primary concern to management requires the collection and interpretation of quantitative data on these changes. By collecting and recording data on a continuing basis (daily, weekly, monthly, quarterly, and yearly) we establish *time series data*. In due time, after several years, it becomes possible to study the behavior of these data in terms of trends, seasonal variation, cyclical patterns (if any), and unanticipated occurrences.

The four-fold objectives of this chapter are to: (1) show the benefits of time series analysis, (2) present the main elements of time

---

[*] Edward E. Lewis, *Methods of Statistical Analysis in Economics and Business,* Houghton Mifflin Company, Boston, 1953.

series, (3) illustrate a simple method of keeping track of an activity's behavior and then forecasting its probable future behavior, and (4) alert the analyst and management of some cautions in the interpretation and analysis of time series data.

Uses of Time Series

Planning

Some famous sayings come to mind when we consider the possible uses of time series data. One saying is: Man* is a planning animal. Another saying is: What is past is prologue.

It is characteristic of intelligent behavior of human beings to plan for the future (even though squirrels generally outdo us in planning for the winter). Advance planning has led to savings for retirement (e.g., IRA's), purchasing a home, taking an enjoyable vacation, and so forth. For business organizations this means planning marketing strategy, planning to assure an adequate supply of raw material, planning adequate facilities and space for anticipated business expansion, planning for anticipated technological developments, or for a possible recession, etc. For government agencies this means budget planning, planning for implementation of new programs, figuring out how to deal with budget or staff cuts or additional mandates, etc.

It may be apparent from these uses of time series that both short-range and long-range planning is an important part of good management.

Forecasting

Planning can be done by relying on good judgment and experience of the past, but more effective planning can be done by also gathering and analyzing quantitative data on the past behavior of the activity being studied. This analysis seeks, and often can discover, a stable pattern of behavior over a sufficient period of time so that, depending on the continuation of this pattern, reasonably accurate predictions can be made of the near future. Activities that may be tracked include sales volume, gross value of sales, or growth of the population in a county or local geographical area; it also can include predicting employment and unemployment rates, budgeting on the basis of public demand for services, etc. Forecasting based on accurate numbers can in many cases be fairly simple, as was demonstrated in the very first chapter of this book, namely by harnessing the *Law of*

---

* Meaning human beings.

Statistical Regularity of Mass Data, if the time series displays regularity and when large numbers are involved.

Facts for rational action

Time series data also provide a basis for systematically studying the influence of various economic, demographic, technological, and other factors on processes of concern to the organization. The mere function of assembling and examining relevant data about an activity over successive intervals of time affords the organization an opportunity to learn more about it than would otherwise be possible, especially when the data are analyzed properly.

By quantitatively measuring the normal growth (trend) of an activity, its cyclical pattern (if any), and the pattern of seasonal variation, management can better understand its behavior, e.g., know whether service demand or costs are greater or less than "normal" and how much the differences are. Thus, mistaken conclusions can be avoided, such as the belief that an upswing in an activity is the result of a real improvement when, in fact, the improvement actually is the result of a normal seasonal high.

Elements Of Time Series

The primary (and probably the sole) objective of time series analysis is to forecast a variable of concern, such as employment or sales, into the unknown future based on data of the past. Thus, time is the independent or influencing variable (x), and the dependent activity variable (y) is the one we wish to forecast. Since forecasting is also one of the objectives of correlation and regression analysis, there is similarity in the primary objectives of the two techniques. Thereafter, however, the objectives of the two techniques differ, because correlation and regression analysis (Chapter 12) serves many other uses besides forecasting.

Another major difference between the two analytical techniques is that in time series we know that the factors which influence the variable of interest are the four so-called *components* of the time series, namely, *trend, seasonal, cyclical,* and *irregular* (or unanticipated) variations. In correlation and regression analysis, on the other hand, the influencing variables usually are not time but others that are considered to be logical influencers of the dependent variable.

Examples of two components of time series analysis are given in Tables 13.1 and 13.2. Glancing at the bottom line of Table 13.1, we see a continuing upward movement in annual average U.S. civilian employment. This upward tendency is called the *trend*. Glancing at the monthly figures in the same table, we see variations in monthly civilian employment. This is called *seasonal variation*. Table 13.2 shows a generally downward trend in annual anthracite coal production, illustrating that some trends are upward and others downward.

Table 13.1
Civilian employment in the United States, by month,
1983-1993 (in millions)

Month	1983	1984	1985	1986	1987	1988	1989	1990	1991	1992	1993
January	97	101	104	107	109	112	115	116	115	115	116
February	97	102	105	107	109	112	115	116	115	115	117
March	98	103	106	108	110	113	116	117	116	116	117
April	99	104	106	108	111	114	116	117	117	117	118
May	100	105	107	109	112	114	117	118	117	118	119
June	102	107	108	111	113	116	119	120	118	119	121
July	103	107	109	112	115	117	120	120	119	120	121
August	103	107	109	112	115	117	119	119	118	119	121
September	102	106	108	110	113	115	117	118	117	118	120
October	103	106	108	111	114	116	118	118	118	118	120
November	103	106	108	111	114	116	118	118	117	118	121
December	103	106	108	111	114	116	118	117	117	118	121
Average	100.83	105.01	107.15	109.60	112.44	114.97	117.33	117.91	116.88	117.60	119.31

Source: U.S. Dept. of Labor, Bureau of Labor Statistics

Table 13.2
Annual production of anthracite coal in the United States,
1984-1994 (in millions of short tons)

Year	Number of tons	Year	Number of tons
1984	4.2	1990	3.5
1985	4.7	1991	3.4
1986	4.3	1992	3.1
1987	3.6	1993	3.4
1988	3.6	1994	3.2 (est.)
1989	3.3		

Source: U.S. Department of Energy

A closer look at the four components of time series

The following expands on the meaning of the four components of time series.

Long-term trend — Trend is the underlying tendency of an activity to grow or decline consistently over a long period of time. Many activities exhibit trends over time. When, for example, the average annual civilian employment figures for each year shown in Table 13.1 are plotted, the general tendency is clearly toward increasing employment in the United States (Figure 13.1). A rising trend represents a positive correlation of the variable with time. Other examples of positive long-term trend in the United States are: population, national income, sales, and prices.

Figure 13.1
Trend in civilian employment in the United States, 1983-1993

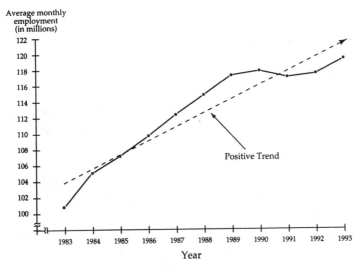

Source: Table 13.1

Most economic series in the United States probably show positive long-term trends because of continuing population growth. There are, however, some series that show a downward or negative long-term trend. The production of anthracite coal in the United States shows a sharply declining trend (Figure 13.2); so is the trend of farm population, or the infant mortality rate in the United States.

Figure 13.2

Trend in anthracite coal production in the United States, 1984-1994

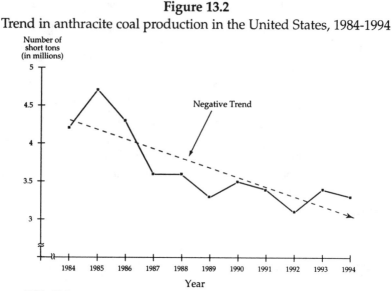

Source: Table 13.2

Seasonal variations — Because of natural and man-made factors, the activities of most organizations vary in some regular pattern during the climatic seasons of the year, hence the term seasonal variations. Examples of natural forces are rainfall, sunshine, cold months, and warm months. Examples of man-made factors are holidays, such as Christmas, New Years, Thanksgiving, etc. These and related customs have caused seasonal variations in different activities that are predictable with reasonable accuracy. Figure 13.3 illustrates the consistent seasonal pattern of variation in total civilian employment in the United States, with the highest employment usually in July and August and the lowest in January and February.

Cyclical variations — In time series we rarely find an unbroken continuous upward or downward movement of the variable over the long run. Generally, the activity described by a time series, while it will show a general straight-line trend, will vary above and below it in *cycles* somewhat like those shown in Figure 13.4.

Because many economic time series have shown a persistent tendency to follow a cycle consisting of periods of prosperity, decline, depression, and recovery, the cyclic component of time series often is defined as the *business cycle*, or simply cyclical variation. Though cycles display a rhythmic pattern, they often last for an unpredictable

Figure 13.3
Seasonal variation in civilian employment in the United States,
selected years, 1983-1993

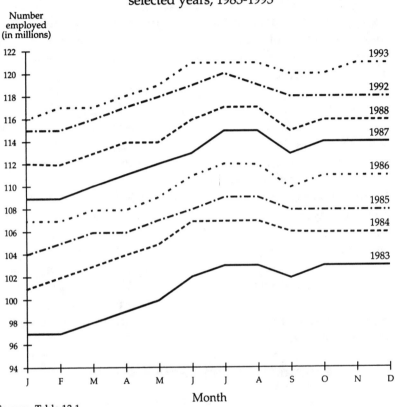

Source: Table 13.1

Figure 13.4
Illustrations of hypothetical cyclical movements over several years

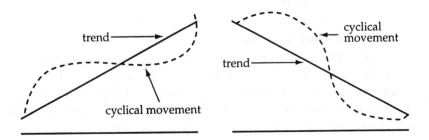

and uneven time period, making forecasts of their behavior more tenuous than forecasts of trend and seasonal variations.

Irregular or unpredictable variations — Another challenge to accurate forecasts is unanticipated occurrences. From time to time unpredictable causes of variation occur either as a result of man-made factors, such as the development of nuclear power technologies, or natural factors, such as a catastrophic earthquake, flood, or drought. These are called irregular or unpredictable variations.

When the history-period data contain such exceptional variations, the analyst must find a way to detect and remove them from the time series to avoid distortion of the trend. Even if removed, their potential for occurring in the future at any given time creates another difficulty in forecasting the future magnitude of the variable of interest. Forecast analysts generally are left the option of making assumptions regarding the time and impact of such occurrences on the forecast, such as technological developments, pending legislation, unexpected policy changes, etc. This component, as well as irregular cycles, make accurate short-range and especially long-range forecasting a difficult task. An article in the Washington Post some time ago on "Why Economists Can't See the Future" had this element in mind — predicting the unpredictable is a major problem in forecasting the future.

Methods Of Time Series Analysis

The main objective in forecasting an activity by time series is to measure, and allow for, the effect on that activity of each of the four components of time series. This analysis is generally called *decomposition* of the time series. By quantitatively allowing for the effect of each of these components, the activity can be better understood and its magnitude predicted with greater accuracy than otherwise. The effect of trend, for example, can be measured readily by holding constant the effect of within-year seasonal, cyclical, and unpredictable factors. The effect of within-year seasonal variations on the annual trend is easily dealt with because it can be accounted for by computing an index of each month's activity based on the "average per month" for the entire year. Dealing with cycles and irregular variations involves making judgmental assumptions regarding their probable magnitude and time of occurrence.

As in correlation analysis, trend analysis may be conducted by the same methods, such as: by logic and judgment, graphically, and by statistical methods. Probably the main contribution to the accuracy of forecasts are the body of data collected over a reasonable period of time combined with good judgment. The quantitative data provide for an objective analysis of trends and seasonal variations. Good judgment helps to account for cycles, if any exist, and the possibility of irregular occurrences. Even the simplest methods of statistical analysis, such as those presented in this chapter, can contribute much to accurate forecasts as long as good historic data are available.

Measuring long-term trend

As in correlation analysis, a first step in the analysis of time series data is a graphic presentation of the data. Thus, Figures 13.1 and 13.2 show a free-hand drawing of the trend line, indicating the direction and general slope of the line. Figure 13.3, on the other hand, shows the existence of a seasonal pattern of variation.

A more precise analysis follows by use of statistical methods of developing the trend line equation and the seasonal index. A graphic analysis of the data, however, is considered a good first start.

The method of least squares — Generally, when the concern is with long-term trend, annual totals or annual monthly averages are used. On this basis, seasonal variations in trend analysis have already been submerged within the year, thereby eliminating the need for accounting for seasonal variations. Special treatment of the data to remove cyclical variations often is not as simple. However, over the long run the problem tends to solve itself, since cyclical variations by their very nature are not one-directional. Their net effect on the trend may therefore be assumed to be compensating or offsetting and relatively small in the long run. The removal of data-points representing unpredictable variations, or *outliers*, is not difficult if one researches the variable under study and discovers when such extreme variations have occurred.* These influences can then be deleted from the time series. Thus, after removal of seasonal variations by using annual data, and after appropriate adjustment of the annual data for known abnormal variations, the resulting data generally can be used to represent long-term trend.

The main idea in *linear trend* analysis is to establish the direction of the trend line and the average rate of its annual growth or decline.

---

*For example, anthracite coal production during the World War II years were extremely out of line in comparison with earlier and more recent years.

Thus, when the graphic picture shows a linear growth pattern, the goal is to fit the most accurate *straight line* to the time series, called the *trend line*, defined by the linear equation $y_e = a + bx$. In this line, y_e is the estimated trend-value of the variable (y) being studied at any given point of time and x is the independent variable representing the year. As in regression analysis, the constant *a* is called the *intercept*, that is, the point where the line intersects the y-axis when the value of x is zero. The constant *b* represents the *slope* of the trend line; it is the rate of increase (or decrease) in y for a given change in x. To determine the value of these constants we will use the *method of least squares* previously demonstrated in Chapter 12.*

An example of determining the trend line — To illustrate the least-squares method of fitting a trend line, we use the data on annual production of anthracite coal from 1984 to 1994, given in Table 13.2. In this case, the dependent variable (y) is tonnage of anthracite coal mined and x is the independent variable representing the year in which it was mined. If possible, abnormal variations (or outlier points) must be removed from the data before the trend line is calculated. The annual anthracite coal data used in our example, however, show no apparent or known reason for such adjustment.

To fit the trend line to the data, we solve the following two normal equations for the constants a and b, using Method #2 in Chapter 12 by the solution of the two simultaneous *normal equations*:

(1) $\Sigma y = Na = b\Sigma x$

(2) $\Sigma xy = a\Sigma x + b\Sigma x^2$.

The calculations are shown in Table 13.3. To solve for the unknown *a* and *b* constant values, we need to calculate from the basic data (of which there are N data-points) the values of Σy, Σx, Σxy, and Σx^2, shown in Table 13.3. Note that the x-variable (time) is changed so that its mean equals zero; this can be done because of the regular spacing (yearly) of the x-values in time series data. This procedure does not distort the results but greatly simplifies the computations. When x is adjusted in this way, the intercept may be called the *pivot point* or the *anchor point* for the trend line.

---

*Only the method of least squares for trend determination is covered in this chapter. Other methods, such as semi-averages or moving averages are not covered.

Table 13.3
Computing a trend line with the coal production data given in Table 13.2

Calendar Year	Numerical order of each year in the series (x)	Modified numerical order of each year * (x)	Coal produced (millions of short tons) (y)	Product of year and tons (xy)	Year squared (x^2)
1984	1	–5	4.2	–21.0	25
1985	2	–4	4.7	–18.8	16
1986	3	–3	4.3	–12.9	9
1987	4	–2	3.6	–7.2	4
1988	5	–1	3.6	–3.6	1
1989	6	0	3.3	0.0	0
1990	7	1	3.5	3.5	1
1991	8	2	3.4	6.8	4
1992	9	3	3.1	9.3	9
1993	10	4	3.4	13.6	16
1994	11	5	3.2	16.0	25
(N=11) Total	$\Sigma x = 0$		$\Sigma y = 40.3$	$\Sigma xy = -14.3$	$\Sigma x^2 = 110$

Substituting the appropriate values from Table 13.3 into the two normal equations, where N = 11 years, we solve for a and b, as follows:

(1) $40.3 = 11a + 0b$

(2) $-14.3 = 0a + 110b$.

Thus, the value of $a = 3.66$ short tons (i.e., 40.3 divided by 11) and $b = -0.13$ (i.e., –14.3 divided by 110). The resulting trend line equation is: $y_e = 3.66 - 0.13x$.

Uses of the trend line — At least four uses can be served by the trend line, $y_e = 3.66 - 0.13x$, as follows:

(1) *Forecasting* — Since a primary objective of the trend line is either or both short-range and long-range forecasting, we can enter

---

*Modified to facilitate the computations without affecting the relationship between x and y. The idea is to assign the middle year a value of zero and successive years on either side similar integers but of differing signs, so as to yield a net total of zero for Σx. When an even number of years is involved, the same objective can be achieved by assigning the two middle years the x-values of –1 and +1, respectively, and successive years above and below the two middle years the x-values of –3 and +3, –5 and +5, etc. This procedure can be used for modifying the x-values regardless of whether the series consists of an odd or even number of years.

into it an x-value representing the next year or two and estimate the expected value of y for these future years. Thus, the first year beyond the history-period, which is 1995, is represented by x=6, and the forecast is y_e = 3.66 − 0.13(6) = 3.66 − 0.78 = 2.9 million short tons. Similarly, when x=7, representing 1996, y_e = 3.66 − 0.13(7) = 2.8 million short tons. These figures, of course, reflect only the effect of trend on coal production. Better forecasts can be made by use of judgment (or knowledge) about the possible effects of cyclical and/or irregular variations on the trend-value of y. For example, impending legislation on the mining of anthracite coal may have a significant effect on the forecast and appropriate judgmental adjustments may improve the forecast.

(2) *Standard error of estimate, σ_e* — By simulating the forecasting equation over its history-period (as was done in Chapter 12), it is possible to measure the average error of the trend-line predictions using the trend line equation, as shown in Table 13.4. The extreme right hand column of the table provides the basic numbers for computing the standard error of estimate by:

$$\sigma_e = \sqrt{\frac{\Sigma\left(y_a - y_e\right)^2}{N}} = \sqrt{\frac{0.7466}{11}} = \sqrt{0.0679} = \pm 0.26 \text{ million short tons.}$$

Since our prediction for 1995 was 2.9 million short tons of anthracite coal, the average error of this prediction can be as large as ±0.26 million short tons, or ±9 percent (i.e., .26/2.9=.09), with a confidence of 68 percent (based on normal distribution theory) that the error is not larger.

(3) *Cycles* — Since prediction errors are most likely to be a result of unexpected occurrences and cycles, we can use the simulation method to research the frequency and length of cycles on one side or the other of the trend line. This is accomplished by examining the prediction errors $(y_a - y_e)$, called *residuals*, for patterns. For example, by examining the residuals in the next-to-the-last column of Table 13.4 (column $y_a - y_e$), we observe a continuous string of four over-prediction errors. This indicates that a cycle of four years of under-average production may have occurred during 1987-1990. Of course, the time series for anthracite coal mining is too short to make a more definitive analysis of cycles. When the time series covers a much longer period of time, the simulation method could provide a basis for analyzing cyclic variation, if it exists. This, in turn, would permit a more

accurate forecast for a year or two by adjusting the trend forecast upward (or downward) as indicated by the expected cycle.

Table 13.4 — Measuring the accuracy of trend-line forecasts of anthracite coal production by simulation

Year (coded) (x)	Actual coal production (y_a)	Trend-line estimate of coal production (y_e)	Deviation from trend (or error) $(y_a - y_e)$	Error Squared $(y_a - y_e)^2$
1984	−5	4.2	4.31	−0.11	0.0121
1985	−4	4.7	4.18	0.52	0.2704
1986	−3	4.3	4.05	0.25	0.0625
1987	−2	3.6	3.92	−0.32	0.1024
1988	−1	3.6	3.79	−0.19	0.0361
1989	0	3.3	3.66	−0.36	0.1296
1990	1	3.5	3.53	−0.03	0.0009
1991	2	3.4	3.40	0.00	0.0000
1992	3	3.1	3.27	−0.17	0.0289
1993	4	3.4	3.14	0.26	0.0676
1994	5	3.2	3.01	0.19	0.0361

Total $\Sigma x = 0$ $\Sigma y_a = 40.3$ $\Sigma y_e = 40.26$ $\Sigma(y_a - y_e) = 0.04^*$ $\Sigma(y_a - y_e)^2 = 0.7466$

(4) *Detection of irregular variations* — As indicated earlier, unpredictable or irregular variations need to be detected, if possible, and eliminated from the original time series data at the outset. This may be done by reference to historic records. Another way of detecting outliers is by ranking the simulated errors of prediction and performing a Z-test of significance on the largest errors. Thus, when the prediction errors or residuals (Table 13.4, column $y_a - y_e$) are arrayed, we single out the largest error (.52 tons) and the time when it occurred. A significance test then can be used to check for possible irregular conditions. For example, a one-tailed Z-test of significance at a 5% risk level would find this error to be a possible outlier, as follows: $Z = \dfrac{(y_a - y_e)}{\sigma_e} = \dfrac{0.52}{0.26} = 2$ standard errors, which is in excess of the critical ratio of 1.65 for a one-tailed test with a 5% level of significance.

---

*Due to rounding, the net error of prediction does not quite equal zero.

Measuring seasonal variation

The preceding section illustrated a method of constructing the trend line and using it to make forecasts for the next year or two. However, when forecasts also are needed for each month, as is often the case, the annual trend forecast needs to be adjusted for seasonal variations within the year. To provide a basis for making these adjustments, an analysis must be made of the seasonal pattern of variation over a reasonable period of time to determine if seasonal variations actually exist. If it is determined that the variable follows a consistently seasonal pattern (as suggested by Figure 13.3, for example), a seasonal index would be constructed.

To establish a *monthly seasonal index* we need to determine how much smaller or larger each month's average figure is than the overall average monthly figure for the entire period of study. Thus, the overall monthly average (covering the entire study period) is established as the base (equal to 100 percent) for comparison with each individual monthly average. For example, we all know that the volume of U.S. mail delivered during the month of December is much higher than the average mail delivered per month for the entire year. The December index would therefore be above 100. Similarly, the sale of ice cream is much greater in the summer months than in the winter months. *The basic idea behind a seasonal index is to determine how much higher or lower each individual month's activity is relative to the overall monthly average of the activity computed for the entire 12 months of the year.*

An example of establishing a monthly seasonal index — The monthly employment figures given earlier in Table 13.1 are used to demonstrate the *method of monthly averages* for obtaining a seasonal index for each month.* The first step is to arrange the 11 years of basic data by year and month as shown in Table 13.5.

Working with the information in Table 13.5, the following steps complete the computation of the monthly seasonal index.

1. The average (mean) per month of the activity over the entire history-period is obtained by dividing the sum of the activity for all months in the history-period (shown on the row labeled "Total" in Table 13.5) by the total number of months in the history-period. In this case, there are 12 months of data for 11 years, so there are 12(11) = 132 months in total. Thus, the overall monthly average is 14,868 million divided by 132 months, or 112.6 million per month.

---

*Other methods of constructing a seasonal index, such as ratio-to-trend and ratio-to-moving-average, are not covered in this book.

Table 13.5
Computation of the unadjusted seasonal index by the method of monthly averages, using data from Table 13.1

Year	Total for year	Jan.	Feb.	Mar.	Apr.	May	June	July	Aug.	Sep.	Oct.	Nov.	Dec.
1983	1,210	97	97	98	99	100	102	103	103	102	103	103	103
1984	1,260	101	102	103	104	105	107	107	107	106	106	106	106
1985	1,286	104	105	106	106	107	108	109	109	108	108	108	108
1986	1,315	107	107	108	108	109	111	112	112	110	111	111	111
1987	1,349	109	109	110	111	112	113	115	115	113	114	114	114
1988	1,380	112	112	113	114	114	116	117	117	115	116	116	116
1989	1,408	115	115	116	116	117	119	120	119	117	118	118	118
1990	1,415	116	116	117	117	118	120	120	119	118	118	118	117
1991	1,403	115	115	116	117	117	118	119	118	117	118	117	117
1992	1,411	115	115	116	117	118	119	120	119	118	118	118	118
1993	1,432	116	117	117	118	119	121	121	121	120	120	121	121
Total	14,868	1,208	1,211	1,219	1,227	1,236	1,253	1,262	1,257	1,245	1,251	1,250	1,247
Average per month 112.6		109.8	110.1	110.8	111.5	112.4	113.9	114.8	114.3	113.2	113.7	113.6	113.4
Unadjusted seasonal index		97.5	97.7	98.4	99.0	99.7	101.1	101.9	101.5	100.5	101.0	100.9	100.7

2.   The individual monthly averages are obtained by dividing the total of the activity for each month by the number of years covered. Thus, the January average is 1,208 / 11 = 109.8; the February average is 1,211 / 11 = 110.1; etc. These numbers are shown on the next-to-the-last row of Table 13.5.)

3.   Now that we have the base of the overall average per month of the activity (112.6), each monthly seasonal index can be computed by dividing each month's average by this base, as follows. The January seasonal index (unadjusted for trend) is 109.8 / 112.6 = .975. Expressed as a percent, it is 97.5%. The February unadjusted seasonal index is 110.1 / 112.6 = 97.8%. The unadjusted seasonal indexes for the remaining months are shown on the last row of Table 13.5.

Adjusting the seasonal index for trend — The index for each month thus far derived is not a true reflection of the "normal" seasonal variation because it was derived from the original basic data (actual monthly employment), which did not allow for the influence of the three remaining components of the time series. While in some cases the seasonal index thus far computed may be in error by a trivial amount, in other instances the error may be substantial. This is especially true if the trend is steep, as, for example, in the case of the anthracite coal series, but not so in the case of civilian employment.

There is a way of readily adjusting the raw seasonal index for trend. However, this is not true for cyclical and unpredictable variations, where the alternative is to assume that cyclical and unpredictable variations tend to offset each other over a sufficiently long period of time and thus would have no serious effect on the resulting seasonal index.

Trend always has some effect on the seasonal index, and this effect must be removed from the original monthly data before an acceptable seasonal index is obtained. Since a trend is either systematically upward or downward, its effect is cumulatively greater on the later months of the year than the earlier months. In other words, even if there were no seasonal variations at all, an upward trend would affect January least and December most in any given year.

If the trend is linear and direct, as in our case, the method of adjusting the raw seasonal index for trend requires that we first compute the annual increase in the activity due to trend, called the *annual trend increment*. This increment (or decrement, if the trend is downward) is represented by the constant b in the trend line equation. As stated earlier, b is the slope of the trend line, or the rate of change in y (employment) as a result of a given change in x (time). It is computed by solving for b in the second of the two normal equations, namely, $\Sigma xy = a \Sigma x + b \Sigma x^2$. In this equation, $a \Sigma x = 0$. Therefore, $b = \Sigma xy / \Sigma x^2$. When the necessary computations are made using the basic civilian employment data shown in Table 13.1, the average annual trend increase (b) in civilian employment is 1.76 million. (The reader may wish to verify this b-value.)

In order to adjust the monthly data for trend, the annual trend increment, b, must be spread over the 12 months of the year. This is accomplished by assigning 1/12th of the annual trend increment to each month cumulatively, resulting in the *monthly trend increment*. In our demonstration problem, the monthly trend increment in employment is the annual trend increment divided by 12 (i.e., 1/12 of b): 1.76/12 = 0.15 million.

The monthly trend increment of 0.15 is added to each successive month cumulatively to account for the effect of the annual trend on the monthly figure. Thus, January, being the first month of the year, has a trend increment of 0.15.* Similarly, the February average includes another 0.15 increment for trend on top of the one for January. Thus, the original monthly average for February is 0.30 million larger because of trend; in other words, trend accounts for 0.30 million of the February average employment. The remaining upward adjustments for trend follow the same pattern, as shown in Table 13.6.

Table 13.6
Illustration of adjusting the seasonal index for trend,
using data from Table 13.5 rounded to two decimal places

(1)	(2)	(3)	(4)	(5)	
Month	Unadjusted seasonal index (From Table 13.5)	Original monthly average (millions) (From Table 13.5)	Average monthly trend increment (millions)	Adjusted monthly average = original average **minus** trend increment (millions) (column 3 – column 4)	Adjusted seasonal index**
January	97.51	109.83	1(.15)	109.68	98.23
February	97.74	110.09	2(.15)	109.79	98.33
March	98.41	110.85	3(.15)	110.40	98.87
April	99.03	111.54	4(.15)	110.94	99.36
May	99.74	112.35	5(.15)	111.60	99.95
June	101.14	113.92	6(.15)	113.02	101.22
July	101.89	114.77	7(.15)	113.72	101.84
August	101.49	114.32	8(.15)	113.12	101.31
September	100.50	113.20	9(.15)	111.85	100.17
October	100.97	113.74	10(.15)	112.24	100.52
November	100.90	113.65	11(.15)	112.00	100.30
December	100.68	113.40	12(.15)	111.60	99.95
Total	1,200.00	1,351.65	11.70	1,339.95	1,200.00
Average	100.00	112.64	0.98	111.66	100.00

Practical uses of the seasonal index

While the trend line is a significant contribution to short-range forecasting and sometimes long-range planning, the resulting trend-adjusted seasonal index is used to make within-year (month-to-month)

---

* It is generally assumed that the y-value for any time period in a time series is located at the end of the period.

** Obtained by dividing each monthly figure in column (5) by the average per month (111.66) at the bottom of that column.

forecasts. Our seasonal index informs us, for example, that January employment is 98.2 percent, i.e., 1.8 percentage points lower than average monthly employment in a year; February employment is 98.3 percent of the annual average (or 1.7 percentage points lower); etc. From an examination of the 12 monthly seasonal indexes it is apparent that civilian employment in the U.S. is seasonally highest in June, July, and August and lowest in January and February. Activities other than civilian employment in the U.S. would display their own seasonal variations and indexes.

One of the ways the seasonal index can be applied in practice is to convert the actual monthly activity under study to what it really would have been (better than usual, the same, or worse) without the effect of normal seasonal variations on the activity. In other words, the index can inform management if an increase in sales (or any other variable being measured) in any given month is a real improvement or simply a normal seasonal increase, and vice versa. If, for example, civilian employment in April 1988 were 114.4 million, we can say that it was much lower than the July (or August) employment because April is a seasonally low employment month. If we wish to remove the seasonal influence, we can *divide* the April employment figure by 0.9936, the April adjusted seasonal index, and say that civilian employment in that month would have been 115.1 million if it weren't affected by seasonal variations. *Deseasonalized* figures, therefore, can be useful to determine the real monthly change in employment (or other variables, such as the Consumer Price Index or the unemployment rate) to assure that seasonal variations do not distort the underlying basic employment figures.

Another use of the seasonal index is in making an estimate of an activity for a specific month of the year after the annual trend-forecast is made. Thus, if a forecast is made of the total sales (or other activity) for a year, the annual figure can be converted to a monthly average by dividing it by 12. The resulting average can then be *multiplied* by that month's monthly index to yield an estimate of the activity for that month; the same can be done for other months. For example, assume a forecast was made that the average monthly civilian employment in 1998 would be 125 million. The April 1998 employment would be estimated as 124.2 million (i.e., 125 times 0.9936). The accuracy of the monthly estimates, of course, depend on the accuracy of the annual forecast as well as the accuracy of the seasonal index.

Some Cautions In Time Series Analysis

Time series data can yield valuable information and provide a basis for sound planning and good forecasts. However, as is the case with other statistical methods, time series analysts must be on guard for problems that may be encountered. The following are some of the problems.

Trend analysis

In establishing the basic long-term trend of a time series, we need to ask ourselves: "What part of the total history-period data should be included in computing the trend line?" "What form of trend analysis should be used — linear or curvilinear?" "What initial adjustment, if any, should be made in the history-period data since they may include abnormal points of data?"

Choice of period covered — The trend line and the resulting trend increment (or decrement) can sometimes be quite different for the same activity, depending on which part of the time series is included to represent the normal trend. If, for example, the anthracite-coal series included data as far back as 1950, the annual decrease in the series due to trend would have been much greater than that for the period 1984-94. As a result, there would be a substantial difference in the trend line of anthracite coal production. In fact, in some time series an upward trend can be obtained from using the data for one period and a downward trend for another period. Which period or part of the potential history-period, therefore, should be used?

There is no general answer to this question; the choice can be based on experience and judgment as to when a normal period of the series began. Usually, but not always, the best results would be obtained by basing the time series on the most recent years to reflect the most recent and relevant factors affecting the series. On the other hand, the series should include a sufficiently long period of time, preferably at least 10 years, to provide a sound basis for trend and seasonal (and possibly cyclical) analysis. Thus, there may be a trade-off between currency of data and a sufficiently long history-period. The choice of the base period to be used for the analysis, therefore, requires experienced judgment.

Choice of trend forecasting method — By plotting the time series data, the path formed by the data will usually become apparent. Caution is necessary, however, because what may appear to be a linear path may occasionally be a different geometric pattern. Moreover, different choices of the scale-values used in plotting the data sometimes can conceal the actual path.

Of the several methods available for fitting a trend line, only the method of least squares is illustrated in this chapter. Other methods include *moving averages, weighted moving averages,* and *exponential smoothing,* as well as more sophisticated methods, such as *autocorrelation* methods, each with its associated qualifications. Of course, the best choice is the one that will give the most accurate forecasts balanced by costs, time, and complexity of the method.

Adjustment for special factors — Occasionally, the basic data will show a figure (or figures) that is strikingly out of line with the others, indicating the probable existence of some special condition. Such outliers must be identified and excluded so that the series used in the analysis represent normal trend points. In other words, by excluding from the trend analysis the data for abnormal years, we deal with an activity influenced by normal or usual conditions. As demonstrated with the data in Table 13.4, simulation and a Z-test of significance can help to detect an irregular point of data.

Choice of seasonal forecasting methods

Several methods of constructing a seasonal index are available. Our illustration dealt with a simple method, the method of monthly averages. As long as the seasonal index resulting from this method is adjusted for trend, it can be considered a reasonably satisfactory method. However, more sophisticated methods, such as *ratio-to-trend, ratio-to-moving-average,* and *link-relative* may yield more accurate seasonal forecasts.

Time interval — The most frequently chosen time interval for analysis of seasonal variation is the calendar month, or sometimes a quarter-year. In some special situations, the choice may be a weekly time interval, depending on the objectives to be served by such a seasonal index. To develop such a seasonal index, basic data, of course, must be available for the desired time intervals.

Alertness to changed conditions

Aside from the need to consider the above factors, time series analysts are aware that both the trend and seasonal patterns may change significantly over time because of the entry of new economic, technological, and other factors influencing the series. Therefore, both long-term trend and seasonal indexes based on past data must be regularly reevaluated to determine if significantly new conditions have emerged to influence the activity in the more recent periods.

Summary

Perhaps the most important point to remember from this chapter is the value of quantifying, on a continuing basis, the activities of concern to management. The mere collection of time series data on an annual and within-year (e.g., monthly) basis forces a deliberate evaluation of the activity on a continuing basis. It also provides a basis for forecasting the probable volume of the activity in future years and during specific time intervals within the year (such as months). The main contribution of quantitative data is objective short-range and long-range planning and budgeting.

In quantitative analysis of time series, whether it be for the purpose of achieving a better understanding of current developments or making forecasts, it is essential to measure the effect of the different components of time series on the activity under study. Thus, methods of measuring the effect of trend, seasonal, cyclical, and unpredictable movements are essential.

When the trend appears to be linear, its direction and annual rate of increase or decrease can be established by use of the method of least squares to fit a straight line with the following linear equation: $y_e = a + bx$, where x = time (preferably coded so that $\Sigma x = 0$). The constants a (the anchor point of the line) and b (the slope of the line, or the trend increment or decrement) can be determined by solving the two normal equations as shown in the chapter.

Once the trend line or forecasting equation is established, it can be used in three ways. (1) Using the history-period data, we can calculate the expected trend value (y_e) for each year in the series. These values are estimates of what the quantities of the variable would have been if no factors except trend affected the series. Differences between the actual values (y_a) and the estimated trend values (y_e) are called residuals or errors; they represent what would have been the errors of prediction due to the effect of cyclical and unpredictable or random movements on the activity. When these errors ($y_a - y_e$) are averaged, using the method of squares and square roots, a useful figure (σ_e) is obtained; it is a general measure of the strength of the forecasting equation should the conditions of the past continue to prevail. (2) The

445

deviation-from-trend (y_a-y_e) values can indicate the extent to which the activity is subject to cycles, their magnitude and duration. (3) The (y_a-y_e) can help to locate points in the time series when irregular occurrences not previously identified exist, thus enabling the analyst to adjust the trend-line by excluding irregular occurrences.

If the history-period data are available by month or quarter, the data can be analyzed to provide an index of seasonal variations. Graphic analysis of the data will show if a seasonal pattern of variation exists. If so, a relatively simple method of measuring the extent of seasonal variation is the method of monthly (or quarterly) averages, as illustrated in the chapter. By using this method, the basic history-period monthly data are not adjusted for trend; therefore, they do not fully reflect the true seasonal variations alone. The effect of trend can be removed from each monthly index, however, by spreading b, the annual trend increment (or decrement), equally over the 12 months. Once the slope (b) of the trend line is computed, it is divided by 12 to obtain the value of the trend increment per month. To adjust for trend, the January average is reduced by 1/12th of b, the February average is by 2/12th of b, and so forth. The trend-adjusted monthly averages can then be converted to an index of the average of the 12 months combined by dividing each adjusted monthly average by the average for the entire 12 months. The 12 percentages thus obtained represent the monthly seasonal index.

The seasonal index is useful in two respects: it can be used to determine whether changes in an activity are above or below those expected from normal seasonal variations, and it can be used to estimate the magnitude of the variable (y) for each month once a forecast has been made of it for the entire year.

Problems

1. List and illustrate the four components commonly recognized in the analysis of time series.

2. Explain the similarity and difference of time series analysis as compared with correlation and regression analysis.

3. What are some possible uses of time series analysis?

4. (a) What is the main objective in the analysis of long-term trend?
   (b) What is the main objective of seasonal analysis?

5. What is the usual definition of the trend line that promises to give the smallest errors of prediction?

6. What is the meaning of each of the terms in the equation $y_e = a + bx$?

7. (a) In the text problem dealing with average monthly civilian employment, it was stated that the annual increment in average annual employment from 1983 to 1993 due to trend was 1.76 million per year. Using the average employment figures for 1983-1993 (given in Table 13.5), verify the constants a and b in the trend line equation $y_e = a + bx$.

   (b) Obtain from the U.S. Bureau of Labor Statistics the appropriate monthly U.S. civilian employment figures for the years since 1993 to supplement the data already shown in Table 13.1 (and Table 13.5). Using the average annual figures, compute the updated trend line equation. (Hint: if there is an even number of years, the coded x-values for the two middle years can best be set to –1 and +1.)

8. Using the trend line(s) determined in problem 7, compute the trend-line values for each of the years in the series and determine the difference between the actual and the trend-line employment figures. What is your interpretation of these differences?

9. Using the monthly data and the results from problem 7, calculate the following:

   (a) the unadjusted (for trend) seasonal index, and

   (b) the adjusted index.

   (c) Explain how you could use the seasonal index in practical situations.

10. The following table shows the size of the farm population in the United States from 1982 to 1991:

Year	Population (millions)	Year	Population (millions)
1982	5.6	1987	5.0
1983	5.8	1988	5.0
1984	5.8	1989	4.8
1985	5.4	1990	4.6
1986	5.2	1991*	4.6

Source: Annual Statistical Abstracts of the U.S.

---

* The Census Bureau descontinued this series after 1991.

(a) Plot a graph of this time series and fit a free-hand trend line to it. What is the direction of the trend?

(b) Using the method of least squares, determine the line of best fit.

(c) Using the trend line, estimate the United States farm population in each of the next three years. (Remember to use appropriately coded x-values for years to make your estimates.)

11. Define the following in your own words:
    (a) annual trend increment   (g) long-term trend
    (b) monthly trend increment   (h) time series
    (c) seasonal index   (i) method of least squares
    (d) linear trend   (j) method of monthly averages
    (e) cycle   (k) annual trend decrement
    (f) irregular variation

12. Bring up to date the series on anthracite coal production (Table 13.2 and Table 13.4) and, by establishing a trend line, prepare forecasts of anthracite coal production for the next two years.
    (Source: Department of Energy.)

13. The following table shows the number of persons aged 85 and over living in the United States, 1980-1992:

Year	Persons (millions)	Year	Persons (millions)
1980	2.24	1987	2.82
1981	2.35	1988	2.89
1982	2.44	1989	2.97
1983	2.52	1990	3.02
1984	2.60	1991	3.15
1985	2.67	1992	3.26
1986	2.74		

Source: U.S. Bureau of Census

(a) Using time series analysis, forecast the population aged 85 and over who will reside in the United States in 1993, 1994, 1995, and 1996, and by the end of the century.

(b) Compare these forecasts with the official estimates of the Census Bureau, and suggest reasons for any large differences over the period covered. The official estimates for 1993 and 1994 are 3.41 and 3.52, respectively (in millions).

Chapter 14

Presenting Statistics in Graphs and Tables

*"The use of statistics presented in well-organized tables, charts and graphs, reduces the tremendous mass of statistical material to manageable proportions."**

....

Chapter 2 indicated that the final step in a statistical investigation is usually the presentation of the data to make clear the facts upon which decisions or actions may be based. It also indicated that statistics may be reported either orally or in writing. Whichever method of reporting is used, primary reliance must be placed on statistical tables and charts to condense quantitative information into a comprehensible form. Well-prepared and carefully chosen charts or tables can reveal in an impressive and clear cut manner the main tendencies, trends, or marked differences in the activities under study, thereby serving the statistical needs of the organization most effectively. The primary purpose of this chapter is to give the highlights of effective graphic and tabular methods of reporting statistical data. The types of tables and charts that may be used, as well as guidelines for their construction, are described and illustrated. Although computers have greatly simplified the construction and presentation of charts, it is still essential to know which types are most appropriate to use in different situations, and some of the advantages and disadvantages of each type.

While the reader, or management, may never have to prepare a single chart or table, he or she frequently may be obliged to direct their preparation, to interpret final results presented by others, or to present prepared data to groups of people. From a number of viewpoints, therefore, an understanding of the main elements of presentation can be useful.

---

* Edwin T. Coman, Jr., *Sources of Business Information*, Prentice-Hall, Inc., 1964.

Tabulation of Data

Before the many questionnaires, or schedules, that are assembled as part of a survey can begin to make sense, the information that they contain must be extracted and grouped in a systematic manner. This organization of data is done by a process of manual, mechanical, or electronic tabulation.

The detailed elements of tabulation of data are not discussed here, not because tabulation is an unimportant part of statistical investigations but because there are ramifications and details in tabulating techniques as applied to large-scale statistical surveys that require separate, intensive study of the subject.* It is enough to say here that, to be able to analyze and present data collected in a survey, the large number of measurements or counts have to be tabulated (i.e., organized and grouped systematically), so that the characteristics and tendencies of the activities being studied will stand out.

Methods of Presenting Data

Effective presentation of statistics is essential for successful completion of a statistical study, for it aids in pinpointing the significance of the findings. Inadequate presentation can squander the efforts and energy expended in planning, collecting, tabulating, and interpreting the statistical results. Of what use is the analysis of a large mass of data if management fails to receive or fully comprehend its message and so does not use it in decision-making?

As indicated earlier, there are two main ways of communicating data — by *oral explanation* or in the form of a *written report*. Regardless of whether the report is oral or written, proper choice of the charts and tables is essential. The particular method used in any one instance is generally determined by the audience, by the nature of the data (such as the amount of detail that needs to be presented), by the type of publication in which the presentation is to be included, by personal preferences, and, above all, by the objectives of the presentation.

Graphic presentation of statistical data

Probably everyone has heard it said that "a single picture is worth a thousand words." This statement is particularly appropriate to the

---

* Many organizations offer training programs in technical tabulation techniques and data processing.

presentation of statistical information, since people in general are apprehensive of statistics. A single, well-chosen *chart* can tell a story more effectively than many words. It can present findings from a survey by means of points, lines, areas, pictures, and other forms that are easy to understand, are impressive, and hold interest more than speeches or many figures.

When graphic methods of presentation are used, there is a choice of many possible charts. A few of the most commonly used types and their principal features are illustrated here.

1. Pie chart — A pie chart presents data in the form of a pie cut into slices. It is usually used to show what percentage of a given entity falls into different classes. Each slice shows what portion of the whole contains specific characteristics. For example, from the pie chart in Figure 14.1, it is clear that Social Security pensions accounted for more than a third of the income of persons aged 65 or older in 1990.

Figure 14.1

Sources of income for persons 65 years of age or older in 1990, United States

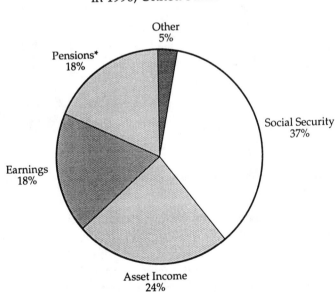

* Includes private pensions, government employee pensions, and Railroad Retirement.

Source: U.S. Department of Health and Human Services, Social Security Administration, Office of Research and Statistics, *Income of the Aged Chartbook*, 1990, September, 1992.

It is also apparent that this type of chart is a simple yet effective way of showing key findings from a statistical survey. It is clear that money income for the population 65 or older comes largely from four sources. Social Security provides the largest portion — 37%. Asset income provides the next largest proportion — 24%. These two sources together account for 61% of the total income of the aged. Smaller, but still important sources are from earnings and from pensions other than Social Security.

Usually, all that is necessary to assure the clarity of the presentation of a pie chart is a complete title of the data being shown, a simple pie broken into appropriate slices, each labeled to identify its characteristics, and a statement of the source of the data. In addition, shading (as shown by Figure 14.2) or color or even artwork can be effective in impressing the results on viewers.

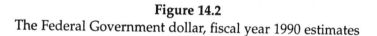

Figure 14.2
The Federal Government dollar, fiscal year 1990 estimates

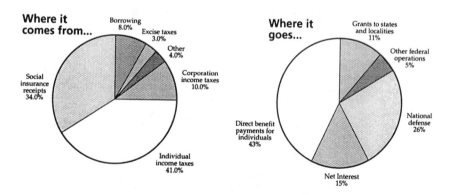

Source: Budget of the United States Government, Fiscal Year 1990, 101st Congress, House Document No.101-3.

While the pie chart has the value of simplicity, it also has some limitations. It can effectively present data for only a few elements — usually no more than six to seven categories. When the number of categories is more than that, it becomes more difficult to observe the differences in magnitude. A second limitation is that it loses its effectiveness when it is used to compare the sizes of the various pieces of the pie in two or more different pies or in cross-classifications. Thus, if we wanted to compare the sources of Federal

Government tax collections in 1980 and 1990, the comparison would require "back and forth" visualization shifts between the two pies. In addition, it would not easily show *how much* of a difference there is between the various categories.

2. **Bar chart** — This chart presents data in the form of columns or bars arranged vertically (or horizontally) on a numeric scale. Often there are two scales, one for the class or group and the other for the number or percentage in each class or group. The vertical height of the bar usually indicates the number or percent of the items containing the characteristics labeled on the horizontal scale. Figure 14.3 is a bar chart showing the number of bedrooms in occupied housing units in New York City in 1990.

Figure 14.3

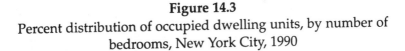

Percent distribution of occupied dwelling units, by number of bedrooms, New York City, 1990

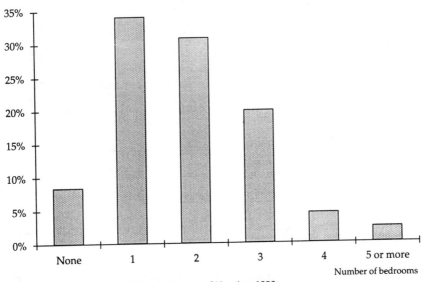

Source: U.S. Bureau of the Census, *Census of Housing: 1990.*

Because of its simplicity and flexibility, the bar chart is probably one of the most frequently used graphic presentations in newspapers, magazines, and other reports. For example, the side-by-side bar chart is an effective extension of the basic bar chart. It is used for comparison of two or three classifications. The side-by-side bar chart is effective for simple comparisons involving two or three groups within each classification because the differences in magnitude of the components are clearly apparent. This is seen in Figure 14.4, which compares over two different years the percentages of households in the U.S. with specified cooking appliances.

Figure 14.4
Comparison of cooking appliances in U.S. households,
1980 and 1990

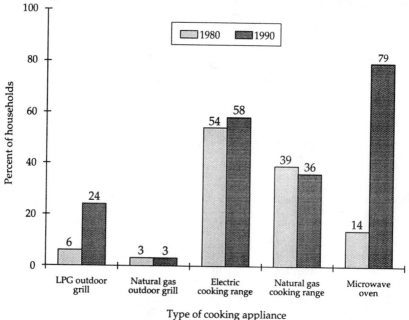

Source: U.S. Department of Energy, *Housing Characteristics: 1990*, Energy Information Administration, Washington, DC, May 1992.

Bar charts can be presented vertically (Figures 14.3 and 14.4) or horizontally, as shown in Figure 14.5. Either chart can be used to present data for a few or several classes, although too many bars can be overwhelming, as illustrated in Figure 14.6. Of the different forms, the vertical bar chart is more common and usually preferred since it focuses attention on the easily-seen vertical scale and therefore on the numeric differences.

Figure 14.5
Foreign visitors for pleasure admitted to the United States, by country of last residence — top ten countries — 1990

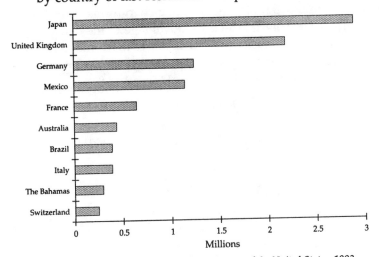

Source: U.S. Bureau of the Census, *Statistical Abstract of the United States: 1993*, Washington, DC, 1993.

Figure 14.6
Death rates for work-related injuries among full-time U.S. workers for selected occupations, 1983-1990 and year 2000 targets for "Healthy People 2000"*

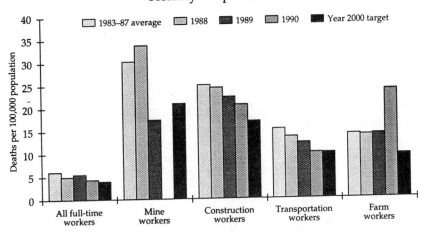

* Targets for health indicators for the nation are established in this report.

Source: U.S. Department of Health and Human Services, *Healthy People 2000 – Review 1992*, National Center for Health Statistics, Hyattsville, MD, August 1993.

3. Histogram — This chart presents data in the form of bars that are touching each other. This is a variation of the bar chart. When the bars in a bar chart are moved or extended to touch each other, a histogram is formed. Because the resulting chart forms steps, this chart is often called a *step chart*. The main advantage of the histogram over the bar chart is that it is easier to see differences in the magnitude of the various categories being studied. It can also show movement up and down the steps, as illustrated by Figures 14.7 and 14.8.

Figure 14.7
Percent distribution of occupied dwelling units,
by number of bedrooms, New York City, 1990

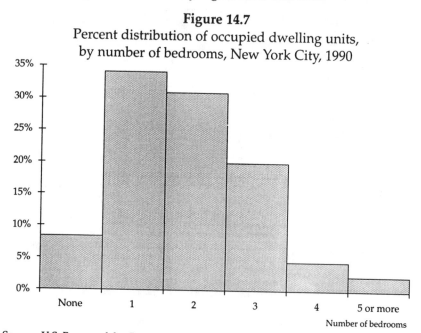

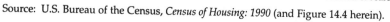

Source: U.S. Bureau of the Census, *Census of Housing: 1990* (and Figure 14.4 herein).

The histogram (with its touching bars) usually is used when portraying data in the form of a frequency distribution (Chapter 3). It is especially appropriate when the variable being presented is *continuous*, since the touching bars give a sense of continuity.*

4. Broken line chart — This chart presents data in the form of a line connecting the plotted points on the scale, thus creating a broken line.

A broken line chart — often called a *line chart* — can portray the same data as a histogram, but the height of each group or category is

---

*For *attribute* data or a *noncontinuous* variable, a bar chart (rather than a histogram) would generally be more appropriate.

represented not by bars but by the midpoint of the class or group shown on the vertical axis. The midpoints are connected by lines to create the line chart, as demonstrated by re-drawing Figure 14.8 as a line chart in Figure 14.9.

Figure 14.8

Distribution of luncheon sales, by cost — histogram

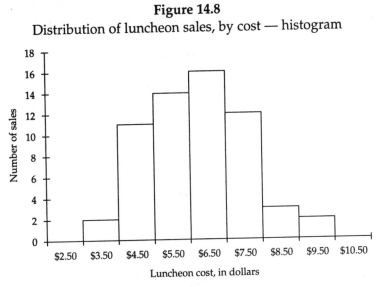

Source: Chapter 3, Figure 3.2 for Restaurant A.

Figure 14.9

Distribution of luncheon sales, by cost — broken line chart

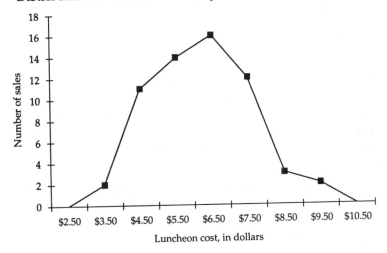

Source: Figure 14.8.

Both the histogram and the line chart are useful in determining the shape or graphic pattern formed by frequency distributions. (See Chapter 3.)

The broken line chart is also effective in displaying variations in an activity over a long period of time, for it gives a sense of the trend or direction of the movement of the variable, as illustrated by Figure 14.10.

Figure 14.10
Resident population of the United States,
all ages and age 85 and older, 1980-1992
(in millions — two scales)

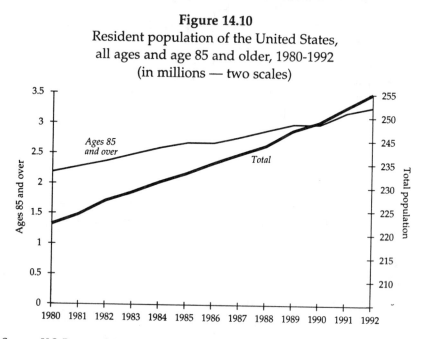

Source: U.S. Bureau of the Census, *Statistical Abstract of the United States: 1994,* Washington, DC, 1994.

5. Smoothed line chart or curve — When a frequency distribution is obtained from a sample and plotted in the form of a broken line graph, irregularities and jagged edges may show up because of chance variations (Chapter 8). To infer the pattern of the frequency distribution of the universe from data based on a sample, the frequency chart is often smoothed, or presented as a graphic curve. *Smoothing* of the frequency distribution is often facilitated by using a histogram or step chart, because the areas under each group or bar are more easily measured and balanced to give a smoothed curve. Figure 14.11 gives an example of a continuous, smoothed curve that was originally a histogram.

Figure 14.11
Distribution of luncheon sales, by cost — smoothed line graph

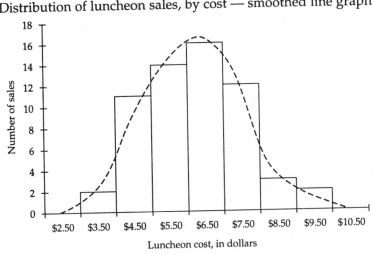

Source: Figure 14.8, based on Figure 3.2 for Restaurant A in Chapter 3.

6. Pictograph — Some people can more readily grasp the meaning of certain statistical findings when they are presented in the form of a picture or pictures. A pictograph presentation may be used to better communicate the meaning of a set of data. This type of chart presents data in the form of pictures drawn to represent comparative sizes, areas, or scales, as demonstrated by Figures 14.12 and 14.13.

Figure 14.12
Estimated number of nuclear weapons held by the United States and the Soviet Union, now Russia, by year

Source: Robert S. Norris and William M. Arkin, Natural Resources Defense Council, 1995.

Figure 14.13
Population of the United States, 1860–1990
Each symbol represents 10 million persons

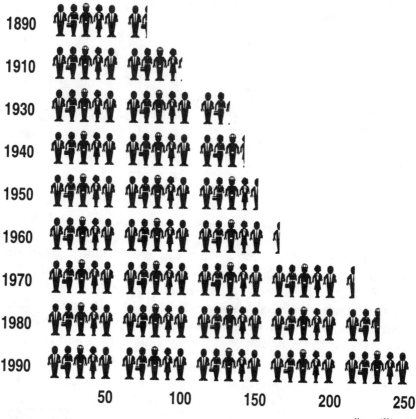

Source: U.S. Bureau of the Census, *Current Population Reports*, P25-1045 and P25-1112.

A number of other types of charts are covered in other chapters of this book, such as control charts (Chapter 11), flow charts (Chapter 11), and scatter diagrams (Chapter 12). Additional types of charts are often used for specialized applications. These include statistical *map charts*, such as the example shown in Figure 14.14. More information about these other types of charts can be found in several texts.*

---

*For example, see Calvin F. Schmid, *Handbook of Graphic Presentation*, Ronald Press Company, New York, 1954; Edward R. Tufte, *The Visual Display of Quantitative Information*, Graphics Press, Cheshire, CT, 1983; and Edward R. Tufte, *Envisioning Information*, Graphics Press, Cheshire, CT, 1990.

Figure 14.14
Center of U.S. population: 1800 to 1990*

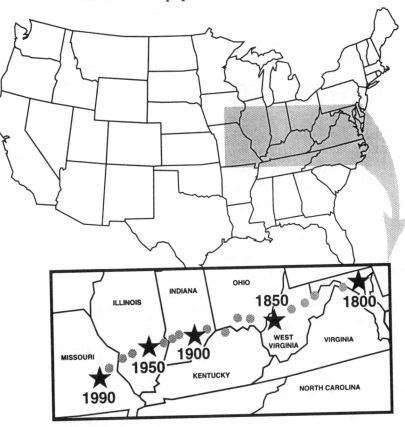

* Center of population is that point at which an imaginary flat, weightless, and rigid map of the United States would balance if weights of identical value were placed on it so that each weight represented the location of one person on the date of the census.

Source: U.S. Bureau of the Census, *Statistical Abstract of the United States: 1993*, Washington, DC, 1993.

In reviewing the variety of charts, it should be noted that every chart, whatever its type, requires a *title* to describe *what* is being presented, *how* the data are classified, to *which* place the data refer, and the *time* period covered. Every chart (except the pie chart and the pictograph) must have a numeric *scale*, as appropriate for that chart, to show the units of measurement by which the data are being presented. In addition, it is always appropriate to show the *source* of the data being presented.

Tabular presentation or statistical tables

While charts are effective in giving a simple and often impressive picture of important facts they have one major limitation. To achieve simplicity, they generally are confined to data for a single classification and a few groups within it. This limitation is overcome by statistical tables, which can be used to present data for at least two or three classifications and cross-classifications and, if properly constructed, can serve many more purposes.

A knowledge of tabular presentation is important for two additional reasons: (1) It is the customary way of presenting quantitative results of statistical surveys. When we examine statistical publications (for example, the *Statistical Abstract of the United States*), by far the greatest part of the data is presented in the form of tables. (2) It is a precise statistical way of expressing quantitative facts about processes or phenomena.

Knowledge of tabular presentation is useful not only in final presentation of data but also in the initial planning of a statistical study involving more than one variable. An essential requirements for conducting a statistical survey is to formulate the problem by identifying the specific data required in advance of actually collecting it. With an understanding of appropriate tabular presentation, researchers can use table formats or *skeleton tables* to clearly communicate the statistical requirements for the survey.*

The rest of this chapter is devoted to a description of the elements of tabular presentation.

Parts of a table — Statistical standards require that an acceptable statistical table be composed of three main parts: (1) a title, (2) the body or format, and (3) explanatory notes where necessary.

Title — As in graphic presentation, the table title must explain clearly and briefly what statistical information is being presented. To be complete, a title must answer the following four questions, generally in the order designated.

(1) *What* is being presented; for example, data on people, workers, or houses.

(2) *How* the data are being classified, or what are the specific *classifications*; for example, workers classified by age or by years of work experience.

---

*This is especially important when specifying data requirements to data-processing staff and others.

(3) *Where*, or which place(s) the data represent.

(4) *When*, or the date to which the data refer.

All four questions must be answered by the title, to assure clarity; they must be answered in the shortest possible way. Unnecessary verbiage (such as "according to") must be removed; subtitles are generally not desirable.

Table format — A table presents data in the form of rows and columns, or in the form of a modified checkerboard. It is therefore necessary to construct (or to imagine) a box with squares (or cells) and to describe the classifications and the sub-classifications that are in the rows and those that are in the columns. The description for the rows is usually called the *stub*, and it is entered in the first column on the left of the box. The classification(s) for the columns are usually called the *captions*, and they are entered in the top row or rows. Proper arrangement of the stub and captions gives clarity to the data being presented and requires good choices of which classifications to enter in the columns and which to enter in the rows.

Explanatory notes — If the title cannot be fully spelled out because of the need for brevity, or if the meaning of a certain term or classification is not entirely clear, explanations are usually given at the bottom of the table in *footnotes*. Examples of the use of footnotes are shown in the Tables 14.1 and 14.2. While a footnote may be necessary only occasionally, a note specifying the *source* of the data is always necessary, both to give credit to the original compiler of the data and to make it possible for users of the data to obtain more detailed information from the original source, if necessary. Sometimes, for reasons of emphasis, a *headnote*, or a note at the top of the table immediately under the title, is given to provide a fuller explanation of the contents of the table.

Steps in preparing a table — The specific steps and requirements in the preparation of a table are illustrated in the following few paragraphs based on the assumption that the U.S. Census Bureau had collected statistics to determine the number of men and women in different classes of work (such as wage and salary work, self-employment, and unpaid family work) in the City of Baltimore, Maryland, in October 1995. How should the data be presented in a final table for publication in the local newspapers?

Step 1 — Planning the table format — The first step is to plan the format of the table. The main idea here is to set up a table format that will yield a checkerboard, with horizontal and vertical descriptions of the figures that are to be entered in each square. Each square is called a *cell*.

Before sketching the table format, it is desirable to:

(a) *List the classifications* for which data are to be presented. In our hypothetical problem they are: (1) class of worker, and (2) gender.

(b) *Decide upon the number of groups or sub-classes* to show for each classification. The classification "class of worker" may be subdivided into many categories, but we will use four groups: (1) total number of workers in the classification, (2) the group of wage or salary workers, (3) the group of self-employed persons, and (4) the group of unpaid family workers. The classification gender is, of course, divided into three groups: (1) total, (2) male, and (3) female. It should be noted that totals are provided for all the groups of a classification. (See section on "Totals and subtotals.")

(c) *Decide where to place the classifications(s)* and their corresponding sub-classifications on the checkerboard to give a description of the figures in each cell when the table is read both downward and across. In other words, the meaning of any figure will be clear from the heading of the rows and columns.

The choice of the classification for the rows (stub) and for the columns (captions) is generally based on considerations of balance — namely, on the arrangement that will best balance the table on the page. When there are only two classifications with a few groups in each, as in our problem, the choice makes little difference. Generally, the classification with the greatest number of groups is placed in the stub (rows), since a page of paper usually offers greater space vertically than horizontally. In our problem we will assign the classification "class of worker" to the stub and the classification "gender" to the captions (columns).

Step 2 — Sketching the format — With the plans for the table completed, sketching of the format can begin:

(a) Draw the checkerboard outline with a line down and a line across, leaving space for entry of the classification and sub-group headings for the stub and captions. This outline may be a square or a rectangular box, depending on the space allotted for the table.

This is the stub   This space is for entry of the caption titles

(b) Enter in the first column the words describing the classification and sub-classes previously planned to be placed in the stub. Also, in the top row, enter the classification and sub-classes previously relegated to the captions. Note that in the caption it is not always necessary to specify the classification itself but simply to show its sub-groups. The stub classification is specified, to fill the space in the upper left-hand corner that would otherwise be left vacant.

Caption classification with its sub-groups

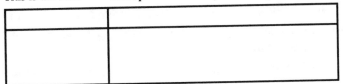

Class of worker	Male	Female
Wage and salary		
Self-employed		
Unpaid family		

This is the stub classification → Class of worker

These are the sub-groups for the stub classification → Wage and salary / Self-employed / Unpaid family

(c) Provide for necessary totals and subtotals both in the stub and captions. Note that statistical standards for final tables (but not necessarily for work tables) call for *totals* to be placed at the *top instead of at the bottom* and to the *left instead of to the right*, contrary to bookkeeping practice. This arrangement gives prominence to the total, which is distributed in both directions in the table and is usually the most important figure in the table. The full format of the table is completed when there is an entry with an explanation for every box or cell in it. For example, the cell containing an X (shown in the accompanying table format) would present a figure on the number of self-employed males.

Class of worker	TOTAL	Male	Female
TOTAL			
Wage and salary			
Self-employed		X	
Unpaid family			

Step 3 — Planning and constructing the title — Prepare the title by answering the questions "what," "how," "where," and "when." Do it concisely, as follows:

(a) What are we presenting? Data on number of workers.

(b) How are the data classified? By class of worker and gender.

(c) Where did this take place? In Baltimore, Maryland.

(d) When did this take place? In October 1995.

The full title, answering the four questions, and usually centered across the page, can now be spelled out as follows:

Number of workers, classified according to class of worker and gender, in the City of Baltimore, Maryland, in October 1995.

Be brief — The above title purposely contains a number of excess words and therefore it does not comply with the requirement of "brevity of the title." This requirement can be met without affecting the meaning and completeness of the title, by deleting a few words and by rearranging others, so that the following, more concise title is obtained:

Number of workers in Baltimore, Maryland, by class of worker and gender, October 1995

Step 4 — Explanatory notes — In our table the title gives a clear statement of the statistics being presented. The requirement of brevity sometimes makes it necessary, however, to rely on footnotes or headnotes to give a fuller explanation of the title. In our problem, for example, it may be desirable to explain in a footnote or headnote that the data are based on a sample and that they are therefore subject to sampling error. It may also be desirable to specify what is meant by "October." In this case, it would be the middle week of October. In other tabular presentations, various occasions for headnotes or footnotes may arise, for clarity and completeness.

In all instances the source of the data must be stated. In our table the source is a publication of the United States Bureau of the Census.

If for any reason the figures in the table have to be rounded (e.g., to the nearest 1,000 workers), the phrase "Workers in thousands" would be inserted between the title and the table format.

Step 5 — The final table — When we have complied with the foregoing requirements for setting up an acceptable table, with all its essential parts as spelled out in steps 1-4 above, the final table shows exactly what data is being (or will be) presented. After the data are collected and verified, the final figures are entered to complete the table, as shown in Table 14.1.

Table 14.1 — Number of workers in Baltimore, Maryland, by class of worker and gender, October 1995*

Class of worker	TOTAL	Male	Female
TOTAL	503,344	265,536	237,808
Wage and salary	433,600	234,864	198,736
Self-employed	67,440	30,240	37,200
Unpaid family	2,304	432	1,872

* Figures are hypothetical.

Source: U.S. Bureau of the Census, *Special survey of workers in Baltimore, Maryland in middle week of October, 1995.*

Primary and secondary classifications — The presentation problem is relatively simple when only two classifications are crossed, as in Table 14.1, because the choice of classifications for the stub is limited to either one or the other. Some tables may occasionally present data for three classifications. How can data with three or more classifications be presented?

The previous guides apply equally well to two or to three classifications except that, when there are three classifications, a choice of one out of six possible combinations has to be made for the classifications to present in the stub and the captions. For example, of the classifications A, B, and C, *either one* of the following six combinations may be chosen for the stub and captions, respectively: A with BC; B with AC; C with AB; AB with C; AC with B; and BC with A. Of course, the number of possible choices increases as the number of classifications to be presented increases, making for complexities contrary to the main purpose of tabular presentation — simplicity.

Suppose that in our table based on the Census Bureau survey we also wanted to include the classification "age" of worker. When there are three classifications, we may present any *one* of the six possible classifications in the stub and captions, respectively, depending on available space and balance.

A third choice is to put no classifications at all in the stub and all three in the captions (or, conversely, all three classifications in the stub and none at all in the captions). However, this would present the data in the form of a *single row* (or, conversely, in a single column). Such a presentation is not considered to be acceptable tabular presentation, except when there is only a single classification of data to be presented, in which case a single column or row of figures is the only possible format.

Suppose, in constructing a table, the combination of classifications chosen is one classification in the stub and the remaining two classifications in the captions. The specific selection and arrangement depends upon a balance of space, visual appeal, and ease of interpretation by the reader. Since the age classification may have more sub-classes (or age groups) than either of the other two classifications, it would appear to be desirable to place it in the stub since on a given page there is more space vertically than horizontally.

The next decision is: Which one of the two remaining classifications (class of worker and gender) that have been relegated to the captions should be made the *primary* (or major) caption and which the *secondary* (or minor) caption? The primary classification is generally the one we wish to emphasize, and it is placed in the very first row. If, for example, we choose "class of worker" as the primary classification, the table format may be presented as shown in Table 14.2.

Experience has shown that a common tendency among some people dealing with two classifications chosen for the captions (or the stub) is to separate them rather than cross-classify one with the other. This practice, while not incorrect, causes a loss of information that may be needed in a full analysis of the problem. The significance of this point will become more readily apparent if Table 14.2 is revised to show a single row for both of the captions, showing the class-of-worker groups and the gender groups in separate columns rather than one crossed with the other. This excercise is left for the reader.

Table 14.2 — Number of workers in Baltimore, Maryland,
by age, class of worker, and gender, October 1995*

Age Group	TOTAL			Wage and Salary			Self-employed			Unpaid family		
	Total	Male	Female	Total	Male	Female	Total	Male	Female	Total	Male	Female
TOTAL												
15–19												
20–24												
25–29												
30–34												
35–39												
40–44												
45–49												
50–54												
55–59												
60–64												
65–69												
70–74												
75 or older												

* Based on a sample; therefore data are subject to sampling error.

Source: U.S. Bureau of the Census, *Special survey of workers in Baltimore, Maryland in middle week of October, 1995.*

Totals and subtotals — Although totals and subtotals are not absolutely necessary for an acceptable final table, it generally is desirable that all totals be shown. Otherwise, the users of the data may be compelled to make their own additions to determine the number of cases in each classification and in all classifications combined. Furthermore, cross-totaling the figures in the table provides a basis for checking the accuracy of the data entered into it.

Four different types of tables

The basic data table — A table with absolute figures (such as the one in Table 14.1) is considered as a basic data table. It may not provide management with all the necessary analytical information. For example, if we had to know the total number of male workers in Baltimore who were self-employed, the table would provide the required information. However, if management needed to know the percentage of male and female workers, the table would not readily provide this information.

The analytical table — In some surveys we need to know not only the numbers involved in different classes but also the relationships between the numbers falling into the various groups. In such instances, the absolute figures need to be presented in percentage or other derivative form. When the original data are converted to derivative figures (such as percentages, ratios, averages, and so forth) and presented in a table, the presentation is called an analytical table. The analytical table gives the user the benefit of some further interpretation of the data. It relieves users from making their own calculations in order to make more complete analyses or interpretations of the information in the table. Table 14.3 shows an analytical table, based on the data shown in Table 14.1.

Table 14.3 — Percent distribution of workers in Baltimore, Maryland, by class of worker and gender, October 1995*

Class of worker	TOTAL	Male	Female
TOTAL	503,344	265,536	237,808
Wage and salary	86.14%	88.45%	83.57%
Self-employed	13.40%	11.39%	15.64%
Unpaid family	0.46%	0.16%	0.79%

* Figures are hypothetical.
Source: Table 14.1.

General-purpose and special-purpose tables — Tables with three or fewer classifications are usually called special-purpose tables. Some tables may be set up with four or more classifications, even though this is contrary to the goal of simplicity. Such tables are generally called general-purpose tables because they provide a large variety of reference data on the subject; they are usually derived by computer processing. For simplicity, it is advisable to present special-purpose tables with not more than three classifications.

Work sheet tables — These tables contain data and computations not generally intended for final presentation. They need not comply with the requirements for final tables, but need to be documented so that a reviewer of the work and all computations can readily identify the various operations and check for possible inaccuracies.

Summary

Effective presentation is essential for successful completion of a statistical survey. Since every survey is designed to provide a basis for action, the results must be clearly communicated to management. There are two main ways of presenting the data — orally or in writing.

Regardless of the method chosen, charts and tables are basic ingredients of presentation. Data may be presented graphically in many ways — in a pie chart, bar chart, broken-line chart, etc. Whatever the method used, the main objective is to gain the interest of the recipient of the data and to communicate the message by presenting simply and clearly the most important facts.

Graphic presentation has one main limitation. Charts, for simplicity, must generally be confined to a single classification. Tabular presentation overcomes this difficulty, since tables can present data distributed by at least two classifications, cross-classified by additional sub-groups within each classification. Elements basic to tabular presentation are: (1) an appropriate title which states in the briefest possible way what is presented, how the data are classified, and the place and time referred to, (2) the table format, which includes a description of the figures entered in each square, (3) the explanatory notes, which supplement the title with any additional explanation that is deemed appropriate to guide users of the data, and (4) the original source of the data.

There are four basic types of tables. A general-purpose table deals with a large variety of data, usually involving four or more classifications. A special-purpose table deals with a limited amount of data, usually fewer than four classifications. A third type is an analytical table, which contains figures that are derivatives (such as percentages and averages) of the original basic data. Finally, there are work tables not designed for final presentation which need not adhere to all of the standards for final tables.

Problems

1. Give and illustrate with a rough sketch three different forms of graphic presentation of data.

2. Define and illustrate the following words: table, chart, scale, footnote, headnote, secondary classification, stub, caption, analytical table, special-purpose table, and general-purpose table.

3. Give two advantages of showing totals and subtotals in a final table; also give a good reason for presenting totals at the top and to the left of final tables.

4. Present the format of a final table that would show the number of Vietnam War veterans living in the United States as of October,

1995, separated into the number of males and females and the number born in the United States and elsewhere.

Assume that the data were supplied by the Department of Veterans Affairs.

5. Set up the table format and all the parts necessary for publishing a final table on the number of persons living in the continental United States in April, 1995, showing the number in each age group, the number of males and females, and the number born in the United States and elsewhere.

(Note: You need not actually locate and fill in figures, although the statistics are available in the various *Statistical Abstracts of the United States*.)

6. (a) Present the data below in a final table.

The total number of workers hired by the ABC Company during 1994 may be summarized as follows:

Number hired:

Men born in the U.S.A. who were married 72
Men born in the U.S.A. who were single 94
Women born in the U.S.A. who were married 81
Women born in the U.S.A. who were single 47
Men born in the U.S.A., not known whether
married or single 8
Women born in the U.S.A., not known
whether married or single 7

In addition, there were 341 foreign-born new-hires. Of the males, 73 were married, 104 were single, and 11 were of unknown marital status. Of the 153 foreign-born females, 97 were married, 44 were single, and the remainder were of unknown marital status.

(b) Illustrate your understanding of an analytical table by presenting the above data as an analytical table.

7. Present a table to show, for the latest census year, the resident male and female population of the various States of the United States. (Data can be found in the *Statistical Abstract of the United States*, published annually by the U.S. Bureau of the Census.)

8. As a special assignment, bring up to date the foreign visitors data shown in Figure 14.5 and present them graphically.

9. The U. S. Bureau of the Census estimated the following resident population of the United States by race as of July 1, 1995, in millions of persons:

    White — 218.3; Black — 33.1;
    Native Americans — 2.2; Asian — 9.8

    Present these data in the form of an appropriate chart.

10. The U. S. Federal Bureau of Investigation reported the following violent crime statistics for the United States during the years 1983–1992 (in millions):

    1983 — 1.26; 1984 — 1.27; 1985 — 1.33; 1986 — 1.49;
    1987 — 1.48; 1988 — 1.57; 1989 — 1.65; 1990 — 1.82;
    1991 — 1.91; 1992 — 1.93

    Present these data in the form of an appropriate chart.

Chapter 15

A Summary of the Book

"The statistical method is more than an array of techniques. The statistical method is a Mode of Thought; it is Sharpened Thinking; it is Power."*

In this chapter an attempt is made to coordinate, in a brief summary, the various parts of the study of statistics presented in the preceding chapters. The chapter is sub-divided into five parts: (1) objectives of the book, (2) statistical principles, (3) statistical methods, (4) variety of uses of statistics, and (5) conclusion — the power of statistics. In addition, a list of practically all the statistical formulas is given in Appendix A.

Objectives of the Book

A primary objective of this book has been, and still is, to instill in the reader an appreciation of the *statistical viewpoint* — that is, the habit of interpreting or looking at phenomena quantitatively. The statistical viewpoint is as important to scientific management as knowledge of the rules of the game is to the baseball player and as knowledge of banking principles is to the bank executive. With the statistical viewpoint we seek the truth in numerical facts and thus deal with problems objectively. Without this viewpoint, the problems of management — involving people, machines, material, methods, and money — are evaluated only from a subjective viewpoint, frequently without knowledge of the appropriate facts. Thus, management is less apt to make correct decisions or take correct action because decisions are not based on objective information. There always will be subjective aspects to any search for truth, but the ultimate truth requires the *combination* of

---

* W. Edwards Deming, *On the Teaching of Statistical Principles and Techniques to People in Industry,* a paper presented at the meeting of the International Statistical Institute, September 1953.

good experience and judgment with sound quantitative facts. Only through the truth can mankind progress, and only through seeking reliable quantitative facts can management be confident that its actions and decisions will be "right" in the long run.

Another objective of this book is to remind the reader that all phenomena on Planet Earth are subject to variation which can be measured by statistical methods, and that variation follows certain basic principles. There are only two broad types of variation. One is caused by chance, or by numerous common or natural factors; the other is the result of non-chance, or unusual factors. In Chapter 5 and in our sampling chapters it was demonstrated that the magnitude of variations due to chance (or sampling variations) can be measured and evaluated by the standard deviation and standard error. Chance variations occur when a process operates under a constant set of conditions and when many small causes of variation exist, none of which alone have a predominant effect on the magnitude of the variable. Non-chance variations are caused by a special factor or factors that have a predominant influence on the outcome of the process being measured.

By statistical methods it is possible to determine, with a high probability of being correct, whether special factors affect a process. Furthermore, when it appears that common or chance factors are affecting the process, management can wisely avoid seeking unnecessarily (and very frequently unsuccessfully) the reasons for that variation; on the other hand, when special factors appear to affect process variations, management is more likely to find it feasible and worthwhile to determine the underlying reasons and take appropriate action. This approach is an efficient way of analyzing variation. It calls for the use of various statistical methods of analysis, particularly statistical control charts (Chapter 11), in controlling and improving the quality of products and services both in the private sector and in government.

Another objective of the book is to offer the reader ways of collecting reliable data, primarily by use of randomly selected samples, and to use and present them properly. Objective decisions with a known risk of drawing a wrong conclusion can be made only when accurate census-type data have been collected or by randomly selected samples.

A still further objective is to introduce the reader to a few of the most basic statistical methods of analyzing quantitative data. Emphasis is placed on the fact that these methods , while powerful, must be used with caution and an awareness of the basic theory and assumptions underlying them, but without discarding common sense and good judgment. By illustrating actual and potential useful applications in the real world, we have aimed at encouraging further study of statistics and the adoption of the statistical approach in efficiently and humanely managing the resources for which management is responsible.

Principles Underlying Statistics

The preceding chapters referred to certain basic principles that underlie the science of statistics; these principles are the source of its strength. They exist whether the statistical method is applied to management, economics, biology, education, medicine, government, or any other field. This book presented both directly and indirectly at least eight basic statistical principles or laws:

(1) *Law of decreasing variation* or statistical regularity, in Chapters 1, 8, 9, 10, and 11;

(2) *Law of probability* and its role in making decisions with a known confidence, in Chapters 1, 6, 8, 9, 10, and 11;

(3) *Law of normal distributions,* including its kin the Central Limit Theorem, relating to the normal distribution of replicated sample-derived estimates, in Chapters 4, 5, 6, 8, 9, 10, 11, and 12;

(4) *The variance principle,* in Chapter 9, of computing the standard error of estimates derived from stratified samples;

(5) *Binomial distribution,* in Chapter 6;

(6) The *t-distribution,* in Chapter 10;

(7) The *Chi-square distribution,* in Chapter 10; and

(8) *Theory of least squares,* in Chapters 12 and 13.

Statistical Methods

In addition to these basic principles, the book presented a variety, but limited number, of statistical methods. These include:

- Quantifying problems
- Collecting data
- Organizing data for analysis
- Analyzing data
- Presenting data

Quantifying problems

As indicated in Chapter 2, problems or processes can be quantified in 7 different ways, depending on the nature of the problem and the fact-finding survey. There is the *mail questionnaire*, with all its attendant problems of obtaining an adequate mailing list of the persons or organizations being surveyed; constructing the questionnaire and adhering to the requirements of brevity and clarity; providing an incentive for reply; dealing with the problem of non-response; and so forth.

There is also the *personal interview*, with its typical problems of developing the interview schedule; obtaining and training interviewers; dealing with the relatively high cost per interview; contacting the appropriate individuals in the sample; etc. A major advantage of the personal interview method over the mail questionnaire, however, is avoidance of the frequently encountered non-response problem.

Quantitative facts are very frequently obtained by *measurement* of physical or mental properties. Here we encounter the problems of errors of measurement and the feasibility of making the measurements.

Another method of obtaining quantified data is through *observation and recording*, as when we count different people, automobiles of different make, etc. The technique of random time sampling (or work sampling) relies heavily on making observations at random moments of time and recording the activities observed to compile reliable data on the amount of time spent and costs incurred to perform the different functions of the organization.

Data tabulated from the *records of the organization* form another source of quantitative information, and *weight or rank assignment* is still another method.

Using *secondary data* by locating statistics already collected by others is a seventh way of quantifying activities or processes.

Collecting data

In collecting data for specific uses , the first requirement is to clarify in precise terms the problem to be investigated — to formulate the problem. While this is not a technical method of statistics, it is a prerequisite in collecting data. Experience has shown that formulation of the problem is a major step towards its solution. As Chapter 2 indicated, frequently the most difficult part of a study is clarifying the requirements and stating the appropriate hypotheses to be tested or questions to be answered. (See also Chapter 7).

There are three ways of collecting data, as follows: (1) a full enumeration or complete count of the universe of interest, (2) a sample selected by judgment, and (3) a sample selected by reliance on the law of probability. Generally, the latter method is preferred over judgment sampling because of the objectivity and validity of its results. It is preferred over full enumeration because of economy, speed, accuracy and general feasibility. (Random sampling is covered in Chapters 7, 8, 9, 10, and 11.)

If each unit in the universe is given a chance of selection equivalent to its importance, the sample is in a sense an "offspring" of the universe as a whole, and is, therefore, representative of it.

There are many ways of selecting samples that adhere to the laws of chance. Chapter 7 covered six well-known single-stage methods: *simple random sampling,* where random numbers, generally generated by computer or taken from a table of random digits similar to the one in Chapter 7, are used to select the sample; *systematic random sampling,* where every k-th unit is selected systematically from the universe after the first case is chosen at random; *cluster sampling,* where batches of the units comprising the universe are selected *systematically* or *randomly; digital random sampling,* where for example, a sample of persons is selected on the basis of randomly chosen digits in their social security account number; and *stratified sampling,* where units are selected by probability methods from judgmentally constructed strata (or sub-universes).

Sample selection that does not rely on the laws of chance is known as *judgment sampling.* When judgment samples are used there is no way of assessing the reliability of the results or to strongly defend them against opposition. The principles which underlie random sampling provide well-established ways of measuring sampling error and stating the confidence in the reliability of the resulting estimates.

One of the problems in defending estimates derived from random samples is the avoidance of serious non-sampling errors in the results. Two types of non-sampling error encountered are: *unsystematic mistakes* or *occasional errors* made by human beings which generally tend to offset each other in the long run; and *systematic mistakes* which are usually one-directional and therefore can cause seriously biased data.

Organizing data for analysis

Except when organized *secondary* (published) data are obtained, the immediate result of the *primary* collected data is a mass of ungrouped and disorganized data. To facilitate the analysis of such raw data it is necessary to organize them in order to extract salient facts from them. A basic method of organizing data for analysis is to condense the raw data into frequency distributions, as described in Chapter 3 and summarized below; also, the array or ranking of the variable values in order of size is useful in many situations.

Important factors to consider in constructing frequency distributions by size are: (1) the number of items involved (i.e., the sample size); (2) the range of values of the variable; (3) the appropriate number of classes (or groups) into which the data are organized; (4) the size or interval of each class; (5) the nature of the variable (whether it is continuous or noncontinuous); and (6) the use of uniform groups and open-end classes.

When plotted, a frequency distribution generally will form any one of five graphic patterns: *a symmetrical graph,* of which the *normal (or bell-shaped) distribution* is a special type; an *asymmetrical graph;* a *rectangular distribution;* a *J-shaped pattern;* or a *U-shaped pattern.* It is important to know which pattern a frequency distribution forms, because this knowledge provides the basis for choosing the methods of analysis, planning the sample-selection methods, and for making other analytical uses of the data.

The shape of the graph helps to determine the nature of the variable. A bell-shaped pattern, for example, often indicates that the variations are caused by many chance, common, natural, or hereditary factors. A pattern showing two or more modes often indicates that the data includes items from two or more different universes which need to be disentangled. The pattern may also be a guide for investigating the possibility of "abnormal" or special factors in a process.

Four special frequency distributions which are used in making inferences or determining significant differences are the *normal distribution, t-distribution, binomial distribution,* and *Chi-square distribution.* These aid in making decisions with a known risk of being wrong.

Analyzing data

Methods of analyzing data include the use of: *percentages or ratios; averages; measures of variation* of items in the universe or of estimates derived from random samples; and the *coefficient of determination* (r^2) which measures the extent (in percent) that variation in a dependent variable is influenced by an associated independent variable. Probably the most important of these analytical methods is the *standard deviation* and the *standard error of estimate,* since practically all processes or phenomena display variation and these provide a sound basis for measuring the extent of variation in them.

Several ways of deriving estimates of different types were presented. Among the most important estimates are those derived from random samples to represent the universe parameters. Two key estimates are the arithmetic *mean* ($\overline{X}$) and the *percentage* (p). These are converted to estimated totals by $N\overline{X}$ and Np, respectively. Other methods include determining the appropriate *size of sample* needed to meet prescribed conditions such as tolerable sampling error, confidence, and costs; forecasting by *regression* analysis the value of a variable that is dependent on one (or more) other variables; and forecasting by *time series* analysis the magnitude of an activity from a study of its four time components, namely, trend, seasonal, cyclical, and unpredictable variations.

Presenting data

An ultimate goal of collecting and analyzing data is their proper presentation. Presentation may be in the form of an *oral report* or a *written report.* In either case, the basic methods of presentation are *graphic* and *tabular.* Both methods may be used in written or oral reports. Charts or graphs are especially effective in oral presentations. Tabular presentations are essential when more than one variable or more than one classification is involved.

Variety of Uses of Statistics

We have tried to live up to one of the main objectives of this book — to illustrate the large variety of practical utility of each statistical method covered, not only in management improvement, but in all fields of human endeavor. Applications were illustrated in quality and productivity improvement, forecasting, marketing, medical research, inventory valuation, financial control, auditing, and inspection. It is appropriate, when referring to the use of statistics, to again quote M.J. Moroney's statement in his book *Facts from Figures:**

---

* M.J. Moroney, *Facts from Figures,* Penguin Ltd., 1951, pages 460-461 (edited slightly).

"A very little consideration shows that there is scarcely a hole or corner of modern life which could not find some applications, however simple, for statistical theory and show a profit as a result."

"It has something to offer the person who specializes in any of the branches of management. If offers assistance to the person responsible for purchasing and quality management. In the hands of the cost accountant or industrial engineer or management analyst, it acts as a hone to sharpen traditional tools and serves as a mechanism for generating additional information and insight. ..."

"In the research laboratory it is a powerful adjunct, offering optimum criteria for the assessment of data, eliminating wishful thinking, and yielding principles of experimental design which face the fact of experimental error and make possible the highly desirable objective of experimenting with a great diversity of combinations of the factors under test. Perhaps most important of all, it enables research to leave the controlled conditions of the laboratory and proceed in the rough and tumble of the real world where, after all, the results of experimental work have finally to be turned into work processes reasonably immune from trouble."

Conclusion — The Power of Statistics

The preamble to this chapter quotes Professor Deming that the science of statistics is not just a series of methods; it is a sharpened way of thinking; it is power. What really makes statistics so valuable? In the authors' opinion, shared by many others, the main power of statistics lies in the objective (honest) point of view that it affords its user in dealing with life's problems. It lies in measuring actual performance of practically all physical and mental processes, thus providing facts for their analysis by objective statistical methods backed by sound principles. It is thus possible to distinguish between important and unimportant causes of variation. The statistical viewpoint recognizes only these two major kinds of variability: unimportant *(insignificant)* or normal types of variation caused by small, chance, common, and natural factors; and important *(significant)* variations caused by unusual or special factors. By distinguishing between important and unimportant influences, statistics gives management and all users of statistics a basis for "managing by exception," that is, to concentrate attention on the exceptional variations and not to waste time on the day-to-day normal or usual insignificant variations.

The statistical viewpoint recognizes further that with statistics it is possible to determine, with a known probability of being right or wrong, when significant factors seem to affect a process. It also recognizes that the exact causes of natural variations are difficult to discover (except by extensive and special research) but that variations caused by outliers can usually be tracked down and eliminated. Discovery of the reason for abnormal variations and prevention of their recurrence is not a statistical problem; it is a problem of management and operations personnel, to be handled primarily on the basis of substantive knowledge and experience in their respective fields.

This book has presented many of the frequently used elements of statistics. Managers and future managers need to appreciate the potential contributions of statistics to humane and efficient management. However, mere appreciation without the actual use of statistics will not yield the benefits it offers. Further, use of statistical methods without an understanding of the underlying principles can lead to misuses. Professor Edward Deming once stated that theory without practice is useless; on the other hand, he said, practice without theory is baseless.

Appendix A

Principle Statistical Formulas, By Chapter

See individual chapters for details about these formulas, and for other formulas and for definitions of terms.

Chapter	*Narrative Statement of Formula*	*Formula*

Chapter 1 Probability of success: $\quad p = \dfrac{s}{T}$

Chapter 4 Sample mean, ungrouped data:*

$$\overline{X} = \frac{\sum x}{n}$$

Sample mean, grouped data:

$$\overline{X} = \frac{\sum f\,m}{n}$$

Sample mean, ungrouped data, short-cut:

$$\overline{X} = \overline{X}_g + \frac{\sum d}{n}$$

Sample mean, grouped data, short-cut:

$$\overline{X} = \overline{X}_g + \frac{\sum f\,d}{n}$$

Median, grouped data: $\quad \text{Median} = L + \dfrac{g\,i}{f}$

Chapter 5 Sample standard deviation, ungrouped data:

$$\sigma_x = \sqrt{\frac{\sum\left(x - \overline{X}\right)^2}{n-1}}$$

also, $\qquad\qquad \sigma_x = \dfrac{\overline{R}}{d_2}$ (in quality control)

---

* n represents use of a sample; for universe data substitute N.

Chapter	Narrative Statement of Formula	Formula

Sample standard deviation, grouped data:

$$\sigma_x = \sqrt{\frac{\sum f(m - \overline{X})^2}{n - 1}}$$

Coefficient of variation: C.V. or V $= \sigma_x / \overline{X}$

Large sample standard deviation, ungrouped data (short-cut):

$$\sigma_x = \sqrt{\frac{\sum x^2}{n} - \overline{X}^2}$$

Large sample standard deviation, grouped data (short-cut):

$$\sigma_x = (i)\sqrt{\frac{\sum (f d^2)}{n} - \left(\frac{\sum f d}{n}\right)^2}$$

Z = Standard normal variate, or difference between a given x-value and the mean in a normal distribution, measured in terms of σ-units (sample data):

$$Z = \frac{x - \overline{X}}{\sigma_x}$$

Chapter 6   Probability of success: $p = s / T$

Number of combinations of n things taken r at a time:

$${}_nC_r = \frac{n!}{r!\,(n - r)!}$$

Number of permutations of n things taken r at a time:

$${}_nP_r = \frac{n!}{(n - r)!}$$

Probability of x successes in n trials, for binomial population with fixed probability or proportion of success on each trial (p):

$$P_x = {}_nC_x p^x q^{n-x}$$
$$\text{where } q = 1 - p$$

Chapter	Narrative Statement of Formula	Formula

Mean successes, for a binomial distribution:

$$\overline{X} = np$$

Standard deviation of successes, for a binomial distribution:

$$\sigma_x = \sqrt{npq}$$

Chapter 9   Standard error of estimated sample mean and total from finite universe:

$$\sigma_{\overline{X}} = \sigma_x \frac{\sqrt{1-f}}{\sqrt{n}} \quad \text{where } f = \frac{n}{N}$$

$$\sigma_{N\overline{X}} = N\sigma_{\overline{X}}$$

Standard error of estimated percentage and total, finite universe:

$$\sigma_p = \sqrt{\frac{p(1-p)(1-f)}{n-1}}$$

$$\sigma_{Np} = N\sigma_p$$

Size of sample required to estimate a mean or total (where E is expressed in decimals):

	Finite Universe	Infinite *(or very large)* Universe
	$n = \dfrac{NZ^2 V^2}{NE^2 + Z^2 V^2}$	$n = \dfrac{Z^2 V^2}{E^2}$

Size of sample required to estimate a percentage (where E is expressed in percentage points):

	Finite Universe	Infinite *(or very large)* Universe
	$n = \dfrac{NZ^2 p(1-p)}{NE^2 + Z^2 p(1-p)}$	$n = \dfrac{Z^2 p(1-p)}{E^2}$

Chapter	Narrative Statement of Formula	Formula

Stratified Sampling:

(1) Variables: *Estimated total:*

$$N_1\overline{X}_1 + N_2\overline{X}_2 + \dots \text{etc.}$$

Estimated mean:

$$\frac{N_1\overline{X}_1 + N_2\overline{X}_2 + \dots \text{etc.}}{N}$$

Standard error of estimated total:

$$\sqrt{N_1^2\sigma_{\overline{X}_1}^2 + N_2^2\sigma_{\overline{X}_2}^2 + \dots \text{etc.}}$$

Standard error of estimated mean:

$$\sqrt{w_1^2\sigma_{\overline{X}_1}^2 + w_2^2\sigma_{\overline{X}_2}^2 + \dots \text{etc.}}$$

where $w_1 = {N_1}/{N}$ and $w_2 = {N_2}/{N}$ ... etc.

(1) Attributes: *Estimated total:*

$$N_1 p_1 + N_2 p_2 + \dots \text{etc.}$$

Estimated percentage:

$$\frac{N_1 p_1 + N_2 p_2 + \dots \text{etc.}}{N}$$

Standard error of estimated total:

$$\sqrt{N_1^2\sigma_{p_1}^2 + N_2^2\sigma_{p_2}^2 + \dots \text{etc.}}$$

Standard error of estimated percentage:

$$\sqrt{w_1^2\sigma_{p_1}^2 + w_2^2\sigma_{p_2}^2 + \dots \text{etc.}}$$

where $w_1 = {N_1}/{N}$ and $w_2 = {N_2}/{N}$ ... etc.

Chapter 10   Number of standard errors separating claimed mean from observed mean (large samples):

$$Z = \frac{\overline{X} - \overline{X}'}{\sigma_{\overline{X}}}$$

Chapter	*Narrative Statement of Formula*	*Formula*

Number of standard errors separating two sample means (large samples):

$$Z = \frac{\overline{X} - \overline{Y}}{\sigma_{\overline{X} - \overline{Y}}}$$

Number of standard errors separating two sample means (small samples):

$$t = \frac{\overline{X} - \overline{Y}}{\sigma_{\overline{X} - \overline{Y}}}$$

Standard error of the difference between two sample means, unpooled method:

$$\sigma_{\overline{X} - \overline{Y}} = \sqrt{\sigma_{\overline{X}}^2 + \sigma_{\overline{Y}}^2}$$

Pooled standard deviation (2 independent samples):

$$\sigma_{pooled} = \sqrt{\frac{\sum(x - \overline{X})^2 + \sum(y - \overline{Y})^2}{n_1 + n_2 - 2}}$$

Standard error of the difference between two sample means, pooled method:

$$\sigma_{\overline{X} - \overline{Y}} = \sigma_{pooled} \sqrt{\frac{1}{n_x} + \frac{1}{n_y}}$$

Number of standard errors separating two sample proportions (large samples):

$$Z = \frac{p_1 - p_2}{\sigma_{p_1 - p_2}}$$

Number of standard errors separating two sample proportions (small samples):

$$t = \frac{p_1 - p_2}{\sigma_{p_1 - p_2}}$$

Standard error of the difference between two sample proportions, unpooled method:

$$\sigma_{p_1 - p_2} = \sqrt{\sigma_{p_1}^2 + \sigma_{p_2}^2}$$

Chapter	Narrative Statement of Formula	Formula

Pooled proportion (2 independent samples):

$$P_{pooled} = \frac{n_1 p_1 + n_2 p_2}{n_1 + n_2}$$

Standard error of the difference between two sample proportions, pooled method (where $p = P_{pooled}$):

$$\sigma_{p_1 - p_2} = \sqrt{pq\left(\frac{1}{n_1 - 1} + \frac{1}{n_2 - 1}\right)}$$

Chi-square test of significance
(two frequency distributions with k cells each):

$$\chi^2 = \sum_{i=1}^{k} \frac{\left(O_i - E_i\right)^2}{E_i}$$

Chapter 11 $\overline{X}$ chart, where m is the number of samples:

Grand mean or norm (Center Line):

$$\overline{\overline{X}} = \frac{\sum \overline{X}}{m}$$

Average range over all samples:

$$\overline{R} = \frac{\sum R}{m}$$

Standard deviation of x, where d_2
is a constant dependent on n
and n is the size of each sample:

$$\sigma_x = \overline{R} \big/ d_2$$

Standard error of $\overline{X}$:

$$\sigma_{\overline{X}} = \frac{\overline{R} \big/ d_2}{\sqrt{n}}$$

Control limits, using 3 sigma limits:

Upper Control Limit: $UCL = \overline{\overline{X}} + 3\sigma_{\overline{X}}$

Lower Control Limit: $LCL = \overline{\overline{X}} - 3\sigma_{\overline{X}}$

Chapter	*Narrative Statement of Formula*	*Formula*

Alternatively, using $\overline{R}$ and A_2, a constant based on n:

Upper Control Limit: $\quad UCL = \overline{\overline{X}} + A_2\overline{R}$

Lower Control Limit: $\quad LCL = \overline{\overline{X}} - A_2\overline{R}$

Range chart:
Norm or Center Line: $\overline{R}$
3 sigma control limits, using D_4 and D_3, constants based on n:

Control limits: $\quad UCL = D_4\overline{R}$ and $LCL = D_3\overline{R}$

p chart for proportion of items with given attribute:

Norm or Center Line: $\quad \overline{p} = \dfrac{\sum p}{m}$

$$\sigma_p = \sqrt{\dfrac{\overline{p}(1-\overline{p})}{n-1}}$$

Control limits: $\quad UCL = \overline{p} + 3\sigma_p$ and $LCL = \overline{p} - 3\sigma_p$

np chart for number of items with given attribute:

Norm or Center Line: $\quad n\overline{p}$

$$\sigma_{np} = \sqrt{n\overline{p}(1-\overline{p})}$$

Control limits: $\quad UCL = n\overline{p} + 3\sigma_{np}$ and $LCL = n\overline{p} - 3\sigma_{np}$

c chart for number of attributes per unit:

Norm or Center Line: $\quad \overline{c} = \dfrac{\sum c}{m}$

$$\sigma_c = \sqrt{\overline{c}}$$

Control limits: $\quad UCL = \overline{c} + 3\sigma_c$ and $LCL = \overline{c} - 3\sigma_c$

Chapter 12 Coefficient of correlation (using universe data):

$$r = \dfrac{\sum (x - \overline{X})(y - \overline{Y})}{N\sigma_x \sigma_y}$$

Explained variation (100 times the coefficient of determination): $\quad 100r^2$

Chapter	Narrative Statement of Formula	Formula

Unexplained variation: $100\left(1 - r^2\right)$

Standard error of estimate:

$$\sigma_e = \sigma_y \sqrt{1 - r^2}$$

Line of best fit (regression or least squares line):

$$y_e = a + bx$$

where $b = \dfrac{r\sigma_y}{\sigma_x}$ and $a = \overline{Y} - b\overline{X}$

Standard error of estimate (simulation method):

$$\sigma_e = \sqrt{\frac{\sum\left(y_a - y_e\right)^2}{N}}$$

Coefficient of correlation:

$$r = \sqrt{1 - \frac{\sigma_e^2}{\sigma_y^2}}$$

Standard error of sample coefficient of correlation (large samples):

$$\sigma_r = \frac{\sqrt{1 - r^2}}{\sqrt{n - 2}}$$

Normal equations, used in algebraically solving for regression equation constants by least squares method:

(1) a and b (for one independent variable, x) in $y_e = a + bx$:

$$\sum y = na + b\sum x$$

$$\sum xy = a\sum x + b\sum x^2$$

(2) a, b_1, and b_2 (for two independent variables, x_1 and x_2) in $y_e = a + b_1 x_1 + b_2 x_2$:

$$\sum y = na + b_1\sum x_1 + b_2\sum x_2$$

$$\sum x_1 y = a\sum x_1 + b_1\sum x_1^2 + b_2\sum x_1 x_2$$

$$\sum x_2 y = a\sum x_2 + b_1\sum x_1 x_2 + b_2\sum x_2^2$$

Chapter	Narrative Statement of Formula	Formula

Chapter 13   Trend line, where x = time period
(preferably coded so $\sum x = 0$):

$$y_e = a + bx$$

Normal equations, used in fitting for trend line
to time series (solved simultaneously for *a* and *b*):

$$\sum y = na + b\sum x$$

$$\sum xy = a\sum x + b\sum x^2$$

Standard error of prediction (simulation method):

$$\sigma_e = \sqrt{\frac{\sum\left(y_a - y_e\right)^2}{N}}$$

Appendix B

Properties of One Half of the Normal Curve

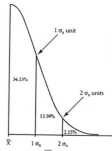

Percentage of all values included within the range formed by the mean ($\overline{X}$) plus (or minus) a specified number of standard deviation (σ) units from the mean.*

σ units	σ value carried to second decimal									
	.00	.01	.02	.03	.04	.05	.06	.07	.08	.09
.0	00.00	00.40	00.80	01.20	01.60	01.99	02.39	02.79	03.19	03.59
.1	03.98	04.38	04.78	05.17	05.57	05.96	06.36	06.75	07.14	07.53
.2	07.93	08.32	08.71	09.10	09.48	09.87	10.26	10.64	11.03	11.41
.3	11.79	12.17	12.55	12.93	13.31	13.68	14.06	14.43	14.80	15.17
.4	15.54	15.91	16.28	16.64	17.00	17.36	17.72	18.08	18.44	18.79
.5	19.15	19.50	19.85	20.19	20.54	20.88	21.23	21.57	21.90	22.24
.6	22.57	22.91	23.24	23.57	23.89	24.22	24.54	24.86	25.17	25.49
.7	25.80	26.11	26.42	26.73	27.03	27.34	27.64	27.94	28.23	28.52
.8	28.81	29.10	29.39	29.67	29.95	30.23	30.51	30.78	31.06	31.33
.9	31.59	31.86	32.12	32.38	32.64	32.89	33.15	33.40	33.65	33.89
1.0	34.13	34.38	34.61	34.85	35.08	35.31	35.54	35.77	35.99	36.21
1.1	36.43	36.65	36.86	37.08	37.29	37.49	37.70	37.90	38.10	38.30
1.2	38.49	38.69	38.88	39.07	39.25	39.44	39.62	39.80	39.97	40.15
1.3	40.32	40.49	40.66	40.82	40.99	41.15	41.31	41.47	41.62	41.77
1.4	41.92	42.07	42.22	42.36	42.51	42.65	42.79	42.92	43.06	43.19
1.5	43.32	43.45	43.57	43.70	43.82	43.94	44.06	44.18	44.29	44.41
1.6	44.52	44.63	44.74	44.84	44.95	45.05	45.15	45.25	45.35	45.45
1.7	45.54	45.64	45.73	45.82	45.91	45.99	46.08	46.16	46.25	46.33
1.8	46.41	46.49	46.56	46.64	46.71	46.78	46.86	46.93	46.99	47.06
1.9	47.13	47.19	47.26	47.32	47.38	47.44	47.50	47.56	47.61	47.67
2.0	47.72	47.78	47.83	47.88	47.93	47.98	48.03	48.08	48.12	48.17
2.1	48.21	48.26	48.30	48.34	48.38	48.42	48.46	48.50	48.54	48.57
2.2	48.61	48.64	48.68	48.71	48.75	48.78	48.81	48.84	48.87	48.90
2.3	48.93	48.96	48.98	49.01	49.04	49.06	49.09	49.11	49.13	49.16
2.4	49.18	49.20	49.22	49.25	49.27	49.29	49.31	49.32	49.34	49.36
2.5	49.38	49.40	49.41	49.43	49.45	49.46	49.48	49.49	49.51	49.52
2.6	49.53	49.55	49.56	49.57	49.59	49.60	49.61	49.62	49.63	49.64
2.7	49.65	49.66	49.67	49.68	49.69	49.70	49.71	49.72	49.73	49.74
2.8	49.74	49.75	49.76	49.77	49.77	49.78	49.79	49.79	49.80	49.81
2.9	49.81	49.82	49.82	49.83	49.84	49.84	49.85	49.85	49.86	49.86
3.0	49.87	49.87	49.87	49.88	49.88	49.89	49.89	49.89	49.90	49.90
3.1	49.90	49.91	49.91	49.91	49.92	49.92	49.92	49.92	49.93	49.93
3.2	49.93	49.93	49.94	49.94	49.94	49.94	49.94	49.95	49.95	49.95
3.3	49.95	49.95	49.95	49.96	49.96	49.96	49.96	49.96	49.96	49.97
3.4	49.97	49.97	49.97	49.97	49.97	49.97	49.97	49.97	49.97	49.98
3.5	49.98	49.98	49.98	49.98	49.98	49.98	49.98	49.98	49.98	49.98
3.6	49.98	49.98	49.99	49.99	49.99	49.99	49.99	49.99	49.99	49.99
3.7	49.99	49.99	49.99	49.99	49.99	49.99	49.99	49.99	49.99	49.99
3.8	49.99	49.99	49.99	49.99	49.99	49.99	49.99	49.99	49.99	49.99
3.9	50.00	50.00	50.00	50.00	50.00	50.00	50.00	50.00	50.00	50.00

*To obtain percentage included on both sides, multiply the indicated percent by two.

Appendix C
The t-Distribution

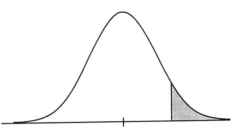

t-distribution values for selected levels of significance, one tail of the distribution for specified degrees of freedom (d.f.)*

d.f.	$t_{.100}$	$t_{.050}$	$t_{.025}$	$t_{.010}$	$t_{.005}$	d.f.
1	3.078	6.314	12.706	31.821	63.657	1
2	1.886	2.920	4.303	6.965	9.925	2
3	1.638	2.353	3.182	4.541	5.841	3
4	1.533	2.132	2.776	3.747	4.604	4
5	1.476	2.015	2.571	3.365	4.032	5
6	1.440	1.943	2.447	3.143	3.707	6
7	1.415	1.895	2.365	2.998	3.499	7
8	1.397	1.860	2.306	2.896	3.355	8
9	1.383	1.833	2.262	2.821	3.250	9
10	1.372	1.812	2.228	2.764	3.169	10
11	1.363	1.796	2.201	2.718	3.106	11
12	1.356	1.782	2.179	2.681	3.055	12
13	1.350	1.771	2.160	2.650	3.012	13
14	1.345	1.761	2.145	2.624	2.977	14
15	1.341	1.753	2.131	2.602	2.947	15
16	1.337	1.746	2.120	2.583	2.921	16
17	1.333	1.740	2.110	2.567	2.898	17
18	1.330	1.734	2.101	2.552	2.878	18
19	1.328	1.729	2.093	2.539	2.861	19
20	1.325	1.725	2.086	2.528	2.845	20
21	1.323	1.721	2.080	2.518	2.831	21
22	1.321	1.717	2.074	2.508	2.819	22
23	1.319	1.714	2.069	2.500	2.807	23
24	1.318	1.711	2.064	2.492	2.797	24
25	1.316	1.708	2.060	2.485	2.787	25
26	1.315	1.706	2.056	2.479	2.779	26
27	1.314	1.703	2.052	2.473	2.771	27
28	1.313	1.701	2.048	2.467	2.763	28
29	1.311	1.699	2.045	2.462	2.756	29
inf.	1.282	1.645	1.960	2.326	2.576	inf.

Level of Significance** (column header spanning $t_{.100}$ through $t_{.005}$)

*This table is abridged from Table IV of R. A. Fisher, *Statistical Methods for Research Workers*, published by Cliver and Boyd, Ltd., Edinburgh, by permission of the author and publishers.

**That is, percentage of items or units falling on one side of the curve.

Appendix D

The Chi-square Distribution*

Degrees of freedom	Probability that chi-square value will be exceeded									
	0.995	0.990	0.975	0.950	0.900	0.100	0.050	0.025	0.010	0.005
1	0.0^4393	0.0^3157	0.0^3982	0.0^2393	0.0158	2.71	3.84	5.02	6.63	7.88
2	0.010	0.0201	0.0506	0.103	0.211	4.61	5.99	7.38	9.21	10.60
3	0.072	0.115	0.216	0.352	0.584	6.25	7.81	9.35	11.34	12.84
4	0.207	0.297	0.484	0.711	1.064	7.78	9.49	11.14	13.28	14.86
5	0.412	0.554	0.831	1.145	1.61	9.24	11.07	12.83	15.09	16.75
6	0.676	0.872	1.24	1.64	2.20	10.64	12.59	14.45	16.81	18.55
7	0.989	1.24	1.69	2.17	2.83	12.02	14.07	16.01	18.48	20.28
8	1.34	1.65	2.18	2.73	3.49	13.36	15.51	17.53	20.09	21.96
9	1.73	2.09	2.70	3.33	4.17	14.68	16.92	19.02	21.67	23.59
10	2.16	2.56	3.25	3.94	4.87	15.99	18.31	20.48	23.21	25.19
11	2.60	3.05	3.82	4.57	5.58	17.28	19.68	21.92	24.72	26.76
12	3.07	3.57	4.40	5.23	6.30	18.55	21.03	23.34	26.22	28.30
13	3.57	4.11	5.01	5.89	7.04	19.81	22.36	24.74	27.69	29.82
14	4.07	4.66	5.63	6.57	7.79	21.06	23.68	26.12	29.14	31.32
15	4.60	5.23	6.26	7.26	8.55	22.31	25.00	27.49	30.58	32.80
16	5.14	5.81	6.91	7.96	9.31	23.54	26.30	28.85	32.00	34.27
17	5.70	6.41	7.56	8.67	10.09	24.77	27.59	30.19	33.41	35.72
18	6.26	7.01	8.23	9.39	10.86	25.99	28.87	31.53	34.81	37.16
19	6.84	7.63	8.91	10.12	11.65	27.20	30.14	32.85	36.19	38.58
20	7.43	8.26	9.59	10.85	12.44	28.41	31.41	34.17	37.57	40.00
21	8.03	8.90	10.28	11.59	13.24	29.62	32.67	35.48	38.93	41.40
22	8.64	9.54	10.98	12.34	14.04	30.81	33.92	36.78	40.29	42.80
23	9.26	10.20	11.69	13.09	14.85	32.01	35.17	38.08	41.64	44.18
24	9.89	10.86	12.40	13.85	15.66	33.20	36.42	39.36	42.98	45.56
25	10.52	11.52	13.12	14.61	16.47	34.38	37.65	40.65	44.31	46.93
26	11.16	12.20	13.84	15.38	17.29	35.56	38.89	41.92	45.64	48.29
27	11.81	12.88	14.57	16.15	18.11	36.74	40.11	43.19	46.96	49.64
28	12.46	13.56	15.31	16.93	18.94	37.92	41.34	44.46	48.28	50.99
29	13.12	14.26	16.05	17.71	19.77	39.09	42.56	45.72	49.59	52.34
30	13.79	14.95	16.79	18.49	20.60	40.26	43.77	46.98	50.89	53.67
40	20.71	22.16	24.43	26.51	29.05	51.80	55.76	59.34	63.69	66.77
50	27.99	29.71	32.36	34.76	37.69	63.17	67.50	71.42	76.15	79.49
60	35.53	37.48	40.48	43.19	46.46	74.40	79.08	83.30	88.38	91.95
70	43.28	45.44	48.76	51.74	55.33	85.53	90.53	95.02	100.4	104.22
80	51.17	53.54	57.15	60.39	64.28	96.58	101.9	106.6	112.3	116.32
90	59.20	61.75	65.65	69.13	73.29	107.6	113.1	118.1	124.1	128.3
100	67.33	70.06	74.22	77.93	82.36	118.5	124.3	129.6	135.8	140.2

*This table is abridged from Table III of R. A. Fisher, *Statistical Methods for Research Workers,* published by Oliver and Boyd, Ltd., Edinburgh, by permission of the author and publishers.

Appendix E

Values of the Simple Linear Correlation Coefficient Needed for Significance at Given Levels

Degrees of Freedom (n-2)	Probability of a Larger Value of r			
	0.1	0.05	0.01	0.001
1	.98769	.99692	.999877	.9999988
2	.90000	.95000	.990000	.99900
3	.8054	.8783	.95873	.99116
4	.7293	.8114	.91720	.97406
5	.6694	.7545	.8745	.95074
6	.6215	.7067	.8343	.92493
7	.5822	.6664	.7977	.8982
8	.5494	.6319	.7646	.8721
9	.5214	.6021	.7348	.8471
10	.4973	.5760	.7079	.8233
11	.4762	.5529	.6835	.8010
12	.4575	.5324	.6614	.7800
13	.4409	.5139	.6411	.7603
14	.4259	.4973	.6226	.7420
15	.4124	.4821	.6055	.7246
16	.4000	.4683	.5897	.7084
17	.3887	.4555	.5751	.6932
18	.3783	.4438	.5614	.6787
19	.3687	.4329	.5487	.6652
20	.3598	.4227	.5368	.6524
25	.3233	.3809	.4869	.5974
30	.2960	.3494	.4487	.5541
35	.2746	.3246	.4182	.5189
40	.2573	.3044	.3932	.4896
45	.2428	.2875	.3721	.4648
50	.2306	.2732	.3514	.4433
60	.2108	.2500	.3248	.4078
70	.1954	.2319	.3017	.3799
80	.1829	.2172	.2830	.3568
90	.1726	.2050	.2673	.3375
100	.1638	.1946	.2540	.3211
125	—	.1740	.2280	—
150	—	.1590	.2080	—
200	—	.1380	.1810	—
300	—	.1130	.1480	—
400	—	.0980	.1280	—
500	—	.0880	.1150	—
1000	—	.0620	.0810	—

Source: R. A. Fisher and Frank Yates, *Statistical Tables for Biological, Agricultural and Medical Research.* Fifth Edition (New York: Hafner Publishing Company, Inc., 1957).

Appendix F

Answers to Problems

CHAPTER 1

1. (a) No; (b) yes; (c) stability of mass data; (d) about 60; applied 2% to 3,000; (e) measurements versus judgments, statistics and reason, use of percentages and averages.

2. (a) The law of statistical regularity. (b) No, because statistical methods are applicable to mass data but not generally to individual cases. (c) By a special case study to determine which accounts are repeatedly service-charged, if any.

3. The probability of survival is 98 percent for each *independent* occurrence, $p = s/T$, or $49/50$.

4. The figure 18.348 gallons is an illustration of spurious accuracy, because the conditions under which such studies are made could not possibly yield accuracy to three decimal places.

5. Indeterminable; the data quoted are incomplete to make a decision; average number of fatalities per 100,000 passenger miles traveled may show a different result.

6. One out of six. The chance remains the same, one out of six, because of independence.

7. $1/50$

8. (b) and (d).

9. Neither; the data are incomplete to make a decision.

10. Probably false; it is not certain that the fourth cycle will duplicate the previous three cycles, since such extreme conditions are usually highly variable and the sample over the time period covered is too short.

11. (a) First column represents automobiles; second column the

remaining manufacturing industries. (b) Stability of mass data; because rates in the second column show greater stability, they probably are based on a larger number of workers.

12. (a) No; sample too small; (b) generalizing or jumping to conclusions; limited data.

13. Variables — weight of students; attributes — gender of students.

14. See section on "Uses of Statistics."

CHAPTER 2

1. Interview a random sample of salespeople; mail questionnaire study of retail outlets; or interview a random sample of present and past customers.

2. c, b or d, a, e.　　　　3. f, a or b, e, d, c.

4. d, b, e or c, f, a.

5. (a) Bad—ambiguous; (b) good—calls for a single answer and is clear; (c) good—easy to answer, diminishes problem of nonresponse by calling for age group.

6. (a) Personal interview or mail questionnaire; (b) mail questionnaire — too impersonal and costly by interview; (c) observation — data in telephone directory; (d) measurement — only way of getting data; (e) company records.

7. Non-response, biased answers, incomplete mailing list, untrained interviewers; sampling error; coding errors.

8. (a) Primary; (b) secondary; (c) primary; (d) secondary; (e) secondary.

9. Observation, measurement, mail questionnaire, personal interview, recording from company records. For second part, see section on Methods of Quantifying a Process or Problem.

10. (a) No; because the captain who wins the toss would select the better player of each two every time.

    (b) Assign a number in rank order to each of the 16 players and select players so that the total team ranks are equal.

    (c) No measurement of the exact quantitative difference between adjacent ranked players.

---

* To be answered by the reader.

11. Cannot tell unless the critical percentage upon which to base the decision is stated.

12. (a) Interview a small random sample of the non-respondents.

    (b) Accept the results if 97 percent response will meet the critical percentage for a decision.

13. Must follow up on non-respondents, since their reply will affect the fifty percent needed for decisions.

CHAPTER 3

1. *

2. (a) and (b)

Grade	Number of students	Percent of total
50-59	2	10
60-69	2	10
70-79	7	35
80-89	6	30
90-99	3	15
Total	20	100

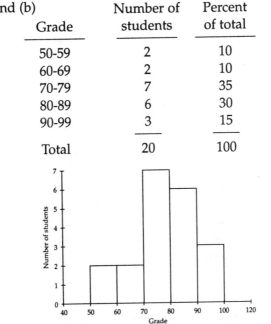

   (c) Approximately a normal distribution, if the number of students in the study were much larger — on the assumption that the grades were obtained under a constant-cause system; otherwise, asymmetrical or skewed.

3. Some of the machines not functioning properly; or not set properly; errors in the measurements; two different grades of raw material fed into the machines.

4. (a)

Size of store — Number of employees	Number of stores (f)
0-9	20
10-19	8
20-29	5
30-39	3
40-49	2
50-59	1
60-69	1
Total	40

(b) 7/40 = 17.5%

(c)

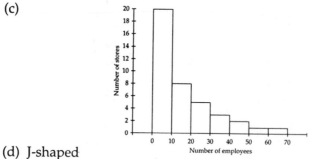

(d) J-shaped

5. (a) $350 (assuming wages can end in $.99, a continuous variable);
   (b) 42.5 inches (continuous variable); (c) 7-1/2 (noncontinuous
   variable); (d) 15 (continuous variable); (e) 33 years (continuous
   variable); (f) 140 pounds (continuous variable).

6. *

7. (a) Yes, if cows were about the same age, number of cows in the
   study were much larger, and cows were treated under the
   same set of conditions;

(b)

Pounds	A.M. (f)	P.M. (f)
2-7	2	1
8-13	3	2
14-19	6	8
20-25	3	3

---

* To be answered by the reader.

(c) More milk yield in evening milking;

(d) Not enough classes; evening — probably skewed;

(e) Wide age differential in cows; too few cases; maybe special treatment given to some cows

8. (a) attributes, noncontinuous
   (b) variables, continuous
   (c) variables, noncontinuous
   (d) variables, continuous for practical purposes
   (e) variables, noncontinuous (no fractional words)
   (f) variables, continuous
   (g) attributes, noncontinuous

9. To determine the cause of a skewed distribution if the expected normal distribution does not show up; also, as explained in Chapter 5, to estimate the percentage of cases which are between the mean and standard deviation units; also, to establish warranties. Other uses given in later chapters.

CHAPTER 4

1. (a) Mode = 30 years; (b) Median = 30 years;
   (c) Mean = 33.1 years.

2. An average of position is one obtained on the basis of frequency of occurrence (mode) or relative position in an array (median). An average of calculation is one obtained by the arithmetic mean.

3. An average very rarely coincides with every value of the variable; hence a value on either side of the average can be perfectly natural as long as it is not "extremely" far away from the average.

4. The two analysts probably used two different averages, e.g., arithmetic mean and median. Therefore, the figures would generally be different. Neither analyst necessarily made a mistake.

5.

Age (years)	f	m	fm
20 - 29.9	6	25	150
30 - 39.9	5	35	175
40 - 49.9	1	45	45
50 - 59.9	3	55	165
Total	15	Total	535

(a) Mean = $\Sigma fm / n$ = 535 / 15 = 35.7 years.

Median = $L + \left(\dfrac{g\,i}{f}\right)$ = $30 + \dfrac{(1.5)10}{5}$ = 33.0 years.

Mode = midpoint of class with greatest frequency = 25 years.

(b) False

(c) In computing the arithmetic mean it is assumed that the midpoint of the items in each class is exactly the value of each item in the class. In computing the median the assumption is made that items in a group are equal spaced. Frequently, neither of these is exactly the case.

(d) No one average is considered more accurate than the others. They are each obtained by a different way and each serves a different use.

6. Machine A is likely to last longer, because its mean life is higher. Total life of all machines is estimated by multiplying the number of machines of the specified brand by its arithmetic mean.

7. Mean of $1,465 times 110 percent = $1,611.50 times 150 = $24,172 (total money needed).

8. 3.47 inches; (a) the data indicate a bell-shaped distribution; hence, $\overline{X}$ would be about the same as the mode which is the midpoint of the class with the greatest frequency, i.e., 3.47 inches.

(b) $\overline{X}$ = $\Sigma fm / n$ = 2508.49 / 723 = 3.47 inches.

9. (a) Median, to overcome problem of open-end class in a frequency distribution by income;

(b) Median, for same reason as (a) above;

(c) Arithmetic mean, because it is the only average which, when multiplied by N gives the grand total;

(d) Mode, to indicate the size most frequently bought;

(e) Mode, to indicate the color most frequently purchased;

(f) Arithmetic mean, because it is the most commonly used average and all the data are available to compute it.

10. Compare the mean daily temperatures; the lower mean would represent the colder winter.

---

* To be answered by the reader.

Special Sections

11. $\overline{X} = \overline{X}g + \dfrac{\Sigma d}{n} = 33.1$ years.

12. $\overline{X} = 151.15$ lbs. (In this case, Short-cut method probably required more time).

13. $\overline{X} = \$119.67$ per week.

14. A, since its mean is 8.10 lbs. and B's mean is 7.72 lbs.

15. Weighted average, Agency A = $3783.33;
    Agency B = $3860.00 per month.

16. 1990 mean = $10.50; 1995 mean = $12.19.

CHAPTER 5

1. (a) 2; (b);* (c);* (d);* and (e).*

2. (a) Operator A appears to be more consistent in making the round trip because his C.V. (7.7%) is less than that of Operator B (10.0%).

   (b) Operator B appears to be faster in completing the round trip because his mean time is 70 minutes compare with 78 for Operator A.

3. Yes, because circumference of heads varies due to hereditary and biological factors.
   (a) 68%; (b) 95.5%; (c) 99.7%.

4. (a) 21.6 years; (b) 2.3 years;
   (c) 10.6 percent, or very little variation.

5. (a) Plant B, because the mean is highest; (b) Plant B, because the C.V. is lowest; (c) Plant A, because the C.V. is highest.

6. Distribution by income is not bell shaped. The estimate is poor.

7. (a) 15.9 percent; (b) 15.9 percent;
   (c) 2.28 percent; (d) 0.13 percent.

8. (a) A; (b) B; (c) The estimates are subject to sampling error.

9. (a) $16.94, but may use $16.50 to simplify computations;
   (b) $2.34; (c) C.V. = 13.8% — fairly uniform.

10. Approximately same as answers to problem 9 (differences due to rounding).

11. (a) Probably grade B, because its mean tearing weight is 43.0 lbs. versus A's mean of 41.25 lbs.;

    (b) Both of about equal consistency:
    C.V. for grade A = 24.7%;
    C.V. for grade B = 25.30%;

    (c) The data are based on random samples, subject to sampling variation; therefore, allowing for possible sampling error, the results could be reversed.

12. $\bar{X}$ for Washington, DC = $820 and σ_x = $198; C.V. = 24.2%
    $\bar{Y}$ for Baltimore, MD = $795 and σ_y = $182; C.V. = 22.8%

    (a) Washington; (b) Baltimore

13. (a) Not normal, because variable is affected by many non-chance factors.

    (b) Normal, because leaf length is primarily affected by natural factors.

    (c) Not normal, because the variable is affected by economic factors.

    (d) Normal, if process is operating under constant set of conditions, equivalent to chance variations.

    (e) Approximately normal when sample size is largest.

    (f) Not normal, because economic and social factors are predominant cause of variation.

14. (a) Grade A

    $$Z = \frac{30 - 41.25}{10.19} = -1.10$$

    Percent = 50.00 − 36.32 = 13.57%
    Number = (25,000)(0.1357) = 3392

    Grade B

    $$Z = \frac{30 - 43}{10.89} = -1.19$$

    Percent = 50.00 − 38.30 = 11.70%
    Number = (25,000)(0.117) = 2925

---

* To be answered by the reader.

(b) Grade A

$$Z = \frac{50 - 41.25}{10.19} = 0.86$$

Percent = 50.00 + 30.51 = 80.51%

Number = (25,000)(0.8051) = 20,128

Grade B

$$Z = \frac{50 - 43}{10.89} = 0.64$$

Percent = 50.00 + 23.89 = 73.89%

Number = (25,000)(.7389) = 18,473

(c) Grade A

$$Z = \frac{70 - 41.25}{10.19} = 2.82$$

Percent = 50.00 − 49.77 = 0.23%

Number = (25,000)(.0023) = 58

Grade B

$$Z = \frac{70 - 43}{10.89} = 2.48$$

Percent = 50.00 − 49.34 = 0.66%

Number = (25,000)(.0066) = 165

(d) Grade B

$$Z = \frac{25 - 43}{10.89} = -1.65$$

Percent = 50.00 − 45.05 = 4.95%

15. (a) $Z = \dfrac{1 - 4.2}{1.3} = -2.46$

Difference in percent = 50.00 − 49.31 = 0.69%

Number = (250) (0.0069) = between 1 and 2 trucks.

(b) $Z_1 = \dfrac{2 - 4.2}{1.3} = -1.69$ $Z_2 = \dfrac{3 - 4.2}{1.3} = -0.92$

Percent = 45.45%   Percent = 32.12%

Difference in percent = 45.45 − 32.12 = 13.33%

Number = (250)(0.1333) = 33 trucks.

(c) $Z = \dfrac{6 - 4.2}{1.3} = 1.38$

Percent = 50.00 − 41.62 = 8.38%

Number = (250)(.0838) = 21 trucks.

16. Every estimate derived from a random sample is subject to sampling error.

CHAPTER 6

1. (a) $\dfrac{1}{1000}$; (b) $\dfrac{1}{500}$; (c) $\left(\dfrac{1}{1000}\right)\left(\dfrac{1}{999}\right) = \dfrac{1}{999000}$;

   (d) $_3C_2\left(\dfrac{1}{1000}\right)\left(\dfrac{1}{999}\right) = 3\left(\dfrac{1}{(1000)(999)}\right) = \dfrac{3}{999000}$;

   (e) (a) simple; (b) addition; (c) conditional;

   (d) multiplication and conditional; (e) d

2. Probability of winning $= \dfrac{1}{1000}$; therefore, when a winning number is picked, \$1,000 should be won; since \$500 is paid, the operator's take is $\dfrac{\$500}{\$1000} = 50\%$.

3. Assuming even odds of each team's winning, fair odds should be $\left(\dfrac{1}{2}\right)^7 = \dfrac{1}{128}$; in other words, \$128 should be paid to the winner; operator's take $= \dfrac{128-40}{128} = \dfrac{88}{128} = 69\%$.

4. (a) Just odds: \$8 for \$1; (b) \$16 for \$1; (c) \$32 for \$1; (d) \$64 for \$1. Operator's take is: 37.5%; 37.5%; 50%; and 53.1%, respectively.

5. (a) $_{26}P_2 = \dfrac{26!}{24!} = 650$; different 3 digit numbers $= 1,000$, i.e., from 000 to 999; total number of different licenses $= (650)(1000) = 650,000$; (b) 15,600,000.

6. (a) 10,000; (b) $_{10,000}C_2 = 49,995,000$;
   (c) $_{10,000}C_3 = 166,616,670,000$.

7. (a) $(1000)(100)(10,000) = 1,000,000,000$;

   (b) $\dfrac{1,000,000,000 - 377,000,000}{7,000,000} = \dfrac{623,000,000}{7,000,000} = 89$ years

   (from 1994 to 2083).

8. (a) 68.3%; (b) 159; (c) 38.3%; (d) 50%.

---

* To be answered by the reader.

9. (a) 0.13%; (b) 99.87%; (c) the distribution of batteries by length of life must be approximately normal.

Special Section

10. Binomial expansion:

	Number of successes		
3	2	1	0

$$(.9+.1)^3 = (.9)^3 + 3(.9)^2(.1) + 3(.9)(.1) + (.1)^3$$

(a) Probability $= (.9)^3 = (.9)(.9)(.9) = 72.9\%$

(b) Probability of at least two successes $= (.9)^3 + (3)(.9)^2(.1) = .729 + .243 = 97.2\%$

(c) Probability of no successes $= (.1)^3 = .1$ of 1 percent

(d) Probability of at least one success = sum of 1, 2 and 3 successes $= 72.9 + 24.3 + 2.7 = 99.9$ percent.

11. (a) $P_x = {_n}C_x\, p^x q^{n-x}$ An example with n=5 follows:

	Number of successes				
5	4	3	2	1	0

$$(p + q)^5 = p^5 + 5p^4q^1 + \frac{5(4)p^3q^2}{2} + \frac{5(4)(3)p^2q^3}{(3)2} + \frac{5(4)(3)(2)p^1q^4}{(4)(3)2} + q^5$$

(b) When $p = .98$, $p^n = (.98)^5 = .904$

(c) $q^n = (.02)^5 = $ practically nil.

12. (a) $(.9)^6 = .631$; (b) $(.9)^5(.1)^1 = .355$; (c) sum of (a) and (b) $= .986$

13.

	Number of defectives			
0	1	2	3	4
$(.97)^4$	$(.97)^3(.03)$	$(.97)^2(.03)^2$	$(.97)(.03)^3$	$(.03)^4$

(a) $(.97)^4 = .885$

(b) $1 - .885 = .115$

(c) $(.03)^4 = $ practically nil $(.0000008)$.

CHAPTER 7

1. Possible simple random samples of n=30 costs:

(a) Simple Random	(b) Systematic	(c) Stratified
$4.41	$4.06	$2.27
$2.88	$2.80	$3.94
$4.75	$5.53	$4.92
$6.01	$4.46	$4.81
$6.30	$4.85	$3.50
$4.04	$2.72	$3.73
$6.40	$3.18	$5.38
$2.52	$3.45	$4.18
$4.80	$4.21	$4.55
$2.85	$6.28	$4.41
$4.48	$4.74	$3.69
$5.23	$4.46	$2.55
$3.06	$3.64	$4.07
$5.27	$3.69	$3.59
$4.16	$4.45	$4.99
$3.86	$5.75	$4.62
$5.24	$5.62	$5.72
$4.94	$4.30	$5.62
$3.35	$6.41	$4.62
$4.54	$6.61	$4.69
$4.24	$3.94	$3.35
$2.61	$3.84	$4.23
$3.09	$4.83	$3.70
$5.96	$4.92	$3.81
$5.43	$2.98	$5.15
$6.48	$2.56	$4.54
$4.92	$3.48	$5.26
$3.64	$2.35	$5.80
$2.97	$5.73	$4.86
$3.04	$3.04	$4.42

2. (a) Simple random: by prenumbering the elements in the universe and then using a random number table to select the units in the sample;

---

* To be answered by the reader.

(b) Systematic random: by selecting every 17-th case after the first was selected from the first skip-interval by use of random digits;

(c) Stratified random: by selecting a 6% sample from each of the four class-year strata, using random digits.

3. Examples: (a) $4.38; (b) $4.30; (c) $4.37.

4. In this case, the systematic random sample, but usually the stratified sample.

5. The stratified random sample usually would yield the most reliable estimate because we are sure that items from each stratum are represented; however, this requires good judgment in stratification and allocating the sample to the strata.

6. Because it is less costly to check for non-sampling errors with a small sample. Checking a large universe on a 100% basis is too costly and more prone to non-sampling errors.

7. The average should be about 6 to 7 letters.

8. Reader's definitions.

9. (a) By use of a table of random digits, examining a 3-digit column (after assigning each card a number from 000 to 999) and following the four steps in simple random selection;

(b) with a skip-interval of 20, select the first from the first 20 cards by use of a table of random digits and every 20-th card thereafter;

(c) since it is a 5% sample, select 5 two-digit terminal numbers at random from the social security account number.

10. (a) One is random selection and the other is judgment selection;

(b) Simple random selection because we can claim validity and measure the sampling error of the resulting estimates.

11. (a) One possible set of samples follows:

Simple Random Sample		Systematic Sample	
$267	294	$257	182
218	167	178	167
263	205	195	131
128	201	224	124
174	151	211	311
121	70	180	217
225	261	145	301
318	379	167	183
301	194	146	327
131	167	136	241
361	88	174	199
168	182	196	379
183	252	266	183
160	265	232	214
167	180	174	240
Sum	$6,241	Sum	$6,280
Mean	$208	Mean	$209
Total	$33,280	Total	$33,440

CHAPTER 8

1. Sampling error (due to chance); systematic error (one-sided errors); unsystematic error (+ or − natural errors which tend to offset each other in the long run).

2. (a) Frequency distribution of many independent random sample estimates based on same n and N sizes and same method of random selection;

    (b) a sample selected by a random selection method;

    (c) caused by random (chance) selection of items;

    (d) a stable process with normal operational causes of variation.

3. A large enough sample ($n \geq 31$) and a large number of replicates ($m \geq 100$).

---

* To be answered by the reader.

4. (a) About 68 times out of 100; (b) about 95 times out of 100;
    (c) about 98.78 times out of 100.

    When expressed as odds: (a) 2 to 1; (b) 20 to 1; (c) 81 to 1.

5. (a) It will approach the bell curve; $\overline{\overline{X}} \pm 1\sigma_{\overline{X}}$ will include about
    68% of all $\overline{X}$ estimates;

    (b) It will approach the the shape of the universe frequency
    distribution; $\overline{X}$ is an unbiased estimate of $\overline{X}'$.

6. σ_x estimates the inherent variation of the original universe of
    x-values from the mean of all values included in the sample;

    $\sigma_{\overline{X}}$ measures the sampling variation of an $\overline{X}$ estimate derived from
    a random sample. Therefore, $\sigma_{\overline{X}}$ is the standard error of the
    sample mean.

7. *

8. Central Limit Theorem, principle of probability, and Law of
    Decreasing Variation.

9. σ'_x , direct; $\sqrt{n}$, inverse.

10. $\sigma_{\overline{X}} = \dfrac{\sigma_x \sqrt{1-f}}{\sqrt{n}}$.

11. (a) 1; 2; 3; 1.65; 2.58; (b) * (use $\pm 1\sigma_{\overline{X}} \pm 2\sigma_{\overline{X}}$ etc.)

CHAPTER 9

1. Solution to the problem given as part of the problem.

2. (a) $f = \dfrac{225}{2000} = .1125$; $\sqrt{(1-f)} = .8875 = .942$

    $\sigma_{\overline{X}} = \pm \$1.57$.

    (b) Practically certain tolerates 3 standard errors.

    $\overline{X} \pm 3\sigma_{\overline{X}} = 60 \pm 3(1.57)$, or $\$55.29$ to $\$64.71$.

    (c) Maximum absolute error = $\pm\$4.71$;
    Maximum relative error = (E) = $\dfrac{\$4.71}{\$60} = \pm 7.9\%$.

3. (a) $N\overline{X} = (40{,}000)(2.4) = 96{,}000$ readers. For 99% confidence, we
    tolerate 2.575 standard errors.

(b) $2.575\,\sigma_{\overline{X}} = \dfrac{(2.575)(.4)\sqrt{1-\dfrac{1600}{40,000}}}{\sqrt{1600}} = \dfrac{\sqrt{.96}}{40} = \pm0.0252;$

S.E. of $N\overline{X} = N\sigma_{\overline{X}} = (40,000)(0.0252) = \pm1,009 \approx \pm1,000;$

$96,000 \pm 1,000$: $95,000$ to $97,000$ with 99% confidence; relative error = 1% (i.e., $1,000/96,000$).

(c) and (d) No; Sales from news stands not included.

4. (a) $\overline{X} = 35.8$ c.f., $\sigma_x = 14.99$ c.f.; $N\overline{X} = (1500)(35.8) = 53700$ c.f.

(b) $\sigma_{N\overline{X}} = \pm4461$ c.f.

Thus, absolute error = ±4461 c.f.; In relative terms,

$(E). = \dfrac{4461}{53,700} = \pm8.3\%.$

(c) 99% or 100 to 1 confidence requires 2.575 S.E.: $(2.575)(4461) =$

$\pm11,487$ c.f.; relative error = $\dfrac{11,487}{53,700} = \pm21.4\%.$

5. $\sigma_p = \pm.0199$; $1.65\sigma_p = \pm0.0329.$

The true percentage is somewhere within 20 ± 3.3 or between 16.7 and 23.3. We are 90% sure that we are right in drawing this conclusion.

6. Alternative #1 – Reduce the confidence to 90%; sample size becomes n = 1,528.

Alternative #2 – Tolerate more error, e.g., 10% at same confidence (Z=3); sample size becomes n = 1,413.

Alternative #3 – Tolerate more error (10%) and reduce confidence to 90%; sample size becomes n = 705.

7. N = 500; p = .333; Z = 1.65; E = .04 (percentage points). This is an attributes problem.

$n = \dfrac{N\,Z^2\,p\,(1-p)}{N\,E^2 + Z^2\,p\,(1-p)} = \dfrac{(500)\,(1.65)^2(.333)\,(.667)}{(500)\,(.04)^2 + (1.65)^2(.333)\,(.667)} = \dfrac{302.35}{1.405}$

$= 215$ loans.

---

* To be answered by the reader.

8. $N = 10000$; $Z = 1.96$; $V = 1.0$; $E = .15$. This is a variables problem. Therefore,

$$n = \frac{N\ Z^2\ V^2}{N\ E^2 + Z^2\ V^2} = 168 \text{ workers (round up to 170).}$$

9. (a) Systematic random;

(b) $n = \dfrac{Z^2 p(1 - p)}{E^2} = 176.$

(Formula for very large population does not require N.)

(c) About 50% or more.

10. $\dfrac{95.4 \text{ confidence}}{4.6 \text{ risk}} = 21$ to 1 (in integers);

$\dfrac{99.73 \text{ confidence}}{.27 \text{ risk}} = 369$ to 1 (in integers).

11. $N = 12,000$; $Z = 1.96$; $V = .5$; $E = .02$. This is a variables problem. $n = 2,001$ accounts.

Note: If this sample size is too costly, increase the tolerable error to 5 percent ($E = .05$); then $n = 372$.

12. $N = 25,000$; $Z = 1.65$; $p = .05$; $E = .01$
$n = 1,230$ recipients.

13. Reduce confidence or increase tolerable error, or both, as indicated in problems 7 and 12.

14. *

15. *

16. *

17. *

18. *

19. *

CHAPTER 10

Note: Answers to many of the computational problems involving Z-tests or t-tests could be different from the one given, depending on the interpretation of the problem (the assumptions used) and the perspective taken (on whom the "burden of proof" is placed).

1. (a) Judgment alone;
   (b) Lack of quantitative knowledge of risk involved.

2. (a) Complete count versus judgment claim;   (b) probably complete count or indeterminate; no statistical basis; (c) make an inventory estimate by an appropriate random sample;
   (d) advantage — no sampling error; disadvantages — subject to non-sampling errors and costly to recount.

3. (a) Universe figure and random sample estimate;   (b) more inclined to accept the sample figures, because of the usual biases of under-enumeration of populations; (c) a post-audit random sample of the census counts with extreme care and well-trained enumerators.

4. (a) $Z_{.10} = 1.282$; $Z_{.05} = 1.645$; $Z_{.02} = 2.054$; $Z_{.01} = 2.327$; $Z_{.005} = 2.575$.

   (b) $Z_{.10} = 1.645$; $Z_{.05} = 1.960$; $Z_{.02} = 2.327$; $Z_{.01} = 2.575$; $Z_{.005} = 2.810$.

5. (a) One-tailed, based on competing claim, which is a smaller percentage;

   (b) $Z = 1.645$; (c) no;

   (d) 97.67% or about 43 to 1.

6. (a) One-tailed (assumes .054 > .05);

   (b) Critical ratio $Z_{.01} = 2.327$;

   (c) Actual ratio $= \dfrac{.054 - .05}{.002260} = 1.77$;
   difference is not significant.

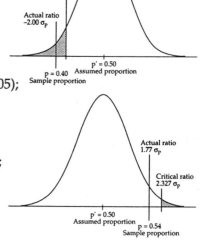

---

* To be answered by the reader.

7. Two-tailed test.

Actual Z-value = $\dfrac{.0214-.0212}{\sigma_{\overline{X}}=.0003} = 6.06$.

Since the Z-test shows Z to be over 6 standard errors, this indicates, with an extremely high probability, that there is a significant difference in quality, worthy of immediate investigation.

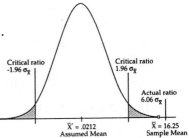

8. $Z = \dfrac{.25-.20}{\sqrt{\dfrac{(.2)(.8)}{625}}} = \dfrac{.05}{.016} = 3.1$.

This is a significant difference even at the .005 significance level. Since the student sample was a judgment sample, and parking lots do not represent all registered cars, the DMV percentage is more credible.

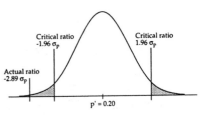

9. (a) One-tailed, with a critical ratio of 1.645, assuming the higher grade should have a greater tearing weight.

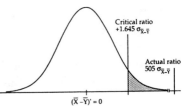

(b) $\sigma_{\overline{X}-\overline{Y}} = \sqrt{\left(\dfrac{.03}{\sqrt{100}}\right)^2 + \left(\dfrac{.02}{\sqrt{60}}\right)^2} = .00396$ lbs.;

Actual $Z = \dfrac{5-3}{.00396} = 505$, a highly significant difference.

(c) $\sigma_{\text{pooled}} = \sqrt{\dfrac{(99)(.03)^2 + (59)(.02)^2}{160-2 \ = \ 158}} = \sqrt{\dfrac{.1127}{158}} = .0267$ lbs.;

$\sigma_{\overline{X}-\overline{Y}} = (.0267)\sqrt{\dfrac{1}{100}+\dfrac{1}{60}} = (.0267)\sqrt{.02667} = .00436$ lbs.;

$Z = \dfrac{5-3}{.00436} = 458.7$, a highly significant difference.

(d) It would not be valid since two *different* grades of paper were involved.

10. Difference in error rates is not significant at 2 percent level of significance (critical ratio = 2.327):

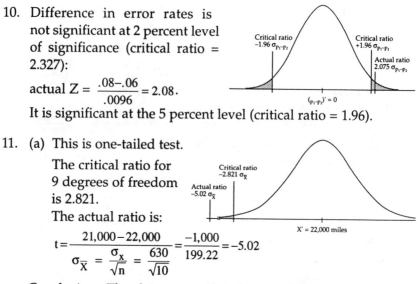

Critical ratio
$-1.96\ \sigma_{p_1-p_2}$

Critical ratio
$+1.96\ \sigma_{p_1-p_2}$

Actual ratio
$2.075\ \sigma_{p_1-p_2}$

$(p_1-p_2)' = 0$

actual $Z = \dfrac{.08-.06}{.0096} = 2.08$.

It is significant at the 5 percent level (critical ratio = 1.96).

11. (a) This is one-tailed test.

The critical ratio for 9 degrees of freedom is 2.821.

The actual ratio is:

Critical ratio
$-2.821\ \sigma_{\bar{x}}$

Actual ratio
$-5.02\ \sigma_{\bar{x}}$

$X' = 22,000$ miles

$$t = \frac{21,000-22,000}{\sigma_{\bar{X}} = \dfrac{\sigma_X}{\sqrt{n}} = \dfrac{630}{\sqrt{10}}} = \frac{-1,000}{199.22} = -5.02$$

Conclusion: The claim cannot be given credence.

12. This is a one-tailed test. The mean breaking strength is estimated to be 530 pounds, with a standard deviation of 32.07 pounds. For a 5% significance level, at 7 degrees of freedom and a one-tailed test, the critical ratio is 1.895.

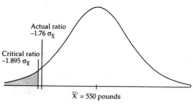

Actual ratio
$-1.76\ \sigma_{\bar{x}}$

Critical ratio
$-1.895\ \sigma_{\bar{x}}$

$\bar{X}' = 550$ pounds

The actual ratio is $t = \dfrac{530-550}{\sigma_{\bar{X}} = \dfrac{32.07}{\sqrt{8}}} = \dfrac{-20}{11.34} = -1.764$.

(a) Conclusion: The claim can be given credence since the actual ratio is less than the critical ratio.

(b) When $\sigma'_x = 25$ pounds is known, the critical ratio would be obtainable from the normal curve table. For a one-tailed test and a 5% significance level, $Z_{.05} = 1.645$.

The actual ratio is $Z = \dfrac{530-550}{\sigma_{\bar{X}'} = \dfrac{25}{\sqrt{8}}} = \dfrac{-20}{8.84} = -2.262$.

Conclusion: The difference of 20 pounds is significant; the claim cannot be given credence.

---

* To be answered by the reader.

13. This is a two-tailed test with a critical ratio of 2.145 (t-table) for a 5% risk level. $\overline{X} = 223.1$ hours; $\overline{Y} = 217.3$ hours; $\sigma_x = 8.46$ hours; $\sigma_y = 21.64$ hours;

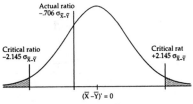

$$\sigma_{\overline{X}-\overline{Y}} = \sqrt{\left(\frac{8.46}{\sqrt{8}}\right)^2 + \left(\frac{21.64}{\sqrt{8}}\right)^2} = \sqrt{8.95 + 58.54} = \sqrt{67.49} = 8.22 \text{ hours.}$$

The actual ratio is $t = \dfrac{217.3 - 223.1}{8.22} = 0.706.$

May be slightly different depending on rounding.

Conclusion: difference is not significant at the stated level of significance.

14. This is a two-tailed test; critical ratio = 2.064.

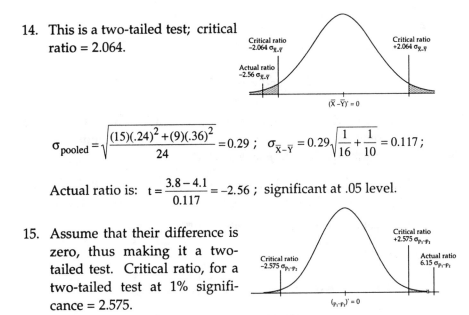

$$\sigma_{pooled} = \sqrt{\frac{(15)(.24)^2 + (9)(.36)^2}{24}} = 0.29 \; ; \quad \sigma_{\overline{X}-\overline{Y}} = 0.29\sqrt{\frac{1}{16} + \frac{1}{10}} = 0.117 \; ;$$

Actual ratio is: $t = \dfrac{3.8 - 4.1}{0.117} = -2.56$; significant at .05 level.

15. Assume that their difference is zero, thus making it a two-tailed test. Critical ratio, for a two-tailed test at 1% significance = 2.575.

$$P_1 = \frac{30}{100} = 0.3; \quad P_2 = \frac{70}{100} = 0.7; \quad \sigma_{P_1-P_2} = \sqrt{(.046)^2 + (.046)^2} = .065 \; ;$$

The actual ratio is $Z = \dfrac{.7 - .3}{.065} = 6.15.$

Conclusion: The difference is highly significant. The coin is warped and leans toward tails. This problem can also be solved by Chi-Square. The reader is encouraged to try it.

16. This is a one-tailed χ^2 test; critical ratio = 16.92.

O	E	O-E	$(O-E)^2$	$\dfrac{(O-E)^2}{E}$
6	10	-4	16	1.6
11	10	1	1	0.1
12	10	2	4	0.4
8	10	-2	4	0.4
7	10	-3	9	0.9
13	10	3	9	0.9
10	10	0	0	0.0
15	10	5	25	2.5
8	10	-2	4	0.4
10	10	0	0	0.0
100	100	0	Total ...	7.2

$$\text{Observed ratio} = \sum \frac{(O-E)^2}{E} = 7.2$$

Since the critical χ^2 value at 9 degrees of freedom is 16.92, the difference is not significant. Conclusion: The roulette wheel is very probably behaving as expected.

17. This is a χ^2 test; critical ratio = 12.83; actual ratio = 13.8. Significant at 2.5% level of significance, where the critical ratio is 12.83.

Conclusion: The die is probably warped.

CHAPTER 11

1. (a) and (d): $A_2\bar{R} = \dfrac{3\sigma_x}{\sqrt{n}}$; both are equal to 3 $\sigma_{\bar{x}}$

2. (a) and (c): $\bar{p} + 3\sqrt{\dfrac{\bar{p}(1-\bar{p})}{n}} = \bar{p} + 3\sqrt{\dfrac{\bar{p}(1-\bar{p})}{\bar{n}}}$

3. $\dfrac{\bar{R}}{d_2} = \sigma_x;\ \dfrac{\bar{R}/d_2}{\sqrt{n}} = \dfrac{\sigma_x}{\sqrt{n}} = \sigma_{\bar{x}}$

---

* To be answered by the reader.

4. (a) 1.96 sigmas;   (b) 2.327 sigmas;
    (c) 2.575 sigmas;   (d) 3.0 sigmas.

5. To control the variation of the process (namely, σ_x) since the $\overline{X}$ chart only controls the process mean.

6. (a) A_2 (when multiplied by $\overline{R}$) is used as 3 standard errors of $\overline{X}$ to compute UCL and LCL of the $\overline{X}$ chart.

    (b) d_2 is used to compute the standard deviation of x by $\sigma_x = \overline{R}/d_2$.

    (c) D_3 is used to compute the lower control limit for the R chart by $D_3\overline{R}$.

    (d) D_4 is used to compute the upper control limit for the R chart by $D_4\overline{R}$.

    (e) σ_p is the symbol used to compute the standard error of p by $\sqrt{\dfrac{\overline{p}(1-\overline{p})}{n-1}}$.

    (f) $\overline{c}$ is used to compute σ_c by $\sqrt{\overline{c}}$ for the c chart.

7. (a) Center line $= \dfrac{\Sigma \overline{X}}{m} = \dfrac{429}{30} = 14.3 = \overline{\overline{X}}$ inches

    $$UCL = \overline{\overline{X}} + A_2\overline{R} = 14.3 + (.58)\left(\dfrac{11.88}{30}\right) = 14.3 + .2297 = 14.53 \text{ inches}$$

    $$LCL = \overline{\overline{X}} - A_2\overline{R} = 14.3 - .2297 = 14.07 \text{ inches}$$

    (b) Center line for R: $\dfrac{\Sigma R}{m} = \overline{R} = \dfrac{11.88}{30} = .396$ inches

    $$UCL = D_4\overline{R} = (2.11)(.396) = .836 \text{ inches}$$

    $$LCL = D_3\overline{R} = (0)(.396) = 0 \text{ inches}$$

    (c) Natural tolerances $= \overline{\overline{X}} \pm 3\sigma_x$;

    Compute $3\sigma_x$ by method #1: $\dfrac{3\overline{R}}{d_2} = \dfrac{3(.396)}{2.326} = 0.51$ inches.

    Also compute $3\sigma_x$ by method #2: $A_2\overline{R} = \dfrac{3\sigma_x}{\sqrt{n}}$:

    so $3\sigma_x = (A_2\overline{R})\sqrt{5} = (.2297)(2.236) = 0.51$ inches.

521

Upper natural tolerance limit:
14.3 + 0.51 = 14.81 inches;

Lower natural tolerance limit:
14.3 – 0.51 = 13.79 inches.

(d) Company specifications of 14.40 inches ± .15 inches give the following:

Upper tolerance limit = 14.55 inches

Lower tolerance limit = 14.25 inches.

Since the company specifications shown above are more demanding than the natural process capability on both limits, the company would have a serious problem in meeting the tighter specifications. The percent of rejects is computed below.

(e) Use : $\sigma_x = \dfrac{\overline{R}}{d_2} = \dfrac{.396}{2.326} = 0.17$

(1) $Z = \dfrac{14.25 - 14.3}{0.17} = \dfrac{-.05}{0.17} = -0.29\,\sigma_x$ which includes 11.41% of the wire strands.

Therefore, 50.0% – 11.14% or 38.59% will be rejects.

(2) $Z = \dfrac{14.55 - 14.3}{0.17} = \dfrac{0.25}{0.17} = 1.47\,\sigma_x$ which includes 42.92% of the wire strands.

Therefore, 50.0% – 42.92% or 7.08% will be rejected.

(3) Altogether, 38.59 + 7.08 = 45.67% of the wire strands would be rejected.

(f) (1) Accept the rejects of 7% and the cost involved;

(2) Adjust the equipment;

(3) Purchase better equipment;

(4) Reduce the cost per item to customer.

8. To detect runs or trends and also to know when (date and time) an assignable cause occurred.

---

* To be answered by the reader.

9. When the process is operating under statistical control or a constant-cause system, the x-values of the product will vary and in the long run will form a frequency distribution shaped like a normal curve. When the process variations display a normal distribution, the resulting averages based on samples of 3 or more items will also form a normal distribution. This has been proven empirically and mathematically by the Central Limit Theorem.

10. (a) $\bar{p} = 0.0843$; $3\sigma_p = 3\sqrt{\dfrac{\bar{p}(1-\bar{p})}{n-1=199}} = 3(.0197) = \pm 0.0591$;

UCL $= 0.0843 + 0.0591 = 0.1434$ } *assignable bad causes -*
LCL $= 0.0843 - 0.0591 = 0.0252$ } May 2 and May 7.

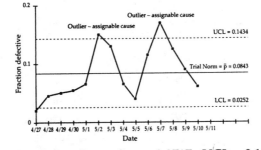

Revised p chart: Center line $= 0.0717$; UCL $= 0.1266$;
LCL $= 0.0168$.

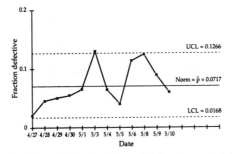

(b) Use the Pareto method to determine which operators made most of the errors and retrain them to improve their work.

11. (a) Estimated percentage miscoded $= \dfrac{174}{(6)(50)(5)} = \dfrac{174}{1500} = 11.6\%$.

(b) With Pareto, found that employees B and D made 67.2% of the errors. Investigate their problem and solve it by training, etc.

12. The specifications are in this interval: 47.875 to 48.125 inches.
We need to establish the natural process capability by $\overline{\overline{X}} \pm 3\sigma_x$.

$$\sigma_x = \frac{\overline{R}}{d_2} = \frac{0.35"}{2.847} = 0.123 \text{ inches and } 3\sigma_x = 0.369 \text{ inches.}$$

The natural process capability = 48 inches ± .369 inches or between 47.631 inches and 48.369 inches.. These are wider than the company specifications and will result in many rejects.

Apply Z-test on the left tail, as follows:

$$Z_1 = \frac{47.875 - 48}{0.123} = \frac{-0.125}{0.123} = -0.125\sigma_x; \text{ includes } 34.61\%;$$

Estimated percent defectives = 50.00% – 34.61% = 15.39% in the left tail.

Right tail gives 15.39% also based on $Z = \frac{48.125 - 48}{0.123} = 1.02\sigma_x$.

Considering both tails total estimated percent defectives = (2)(15.39%) = 30.78%.

Recommendations: (1) Change specifications,
(2) Improve process capability,
(3) Reduce cost to purchaser,
(4) Apply Pareto analysis.

13. (a) Use a c chart;

(b) Yes, with 3 sigma limits shown below, day 6 and 7 are outliers (due to a strike).

$$\overline{c} = \frac{255.71}{21} = 12.18; \quad UCL = 12.18 + 3\sqrt{12.18} = 22.65; \quad LCL = 12.18 - 3\sqrt{12.18} = 1.71.$$

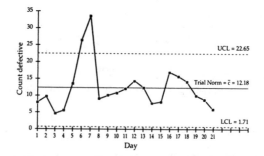

---

* To be answered by the reader.

(c) Revised $\bar{c} = \dfrac{255.71 - 60.23}{19} = \dfrac{195.48}{19} = 10.29$;

$UCL = 10.29 + 3\sqrt{10.29} = 19.91$; $LCL = 10.29 - 3\sqrt{10.29} = 0.67$.

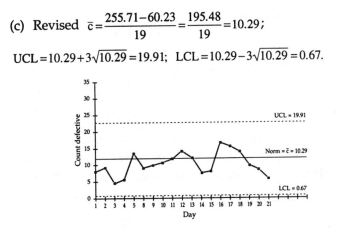

14. Determine each employee's percent contribution to the 77 errors. It is found that employees 2, 5, 8 and 12 made 67.6% of all errors. Investigate the reason for their high error rates and take steps to improve their performance.

15. (a) $\sigma_{\bar{X}} = \dfrac{12}{\sqrt{9}} = 4$; $UCL = 106 + 3(4) = 118$; $LCL = 106 - 12 = 94$;

(b) Sample #4 is below LCL.

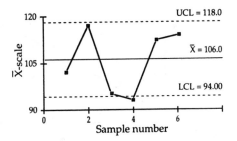

16. (a) $UCL = \bar{p} + 3\sqrt{\dfrac{\bar{p}(1-\bar{p})}{n-1}}$; $LCL = \bar{p} - 3\sqrt{\dfrac{\bar{p}(1-\bar{p})}{n-1}}$;

   (b) $UCL = \bar{p} + 3\sqrt{\dfrac{\bar{p}(1-\bar{p})}{\bar{n}-1}}$; $LCL = \bar{p} - 3\sqrt{\dfrac{\bar{p}(1-\bar{p})}{\bar{n}-1}}$;

   (c) $UCL = n\bar{p} + 3\sqrt{n\bar{p}(1-\bar{p})}$; $LCL = n\bar{p} - 3\sqrt{n\bar{p}(1-\bar{p})}$;

   (d) Preference for an np chart is to avoid computing percentages; an objection to the np chart is that any change in sample size requires recomputation of the center line and control limits.

17. (a) $\bar{X}$ and R charts; (b) p or np chart; (c) c chart.

CHAPTER 12

1. Seek out the definitions in the text.*

2. Forward method (Method #1) using $\bar{X}$, σ_x, $\bar{Y}$, σ_y, and backward solution (Method #2) using two algebraic equations, so-called normal equations, to solve for a and b.

3.* (a) About 0.8;

   (b) Linear, direct;

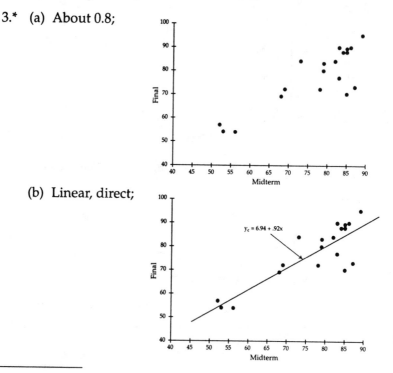

---

* To be answered by the reader.

(c)

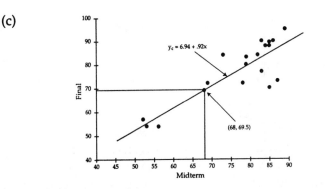

$$y_c = 6.94 + .92x$$

(68, 69.5)

(d) About 70 (passing grade).

4. (a) r = 0.85; (b) y_e = 6.937 + 0.921x; (c) y_e = 70 (rounded);

(d) 72.8% and 27.2%; (e) Time spent on studying, extra help (e.g., tutoring); (f) Multiple linear correlation and regression analysis.

5. (a) σ_e = 6.372 points;

(b) Except for differences due to rounding, they should be the same;

(c) (1) Z = -2.37 for largest error (-15);

(2) 75%, as compared to expected 68% (difference due to rounding and small universe of N = 20).

6. (a) Yes; the more income available for use, the more likely some of it will be spent;

(b) income is the independent variable;

(c) *;

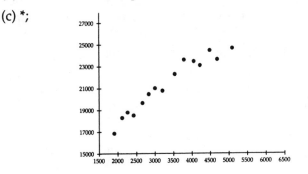

(d) linear;

(e) direct;

(f) *;

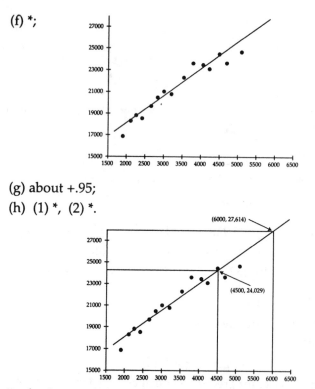

(g) about +.95;

(h) (1) *, (2) *.

7. By further rounding of the figures, e.g., to trillions and billions of dollars, with (perhaps) one decimal place; or use of a computer with the appropriate software programs; or use of a pre-programmed calculator.

8. (a) $r = 0.97$; $r^2 = 0.94$; $y_e = \$13{,}274 + 2.39x$, where $y_e =$ annual total store sales (in millions of dollars) and $x =$ total disposable personal income (in billions of dollars); $\sigma_e = \$653.34$;

(b) (1) $y_e = \$24{,}029$ million when $x = \$4.5$ trillion;

(2) $y_e = \$27{,}614$ million when $x = \$6.0$ trillion, although this figure ($x = \$6.0$ trillion) is beyond the range of the available data, so y_e must be used cautiously.

9. (a) About 68%; about 95.5%;

(b) 94% ($r^2 = 0.94$) and 6% ($1 - r^2 = 0.06$);

(c) 3% $\left(\dfrac{\sigma_e}{\overline{Y}} = \dfrac{\$653}{\$21{,}296} = 0.03 \right)$.

---

* To be answered by the reader.

10. (a) zero ; (b) 81%.

11. An error in arithmetic (or a wrong formula) is causing it because r cannot be negative.

12. We must first establish that a logical cause and effect relationship exists. Also, we must determine if the scattergram shows a linear path or not.

13. False, $r^2 = 81\%$.

14. False; $r^2 = 81\%$ for $r = .90$ and $r^2 = 20\%$ for $r = .45$.

15. *

16. *

17. (a) *; (b) $r = 0.686$;
    (c) $y_e = 0.74x - 15.9$;;

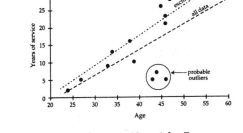

(d) age 46 with 5 years of service and age 43 with 5 years of service
(e) *; (f) revised $r = 0.85$.

18. (a) $y_e = 2.25 + 0.144x$;
    (b) Simulation checks it out;
    (c) ±7 hours.

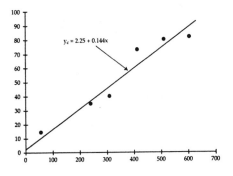

CHAPTER 13

1. Trend, seasonal variations, cycles and irregular (or unpredictable) variations.

2. Time series analysis deals with but one independent variable — time. Correlation and regression analysis can deal with many variables which logically influence the dependent variable.

3. Short-range planning and forecasting; long-range planning; better interpretation of the real magnitude of an activity within the year by use of a seasonal index.

4. (a) To forecast the magnitude of an activity, such as sales, a year or two hence, for budgeting and short-range planning.

   (b) To construct a seasonal index adjusted for trend and use it to forecast the real magnitude of a seasonal activity.

5. Line of least squares.

6. *

7. (a) Solve the two normal equations shown in the text
   for b by $\Sigma xy = b \, \Sigma x^2$.

   (b) *

8. There are errors of prediction due to irregular occurences and/or cyclical variations.

9. *

10. In starting the time series, delete the 1982 figure as an outlier:
    (a) *
    (b) $y_e = 5.13 - .16x$;
    (c) 1992 = 4.3; 1993 = 4.2; 1994 = 4.0; 1995 = 3.8 (all in millions).

11. *

12. *

13. *

CHAPTER 14

1. *

2. *

3. *

---

* To be answered by the reader.

4.

Table 4
Number of Vietnam War veterans living in the United States, by gender and country of birth, October, 1995

Gender	Country of birth		
	TOTAL	United States	Other Countries
TOTAL			
Male			
Female			

Source: Department of Veterans Affairs.

5.

Table 5
Number of persons residing in the United States, by age, gender, and country of birth, April, 1995

Age	TOTAL			Male			Female		
	TOTAL	United States	Other Countries	T	US	O	T	US	O*
TOTAL									
Under 20									
20 – 39									
40 – 49									
50 – 59									
60 and over									

* In the actual table, these subclass names should, of course, be spelled out.
Source: U.S. Bureau of the Census, *Statistical Abstract of the United States.*

6. (a):

Table 6
Number of workers hired by the ABC Company during 1994, by marital status, nativity, and gender

Marital Status	TOTAL			USA-born			Foreign-born		
	Total	Male	Female	Total	Male	Female	Total	Male	Female
TOTAL	650	362	288	309	174	135	341	188	153
Married	323	145	178	153	72	81	170	73	97
Single	289	198	91	141	94	47	148	104	44
Unknown	38	19	19	15	8	7	23	11	12

Source: ABC Company records.

6. (b) *

7.

Table 7
Resident population of the United States,
by State and gender, April 1, 1990

State	TOTAL	Male	Female
TOTAL U.S.A.			
Alabama			
Alaska			
Arizona			
Arkansas			
California			
Colorado			
etc.			

Source: U.S. Bureau of the Census, *Statistical Abstract of the United States: 1993,* Washington, DC.

8. *

9. * Hint: Complete the percentage that each population classification is of the total resident population.

10. *

---

* To be answered by the reader.

Index

A

A Million Random Digits with 100,000 Normal Deviates, 184–185
Absolute value, 112
Acceptance sampling, 163
Accuracy in Collecting Data, 40
Actual Z-ratio, 285
Adjusting the seasonal index for trend, 439
Analytical table 469
Anchor point, 434
Annual trend increment, 440
Arithmetic mean, 78
    distribution of, 120-121, 218, 226
    of grouped data, 83–85
    of ungrouped data, 80–81
    short-cuts, 95–100
Arkin, Herbert, 261
Arkin, William M., 459
Arnauld, Antoine, 277
Array, 330, 356-357
Assignable causes, 321, 332, 344, 349-350, 362
Asymmetrical distributions
    See Skewed
Attributes, 4, 234-235, 333–334
    frequency distributions, 59
Average, 77
    concepts, 79-80
    uses, 89-91
    weighted, *See* Weighted mean
Average deviation, 111-112
Average of extremes, 78, 93

B

Bar chart, 61-62, 453
Bell curve, *See* Normal distribution
Best fit, line of
    See Correlation and regression
Bias, 211
Bimodal distribution, 71
Binomial distribution, 159–165, 363
Broken line chart, 456
Business cycle, 430
Butler, Joseph, 145

C

Captions, 463
Cell, 464
Cell counts, 316-318
Central Limit Theorem, 216-219, 223, 224, 289, 295
Central tendency, *See* Average
Charts, *See* Graphs
Chi-Square test, *See* Significance
Class interval, 50–56
Class midpoint, 56
Classifications, 17, 23, 28, 44, 60, 76, 106, 179-180, 453-454, 462-465, 467-471, 481
Cluster sampling, 194-195
Cochran, William G., 173, 195
Coefficient of correlation, 390
Coefficient of determination, 392
Coefficient of variation (C.V.), 117, 331
Coefficients of the regression line, 396
Coman, Edward T., Jr., 449
Combinations, 152-154
Components of time series, 427-432
Conditional probability, 159
Confidence level, 181, 221, 223-224, 332
Confidence interval, 241, 244
Confidence interval tests
    See Significance
Constant-cause system, 64, 67, 332
Contact list, 28
Continuous variable, 57
Control charts
    a process for constructing, 342
    averages ($\overline{X}$ chart), 342
    factors
        d_2, 347
        D_4, A_2, D_3, 354
    fraction defective (p chart), 362
    individual items (x chart), 372
    management action, 352, 361
    management specifications, 358-361
    number of defectives (np chart), 369
    number of defects
        per unit (c chart), 370
    productivity control chart, 408
    provisional, 343
    quality, 331
    ranges (R chart), 353
    regression, 372

Correlation and regression analysis
  backward solution (Method #2), 405
  cautions in use of, 410-415
  coefficient of correlation, 392, 397, 497
  coefficient of determination, 392
  coefficients of regression line, 396
  forward solution
      (Method #1), 397, 405
  graphic, 387-390
  linear, 395, 411
  logical, 386-387
  multiple, 382, 393, 411
  outliers, 390, 404, 415
  r, *See* Coefficient of correlation
  r², *See* Coefficient of determination
  simple, 382, 410
  simulation, 401, 404
  spurious, 412
  standard error of estimate, 396-397
  uses, 383-384, 408-410
Critical ratio, 285, 305, 322
Cumulative distribution, 88
Cyclical variations, 430, 436

D

Data
  accuracy, 11, 40-41, 210-211
  analysis, 30-31
  collection, 26-28, 40-41
  organization, 47, 52-55, 464, 469-470
  presentation, 31-32, 450-470
  primary, 27
  secondary, 27
  tabulation, 30, 450, 462-470
Data entry sheet, 343-344
Data processing, 3, 29
Decomposition, *See* Time series
Degrees of freedom, 292, 311,
  316-317, 412-413
de Mere, Chevalier, 146
Deming, W. Edwards, 1, 23, 233, 475
Dependent variable, 383
Deseasonalized figures, 442
Digital random sampling, 193-194
Dix, Arthur H., 38

E

Edwards, G.D., 47
Error, *See also* Sampling
      and Standard error *and* Variation
  and risk, 12
  non-sampling, 211

  sampling, 181, 210
  tolerable, 253
  stratified sample, 264
  systematic, 211
  Types I and II, 279, 280
Estimation procedures, 234
Explained variation
      See Coefficient of Determination
Explanatory notes, 463

F

Factorial, 153
False accuracy, 11
Finite correction factor, *See* Sampling
Forecasting, 396, 414, 425, 426,
  435-436, 443-445
Formulas, summary, 485
Frequency distribution
  asymmetrical distribution, 92
  bimodal distribution, 71
  binomial distribution, 296
  class interval, 50
  class midpoints, 50
  continuous variable, 57
  cumulative distribution, 88
  defined, 47
  graphic patterns, 60
  noncontinuous variable, 58
  normal distribution, 5, 18, 47, 62-64,
      94-95, 126, 218-219, 283-284, 385
  organizing a variable for analysis, 52
  percentage frequency
      distribution, 51
  uses of, 48

G

General-purpose tables, 470
Generalizing, 7, 10
Goodness-of-fit test, 319
Grand mean, 219, 346
Grant, E. L., 107
Graph, 60, 450
  bar chart, 61, 453-455
  broken line chart, 61, 456-458
  cumulative curves, 88
  histogram, 456
  pictograph, 459-460
  pie chart, 451-453
  scatter diagram, 387-390
  smoothed curve, 62, 458-459
Grieves, Howard C., 209
Griffith, Kenneth F., 384
Grouped data, 83

H

Histogram, 456
Huff, Darrell, 10
Hyman, Herbert H., 35
Hypothesis testing
   See Significance testing

I

Incomplete data, 10
Independent event, 157
Independent variable, 383, 414
Inferences, 233
Insignificant difference, 279
Insignificant variations, 332
Intercept, 396, 434
Interviews, personal
   See Personal interviews
Inverse correlation, 417
Irregular variations, 427, 432, 437

J

Jahoda, Duetsch, and Cook, 35
J-shaped curve, 64-65, 73, 224, 480
Journal of Quality Technology, 373
Judgment samples, 202
Jumping to conclusions, 10

K

Kleinbaum, David, 411
Kupper, Lawrence, 411

L

Law of
   Decreasing Variation, 213, 219
   probability, 5, 214
   Stability of Mass Data, 6-7, 219
   Statistical Regularity
      of Mass Data, 6-7, 426
   Universal Variation, 6, 212
Level of significance, 279
Lewis, Edward, E., 425
Likelihood, 147
Line graph, 61, 456-458
Line of average relationships, 396
Line of best fit, 390, 396
Line of least squares, 396, 399
Linear correlation, 395, 411

Linear regression analysis
   See Correlation and
   regression analysis
Linear trend, 433-434
Logical correlation analysis, 386-387

M

Mail questionnaires, 34-35, 38
   comparative advantages
      relative to personal interview, 41
   non-response, 40
Mailing list, 28
Management specifications, 358-361
Mandel, B.J., 371
Map charts, 460
Maximum absolute error, 246
Maximum relative error, 247
Mayer, Raymond, R., 344
Mean, *See* Arithmetic mean
Median, 81-82
   graphic determination, 88
   grouped data, 85-88
   use of, 91-94, 110
Midpoint of frequency classes, 56
Mode, 78, 80, 82
   grouped data, 89
Moment-of-force, 92
Monthly seasonal index, 438
Monthly trend increment, 440
Moroney, M. J., 18, 481
Multiple correlation, 384
Mutually exclusive, 156

N

Natural process capability, 358-359
Noncontinuous variable, 58
Non-sampling errors, 176, 211
Nonproportional stratified
   sampling, 197, 200
Norm, 346
Normal distribution, 62, 494
   properties, 120-121, 155
   uses of, 66-69
Normal distribution principle, 219
Normal equations, 405, 434
Normal variate, standard, 284, 360
Norris, Robert S., 459
Not significant, 306
np control chart, 369
Null hypothesis, 303

O

One-Sided Tests, 301
Open-ended class, 56
Optimum allocation
    in stratified sampling, 267
Oral presentation, 450
Organizing a Variable for Analysis, 52
Outliers, 344, 390, 404, 415, 433
Overlapping-confidence-interval, 287

P

p control chart, 362
Parameters, 233
Pareto method, 336
Partial correlation analysis, 386
Parts of a table, 462
Pascal, Blaise, 146
Pearsonian correlation coefficient, 397
Percentage frequency distribution, 51
Percentages or rates, 7, 234, 330
Permutations, 154
Personal interviews, 35
    comparative advantages
    relative to
        mail questionnaire, 41
Pictograph, 459-460
Pie chart, 451-453
Pilot study, 29, 181
Pivot point, 434
Point estimate, 244
Poisson Distribution Theory, 370
Pooled standard deviation, 292
Power, statistical, 291
    See Significance
Preliminary control chart, 347, 349
Presentation of data
    graphic, 450
    tabular, 463
Presenting Sample-Derived
    Estimates, 242
Primary data, 27
Principles of Statistics, 5
    See also Laws
Probability, 5, 147
    basic rules, 156-159
    conditional, 159
    measurement, 147, 150
Product-moment correlation, 397
Productivity control chart, 408
Proportional stratified sample, 197
Provisional $\overline{X}$ control chart, 350-351

Q

Quality, 331
Quality control, 120, 331
    of basic data, 29
    process control, 329
Quantifying, 4
    by observation, 34
    records, 33
Quantifying a Process or Problem, 33
Questionnaires
    See Mail questionnaires

R

r, *See* Correlation and
    regression analysis
Random Sampling, 151, 174
    digital, 193-194
    simple, 173-174, 181-182, 184-190
    stratified, 196-202, 264
    systematic, 190-193
Random time sampling
    See Work sampling
Random variable, 151
Range, 9, 53, 116, 331
Range Chart (R Chart), 353
Ranking, 38
Rectangular distribution, 64
Regression analysis
    See Correlation and
    regression analysis
Regression control chart, 372, 408
Regression line, 396, 399
Relative error of estimate, 247, 403
Reliability, 118, 181, 233
Replicated sample estimates, 216, 219
Replication, *See* Sampling
Representiveness of results, 11, 174
Residuals, 436
Risk, 5, 12, 224, 332
    See Probability *and* Significance
Romig, Harry G., 245
Rounding, 11
Run of points, 344, 351

S

Sample standard deviation
    See Statistical tools
Sampling
    advantages (SAFE), 175-178
    a controlled experiment in, 214

acceptance, 163
confidence, 181, 223, 233
distribution, 217, 236, 243, 278
efficiency, 198
error, 181, 210, 211
 See also Standard error
estimation, 234, 236, 264
judgment, 202
fraction (finite correction factor),
 213, 237, 252, 260
frame, 180
methods of random selection,
 See Random sampling
pilot study, 29, 181
probability, 173
 See Random sampling
random time, *See* Work sampling
replication, 215, 236
risk, 12, 224
sample size formulas, 250-260, 266
sample size tables(attributes),
 261,-263
spot-check, 203
steps in conducting a survey, 25, 28
system, 178
unit, 180
variance, 210, 265
with replacement, 216
Sampling and the Three
 Fundamental Frequency
 Distributions, 224
Scattergram, 387-390
Schmid, Calvin F., 460
Scientific Method, 33
Seasonal variation, 430, 438
Secondary data, 27
Siegel, Andrew F., 159
Significance, statistical
 and power, 291
 and risk, 279-280
 assumptions underlying test of, 294
 Chi-square test of, 314
 confidence interval tests, 283,
  287, 297, 299
 level of, 279
 of correlation, 412, 497
 procedure, guidelines, 304-306, 317
 t-test of, 295, 310
 tests for means, 284, 310
 tests for percentages, 296
 two-sided tests (*v.* one-sided), 301
 variations in control charts, 332
 Z-tests of, 284, 288, 297, 300

Simple correlation analysis, 386, 410
Simulation method, 401, 436, 437
Single-stage cluster sampling, 195
Size of Sample, 250
Skeleton tables, 462
Skewed distribution, 62, 64
Skip-interval, 191
Slope, 396, 434
Smally, C.W., 384
Smoothing, 62, 458-459
SPC, 329
Special-purpose tables, 470
Specifications, 358-361
Spot-check sampling, 203
Spurious correlation, 412
Stability of mass data, 6, 219
Standard deviation, 9, 112-115,
 120-121, 132
 compared to standard error,
  220-221, 224-228
 short-cut, 133
 uses, 116-120, 124-125, 126
Standard error,
 compared to standard
  deviation, 220-221, 224-228
 of difference between
  two means, 288-292
 of estimated mean, 220-221,
  236, 264-265
 of estimated number of items
  possessing an attribute, 241, 266
 of estimated percentage, 331
 of estimated total, 239
 of regression estimate, 397
 of trend estimate, 436
Standard normal variate, 128, 284
Statistical control, 332
Statistical Formulas, By Chapter, 485
Statistical process
 control (SPC), 329
Statistical regularity, 7, 426
Statistical significance
 See Significance
Statistical tools, 7-10
 arithmetic mean,
  See Arithmetic mean
 average deviation, 111
 average, *See* Average
 coefficient of variation, 117
 formulas, 485
 median, *See* median
 mode, 80, 82, 89
 standard deviation,
  See Standard deviation
 uses, 13-17

Strata, 196
Stratified random sampling,
    estimation, 264
    sample size, 266-268
    sampling error, 264-266
    selection, 196-202
    TASK, 201
Strength of correlation, 389
Stub, 463
Sub-universes, 196
Survey, statistical, 23
Symmetrical distributions, 62
Systematic mistakes, 211
Systematic random sampling,
    See Random sampling

T

Tables, types, 469-470
*Table of 105,000 Random
    Decimal Digits*, 184
Tabular presentation of data, 450, 462
Tchebycheff, P.L., 126
Tests of significance, *See* Significance
Time lag, 414
Time series analysis, 425
    components of, 427
    methods of, 432
    seasonal measurement, 438
    some cautions in, 443
    uses of, 426-427, 435-437, 441-442
Tippett, L.H.C., 77
Total Quality
    Management (TQM), 67, 14, 329
Trend
    t-distribution, 310
    t-test of significance, 295, 310
Trend, in control charts 351
Trend line
    increment, 440
    long-term trend, 429
    measurement methods, 433-435
    uses, 435-437
Tufte, Edward R., 460
Two-Sided Tests, 301
Two-stage cluster sampling, 195
Type I error, 279
Type II error, 280

U

u-chart, 372
U-shaped curve, 64
Ungrouped data, 83
Uniform classes, 52
Uniform distribution, 64
Universe, 174, 180
Unpredictable variations, 432
Unsystematic mistakes, 211
Unwarranted generalization, 10

V

Validity of the results, 11
Variables, 5, 49, 234
    continuous, 57
    noncontinuous (discrete), 58
Variance, 265
Variation, 9, 109, *See also* Error

W

Weighted mean, 100-101
Weights, *See* Ranking
Work sampling, 16-17, 151, 299
Work sheet tables, 470

X

$\bar{X}$ chart, 342
x chart, 372

Z

Z-test, *See* Significance
Z-variate (Z-score), 128